Bárbaros:
Spaniards and Their Savages
in the Age of Enlightenment

Bárbaros:
Spaniards and Their Savages
in the Age of Enlightenment

DAVID J. WEBER

YALE UNIVERSITY PRESS

NEW HAVEN AND LONDON

Published with assistance from the Annie Burr
Lewis Fund and the Program for Cultural Cooperation between Spain's Ministry of Culture
and United States Universities.

Set in Monotype Janson type by Duke & Company,
Devon, Pennsylvania.
Printed in the United States of America by Hamilton
Printing Company, Castleton, New York.

Library of Congress Cataloging-in-Publication Data

Weber, David J.
  Bárbaros: Spaniards and their savages in the
Age of Enlightenment / David J. Weber.
      p. cm.
  Includes bibliographical references and index.
  ISBN 0-300-10501-0 (alk. paper)

  1. Indians—Colonization. 2. Indians—Missions.
3. Indians—Government relations. 4. Spain—
Colonies—America—Administration. 5. New
Spain—Colonization. 6. America—Discovery
and exploration. 7. America—History—To 1810.
I. Title.
  E59.C58W43 2005
  323.1197′0171246′09033—dc22
                                        2004030553

A catalogue record for this book is available from
the British Library.

10   9   8   7   6   5   4   3   2   1

Only with kindness, impartiality, and good faith
can we achieve peace and commerce with the fiercest
and most valiant Indians.
Miguel Lastarria
Río de la Plata, 1804

So much blood, so much fear, so much weeping.
An Indian woman, remembering
Nuevo Santander, ca. 1795

Contents

CONTENTS

Illustrations

Maps

Acknowledgments

Impetus for this book came from John Lynch, a distinguished historian of Latin American history whom I have never met. In a review of my book *The Spanish Frontier in North America* (Yale University Press, 1992) Professor Lynch gently chided me in the *Times Literary Supplement* for failing to compare Spain's North American frontiers with its Central and South American counterparts. His criticism struck a chord. While working on *The Spanish Frontier* I had wondered how some of the Spanish policies and practices that I saw on the northern frontiers of the empire played out on other Spanish frontiers. Seen from a distance, Spain's imperial system appears to have been a monolith, applying its policies equally throughout the Americas. Closer inspection, however, suggested that local forces shaped implementation of imperial policies. That being the case, were practices that I saw on North American frontiers commonplace to the frontiers of the empire? or anomalous? If local conditions on Spanish-American frontiers shaped the implementation of imperial policies, did they also influence the officials who crafted them in Spain's Iberian center of power? Could Spanish policy be understood adequately by looking at its parts? or did one have to see it whole? Such questions had aroused my curiosity, but I yielded to the realities of time and space, kept my focus squarely on North America, and finished the book. Then came Professor Lynch's review, which reminded me that the bigger picture of Spain's American frontiers still needed exploring and assured me that someone other than myself would be interested in the journey.

As I looked at the large literature on Spain's many American frontiers, it quickly became clear I would have to narrow my focus to a single subject. I chose Spanish relations with unconquered Indians, or savages, as the Spaniards called them—the most consistently vexing challenge Spain faced on the frontiers of America. It also became evident I would have to narrow my subject chronologically if I was to expand it geographically. I settled on the late eighteenth century, from 1759, the year Carlos III acceded to the Spanish throne, to the 1810s, when the Spanish-American colonies began to break away. Those years saw the effects of the Spanish Enlightenment come to full flower in Spanish America. During that time of enlightened despots, I supposed that Spain would both pursue and practice a kinder, gentler Indian policy and implement it with some uniformity throughout its American empire.

Even by limiting my story to a specific subject and half a century, I could not hope to do comprehensive archival research. Luckily for me, several generations of scholars in Europe and the Americas have studied Spanish relations with Indians. Those scholars have edited and published volumes of original documents and quoted from them extensively in monographs and articles in scholarly journals. Along with their interpretive pieces, then, they have brought a large number of primary sources into print, facilitating the work of those of us who have followed them.

In my quest for sources, I have profited from the unfailingly kind assistance of scholars, archivists, and librarians. In Argentina, I am especially grateful to my colleague and friend Professor Raúl Mandrini, Director of the Instituto de Estudios Históricos, Universidad Nacional del Centro de la Provincia de Buenos Aires in Tandil, who introduced me to Argentine institutions and scholars, including his affable, helpful, and informed protégés, Sarah Ortelli and Carlos Paz. In Buenos Aires, the extraordinarily knowledgeable and generous staff of the library of the Instituto de Historia Argentina y Americana "Dr. Emilio Ravignani," especially Marcelina Jarma and Abel Roth, gave me convenient access to regional journals. The remarkably prolific legal historian Abelardo Levaggi of the Instituto de Investigaciones Jurídicas y Sociales in Buenos Aires kindly shared much of his work on treaties with Indians prior to its publication. When I began this project, I intended to devote more space to those treaties, but don Abelardo has covered the field. In Buenos Aires, Silvia Ratto and Jorge Gelman have also graciously shared their work. In Jujuy, Marcelo Lagos, Ana Teruel, and Daniel Santamaría introduced me to regional historiography and welcomed my wife and me to their homes. Don Daniel guided us into the Quebrada de Humahuaca on a memorable day. At the Universidad del Sur in Bahía Blanca, Juan Francisco Jiménez and Daniel Villar have been the most gracious of collaborators, and the Argentine historian Florencia Roulet has shared her work with me from her distant post at the University of Lausanne in Switzerland.

In Bolivia, I owe a debt to the hospitable Josep Barnadas, the former director of the Archivo Nacional de Bolivia in Sucre, and to two erudite, hospitable historians in Santa Cruz, Alcides Parejas Moreno and Gustavo Prado Robles.

In Chile, Jorge Pinto received me graciously at the Universidad de la Frontera in Temuco, introducing me to the latest scholarship, including his own, and patiently disabusing me of misconceptions. Leonardo León Solís of the Universidad de Valparaíso gave me copies of his remarkable publications that would have been difficult for me to find in other ways. From the Université d'Angers in France, the Chilean historian Fernando Casanueva generously shared ideas and offprints of his publications with me.

In Mexico, Ignacio del Río at the UNAM and the accomplished Argentine scholar Sara Ortelli, who recently completed her doctorate at the Colegio de México, located key documents for me.

In Venezuela, I received a warm welcome in Caracas from Vilma Lehmann and other members of the fine staff of the Biblioteca Nacional, Rafael Fernández Heres, Director of the Academia Nacional de la Historia, and Guillermo Briceño Porras, Director of the Archivo General de la Nación. For extraordinary help I am especially indebted to Susan Berglund, professor of history at the Universidad Central de Venezuela.

In Spain, Douglas Inglis, one of the preeminent *ratones del archivo,* oriented me both in and beyond the Archivo General de Indias, and Alfredo Jiménez Nuñez, that courtly polymath in the Departamento de Historia de América at the Universidad de Sevilla, offered wisdom and friendship. In Madrid, I continue to be grateful to the dynamic Sylvia L. Hilton of the Departamento de Historia de América at the Universidad Complutense, with whom I have enjoyed a long collaboration, and to the irrepressible Salvador Bernabéu, who has since moved from the Consejo Superior in Madrid to the Consejo Superior's Escuela de Estudios Hispano Americanos in Seville. The Argentine expatriate Beatriz Vitar, whom I first encountered in Madrid, has generously shared her knowledge of the Chaco. Finally, I owe much to a member of our family in Madrid, *el sabio* Federico Jiménez García.

In the United States, a number of scholars generously introduced me to their Spanish-American counterparts, oriented me to archives and bookstores in the areas of their specialties, and answered a myriad of questions: Arnold Bauer (University of California at Davis), Charles Cutter (Purdue), Judy Ewell (William and Mary), Donna Guy (Ohio State), Kristine Jones (Associate Director, Center for Latin American Studies, University of Chicago), Erick Langer (Georgetown), Michael Perri (Emory), Cynthia Radding (University of New Mexico), and Jane Rausch (University of Massachusetts). James Saeger (Lehigh) not only guided me into the literature of the Chaco, but also shared notes from archival sources.

In the United States I profited from the collections of several libraries, including the Zimmerman Library at the University of New Mexico, whose riches and convenience I have enjoyed since the early 1960s. I especially appreciate the kindness of Walter Brem at the Bancroft Library at Berkeley and of Adán Benavides at the Benson Latin American Collection at the University of Texas, Austin. A Times Mirror Fellowship from the Huntington Library for 2000–01 enabled me to extend a one-semester university leave into a year-long residence in San Marino, California. In that nirvana I enjoyed uninterrupted time to write under the watchful but benign eye of the Director of Research, Roy Ritchie, and the Huntington's ever-attentive staff. A semester of teaching as a visiting professor at Harvard in the autumn of 2002 gave me access to its incomparable library, allowing me to scour publications from Latin America that I could not have found so readily at any other location in the United States. There, for many favors, I am grateful to John Coatsworth and Aaron Navarro, but particularly to Brian De Lay and Diliana Angelova for reasons they know best.

My own institution has facilitated my work in many ways. I could not have written this book without the broad collection of our Fondren Library, the deep holdings of the DeGolyer Library, directed with unfailing good cheer by David Farmer and now Russell Martin, and our fine interlibrary loan department, run so efficiently by Billie Stovall. I would not have undertaken a project of this scope without the generous resources of the Robert and Nancy Dedman Chair in History, which supported my research travel and a part-time research assistant—Jane Elder in the early stages of the book, Andrea Boardman in the middle phase, and Dionne Procell and Ruth Ann Elmore toward the end. I am indebted to each of them. The Dedman Chair in History has also provided me with essential research leaves. Two colleagues who presided over Southern Methodist University's Clements Department of History while I wrote this book, Daniel Orlovsky and James Hopkins, have given me their friendship as well as departmental support.

Midway through this project I tested one of its themes at a conference organized by Amy Turner Bushnell and Jack P. Greene at Michigan State University in 1997. That essay appeared first in Spanish, published in Tandil, Argentina, as "Borbones y bárbaros: Centro y periferia en la reformulación de la política de España hacia los indígenas no sometidos," *Anuario del IEHS* 13 (1998): 147–71; it appeared several years later in English as "Bourbons and Bárbaros: Center and Periphery in the Reshaping of Spanish Indian Policy," in *Negotiated Empires: Centers and Peripheries in the New World, 1500–1800*, ed. Christine Daniels and Michael Kennedy (New York: Routledge, 2002), 79–103 (prose and ideas from that essay are reproduced here with permission of the *Anuario del IEHS* and Routledge/Taylor & Francis Books, Inc.). As the work moved toward completion, I had the privilege and honor of trying out other ideas on other university campuses, most memorably at Cornell, where I gave the three-part Carl Becker Lectures in 2003, and at Baylor in 2004, where I gave the two Edmondson lectures. The latter were published as *Spanish Bourbons and Wild Indians* (Waco: Baylor University Press, 2004). (Parts of these lectures have found their way into *Bárbaros: Spaniards and Their Savages* and appear here with permission of the publisher.)

I am beholden to generous colleagues who have read portions of the manuscript for me: Gary Anderson (University of Oklahoma), Stephen Hackel (Oregon State), Pekka Hämäläinen (University of California, Santa Barbara), Robert Lane Kauffmann (Rice University), Florencia Roulet (University of Lausanne), James Sandos (University of Redlands), Refugio de la Torre (University of California, Berkeley and the Colegio de Michoacán), Sam Truett (University of New Mexico), and members of my own department, particularly Peter Bakewell, Edward Countryman, and Kathleen Wellman.

Several stalwarts read the entire manuscript: Matt Babcock (a superb Ph.D. candidate and ethnohistorian at SMU), James F. Brooks (School of American Research), Amy Bushnell (retired at an early age and now associated with the John Carter Brown Library), James Hopkins (SMU), Peter Onuf (University of Virginia), Cynthia Radding (University of New Mexico), James Saeger (Lehigh University), Stuart Schwartz (Yale), and William Taylor (my former colleague at SMU now at the University of California, Berkeley, who encouraged this project from the beginning). Each has saved me from errors of commission and omission, forced me to question assumptions, and earned my deep gratitude. I have only myself to blame, of course, for the errors and oversights that remain.

Over a decade ago, my editor Chuck Grench, now at the University of North Carolina Press, introduced me to the pleasures of working with the extraordinary staff at Yale University Press, from the designer Nancy Ovedovitz to the head of marketing, Tina Weiner. It is a privilege to have them turn another of my manuscripts into a book and get it into readers' hands, and it has been a distinct pleasure to work with Chuck's smart, buoyant successor, Lara Heimert, and with the astute Lawrence Kenney, whose copyediting saved me from errors in two languages. Jerome N. Cookson of Pensacola, Florida, made the maps with a sharp eye toward contradictions and ambiguities. Laura Moss Gottlieb of Madison, Wisconsin, who produced a spectacular index for my *Spanish Frontier in North America*, has repeated her performance with *Bárbaros: Spaniards and Their Savages*.

As she has with all of my previous books, my best friend, Carol Bryant Weber, read the final version of the manuscript. It has benefited from the sensibilities she has acquired over the years as a former English teacher, editor, and now attorney. But however much the manuscript has profited from her critical eye, I have gained infinitely more from her love, her intelligence, and her sunny disposition.

A Note on Translation

Translations of quotations in the text are my own, except where the citation is to an English-language source (some Spanish-language documents are available in print only in English). I have tried to translate passages into clear and graceful English without sacrificing what I took to be the author's intention. In so doing, I have taken liberties with individual words and phrases. Those who wish to consult the original Spanish wording can find it in my notes. In general I have modernized spellings and diacritical markings in Spanish-language quotations, although in some cases I have left infelicities in the original Spanish to retain its flavor—as in the words of Alejandro Malaspina, whose native language was not Spanish.

Bárbaros:
Spaniards and Their Savages
in the Age of Enlightenment

Introduction

I want to know, and to write, about the places where disparate
points of view rub together—the spaces between.
Barbara Kingsolver, writer, 1995

In 1794, as he prepared to retire after a decade in office, America's first secretary of war, Henry Knox, deplored the catastrophic results of his countrymen's treatment of Indians. Westward-moving Americans, he said, had brought about "the utter extirpation of nearly all the Indians in the most populous parts of the Union." Along the nation's western borders, Americans continued to encroach on Indian lands, inciting "savages" to retaliate and dragging the United States into wars. His fellow Americans, Knox declared, "have been more destructive to the Indian natives than the . . . conquerors of Mexico and Peru."[1]

Under Knox's direction, the United States had tried to fashion an Indian policy based on conciliation rather than confrontation. Knox believed that Indians themselves, if given the opportunity, would eventually "see the desirability of an end to savagery and their acceptance of civilization."[2] Conciliation had two other advantages over war: it cost less and it would not sully the nation's honor.[3] On the other hand, Knox told one of his generals, if Americans continued to "destroy the tribes, posterity will be apt to class the effects of our Conduct and that of the Spaniards in Mexico and Peru together."[4]

Knox's countrymen would have readily understood his allusion to the Spain of Hernán Cortés and Francisco Pizarro. Like their English and English-American forebears, citizens of the young

1

United States deplored what one Anglophone writer described as the Spaniards' "un-paralleled inhumanity to the unhappy Indian nations they conquered, their extirpation of the inhabitants of whole kingdoms, and other horrid excesses."[5] Spain, then, had long served English speakers as a model to avoid rather than to emulate, but the Spain of the conquistadors had ceased to exist. Throughout the Spanish-American mainland by the 1790s, numerous indigenous peoples had been incorporated rather than eliminated, and most of the Natives who still lived independently along the borders of Spain's American empire had come to some form of accommodation with the Hispanic world, and it with them.

In Knox's day, men imbued with the learning and sensibilities of the Enlightenment governed Spain as they did the United States. Early in the century the tired dynasty of the Habsburgs had yielded to dynamic Bourbons. Beginning with the reign of Felipe V (r. 1700–46), the Bourbons brought fresh ideas from France to make Spain a more unified and prosperous state. To reform public administration they preferred men of ability and knowledge over nobles with pedigrees. Many members of the new governing class had training in the law and deep learning in other disciplines.[6] The economist Pedro Rodríguez Campomanes, the conde de Campomanes (1723–1802), studied Greek, Latin, and Arabic as well as the law. He published works in ancient history, modern history, archaeology, and empirical science and won membership in scholarly academies in Spain and France and in Benjamin Franklin's Philosophical Society of America. Like other Spanish intellectuals of his day, Campomanes knew the influential European books of his era and found good conversation in the salons of Madrid, eventually establishing one of his own.[7] The brilliant, dynamic José de Gálvez, who presided over Spain's American empire as minister of the Indies from 1776 to 1787, overcame his humble birth by distinguishing himself in the law and immersing himself in affairs of state. Although not Campomanes's equal as a scholar, Gálvez possessed an impressive library for his day. It included titles in history, geography, and science. Gálvez's command of French allowed him to read the works of René Descartes and the French encyclopedists in the original and gave him access to works translated into that language, like William Robertson's *History of America* (1777). Harshly critical of Spain as a colonial power, Robertson's *History* occupied a place on the Bourbons' list of prohibited reading, as did some of the other titles in Gálvez's library.[8]

Spain's Bourbon reformers, like their enlightened counterparts elsewhere in Europe and America, hoped to bring about progress by applying the methods of science to society. They streamlined administrative structures, sought ways to promote economic growth, and gathered and analyzed data. Some, like Campomanes and Gálvez, took self-conscious pride in the rationality and spirit of reform of their age. The jurist Victorián Villava understood that he lived "in the most enlightened century" and was informed by "the philosophy . . . of its brilliant writing."[9] Others, like Eugenio Espejo, regretted the limited impact of enlightened ideas. Born in Quito in 1747 to an Indian father and a mulatto mother, Espejo earned degrees in the law and medicine and steeped himself in the ideas of enlightened thinkers, including foreigners like Adam Smith, John Locke, Jean-Jacques Rousseau, and Charles de Secondat, the baron de Montesquieu, and Spaniards such as Benito Jerónimo Feijóo and Gaspar Melchor de Jovellanos. Bitterly disappointed by the slow pace of reform in Spanish America, Espejo turned to writing satire. One of his characters thought it paradoxical to live in what he called "the era of idiocy and . . . the century of ignorance" and yet refer to it as the Age of Enlightenment.[10]

As in other eras, the Age of Enlightenment or the Age of Reason was riven by intellectual crosscurrents. Then as now, data gathered through the use of empirical methods could be read in different ways, and ends could be achieved by different means. One man's rationality might be another's "idiocy." Gálvez, for example, defined Spain's American provinces as "colonies." In 1768, he apparently became the first Spaniard to use the word in an official document. Campomanes, on the other hand, wished to put Spain and its American provinces on an equal footing, erasing the distinction between metropolis and colony. Each man championed a different means toward the same end. Each saw his strategy as the best way to serve Spain's absolutist monarchy and to preserve Spain's position in America.[11]

At the same time that they differed over ideas, Spain's enlightened government ministers jockeyed for political influence for themselves, their regions, and their class. They formed political factions that coalesced and split and rose and fell from power within the enlightened regimes of King Carlos III (r. 1759–88) and his less than able son Carlos IV (r. 1788–1808). Whatever their intellectual and political divergences, however, enlightened Spaniards, like their opposite numbers in Europe and America, shared a belief in the application of reason to society. Nothing was to be taken on faith, except perhaps the faith that rational testing of old assumptions about politics, economics, and society would result in the further progress of humankind.[12]

As they sought to promote progress through reason, enlightened Spanish officials debated the status of the crown's impoverished Indian vassals. Were subjected Indians naturally degraded? or degraded because Spaniards had exploited them? Were Indian vassals naturally inferior and resistant to progress? or inferior and unprogressive because they lacked opportunities? The answers to those questions determined the answers to others. Should Spain's Indian vassals be maintained as a separate class that would provide cheap labor and pay tribute? Or would Indians be more productive if they were integrated into Spanish society and enjoyed the same opportunities and incentives as Spaniards? Each path promised to lead to greater economic progress for Spanish America and Spain, and each path had influential supporters among enlightened bureaucrats. Neither proponents of integration nor supporters of segregation, however, could translate their principles into enduring policy. The crown had the authority to end the impasse but vacillated and left the question unresolved. In the end, pragmatism and power usually prevailed over ideas. Spanish officials were no more consistent in acting on their convictions than Virginia planters who deplored slavery but held onto their own slaves.[13]

Although they disagreed about the best way to incorporate Indians, enlightened

1. Carlos III, 1784. Retrato de S.M. el Rey
Carlos III, *oil by Mariano Salvador Maella.*
Courtesy, Patrimonio Nacional, Madrid.

Spaniards like Victorián Villava believed they lived in an age of "equality and fraternity" that required humane treatment of Indians.[14] Spaniards could not "impose respect with force, nor achieve it with fear," Miguel Lastarria wrote in 1804. A Peruvian-born doctor of sacred law and legal advisor to the viceroy of the Río de la Plata, the marqués de Avilés, Lastarria rejected the past use of force against Indians as counterproductive: "Only with kindness, impartiality, and good faith can we achieve peace and commerce with the fiercest and most valiant Indians . . . and conduct to the contrary will change the most languid and timid . . . into ferocious Indians."[15]

Enlightened Spaniards resented outdated depictions of their cruel, dagger-carrying countrymen conquering Indians with dogs in a "sea of blood" (as they were represented in a book written at the time of the American Revolution by an anonymous author pretending to be an aggrieved Iroquois Indian).[16] In the late eighteenth century, the Spanish crown and the Inquisition launched a counteroffensive against writers who disparaged

Spain's sixteenth-century conquest of America, suggesting that the Indian population of America was low and denying that a holocaust had occurred. The Spanish polymath Félix de Azara, who candidly described the age of Cortés and Pizarro as a "backward time," wondered why other countries continued to vilify Spain for its treatment of Indians. Among European powers, Azara observed, only Spain had embraced "millions of civilized and savage Indians" within its colonial society, transformed an "infinity" of Indians into Spaniards through racial mixture, and adopted "a voluminous code of laws in which every sentence and every word breathe an admirable humanity and grant Indians full protection."[17] Other European nations had driven Natives off their lands, the conde de Campomanes noted, but Spain had transformed them into useful subjects.[18]

If Campomanes intended to draw an unfavorable comparison with the British colonies, he was on the mark. Incorporated Indians constituted over half of the population of the colonized areas of Spanish America, but Indians amounted to less than 6 percent of the population of English America east of the Mississippi in 1770.[19] The nature and numbers of Indians that Englishmen and Spaniards encountered in their respective parts of America help explain this stark contrast, but so too does the behavior of the colonists themselves. Initially, all the colonial powers intended to turn Indians into Europeans and incorporate them peacefully. In practice, however, Englishmen proved less interested than Spaniards in converting or intermarrying with Indians. Englishmen tended to exclude Indians from their society; Spaniards to include them.[20]

Prior to 1700, the Habsburg dynasty had enforced Spain's humane and paternalistic laws unevenly, never resolving the tension between its wish to protect Indians and its interest in exploiting Indian labor. After 1700, Bourbon Spain narrowed, but never closed, the still sizable gap between policy and practice. During the reign of the most American-oriented of Spain's enlightened despots, Carlos III, the Bourbons' administrative reforms began to be felt intensely in Spanish America. Carlos III filled the Council of the Indies, which governed American affairs, with men who had firsthand knowledge of America.[21] Like their British counterparts of the 1760s and 1770s, Bourbon officials took measures to strengthen the colonial system and make it more efficient, secure, and profitable for the mother country. In Spanish America, however, the Bourbon reformers continued their work until the 1810s, when Spain's American colonies began to slip away—a generation after England had lost most of hers.

The Bourbon reforms reached to the very edges of Spain's colonies, affecting even Indians who lived beyond Spanish political control. In the late eighteenth century, the borderlands of the Spanish Empire acquired heightened strategic importance as they gained the attention of Spain's European rivals or, in the case of North America after 1783, the young United States. Bourbon officials hoped to consolidate political control over some of those strategic frontiers, secure them from Indian raiders and foreign interlopers, and make them more productive.[22] Accordingly, Carlos III sent a wave of trained scientists and explorers to gather intelligence about resources, geography, and peoples in the poorly understood spaces beyond the edges of the empire. He also sent professional bureaucrats to reform the two traditional frontier institutions—the military and the missions—promote civilian settlements, foster economic development, and forge alliances with Native leaders who wielded local power.

To oversee frontier defense and development, the Bourbons established new administrative structures. In the single year of 1776, New Spain's northern frontier, once governed entirely by the viceroy in Mexico City, became a semiautonomous *comandancia general* under the authority of a military commander; much of today's Argentina, Uruguay, Paraguay, and the mineral rich area of Upper Peru (in today's Bolivia) were separated administratively from Lima and placed under a new viceroyalty, with its seat in Buenos Aires on the Río de la Plata. In that same year a half dozen provinces along the northern coast of South America were consolidated fiscally into the *intendencia* of Venezuela, with its headquarters in Caracas, and then refashioned politically and militarily as the *capitanía general* of Venezuela in 1777. Chile, governed from distant Lima by the viceroy of Peru, acquired greater autonomy as a *capitanía general* in 1778. These efforts to consolidate control over peripheral areas support the contention of some scholars that the Bourbon reforms represented a "revolution in government" that led to the "second conquest of America" and may better exemplify an effective "reconquest" than did reforms in the empire's heartlands.[23]

In the *un*conquered lands beyond the edges of empire, however, there could be no *re*conquest. Autonomous Indians inhabited those lands and had embarked on their own experiments at political, economic, and military reorganization. Some societies of independent Indians had forged commercial relations with Spaniards, thus obtaining European goods through peaceful means. Other Natives societies, each for their own reasons, favored the use of force. The latter raided Spanish farms and ranches, destroyed Spanish property, took Spanish lives, and blocked the arteries of commerce that kept the empire alive. In the area of the Río de la Plata alone, the French explorer Louis-Antoine de Bougainville observed in 1767, "wild Indians" were so numerous that Spaniards could not subjugate them. They stole Spanish livestock and attacked haciendas and caravans, capturing those Spaniards they did not kill. "These Indians are brave, warlike, and the time has passed," Bougainville observed, "when a single Spaniard can make a thousand Indians flee."[24] But Spaniards did retaliate or launch provocative sorties of their own into Indian territories. By the mid-1700s, many of Spain's American frontiers had become the scene of endless raids and counterraids. Periods of conflict alternated with times of peace and accommodation, to be sure, but as in other empires around the globe, the edges of the Spanish-American empire were more violent than its heartlands. Violence, one historian has reminded us, characterizes frontiers "where rival groups, tribes, nations, and states meet and compete for resources and space."[25]

The most progressive Bourbon officials hoped to bring peace to the ragged edges of empire by replacing war with commerce, colonists, and diplomacy. Like Henry Knox,

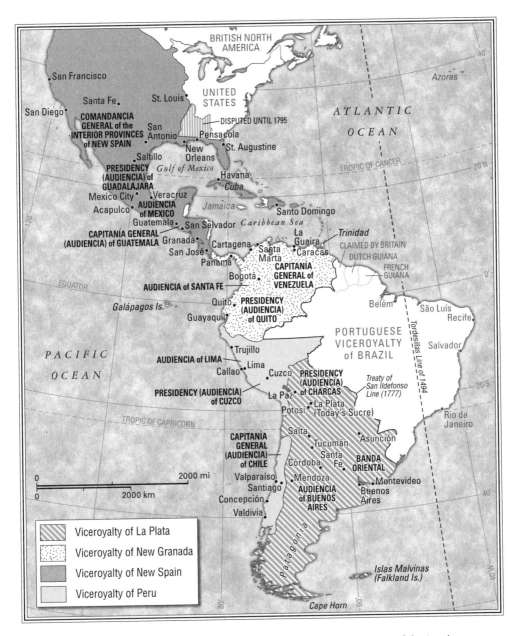

Map 1. Spanish America, 1783. Although independent Indians controlled most of the Americas, state societies created political jurisdictions and drew boundaries through their territories as if they did not exist. In the Treaty of San Ildefonso of 1777, Spanish and Portuguese negotiators recognized the irrelevancy of the last great Spanish-Portuguese division of America in 1494, the Treaty of Tordesillas. In North America, the Mississippi became Spain's boundary with the newly independent United States by terms of the treaties of Paris of 1783, but Spain also emerged from those negotiations with both of the Floridas, thus giving it control of both sides of the lower Mississippi. Adapted from Brading, 1984, 398.

these Spanish officials believed that peaceful means of neutralizing peoples they called savages would be less costly than war and, in the long run, more effective and humane. Also like Knox, however, they could not fully control their more aggressive countrymen, some of them military officers, who preferred war to peace.

Following Spain's initial military conquests of the early 1500s, the task of moving into new Indian territory and bringing Natives under Spanish control had fallen heavily on missionaries. The Bourbons continued the Habsburg policy of relying on missionaries to pacify Indians, but where Indians proved especially resistant to missionaries' initiatives, liberal policymakers believed that merchandise would be more likely to win Natives' allegiance than would promises of salvation. In some places, Spain turned to private merchants to control Indians through trade. In other areas, it relied on military officers to serve as Indian agents and to enter into treaties of friendship and commerce with Indians.

Trade and treaties do not fit the image Knox and his contemporaries had of Spanish policy toward so-called savages. Neither do they fit the image still projected by some North American scholars who tend to regard Spanish policy toward Indians as timeless. "To a large extent, the major outlines of the Spanish program for civilizing the Indians remained the same from the early 1600's to the early 1800's," one respected specialist has observed.[26] "Despite tactical shifts," another scholar has noted, "Spanish grand strategy on the frontier ossified during the colonial period. . . . Over the centuries, Spanish officials seemingly forgot little and learned little."[27] These and other familiar oversimplifications resonate through our literature: the idea that the Indian policy of England and France "was based on trade . . . and Spain's was based on the vain hope of mass conversion to Catholicism";[28] the generalization that "a logic of territorial conquest rather than economic exploitation underpinned the subjection of frontier indigenes and posited their social exclusion, that is, their extermination or segregation";[29] the notion that "there were no Spanish-Indian treaties";[30] and the commonplace comparison that "while the French sought a consensual 'alliance' with the natives, Spaniards sought submission. Even the most benevolent methods of enacting Spanish authority *never* sought consent from natives."[31]

Spanish policymakers of the late colonial period did in fact seek consent from Natives. Following the enlightened formula of the late 1700s, military officers who governed frontier zones often courted autonomous Indians with gifts, generous terms of trade, and friendly alliances even as they strengthened their own military position. In some documents of the era, discussions of trade, diplomacy, and gentle treatment of Indians are so pervasive that one might conclude, as did one historian, that Bourbon policy represented a "reaffirmation of the [crown's] policy of peaceful conquest."[32]

It would be a mistake, however, to assume that the Bourbons embraced a single Indian policy. In hawkish military circles the newly popular discourse of trade and diplomacy did not replace the language of all-out war. Thus, even as some Bourbon officers extended the olive branch, others moved vigorously to meet violence with violence and to end

Indian raids by killing or exiling Indian raiders. In the Age of Reason even the hierarchical and professionalized Spanish military spoke with many voices.

The Spanish military represented one of several competing interest groups, each divided into reformers and defenders of the status quo, who shaped and reshaped Indian policy into the twilight years of the Spanish Empire.[33] Spain's enlightened despots, operating from the empire's peninsular center and possessed of unprecedented regal power, did not so much dictate policies as negotiate them in ongoing dialogues with their own colonial subjects—ecclesiastics, military officers, bureaucrats, common folk, and elites. Indeed, local oligarchs and officers close to the scene often had a greater impact on policy than did Bourbon officials in Madrid. A Franciscan in Chile, Francisco Javier Alday, discovered this to his sorrow in 1804 when he tried to forward a petition to Spain to reverse a series of local decisions that had gone against him. Fray Francisco had hoped government officials would force obdurate Araucanians into missions, but the governor of Valdivia, the intendant of Concepción, and the *audiencia* of Santiago all denied his request. Fray Francisco then asked a royal inspector to send his petition on to Spain. The inspector replied that it would not be wise "because the Council of the Indies cannot make any determination without asking for a report from the government of Chile, which will have to defend its decisions, and what will come of that? More damage than advantage. . . . With patience, that which cannot be done in one year can be done in another, and that which cannot be done during one administration can be done during another."[34]

The Spanish crown itself, then, was just one of several players in the formulation and implementation of Indian policy. In this respect, absolutist Spain resembled other early modern states, including the United States, whose governments could not control the actions of local officials or individual frontiersmen.[35] When it came to dictating the way a society would relate to independent Indians, enlightened despots were no more successful than republicans.

If a variety of Spanish interest groups remained in lively and often tense conversation about the nature of Indian policy, independent Indians shaped their conversation in a number of ways. Some Indians succumbed to a handful of soldiers and a few missionaries, suggesting the efficacy of peaceful conquests. Some had sufficient power to force Spaniards to abandon all efforts to conquer them. Some independent Natives, particularly those with access to guns and ammunition from Spain's rivals, could make Spaniards pay tribute to them and to recognize their autonomy—that is, to invert the relationship that Europeans imagined as proper and normal. The policies Spaniards employed toward independent Indians depended as much on Indian responses as on Spanish initiatives, and Indians often took the initiative, forcing Spaniards to respond.

In places where independent Indians found it in their interest to cooperate with Spaniards and where Spaniards found peaceful relations more valuable than conquests, conciliation prevailed over conflict. One such place was the broad region where Spain's colonial empire bordered the young United States. After 1783, Spain and the United

Map 2. *Disputed Spanish-American borderlands, 1783–95. Spain acquired the Floridas from Britain in the treaties of Paris of 1783, but the treaties failed to specify West Florida's northern boundary. Spain claimed that it extended at least to 32° 28', at present Vicksburg. Spain also asserted that East Florida extended to the Ohio and Tennessee rivers by virtue of Spain's successful military operations against the British in that region during the American Revolution. The United States, heir to British claims, put the border at the 31st parallel, which had once separated British West Florida from Indian territory. The dispute ended in 1795 when Spain abandoned its claims to the area north of the 31st parallel. Map adapted from Weber, 1992, 277.*

States vied with one another for control over a large zone that stretched across present-day Mississippi, Alabama, and Georgia. In that disputed territory each tried to win the allegiance of Indian leaders, and Indian leaders tried to profit from their rivalry. As Spaniards understood it, the southeastern tribes had developed an "irreconcilable hatred" toward Anglo-Americans, who were "waging a cruel and continual war [against the Indians] in order to penetrate the country and advance their settlements."[36] The high point of Spanish–Indian diplomacy in this region came in the fall of 1793, when Spanish agents brought representatives of the Cherokees, Chickasaws, Choctaws, and Creeks to the Spanish fort of Nogales (today's Vicksburg, Mississippi). There the tribal leaders formed an alliance and swore "to contribute . . . to the preservation of [Spain's] dominion throughout all the provinces of Louisiana and both Floridas."[37] Spain, however, quickly lost the advantage. Struggles with France (1793–96) and Britain (1796–1802 and 1804–8) diverted Spain's attention and resources to Europe, left its navy in shambles, and crippled its ability to govern its American colonies.

Before things fell apart, Spain's influence over independent Indians had caused Henry Knox considerable concern during his tenure as secretary of war, but he probably knew little about the policies or practices of his Spanish counterparts anywhere in the hemisphere except in North America. Americans of his day had scanty information about the internal workings of the Spanish Empire. Indeed, what most Americans knew about Spanish relations with Indians began and ended with the conquistadors. Stories of Columbus's discoveries and the sensational conquests of Mexico and Peru captured the American imagination and reinforced a strong anti-Hispanic and anti-Catholic strain in American thought. Over the intervening centuries, however, Spain and Spanish Americans seemed to have taken a long siesta. "Naturally weak and effeminate," one popular American schoolbook of the 1790s observed, "[Spaniards] dedicate the greatest part of their lives to loitering and inactive pleasures."[38]

Today, although American scholars have moved beyond such caricatures, and their knowledge of the Spanish Empire runs broad and deep, most historians of Spanish–Indian relations have overlooked the impact on Indians of Bourbon Spain's enlightened reforms. The most important exceptions are studies of two dramatic episodes that involved Indians living under Spanish control: the expulsion of the Jesuits in 1767 and the great Andean revolts of Tupac Amaru and others in the early 1780s.[39] Instead, students of Spanish–Indian relations have focused on the Habsburg era and have sought to explain how a small number of Europeans prevailed over numerous Native Americans. These historians have described the roles of disease, of weaponry, and the articulations of European and Indian political, economic, and cultural systems; they have demonstrated how Europeans and incorporated Indians came to understand and misunderstand each other; they have examined relations of power and the variety of ways in which conquered Indians responded to the exigencies of Spanish rule.[40]

This book looks at the late Bourbon era and draws from a different historical literature, much of it written by Latin Americans in the past few decades.[41] It leaves behind the familiar worlds of conquered and incorporated Indians and their descendants—those Indians whom Spaniards knew as *indios sometidos, reducidos, tributarios,* or *domésticos.* It directs our gaze beyond the roads that connected Spanish towns, villages, missions, and haciendas to the less explored terrain where Spaniards met unconquered Indians: *indios no sometidos.* These frontiers, it would appear, had more in common with one another than with the colonial core regions with which one usually associates them.[42]

Although Spaniards had annihilated Indians on the major Caribbean islands, replacing them with laborers from black Africa, in the late 1700s independent Indians still held effective dominion over at least half of the actual land mass of what is today continental Latin America, from Tierra del Fuego to present-day Mexico.[43] North of Mexico, in the vast expanses claimed by Spain but now in the United States, independent Indians also held substantial territory. Comanches alone dominated most of the southern plains, a region of some 240,000 square miles, larger than all of Central America (see map 6).[44]

The number of Indians who lived independently within territories claimed by Spain remained substantial two centuries after Spain's conquest of America.[45] Initially, European diseases, particularly smallpox, had penetrated far beyond areas visited by Spaniards and had carried away high percentages of Natives on the peripheries of the empire—perhaps as high as 90 percent in areas of sustained contact. During the eighteenth century, however, Indian populations began to stabilize or rise, partly because Indians acquired greater immunities to disease. One scholar estimates that by the late eighteenth century independent Indians numbered perhaps 2,700,000, which would represent nearly 22 percent of the total population of what was then the Spanish-American mainland.[46] His estimate is low, however, for it does not include independent Indians living in Chile, along the Caribbean coast of Central America from Darién to Honduras, and in the area of the present-day United States that then lay within the Spanish Empire. In comparison, the number of Indians who resided along the western borders of the United States in the late 1700s seems paltry. Knox estimated their fighting force at 15,000 to 16,000.[47]

Clearly, Spain had not completed the conquest of America in the Age of Conquest. Two and a half centuries after Columbus's discovery, Spain continued to claim dominion over peoples it neither conquered nor knew, basing those claims on the so-called papal donation of 1493 that divided the non-European world between the Spanish and Portuguese crowns. The Spanish author of the impressive *Atlas geográphico de la América* (1758), for example, described the district of Mainas, on the eastern slope of the Andes in the Audiencia of Quito, in these terms: "The extent of this jurisdiction is not presently known because it borders upon various undiscovered lands inhabited by wild Indians." Nonetheless, "savages," "wild Indians," and "ferocious and indomitable [Indian] nations" appear in this atlas as residents of virtual Spanish territories, together with lions, tigers, and crocodiles.[48]

Bárbaros: Spaniards and Their Savages has nothing to say about lions, tigers, and crocodiles, but it does try to explain Spaniards' attitudes toward and relations with "wild In-

2. *In the late eighteenth century, Spanish artists produced stylized representations of the hierarchy in the racially mixed colonial society. These "casta paintings" usually presented races and racial mixtures in sixteen panels, with "pure-blooded" Spaniards occupying the highest position and "savages," or* indios bárbaros, *at the bottom. The artists included "savages" within the* sociedad de castas, *but by depicting them as semiclothed and with few material possessions, the artists made clear that savages inhabited a world apart (Katzew, 2004, 136–37, 146–47). Yndios Bárbaros/ Savage Indians. From O'Crouley, 1972 (first published in 1774), opposite page 115.*

dians" throughout the Americas in the late eighteenth century. The book includes a variety of people and places, from Araucanians in southern Chile to Tlingits in the Pacific Northwest, and from Chiriguanos on the western edge of the Gran Chaco to Comanches on North America's southern plains. Yet it cannot be comprehensive. Like officials in Spain who were overwhelmed by reports from America, I focus on the groups that seem to have had the greatest strategic or economic value for the empire. Some Native peoples inevitably receive short shrift. In North America, for example, I have more to say about Apaches and Comanches than about Osages and Utes. In South America, Araucanians and Pampas have drawn my attention more than Matacos and Mataguayos.

In this panoramic view, then, some people are less sharply drawn than others, but whatever its limitations the larger perspective effectively suggests the immensity and complexity of the frontiers where Spaniards and independent Indians came together in late eighteenth-century America. Historians who have examined Spanish–Indian relations from a purely local perspective have often failed to appreciate the scope and variety of

the challenges that independent Indians posed for Spain's Bourbon rulers, who continued
to hold their American empire for two generations after first France and then England
had lost most of theirs. One American writer, for example, concluded from his understanding of Spain's efforts in North America that Spaniards seemed "flummoxed by practical
tasks" and that Spain "never understood" that sovereignty required the occupation of
land. Spain, he said, represented "a complete failure."[49] Had he placed North America
in the context of Spain's entire empire, with its priorities and exigencies, his picture
might have been less bleak.[50]

From Madrid the king and his Council of the Indies looked out over a vast American
empire. From their vantage point, Indians who remained independent in the 1700s often
held the lands with the least economic value, some of it ruggedly mountainous and much
of it drylands and tropical forest, including the present-day American Southwest and
northern Mexico, the Central American lowlands, the Amazon and Orinoco basins, the
Gran Chaco, the pampa, Patagonia, and Tierra del Fuego. As a viceroy of Peru, the
conde de Superunda, explained in the mid-1700s, "The unconquered country is jungle
and mountains, difficult to traverse, and plains are humid, swampy, and hot, and so Spaniards cannot support themselves."[51] Yet ecology, topography, and climate do not fully
explain Spain's failure to conquer these areas. With the right enticements, Spaniards
pushed into forbidding terrain and lived under inhospitable conditions, as in high-altitude
Potosí with its thin, cold air and rich silver mines. The absence of readily exploitable
gold, silver, or other valuable resources, then, as much as the physical environment, dis-
suaded Spaniards from taking control of some areas.[52]

The nature of Native societies in lowland regions and in arid, rugged mountains also
discouraged Spaniards from subduing them, just as it had deterred Native imperialists,
Incas and Aztecs, before the arrival of Europeans. With notable exceptions—such as the
cacao-producing area of Venezuela, the Cauca and Magdalena river valleys in present-
day Colombia, parts of Paraguay, and central Chile south to the Río Biobío—Spaniards
settled for subjugating prosperous highland farmers, whose labor they could exploit and
whose hierarchical governments they could control. Indians who farmed, hunted, or
gathered in marginal lands had little surplus production to exploit, and their small-scale
political organization, usually centering on the family, afforded Spaniards no leaders
through whom they could exercise control. Harsh, sparsely populated lands also contained vast spaces where Indians could often take refuge from Spaniards. The conde de
Superunda expressed a common Spanish view when he described the inhabitants of
such lands as people who "do not cover their nakedness, and their houses are so poor
they lose nothing when they leave them. . . . To conquer them by force always has been
impossible."[53] His judgment, minus the hyperbole, has echoed in the work of modern
social scientists, one of whom has observed that "the simpler and poorer the native sociocultural system, the more difficult it can be [for Europeans] to dominate them effectively
without exterminating them."[54]

To Spaniards of the eighteenth century, Indians who remained unconquered were not simply Indians, or *indios*. Instead, Spaniards described them as wild Indians (*indios bravos*), wild and ignorant Indians (*indios bozales*), heathen Indians (*indios infieles* or *gentiles*), and savage Indians (*indios salvajes* or *indios bárbaros*).[55] These adjectives held diverse meanings for Spaniards, and the meaning of "savage" changed over time.[56] Close observers of Indians, such as the learned Miguel Lastarria, understood that not all *salvajes* were alike. They differed not only in language and culture, but in what he imagined to be their stages of development. In 1804, drawing examples from the viceroyalty of Buenos Aires, he divided Indians into fourteen degrees of progress toward what he called the "adult stage of civilization." Spaniards, of course, occupied the top position, number fifteen. At "the lowest level of rationality" Lastarria put "savages from the lands we have not conquered": Tupis, Charrúas, and Chiriguanos. Wandering Mocobíes and Tobas from the Chaco, who had some dealings with Spaniards, occupied the next highest step. Mbayás, Guanás, and Payaguás, who emerged from the Chaco to work occasionally for Spaniards, stood on the third rung, and Indians whom he termed "savage merchants"— Puelches, Pehuenches, Pampas, and some Patagonians—held the fourth position. Unlike the "savages" in the first four stages, who "had not progressed to the point of declaring in public their recognition of Divine Providence," the remaining Indians were ranked according to the degree to which they had absorbed Christianity and other Spanish ways, beginning with Indians who had accepted baptism but fled the missions and thus became "wild Christians."[57]

While Spanish scholars created taxonomies and examined shades of meaning, in popular parlance Spaniards of the late eighteenth century used *bárbaros, salvajes, bravos,* and *gentiles* interchangeably to describe Amerindians who lived beyond the pale of Christendom. To convey in English what the Spaniards actually meant, I often use the English word *savage* in this book. *Bárbaro,* or "barbarian," translates poorly into English, where it suggests Goths, Ostrogoths, and Vandals. *Gentil,* or "heathen," refers only to the Indians' religious state in relation to Christianity. *Savage,* more than any other word in English, corresponds to the time and place this book examines—as does its Spanish cognate, *salvaje.* As one Spanish savant noted in the 1790s, the word *salvajes,* "taken from the French, *les sauvages,* seems the most suitable for characterizing all tribes not subject to the [Spanish] monarchy."[58]

Spaniards, of course, knew these unsubjugated peoples by the names of specific bands, tribes, or chiefdoms,[59] but outsiders had usually bestowed those names and thus ascribed identities rather than describing them. Picunches in Chile, meaning "people of the north," was clearly coined by Indian peoples who lived to the south of them. Labels indicating a group's geographical location, such as Serranos in Argentina, the mountain people, or the Gileños, "people who live along the Gila River" in Arizona, originated with Spaniards who did not live in those places. Still other ascribed identities referred to the degree to which outsiders perceived a group as hostile or friendly, as with the Aucas (in southern South America) or Comanches (in southwestern North America), whose names meant "enemy" in Quechua and Ute, respectively. Or a name might refer to the appearance of Indians, as in the case of various peoples to the south of Lake Maracaibo in today's Venezuela, whom Spaniards called Motilones (from the Spanish verb *motilar*, "to cut the hair") because, in contrast to their neighbors, they wore their hair cropped short.[60]

Applied to peoples whose own name for themselves was usually "the people," these ethnic labels were often capricious and imprecise as well as counterfeit. Outsiders might give the same people a multiplicity of names or apply the same name to several groups, depending on their physical location or relationship at a given time. Who the "people of the north" were depended on how far south the observers were. The groups themselves, whatever name they went by, generally represented mixtures of people who did not see themselves as the single people that outsiders imagined them to be. As is usually the case, ethnic labels suggest a false sense of ethnic purity or ethnic continuity. People met and mingled, became bilingual or multilingual, and moved in and out of ethnic groups. Athapascan speakers of the eighteenth century, for example, did not all derive from Athapascan stock. Navajos, Athapascans of Apache origin, seem to have absorbed some Pueblos and Paiutes who became Navajos, and the number of Pueblos living among Navajos was so great that one scholar has suggested that Navajos "may have been Puebloans for part of their history."[61] By the eighteenth century, many communities of independent Indians had also incorporated individual Africans and Europeans, along with aspects of their cultures and their genes—racially, but not ethnically, many Indians were, like Spaniards, mixed bloods, or mestizos. Just as they conceal racial and ethnic mixtures, ethnic labels obscure local politics and local identities. By the 1700s, for example, a clear division existed between supposed ethnically pure Miskitos and Zambo-Miskitos who had absorbed black African slaves. Nonetheless, in juxtaposing Indians against Spaniards, I often refer to Miskitos as if they were a single society.

Today many Indian peoples prefer to identify themselves in their own languages, but I have chosen to retain the historical names by which Spaniards knew them and with which modern readers are more likely to be familiar. For example, I use Tarahumaras instead of Rarámuris, Seris instead of Comcáac, Pápagos instead of Tohono O'odhom, Cunas instead of Tules, Guajiros instead of Wayús, Matacos instead of Weenhayek, Guahibos instead of Wayapopihíwis, Chiriguanos instead of Avas, Payaguás instead of Evuevís, and Patagonians rather than Tehuelches.

If the words for Indians and their tribal names require explanation, so does the word *Spaniard*, a label that was also originally applied to them by outsiders and whose meaning, like that of all ethnic markers, depends on context.[62] In the narrowest sense of the word, a Spaniard, or *español*, in eighteenth-century Spanish-American society was a *peninsular*, that is, a person born in Spain of Spanish-born parents, or a *criollo*, a person born in America to Spanish parents. Other words, like *mestizo*, *lobo*, and *coyote*, applied to American-born mixed bloods. Yet all Hispanicized peoples, whatever their place of birth or racial composition, became "Spaniards" when they sought to distinguish themselves from *indios domésticos* or *indios salvajes*. As one missionary wrote in 1788 from the Indian country of Texas, "When I say Spaniard I mean a non-Indian; this is the usage here."[63]

In writing about Spaniards and their savages, I do not mean to imply that these were mutually exclusive groups. Just as the category of Spaniards included acculturated persons of Indian and African ancestry, so, too, did the category of savages include Hispanics and Africans and their descendants who lived among Natives. Moreover, the interests and circumstances of peoples *within* the categories of Spaniards and savages commonly diverged. Each had family loyalties, communities of interests, and ideologies that divided them. Conflict, then, could be intramural as well as extramural. So, too, could cooperation and reciprocity take place within or across ethnic and political boundaries. At the local level, peaceful economic transactions occurred between groups of Spaniards and independent Indians even when their respective societies were at war, and economic relations often result in harmonious social relations.[64]

If the distinctions between Spaniards and independent Indians often blurred, so did the line between *indios domésticos* and *indios bárbaros.* Small communities of Pápagos and Sobaipuris, for example, settled near Tucson in today's Arizona, where they tilled their fields and seemed to submit to the authority of the missionary at nearby San Xavier del Bac. Yet when the time came for harvesting the fields of the mission itself, these "wandering communities," to the dismay of missionaries, returned to the wilds.[65] Tribute-paying Indians in the area of Cochabamba in today's Bolivia appeared to one Spanish official in 1780 to be among "the most civilized," yet he lamented their failure to escape from "barbarism" because they continued to speak their own language and use "their ancient customs and clothing" for fiestas and other celebrations.[66] Along the north coast of present-day Colombia, where independent Chimilas and Guajiros menaced Spanish shipping up the Río Magdalena, tribute-paying Indians from the town of Talaigua posed as savages, "disguised with feathers and colors," to rob and murder Spaniards.[67] Spaniards and independent Indians, then, can be understood only in the plural. Their relations with and among one another took many forms, changing with time and circumstance.

It has become a cliché to note that modern efforts to reconstruct Native peoples' histories are highly imperfect. Most of what we know of eighteenth-century Amerindians has come to us through the haze of linguistic and cultural assumptions of non-Indians. In the time and place that I treat, the one-sided written record contains much about Indians whom Spaniards incorporated into their society but relatively little about Indians who remained independent on the margins of the Spanish Empire.[68] I make no claim, then, to write Indian history. I cannot illuminate Indian societies from within or confidently explain events or processes from the manifold cultural and material perspectives of a great variety of Native peoples, some of whom comprehended reality in ways quite foreign to the Western rationalism that has shaped my own thinking.[69] Thus, although I write at a time when, as the historian J. H. Elliott lamented, "the observed have been accorded a privileged status that has been denied their observers," I unfashionably focus more on the record-keeping observers than on the observed.[70]

If my sources are largely those of the record-keeping observers, I hope my interpretation of those sources is not entirely Eurocentric. This is a story of relationships. I try to explain how the actions of people Europeans called savages shaped Spaniards' policies and behaviors, as well as how Spaniards' actions shaped the policies and behaviors of independent Indians. Throughout I have tried to follow the wise advice of the ethno-historian James Axtell, "to give proper agency" to Indians and non-Indians alike "without minimizing or ignoring the constraints of power, culture, and biology within which both groups operated."[71]

1

Savants, Savages, and New Sensibilities

*Happy will they be if content with the situation in which
Nature placed them, without enmity with their neighbors, without
disputes over property, and free from the ambition that torments
cultured Europe, they live for a long time in peaceful state
the beneficent Mother of Morals granted them.*
Report from the Malaspina expedition, 1791, speaking of
Chumash Indians in California

*. . . wandering through the forests, without enlightenment,
without religion, given over to the impulse of their passions
and the misery of savage life.*
Anonymous report of the *Sutil* and *Mexicana*, 1792,
describing California Indians

In September 1788, within months of his return from an arduous
two-year voyage around the world, Alejandro Malaspina, a young
Spanish naval officer, made plans to circle the globe again. This
time, instead of serving as captain of a single ship on an errand,
he hoped to lead a scientific and commercial reconnaissance. With
a colleague five years his junior, José Bustamante y Guerra, the
thirty-four-year-old Malaspina composed a "Plan of a Scientific
and Political Voyage around the World." They drew inspiration
from the voyages of the Englishman James Cook and the Frenchman Conte de La Pérouse, whose recent discoveries had enriched
understanding of human and natural history.[1]

The plan won the immediate support of the Spanish crown, which put Malaspina and Bustamante in command of two newly built corvettes. The two commanders hired scientists, artists, officers, and crew and stocked the vessels with books, manuscripts, and scientific equipment. On July 30, 1789, the corvettes set sail from Cádiz, each carrying 102 men. Instead of bearing the names of saints, as Spanish vessels often did, the identical three-masted corvettes bore distinctly secular names—the *Atrevida* (the audacious) and the *Descubierta* (the act of scanning the horizon at sunrise and sunset)—perhaps in homage to Captain Cook's *Resolution* and *Adventure*. The Spanish commanders planned a voyage of three and a half years, but five years passed before they returned to Cádiz. Circumstances prevented them from circling the globe, as intended, but in all they traveled an even greater distance. They traced the Pacific coast of the Americas from Chile to Alaska and explored a number of South Pacific islands before returning to South America and recrossing the Atlantic to Spain. It was Spain's most ambitious scientific expedition in the Age of Reason.[2]

Malaspina Among the Savages

The Malaspina expedition, known by the name of its meticulous architect, reflected the most sophisticated thinking of the age. It set out at a time when intellectuals, under the influence of Enlightenment thought, questioned the authority of ancient texts and sought knowledge based on observable evidence. The measuring and inventorying of artifacts, the taking of plant and animal specimens, and the describing of people in their natural and social worlds had become the rage among enlightened intellectuals. Colonial governments sponsored this scientific work in the expectation it would produce economic and political benefits. Thus, Malaspina's expedition surveyed the natural world —its geography, geology, astronomy, botany, and zoology. More intensely than any other Spanish scientific expedition of its day, Malaspina's party also studied the characteristics and needs of humankind, seeking information that might make Spain's overseas colonies more profitable.

American Indians held special interest for Malaspina, as they did for other enlightened Europeans.[3] As he saw them, Indians in America fell into two broad categories: those who had submitted to Spaniards and those who had not. In the second group, he included Patagonians of southern Argentina, Araucanians on the southern edge of Chile, and Indian "nations" that bordered on the United States and Canada, nations "whose speeches, ideas, and customs indicate their civil principles."[4] These independent Native Americans gave Malaspina an opportunity to study humanity in what he perceived to be its earliest stage of development, close to a state of nature. Out of his brief stays among these peoples came lasting contributions to ethnography and ethnology, studies which also reveal much about the ways educated Spaniards of Malaspina's day understood themselves and their society.[5]

In diaries, Malaspina and several of his scientists, artists, and well-schooled officers

Map 3. Malaspina in America, 1789–91. Adapted from Higueras, 1988b, 149.

recorded their observations about the language and customs of independent Indians. In his final report, Malaspina summarized or quoted from those diaries and from published and unpublished sources he consulted along the way. Much of what Malaspina had to say about Indians was, as he noted, "a compilation of the works of others, rather than an original work."[6] In this sense, Malaspina's report represented a distillation of the conventional wisdom of educated Spaniards of his day.

Typical of intellectuals of their age, members of Malaspina's cosmopolitan team had eclectic interests.[7] Malaspina himself was born into a noble family in the Italian duchy of Parma in what would become Italy, and he was raised in the Spanish Bourbon kingdom of Sicily. He studied physics at an elite school in Rome, where his empirical training included ample exposure to major writers of the Enlightenment, including Voltaire. In 1774, at the age of twenty, he moved to Spain. There he entered Spain's proud navy and broadened his training at the elite midshipmen's school in Cádiz, the Escuela de Guardiamarinas.

3. Alejandro Malaspina. Profile by Bartolomé Maura,
from Malaspina, 1885.

An inquisitive and ambitious junior officer, Malaspina continued to read widely in the sciences, literature, and economics after his formal training ended. He sought knowledge, he told a friend, "of the Creator, of man, and of the environment he inhabits."[8] In Cádiz he taught a weekly seminar for young officers and studied works in French and English —including those banned by the Inquisition but readily available in that port city.

The Royal Navy stood at the forefront of Spanish science in Malaspina's day. Its energetic director, Antonio Valdés, who served as secretary of the navy as well as head of the office in charge of Spain's American colonies, had personally promoted scientific training for naval officers. Some of the officer-scientists who served on Malaspina's expedition, notably José Espinosa and Dionisio Alcalá Galiano, benefited from that training.[9] Other Spanish scientists who served under Malaspina received their schooling outside naval circles. Lt. Antonio de Pineda, for example, one of the expedition's naturalists, studied in the French-inspired Real Seminario de Nobles in Madrid, where the works of Descartes, Newton, Copernicus, and Leibnitz first came to his attention. After entering the Spanish royal guard, Lieutenant Pineda continued his studies in mathematics,

4. Puerto Deseado, as depicted by the expedition's artist, José del Pozo, 1789. Vista del Puerto Deseado, *a watercolor, from Carril, 1964, plate 15, original in the Colección de Bonifacio del Carril, Argentina [Colección Bauzá, I-14] (Sotos Serrano, 1982, 2:22).*

anatomy, physics, chemistry, and natural history, and the languages necessary to read what non-Spaniards had to say about those subjects, including Latin, Italian, French, and English.[10] Some of Malaspina's scientists received training abroad, notably the French-born botanist Luis Née and the Bohemian naturalist Tadeo Haenke—both of whom missed the boats' sailing from Cádiz but caught up with the expedition in America. Nearly all of Malaspina's scientists studied in Europe rather than in America. Even Lt. Francisco Xavier de Viana, born in Montevideo and raised in Buenos Aires, received his naval training in Spain, where his parents sent him at the age of ten. Viana, who served as one of Malaspina's principal diarists, would return to Uruguay in the early 1800s to fight Indians and Portuguese and become a hero of Uruguayan independence.[11]

In the summer of 1789, the *Atrevida,* commanded by Bustamante, and the *Descubierta,* commanded by Malaspina, crossed the Atlantic to Montevideo, on the north shore of the great estuary of the Río de La Plata. From there, the corvettes traveled south to the mouth of the Río Deseado, the site of a short-lived Spanish military colony (1780–81) on the Patagonian coast more than a thousand miles from Buenos Aires. The explorers had arrived in early December, toward the beginning of South America's summer, at a place where Spain's presence lay lightly on the land.

Spain believed that all of Atlantic Patagonia, the area below the Río Negro to the Strait of Magellan, fell within its political jurisdiction, but Spaniards had scarcely penetrated this stark, dry coast. A map commissioned by Madrid just three years before noted that the Patagonian interior was "inhabited by various nations of Indians, barbarous and ignorant of Spaniards."[12] Nonetheless, some Patagonians had direct contact with small

5. The expedition's artist, José del Pozo, painting a Patagonian girl, 1789. José del Pozo, sepia wash. From Carril, 1964, plate 17, who identified it as residing in the Colección of Germán Vergara Donoso, in Chile. Its present location is unknown (Sotos Serrano, 1982, 2:24, fig. 38).

groups of Spaniards at the fort of Nuestra Señora del Carmen at the mouth of the Río Negro, at Puerto Deseado, and at several other temporary Spanish outposts on their coast. Patagonians, Malaspina learned, also had indirect contact with Spaniards beyond the Andes in Chile by way of independent Indians whom he understood to be Huilliches.[13]

Malaspina sought out a small band of Patagonians in the hope of observing them first-hand. Before he left Spain, Malaspina's reading had led him to conclude that Patagonians were "wanderers but civilized nonetheless," and so he found them, a people so generous, affable, and peaceful they did not deserve "the old name of savages."[14] Initial encounters were peaceful. Indians and Spaniards sat in a circle, he said, and "suspicion began to give way to the desire, innate in man, to want to know more about his fellow man."[15] The Spaniards presented the Patagonians with gifts, asked them about their customs, and took notes on their vocabulary. Although the Bourbons had pushed vigorously to make Castilian the lingua franca of America and slowly eradicate Indian languages, savants of that era continued Spain's long tradition of compiling Native vocabularies. Like other forward-thinking Europeans, they believed that by studying languages they would understand more clearly the prehistory of nations and that relationships between languages offered clues about the origins of man.[16]

6. *The cacique Junchar, whom Pineda measured,*
holding his cape in his left hand and a walking stick
in his right. A pencil drawing by José del Pozo, 1789,
entitled El Cacique Junchar. *From Carril, 1964,*
plate 16, and original in the Colección de Bonifacio
del Carril, Argentina [Colección Bauzá, tomo II-95].
(Sotos Serrano, 1982, 2:25).

Earlier European visitors had described Patagonians as giants.[17] They were, Malaspina told a fellow scientist, "of considerable importance for the history of the propagation of the human species."[18] He promised to describe them with "accuracy, as the present state of philosophical science in Europe should demand."[19] Reflecting the empirical impulse of the era, Antonio de Pineda took the measurements of one Junchar, whose age Spaniards estimated at sixty. The expedition's artist, José del Pozo, sketched a standing Junchar and then apparently painted his portrait (see figs. 6, 10).[20]

In mid-December, Malaspina set sail from Puerto Deseado, taking a detour to inspect the Islas Malvinas (also known today as the Falkland Islands) before rounding Cape Horn into the Pacific. He had another chance to observe independent Indians when his vessels dropped anchor on February 5, 1790, at the little port of San Carlos (today's

7. *An oil painting of the son of Catiguala, an independent Huilliche chief, attributed to the artist José del Pozo, 1789. Courtesy, Museo Naval, Madrid (A-642). In December 1792, three years after Malaspina's visit, Catiguala's son returned to Chiloé, following a Huilliche uprising against Spaniards on the mainland, on the Río Bueno. Spanish forces from Valdivia, led by Capt. Tomás Figueroa, took reprisals by marching deep into Huilliche country, killing rebel leaders, burning houses and fields, and taking women and children captive. Catiguala and his son demonstrated their loyalty to the Spaniards and escaped Figueroa's wrath by agreeing to his demand that they cede lands around the long-abandoned Spanish town of Osorno. Catiguala then sent his son to guide one of Figueroa's officers to Chiloé with the news. Figueroa, 1884, 49–54.*

Ancud) on the north end of Isla Grande de Chiloé, a mountainous, rain-soaked island of forests and fjords. Spaniards had conquered the island's native Huilliche population in the sixteenth century, but during Malaspina's stay a delegation of independent Huilliches who lived on the mainland south of Valdivia had come to San Carlos to visit the Spanish governor. An Araucanian-speaking people of ferocious appearance, the Huilliches impressed Lt. Francisco Viana as "warlike by necessity." A "free, independent, and happy nation" before Spaniards enslaved them in the sixteenth century, as Viana put it, the Huilliches had regained their freedom by bringing "destruction, desolation, and death" to Spaniards.[21] Now, to maintain the right to pass through Huilliche lands en route to Valdivia on the mainland, Spaniards needed to pay tribute to the Huilliches. The governor at San Carlos saluted the arriving delegation with cannon fire, gave them gifts, and negotiated with them through their interpreter. In contrast to these independent mainland Huilliches, the Christianized Huilliches and other converted Indians on the islands, who numbered 11,794 according to a Franciscan census, seemed lazy, stupid, servile, thieving, alcoholic, and licentious to Viana. The "crudeness" of the native Chilotes made them easy victims for rapacious local officials, whose behavior scandalized the expeditionaries. The impoverished Chilotes had become "imprisoned in their own country."[22]

After two weeks on Chiloé, Malaspina sailed northward, stopping at Pacific ports. His itinerary made it unlikely he would encounter more independent Indians before setting out across the Pacific to Hawaii. At the Mexican port of Acapulco, however, surprising new instructions diverted the expedition to Alaskan waters. The crown ordered Malaspina to inspect a newly established Spanish military post on Vancouver Island and investigate rumors that a water route crossed the far northern reaches of the North American continent. Spain feared that Britain had discovered and would monopolize this long-sought waterway, known to the British as the Northwest Passage and to the Spaniards as the Strait of Anián or the Strait of Juan de Fuca.

Although geopolitical concerns had changed the expedition's itinerary, science would still benefit. At Yakutat Bay in Alaska and at Nootka Sound on Vancouver Island, Malaspina's expeditionaries had the opportunity to study Indians who not only lived beyond European overlords, but had little prior contact with Europeans.

Leaving a small detachment of officers and scientists to investigate the heartland of New Spain, Malaspina set sail from Acapulco on May 1, 1791, heading directly for Alaska. A Spanish atlas, published a generation earlier, imagined that in that region there existed the Province of Anián, whose "inhabitants have neither law nor religion, nor do they have any town, and it is a little-known land."[23] The twin corvettes put in first at Yakutat Bay, where the native Tlingits at Port Mulgrave had only recently encountered Europeans. As the Spanish vessels approached Port Mulgrave, Tlingits raced out in canoes to meet them. Dressed in skins, their faces painted "in the ordinary custom of all savages," and their hair covered with grease and red ochre, the Tlingits presented a wild aspect. As they drew close to the *Atrevida* and *Descubierto* the Tlingits rose to their feet. One shouted

8. On Vancouver Island, Spaniards set up camp at Cala de los Amigos, remembered yet today as Friendly Cove. In this ink-and-wash drawing, the artist Tomás Suria shows the tents on the beach that housed observatory equipment and Nootka women and Spaniards watching male Nootkas dance. Courtesy, Museo Naval, Madrid [MS 1723–7].

a signal, and the Indians raised their arms and began to sing.[24] Spaniards found the Native music agreeable but possessed of a "savage character, more appropriate for arousing passions of war than for stirring sweet and tender sentiments."[25] Realizing, however, that the Tlingits offered song as a sign of peace, the Spaniards returned song with song.[26]

In contrast to the small bands of Patagonians and Huilliches whom the explorers had to seek out, Tlingits vastly outnumbered the Spaniards and approached them to trade. Skilled woodworkers and sculptors, like other peoples of the Northwest Coast, Tlingits lived in wooden houses, fished from great canoes dug out of red cedar, and enjoyed a rich material and ceremonial life. To the Spaniards, Tlingits also seemed unpredictable, given to theft, and warlike—characteristics that Malaspina and his scientists sought to explain. Why, for example, did Tlingits value warfare when they lived in a land of abundance? Although Tlingits did not need to fight to expand their territory, the scientists hypothesized, they did need to defend it, and that led them to place a premium on war.[27] The wary Spaniards took their own defensive precautions. Malaspina issued stern orders against provoking Indians. When he tried to intimidate them with displays of firearms, the "warlike" Tlingits again responded by singing.[28]

Leaving Mulgrave after ten days, the Malaspina expedition continued north to Prince William Sound to search for the Strait of Anián. Seldom touching land, the expeditionaries did not resume their study of Northwest Coast Natives until they returned south and dropped anchor on August 10 at Nootka Sound on Vancouver Island's west coast. There, Spain had established the military post of Santa Cruz de Nutka just two years before. Since its discovery in 1774 by Juan Pérez, English and American mariners had frequented the sound, making it a focal point for a profitable European sea otter trade with the Chinese port of Canton. Foreigners had made themselves at home among the genial Natives, whom Captain Cook, on a visit in 1778, had misnamed Nootkas. He had mistaken a word in their language, meaning "going around," for their name. In actuality, the so-called Nootkas represented perhaps two dozen distinct groups, each with different names. At Nootka, Malaspina welcomed the unusual opportunity to compare his observations of Natives with the written commentaries of foreigners like Cook, whose printed works he carried.[29]

Malaspina arrived at Santa Cruz de Nutka amidst high tensions over the fatal shooting of a Nootka leader, but he apparently won the confidence of the Nootka's principal chief, Maquinna, and proceeded to quiz him for ethnographic information. In particular, the Spanish scientists hoped to explain the workings of the Natives' government. The clan and kinship system that held Nootka society together eluded the Spaniards' understanding. Instead, they imagined a system resembling their own. They supposed that a benign Nootka monarch succeeded to power through primogeniture or, if a ruler died without a successor, through election by an assembly. Then, building on that misunderstanding, the scientists conjectured that the Nootkas possessed a high level of civilization because the mass of their plebeians esteemed their rulers and submitted to them with docility.[30] This Eurocentric construction, however, raised another question. Why did the Nootkas possess a more "advanced level of civilization" than any other group on the Northwest coast? Malaspina hypothesized that it might have resulted from the moderate climate, the influence of peaceful Indian trading partners, or recent contact with Europeans.[31] After an eighteen-day visit, the Spanish scientists left Nootka pleased with the information they had gathered and wondering how to fit their findings into general theories about the development of man.

From Vancouver Island, the expedition sailed south for a stopover in Monterey, the capital of Alta California. In this youthful Spanish province, which Spaniards had begun to settle in 1769, the scientists could study Indians recently come to Franciscan missions as well as Indians who refused mission life. After listening to Franciscans whom he met in Monterey and reading reports of Jesuits who had long labored in Baja California, Malaspina concluded that Indians in both Californias had endured a miserable existence before Spaniards arrived to rescue them. Relying on authority rather than firsthand observation, Malaspina accepted the judgment of the Jesuit Miguel Venegas, who in 1739 had described Indians of Baja California as living "in perpetual inaction and idleness, in horror of every kind of work or ambition."[32] Malaspina did not question the source, and he took the part for the whole. He described Indians from Cabo San Lucas to San Francisco as homogeneous but bitter enemies engaged in internecine

9. Maquinna, the principal chief at Nootka,
as sketched in pencil by the artist Tomás de Suria.
Courtesy of the Museo Naval, Madrid (1–27).

wars. The only exceptions for Malaspina were Chumash Indians, about whom he also had secondhand information. The Chumash, who inhabited the islands and mainland near the Santa Barbara Channel, lived harmoniously with nature and "free from the ambition that torments cultured Europe" Malaspina concluded.[33] As for the rest, "the arrival of the Spaniards has brought to these Natives, without the least spilling of blood, the cessation of numerous wars that destroyed them, social principles, a pure and holy religion, and healthy and dependable food."[34]

On September 26, after fifteen days in Monterey, the twin corvettes set sail for Acapulco. There, rejoined by the men they had left behind the previous spring, they sent boxes of reports, charts, and specimens back to Madrid before setting out across the Pacific, where the expedition continued its work in Guam, the Philippines, Macao, Australia, New Zealand, and Fiji before returning to South America and Spain. Malaspina was not through entirely, however, with North America. Under a special arrangement with the viceroy of New Spain, he left two officers behind to head a detailed reconnaissance of the Pacific Northwest and its Native peoples. In the spring of 1792, Dionisio Alcalá Galiano and Cayetano Valdés sailed northward on two specially built shallow-draft vessels, the *Mexicana* and the *Sutil*, which could explore coastal waters that Malaspina's corvettes could not have entered.

Malaspina's expedition had left American shores with abundant data, drawings, and artifacts gathered from visits with independent Indians, and its officers congratulated themselves on their enlightened conduct. "We abandoned these rustic places," Lieutenant Viana exclaimed, "with the sweet satisfaction of not having produced the least harm to their inhabitants."[35] Malaspina put it less poetically: "Our peaceful contact with the natives had put down solid roots at that time, even at the cost of various gifts . . . [and] a steady contribution of biscuits."[36]

Malaspina and the scientists who sailed with him represented a new Spanish sensibility toward those peoples they and their countrymen regarded as savages. Like other European thinkers inspired by the Enlightenment, Malaspina and his team found savages of interest both as specimens and as symbols. As living specimens, savages offered Europeans an opportunity to deepen their understanding of the origins of human society and the impact of culture and environment on social arrangements. As symbols, savages offered European social critics a ready foil they could use to draw sharp comparisons with European societies. Neither the idea of the savage-as-specimen nor that of the savage-as-symbol was entirely original to eighteenth-century Spanish thought, but in the Age of Reason some Spaniards found fresh ways to think about them and to apply them.[37]

Savages as Specimens

Interest in the savage-as-specimen grew out of the Europeans' supposition that fundamental principles like those that ordered the natural world governed human society and only awaited discovery. Humanity at its most basic level, before the artificiality of civilization influenced or corrupted it, seemed to hold a key to finding those principles and unlocking the secrets of how and why elaborate societies developed. The answer, men such as Malaspina believed, would be found in personal observation rather than in ancient texts. America, then, became "the prime source for new theories about society," as one historian put it, and within America, Indians took on new significance.[38] "The Indian, the more savage he may be, is the principal and most interesting part of America," declared the Spanish military engineer, officer, and naturalist Félix de Azara, who spent much of the 1780s and 1790s studying "wild Indians" from Paraguay to Patagonia.[39] Out of the observations of scientists like Azara, enlightened philosophers believed, practical benefits would flow. If rules that governed social affairs could be ascertained and governments could make better-informed decisions, humanity would progress from what Europeans termed savagery to what they imagined to be civilization.

Malaspina understood his "Scientific and Political Voyage" as a contribution to the systematic, comparative study of human society that enlightened philosophers espoused.

The accumulation of knowledge about the characteristics of the Natives in different areas, he supposed, "could ultimately guide us to other, more important inquiries for the history of society."[40] Malaspina pronounced himself less interested in the physical characteristics of mankind than in moral qualities. The values of savages, he believed, gave the "philosopher" clues about "the natural vices and virtues of man, the innate inclinations . . . the inchoate principles of society."[41] Some of those principles seemed clear on the Northwest Coast of North America, where he found that the Natives heeded "the melodious laws of nature relative to paternal care and respect and to conjugal and filial love."[42] Like scientific principles, laws of nature could not be broken without damaging society. "We should not violate nature," Malaspina noted, "lest we destroy the laws that she herself has prescribed. Instead, we should put social measures in the proper balance that always must be maintained by man, with his inconstant nature."[43]

Malaspina's government-sponsored expedition exemplifies the European states' quest for useful knowledge in the Age of Reason. Malaspina himself, the cosmopolitan, learned, liberally minded man of action searching for useful knowledge through firsthand observation, represented the ideal of the French philosophes, or of their Spanish counterparts, the *ilustrados*. Drawing from the works of trained travelers, philosophers would discover principles that governed both the natural world and human society, and enlightened monarchs, informed by those principles, would use the power of the state to promote progress and the happiness of their peoples.[44] Europe's monarchs adopted this strategy with alacrity, fearful their rivals would outstrip them. As the enlightened Portuguese minister the marqués de Pombal observed, "All the nations of Europe are today augmenting themselves by reciprocal imitation, each carefully watching over the actions of the others."[45]

European states had long obtained useful knowledge about their colonies from travelers and from their overseas officials. Spain traditionally required its bureaucrats in America to respond to a series of formal questionnaires that became more elaborate in the eighteenth century. To some skeptical minds in the Age of Reason, however, the reports of untrained observers seemed unreliable. In 1763, when a hiatus in a string of costly wars freed up resources, European monarchs began to send expeditions of specialists to scour the remote corners of the world. From Spain, Carlos III (r. 1759–88) and Carlos IV (r. 1788–1808) sent scientists to their American possessions and beyond, and travel literature found a growing market among the Spanish elite.[46] Working in Chile and Peru under royal patronage, two young pharmacists from Madrid, Hipólito Ruiz and José Pavón, searched the countryside for plants for a decade, from 1777 to 1787. Carlos III approved the appointment of a persistent and experienced physician-botanist from Madrid, José Celestino Mutis, to head a royal botanical expedition in 1783 in today's Colombia. Following orders from Carlos III, who wished to fulfill a request from Catherine the Great, Mutis also searched for grammars and dictionaries in native languages. In New Spain, the Royal Scientific Expedition (1787–1803), directed by another Spanish-born physician, Martín Sessé, organized surveys throughout the viceroyalty and trained Mexican-born botanists, including the very able and productive José Mariano Moziño, who linked up with Malaspina's expedition.[47]

For the Spanish crown, these expeditions represented investments in "useful knowledge," the mantra of enlightened thinkers. Botany was the science of choice not simply because Carlos III wanted specimens for his new Royal Botanical Garden, but also because products from plants had practical use as foods, in medicines, and in manufacturing.[48] Like their European contemporaries, however, Spain's scientists rarely restricted themselves to a single discipline. Whether botanists, zoologists, or astronomers, they understood themselves as advancing the natural sciences, which then included the study of all humankind.[49]

It was in this context that Malaspina studied independent Natives, gathering data and subjecting it to "philosophic inquiry" in order to understand more clearly "the progress of the human species."[50] Like other enlightened Europeans who traveled to distant lands, he believed one could observe the course of human progress because the past lived on in the form of present-day Patagonians, Huilliches, Tlingits, and other Indians who inhabited realms beyond Christendom. "Savages," by definition, "are still in the first stages of social life," one Spanish intellectual noted in 1781. Or, as the foremost Spanish reference work on America of that day put it, Indians "formed a lively picture of the most remote antiquity."[51] Through Indians, enlightened Europeans imagined they could see, in the vivid phrase of Edmund Burke, "the Great Map of Mankind . . . unroll'd at once."[52] Knowledge of that "Great Map," however, required that wise men travel to the savage lands and study the Natives firsthand. "Such a journey," Jean-Jacques Rousseau had declared, "would be of more importance than all others." Upon their return, "these new Hercules" would write "a natural, moral, and political history of what they had seen, then we would see for ourselves a new world arise from their pens, and we would learn to know our own."[53] Whether or not Malaspina fancied himself a new Hercules, he knew of Rousseau's ideas and clearly intended to write the kind of history that Rousseau imagined. He and his chief officers kept copious notes of what they observed, heard, and read —including "the customs of the savages."[54]

Malaspina and his team tested their firsthand observations of Natives against popular social theories of the day, finding ways to reconcile their observations with their expectations. Swayed apparently by Rousseau's argument that man in a state of nature "is naturally good," peaceable, and possessed of an "innate abhorrence to see beings suffer that resemble him," Malaspina offered explanations for bellicosity among the Patagonians, Huilliches, and Nootkas.[55] Believing that property was the source of social inequality (as Rousseau and others argued), Malaspina's scientists tried to account for the hierarchical structure of the Tlingits. "Among men whose necessities are so limited and whose means of satisfying them are equally so," how could there be differences in rank?[56] Malaspina advanced environmental explanations. The Tlingits at Mulgrave lived on a harsh coast where fishing provided subsistence for only half the year; they needed to store fish for the other six months as well as defend themselves from invaders. Both activities required a high degree of social organization and, he presumed, strong leadership.[57] In support of another argument, however, Malaspina overlooked his own observations of the Tlingits' inequalities of rank and wealth and instead represented them as symbols of a salubrious egalitarianism that Europeans might admire: "We cannot but envy this rude stage of nations, in which the lack of property itself makes man work for all and be useful to all."[58]

Malaspina and his cosmopolitan officers knew the works of the principal non-Spanish social theorists of their day, whether they mentioned them explicitly (as they did the French naturalist Louis Leclerc, Comte de Buffon, the political philosopher the Baron de Montesquieu, the French writer and naturalist J.-H. Bernardin de Saint-Pierre, the Scottish economist Adam Smith, and the Scottish philosopher Adam Ferguson) or referred to them indirectly (as in the case of John Locke and Rousseau).[59] Malaspina had insisted on stocking the *Atrevida* and the *Descubierta* with libraries that included works by two Jesuits recently expelled from Mexico and Chile, Francisco Javier Clavigero and Giovani Ignacio Molina, by the Scotsmen David Hume and William Robertson, by the American Thomas Jefferson, and by the Italian Gian Rinaldo Carli, who wrote the *Lettere americane* (1780).[60] In addition to published works of foreigners, the expedition carried private letters of advice sent to Malaspina from leading scientists in London, Paris, and Turin. Malaspina also knew key works by Spanish authors, whether or not he had their books aboard. He had studied the public report of two prominent Spanish naval officers and scientists, Lts. Jorge Juan and Antonio de Ulloa, who conducted an ambitious reconnaissance of America earlier in the century (1735–45), and tracts by at least two influential ministers of Carlos III, Pedro Rodríguez Campomanes, the conde de Campomanes, and Pedro Pablo Abarca y Bolea, the conde de Aranda. Malaspina also traveled with manuscripts copied from public and private archives in Spain, and he had documents copied from American archives to carry back to Spain.[61]

Conventional wisdom once held that Catholic Spain and its American colonies served as stout redoubts against Enlightenment rationalism, but scholars have long since put that notion to rest. As in other Catholic countries, the institutional church in Spain vigorously resisted the circulation of ideas that separated epistemology and natural science from theology, for such notions implicitly questioned basic Catholic beliefs, such as transubstantiation.[62] Nonetheless, a critical and empirical attitude toward knowledge, characteristic of the Enlightenment yet compatible with Spanish Catholicism, began to gain currency among a small circle in Spain in the late 1600s. In the first half of the 1700s, the intellectual underpinnings for this shift came largely from the encyclopedic and influential essays of a Benedictine professor at the University of Oviedo, Benito Jerónimo Feijóo. In the last half of the 1700s, the circle of writers widened. Metaphysics began to make room for physical sciences, and faith came to accommodate empirical epistemologies throughout the Hispanic world.[63]

The change in intellectual climate occurred during the lifetime of Lieutenant Juan, whose work Malaspina admired and emulated. Returned to Spain in 1746 after a decade of scientific study in the Indies with Lieutenant Ulloa, including a stint in Ecuador with the French scientist Charles Marie de la Condamine, Juan feared that his espousal of new theories would leave him vulnerable to charges of heresy. Thus he took the precaution of prefacing his *Observaciones astronómicas* (1748) with a denial that the earth rotated on its axis. His French translator offered an apology: "The author of this work does not speak as a mathematician . . . but as a man writing in Spain, that is to say, in a country where the Inquisition exists." By 1774, however, Juan could ask critically, in an essay published in Spain, "Will it not insult [the Sacred Scriptures] to pretend that they oppose the most exacting proofs of geometry and mechanics?"[64]

In the late eighteenth century, the ideas of the philosophes reached the Spanish-speaking world directly as Spaniards like Juan traveled abroad, as foreigners visited Spain, and as books and essays, even those forbidden by the Roman Index and the Inquisition, circulated among some members of the small but highly influential elite. Indirectly, too, the ideas of the Age of Reason circulated widely in the form of translations, paraphrases, and plagiarisms.[65] Rousseau's works, for example, entered Spain soon after their publication in France. The Spanish Inquisition received a copy of his *Discourse on the Origin of Inequality* so quickly that it banned it in 1756, just a year after its appearance in France—the ban apparently stimulated rather than discouraged Iberian readers.[66] Rousseau's *Émile*, which the Inquisition banned as well, also circulated in Spain. In December 1762, just months after its appearance in Paris, the editor of a popular periodical in Madrid published *Émile's* opening lines in Spanish, attributing them to "a famous author": "Everything is good as it leaves the hands of the Author of things; everything degenerates in the hands of man."[67] For those who could not read *Émile* in French or who would not read a book on the Index of prohibited titles, some of Rousseau's ideas circulated in a popular novel, *Eusebio* (1786), whose author, Pedro Montengón, modeled his protagonist after *Émile*.[68] Rousseau may have been the best-known foreign author south of the Pyrenees in the last half of the eighteenth century.[69] While officials continued to impose restrictions, such as banning the publication of novels in 1799, Spaniards continued to read forbidden texts.[70]

From foreign sources and from Spain itself, the empiricism of the Enlightenment spread easily to the Spanish-American elite, often through legal channels. At the University of San Carlos de Guatemala in the last half of the eighteenth century, one scholar has suggested, a professor could introduce his students to contemporary European thought "without dependence upon prohibited books."[71] A high-ranking Spanish official, Francisco de Saavedra, on an official mission that took him to Cumaná, Havana, Pensacola, and Mexico City in 1780–81, observed that among the *criollos* "the new philosophy goes forward, making more progress there than in Spain." He ascribed this to the impact of foreigners, who had introduced "new ideas concerning the rights of man and of sovereigns" and the introduction of "French books." He confidently announced that thousands of copies of the works of "modern philosophers" such as Voltaire, Rousseau, Robertson, and the French historian G. T. F. Abbé de Raynal circulated throughout Spanish America. Read with "enthusiasm," these works were bringing about a "revolution" in thought.[72]

On occasion, possession of a forbidden work brought retribution, some of it terrible, but more often officials could not or would not enforce prohibitions. Inquisitive, well-connected individuals could obtain dispensations to read prohibited literature even in places as remote as Chile. Indeed, one historian has argued that the Enlightenment in Spanish America went beyond "mirroring or contesting European ideas" and was itself "a deeply original and creative movement."[73]

Like intellectuals elsewhere, Spaniards who considered themselves enlightened rejected some enlightened ideas. If Spanish intellectuals wrote frequently about Rousseau's *Social Contract*, it was usually to repudiate it. "The mere dreams of a man awake," one Spanish critic noted with sarcasm.[74] Only an imprudent Spaniard would have joined Denis Diderot in asking if Spain's occupation of America was "not as unjust, as senseless, as if some savages were to land by chance on European shores and write on sand or on the bark of trees: 'This country is ours.'"[75]

Like the French philosophes, Spanish and Spanish-American *ilustrados* held widely divergent and often contradictory views. Through the crosscurrents of the Enlightenment, however, ran a strong belief in the power of human observation and reason unaided by either divine revelation or the authority of the ancients. Among modern, educated Spaniards, belief in research and reason came into full flower in the late eighteenth century, when it manifested itself in the study of political economy and its practical application at the highest levels of government.[76]

The reign of Carlos III, one of Europe's most enlightened despots, brought to power men swept up in the optimism of the Enlightenment.[77] Heading key government ministries, they took what they believed to be rational, scientific approaches to political, economic, and social problems. Their solutions seemed certain to lead to humanity's progress and break old cycles of rise and decline. A judicious application of reason, these officials believed, would increase trade, industry, agricultural production, and, not incidentally, public revenues. At the same time, rational, scientific restructuring promised to liberate the king's vassals from poverty, ignorance, and oppression, making them more productive taxpayers in the American colonies as in Spain itself.[78]

In the Americas, the king's vassals included Indians, many of them long subjugated. Enlightened Spanish policymakers hoped not only to turn those Indian vassals into more productive taxpayers, but also to have peaceful and profitable commercial relations with independent Natives as well, eventually bringing them under the protection of the Spanish crown. The institutions that traditionally worked toward that end, missions and the military, seemed stalemated along many frontiers of the empire, however, and some *ilustrados* called for fresh approaches. But in the Age of Reason, fresh approaches had to be built on a firm grasp of the basic principles that governed human societies in general and Indian societies in particular. Those principles still awaited discovery; they would reveal themselves only after scientists had gathered sufficient sociological and anthropological data.

The intellectuals of Malaspina's generation who attempted to understand the nature of Indian societies joined a debate that had sixteenth-century origins. Was the alleged barbarism of American Indians innate—a natural condition? or was it an accidental result of environmental circumstances? Much hung on the answer. If barbarism was natural and thus immutable, then Indians were a defective form of mankind, natural slaves who could be justifiably forced to serve fully formed members of the human race.

The most sophisticated and influential Spanish thinkers, those whose works shaped humane Spanish policy in the sixteenth and seventeenth centuries, rejected the view that savages were less than rational beings. Some Spanish scholars who never visited the so-called New World came to that conclusion through deduction, as did the Dominican Francisco de Vitoria at the University of Salamanca. Others with experience in the New World gathered empirical evidence, in the manner of Bartolomé de Las Casas, the Dominican famous for his vigorous defense of American Indians, and José de Acosta, a Jesuit whose systematic, comprehensive work on America would dominate the debate through the seventeenth century. All Indians, those scholar-priests concluded, even nomads, were fully rational (Las Casas did, however, allow for some anomalous creatures). Las Casas and Acosta argued that the barbaric characteristics of some Indians resulted in part from their physical environment, but only in part. For them, environment influenced but did not determine culture. Of equal if not greater importance was a people's position on a historical continuum. All peoples, Las Casas and Acosta supposed, had once been savages, beings without culture; some societies were simply younger than others and needed to grow to adulthood.[79]

In their emphasis on environment and stages of human development, these scholar-priests of the Renaissance anticipated enlightened thought. At the same time, they occupied a mental universe in which articles of faith, such as the belief in men's and women's descent from Adam and Eve, put boundaries on reason and in which two powerful metaphysical forces, a god and a devil, shaped human societies.[80] Argue as he might that Indians needed to be understood on their own terms and not through simple analogy with other peoples, a sixteenth-century priest could not write of pagan religion with detachment. Acosta's attempt to understand different belief systems did not mean he condoned them; on the contrary, he and his contemporaries studied the beliefs of pagans in order to convert them to Christianity.[81]

In the Age of Reason, Spaniards still sought to turn Indians into Christians, but Malaspina and others of like mind acquired knowledge of Natives more to serve humankind than to advance their religion. In that sense, they represented a break with the past. So, too, did their abandonment of supernatural explanations, including the devil, in favor of analysis rooted in the natural world.[82] Empirical scholars of the late eighteenth century generally rejected the view that either a god or a devil shaped human events. Instead, influenced by Montesquieu, they looked for physical laws. Much as they began to believe that the roots of insanity had social or medical rather than transcendent causes, so the *ilustrados* sought worldly explanations for Indian behavior and beliefs. Lieutenant Viana, for example, postulated that the Huilliches believed in a "creator" who was "an evil force" because they inhabited a rocky, volcanic homeland, where one could feel "the apparent disorder of the universe."[83]

The enlightened argument that natural forces and basic principles governed human behavior rested on the assumption that humans behaved in rational ways.[84] There could be no laws governing political, economic, and social behavior if the species behaved irrationally. Thus, Malaspina and his scientists tended to portray Indians' behavior as rationally adaptive and often virtuous, no matter how much their societies differed from European norms.[85] An incident that suggested exemplary Patagonian honesty to Malaspina, for example, led him to exclaim that integrity among "a people almost naked and barbarous" like the Patagonians would force "the moral philosopher and the lover of our species" to conclude that humankind was not "vicious and disposed by nature to the bestial life."[86] Similarly, Lieutenant Viana noted that although the *patagones* lived "alone in the remote and sterile depths of South America, buried in pitiable ignorance," they nonetheless displayed "good faith, honesty, and probity."[87] That the Patagonians were also "humane and decent" was all the more extraordinary to Viana since they were surrounded by Pehuenches, Huilliches, Aucases, and Pampas, whom he characterized as "cunning, perfidious, sanguinary nations . . . among whom robbery, drunkenness, and deceit substitute for virtues."[88]

Even the apparent vices of Natives had rational causes. If Patagonians, Huilliches, and Tlingits made war, it was because aggressive neighbors or invaders forced them to behave in ways that ran counter to their peaceful natures (the question of why the neighbors or invaders were warlike, however, went unasked). If Indians on the Northwest Coast had the unfortunate habit of offering women to Europeans, those women often were slaves and not the wives or daughters of those who gave them away. If parents sold their daughters, it was because girls were liabilities in societies that needed men to maintain them through fishing and war.[89] If some Indians who lived in nature possessed what Malaspina termed "a certain foolish indolence," the cause might be a comfortable climate that provided abundant food year-round or an enervating climate that caused Indians to sweat too rapidly.[90] Such explanations would have pleased Montesquieu.

One vice, cannibalism, seemed so odious to Malaspina that on one occasion he denied its existence rather than try to explain it. He devoted considerable time to tracing the source of the European idea that Nootkas ate human flesh, an idea that circulated among European visitors, including Captain Cook. Unconvinced, Malaspina declined "to admit such an ignominious truth about our species" and concluded that Europeans had misread the evidence.[91] Another Spanish explorer of Malaspina's generation, however, readily acknowledged the existence of anthropophagy as an "ignominious truth" but explained what he believed to be Indians' tendency to eat flesh in rational terms. Exploring the Río de Engaños in what is today Colombia's Amazon basin in 1781, the engineer Francisco de Requena noted that local Indians had "the bad habit of eating their prisoners, a vice they must commit perhaps more due to necessity than out of gluttony, given the lack of meat in this region."[92]

Enlightened thinkers, then, sought explanations for Indians' behavior in their physical and human environments rather than attributing it to an innate depravity or perversity.[93] Lieutenant Viana employed what modern anthropologists might call a theory of functional ecology to explain how subsistence shaped the social life of wandering Patagonians. In the summer, he observed, Patagonians moved south to fish; in the winter, when streams froze in the south, they moved north to hunt *guanacos*, a mammal closely related to the camel. Abundant fish in the south enabled the Indians to live together in large groups under powerful chiefs during the summer, but scarcer game on the treeless plains in the north could not support the same large concentrations of population. In the winter, then, Patagonians dispersed in smaller groups under the leadership of lesser figures. Malaspina offered a similar environmental explanation for the Patagonians' mobile lives. Neither he nor Viana followed the lead of earlier writers who attributed the Patagonians' seasonal migrations to "a disposition to roving" or "an inclination to wander" or a "natural restlessness."[94]

The expeditionaries' observations suggest that on this occasion they were more astute than most Europeans of their era, who failed to see the underlying order and highly structured lives of nomads or seminomads and who instead assumed the existence of what one scholar has termed "a cultural dichotomy between 'savage' (lack of order) and 'civilized' (order) that did not, in fact, exist."[95] That fictitious dichotomy had served Spaniards and other Europeans well. They regarded a mobile people's lack of a permanent, fixed place of residence as a sign of their barbarity and fastened on that as a pretext for conquering, exploiting, and "civilizing" them. Malaspina and his researchers, however, had come only to observe; they had no need to concoct rationalizations for conquest and exploitation.

Like many of their progressive contemporaries, however, Malaspina and his officer-scientists were not slaves to consistency. The American-born Viana, who offered environmental explanations for some Indian behavior, also believed Native Americans possessed an indolent character. Patagonians overcame their natural indolence only because a harsh environment forced them to exceptional industry.[96] Malaspina described a small group of Patagonians who lived in the inhospitable climes of Tierra del Fuego as "seeming to subsist there against the dictates of Nature itself." Rather than remark on their successful adaptation, he pronounced those Patagonians as fallen into an unnatural "stupidity." Otherwise, he said, they would have emigrated.[97] The same Malaspina who explained Patagonian mobility as an environmental adaptation regarded the seasonal movements of some California Indians as a social defect. The "wandering life," he opined in the California case, was "always the source of depopulation or of discord."[98]

Inconsistencies aside, Malaspina and his scientists tended to view human society through the evolutionary lens of Étienne Bonnot de Condillac, Montesquieu, Rousseau, and others.[99] Malaspina knew the work of Adam Ferguson, one of the most sophisticated proponents of the theory that societies in general progressed naturally over time through four stages, each reflecting and shaped by a distinct mode of subsistence: hunting, pasturage, agriculture, and commerce.[100] In Malaspina's own formulation, Indians who lived in the most basic fashion occupied "the earliest stages of society."[101] Humankind in the later stages, in his view, included complex Indian societies like the Aztecs and Incas, who were "civilized, united, lovers of order and government." Malaspina judged them inferior to Europeans only in their lack of knowledge of gunpowder, iron, horses, and navigation.[102] Malaspina did not take Ferguson entirely to heart. Ignoring the philosophe's injunction "to collect facts, not to offer conjectures,"[103] Malaspina consciously or unconsciously followed Rousseau's stages of human development and imagined that the earliest humans lived like wandering beasts. Early man, he postulated, was a naked hunter who lacked rules of social conduct, laws, hierarchy, and religion.[104] Ferguson, on the other hand, saw man as inherently social and rejected the idea that "a supposed state of animal sensibility" once existed.[105]

Malaspina's analysis of the savage-as-specimen belongs to a shift in European thought that some scholars identify as the beginnings of social sciences in general and modern anthropology in particular. Eighteenth-century theorists did not invent the study of physical and cultural differences among human populations,[106] but they applied scientific thinking to the study of human societies with a rigor that many twentieth-century scholars recognize as modern.[107] By some measures, Malaspina's scientists exemplified modern ethnologists at work: gathering empirical data, classifying and comparing those data to produce larger generalizations, explaining cultures as shaped by environmental and social forces, disagreeing about those explanations, and, on occasion, tolerating difference.[108] Viana, for example, described but did not condemn the Tlingit women's use of the labaret, a conical piece of wood inserted in an incision in the lower lip that exposed the teeth of the lower jaw. "How men's ideas of beauty vary," Viana wrote. "As the opinion of Mr. Buffon asserts, taste is pure convention."[109]

Measured by today's standards, however, Malaspina's scientists practiced a primitive or protoanthropology. Modern anthropologists live among the peoples they study long enough to learn their languages and reckon with their cultures as participant-observers. The Spanish explorers, in contrast, stayed briefly and warily among Natives, taking precautions to defend themselves from attack. They lacked languages to communicate with their subjects and, one modern scholar has argued, lacked a scientific method "to structure and systematize rigorously the body of information they gathered."[110] Moreover, the Spanish observers lived in a pre-Darwinian, prerelativistic era. Their idea that man developed in stages and that hunter-gatherers represented the childhood of society runs counter to the modern notion that societies mature in diverse ways and that nomads as well as pastoralists and farmers occupy a fully developed world of their own.[111] The Spaniards' expressions of toleration of other cultures were tempered by their certainty that reason and progress, as Europeans understood them, were universal values. European notions of reason and progress became the standards against which they measured all other cultures. Enlightened Europeans' expressions of toleration did not approximate the moral indifference of modern cultural relativism.[112]

Arguments about the limitations of Malaspina's anthropology, however, rest on dis-

tinctions between eighteenth- and twentieth-century scholarship that are more of degree than of kind, as is apparent from the lively criticism that today's ethnographers and
ethnologists offer of their own work.[113] Questions that engaged and sometimes perplexed
Spanish theorists, such as the relationship of written language to the development of
cognitive processes and the nature of the mind of the so-called savage or the primitive,
remain in spirited contention among present-day social scientists. Moreover, few would
argue that present-day representations of the Other have moved entirely beyond self-
representation.[114]

Savages as Symbols

Independent Indians whom Malaspina and his expeditionaries studied as specimens
also had heuristic value as symbols, both positive and negative. Critics of European institutions and values represented Indian communities as ideal societies whose members
lived the pure, simple lives Europeans might have enjoyed if civilization had not corrupted
them. Celebrators of European culture represented Indians as the embodiment of man's
base or brutal nature, unrefined by the benefits of European institutions and values.
Malaspina employed each of these contradictory tropes, but idealizing "savages" generally
suited his purposes better than negating or debasing them.

The idea that humans in a state of nature lived a good and rational life had a long
history in classical and Christian thought, but the discovery of America offered a new
set of "savages" whom critics of European civilization could idealize and offer as exem-
plars. Sixteenth-century Spanish chroniclers like Peter Martyr and Francisco López de
Gómara, who never visited America, romanticized Indians when it suited their purposes.
Most famously, Bartolomé de Las Casas, who knew America firsthand, evoked countless
"humble, patient, and peaceable" Indians in his withering polemic against the conquistadors' abuses. Las Casas's *Brief History of the Destruction of the Indies* (1552), became a *succès
de scandale* as it circulated throughout Europe in various languages and, together with
other Spanish chronicles, left an imprint on successive generations of European writers.[115]
Among them was Michel de Montaigne (1533–92), whose arresting claim that "in every
kind of barbarity" Europeans surpassed even cannibals echoed loudly in the seventeenth
and eighteenth centuries. The New World's Natives, Montaigne asserted, were superior
to Europeans in "devoutness, observance of the laws, goodness, liberality, loyalty, and
frankness."[116]

The term *noble savage* was not current among the philosophes—it did not come into
vogue until the last half of the nineteenth century. Rousseau, long credited with establishing the myth of the noble savage, apparently never used the term. Rousseau did suppose
that Indians were freer and in some ways happier than Europeans, but he did not present
Indians as noble or urge a return to a "state of nature."[117] Nonetheless, French essayists
and fiction writers of Malaspina's era did employ the trope of *les bons sauvages.* In Spanish novels of the era, on the other hand, "good Indians" never appear, and enlightened

*10. Attributed to José del Pozo, this oil painting shows a Patagonian
man, apparently Junchar, in a state of "savage" undress
(notwithstanding the animal skin draped over his shoulder),
but serene, self-confident, and a specimen of robust health.
Courtesy, Museo Naval, Madrid (1–474).*

Spanish essayists usually described all but the most cultured Indians, such as Incas and Aztecs, as mired in woeful barbarism.[118] Perhaps eighteenth-century Spanish writers supposed that idealized Natives would not make plausible characters for a readership that knew so much about American Indians. Then, too, Catholic Spain had rejected the deism that allowed some European intellectuals to believe in the natural virtue of pagans. In the chaos that followed the French Revolution of 1789, romanticizing primitive man seemed especially repugnant to some Spanish intellectuals. In 1802, in an apparent rebuke to some of the French philosophes, the prominent Spanish liberal jurist and statesman Gaspar Melchor de Jovellanos condemned the idea of celebrating man in "his primitive barbarism," which he saw as "a chaos of absurdities and blasphemies."[119]

Influenced by the larger European Enlightenment rather than its Spanish variant, Malaspina and his officers did idealize some aspects of Native behavior and suggested that their compatriots would profit from emulating Indians. Lt. Antonio Tova y Arredondo, one of Malaspina's official diarists, argued that the honesty and mutual affection Patago-nians showed toward one another "can serve as a model for more civilized peoples."[120] Malaspina himself observed that independent Indians such as Patagonians and Arauca-nians resisted living in Spanish society, although they saw only "its agreeable exterior." Had they understood European society from the inside, he asserted, they would have found it odious: "the inequality between classes and in wealth, the pernicious ideas of comfort and of indolence, the conflicts that result from those causes and from becoming involved in all the wars in Europe."[121] In one of his rosiest formulations, Malaspina de-clared that before the arrival of Spaniards the American Indian was "tranquil, not know-ing the value of silver and gold, or needing to perform hard, persistent work in order to enjoy a comfortable subsistence."[122] Native societies, he wrote, lived happily in a state of nature until envy and war and other artifacts of civilization led to "the social corruption that prevails today."[123] At Nootka in 1792, the botanist Moziño offered similar reflec-tions on the virtues of a simple savage life: "Since vices increase with desires, and desires increase with the luxuries of sophisticated nations, no one will say I exaggerate when I affirm that the vices of these savages are very few when compared to ours. Here one does not see greed for another man's wealth, because articles of prime necessity are very few and all are common. Hunger obliges no one to rob on the highways, or to resort to piracy along the coasts . . . . The trade with Europeans has allowed them to become acquainted with various things they would have been better off without forever."[124] Moziño's Nootkas found Europeans vulgar and lacking in spirituality. Upon learning the meaning of the lyrics to Spanish and Indian songs, one chief reportedly asked Moziño, "Do not the Span-ish or the English have a God, since they celebrate only fornication and drunkenness?"[125]

In general, Malaspina and his chroniclers drew such flattering portraits of Indians that they prompted a rejoinder from at least one dissenting member of the expedition. The Spanish-born artist Tomás de Suria, who had studied at the Royal Academy of Fine Arts in Madrid but who had lived in Mexico for thirteen years before joining Malaspina at Acapulco, believed that his firsthand observations of Indians over his long residence in Mexico gave him a realistic if less rosy picture. Malaspina and his fellow scientists, Suria complained, presented "a sublime idea [of Indians] . . . as different as possible from what is seen by the eyes."[126]

Malaspina's use of sublime savages as a metaphor did not mean that he, any more than Rousseau, actually believed that the savage state was superior to European civiliza-tion or that all savages were noble. All of the Indians of Baja and Alta California, save the Chumash, seemed to him thoroughly disagreeable and led him to reflect that "leaving man to his own passions and to care exclusively for his animal needs degrades him, numbs him, and almost converts his life into a living representation of the life of irra-tional beings."[127] Perhaps Malaspina saw no contradiction between his dark view of Cali-fornia Indians and his brighter pronouncements, such as his thought, inspired by the Patagonians, that humans were not "disposed by nature to the bestial life."[128]

When Malaspina and his diarists were not extolling Indians to make a point about the decadence of European society or the errors of Spanish policy, they made it clear that independent Indians needed contact and commerce with other people or they would "never be able to become civilized."[129] When it suited their purposes, Malaspina and Viana agreed with the baneful view of savage life that appeared in the report of the *Sutil's* and *Mexicana's* voyage to California and the Pacific Northwest in 1792. The author, whose identity is not clear, contrasted the happy lives of Indians living at the mission in Monterey, California, with the miserable existence of "their companions wandering through the forests, without enlightenment, without religion, given over to the impulse of their passions and the misery of savage life." Approvingly, the author of the report quoted the British naturalist William Nicholson: "Man in a rude and savage state ... is an object of pity, when compared to a man enlightened and assisted by philosophy."[130] Similarly, another member of Malaspina's team, Lt. José de Espinosa y Tello, who traveled overland from Chile to Buenos Aires in 1794, described the Chaco as "the nursery and breeding place of the savages," a place in which man was not "king of Nature" but rather "many Indians live in the manner of animals ... crude, uncontrollable, vagrant, lazy, stupid in their ideas, and great warriors."[131]

The image of savages as beasts had a long tradition in European thought, and even the most enlightened of Spanish scientists continued to entertain it. The studious Félix de Azara, who knew Indians of the Río de La Plata firsthand, could not decide if Indians had developed separately from Europeans or if they, too, had descended from Adam. Reviewing the arguments on both sides, he noted that supporters of the first position described the "savages of America" as people with unusually sensitive hearing and eyesight and white, clean, regularly formed teeth; they seldom spoke or smiled. They had sexual relations "without preambles or ceremonies," gave birth easily, recognized no superior authority, had no games, dances, or songs or instruments of music, patiently endured bad weather and hunger, did not wash or clean themselves or sew, did not instruct their children, and had no religion. "All these qualities seem to approximate the quadrupeds, and they seem even to have some relation to birds, because of the strength and sharpness of their vision."[132]

Even when they emphasized the bestiality or "misery of savage life," Malaspina and his companions generally adhered to the idea that Indians who lived in a state of nature occupied an early stage in human development, one comparable to childhood. Circumstances shaped them, and circumstances could improve them. In particular, exposure to the best of European society would lead them to progress to adulthood. In adopting the position that American Indians were temporarily immature, Malaspina and his expeditionaries implicitly rejected the argument that indigenous peoples were inherently degenerate —an argument advanced by some of his enlightened contemporaries who saw America itself as the cause of the Natives' inferiority.

The idea that the American continent corrupted humankind, Indians and Spaniards alike, had enjoyed popularity since the early 1600s among Spaniards born in the Iberian Peninsula. As one Spanish priest put it in 1612, "The earth and sky of America are not as good for men as they are for Paraguayan tea and [precious] metals."[133] But American-born Spaniards (like American-born Englishmen of a later generation) could not accept the view that the Western Hemisphere's environment caused Indians to degenerate without casting aspersion on themselves.[134] Initially, many Spaniards born in the New World recoiled against this notion by distancing themselves from Indians. Slowly they ceased identifying themselves as *indianos,* a word used in the 1500s to identify Spanish residents of the Indies. To avoid the association that the similarity of the words *indianos* and *indios* ("Indians") might suggest, American-born Spaniards came to call themselves *criollos* in the 1600s.[135] Nonetheless, the idea that *indios* and other persons born in America were inferior lingered into the eighteenth century, when some enlightened thinkers, *criollos* among them, gave it new respectability. It was not just prejudiced foreigners who pronounced Indians "incapable of reason," the military engineer Pedro Andrés García declared, but men with the same view could "also be found in the major cities of America." García, who knew Indians of the Argentine pampas firsthand, attributed this to "common ignorance," while praising the "sagacity" of Indians.[136]

Malaspina probably encountered the idea of Indians' degeneracy in Robertson's widely popular *History of America* (1777) or in the more vehement prose of the Prussian philosopher abbé Cornelius de Pauw, whose sensational *Recherches philosophiques sur les Américains* appeared a decade earlier. Expanding on an argument that Buffon had applied principally to flora and fauna, de Pauw attributed the source of American Indians' supposed inferiority to the New World's climate. The Western Hemisphere, he asserted, had been "so thoroughly maltreated by Nature that everything in it was either degenerate or monstrous." In the Americas even iron lost its strength.[137] But Malaspina need not have read de Pauw or Robertson to know their arguments. The library he carried on shipboard included several writers who summarized them in order to refute them, including Clavigero, Molina, Jefferson, and especially Carli.[138] In New Spain, the Mexican-born scholar José Antonio de Alzate wrote a treatise for the Malaspina expedition that explicitly refuted Buffon and lauded Indians as peaceful, honest, hardworking, patient, and docile. Their vices, he suggested, came not from the American environment, but from their contact with Spaniards.[139]

Alzate's views enjoyed currency among enlightened *criollos* in New Spain. If Indians occupied the lowest rungs on the social ladder in the late eighteenth century, the argument went, it was because conquistadors and their descendants had treated them harshly, not because Indians were innately inferior. "For *criollos,* with Indian blood flowing deeply in their veins," one historian has argued, "it was important to present Indians as gifted as any whites."[140] The many Indians who learned to live like Spaniards provided empirical evidence of Indians' intellectual capacities. Antonio Alcedo, an Ecuadoran who wrote a multivolume encyclopedia on the Americas in the tradition of the philosophes, praised an Indian from Oaxaca, Nicolás del Puerto, to make that point. A "celebrated jurist" who became the bishop of Oaxaca, Puerto was "a man of such virtue and science that he destroys the opinion that Indians are not capable of the understanding of Europeans."[141]

In central Mexico especially, where danger of Indian revolt seemed slight, enlightened *criollos* tended to romanticize Indians but did so selectively. Mexican *criollos* glorified the cultured Aztecs, whose descendants seemed safely subservient or long gone, rather than Apaches or Seris, who continued to resist Spanish domination. As unhappiness with Spanish administration deepened in the twilight of years of the empire, some *criollos*, in the words of one historian, "came to regard the plight of the Indians as a metaphor for their own oppressed condition."[142] Literally or metaphorically, some *criollos* revived the memory of their own distant Indian ancestry as a source of status. In an epistle to Ferdinand VII that he wrote from prison in 1817–18, the Mexican-born *criollo* Carlos María de Bustamante appealed to an incipient Mexican nationalism by signing himself a "Mexican Indian."[143]

On both sides of the Atlantic, some enlightened Spaniards found reasons to continue to portray Indians as lesser beings, but others rejected the idea of Indians' inferiority and emphasized their virtues.[144] Spanish reformers such as Malaspina could not reconcile the idea of the inherent inferiority of Indians with their interest in turning American Indians into productive vassals of the crown. Innately inferior people could hardly be expected to behave like the rational economic actors that enlightened Spaniards wanted them to be.

From Malaspina's viewpoint, if independent Indians did not wish to join Spanish society or if conquered Indians did not thrive within the Spanish Empire, the fault lay more with Spain's colonial system than with Indians. Spaniards, he said, depended on Indians to work mines, cultivate crops of value to Europeans, and consume manufactured goods they did not need. Spaniards sought to deprive Indians of a life of ease so that they themselves might enjoy a life of indolence. Indians who resisted working for Spaniards for a pittance, then, were sagacious rather than lazy. Because they lived amidst abundant fish and game, it made no sense for them to abandon "an idle and almost wandering life for a laboring life in a well-ordered [Spanish] society."[145]

The "continual struggle" between Indians and Spaniards, which led to "the true debilitation of all," would not cease until Spain ended what Malaspina called "political and mercantile slavery" and allowed Indians to enjoy the fruits of their labor.[146] For Malaspina, as for other enlightened philosophers, this was axiomatic. It reflected the influence of Locke's famous argument that man had a natural right to own as property the products of his labor. Locke's argument had adherents in Spain, including Jovellanos, who held that individual prosperity led to the national good and that wise governments did not adopt regulations that discouraged individuals from pursuing their own interests.[147] The idea that Indians should profit from their work took on new urgency when the great rebellion of Andean Indians in 1780–83, led by Tupac Amaru, forced Spanish policymakers to rethink their relations with Indians.[148]

Although Malaspina and many of his forward-thinking counterparts in Spain rejected the idea of an abiding inferiority of American Indians, they nonetheless invoked antithetical images of Indians. "Intellectuals of the Enlightenment," as one historian has put it, "wrangled bitterly about the capacity, character, and achievement of the Indian."[149] So long as the metaphors of good and bad savages proved useful, they could exist side by side, even in the rhetoric of a single enlightened thinker, as Malaspina illustrates.[150]

Humanity and Compassion

Whether they idealized or demonized independent Indians or presented them as some combination of the two, enlightened Spaniards argued that even the basest barbarians deserved humane treatment. When Viceroy Revillagigedo (the younger) sent an expedition to the Pacific Northwest to follow up on Malaspina's work, he issued stern instructions that firearms were to be used only in self-defense. Even then, he warned, the mariners would have to justify their use upon return to Mexico. The explorers were to lay "a foundation for a friendship perhaps very useful in the future to religion and the sovereign." Toward that end, they were to give Indians gifts and treat them with "gentleness." They were to ignore offenses that Indians committed against them and assure that members of the crew did not cheat or insult Indians. The expeditionaries should carry out their work, the viceroy wrote, "without offending in the slightest degree those unhappy beings who in their ignorance clamor for my humanity and compassion."[151]

Since the days of Ferdinand and Isabel the Spanish crown and its highest representatives had expressed similar sentiments, but in the late eighteenth century enlightened Spaniards were more likely to act on them. In part this reflected the humanitarianism that ran deeply through Enlightenment thought. "I can flatter myself," wrote a naval commander after an epic journey into Alaskan waters, "that treating these Indians as men ought to be treated, and not like individuals of inferior nature, I have lived in the very breast of tranquillity."[152] At Nootka in the summer of 1792, Dionisio Alcalá Galiano added a philanthropic twist: "Europeans who trade with barbarous nations and bring to them all the evils of civilization . . . must try to recompense them with whatever physical and moral benefits lie within their reach."[153]

For Spaniards of the late eighteenth century, humane treatment of their savages would also demonstrate to foreigners that Spain had moved beyond the cruelties of the sixteenth century that had blackened its reputation. In the eyes of its foreign enemies, Spain's conquest of America and treatment of Indians were barbaric. Foreigners had found ample evidence of Spanish savagery in the critical writings of Spaniards themselves, most notably in Las Casas's *Brief History*, a work so critical of Spain that the crown kept it on the Index of prohibited books.[154] Spanish cruelty had become part of the lore of the European elite, a fact no educated Spaniard could ignore, especially in the late eighteenth century as ideas of the philosophes filtered south across the Pyrenees into Spain and on to its New World empire.[155] In the Age of Reason, Spain represented the epitome of the obscurantist, ecclesiastical government—a case Voltaire famously made in *Candide* (1759)—and Spain's Indian victims symbolized Iberia's excesses.[156]

The idea of unique Spanish cruelty toward Indians, one of the cardinal tenets of that

11. Early European illustrations of Native Americans, which came largely from non-Spanish graphic artists, spread a message inspired by the Protestant Reformation: Indians were noble and Catholic Spanish conquistadors were savages. Illustration from Bartolomé de Las Casas, Narratio Regionum Indicarum Per Hispanos quosdam deuastatarum verissima. . . . *Francofurti: Sumptibus Theodori de Bry . . . , 1598. Courtesy, DeGolyer Library, Southern Methodist University.*

cluster of anti-Spanish beliefs known collectively as the Black Legend, appeared in European popular literature as well as in the ruminations of philosophes. In the *Life and Strange and Surprising Adventures of Robinson Crusoe* (1719), the only book in the possession of Rousseau's fictional Émile and one of many books in the library of Spain's minister of the Indies, José de Gálvez, the protagonist pondered the question of killing cannibals who have done him no harm. Crusoe turned his moral compass toward the Spaniards, whose conquest of America, he said, "is spoken of with the utmost Abhorrence and Detestation, by even the Spaniards themselves, at the Time; and by all other Christian Nations of Europe, as a meer Butchery, a bloody and unnatural Piece of Cruelty . . . for which the very Name of a Spaniard is reckon'd to be frightful and terrible to all People of Humanity."[157]

Enlightened Spaniards responded to charges of Spanish cruelty in several ways. Some took them as truth and lamented the damage done to Indians as well as to Spain's reputation. Benito Jerónimo Feijóo, Spain's most influential philosopher of the first half of the eighteenth century, set the tone when he deplored the "wretches who violently oppress Indians [and] make all the nation suffer." Who, he asked rhetorically, would burn in the hottest flames of hell, "the ignorant Indian idolater, or the cruel and bloody Spaniard?"[158] Lieutenant Viana celebrated the Araucanians' overthrow of their Spanish oppressors in the sixteenth century, describing them as "heroic savages."[159] For some enlightened American-born Spaniards, the Black Legend became an article of faith. By blaming Spaniards for Indians' impoverished condition, *criollos* also undermined the argument that the New World environment had debilitating effects on its residents.[160]

Other enlightened Spaniards tried to defend their nation's honor. Some charged that Spain's critics exaggerated the cruelties of their countrymen or inflated the number of Indians whom Spaniards killed. Foreigners' accounts of "oppression, tyranny, and violence committed by Spaniards are hoaxes," one of Malaspina's officers asserted, "and do not merit public faith and credit."[161] Other apologists asserted that excesses resulted from actions of individuals rather than royal policies, pointing out that the crown had prevailed in the end and rescued Indians from their barbarity and idolatry.[162] Spanish patriots put Spanish violence in perspective by arguing that representatives of other nations also "commit incredible cruelties, not in the century of ignorance in which the conquest was carried out, but in this enlightened century."[163] The erudite Spanish-born Azara, working in the interior of what is today Argentina and Paraguay in the 1790s, challenged foreign philosophers to present him with another example of a colonial power that had saved the lives of so many Indians, allowed Indian populations to grow since the conquest, and transformed Indians into Europeans through racial mixture.[164] Antonio Alcedo, the Ecuadoran encyclopedist, noted that colonists in Massachusetts offered bounties for killing Indians and in 1724 paid one John Lovewell a large sum for killing ten sleeping Indians. "The English boast of this stain on humanity," Alcedo wrote, "and they attack the cruelties of the Spaniards in America, which certainly occurred but did not reach that level of barbarism."[165]

Acutely aware of Spain's reputation, Malaspina and his principal officers took pains to avoid offending Indians and to portray themselves in a different light than their sixteenth-century predecessors.[166] As they departed from Port Mulgrave, where Malaspina's scientists took pride in their kindness, generosity, and restraint toward the Tlingits, Lieutenant Viana observed that the expeditionaries' conduct, "so in conformity with the beneficent and humane character of the Spaniards, will some day confound a certain class of writers who have dedicated themselves to defaming an illustrious and honourable nation that, despite their ridiculous and extravagant statements, will always occupy a distinguished place in the annals of the universe."[167]

Malaspina's chroniclers drew invidious comparisons between their humane behavior toward Indians and the villainous conduct of Englishmen and Americans who sailed the same waters. Viana described Patagonians' bitter memories of an English vessel that fired its cannons at them on the beach, with fatal results. He expressed shock and surprise at this "inhumane act" committed by representatives of a nation he described as "wise, generous, and honored," but he also noted that British whaling ships were "commanded by brutal men, without education or sentiment, whose operations usually contain a larger portion of liquor and beer than of feelings of the heart."[168] As for Anglo Americans, the botanist Moziño criticized their "perverse idea of teaching the savages the handling of firearms—a lesson that could be harmful to all humanity."[169] Another of Malaspina's officers deplored the treatment of Indians by both British and American fur traders in the Pacific Northwest: "Impiously, they rob these unfortunates and they force them with superiority of arms to give their furs . . . or to defend their possessions at the cost of their lives and the ruin of their temples and houses."[170]

Malaspina's officers had reason to take pride in their conduct at Nootka. In contrast to their sixteenth-century predecessors, they had not tried to conquer Indians or subject them to systems of forced labor. Nonetheless, some of the crew of the vessels associated with Malaspina's expedition did not share their officers' lofty sentiments and self-congratulatory humanitarianism. As Moziño described it, "The sailors, either as a result of their almost brutal upbringing or because they envied the humane treatment the commandant and other officers always gave the natives, insulted them at various times, crippled some and wounded others, and did not fail to kill several. Humanity is the greatest characteristic of civilization. All the sciences and arts have no value if they serve only to make us cruel and haughty."[171]

Sailors, of course, outnumbered savants, just as common folk Spaniards outnumbered the enlightened elite in Spain and its colonies. In Spain itself, by one estimate, the ideas of the Enlightenment directly informed no more than 5 percent of the population—a few hundred thousand people.[172] And the enlightened few did not hold uniform opinions about Indians. Even scientists who sought empirical evidence to sustain generalizations about natural phenomena fell back on stereotypes in discussing Indians. The *ilustrado* Antonio de Ulloa, for example, who had explored America with Jorge Juan and governed Spanish Louisiana in 1766–68, continued to hold that laziness, deceitfulness, and rebelliousness constituted an innate part of the Indian character and that Spaniards had to force Indians to work for their own good.[173] The botanist Hipólito Ruiz, who traveled into Indian country in Chile in 1782 to witness negotiations between the governor of Chile and some Araucanian leaders, persuaded himself that the Araucanians were "sullen and warlike by nature" and needed to be pounded into submission rather than treated "with kindness and tolerance . . . as commanded by the Spanish sovereigns."[174] When two Indians whom his exploring party had rescued from slavery fled to return to the wilds, the engineer Francisco de Requena abandoned empiricism: "The devil induced the desertion of these poor wretches" to stop them from becoming Christians.[175]

New ways of thinking about Indians, then, did not supplant the old during the Enlightenment—even among the most enlightened. As in other spheres of thought, contradictory ideas about Indians coexisted in late eighteenth-century Spain and its American colonies (as they had from the beginning among Englishmen as well as Spaniards).[176] That portion of the enlightened minority, however, that saw Indians as rational beings capable of acting like European consumers and producers would have remarkable influence on Spanish relations with independent Indians in the realms of religion, war, commerce, and diplomacy.

Alejandro Malaspina himself had little impact on the course of Spanish relations with Indians. The crown honored him when he returned to Spain from his great voyage in 1794. Carlos IV and his queen, María Luisa, received him at the Escorial outside of Madrid, and the navy promoted him to brigadier. Eighteen months after his return, however, the skillful mariner crashed clumsily on political shoals. The crown had ordered him to confine his political advice to secret memoranda, but Malaspina had urged a public examination of Spain's shortcomings in governing its empire. He suggested that Spain grant its colonies substantial independence and reduce the tariffs and trade restrictions of the sort that had provoked the English colonies to rebellion. "Pettiness and ignorance surround us on all sides," Malaspina wrote to his brother a few months before he unwisely wrote to the king and queen to urge that they replace their principal advisors. His letters fell into the hands of the king's chief minister and the queen's lover, Manuel Godoy, whom Malaspina apparently hoped to unseat. Malaspina's arrest and imprisonment followed. He served nearly seven years in prison before influential friends won his release in 1803 and authorities sent him into exile. Malaspina's papers were scattered, and no published narrative of his voyage appeared in his lifetime. He died in obscurity in Italy in 1810.

Malaspina's journey had allowed him to see remarkable things and gave him, as he put it, "occasion to compare at each step the savage, the plebeian, and he whom we call civilized." His failure to publish his observations, however, robbed Spain of the glory that the publications of Cook and La Pérouse earned for Britain and France in their lifetimes.[177]

2

Savages and Spaniards: Natives Transformed

"Cultures" do not hold still for their portraits.
James Clifford, anthropologist, 1986

On a mission to map the southernmost shores of the continent, the Spanish frigate *Santa María de la Cabeza* approached the Strait of Magellan in December 1785. As the ship dropped anchor at Cabo Vírgenes, its crew spotted fires on the shore, and the captain sent a small boat to investigate. Patagonians on horseback rode down to the beach to meet the visitors. The Natives' leader, who spoke Spanish well, introduced himself as Francisco Xavier. In the manner of Indians of the region, he wore a cape made from the thick, fawn-colored coat of the guanaco, a South American hoofed mammal closely related to the llama, and he carried *bolas,* a weapon made of small, weighted balls on the ends of leather cords that Natives in the pampa and the Chaco had used long before the coming of Europeans. Beneath the guanaco cape, however, he was dressed in the style of a *criollo.* Along with the *bolas* he sported a Spanish saber, which hung in a scabbard from his side, its blade engraved in capital letters with "POR EL REY CARLOS III." Invited aboard the *Santa María,* Francisco Xavier accepted with alacrity. Aware of the ways of Spaniards and eager not to alarm his hosts, Francisco Xavier instructed his companion, a giant of a man, to remove circles of black and white paint from around his eyes. Aboard ship, the two Patagonians smoked and shared a meal with their hosts. They sat at the table, one observer noted, "dexter-

12. The French explorer Alcide d'Orbigny sketched these Patagonians breaking camp in 1829,
at San Javier, a small military post on the south side of the Río Negro, about fifteen miles upriver from
Carmen de Patagones. Long before, horses had become the major mode of transportation for these
northernmost Patagonians, whose toldos, *or tents, of hides and sticks can be seen in the background.*
Départ des Patagons. *Lithograph from Orbigny, 1835–47, vol. 3, ser. 2, no. 5. Courtesy,*
John Carter Brown Library at Brown University.

ously using fork and spoon" while declining wine and brandy because of its ill effects.[1]
Francisco Xavier and his companion seemed entirely at ease. Perhaps it was not their
first visit to "a house of wood, which traveled on the water."[2]

Just as Spaniards had deepened their knowledge of independent Indians over the
course of two and a half centuries, so too had independent Indians become more sophisticated in their understanding of Spaniards.[3] The Indian who introduced himself as Francisco Xavier lived far beyond the regions controlled by Spain. The nearest Spanish settlement of any size on that coast lay over one thousand miles to the north, on the Río de
la Plata. Francisco Xavier, however, had spent time with Spaniards who, in 1779–80, had
established several military posts in northern Patagonia, midway between Buenos Aires
and the Strait of Magellan.[4] Spaniards had clearly influenced his dress and his speech, and
the horse he rode, also introduced by Spaniards, had altered his society. A similar transformation had taken place on the Pacific Coast of Patagonia below Chile; the French
explorer La Pérouse noted in 1786 that independent Indians "are no longer those Americans of old in whom European weapons struck terror." Horses, cattle, and sheep "have
transformed these people into real Arabs. . . . They travel with their herds and feed on

their flesh and milk, and sometimes on their blood; they dress themselves in their skins of which they also make helmets, breast plates and shields .... They follow almost none of their ancient practices, no longer live on the same fruits, no longer wear the same clothes."[5]

By the eighteenth century, direct contact with occasional Spanish visitors and the indirect influences of Spanish trade goods, livestock, crops, and disease had altered the societies of independent Indians beyond the frontiers of the empire, from Patagonia to the Great Plains of North America.[6] In many cases, conflict with Spaniards and diseases introduced by the Spanish had fatal consequences for Indian societies. Some ethnic groups vanished, swept away by epidemics or crushed militarily and subordinated by Spaniards or by even more powerful Native neighbors. Other independent Indians not only survived but reinvented and strengthened their societies. Some retreated; others held their ground; some allied themselves with Spaniards or other Europeans; others expanded at the expense of Spaniards. Some Indians adapted by fission, splitting into smaller units that could more easily elude Europeans; others underwent a process of fusion, absorbing members of other Indian communities, along with Spaniards and blacks who willingly or unwillingly "went native."[7]

We know little about the journeys independent ethnic groups followed on their way to extinction or reinvention, or of the environmental and cultural imperatives that pushed them. We can imagine, however, that in their earliest encounters with Spaniards, those Natives who lived in small, mobile family units, or bands, had the best chance of avoiding conquest. Distance and dispersal made them less susceptible to the European infectious diseases that devastated many sedentary societies.[8] We can also imagine that ethnic and political boundaries were drawn and redrawn more rapidly than ever before in the face of unprecedented changes that Spaniards and other Europeans provoked. In many places once populated by societies organized in bands or loosely knit networks of related families, eighteenth-century Spaniards faced tribes. Their leaders, like Francisco Xavier, knew the ways of Spaniards—both how to cooperate with them and how to resist them.

"Wild Men Extraordinary": Araucanians

Perhaps no Native Americans developed the military capability of maintaining independence from Spaniards more rapidly or effectively than the Araucanian-speaking peoples of south-central Chile. Spaniards invaded their country in the mid–sixteenth century and reduced many to servitude, but Araucanians mounted fierce resistance. In a large-scale counteroffensive of 1598–1603, they destroyed six substantial Spanish towns and took hundreds of women and children captive. Spaniards withdrew from remaining settlements below the Río Biobío, maintaining only an offshore presence on the great island of Chiloé.

In the years that followed, Araucanians frustrated repeated Spanish attempts to regain control over their heartland. By the 1640s Araucanians had won what Spaniards called the War of Arauco. They forced Spaniards to recognize the Río Biobío as a permanent border. Some Araucanians had remained north of the river and succumbed to Spanish overlords, gradually becoming Hispanicized. Araucanians south of the Biobío despised them. They called them *zapatudos* because they wore shoes (*zapatos*) or *reyunos* because they served the king (the *rey*).[9]

Even as independent Araucanians lost respect for their brethren who fell under Spanish control, Spaniards gained respect for Araucanians who remained independent south of the Biobío. One Spanish soldier who fought in the bitter War of Arauco, Alonso de Ercilla y Zúñiga, returned to Spain to craft an epic poem that immortalized Araucanian valor, as these lines suggest:

> Wild men extraordinary,
> Brazen, scorning earth and heaven,
> . . . .
> Stalwart limbs and steely sinews;
> They are confident, emboldened,
> Dauntless, gallant, and audacious,
> Firm inured to toil, and suffering
> Mortal cold and heat and hunger.[10]

Read throughout Europe, Ercilla's *La Araucana* spread the reputation of Araucanians as an indomitable people and gave currency to the name Araucanian. Ercilla used the word *Araucanian* (*araucano*) to denote Indians in the locality of Arauco, an Araucanian word meaning "muddy water." The word came to signify the Natives' language (what specialists today call *mapudungún* rather than Araucanian) and one of the ethnc groups who spoke it—the peoples who lived between the Toltén and Biobío rivers.

Following the Araucanians' stunning victory, Spaniards tried again to resettle the lands below the Biobío, but Araucanians forced them to retreat. Finally, in 1745–47, almost a century and a half after its abandonment, Spaniards reconstructed Valdivia as a fortified garrison when Dutch pirates threatened the coast.[11] Supplied by sea from Peru, Valdivia remained the only significant Spanish enclave on the mainland below the Biobío until 1796, when Spaniards reestablished Osorno, which Araucanians had forced them to abandon in 1600.

Indians everywhere had powerful reasons to avoid falling under Spanish domination. At worst it meant slavery, at best heavy payments of tribute and personal service. Araucanian-speaking peoples, however, had unusual success at regaining and maintaining their freedom, and they owed that achievement to a lucky combination of circumstances.[12] Their dense population gave them a numerical advantage over the Spaniards. Their dispersed social organization made it impossible for Spaniards to negotiate with a central authority or conquer them as a single people by seizing a leader. Their economy, characterized by a mixed subsistence system that depended more on hunting and gathering than on farming, articulated poorly with that of the Spaniards during the early years of contact. Their lack of complete dependence on formal agriculture denied Spaniards the opportunity of forcing them to the bargaining table by destroying their crops. Their climate, characterized by an eight-month rainy season, gave them respite from Spanish troops, who preferred to fight during the four-month dry season. Their geography, which included rugged mountains, dense tropical forests, and swamps, afforded refuge from Spanish forces. Moreover, they fought to defend familiar terrain against poorly equipped and undercapitalized private armies that could not sustain a long war without assistance from the Spanish state—assistance that did not come until the early 1600s and then modestly.[13] Chile, which lacked precious metals, stood low on the list of imperial priorities.

Favorable circumstances helped Araucanians gain and maintain their freedom, but they also capitalized on their advantages. Their resistance to Inca attempts to incorporate them (Incas knew them as *aucas*, or savages) had honed their skill at warfare long before the arrival of Spaniards.[14] Araucanians came to see war as central to maintaining social, political, and even cosmic equilibrium.[15] When Spanish intruders presented a new challenge, Araucanian warriors—like Indians on other frontiers of the empire—adopted new strategies and technologies and married them to tactics and weapons that had worked well in the past.[16] Even before Spaniards fled the Araucanía in 1603, leaving many of their possessions behind, Araucanians had acquired a considerable number of Spanish horses, helmets, armor, and iron weapons, together with lessons on how to use them from Spanish deserters. Stockmen who raised guanacos and llamas before the coming of Europeans, Araucanians readily augmented their livestock with cattle, sheep, pigs, and horses introduced from Europe. By 1600, they possessed large horse herds and had become excellent horsemen. They mobilized units of light cavalry in their successful struggle against the new Iberian overlords.[17]

Spanish iron made Araucanians' traditional lithic weapons—lances, clubs, and hatchets—more deadly and durable. To these, Araucanians added Spanish pikes, sabers, swords, and machetes.[18] Until late in the colonial period, Araucanians made little use of Spanish firearms that fell into their hands. They could not easily obtain ammunition, and their own tactics and weaponry proved so effective that they may have had little incentive to make gunpowder and shot. Then, too, limited range, accuracy, and rate of fire of European matchlock or flintlock weapons offered little advantage. Difficult-to-ignite firearms left their users vulnerable in lengthy intervals between shots. A Pehuenche told a Spanish officer in 1792 that Indians had "no need to fear Spaniards because they can do no more damage than get off the first shot, and after that . . . they are defeated."[19]

Disdain for firearms, however, was unusual among Indians. Most tried to obtain guns to augment, but not to replace, their traditional weapons. Natives with firearms had an edge over neighbors who lacked them. Firearms offered psychological advantages and greater penetrating power than bows and arrows. Warriors trying to take or defend a fortified place found firearms especially effective. Some Spanish officials regarded firearms as inferior to Indian bows and arrows (weapons little used by Araucanians), but their views did not represent the conventional wisdom. Until late in the colonial period, Spanish law prohibited Spaniards from supplying Indians with firearms. Officials' repeated injunctions to Spaniards to follow the law, however, suggest that scofflaws continued to ignore it.[20]

A. Indienne du Chily broyant du mays pour en faire de la farine.
B. Indien en Poncho et Polainas
C. Indienne en Choñi et yqüella
D. Indien jettant le laqs au taureau pour l'arreter

13. *The French explorer Amedée Frézier included this didactic image
of Araucanians in his* A Voyage to the South-Sea and Along the Coasts
of Chili and Peru, in the Years 1712, 1713, and 1714,
*published in London in 1717 with plates from the original French edition.
Here (in plate 10, facing p. 71), he shows*
A. *Indian woman grinding Maiz, or Indian corn, to make Meal*
B. *An Indian in his loose Garment, call'd Poncho and Buskins [leather boots]*
C. *An Indian woman in her Chonni and Iquella, the names of her cloak and coat*
D. *An Indian casting a Noose at a Bull, to stop him*
He goes on to explain, "The Spaniards have taken up the Use of the Chony, *or*
Poncho, *and of the Buskins, by them call'd* Polaina's *[sic:* polainas *in Spanish],
to ride in, because the* Poncho *keeps out the Rain, is not undone by the Wind,
serves for a Blanket at Night, and for a Carpet in the Field." (p. 71).
The women, he says, wear a "little square Piece of Stuff call'd Iquella [a shawl],
the two Sides whereof are made fast on the Breast with a great Silver Pin,
which has a flat Head four or five Inches diameter, by them call'd* Toupo
*[tupu in Mapuche]" (p. 71). Courtesy, Huntington Library,
San Marino, California.*

Once acquainted with Spanish military organization, strategy, and tactics, Araucanians adjusted their fighting style to counter them, not merely imitate them. They invented a hybrid cavalry-infantry in which each horseman carried a footman to the scene of a battle. They burned fields to deny pasture to Spanish horses; they lured Spanish soldiers to watery or hilly terrain to neutralize the effectiveness of horses and guns; they attacked in the rain when Spaniards could not strike the matchlocks on their muskets. Annually, in the early 1600s, Spanish forces entered the Araucanía and returned empty-handed. "The Indians," wrote one embarrassed official, "died of laughter."[21]

Protracted war with Spaniards changed more than tactics, it also changed social relations at all levels of Araucanian society. As Araucanians, particularly those closest to the Río Biobío, resisted a state society that sought to dominate them, social relations within and between Native communities became more stratified. Endemic warfare gave the most skillful or aggressive warriors greater opportunities to obtain power, status, and wealth, measured in these cash-free societies by the possession of goods, livestock, and women. In the polygamous, patriarchal Araucanian society, the most successful warriors acquired surplus women as battlefield fatalities reduced the number of men in proportion to women or as raiders seized Spanish women and women from other tribes.[22] Indian warriors who possessed European goods and wives taken in warfare valued them as much for their symbolism as for their utility. These visible signs of their fighting prowess raised their status among their peers.[23] An Indian on the upper Orinoco who asked a friar "how many wives our king had" must have been amazed to learn he had but one.[24]

Among those who achieved high status as war leaders among Araucanians were white captives or white fugitives and their mestizo children. Possessed of special knowledge of Spanish society, these so-called white Indians often parlayed that knowledge into power and became chiefs or caciques. In one remarkable case, the descendants of Rodrigo de las Cuevas, captured in Valdivia about 1600, served as the principal leaders of an Indian community at the mouth of the Río Toltén for the next two centuries.[25]

To fend off their Spanish adversaries, Araucanian military leaders also formed new political structures. Before the arrival of Iberians, a small band consisting of several extended families presided over by an elderly, respected male cacique (a *lonco* or *ulmen*) had been the common sociopolitical unit among Araucanians. Termed *lebos* or *rehues* (the name of the sacred space of each *lebo*), these units came together to form an *ayllarehue* (*aylla* means "nine," the number of *rehues* it apparently took to make an *ayllarehue*). By the mid-1600s, however, it appears that the need to coordinate a large number of combatants in a collective military response to Spaniards had pushed the *loncos* to form even larger entities. Araucanian leaders, from the Biobío south to the Toltén, organized loose communication networks, or *butalmapus*, a word meaning "large lands." In the mid-1700s, three *butalmapus* ran north and south in long strips between the Biobío and the Toltén. Each corresponded roughly to a physiographic region—the coast, the coastal range, and the central valley, or *llanos*. A war chief, or *toqui*, headed each *butalmapu* and apparently coordinated military strategy with his counterpart in the other *butalmapus*.

These loose confederacies lacked clear boundaries, changed over time, and existed largely as units of communication when Araucanians mounted resistance to Spaniards or negotiated with them. For their part, Spaniards understood *butalmapus* to be the equivalent of provincial governments and welcomed them as useful administrative units through which they might control Araucanians.[26]

Sociopolitical changes provoked by war with Spaniards extended to the Araucanians' very identity. Like many other Native groups, the peoples Spaniards knew as Araucanians called themselves as the *che* (the "people") or the *reche* ("the authentic people"). One way they distinguished between themselves and their neighbors was by the cardinal points of the compass. They referred to peoples to their north as Picunches and peoples to their south as Huilliches. Initially, these names signified only relative location, not ethnicity—north or south depended on where the person using the descriptive label was standing. With the passage of time, Spaniards applied these relational names to Indians who lived in specific regions. Meanwhile, Indians themselves adopted these names to identify themselves as belonging to a group larger than their immediate family or their clan. Although they masked a degree of cultural diversity within each group and papered over deep political divisions, these names distinguished Indians from Spaniards and from other Indians.[27] *Picunches* came to signify all Araucanian speakers who lived to the north of the Biobío and who, by the 1700s, had been absorbed by Spanish society and disappeared as an ethnic group. *Huilliches* denoted those who lived south of the Río Toltén, farthest from Spanish influence. Spaniards usually restricted their use of *Araucano* to the Natives who lived between the Biobío and the Toltén—although by the mid-1700s Spaniards began to refer to Araucanians in this region as Mapuches, meaning "the people of the land." Beyond that, Spaniards made still finer distinctions, referring to Mapuches who lived by the sea, for example, as *costeños* (from *costa*, meaning "coast") and to those who lived in the central valley as *llaneros* (from *llano*, meaning "plain").[28]

To defend themselves from Spanish aggression, then, small family bands of Araucanian speakers, the *che*, amalgamated into larger social and political units whose structures, values, and ethnic identities differed from those of their forebears. This phenomenon of "tribalization" was a commonplace response of kin-based peoples to political and economic pressures from state societies and suggests to one student of violence that "it is not ethnicity that determines war but conflict which creates ethnicity, and . . . *colonial conflict creates 'tribes.'*"[29]

As the once-segmented societies of the *che* merged into new, more powerful ethnic polities, they influenced or absorbed non-Araucanian speakers. The prosperous mountain-dwelling Pehuenches, who occupied a vast Andean region of humid forest, offer the best-known example. They represented diverse ethnic groups, but by the eighteenth century they had taken on many of the characteristics of Araucanians as well as the Araucanian language and an Araucanian name. A Spanish officer who visited them in 1760 described them as a single people. They lived in tents made from animal skins, raised horses, cattle, oxen, sheep, and goats, and crafted products from ostrich feathers, leather tanned by the

PACIFIC
OCEAN

Santiago

Mendoza

San Luis

MELINCUÉ

MERCEDES   ROJAS

SALTO   ARECO   Buenos Aires

LUJAN
NAVARRO   LOBOS
MONTE

RANCHOS
CHASCOMÚS

SAN CARLOS
(1770)

Río Diamante

Pehuenches

Ranqueles

Talca

*Pehuenches
de Malargüe*

Río Maule

Chillán

*Pehuenches
de Balbarco*

CONCEPCIÓN

*Río de
la Laja*

ARAUCO

Río Biobío

LOS ÁNGELES

Mapuches

Río Toltén

VALDIVIA

Río Bueno

OSORNO
(ABANDONED
1600-1796)

Huilliches

SAN CARLOS
(TODAY'S ANCUD)

CASTRO

Isla de
Chiloé

Río Atuel

Río Salado

Río Neuquén

Río Limay

Choel Choel

*Lago
Nahuel Huapí*

Pampas

*Sierra de
la Ventana*

*Sierras del
Tandil*

Río Colorado

Río Negro

Río Salado

Río Paraná

Río de la Plata

CARMEN DE
PATAGONES

Patagonians

*Golfo de
San Matías*

SAN JOSÉ

ATLANTIC

OCEAN

40°S

*Archipiélago
de los
Chonos*

*Golfo de
San Jorge*

0   300 mi

0   300 km

PUERTO DESEADO

45°

*Golfo de
Penas*

*Archipiélago
de Guayaneco*

• Town

■ Fort

♱ Fort and mission

Present-day
international boundary

Spanish road

PUERTO SAN JULIÁN

50°

Cabo Vírgenes

*Islas Malvinas
(Falkland Is.)*

75°   65°   60°   55° W

Map 4. The Araucanía, the pampa, and Patagonia, 1781. Adapted from Villalobos R., 1989, 177;
Marfany, 1940, 329.

women, and wool that women spun and wove. Women as well as men traded these items to Spaniards in exchange for Spanish manufactures and agricultural products, such as wheat and indigo.[30] Because their diet depended heavily on nut-bearing pine trees called *pehuenes,* these mountain dwellers came to be known as the "people of the *pehuén,*" or Pehuenches. Eighteenth-century Spaniards saw them as a single ethnic group divided into subgroups based on locale—for example, the Pehuenches de Malargüe or Pehuenches de Balbarco—but erroneously imagined that Pehuenches had always been a culturally homogeneous people or nation.[31] For Spaniards of the eighteenth century, the word *nation* might mean the nation-state, but when they used it in reference to Indians it commonly meant a group. In the words of Félix de Azara, *nation* referred to a group of Indians who are "free or savage" and who "may consider themselves as forming a single . . . nation and who may have the same spirit, the same forms, the same customs, and the same language."[32]

The horse, which made Araucanian speakers more mobile, contributed to the homogenization and expansion of Araucanian culture. Horses improved communication between isolated communities, facilitated the spread of ideas as well as material goods, and helped forge new identities.[33] These regionally based identities took on additional meaning in the presence of an external force. Pehuenches, for example, seem to have formed their own *butalmapu* by 1760, if not before. Endemic war with Huilliches as well as pressure from Spaniards had impelled Pehuenches toward a more centralized political structure. In turn, groups of Huilliches, often at war with one another as well as with Spaniards and Pehuenches, forged their own political alliances south of the Río Toltén. Intertribal war, then, as well as the influences of Spaniards galvanized Indian peoples into larger political units which became new loci of their identities.[34]

Like other independent Indians around the edges of the Spanish Empire, Mapuches, Pehuenches, and Huilliches adopted the material culture of Spaniards. Observers often described their leaders, even in the most remote areas, as being dressed "in the Spanish manner." Some became Spanish allies and fought alongside them against other Araucanians.[35] Most of the *che,* however, adapted in ways that strengthened their ability to remain independent of Spaniards. As late as 1780, a Franciscan, Antonio Sors, estimated that two-thirds of the Chilean Indians "do not recognize our Sovereign."[36] He had in mind Mapuches, who numbered at least 80,000, Pehuenches, whose population easily exceeded 10,000, and the more remote and difficult-to-count Huilliches, who may have totaled 20,000—this at a time when the entire Chilean population north of the Araucanía was about 310,000.[37] Had he looked eastward across the Andes, fray Antonio would have found more "Chilean" Indians who did not recognize Spanish sovereignty. Having assimilated aspects of the culture of invading Spaniards in Chile, Araucanian speakers had spilled over the mountain passes into lands that would become Argentina, where they made a deep imprint on the cultures of its indigenous peoples.

Araucanizing the Pampas and the Patagonians

The eastern slope of the Andes had attracted Araucanians before the coming of Euro-peans, but horses, which shrank time and space for travelers, eased trans-Andean travel over ancient trade routes.[38] Spanish-introduced horses and cattle had spread rapidly on the grass-rich Argentine pampa and gave Araucanians additional motive to travel east-ward. Horses, introduced at Buenos Aires in 1537, could be found at the Strait of Magel-lan by 1580, and by the mid-1700s one observer noted that livestock covered the pampa "as if it were an hacienda or estancia."[39] With Pehuenches in the vanguard, Chilean In-dians began in the 1600s to avail themselves of feral horses and cattle that could be had for the taking on the pampa. They drove the livestock back over the Andes, following well-worn trails, or *rastrilladas,* such as those that crossed the well-watered eastern pampa —the *pampa húmeda*—to the Río Colorado and the Río Negro. From there, the *rastrilla-das* led them westward across the higher and drier *pampa seca* and over ancient mountain passes. In Spanish Chile, decades of war had created shortages of livestock, and demand in Chile and the Araucanía would continue to outstrip supply even in times of peace. By the early 1700s, one observer reported, most of the cattle consumed in Chile came from the eastern side of the Andes.[40]

In the eighteenth century, Araucanians' forays onto the pampa brought them into conflict with Spaniards as overhunting decreased the numbers of wild horses and cattle at the same time that the Spanish population rose. In towns along the eastern edge of the cordillera, from Tucumán to Salta, in the mines of Peru, and in Chile itself, heavy demand for beef, hides, and tallow encouraged overhunting. In 1715, the city council of Buenos Aires announced that wild cattle were nearly extinct in the province. No longer able to round up wild animals, Spanish ranchers began to domesticate their herds.[41]

Chilean Indians responded to the decline in wild animals by stepping up raids on Spaniards' domestic herds and on Spaniards themselves. In the late 1600s, Pehuenches had begun to attack estancias in the arid country near the oasis cities of Mendoza and San Luis in the province of Cuyo. By 1711, Araucanian raiders reached the rich grasslands in the province of Buenos Aires.[42]

Araucanian speakers did not cross the Andes to defeat an enemy; they went on hunting and looting expeditions, which local Indians joined. A pattern emerged early in the cen-tury. Traveling in small numbers on horseback, Indian raiders staged surprise attacks on Spanish estancias in which they not only drove away cattle and horses, but carried off women, children, and portable European goods ranging from tools to jewels. Span-iards in Argentina knew these raiders by the name *Aucas,* a word Incas had used to de-scribe these "savages." Argentines understood, as Azara explained, that Aucas were "a division or faction of the famous Araucanians of Chile."[43] By the mid-1700s, as Auca raids intensified, the Araucanian word for raiders—*maloqueros*—and the Araucanian words for raids—*malocas* and *malones*—entered the vocabulary of Spaniards in Buenos Aires, where they spelled terror.[44]

14. *A surprise attack, or* malón. *An engraving based on an oil painting by the Bavarian artist Johann Moritz Rugendas, who traveled into Araucanian country below the Biobío in 1835, in Gay, 1854. A color reproduction of the painting is in Bindis, 1989, 46. Courtesy, John Carter Brown Library at Brown University.*

While some of the Araucanian *maloqueros* who struck on the eastern side of the Andes pushed stolen herds homeward, other Araucanians crossed to the Argentine side of the Andes and never returned. By the mid–eighteenth century, mountain-dwelling Pehuenches, joined on occasion by Mapuches, had expanded northeast to the Río Diamante, east to the Río Salado, and southeast to the Río Neuquén. Pehuenches, who had become excellent horsemen, might have pushed farther east into the *pampa húmeda,* but other Araucanian speakers, particularly Huilliches, blocked their way. Drawn by horses and cattle to the Argentine pampa, Huilliche raiders gradually pushed northeasterly from their lands below the Río Toltén on the Pacific side of the Andes to extend their influence over northern Patagonia and the pampa from the Golfo de San Matías to the province of Buenos Aires. In 1765, a Spanish war council meeting in Concepción characterized Huilliches as "the most rebellious and obstinate nation who inhabit the other side of the Cordillera Nevada [the Andes], committing continuous hostilities, murders, and robberies against Spaniards who travel from Chile to Buenos Aires."[45]

Across the Argentine pampa, south of the road running from Buenos Aires to Mendoza, Araucanians flowed into lands that Spaniards had never effectively conquered. As late as the 1780s, Spanish estancias remained north of the Río Salado, less than a hundred miles from Buenos Aires. Nowhere else in the late eighteenth century did a viceregal capital come so close to the lands of independent Indians. Beyond the Salado lay what Spaniards called the *tierra adentro* or *tierra del enemigo*. To casual observers, oblivious to the variety of ecological niches on the pampa, the region seemed both uninhabitable and nearly devoid of people. In the early nineteenth century, Argentines would call it a desert, much as North Americans mistook their Great Plains for the "Great American Desert."[46]

In the eighteenth century, Indians known to Spaniards by a variety of names, but often called Pampas, inhabited the lands south of the Salado to the Río Negro; Patagonians dominated the region from the Río Negro to the Strait of Magellan. (Araucanians knew both Pampas and Patagonians as Tehuelches, or "wild people," a word also adopted by Spaniards and used today by some ethnologists.)[47] Denizens of harsh lands, Pampas and Patagonians migrated with the seasons, making their homes along the shores of lakes and streams where they found firewood as well as water.

With the coming of Spaniards, Pampas and Patagonians became mounted hunters of cattle and horses, their societies transformed in ways that made them, like the Araucanians, more formidable warriors. Horses increased their range, facilitated their consolidation from small family groups into larger bands and tribes, and made it possible for their leaders to command larger forces than ever before. Horses, cattle, and sheep provided a steady supply of protein, and an enriched diet probably contributed to an increase of population among these Natives who previously hunted guanacos and ostrichlike rheas on foot. With the coming of European livestock, Pampas and Patagonians no longer had to move with the seasons to follow game. Owners of European animals could also use them in trade and so had additional motives to acquire them. In exchange for horses or hides, for example, Pampas obtained woven blankets and silver jewelry from Huilliches and pine nuts, ponchos, hard cider (*chicha de manzana*), and Spanish-made liquor from Pehuenches, who traded it from Spaniards in Chile and the Andean province of Cuyo.[48]

The Pampas and northernmost Patagonians experienced Spanish-induced change earlier than Patagonians who lived farther south. The more northerly people lived in a temperate zone below the Río de la Plata where horses thrived and where they had more direct access to Spanish goods and livestock. Southernmost Patagonians inhabited arid steppes, where feral cattle and horses did not multiply as rapidly, and may not have become horsemen in meaningful numbers until the mid-1700s.[49]

Whatever the variations in time and place, the grassy plains of Argentina became the site of intense competition among Indians as well as between Indians and Spaniards. Some smaller ethnic groups, such as the mountain-dwelling Huarpes (a subgroup of Pampas in the area of Mendoza), seemed to disappear, their numbers already thinned by disease and Spanish demands for labor. Others, like the Puelches, remained identifiable as a group but came to speak the Araucanian language (*mapudungan*) by the mid-1700s, along with their own idiom (Native Americans were commonly bilingual or multilingual in areas where they lived close by members of other language groups).[50]

To different degrees, Pampas and Patagonians became Araucanized as they vied with

Araucanians pushing over the Andes. They gradually adopted many of the cultural traits and religious beliefs of the more numerous and militarily experienced Araucanians, including weaving, metalworking, and language itself. Pampas, for example, began to refer to non-Indians as *güincas,* the same word Araucanians used for them in Chile.[51] The phenomenon of Araucanization is well known but the process is dimly understood, perhaps because it took many forms. On some levels, cultural and societal changes occurred peacefully, as Pampas, Patagonians, Huilliches, Mapuches, and Pehuenches formed alliances and intermarried; at other levels, violence or force induced societal changes, as bands of different ethnic groups contested with one another for resources and power.[52] By the late eighteenth century, the Araucanians' language had become the lingua franca of the pampa, and Araucanians had influenced Argentine peoples in a territory ten times larger than the region in Chile from which they had come. The Araucanization of the pampa continued into the first half of the nineteenth century as Araucanian speakers continued to migrate across the Andes.[53]

Cultural traits did not move in one direction only, as the word *Araucanization* suggests. Araucanians also felt the influence of the Tehuelches, as they called Pampas and Patagonians. Araucanians living on the pampa, for example, adopted portable tents (*toldos*) of animal skins and riding boots made from the skins of horses' legs, and words from Tehuelche, the language of Pampas and Patagonians, entered the vocabulary of Araucanians.[54]

In economic terms, Araucanization took place more gradually and with greater local variations than scholars once supposed.[55] Not all Araucanized Pampas or Patagonians became hunters on horseback who preyed on Spaniards and their livestock. To the contrary, as herds of wild animals diminished and as Araucanians introduced agriculture, animal husbandry, and European crops such as wheat and barley, some "wild" Tehuelches took up farming and ranching. Among Pampas, as among Araucanians, farming, sheep raising, and weaving became principally the work of women, whose lives also were transformed by the spread of sheep, growing markets for textiles, and the demands of specialized production for those markets.[56]

Some Araucanians and Araucanized peoples abandoned agriculture to become stock raisers for Spanish markets, unaware that they were moving backward on the evolutionary scale that, according to some European theorists, placed agrarians ahead of herding peoples. Pehuenches who inhabited the eastern foothills of the Andes south of Mendoza in today's Argentine province of Neuquén, for example, gave up farming in favor of more profitable ranching. They domesticated herds and flocks, maintained them in corrals, rotated pastures, and practiced transhumance. Then they drove their fattened horses, cattle, and sheep across the Andes, where they traded them for grains and other goods at markets in Chile.[57]

Whatever the local economic variations, however, the outlines of larger sociopolitical transformations on the pampa and in Patagonia seem clear. As among Araucanians, small, family-centered bands of Pampas and northern Patagonians coalesced into larger political units.[58] This hierarchical restructuring took place later than on the Chilean side of the

15. As Araucanians and their influences spilled eastward onto the pampa, Indians of the pampa increasingly resembled Araucanians in dress. This elegantly appointed woman—a Pampa, or Auca (words used interchangeably by Spaniards in Buenos Aires)—wore massive Chilean-style silver earrings (the style, rendered in copper, had pre-Hispanic origins), a necklace of silver and glass beads, and a woolen shawl. This lithograph, based on a sketch made in 1828 by the surveyor Narciso Parchappe, shows Araucanized Pampas, or Aucas, and their tents, viewed from Bahía Blanca, with the Sierra de la Ventana in the background. Aucãs et leurs toldos. From Orbigny, 1835–47, vol. 3, ser. 2, no. 3. Courtesy, John Carter Brown Library at Brown University. For the silver and beadwork, see Morris von Bennewitz, 1997, 72, 86–87.

Andes, but it was well under way by the mid–eighteenth century and continued into the mid–nineteenth, when the militarization of Native societies reached its apogee on the pampa. Like Araucanian leaders, the caciques, or *conos,* who headed tribes, or what Spaniards called *cacicatos,* or chiefdoms, possessed more wealth, status, power, and women than their predecessors. The new rich, men and women alike, displayed their wealth with ornaments, decorating their ponchos with round, thin copper pieces, their boots with copper nails, and their bridles and spurs with silver plate. Even their horses' halters glittered with silver trim. Azara, who traveled extensively among various peoples in the littoral of the Río de la Plata, noted that he had not seen "this inequality of wealth, nor similar luxury in dress and adornments among any other wild nation," although he imagined correctly that well-to-do Aucas, or Araucanians, whom he had not visited, made similar displays.[59]

16. *Cangapol and his wife, Huennee, drawn by the English-born Jesuit Thomas Falkner, who "endeavoured to draw his likeness, as well as I could by memory." Falkner estimated that Cangapol was over seven feet tall, "because, on tiptoe, I could not reach to the top of his head." From Falkner, 1935, 26.*

The new aristocrats gained authority over large numbers of their people and territory —authority that Spaniards often recognized. In 1806, as Luis de la Cruz traveled from Chile in search of a new overland route between Concepción and Buenos Aires, he approached the territory of Carripilún, a powerful cacique of the Ranqueles, a splinter group of Pehuenches. He told the caciques from neighboring territory, "I know Carripilún is the governor of these lands . . . and it would be imprudent for me to arrive at his house without first announcing my arrival in his lands."[60] Four years later, Carripilún reprimanded Pedro Andrés García, a Spanish-born military engineer, for failing to alert him of his expedition to the Salinas Grandes, on the pampa deep in Indian country to the southwest of Buenos Aires. Carripilún explained to García that he was "the lord, the viceroy, and king of all the Pampas." García replied, "I am not going to dispute your viceroyalty or the legitimacy of your properties."[61]

On occasion, leaders of various *cacicatos* united under a single leader, notwithstanding that, as one Jesuit observed, "the different nations are at continual variance among themselves."[62] Even temporary alliances gave caciques enormous power. In 1739, for example, the aged Pampa cacique Cacapol, angered at a Spanish slaughter of a group of unarmed Indians, united bands of Pampas and Huilliches into a fighting force of more than one thousand men. Leading his forces into the province of Buenos Aires, Cacapol came within some ten miles of the capital. He reportedly made off with a great number of women and children, twenty thousand head of cattle, and various horse herds, leaving a number of dead Spaniards in his wake. His only casualty, it was said, was a single warrior who became separated from his companions and was taken prisoner. The next year Cacapol's son Cangapol, a giant of a man whom Spaniards knew as cacique Bravo, or "wild," raised an army said to have numbered four thousand. Fearful of another slaughter, Spaniards negotiated with him rather than fight.[63]

Cacapol's offensive in 1739 ushered in nearly a half century of intermittent war on the pampa, war that put Spaniards largely on the defensive. Along the road that stretched westward from Buenos Aires through Luján, San Luis, and Mendoza before descending the Andes into Santiago, mounted Indian raiders whom Spaniards knew by a variety of local names made life uncertain for ranchers, townspeople, and travelers. They frustrated Jesuit efforts to build missions south of the Río Salado, and they forced Bourbon officials to reconsider the way they defended the region against what one officer called "the savage hordes."[64] Indian raiders, the governor of Buenos Aires wrote in 1770, had left the residents of the countryside "in the greatest distress, many crying for the loss of their families, for the captivity of others, and most of them for the destruction and pillaging of their haciendas."[65]

Indomitable Equestrians: The Chaco, the Comanchería, the Apachería, and North America's Southeastern Woodlands

The restructured societies of Araucanians and Araucanized equestrians who controlled much of the cone of South America by the mid–eighteenth century had counterparts throughout the hemisphere. Where Spain's sixteenth-century explorers had used the novelty of guns and horses to intimidate small bands of nomads and seminomads, eighteenth-century Spaniards often faced savvy and formidable Native societies who intimidated them. Refashioned by their adoption of horses and Spanish trade goods, these societies controlled many of the lowland peripheries of the empire from South America to North America and continued to avoid Spanish subjugation.

Some of the most indomitable Indians lived in the Gran Chaco, a lowland plain of some one hundred thousand square miles, half the size of Spain (or about the size of Wyoming).[66] Embracing much of today's northern Argentina, western Paraguay, and southeastern Bolivia, the Chaco took its name from the Quechua word *Chacu*, meaning "great hunting ground" to the Incas. With its thickets of scrubby, thorny woodland alternating with grassy savannas, unnavigable rivers, parched winters, and steaming, rain-drenched summers, the Chaco had little to recommend it to Incas or Spaniards. Hunters, gatherers, fishers, and slash-and-burn farmers, on the other hand, found it a land of plenty as they moved with the dramatically changing seasons from one food-rich ecological niche to another. They made it "their Palestine and Elysium"—"a refuge of liberty and a palisade against servitude" in the words of one Jesuit. "The highest hills served them as

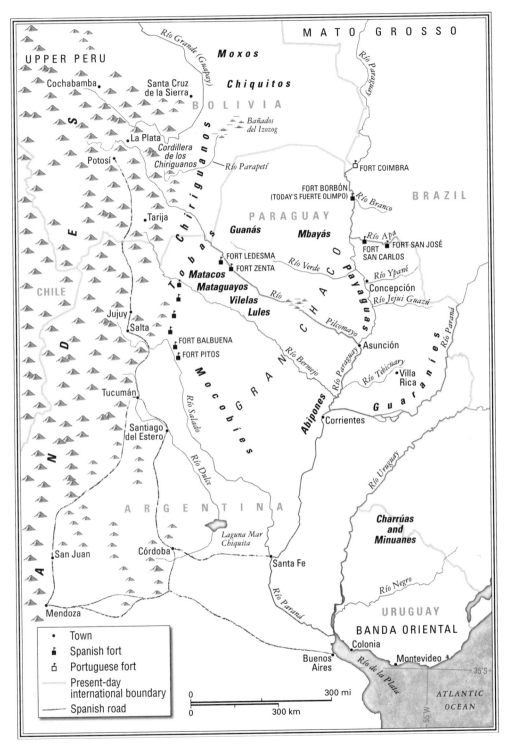

Map 5. *The Chaco, Paraguay, and Upper Peru, 1794. Adapted from Saeger, 1999, 259, the 1774 "Mapa del Chaco" by Antonio Josef del Castillo, in Saignes, 1974, and Brown, 1979, 13.*

watchtowers, the impenetrable woods took the place of a wall, the rivers and marshes a kind of ditch, the countryside, replete with wild animals and fruit trees, a storehouse."[67]

Spaniards knew residents of the Chaco collectively as *guaycurúes,* a Guaraní word for residents of the eastern Chaco that Spaniards applied collectively to different equestrian peoples of the entire Chaco.[68] They also knew the Guaycuruan speakers of the Chaco by the names of their individual nations, such as Abipones, Mbayás, Mocobíes, and Tobas. Like Araucanians and Pampas, these groups quickly lost their fear of Spaniards and their weapons. "They began," one observer noted, "to consider the thundering barrels of the guns of little danger, knowing that they frequently misfired and that if they did fire they would produce a harmless noise."[69] Beginning in the late 1500s, the Guaycuruans began to acquire horses and to dominate their nonequestrian Indian and non-Guaycuruan-speaking neighbors, such as Lules, Vilelas, Matacos, and Mataguayos. The Guaycurúes augmented their diet with cattle and sheep that they appropriated from Spanish missions, ranches, and towns on the perimeter of the Chaco when the annual drought cycle pushed them farther afield in search of game.[70] Unlike Araucanians and Pampas, none of the Guaycuruan groups developed centralized leadership or political structures beyond the level of the band. Once they adopted the horse, however, their bands and raiding parties grew larger and put Spaniards on the defensive.

Employing "great soldiers who certainly competed in their way with those of Flanders," as one Jesuit put it, the fearsome-looking scarred and tattooed Guaycurúes effectively slowed the advance of Spanish missionaries and cattlemen well into the 1720s.[71] In the foothills of the Andes on the Chaco's western edge, Guaycuruan horsemen, especially Mocobíes and Tobas, raided estancias near Córdoba, Santiago del Estero, Tucumán, Salta, and Jujuy, forcing Spaniards to retreat by the early 1700s. They also disrupted commerce along the road that linked those communities to Potosí and other markets in Upper Peru (today's Bolivia).[72] On the eastern side of the Chaco, Abipones, Mbayás, and far-ranging Tobas caused similar disruption. Throughout the Chaco, Guaycurúes frustrated early Jesuit efforts to convert them and eluded Portuguese slave hunters, or *bandeirantes,* who tried to capture them. Mbayás, accustomed to employing their own Indian slaves (the relatively docile Guanás, or Chanés), responded to a suggestion by the Portuguese governor of Mato Grosso that they settle down and take up farming by asking "how many slaves His Excellency was going to send" to help them.[73] Guaycuruan power peaked, however, in the 1720s when disease, intensified internecine warfare, and an environmental crisis combined to decrease the population and weaken the survivors. The once-numerous Guaycurúes, who may have numbered as many as five hundred thousand at the time of their first contact with Europeans, had declined to thirty-five to forty-five thousand by the mid-1700s.[74]

On the northwestern edge of the Chaco, another ethnic group, the Chiriguanos, resisted Spanish efforts to subdue them and expand into their territory.[75] Some submitted to missions, and others found a way to coexist with Spanish neighbors, but most, one Jesuit wrote in 1767, "are today the most decided enemies of the Spaniards and feared throughout the entire region."[76] The Chiriguanos had their genesis in waves of Guaraní immigrants who crossed the Chaco from the east and settled in what came to be called the Cordillera de los Chiriguanos—spurs of the Andes between Tarija to the south and Santa Cruz de la Sierra to the north. The Guaraní newcomers, mostly males, conquered and absorbed members of more numerous highland tribes, especially the Chaneses, Arawak-speaking agriculturalists whom they enslaved. The Guaraní newcomers also incorporated blacks, mulattos, and Spanish captives into their small family bands. Out of this ethnic mixture emerged a people who called themselves Ava, meaning "the people par excellence," but whose neighbors came to know them contemptuously as Chiriguanos, a word that appears to have meant "cold shit" in Quechua.[77]

Through natural increase and continual absorption of Guanás and other peoples, the Chiriguanos' numbers continued to rise, notwithstanding losses they incurred in cycles of raids and reprisals they carried on with Spanish settlements in the province of Upper Peru to the west. By the mid-1700s their population reached its apogee at some two hundred thousand, double that of the late 1600s.[78] Mounted on horseback, their bodies painted red with black stripes and their teeth blue, Chiriguano warriors controlled a swath of mountainous country between Upper Peru and the Chaco, running some three hundred miles between the Río Grande (or Río Guapay) to the north and the Bermejo River to the south.[79]

A continent away, across the vastness of northern New Spain, Spaniards also faced large numbers of Indian raiders on horseback. After two centuries, many Indians had been forced to work in mines or had been drawn into missions. Some, like Yaquis in Sonora, had accommodated to Spanish society while others, like the Tarahumaras in Chihuahua, had retreated peacefully into mountainous regions. In the mid-1700s, however, much of northern New Spain was controlled by independent Indians whose raids made life tenuous for Spanish ranchers, miners, and missionaries. These peoples included remnants of many small groups, such as Seris and Pimas in Sonora and Chichimecas in Coahuila, but they also included Comanches and Apaches, whose numbers had grown to formidable proportions and whose societies had undergone transformations that resembled those of Araucanians, Pampas, and Guaycuruans.[80]

Comanches had their origins in small groups of Shoshone-speaking hunters and gatherers who had spilled out from the Great Basin and, in fits and starts, filtered eastward through the Rocky Mountains in the late 1600s. Horses, bison, and Indian slaves drew them to the central plains, and the opportunity to appropriate livestock and manufactured goods from Spanish settlements drew some of them to the southern plains of New Mexico and Texas. These mounted Shoshone speakers called themselves Nemenu, meaning "the people," but Spaniards knew them as Comanches, from the Ute word *Komántcia,* meaning "the enemy."[81] By the 1760s, the Comanches' dominion ran from the Arkansas River south some six hundred miles to the outskirts of San Antonio and east over four hundred miles from the Sangre de Cristo Mountains of northern New Mexico to the Cross Timbers of today's central Texas. There, in a region of mild winters and abundant grasses, they raised fine horses and mules. They traded the surplus to the agricultural peoples who lived to their east and west—including Spaniards in New Mexico—and to plains peoples farther north, where hard winters took a heavy toll on horses. The Comanche country—the *comanchería*—exceeded Central America in size and stood as a formidable barrier against Spanish efforts to expand to the north and west of San Antonio.[82]

In the late 1700s, Spaniards understood that Comanches fell into four large divisions: western Comanches, made up of Jupes and Yamparicas, and eastern Comanches, consisting of Kotsotekas and Orientales. Within these large divisions were clusters of family groups, tenuously connected into bands. The Comanches' numbers grew throughout the 1700s as they absorbed members of other tribes, including Apaches, Caddos, Osages, Pawnees, Pueblos, and Wichitas. Spanish captives and renegades also added to their numbers. From a population of about eight thousand in 1750 they grew to twenty thousand in 1780, partly by absorbing captives. Comanche women gained status by indoctrinating captives, and senior Comanche men acquired additional wives as status symbols and domestic laborers. As they incorporated other peoples, one historian has suggested, Comanches became more polyglot, cosmopolitan, and better informed about their neighbors.[83]

Along with an increase in prosperity, Comanche society became more hierarchical and adept at large-scale raiding and military operations. Unlike Araucanians, however, whose political structure began to resemble a state, horse-dependent Comanches seem to have reached a critical mass and then become more decentralized as the need to find forage for their ever-growing horse herds forced them to disperse. When the situation demanded it, however, disparate Comanche bands and divisions cooperated. The four divisions, one New Mexico governor observed in 1794, "agree among themselves perfectly. . . . Their interests are common and they have a common destiny."[84]

Apaches had undergone similar migrations and transformations, but Comanches forced them to scatter across much of northern New Spain, where they became a powerful obstacle to Spanish expansion. Athapascan-speaking peoples linguistically associated with Native peoples in Alaska and Canada, Apaches appear to have established themselves in northern Arizona and New Mexico by the 1400s, if not before.[85] Like Comanches, they called themselves "the people," and Spaniards knew them by a word that meant "enemy," the Zuni word *apachú*, with multiple adjectives denoting individual bands.[86]

Like other Native Americans who acquired horses and new external enemies, Apaches coalesced, at least initially, into larger political units. By the mid-1700s, Apaches whom Spaniards identified as Navajos, Chiricahuas, Gileños, Mimbreños, and others came to dominate parts of present-day western New Mexico and southern Arizona. Others, known to Spaniards as Jicarillas, Mescaleros, and Lipanes, flourished to the east of the Río Grande. There they hunted buffalo on the high plains and alternated raiding and trading with Spaniards and sedentary Pueblo Indians in the Río Grande Valley of New Mexico. Spaniards understood that these Apache bands spoke the same language but did not constitute "one uniform nation in their customs, habits and tastes." Indeed, Apaches remained organized in small bands, each led by a chief who did not recognize

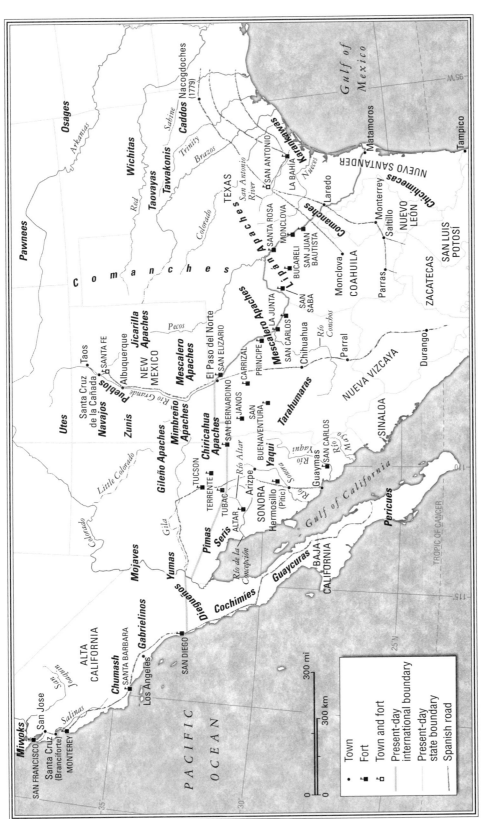

Map 6. Northern New Spain, 1776. On the northernmost reaches of New Spain, Spaniards and their Indian allies, such as Pimas and Pueblos, occupied islands of settlement in a sea of independent Indians, such as Apaches and Comanches. In 1776, Spain responded to the peculiar defensive needs of this region by separating it from the viceroyalty of New Spain and putting it under the direct control of a military commander. Adapted in part from Moore and Beene, 1971, 275, and Weber, 1982, 2–3, 90–91.

the superiority of any other chief, but who might come join others to raid or confront Spaniards. Apache political structure, like that of some other equestrians, was both centralized and decentralized, depending on the demands of the moment.[87]

Although the horse made them more robust warriors and raiders, Apaches who hunted buffalo on the southern plains lost ground to southward-moving Comanches in the early eighteenth century. The plains of today's eastern Colorado, eastern New Mexico, Kansas, and West Texas would seem to have ample space for both groups, but in wintertime each depended on narrow river valleys for water, wood, and shelter. In the summer, Apache farmers needed those valleys to sustain their crops; Comanches, who did not farm, needed them for water. Comanches and Apaches also competed in the same markets for trade goods and corn. In the end, Comanches won. More mobile than the semi-sedentary plains Apaches and possessed of larger horse herds, Comanches drove Apaches south and west, hard against Spanish settlements in Coahuila, Chihuahua, and Sonora.[88]

Comanches also prevailed over Apaches because they had greater access to European firearms, which they obtained from the French via Kansas, Wichitas, and other intermediate Indian peoples, and they stood between Apaches and their principal sources of firearms to the east. Guns and ammunition, it would seem, could not gain widespread currency far beyond their sources because Indians depended on Europeans for a steady supply of gunpowder and lead shot. Nonetheless, Indians who lived at some remove from Europeans might obtain guns and ammunition through Native middlemen. At mid-century the governor of New Mexico warned presciently that Comanches were acquiring such large quantities of firearms, powder, and shot that "they will be greatly feared in this province."[89] Soon they were. By the 1760s, firearms had shifted the balance of power on the southern plains to the well-armed Comanches and their Wichita allies. "The old conquistadors," the leading military officer in northern New Spain observed in 1780, "fought with peoples who had not seen horses or firearms, but Apaches, Comanches, and the other Indians of the North employ them skillfully."[90]

Forced by Comanches into arid areas of Sonora, Nueva Vizcaya, and Coahuila, where other peoples already controlled the best grazing lands and the watercourses that sustained agrarian life, Apaches made their livelihood by appropriating horses, cattle, and crops from their sedentary neighbors—Indians and Spaniards alike. Much like Araucanians, who stole horses from the pampa and drove them to markets in Chile, Apaches became the suppliers for a long-distance trading network. They stole or traded horses in Nueva Vizcaya and Coahuila, for example, and drove them to markets in New Mexico, Texas, and Louisiana; or they obtained horses in Sonora and marketed them in Chihuahua. As they moved deeper into northern New Spain, Apaches also continued a decades-old process of absorbing members of other ethnic groups. Now it would be remnants of groups diminished by their exposure to Spanish arms and disease: Janos, Jocomes, Mansos, Pelones, Sumas, Sobaipuris, and Tobosos. Indeed, one scholar has suggested that the absorption and renaming of these peoples as Apaches was as important to the Apache diaspora as the expansion of Apaches themselves.[91]

Much as Araucanian speakers Araucanized the pampa, Athapascan speakers extended their influence over northern New Spain. What had been a region of great tribal heterogeneity became in the Spanish mind the *gran apachería*, extending from today's northern Sonora and southern Arizona to West Texas and Coahuila—750 miles from east to west and up to 550 miles from north to south.[92] "Their field of action," one Jesuit noted in 1764, "is much greater and extends over a larger area than many of the European kingdoms."[93] "Under the name of Apache are an infinity of nations," Viceroy Antonio María de Bucareli y Ursúa reported to the crown in 1772. "There is no place free from their outbursts."[94]

With some exceptions, like Jicarilla Apaches who went over to the Spanish side in New Mexico, Apaches formed a barrier that blocked Spain's northward advances at mid-century. They isolated New Mexico from northern Sonora and Chihuahua and made travel dangerous throughout northern New Spain. In some areas, like northeastern Sonora, the Spanish frontier receded as the *apachería* expanded. "Apaches and other perfidious and warlike nations," a Spanish investigator reported in 1750, had left Sonora in a state of "deplorable destruction and decay." One out of every four Spaniards had left the province as Apache raiders forced Spaniards to abandon ranches and mines.[95]

From East Texas to Spanish Florida, the woodlands of southeastern North America also saw the genesis of powerful societies of independent Indians, whom eighteenth-century Europeans called Chickasaws, Choctaws, Cherokees, Creeks, and Seminoles (see map 2). These new Indian groups rose from the ashes of the large, socially stratified, and hierarchically organized precontact polities that anthropologists term chiefdoms and associate with a Mississippian tradition. The new came into being after Europeans and their microbes triggered the collapse of the old. Although horses never became central to their economies, these southeastern agrarians nonetheless relied heavily on Spanish-introduced horses and European markets to become commercial hunters. The ways in which they reconstructed their societies, however, varied with their geographical location relative to other Indian and non-Indian groups and by each culture's manner of adapting to or resisting change.[96]

Some newly powerful Indian nations came into being by absorbing other displaced peoples. The Creeks, who had been devastated by European disease in the sixteenth century, assimilated Alabamas, Hitchitis, Apalachees, Chickasaws, Shawnees, Natchez, Uchis, and Yamasees. By the mid-1700s, the ethnically mixed Creeks had reached perhaps thirteen thousand people and continued to grow through natural increase and further absorption of remnants of other Indian societies as well as blacks and whites. By the 1790s, they had a population of more than twenty-five thousand, including four thousand to five thousand "gunmen."[97] By then, what outsiders described as the Creek Confederacy had begun to emerge. Previous to the 1780s, Creeks identified themselves with their towns or clans, but pressure from the neighboring United States in the 1780s and 1790s pushed some Creek leaders, many of them mestizos, to try to centralize power in order to control individuals and protect property. In the late 1700s, the confederated Creeks became the most powerful polity in southeastern North America, controlling a wide swath of Alabama and Georgia from the Tombigbee River to the Spanish settlements in northern Florida. The new confederate governing structure, however, met staunch resistance from those Creeks who defended traditional values; the tensions erupted into civil war in the early nineteenth century.[98]

In contrast to the Creeks, who augmented and modified their society by absorbing smaller groups, other independent peoples of the woodlands represented a blending of ethnic groups, each contributing ingredients to a new political and social unit. That was the case with the Choctaws, who emerged in Mississippi from the remnants of several societies that had withered under the onslaught of European microbes—a time, as elders of one of those groups recalled, when "the earth ate their children." Before the late 1600s, no people recognizable to Europeans as Choctaws existed. By the 1700s, Choctaws dominated the gulf region between the lands of the Creeks and the Caddo country of Louisiana and East Texas. Like Creeks, distinctive Choctaw groups, each with its own concerns and strategies, organized into a loose confederacy in response to European threats. Contemporaries estimated their numbers at thirty thousand by 1775.[99]

From "Petty Thieves" to "Astute Warriors"

Indians were skilled in the martial arts long before the arrival of Europeans, fighting with one another for land, water, hunting privileges, trade routes, women, slaves, and intangible benefits like masculine prestige, revenge, and spiritual rewards. The most militarized societies, however, may have been those that honed their skills by resisting pre-Columbian conquest by state societies. This appears to have been the case with peoples who withstood Inca expansion—Araucanians, Chiriguanos, and Guaycuruans, and with Chichimecas, who defied the Aztecs and perhaps the Aztecs' predecessor states.[100]

Some scholars have argued that precontact kin-based societies were, by definition, warlike and violent and that "primitive man is . . . a warrior." They see war itself as an expression of culture, if not of human biology.[101] At the other end of the spectrum are those who see war in the Western Hemisphere as the result of European expansion. They do not deny the existence of violent conflict in pre-Columbian America but argue that so-called primitive peoples raided one another for limited objectives: to gain status, women, resources, or revenge. They did not fight to gain hegemony over their enemies or to seek to destroy them because without enemies there could be no future raids in which young men might gain status as fighters. Through raids (or limited, ritualistic wars), this argument goes, small egalitarian Amerindian societies kept one another in check. Then Europeans arrived and created real "war in the tribal zone." War, in this view, is not an expression of culture, but rather a response to material conditions in general and to European influences in particular.[102]

We have ample evidence to discredit the romantic notion that organized violence in pre-Columbian America was little more than a lethal ritualistic game. It produced large-scale dislocations and human suffering that a reasonable person would describe as war.

At the same time, we do not need to explain precontact warfare with the reductionist argument that "primitive" man was predisposed to war.[103]

Whatever the extent of precontact warfare, however, it takes no stretch of the imagination to suppose that Spaniards, like other Europeans, pushed indigenous conflict to new levels, sometimes to the point where war became an end in itself.[104] Indirectly and unintentionally, Spaniards altered the balance of power between Native peoples and raised the level of violence by introducing horses and metal tools that Indians coveted so strongly that they would fight Spaniards, or one another, to gain them. Directly and intentionally, Spaniards also drew Indians into war by identifying them as allies or as enemies or by intruding into their space. As conflict became commonplace, it often altered Indian societies in ways that increased their abilities to resist Spaniards. That fact did not go unnoticed by contemporaries. "From the petty thieves they were at the beginning, we see them converted into astute warriors in proportion to the length of our effort to make war against them," the Minister of the Indies, José de Gálvez, said of the *indios bárbaros* in northern New Spain in 1779.[105]

Reasons for the initial outbreak of hostilities between Spaniards and Indians were usually lost to memory, but Spaniards certainly provoked hostilities when they tried to seize control of resources, including Indians themselves, whose labor Spaniards regarded as theirs to exploit.[106] As Spaniards taxed the surplus production of Native farmers, they left them with nothing to trade to nomads. Spaniards, then, gave nomads reasons to take by raiding what they could no longer obtain by trading and gave Native farmers reasons to turn against them. Indians like the Tobosos, in Nueva Vizcaya, whom Spaniards first described as peaceful farmers, responded to Spanish provocations by becoming "Indians of war."[107] As Spaniards occupied lands where Indians once hunted, fished, gathered food, and cut wood, they deprived hunters and gatherers of their resource bases. From the Argentine pampa to the Texas coastal plains, Indians changed their subsistence strategies and raided agricultural neighbors or "hunted" Spanish livestock.[108]

Indians with strong hunting traditions readily transferred their skills to bagging horses, cattle, and sheep. In dry lands or lands subjected to periodic droughts, Spanish ranchers could not maintain their livestock in corrals and had to let the animals range far and wide. It seems unlikely that Indian hunters paused to distinguish between feral stock and untended Spanish-owned stock. Horses, cattle, and sheep must have seemed indistinguishable from other large game animals, although slower cattle and sheep would have made easier targets. Some Indians simply refused to recognize Spanish ownership of livestock. Spanish cattle, a group of Abipones told one priest, "belongs to them" because they were born on lands that their elders occupied and that Spaniards took "without any right." Or, once they had developed their own herds, Indians like the Guajiros might see the seizure of Spanish stock as a way of defending their own pastures and water from Spanish encroachment.[109]

Even members of an Indian society with what one scholar terms an "antiviolent value system"[110] might still search out Spanish livestock during a time of hunger or attack Spaniards who threatened to punish or enslave them. They would also make off with the spoils of war—just as Spaniards did. Apaches and Comanches apparently regarded the appropriation of the property of strangers or persons hostile to them as justifiable, even admirable, acts. In the value-neutral and bloodless language of anthropology, these Indian raiders were "production units," engaged in "negative exchange" or "negative reciprocity."[111]

Once begun, wars maintained themselves. Each side sought revenge and demonized the other. As war became endemic, it strengthened war leaders on both sides, Indian and Spanish, whose status depended on the continuation of war and who served their interests by promoting it.[112] The prospect of spoils and status raised the expectations of young males, who commonly abandoned peacemakers or irresolute war leaders and threw their support to the most bellicose among them. As the ethos of the warrior grew stronger in a society, it became more difficult to maintain peaceful relations with neighbors, be they Spaniards or Indians.[113]

Some societies may have venerated warriors long before contact with Europeans, but postcontact sources certainly make clear that some independent Indians placed high spiritual value on martial valor. Comanches, according to a Spaniard who lived among them, believed that a warrior who died in battle went to a paradise, where he lived happily ever after as "a child of the sun."[114] Cunas, who dominated Darién (the eastern portion of the Isthmus of Panama), believed that those they defeated in combat would become their slaves to serve them throughout eternity, "the Indian equivalent," one historian acidly noted, "of the Masses that Catholics purchased from the church . . . to enjoy eternal happiness."[115] When warriors had such strong spiritual incentives to fight, peacemakers had little to offer to discourage them.

With or without an ethos that exalted the warrior, Indians who coalesced into so-called tribes and adopted a hierarchical command structure increased their ability to marshal men and resources to resist the forces of the Spanish state and to raid Spanish neighbors. Much as nomadic Mongols on the steppes of inner Asia formed state societies as a way of dealing more effectively with sedentary Chinese neighbors, Native-American societies such as Araucanians, Pampas, Comanches, and Apaches consolidated into larger bands or tribes or found new mechanisms to cooperate when the occasion demanded it. Coalescing, even temporarily, could make them more effective at defending themselves from Spanish encroachment, appropriating property from Spaniards, or negotiating the terms of trade or peace.[116]

By making themselves the conspicuous common enemy, Spaniards themselves may have encouraged intratribal if not intertribal unity, but forces within Indian societies also determined if they would coalesce or remain fragmented. In the Chaco, a fractious political culture prevented Abipones, Mbayás, Mocobíes, and Tobas from creating governing structures beyond the level of the band. Initially, their lack of centralized leadership served them well against Spaniards, but factionalism left them at a disadvantage as their Spanish adversaries gained strength.

In some of the restructured Indian polities, authority concentrated in the hands of a small number of leaders in times of peace as well as war. In those cases, what had been tribes—aggregations of bands with no permanent centralized political hierarchy—moved in the direction of becoming chiefdoms, as a paramount chief rose to the position of permanent leader and their societies became more stratified. Among peoples as various as Araucanians, Pampas, Mocobíes, and Comanches, some leaders possessed sufficient authority to pass their position on to their heirs.[117]

Previously, bands came together temporarily under a single leader to make peace or war, as Spaniards well understood. "They elect a chief to lead them in war; otherwise, each family is ruled by its head," one Franciscan noted of the Apaches.[118] Even in wartime, leaders of these tribal societies often had little coercive power. Instead, they derived authority from their ability to maintain harmony and consensus within the group through rhetorical eloquence and generosity.[119] As the Ranquel cacique Carripilún explained, "I don't have the means to be arrogant, since I don't possess more property than my vassals, nor have more wealth or protection than they do. . . . I need to consult them to proceed firmly on any matter of state."[120] A state of permanent war, however, pushed tribal peoples toward accepting permanent leaders.[121]

None of the new polities of independent Indians in America came to constitute a nation-state or to possess the substantial political structures and professional bureaucracies that we associate with states. Thus, although Indians improved their chances of resisting Spanish domination by amalgamating into larger units, they could not defeat Spain when it brought its full resources to bear against them. "To defeat a state," one scholar has suggested, "takes an organization that functions on its level."[122]

Among some Native people, no single powerful leader seems to have emerged. Instead, cultural forces like a strong sense of competition among warriors or physical restraints like a harsh environment pushed people toward dispersal and factionalism. Even when taken to the extreme of fratricidal internal wars, however, factionalism did not necessarily weaken these societies to the point that Spaniards could defeat them. Some deeply divided ethnic groups, such as the Chiriguanos, Guaycurúes, and Apaches, frustrated Spanish attempts to conquer or co-opt them precisely because they lacked a single authority figure with whom Spaniards could negotiate or whom they could force to surrender.[123] No less than other state societies throughout the world, Spain found it difficult to control seemingly leaderless nomadic and seminomadic people who, as a military junta in Argentina lamented in 1778, "form wandering groups, without fixed settlements or homes."[124] Spaniards, then, could not easily defeat independent Indians, and independent Indians could not defeat the Spanish state.

Throughout the edges of the empire, however, Indians wrought havoc on other Indians in ever more bitter intratribal and intertribal wars, which Spaniards encouraged or discouraged depending on their interests. Some of these internal wars were horizontal, as leaders fought other leaders. Others were vertical, as young warriors fought against senior chiefs and chiefs tried to maintain the traditional social order against upstart young warriors who concentrated and personalized power rather than ruling by consensus. As personal rivalries and power struggles split them into factions, some leaders strengthened their position by allying themselves with Spaniards or with leaders of other ethnic groups, thus widening the scope of war still further. Leaders of losing factions might be killed, their women and children enslaved, and their settlements destroyed.[125] Native groups that avoided fratricidal wars, such as the Comanches, seem to have enjoyed an advantage over their more fractious neighbors.[126]

Where Spanish intruders pushed Indian peoples to coalesce into larger and more bellicose political units, horses facilitated that process enormously. Large numbers of wild horses could be had for the taking, especially on American grasslands in temperate zones where they reproduced profusely. Horses also thrived in the stubby forests of the Chaco and amidst the pines, cypress, and live oaks of what is today the southeastern United States. If Indians feared horses initially, they quickly came to covet and acquire them as a source of food, a means of transportation, a trade item, and as symbols of status and power. When warriors died, Indians as various as Abipones in the Chaco and Blackfeet, Crows, and other peoples of the North American plains sacrificed their horses to accompany them into the afterlife.[127]

Spaniards understood that Indians on horseback (*indios de a caballo*) had a great advantage over Indians on foot (*gente de a pie*).[128] Fearing the dangers posed by mounted Indians and eager to keep them in a subordinate status, the crown had prohibited Indians from traveling on horseback—as it had prohibited conquered Muslims in Iberia. As horses proliferated, however, Spaniards saw their worst fears realized. "Pizarro and Cortés," one missionary noted in the mid-1700s, "subjugated innumerable Indians, killing them or causing them to flee, but they dealt with Indians on foot. If these same heroes returned today to face the Abipones, Mocobíes, Tobas, Guaycurúes, Serranos, Chiquitos, and other equestrian people of Paraguay, I would not venture to assure them the same glory."[129] Indeed, by the mid-1700s, independent Indians in some areas may have possessed more and better horses than the Spaniards who introduced them.[130]

In some respects the horse transformed Araucanians, Pampas, Guaycuruans, Chiriguanos, Guajiros, Apaches, Comanches, and other Indian people in strikingly similar ways. "Once on horseback," as one historian has put it, "whole peoples see entirely new potential both in the land they ride above and within themselves." Indirectly, horses allowed Indians to draw energy from grasslands, a seemingly inexhaustible source previously unavailable to them.[131] With grass-fueled horsepower, Indians became more efficient hunters; infantrymen became cavalrymen who could make deeper forays into enemy territory; Indian raiders could leave women and children at a safe distance from the scene of combat; successful raids against sedentary peoples seemed assured, and raiding became a primary means of subsistence, if it had not been before. Mounted Indians also expanded their ranges into territory traditionally hunted by other Natives, and intertribal conflicts intensified. As it did, institutions of war became more fully developed and war leaders gained prestige and authority to unite small family-oriented bands into larger units to raid or make war.[132]

Indians who built hunting or trading economies based on horsepower, then, found themselves pushed toward residential decentralization and political centralization. Because horses quickly consumed all nearby pasturage, Indians with large horse herds had no choice but to live in small, dispersed bands and to keep on the move. Yet even as horses encouraged dispersal, conflicts with Europeans and with one another pushed these Indian societies to become more effective fighters with more centralized political structures and to invest war leaders with greater authority.[133] Moreover, the very horses that accelerated intertribal conflict also extended intertribal contacts and helped diffuse cultural traits that further united what had been small bands of disparate peoples into Apaches or Araucanians.

The characteristics that militarized "horse cultures" had in common have tended to obscure their differences. The impact of horses on Indian societies depended in part on each group's prehorse economy and culture, the ecological niche that a group occupied, the way it interacted with neighboring peoples—other Indians as well as Spaniards—and the extent to which a group embraced equestrianism.[134] Paiutes in the North American Great Basin ate horses rather than using them for transportation. Pampas used horses for transportation, but also ate them and used their hides for shelter. They renewed their supply of horses through raiding or by rounding up wild horses. Guaycuruans of the Chaco neither ate horses nor sheltered themselves with their hides.[135] Apaches, who continued to farm, had to limit the size of their herds to the amount of nearby pasturage. Moreover, their fixed location left them vulnerable to attacks by fully equestrian Comanches, who maintained larger herds and ranged more widely.[136] Gender roles seemed to change profoundly in some societies that adopted the horse, as among Araucanians and in small ways among Creeks, who replaced women with horses as baggage bearers. Among Cherokees, on the other hand, gender roles apparently remained much the same.[137]

In North as well as South America, independent Indians who adopted the horse did not all become raiders or nomads. Apaches in north central Arizona, who called themselves *diné* (the people) and whom Spaniards came to know as Navajos, acquired sheep as well as horses. They used horses to raid but did not develop a war cult. Instead, influenced in part by nearby Pueblos, some became stockmen and diversified their farming to include cotton. By the late 1700s, they lived in rich farming communities amidst large herds of sheep, goats, and horses. They processed wool and wove fabrics, a governor of New Mexico observed, "with greater care and taste than the Spaniards," and they dressed "decently," adorned with jewelry made of Spanish-introduced silver.[138]

Thus, no single horse culture emerged from Indians' adoption of horses, but rather a variety of cultures that continued to change over time as they competed and collided with Spaniards and with one another. Whatever the case, Indian societies that adopted horses lost even as they gained. Horses, as one astute historian observed, helped Indians "move, hunt, trade, and wage war," but in some Native societies the incorporation of horses also "disrupted subsistence economies, wrecked grassland and bison ecologies, created new social inequalities, unhinged gender relations, undermined traditional political hierarchies, and intensified resource competition and warfare."[139]

Just as the horse was a powerful agent for change in Indian societies, so too were Spanish manufactures and markets. When used for trading or raiding, horses were often just the means to obtain goods that Indians could not manufacture for themselves. Metal objects like spurs, bits, knives, and hatchets, Spanish cloth and clothing, and luxury items such as flour, sugar, tobacco, liquor, and playing cards in themselves generated profound social and political changes in Native societies.[140] Some nouveau riche war leaders enhanced their status as much through trade as through war by redistributing goods and captives and by mediating between the market economy of the Spanish world and the barter economies that characterized many Native societies.[141] Efforts by some chiefs to control trade in foreign goods could itself lead to intratribal wars—wars made all the more deadly as Natives added metal-tipped lances, swords, and firearms to their arsenals.[142]

Independent equestrian societies did not depend solely on raiding and warfare to acquire European-introduced goods. Their transformation through years of contact with Spaniards and things Spanish opened the way for a range of relationships, including commerce. Some raised horses, cattle, sheep, and goats that they traded to Spaniards "on the hoof." Comanches and Araucanians who traded surplus horses *to* Spaniards inverted the traditional role of the European as supplier. Other Indians traded surplus grain they had produced, fruit and nuts they had gathered, or silver or leather they had worked.[143]

Vast trading networks developed in frontier zones where the economies of Spaniards and independent Indians articulated with one another. In such places, the stabilization of economic relations promoted peace, borders became diffuse, and trade became the norm.[144] We often fail to see the extent of those peaceful relations between Spaniards and their savages. Indian traders inspired fewer governmental reports than Indian warriors, and Spanish record keepers often found it to their advantage to portray Indians as menacing rather than peaceful. Along the Spanish–Mapuche frontier, for example, military officials commonly overstated the danger posed by Indians. José Perfecto de Salas, a royal official who traveled apprehensively through Mapuche lands en route to Valdivia in 1749, was surprised to find himself amidst a peaceful people. Spanish officers, he concluded, had exaggerated the Araucanian threat so they could keep their budgets and positions and so they could control the profitable Indian trade below the Biobío.[145] Missionaries also inflated the Indian menace as a way of extracting greater support from the crown, and ranchers, miners, and merchants won tax breaks from the crown on the grounds that they inhabited a war zone.[146]

Influenced by their sources, historians long viewed the Araucanía as a place where Indians struggled heroically against whites for 350 years, from their first contact with Spaniards in 1536 until their crushing defeat in 1883. Closer study of these years, however, has suggested that Spanish–Mapuche relations entered a relatively peaceful phase in the mid-1600s that lasted until the end of the colonial era. Although relations were often tense, complementary economies and the high costs of war created the conditions for peace. Spaniards provoked two so-called Araucanian rebellions, in 1723 and 1766, but those outbreaks were exceptional. Years of close contact between Spaniards and Indians in the broad zone on both sides of the Río Biobío had broken down racial and cultural distinctions. Spanish slaving, which inevitably brought Indian reprisals, had diminished. Meanwhile, each side had come to depend on the other for trade goods. Araucanians needed iron and silver; Spaniards needed horses, agricultural products, textiles, and the labor of independent Indians. In the mid-1700s, then, peaceful commercial relations prevailed between Spaniards and Mapuches in Chile, even as Huilliches and Pehuenches fought one another for control of trans-Andean passes and even as the Araucanized Indians intensified their raids on Spanish trade routes and settlements in Argentina, sending stolen livestock westward over the Andes into Chilean markets.[147]

On a day-to-day basis, however, neither absolute peace nor unqualified war characterized relations between independent Indians and Spaniards, even during times of peace and times of war. Some Natives, like Navajos, raided and traded simultaneously, for no central authority dictated a single Navajo way of interacting with Spaniards.[148] In other areas, outbreaks of violence punctuated long periods of peace or outbreaks of peace punctuated long periods of raiding. Factions of tribes and tribes who made war on Spaniards halted hostilities from time to time in order to trade, sometimes on a regular schedule. As one chronicler noted of the Indian nation in New Mexico in the mid-1700s, "All ask for peace when they find it advantageous, and start war when they find it convenient, every year at a certain time."[149] Some Indians made war on one province while maintaining peace with another. The Abipones, one Jesuit observed, robbed Spaniards on the western edge of the Chaco but took care to maintain peace with one city where they could trade the booty from war for the "utensils necessary for war."[150] Although Indians who alternated raiding and trading struck Spaniards as faithless, they may simply have extended a normal way of dealing with one another into their relations with Spaniards.[151]

Throughout the empire, Spaniards proved to be some of the best customers for manufactured goods and livestock that Indians took from other Spaniards—an irony deplored by some Spanish officials. Notwithstanding frequent orders against trade with *indios bárbaros* in northern New Spain, New Mexicans bought branded livestock from Apaches and Comanches who had driven them north from other provinces. Chileans, at peace with their immediate Mapuche neighbors, traded for livestock stolen on the other side of the Andes. Residents of Corrientes and Santa Fe bought goods and livestock that Guaycuruans had plundered in raids on Córdoba and Asunción.[152]

From the viewpoint of frontier Spaniards, trading with independent Indians bought local peace and profits. From the imperial perspective, on the other hand, Spaniards who bought stolen goods gave Indians incentives to steal and so contributed to the destabilization of the empire's frontiers. In frontier zones where the Spanish demand for labor was high and Spanish institutions weak, Spaniards' trade in one commodity alone, human captives, raised the level of violence. Beginning in the 1580s, at the height of war against the Chichimecas, successive viceroys of New Spain moved to halt slave taking. The practice not only infuriated Indians, but, as the crown understood, soldiers had found slaving so profitable they did not want to end the war and lose their pretext for enslaving Indian "rebels." A century later, in 1683, the Spanish crown abolished Indian slavery in Chile when it recognized that enslaving Araucanians intensified Indian resistance rather than cowing them into submission.[153] Despite these royal prohibitions, Spaniards continued to poison relations with Natives by seizing Indian men, women, and children and forcing the captives to work in mines, haciendas, households, and workshops.[154]

Spaniards did more than seize Indian captives. They also bought Indians from other Indians. By providing a market for Indian captives, Spaniards gave some Native groups incentive to attack and seize their neighbors, thus intensifying intertribal warfare and further destabilizing frontier regions. Yumas, who lived along the Colorado River on the northern reaches of the Sonoran desert, fought with their neighbors before the coming of Spaniards, but their aggression apparently increased in the 1700s as the Spanish market for captives moved northward. Captives were the only commodity Yumas could offer Spaniards for the metal tools and other merchandise they sought. "What wars they have among themselves are born of the interest created by the captives which they seize," a Franciscan noted in 1780. "The profits which are seen in their [the captives'] sale necessitate the continuation of war."[155]

If the desire for manufactured goods led some Indians to bring captives into the Spanish marketplace, Spaniards' treatment of those captives probably strengthened the resolve of many Indians to live apart from the Spanish world. In the early 1740s, for example, two Jesuits tried to persuade a Mocobí cacique, Ariacaiquin, to accept missionaries. Seated on a tiger skin, the cacique told the black-robed Jesuits, "The Spaniards have deceived our ancestors excessively. Their kindness was a falsehood and their friendship feigned. Of course, they only tried to make us slaves and kill us with whips, as if we were not human beings like them and did not have understanding. They used us as beasts of burden."[156] We might discount this putative speech as a missionary's critique of Spanish secular society, but Spaniards who entered Indian territory often heard similar complaints. "We Indians were always suspicious of Spaniards," Carripilún explained in 1806, "because many times they deceive[d] us. Since a single deception is enough to arouse distrust, it does not take much to harbor suspicion in our hearts. You cannot, my friend, deny me this truth."[157]

By the eighteenth century, independent Indians throughout the edges of the empire had good reason to regard Spaniards with suspicion. Those in touch with the Spaniards must have known that they built their colonial empire on the sweat and muscle of Indian laborers. Directly or indirectly, independent Indians had received reports from Indians who had fled Spanish masters, Spanish tribute, Spanish prisons, and Spanish missions, where overseers commonly applied the lash to neophytes who refused to accept what Spaniards called the "gentle evangelic yoke."[158] Spaniards correctly regarded these "apostates and fugitives" as especially dangerous. Spanish-speaking Indians, or *ladinos,* who fled from Spanish towns and missions possessed special knowledge as well as a desire for revenge. Spanish authorities regarded them, along with renegade Spaniards, as the enemy within—as "domestic enemies," in contrast to independent Indians, whom they conceived of as external enemies. Spaniards often blamed independent Indians, such as Apaches, for thefts of livestock that domestic enemies actually carried out, and Spanish officials went on heightened alert when they suspected collaboration between their internal and external enemies.[159]

Strategic Frontiers: Markets, Merchandise, and Autonomy

As much as independent Indians might wish to maintain their independence from Spaniards, the very livestock and Spanish trade goods that helped them strengthen their societies might also weaken them and lead to their subjugation. Indians who came to see Spanish manufactures as necessities rather than luxuries developed a powerful dependency on Spaniards that, in time of crisis, could force them to compromise their autonomy, if not surrender it entirely. As with their adoption of the horse, then, Natives' acquisition of European trade goods had drawbacks as well as benefits.

Mbayás, Guaycuruan speakers who dominated the Río Paraguay above Asunción in the mid–eighteenth century, had acquired horses and used their new mobility to expand their area of influence. They subjugated neighboring farmers, the hapless Guanás, reducing them to a servile class. With metal cutting tools, the Mbayás also became more efficient harvesters of nuts, dates, oil, and hearts of palm from the palm trees that had been the staple of their diet. Indeed, they knew themselves as *eyiguayegis,* or "people of the palm." Spanish-introduced horses and iron lance points also made Mbayás more efficient killers of deer and other game animals and ushered in a period of great prosperity. By the early 1700s, however, they had become victims of their own success. Trade in animal skins with Spaniards spurred them on to hunt more game than they needed for their own use, and their overhunting made animals scarce. The people of the palm also devastated their palm groves with more efficient metal tools. As their subsistence base deteriorated, some welcomed missionaries as a reliable source of tools, clothing, and livestock or made accommodations with Spanish civil society.[160]

Independent Indians who inhabited the strategic frontiers of the Spanish Empire—areas that faced the possessions of other European powers—had greater leverage. The Mbayás' fortunes improved, for example, when Portuguese traders moved closer to their territory in the eighteenth century and eased their dependence on Spaniards.[161] In areas where two or more European nations vied for influence, Indians could play one power off against the others. In the La Plata provinces of Entre Ríos and the Banda Oriental, the Charrúas maintained a precarious balance between Portuguese and Spaniards, and in the borderlands between Texas and Louisiana, Caddos held their own by dealing alternately with Frenchmen, Englishmen, and Spaniards.[162] When one European group became dominant, however, Indians were often forced into alliances with a single European nation. Yamasees and Creeks, for example, embraced Spaniards in Florida as a counter-weight against English slave hunters from Carolina, and Guaraníes preferred Spanish missions to Portuguese slavers.[163]

Until the Bourbons reformed the system in the late eighteenth century, Spain's European rivals usually had more to offer Indians than did Spaniards. The English and the French in particular neither shared Spain's scruples about arming independent Indians, nor suffered from the chronic shortages of guns and ammunition that plagued Spanish officials in America. Thus, Indians who lived on or near the empire's strategic frontiers had greater access to firearms, powder, and shot than those who lived on internal frontiers. The circum-Caribbean alone was an area of multiple points of contact with non-Spanish Europeans: for Creeks along the gulf coast in North America, Miskitos in Nicaragua, Cunas on the coast of Darién, Guajiros who controlled the Guajira Peninsula that straddles the present-day border of Venezuela and Colombia, and Caribs in what is today Venezuela, Guyana, Surinam, and French Guiana (see map 7).[164]

To the distress of their Spanish neighbors, Indians used European firearms skillfully. One Spanish officer admired the speed with which equestrian Guajiros reloaded their muskets. "They take two cartridges from the cartridge holder and load the musket with one and keep the other in their mouth, and as soon as they have shot they reload again."[165] With the booty seized from raiding Spanish settlements, Indians could barter for more weapons and other manufactured goods from their foreign trading partners. Foreigners, then, offered Indians means and motive to raid Spanish settlements. Moreover, Indians who enjoyed access to non-Spanish European weapons and markets rarely succumbed to Spanish arms or the blandishments of Spanish missionaries, although they might instead become dependent on their English, French, or Dutch patrons.

Miskito Indians, who came to dominate the Caribbean coast of Central America from the Bay of Honduras to Costa Rica, are a case in point. Spaniards had known the Caribbean waters of Costa Rica, Nicaragua, and Honduras since Columbus explored them, but Spain had no compelling motive to try to conquer the small groups of Natives who hunted and fished along the winding rivers and lagoons of those hot, humid, insect-infested shores. While Spaniards extracted profits from the labor of sedentary peoples in the hospitable temperate zones of Central America—peoples like Pipiles in El Salvador's piedmont and Mayans in the upland valleys of Chiapas and Guatemala—they left a vacuum on the Caribbean coast. English traders in search of slaves, and pirates in search of safe harbors, began to fill it.[166]

Early on, a small number of Englishmen established a beachhead in the region of Cabo Gracias a Dios, where they formed relationships with Natives whom they came to call Mosquitos or Moscos (we know them today as Miskitos). Although their name does not derive from their possession of muskets, or *mosquetes,* as some scholars have asserted, access to European guns and gunpowder did give Miskitos the means to expand along the coast at the expense of their neighbors.[167] From their first recorded contact with Englishmen in 1633, Miskitos gradually extended their influence along what would come to be known as the Mosquito Coast—the Caribbean side of today's Honduras and Nicaragua. By the early 1700s, their fishing and slaving expeditions took them to Costa Rica and Panama, as far as the Río Chagres. To avoid capture by Miskitos, independent Indians like Sumus and Matagalpas in Nicaragua and Doraces in Panama fled into the interior. Members of other tribes that had remained free of Spanish dominion, such as Caribs in lowland Nicaragua and Jicaques in rugged northern Honduras, remained in the Miskitos' sphere, where they had to pay tribute or risk enslavement. One scholar estimates that Miskitos enslaved some two hundred thousand Indians in the 1700s and sold them to English traders who, in turn, shipped them to Jamaica, Belize, and the English colonies on the North American mainland.[168]

The slave trade with the English brought new products and prosperity to the Miskitos, whose opportunities continued to increase as the foreigners diversified their activities in the eighteenth century—planting indigo and sugar cane, raising cattle, exporting mahogany, and smuggling contraband into the Spanish settlements.[169] The new prosperity came with a price. Accustomed to using firearms, Miskitos lost their skill with lances and bows and arrows. Dependent on English suppliers for their weapons, they also lost a measure of autonomy. Then, too, contact with the Europeans brought measles and smallpox, which diminished the Miskito population.[170] New arrivals, though, augmented the tribe. Black African slaves, introduced by the English, together with blacks shipwrecked along the coast adopted Indian customs and language and melded into the Miskito world. Along the coast of Honduras and down the Nicaraguan coast to Sandy Bay below Cabo Gracias a Dios, which saw the greatest racial mixture between Indians and black Africans, Europeans termed the Natives Zambos, from the Spanish word for children of a union between blacks and Native Americans, or Zambo-mosquitos. From Tuapí Lagoon south, the name Mosquito obtained for the "pure" Miskitos, whom some would later call straight-hair, or Tawira, Miskitos. Although some outsiders characterized Miskitos as a single nation sharing a common language and culture, rivalries between Zambos and Tawiras erupted into war on occasion. Zambos fell deeply under English influence, even welcoming Protestant missionaries. Tawiras resisted Protestant missionaries, and their hunts for hawksbill turtles along the shores of Costa Rica and Panama made them more inclined than Zambos to find some accommodation with Spaniards who patrolled those waters.[171]

Just as contact with foreigners refashioned the Miskitos' economy and their racial composition, so it reshaped their politics and social order. Traditionally, Miskitos had no authority higher than headmen and elders who ruled individual villages. After 1687, however, when an Englishman placed a crown on the head of one Zambo-Miskito, a king ruled the Mosquito shore from his headquarters at Sandy Bay on Cabo Gracias a Dios. Over the years the British anointed a Tawira-Miskito as governor and other Zambo- and Tawira-Miskitos as generals, admirals, princesses, dukes, and colonels. Each of these Indian officials held a separate commission from English officials in Jamaica and went by English names. In 1780, for example, the Zambo-Miskitos' leaders included King

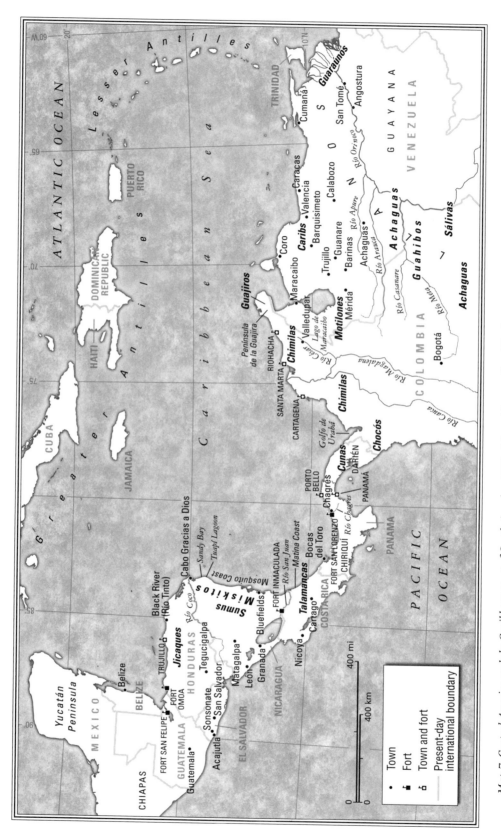

Map 7. *Central America and the Caribbean coast of South America, 1777. Adapted in part from Floyd, 1969, 219, 222, Lombardi, 1982, 111, and Rausch, 1984, 3.*

George II, his brother, Duke Isaac, Admiral Dick Richards, and Col. Julius Caesar. Gov. Colville Briton of Tuapí Lagoon, Gen. John Smee, and Admiral Alparis Dilson, among others, headed the Tawira-Miskitos. Headmen and elders continued to govern villages in time-honored fashion, but the figures in charge of the British-inspired Kingdom of Mosquitia became more than figureheads in the late 1700s. They enjoyed special access to British arms, clothes, and rum and had power to exert authority over villages and raise fighting forces when times demanded it.[172]

Miskitos reached their apogee at some ten thousand by the mid-1700s, Zambo-Miskitos outnumbering the Tawira-Miskitos about two to one.[173] Although Miskitos allowed Spanish smugglers to purchase British goods at Black River and Cabo Gracias a Dios, assuring them safe passage for a price, they blocked Spanish attempts to expand toward the Caribbean coast and shielded English coastal operations. With the aid of their English patrons, Miskitos frustrated the attempts of Spanish soldiers and priests to gain control over Jicaques in Honduras, Caribs in Nicaragua, and Talamancas in Costa Rica. Taking the offensive, Miskitos also crossed over to the Pacific slope and raided Spanish settlements in Nicaragua and Panama. Armed with English firearms, they usually defeated Spanish forces, as in 1756 when they killed Gov. Francisco Fernández de Pastora as he led an expedition to interdict English smugglers along Costa Rica's Matina Coast.[174]

As the case of the Miskitos suggests, access to trade goods and markets from Spain's European rivals strengthened Indians' abilities to maintain their independence from Spanish sovereignty, but it could also exacerbate inter- and intraethnic strife. European gun merchants often set off arms races and increased slave taking, setting tribe against tribe or members of the same tribe against one another. Caribs, whose name for themselves, *Kari'ñako*, meant "the people" and whose name for non–Carib speakers, *itoto*, meant "the enemy," developed a heightened sense of unity and ethnic identity in response to Spanish intrusions into the Orinoco basin and what would become Venezuelan Guayana. Initially the Caribs aligned themselves with the Dutch. Carib unity shattered, however, as rival chiefs pursued their own alliances with Europeans. Even as they maintained their political autonomy, some became known as Spanish Caribs and others as Dutch Caribs. Caribs from one group enslaved those from another and exchanged them for European manufactures. Caribs also turned on their sometime allies, the Guahibos, capturing them and selling them to Europeans. Guahibos, in turn, betrayed their former trading partners, Achagua and Sáliva agriculturalists, and seized their children to sell as slaves.[175]

Access to European goods did not always produce betrayal and human misery. Under certain conditions it could foster stable intertribal trade and often-friendly relationships between peoples with complementary economies. At various times, for example, Kiowas, Cheyennes, and Arapahos, who had access to guns, traded them to Comanches in exchange for horses, which Comanches had in abundance.[176]

By the mid-1700s, a sizable number of independent Indian societies had undergone deep political, social, and cultural transformations in response to Europeans and to elements introduced into their worlds by Europeans. Those transformations took different forms depending on such variables as ecology, geography, intertribal rivalries, intratribal factionalism, propinquity of other European powers, and the cultural values of individual Native groups. On the empire's strategic frontiers, Indians such as Miskitos not only had access to guns and ammunition from Spain's rivals, but provided weapons to Indians who lived in the interior. On the internal frontiers of the empire, from the Araucanía to the Apachería, some equestrian Indians developed highly mobile fighting units that coalesced in time of war but dispersed in times of peace or when Spaniards gave chase. On still other internal frontiers, equestrians and nonequestrians alike forged commercial relations with Spaniards and preferred peace to conflict. These transformed societies of alleged savages posed serious challenges and opportunities for Spain's Bourbon administrators when they turned their full attention to the American colonies in the reign of Carlos III. Could enlightened Spaniards convert them, defeat them, or coexist with them?

3

The Science of Creating Men

The art of making Christians is the science of creating men.
Viceroy Castelfuerte, Lima, 1736

Though our missionaries sometimes make Christians,
they never make civilized men of them.
Jean-Jacques Rousseau, 1755

In 1776, when Carlos III appointed Teodoro de Croix as the
commander in chief of the newly autonomous Comandancia General of the Interior Provinces of New Spain, he instructed him to
make "the conversion of the numerous nations of heathen Indians" his highest priority. In the time-honored formulation of Spanish monarchs, Carlos III ordered Croix to see that the Indians
were brought to Christianity with "the gentle and effective means
that the Laws of the Indies provide: cajolery, good treatment, persuasion by missionaries, gifts, and secure offers of my sovereign
protection."[1]

After surveying the vast jurisdiction of his quasi-viceroyalty,
which included much of what is today northern Mexico and the
southwestern United States, Croix concluded that conversions were
neither gentle nor effective. In Texas, he reported to the crown,
soldiers forced Indians into missions, and Franciscan missionaries
would not let them leave without a permit. Inside the mission an
Indian "has nothing to aspire to for the rest of his life; continuous
work, nakedness, hunger, lack of liberty, and bad treatment are
his fortune."[2] Threatened by whipping, Indians worked from sunrise to sunset. Their labor adorned the churches but produced

nothing for them. Slaves were better off, Croix concluded, because their owners took care to protect their costly investments. Missionaries, on the other hand, could over-work "heathens," or *gentiles,* as missionaries called non-Christians, then send soldiers to recruit a fresh supply.[3]

Croix also indicted the Franciscans for instructing Indians "in Spanish, which they do not understand," so that Indians neither grasped nor appreciated Christianity.[4] After submitting uncomprehendingly to the ritual of baptism and receiving "the name of some saint," Croix said, many Indians fled missions to rejoin their families and other relatives. From these "apostates" and from Apaches and others who visited the Texas missions, other Indians learned that "it is the greatest misfortune to settle in a mission."[5]

Much of what Croix said was true. Franciscans themselves acknowledged that some of their brethren in Texas deprived Indians of their freedom and forced them to work. Most Indians in the San Antonio missions either succumbed to disease or stayed just long enough to regroup and flee. For some Indians, as one scholar has put it, missions "were refugee camps to be quitted when life returned to normal."[6] At the mission of La Bahía del Espíritu Santo, down the river from San Antonio, Indian fugitives kept the missionaries busy "almost continuously . . . like hunters in search of wild animals, search-ing for Indians," one Franciscan complained.[7]

Similar criticisms of missionaries could be heard from many quarters of Spain's Ameri-can empire. Antonio Caballero y Góngora, an enlightened, Spanish-born priest who rose to become both archbishop of Bogotá (1778–89) and viceroy of New Granada (1782–89), leveled a withering assessment of missions in his province. He accused missionaries of using "force and fear" to compel Indians to accept "society and religion," and of teach-ing Christian doctrine by having Indians "repeat in precise order an infinite number of words" in a language they did not understand. The results, he said, were counterpro-ductive. The coercive missionary system was "better suited to make [Indians into] fak-ers and hypocrites than faithful subjects of the State and of Religion."[8]

Critics like Croix and Caballero y Góngora told only part of the story. Even as some Indians escaped from missions, others willingly remained. A small number made mis-sions their permanent homes, using a Spanish institution to reconstitute or reinvent shattered Indian communities or to resolve individual problems. In Texas, Coahuilte-cans who sought refuge in missions from their more aggressive neighbors received food and clothing and learned the Spanish language and Spanish trades so well that they or their descendants ultimately merged into Hispanic society. Not all missions worked alike. If some missionaries kept Indians confined, others allowed them to come and go freely. But Croix had less interest in nuances than in advancing an argument. Reform-minded Bourbon administrators like Croix demanded that missionaries change the way they did business, and the crown echoed their concerns.[9]

"Neither by Arms nor with Gifts"

Legally and morally, Spain regarded the conversion of Indians to Christianity as its central enterprise in the New World. Spain's claim to its American empire rested in part on edicts, or bulls, issued in 1493 by Pope Alexander VI, the head of the Christian church in the west. In exchange for papal recognition of Spain's title to its discoveries in America, the pope required Spanish monarchs to instruct Native Americans in Christianity—a faith predicated on the idea that an almighty god had revealed absolute truths to some members of the human race and charged them to spread those truths to others. Some Spanish jurists maintained that Spain had to justify its conquest and colonization of the New World by spreading Christianity.[10]

To fulfill its obligation to the pope, the crown turned to male missionaries from religious orders. Drawing from long experience at converting heathens in the Old World, missionaries made rapid strides in America. Offers of new technology, crops, and livestock helped them draw Indians to missions. Missionaries had their greatest success, however, when they convinced Indians that the god of the Christians would protect them from the ravages of strange new diseases and from drought and famine or that mission life would shield them from intertribal wars, intratribal power struggles, or Spanish exploitation.[11]

Protestant Englishmen, less enthusiastic than Spaniards about converting Natives, generally declined to bring Indians into their community of faith until they had acculturated them and fully instructed them. In contrast, Spanish missionaries often turned Indians into Christians before acculturating them. The ritual of baptism alone brought children or dying adults into the fold; brief religious instruction and the baptism together sufficed for adults. At a California mission, for example, a priest baptized two young Native men and immediately afterward presided over their Christian marriages. In practice, however, Spanish missionaries generally regarded baptism as an initial step in a long journey. In word and deed, eighteenth-century missionaries made it clear that baptized Indians could become fully Christian only when they lived like Spanish Christians. Until then, baptized Indians remained neophytes or children, in need of the missionaries' tutelage and fatherly care. As one Franciscan explained, "Savages . . . needed to be made rational men before being made Christians."[12]

For Spaniards, making Indians rational meant putting them in order—*ponerlos en policía* in the phrase of the day—by congregating them in Spanish-style communities, or *reducciones.* Indians who did not live in settled communities appeared to Spaniards as "vagabonds" who lived a "licentious and brutal life, without a trace of order."[13] For Spaniards, the town, or *civitas,* was the locus of civilization. Only in urban settings, where law, order, and morality flourished, could Indians learn to live like Spaniards, receive religious instruction, and forget "the errors of their ancient rites and ceremonies."[14]

Spanish missionaries often succeeded at planting seeds of Spanish culture in Native

17. Experienced missionaries understood that Indians came to missions for worldly reasons, including gifts, food, and protection. In the missionaries' ideal world, however, Indians would have flocked to them simply because they brought word of a one true god. Here, before a saintly fray Antonio Margil de Jesús armed only with a cross, two Indians kneel and utter the words, "Yes, I believe." From an engraving attributed to Francisco Sylverio (Katzew, 1998, 64), in Vilaplana, 1763. Courtesy, DeGolyer Library, Southern Methodist University.

soil. Like early Christians who spread features of Mediterranean life throughout Europe, Spain's missionaries brought Spanish law, language, government, architecture, urban design, and European foods, animals, and manufactures to America. Many Indians found reasons to embrace these innovations, along with some of the external, if not the internal, manifestations of Christianity.[15]

Missionaries understood full well that they served the interests of the state. They sought to convert Indians "for God and for the King" or to make Indians "sons of God and vassals of Spain."[16] The state, in turn, provided resources that made hemispheric-wide missionary work possible. Unlike Protestant missionaries in English America, who depended heavily on their small congregations to support them and their families, Spain's unmarried Catholic missionaries received salaries, supplies, and military protection from the government. With the support of the Spanish crown, a small number of missionaries played a key role in bringing an area twenty-nine times the size of Spain under Spanish rule by the end of the colonial era.[17]

Early on, the crown recognized missionaries' singular capacity to advance imperial goals without great expense or bloodshed. Under the Royal Orders for New Discoveries, promulgated in 1573, the crown designated missionaries as the primary agents for extending the empire. In the royal orders, the crown sanctioned only peaceful expansion carried out by missionaries and prohibited unlicensed parties from entering the territory of unpacified Indians. Never repealed or modified and still invoked in the late 1700s, the royal orders prohibited the conquest of Indians. Under these orders, one historian has explained, "The military's mandate was not to advance the frontier, but to defend the advancing missionary."[18] In practice, however, the distinction between military conquest and missionary pacification often blurred. When Indians declined to hear the gospel in the Costa Rican province of Talamanca, Carlos III prescribed military force. "The Gospel could spread *without* armed force," he acknowledged, and yet "the Church often resorted to the arms of the Catholic princes to oblige the heathen to hear the word of God."[19]

By the eighteenth century, when Carlos III defended the use of force to spread the gospel in a land of war, missionaries had found that independent Indians had become less tractable and the task of pacification through persuasion more difficult. In contrast to the hierarchically organized agriculturists of the highland communities in Mexico and Peru, among whom the first generations of missionaries worked, the remaining heathens lived in small, often mobile family groups in regions remote from Spaniards. Infectious diseases from Europe, which once devastated entire societies and pushed survivors toward missions, took less of a toll by the 1700s as Natives acquired immunities and their populations began to recover. Epidemics of smallpox and measles still devastated Indians in the eighteenth century, but higher death rates occurred among people living in dense communities, such as missions, than among seminomadic people. Missionaries ministered to the ill, but dimly understood the cause of these diseases, sometimes regarding them as the will of their deity.[20]

By the mid-1700s, many groups of independent Indians had found ways to acquire Spanish-introduced products and yet maintain autonomy from missions. By raiding Spanish settlements, sometimes as part of their seasonal migrations, independent Indians gained direct access to European technology, livestock, and captives.[21] Other independent Indians obtained European manufactures by trading with individual Spaniards or with Spain's European rivals. So long as no natural disaster or formidable adversary pushed them into the Spanish sphere, powerful horsemen like the Pampas, the Abipones and Tobas of the Gran Chaco, and Apaches of northern New Spain tended to keep their distance from missionaries. The Abipones, one Jesuit missionary noted in 1784, "would not permit themselves to be conquered, neither by arms nor with gifts."[22] The result was a stalemate. "I have … heard much about uprisings of Indians and very little about new conversions," the bishop of Durango, in northern New Spain, lamented to the king in 1754.[23]

On the edges of the empire, where it seemed as though "all the horizon was covered with infidelity and savagery," missionaries often blamed Spanish colonists for their failure to reduce wild Indians to "a sociable life."[24] Spaniards' bad example and exploitation of Indians, missionaries said, turned Indians away. Missionaries labored to persuade Indians that Christianity was good even if the flock had a few bad sheep, but the actions of Christians behaving badly spoke more loudly than words. "I want to live and die as a good Pampa and not as a bad Christian," one Indian explained to a Jesuit.[25] In blaming fellow Spaniards for Indians' distrust, missionaries found allies among high-ranking Bourbon officials who knew the familiar dictum that in the Indies, "the shadow of a Spaniard kills the Indian."[26] Harsh treatment of converted Indians, observed Francisco Antonio Moñino, conde de Floridablanca, the powerful secretary of state from 1776 to 1792, "makes the name 'Spaniard' abhorrent to Indians … whom we try to attract to our holy faith."[27]

Missionaries also blamed their failures on Indians themselves, dismissing some of them as hopeless candidates for conversion. One clergyman described the Charrúas in today's Uruguay as "so savage they have not been able to support a priest who might instruct them."[28] A Jesuit, writing in frustration from the Río de la Plata, wondered if "Christian morality might seem excessive and unattainable" to a people as "depraved" as the Pampas.[29] Another Jesuit, frustrated at his efforts to convert Chiriguanos, supposed them possessed of "an unbelievably fickle disposition, changeable with the wind. They don't keep their word. Today they appear to be men and Christians, and the next day apostates and animals."[30] "The Indian is a monster of human nature," a frustrated Franciscan wrote in 1765, as he sought to explain why some Amazonian Indians regarded mission life as "hellish."[31]

Even as they condemned intractable Indians, missionaries expressed respect for compliant Indians. Missionaries who lived amidst "friendly" Indians for years at a time had the opportunity to do more sophisticated ethnographic work than Alejandro Malaspina and his scientists. With ready access to informants, they often learned Native languages and had come to understand Indian economies, living arrangements, dress, tools, and details of daily life. These missionaries, like some Spanish scientists, might also have idealized Indians in order to dramatize Europeans' moral failings. One Jesuit described the Abipones of the Chaco as so honest they had no need for the "doors, locks, bars, safes, and guards with which Europeans protect their possessions from thieves." His Abipones fought against Spaniards only in self-defense and perhaps as instruments of a divine plan. "It occurs to us to think that the Abipones and their allies, the Mocobíes and Tobas, have been reserved by divine justice to punish the crimes of the Christians."[32] A Franciscan suggested that the "savages" of the Amazon had much to teach the "pernicious and perverse deists of our century," for the idolatrous Indians, unlike the "false fathers of philosophy," had sense enough to recognize the connection between a Divine Providence and the well-being of humankind.[33]

Although they highlighted the attributes of so-called savages to rebuke the behavior or beliefs of their fellow Europeans, missionaries with firsthand experience with Indians had no illusions about their nobility. Domingo Muriel, a Jesuit who had taught at the University of Córdoba de Tucumán, for example, took issue with an entry on the Río de la Plata in Denis Diderot's *Encyclopédie,* in which the region appears as "the seat of Pan [the Greek Arcadian god of fertility] who has lived there for centuries without being troubled by the crimes of the cruel Europeans."[34] "Whether these considerations are sincere or ironic, whoever makes them ignores entirely the nature of the place," Muriel wrote in 1790.[35] In a direct rebuttal to the "philosophes of our century," a Franciscan *criollo* from New Spain, Vicente de Santa María, described the "American savages" as degraded children of Noah who, with the passage of each generation, had become more ferocious, passive, unfeeling, irreligious, and barbarous—"the disgrace of the human species." Indians living in a state of nature, he argued, lived in "true anarchy."[36]

As fray Vicente's assessment suggests, late eighteenth-century Spanish missionaries tended to judge Indians more by their behavior than by their ethnicity or race. Indians, one Franciscan in Chile noted, "are men like Spaniards and other vassals [of the king], and no different from them, not even from the [skin] color of Spaniards who work in the open as herders or farmers." Another Franciscan in Texas declared, "Some are good and some are bad, as in all the world."[37] By definition, bad Indians were those who resisted the Christian life. Missionaries might describe the very same group of Indians as "tame and affable" when they cooperated with priests, yet "crude, wild, bold, and inclined to theft" when they did not.[38] Thus, the bipolar categories of good and bad Indians, which had remained constant since the sixteenth century, tell us more about missionaries' hopes and frustrations than about Indians.[39] For example, the Pueblos in arid New Mexico and the Huilliches on the inclement island of Chiloé won praise for their "docility" because they welcomed missionaries. Their docility, however, probably owed less to their character than to the fact that they had no place to flee from Spaniards and no ready means to drive them away (a handicap the Pueblos overcame only momentarily in their remarkably successful revolt of 1680).[40]

Even Indians they regarded as good, however, often seemed childlike or perverse to missionaries. Following a tradition that reached back to the sixteenth century, Franciscans likened mission Indians to children in need of strict parental control lest they become "corrupted with gambling, drunkenness, and other evils."[41] Missionaries who saw baptized Indians as childlike regarded themselves as their fathers, legal guardians who would provide much-needed guidance. Over and over again, missionaries described Indians as congenitally lazy. In the fertile Chaco, one priest lamented, Indians preferred hunting, fishing, and gathering to sowing and reaping. Only the young and the old came to the mission.[42] Left on their own, said one veteran Franciscan missionary, Indians would not work without prodding, look for food unless they were hungry, or clothe themselves until they were cold. They could not govern "four chickens" much less govern themselves. "Experience has taught this science, which seems to refute natural reasoning."[43]

18. Representations of martyrs, a popular genre,
left no doubt about the murderous intentions of
"bad" Indians or about the sanctity and innocence
of their victims. The inscription under this oil
painting by Diego de Sanabria (late eighteenth to
early nineteenth century), identified the victim,
fray Francisco de Jesús María, as having been
killed "inhumanely" by Indians in New Mexico
in 1696. In the background, Indians club another
Franciscan to death as he kneels before a cross.
Courtesy, Museo Regional del Colegio de
Guadalupe, Zacatecas, and reproduction
authorized by the Instituto Nacional de
Antropología e Historia, Mexico.

In comparing recalcitrant Indians to children, animals, and monsters, eighteenth-century missionaries echoed a discourse they had applied to the popular classes in Europe. Missionaries who described Indians as beastlike did not mean to suggest that Indians were beasts, any more than they questioned the humanity of Italian peasants, whom they also compared to animals. The question of Indians' humanity had been officially settled by the papacy in the sixteenth century, if it was ever in doubt.[44] As the bishop of Charcas (today's Bolivia), writing to the Chiriguanos in 1787 in their own language, told them, "You are our brothers, and we recognize you as such, because we are all works and creatures of God and we all descend from one man, that first man, whom God created from nothing and named Adam, at the beginning of the World."[45] Whatever their private misgivings, missionaries in general did not openly challenge the idea that Indians were human, rational, or capable of Christian salvation. Many did, however, believe that Indians could never function fully as Spaniards.[46] In this, members of the religious orders, dominated by racially pure Spaniards, reflected their ethnicity. Even in the Age of Reason and in the face of evidence to the contrary, those Spaniards who occupied the highest rungs on the social ladder commonly imagined that mixed bloods and Indians were innately inferior.[47]

If Indians were creatures of the Spaniards' god, they were also susceptible to the temptations of the Spaniards' devil. In the late eighteenth century, the devil remained a vital force in the minds of rank-and-file missionaries who had not drunk deeply from the Enlightenment's cup of rationality. At a time when educated churchmen and laymen alike turned to social and environmental explanations of Indian behavior, many missionaries still described themselves as engaged in a struggle with an extraterrestrial "prince of darkness and error" who held hapless Indians in his "claws."[48] In 1799, when a group of Guaycurúes who settled into a new mission at San Pablo between Moxos and Chiquitos rebelled after seven years of mission life, the Franciscan in charge blamed a shortage of supplies and the inspiration of the devil.[49] Indians who ignored missionaries' preaching had "impenetrable hearts possessed completely by Satan."[50]

Defeating the devil, some missionaries believed, justified any measures that would extirpate Indians' "vices" and make them less "brutal."[51] So, too, did the seeming brutality of Indians justify the use of force against them. "All men were born to live in society," a friar wrote in 1795, and Indians should be brought into society by "all imaginable means, without excepting the most rigorous punishments."[52] Only through forcible means, the head of the Franciscan contingent in Alta California argued in 1801, could friars rescue a people "of vicious and ferocious habits who know no law but force."[53] Although Catholic doctrine required that adults voluntarily accept baptism or conversion, some missionaries crossed the thin line between forcing Indians to "*hear* the word of God," as Carlos III advocated, and forcing them to *become* Christians.[54] In eastern Venezuela, for example, where peaceful persuasion had borne little fruit, Franciscans sent soldiers and Indian allies on bloody *entradas* to capture potential Carib converts. These military campaigns went on for decades, culminating in the 1770s. European microbes, however, had accompanied the missionaries' forces, sweeping away 80 percent of the Carib population between 1730 and 1780. It was a hollow victory for the friars.[55]

Once Indians received baptism, voluntarily or involuntarily, missionaries had no more compunction about using physical punishment to keep them in the Christian fold than they did about using it to keep Spaniards from straying or about flagellating themselves to atone for their sins. Indians who lapsed into apostasy or other mortal sins might infect an entire mission community with their wicked ways, and the souls of sinful Indians would "suffer eternally in the company of devils."[56] Thoughtful missionaries also imagined a danger to their own souls, for their theology suggested, in the words of one Franciscan historian, that "he who could prevent a given sin and failed to do so was actually cooperating in the offense committed against God and therefore shared in the guilt."[57] Numerous royal edicts prohibited the harsh treatment of Indians, even to the point of proscribing their use as unpaid laborers. Missionaries such as Rafael Verger, the head of the Franciscan College of San Fernando in Mexico City, took the position that the laws applied only to "ministers of civilized Indians," not to missionaries who worked among the "unfortunate, savage heathen."[58] "The Pope as well as the King," the head of the missionary college at Tarija, in today's Bolivia, wrote in 1800, "has conferred upon the friars all the authority and power that may be necessary to make their Indians Christian, political, and economic men."[59] He had a point. Authorities at the highest level authorized the modest use of force when exhortation failed. In their life-or-death contest with the devil, then, missionaries regarded the use of stocks and whips as necessary to make Indians fulfill their spiritual "duties," and Bourbon officials gave qualified approval.[60] Whether mission Indians regarded corporal punishment as cruel or not, one historian has suggested, may have varied with different cultures and with the amount of pain Indians had inflicted on one another in their premission lives. It also varied with the degree of punishment: Andaquíes drove the Franciscans away from the mission when one of their number died after receiving fifty lashes from a friar.[61]

In the Europeans' Age of Reason, with its appeals to rationality and self-interest, missionaries' use of corporal punishment as an instrument of social control seemed anachronistic to some Spanish reformers. It is true that the utilitarian Bourbon state forced Spanish vagrants, petty criminals, social outcasts, and the unemployed to work for the common good and that employers used physical punishment to maintain discipline among lower-class Spanish workers. However, in the last two decades of the eighteenth century the trend in Spanish society was away from punishments that seemed excessive or cruel and toward rehabilitation through compulsory but useful work.[62]

In the missionaries' ideal but seldom realized world, baptized Indians would remain within the mission boundaries unless they had a written pass to leave.[63] But missionaries often lacked the power and resources to stop Indians from slipping out to reunite with heathens or from using the missions as safe havens from which to launch raids.[64] Where missionaries operated alone, without military force, Indians did as they pleased.[65] Where European cultigens and livestock did poorly, as in the tropics, missionaries often yielded to economic realities and permitted Indians to hunt or gather or practice slash-and-burn agriculture beyond mission compounds. Where missionaries needed an infusion of funds, mission Indians might be released to work as contract laborers at nearby presidios or haciendas. Or mission Indians might steal away and work covertly for wages at a presidio or in town.[66]

In the late eighteenth century, *love* and *kindness* became fashionable watchwords in the missions and Indian parishes of Spanish America. This new discourse may have reflected an enlightened sensibility toward Indians, but it was also the case that priests who lacked the power to coerce had no choice but to rely on love and kindness to entice rather than force Indians to receive Christian sacraments and live Christian lives. Where priests had little power, as in the Araucanía, love and kindness became the favored idiom. In contrast, missionaries who enjoyed authority over Indians' lives and property, such as those whom Croix condemned in Texas, continued to depend on force and fear.[67] Even when clerics emphasized love and kindness, however, they never let their potential converts lose sight of the fearsome consequences of failing to accept Christianity. In an exhortation to Chiriguanos to accept baptism, the bishop of Charcas explained in 1787 that his religion was one of "peace and gentleness." It required all believers to treat their enemies with benevolence, and its "weapons are nothing more than the truth, persuasion, and kindness"—but Indians who died outside the bishop's gentle religion would be "condemned eternally to hell."[68]

Some Indians who entered traditional missions as adults may have thought they had already gone to hell. As residents of mission communities that restricted their mobility, Indians often became vulnerable to demands for forced labor from Spanish ranchers or farmers.[69] The neophytes also had to sacrifice autonomy, divorce themselves from their cultural and physical environments, and submit to the regimentation of ordered spaces, linear time divided into hours on the days of a Roman calendar, physical punishments, a strange and often inferior diet, and an alien religion.[70] Both sexes had to adapt to new gender roles, too, which included restraints on sexual expression. Men, who often regarded farming as women's work, entered a radically new work regimen. Conversely, women usually found continuity in food preparation and household chores. Women, however, often had to leave the security of familiar matriarchies to conform to the patriarchal values of the fathers.[71]

With its prohibition of multiple marriages and its devaluation of Native religious leaders, Christianity threatened established social and political orders, which Indians often understood in religious terms.[72] "In no way should you wish to become Christian," one Chiriguano leader told his band in 1767, "because that is a trick to bring us priests and make us live the bitter life of oppression that we know and see among Christians. . . . to be a servant of the Spanish."[73] A Carib leader, Oraparene, explained to a Spanish official in 1754 that he would not give up his position as "king" of his people to enter a mission "where he could not rule, have women, or liberty to raid or to trade with his friends the Dutch." The uncomprehending official described Oraparene as a paradox—

a "man of advanced reason" who nonetheless stubbornly insisted on maintaining his "animal life."[74] When missionized Indians revolted, their actions spoke loudly of their contempt for Christianity. Guajiro converts, who rebelled in 1769, burned mission churches and, in the words of one missionary, "profaned the sacred vessels, drinking from the holy chalices their evil *chichas* and liquor . . . and [sharpening] their tools on the altar stones."[75]

Although missionaries attributed their failures to the pernicious influence of Spanish civil society, to the innate perversion of bad Indians, and to the devil, it seems clear they also had themselves to blame. Teodoro de Croix was on the mark in charging that reports of mission life repelled independent Indians in Texas, and he could have found similar cases elsewhere on the edges of empire. Indians who had viable alternatives tended to avoid life in missions.[76]

The New Method

At the same time that many Indians grew more determined to maintain their independence from missionaries and more adept at doing so, Spanish support for traditional missions began to waver. Bourbons continued to provide missionaries with military and financial support (sometimes drawing from the war fund since missionaries helped subdue Natives) and to insist, as the viceroy of Mexico declared in 1772, that the "pious goal" of future conquests remained the conversion of heathens "to the gentle yoke of our Holy Religion."[77] Indeed, royal policies supported the conversion of heathens so wholeheartedly that one high-ranking military officer complained in 1772 that the king and his predecessors favored the interests of the "infidels and neophytes over those of the other vassals of these kingdoms."[78] Even as they offered moral and material support for new conversions, however, Bourbon administrators questioned the padres' skill in "the science of creating men" and sought new ways to integrate Indians into the religious, economic, and social life of the empire.[79]

In contrast to the Habsburgs, who gave missionaries a privileged position on the frontiers of the empire, the Bourbons relied on professional officers like Croix to promote frontier development and gave them authority over missionaries.[80] Many of these officers believed that traditional missions contributed to economic stagnation by robbing Indians of the incentive to work, limiting Spanish colonists' access to Indian labor, tying up desirable grazing and farming land, and hindering the integration of Indians by isolating them in segregated communities. The early Habsburgs had hoped that Hispanicized Indians and Spaniards would occupy separate Christian towns, or *repúblicas*. In the words of one historian, "Indians were to be incorporated into, but not integrated with, the newly evolving colonial society." By the eighteenth century, however, integration had become widespread throughout the empire, including at many missions. Bourbon reformers hoped to accelerate that process of integration by breaking down barriers that some missionaries still maintained between mission Indians and non-Indians.[81]

The reformers condemned traditional missions in strong language. Life in a mission, wrote the progressive military governor of the Venezuelan province of Guayana, Lt. Col. Manuel Centurión, left Indians "almost as naked, savage, and useless to the State as when they lived in the jungles before their reduction [to mission life]."[82] Missionaries, said Vicente de Emparán, the military governor of another Venezuelan province, kept Indians in "stupidity and savagery." Capuchin missionaries in Cumaná, he charged, preferred to have "the authority to govern Indians as idiots, over the progress that Indians would make in the society . . . of Spaniards."[83] Even some reform-minded clergy agreed. In a scathing critique of the missionaries' practice of baptizing unacculturated Indians, Archbishop Caballero y Góngora wrote in 1789 that Indians needed to "stop being brutes and begin to be men, and afterward elevate themselves to become Christians." The "sublime truths of Christianity," he said, were wasted on Indians' "brutalized souls." "God save a bishop of the Catholic Church from preferring anything over the spread of the Gospel, but the interest of religion itself requires that you do not throw pearls before swine."[84]

Philosophically, communal missions ran counter to emerging liberal ideals of private property, individual liberty, and rewards to individuals for their labor, which resonated among some enlightened Spanish military officers. As he criticized the oppression that Indians suffered in the missions of Moxos and Chiquitos in the Bolivian lowlands, Francisco de Viedma, the naval officer and intendant of Cochabamba, observed that "nothing is more precious to man than the liberty in which God has made him."[85] Félix de Azara, who rose through the ranks to become a brigadier general after two decades in the Río de la Plata, made the case squarely. Traditional missionary activity among many Indians had been "useless" and "has not had nor will ever have good results."[86] Indians living in mission communities lacked incentive "to develop their talent or reason, because neither the most able, nor the most virtuous, nor the most energetic is better fed or better dressed than the others."[87] "There will never be civilization, sciences, nor arts where communal government exists."[88]

While reform-minded officers urged that Indians be left in their "natural liberty" so they might become rational economic actors, Franciscans condemned Indians' natural freedom as "false liberty." True liberty could be achieved only by subordinating oneself to the rules of the Catholic Church. Those rules might seem heavy, the bishop of Charcas wrote to the Chiriguanos in 1787, but they offered a way to freedom, much as wings that "are heavy for a little bird" allow it to fly. Complete "liberty," on the other hand, would give Indians freedom to practice "brutal customs," and make them "incorrigible."[89] Taken to excess, liberty was "religion in the French-style," another bishop intoned in 1791, two years after the French Revolution.[90]

Critics of traditional missions did not wish to dispense with missionaries. They recognized that regular clergy could accomplish much at little cost. As a Spanish naval officer and scientist who traveled with Malaspina put it, "One man with a breviary, a crucifix, a small military escort and 300 pesos a year, passes through vast lands, among the multitude of savages."[91] Thus, even officers hostile to traditional missions continued to provide supplies and military escorts in support of missionaries' initial efforts to convert Indians to a "civil and Christian society."[92] At the same time, however, they tried to limit missionaries to the purely spiritual realm and relieve them of their control over Indian labor and property. Spain, observed Juan Bautista de Anza, the veteran commander of a presidio in northern Sonora, needed to "destroy and reform the system up to now observed in the missions as useless and prejudicial."[93] There is a clear difference "between an empire and a priesthood," Governor Centurión declared to the viceroy of New Granada in 1774.[94]

Rather than rely entirely on missionaries to prepare Indians to take a place in Hispanic society, advocates of mission reform urged what some called the "new method of spiritual government," which would put mission Indians "in liberty . . . . that they may govern themselves without a tutor, that they may trade, that they may travel, that they may deal, because only in this way will they progress."[95] The reformers put their faith in the acculturating influence of Spanish colonists, Spanish towns, and Spanish markets. "It is well known how much the contact of certain peoples with others advances them no matter how stupid they are," Captain Anza told the viceroy. Like reformers in the late nineteenth-century United States who pushed for the destruction of Indian reservations as impediments to the assimilation of Indians, eighteenth-century Bourbon reformers saw missions as places that isolated rather than integrated Indians. Colonists could bring about the salvation of Indians by "making them men, and Christian men," Viedma argued. Mission Indians needed to learn arts and industry from Spanish colonists or they would "never be able to be men or useful vassals," declared a military engineer in California.[96] One key to making Indians "useful vassals" was the Spanish language itself. That the crown continued until the end of the colonial era to issue orders that missionaries teach Indians Spanish underscores the failure of many missionaries to do so. That failure, from the point of view of the crown, offered a further argument for weakening missionary control over Indian communities.[97]

Bourbon reformers and missionaries shared the goal of turning Indians into "rational men," but the reformers thought it best, as Azara put it, to begin by making an Indian a "useful vassal and sociable man" before trying to turn him into a Christian. Missionaries, Azara argued, had erred in assuming that "civilization" would follow conversion. "I believe the contrary," he declared. "The government, not the ecclesiastics, should civilize these savages."[98] The reformers, then, sought to break the missionaries' monopoly over the lives, land, and labor of mission Indians and limit missionaries' responsibilities solely to the care of Indians' spiritual lives.[99] To the extent the reformers succeeded in imposing this "new method" on the missionaries, they weakened missions as effective institutions for frontier expansion and defense.[100]

The New Method on a New Frontier

Bourbons' doubts about the wisdom of using traditional missions to advance into Indian-held lands had first translated into practice in 1749. That year, Spaniards began to colonize the gulf coast of New Spain from Tampico to the edge of Texas at the Nueces River, a band 150 to 200 miles wide and some 250 miles long that they called Nuevo Santander (see map 6). The humid, inhospitable coastal strip, together with the Sierra Madre to the west, had remained the domain of "savage nations of enemy Chichimecos, heathens, and apostates," as one Spanish document termed them. These people attacked the neighboring jurisdictions of Tampico, Pánuco, Nuevo León, Coahuila, and Texas, leaving in their wake "fires, deaths, robberies, and all manner of inhuman atrocities." They destroyed towns and ranches, hindered commerce, "perverted" Christian Indians, and cost the Royal Treasury millions of pesos.[101] The Indians whom Spaniards labeled *Indios Chichimecos* actually represented a variety of Native peoples, many of whom had fled from Spanish forced labor and missions in neighboring Nuevo León. Here as elsewhere, fugitives and apostates seemed especially dangerous to Spanish officials, who feared that their knowledge of the Hispanic world made them "irreconcilable enemies ... against their former masters" and gave them skills "to lead the other heathen Indians in their robberies, murders, arson, and all kinds of atrocities."[102]

Influenced by the English model of revenue-producing colonies and eager to occupy the gulf coast for geopolitical reasons, Viceroy Revillagigedo (the elder) had authorized a radical experiment—one that Spain never repeated in America. Nuevo Santander was to be settled by colonists as a *colonia* instead of a *provincia* pacified by missionaries and soldiers.[103] To head the enterprise, the viceroy turned to José de Escandón, a popular and prosperous military officer whose ranches, textile mills, and merchandising had made him rich. Beginning in the 1720s, soon after his arrival in America from his native Santander, Escandón won a reputation as an Indian fighter in the Sierra Gorda, a mountainous region that arcs across the modern Mexican states of Querétaro, Hidaglo, and San Luis Potosí, where Natives had long resisted the cross and the sword.

Between 1749 and 1753, Escandón moved with remarkable speed to direct the settlement of more than six thousand colonists into the Colonia del Nuevo Santander and to found twenty towns.[104] Franciscans accompanied the colonists, but Escandón made it impossible for the padres to build thriving mission communities. First, he denied them juridical and economic power over Indians, lest the missionaries turn Indians "into perpetual slaves on the king's account." Second, he obliged the padres to establish missions on the edge of the new Spanish towns rather than apart from them and demanded that the missionaries serve the spiritual needs of the colonists at the same time they ministered to Indians. Escandón intended to use friars as parish priests and to rely on markets rather than missions to draw Indians into the Spanish world. He ordered that Indians receive a wage for their labor and that Spaniards who employed Indians "teach them to pray and to go to mass every Sunday and submit to their missionary."[105] He had experimented with this system in the Sierra Gorda and won the praise of reformers. Here was a way to end the isolation of mission Indians, integrate them into the work force, and gain access to their lands without having to challenge meddlesome missionaries.[106] A supply of cheap Indian labor for Spanish colonists would also advance the Bourbons' goal of occupying the gulf coast rapidly and inexpensively.

Escandón knew that some Indians would not work for wages, and he planned to eradicate them. Experience had convinced him it was "useless" to try to pacify Indians who resisted Spaniards, and he had the blessing of the viceroy's influential legal counselor, the marqués de Altamira, who authorized him to wage a war "of fire and blood" against Indians who would not submit. "If only one remains alive," Altamira wrote, "it will be enough to upset all." Many Indians, however, chose to submit—particularly sedentary peoples like Huastecos and Pames, whose descendants, it would appear, were absorbed into Spanish society. Others fled to a new region of refuge or were eradicated. When Escandón began colonization of Nuevo Santander, the region held some thirteen thousand Indians, a number already much reduced by disease and slave raiders from Nuevo León. In 1821, when Mexico became independent, perhaps two thousand Indians remained.[107]

The use of colonists instead of government-supported troops or priests and harsh treatment of unmanageable Indians seemed a throwback to Spain's sixteenth-century reliance on privately financed *adelantados* to carry out conquests. It also violated the Royal Orders for New Discoveries and laws that required the peaceful reduction of Indians into segregated towns, or *repúblicas de indios,* where missionaries could teach them the faith free of the baneful influences of Spanish civil society.[108] From Mexico City to Madrid, however, officials turned a blind eye to the law when it stood in the way of Escandón's progress. So long as Escandón and other investors paid the bill, settled new lands, and brought in new tax revenues, higher officials lodged no complaints. Authorities explained away the irregularities by arguing that Indians needed exposure to Spanish towns: "The Indians, even the least savage, are only impressed with what they see . . . they need settlements of Spaniards close by . . . to contain them, tame them, and protect them." Although authorities deplored the notorious system of *congregación* or *congrega* which Spaniards in northeastern Mexico used as legal cover to enslave Indians, authorities at the highest levels also recognized that Nuevo Santander's success depended on attracting colonists with cheap Indian labor.[109]

Escandón's system infuriated the Franciscans. The Franciscan College of San Fernando in Mexico City protested its illegality and refused to participate in the venture. Franciscans from the College of Guadalupe de Zacatecas did sign on and established a dozen missions in Nuevo Santander but soon came to regret their decision. They could not compete with officials and colonists who paid Indians for their work, and they lacked authority to keep baptized Indians in mission compounds to till the fields, tend the orchards, watch the flocks and herds, and receive religious instruction and the sacraments. From the point of view of the friars, Escandón had deprived them of the tools of their trade. Although many Franciscans regarded the management of a mission's business affairs as a burden, they also knew they could not succeed without control over the income that missions produced. As one Franciscan in Sonora put it some years later, "Once the Indians see that the Father . . . has nothing to give them, it will not be very easy to keep them in subjection and due subordination to the law and to the king."[110]

In 1757, an official investigation of Escandón's stewardship took the side of the missionaries, but nothing came of its recommendation that they be granted authority to hold Indians in missions.[111] Unable to sustain viable mission communities in Nuevo Santander, the College of Zacatecas asked to withdraw from the *colonia* in 1765. The college excoriated Escandón for using missionaries as mere parish priests and for wasting the alms that the king had designated for missions.[112] Late in life, following a massive inquest, Escandón had to answer to thirty-eight charges against him, including failure to congregate and convert Indians. He was absolved posthumously.[113]

By declining to establish traditional missions, in which priests had control of Indian lives and property, Escandón had violated the law and parted from tradition. Nonetheless, he was a harbinger. Some officials approved of Escandón's experiment in the "science of creating men" and hoped his practice would become Bourbon policy. First, however, Bourbon reformers moved to assert their authority over the missionary orders and the church itself.

Secularizing Missions on Older Frontiers

José de Escandón and the Bourbon officials who initially supported his efforts to limit the temporal power of missionaries in Nuevo Santander had the advantage of operating on a new Indian frontier, one largely devoid of prior Spanish missions and established precedents. On older frontiers, however, Bourbon reformers often found missionaries well entrenched, with substantial political, economic, and social control over Indians. In such places, Bourbons had to reform the old order before they could create a new one.

The crown had always regarded the mission as a transitory institution, one whose purpose was to convert "those who were wild or infidels, enemies and savages" into "Christians and vassals of the King."[114] Early on, the crown assigned the task of converting Indians to the regular clergy—those who lived by the *regula,* or rule, of their religious order, such as Franciscans, Jesuits, and Dominicans. In theory, once these missionaries taught Indians to embrace the tenets of Catholicism and live like town-dwelling Spaniards, they had completed their work. At that stage, the regular clergy, or missionaries, were to turn the mission (*misión, conversión,* or *reducción*) over to secular clergy, that is, parish priests or *curas* who worked under the direct authority of bishops rather than of a religious order. Secular clergy had responsibility for preserving the faith, while missionaries propagated the faith.[115] Freed from their missions by secularization, regular clergy and their Indian collaborators could move to new frontiers. There, with continued financial support from the crown, they could begin again, in the words of one Franciscan in California, "to transform a savage race ... into a society that is human, Christian, civil, and industrious."[116]

The crown had strong economic reasons to turn missions into self-supporting parishes (*parroquias* or *curatos*). With the secularization, mission-held properties were to revert to the Indians; former mission Indians would come under the authority of civil officials and lose the exemption from taxes, tithes, and other fees the missions had afforded them; the *cura* would be paid by tithes from Indian parishioners rather than by the crown. The crown, then, sought the rapid conversion of heathens. As early as 1607, a royal edict implied a time frame when it offered a ten-year exemption from taxes to Indians who "submit voluntarily to our Holy Faith."[117] With the passage of time, authorities began to think of ten years as the ideal length of time to keep Indians in missions before making them parishioners.[118]

Bourbon officials who favored speedy secularization of missions enjoyed the support of those Spaniards who lived in proximity to missions and who saw missions as hindrances to local economic development. Missions blocked Spaniards' access to Indian lands, water, and labor, prevented local officials from collecting taxes from Indians, and deprived the church of tithes. Although Indians were to take possession of secularized mission lands, so-called excess mission land often went to Indians' Hispanic neighbors. Thus, the possibility of gaining former mission lands along with access to the labor of former mission Indians gave Spanish colonists an intense interest in promoting the secularization of missions.[119] In northern New Spain, for example, the Jesuit and Franciscan missions that dotted the landscape from Sonora and Sinaloa to Nuevo Santander and Texas drew the attention of Spaniards who moved into the region in the 1700s, and officials at the highest levels listened to their complaints. Viceroy Revillagigedo took the colonists' side in 1754, arguing that missions retarded economic and territorial growth in northern New Spain by confining Indians in segregated communities under a "despotic rule." Had they been open to Spanish colonists, he said, "within a few years the missions would have become extinct, the Indians enjoying liberty, the proceeds from ... their own work, and the King the payment of their tribute."[120] Missionaries, the viceroy said, would also benefit from the dissolution of their mature missions: they could return to lives of contemplation or go on to new territory to win additional souls.

Revillagigedo's views reflected a renewed interest in the secularization of missions, one that emanated from the highest level of government. Although the crown did not press regular clergy or missionaries to surrender youthful missions, it had long demanded secularization of self-supporting Indian parishes (*curatos*) and of mature missions that seemed ready to support themselves (*doctrinas*). In the mid-1700s, the Bourbons reinvigorated that campaign. In 1749, the same year that Escandón moved into Nuevo Santander, the crown had ordered that regular clergy in the archdioceses of Mexico and Lima to complete the secularization of mature Indian missions and Indian parishes. Members of religious orders had continued to maintain spiritual control over some self-supporting Indian communities, and the crown wanted the secular clergy to replace the regular clergy. Four years later, in 1753, the crown extended the order to its dioceses throughout the Americas.[121]

The Bourbons' new push to secularize missions reflected the crown's larger interest in reducing the wealth and power of the Catholic Church. In general, Spain's enlightened government ministers did not embrace the anti-Catholicism or skepticism characteristic of some French philosophes but did share their anticlericism. One bureaucrat, for example, accused Franciscans of wanting "to be absolute deities" and live among Indians "in unbridled polygamy."[122] Ad hominem attacks aside, the utilitarian Bourbons saw clerics as too powerful and the church's untaxed wealth as excessive, unproductively idle, a drain on Spain's treasury, and an obstacle to economic progress. Instead of maintaining a relationship with the church as an equal partner of the state, as had been the policy if not always the practice under the Habsburgs, the Bourbons sought to subordinate the church to the state and restrict the clergy's activities to the spiritual and pastoral. In the view of many reformers, the papacy itself stood in the way of change, and they aimed to wrest control of the church in Spain from Rome and bring it under the control of the Spanish crown. They justified their "regalism"—their assertion of royal supremacy over the church—on the grounds that Spanish monarchs ruled by divine right.[123]

In their efforts to assume autonomy from Rome, the regalists found an ally in a small group of reform-minded clerics within the Spanish church itself. Identified with what has since been called Enlightened Catholicism, these clerics hoped to turn the church toward what they believed to be a purer form of Christianity, one that emphasized the spiritual over the material.[124] They, too, saw papal control as an impediment to reform and so found it useful to subscribe to the doctrine of divine right of kings.[125] As one enlightened Spanish catechism asserted, "In their kingdom, the monarchs are the visible images of God."[126]

Enlightened Spanish bureaucrats and enlightened Catholics also found common ground in their criticism of religious orders. It appeared to Catholic reformers that too many of the regular clergy stayed in the cities, failed to contribute to the church's pastoral mission, and drained resources badly needed by parish priests. Liberal bureaucrats went further, condemning regular clergy as unproductive members of society who had forgotten their vows of poverty and as unthinking defenders of tradition who opposed reason and progress. By the Bourbons' calculations, Spain had more ecclesiastics than it needed to serve the religious needs of its people,[127] so authorities took measures to reduce the number of regular clergy on the utilitarian grounds that they, like beggars and idle noblemen, contributed nothing to the kingdom's economic growth.[128]

The Reformers and the Former Jesuit Missions

The Bourbons' quest to rein in the religious orders reached its apogee when Carlos III expelled the Jesuits. In 1767–68, in stunningly swift and secret operations, the Bourbons removed 2,800 Jesuits from Spain and another 2,200 from America, sending all into exile.[129] Although some Jesuits were regalists, most were devoted to the pope, to whom they took a special vow of loyalty. Thus, the well-trained, disciplined, and affluent Society of Jesus had seemed a formidable obstacle to the state's ability to gain further control over the church. Portugal and France had expelled the Jesuits in 1759 and 1764, respectively. The Spanish Bourbons followed suit in 1767, with the support of reformist elements within the Spanish church who regarded Jesuits as reactionary or who viewed their power and wealth with envy.

Along with schools, colleges, universities, and estates, Jesuits had ministered to some 300,000 Indians in 220 missions in Spanish America at the time of their expulsion— more than any other religious order. Most of the Jesuit missions, as one official put it, stood on the frontiers with "wild Indians."[130] One hundred and two of those missions operated in northwestern New Spain, from the Sierra Madre Occidental to Baja California. The second largest number, seventy-eight, were in the viceroyalty of Peru and included thirty Paraguayan missions, twenty-five missions of Moxos and Chiquitos in the lowlands of today's Bolivia, fifteen missions on the eastern and western edges of the Chaco, and a scattering of missions among the Araucanians in Chile. The viceroyalty of New Granada had forty-two Jesuit missions, twenty-five of them in Mainas on the Upper Amazon and the other seventeen distributed in three locations: the llanos of Casanare, the valley of the Río Meta (in present-day Colombia), and the basin of the upper Orinoco (today's Venezuela).[131]

The Jesuits' ambitious program to convert Indians in America had no direct bearing on the crown's decision to expel them, but it did offer a splendid pretext—one that the regalistic conde de Campomanes, the *fiscal*, or attorney general, of the Council of Castile, had seized upon in a secret investigation designed to justify the Jesuits' ouster.[132] Beyond his charges that Jesuit missionaries treated Indians like slaves and deprived the crown of revenue from unpaid tithes and taxes—charges he might have leveled against other religious orders as well—Campomanes had accused Jesuits of operating their missions "like an independent and absolute monarchy," acquiring power and wealth at the expense of Indians.[133]

The Bourbons offered a new kind of mission. The president of the Council of Castile, the conde de Aranda, announced that the crown itself would assume control of the property of the former Jesuit missions' "temporalities," which contemporaries understood as "the communal property of the Indians," and that a civil administrator would manage them.[134] Either secular priests or regular clergy could provide spiritual leadership, but in either case they would work under the direction of bishops, who owed their appointments to the crown, rather than take instructions from the independent-minded religious orders.[135] Under this system, then, the state would control mission properties and, through its bishops, control the secular clergy or regular clergy who might remain in charge of a secularized parish. Members of religious orders would no longer manage all aspects of life in the former Jesuit missions or have the opportunity to commit a "scandalous seizure of the property of the Indians," as Campomanes charged the Jesuits had done.[136]

Map 8. Jesuit missions in Spanish America, 1766,
adapted from Merino and Newson, 1995, 136.

Indians whom missionaries once taught to venerate a divine being would now recognize the divine right of kings. When the bishop of Charcas sent emissaries on a peace mission to the Chiriguanos in 1787, he explained that his representatives came in the name of Carlos III, "the Great one above all Great Ones," who enjoyed "the power and the authority that God and the Laws have deposited in his Royal Hand."[137] In some former Jesuit missions, as at Moxos in the Bolivian lowlands, portraits of the king and queen were displayed and the sovereigns' birthdays celebrated as major holidays. A secular catechism made the new arrangements clear:

Question: Who are you?
Answer: I am a loyal vassal of the King of Spain.
Q: Who is the King of Spain?
A: He is a Lord so absolute that he recognizes no greater temporal authority.

Q: And where does the King derive his royal power?
A: From God himself.[138]

Whether the source of royal power was divine or earthly, implementation of the new policies floundered on hard American realities, frustrating policymakers. The Bourbons' efforts to secularize the Jesuits' celebrated Guaraní missions exemplify the reformers' difficulties and their pragmatic yet inconsistent efforts to surmount them.

The disposition of thirty Guaraní missions on the middle and upper Paraná and Uruguay rivers fell to the governor of Buenos Aires, Francisco de Bucareli y Ursúa. A career military officer who had overseen the expulsion of the Jesuits from the Río de la Plata in 1768, Bucareli had condemned them for their paternalism and urged the assimilation of the Guaraníes. He ordered civil administrators to "take every measure to end the odious separation that has been maintained between Indians and whites up to now" and to encourage Indian women to marry Spanish men. This went beyond Aranda's orders that Spaniards be permitted to settle and obtain property in Guaraní towns and departed sharply from previous policies designed to keep Indians in *repúblicas de indios*.[139]

Although Bucareli championed the cause of Indian liberty, his own plans for the Guaraníes' orderly transition to secular life offered them little freedom. He appointed civil administrators to oversee the temporalities, as Aranda's instructions required, and empowered administrators to force Indians to work communal lands. He also invoked an old law that required mission Indians to remain in missions and defined Indians who left as fugitives.[140] Bucareli justified his own paternalism on the grounds that the Jesuits had failed to prepare Guaraníes to manage their own affairs. They needed protection until they could be assimilated into Spanish society.

Rather than accomplish his goal of liberating Indians from Jesuit paternalism or slavery, Bucareli made the Guaraníes vulnerable to exploitation by new and harsher masters. Bucareli had charged civil administrators with "maintaining and increasing the property of these Indians," but many of the untrained and poorly prepared administrators proved either inept or dishonest or both.[141] The worst of them used their new offices to enrich themselves. They sold mission property, slaughtered mission herds to supply a growing market for hides in Buenos Aires, and obliged Indians to work for them despite government orders against forcing Indians into personal service.[142] In 1800, the viceroy of the Río de la Plata condemned the administrators as vampires, who "suck the blood of the helpless." Similar charges were heard wherever civil administrators took control of Jesuit properties.[143]

Boats continued to sail down the Río Paraná to market in Buenos Aires bearing Indian-made cotton cloth and Indian-harvested Paraguayan tea, or yerba maté, but profits that Jesuits once poured back into Indian mission communities now went largely to the civil administrators. Capital, which Jesuits had drawn from their estates and investments, no longer arrived to subsidize missions.[144] Food production dropped as administrators focused on cash crops, and the land base that once supported mission Indians shrank as Spaniards in search of new grazing lands pushed into Guaraní country that Jesuits had once protected.[145] Inspecting the mission town of Mártires in 1776, just eight years after the Jesuits' abrupt departure, Lt. Juan Valiente found it "in the most deplorable state of need that can be imagined, with such hunger that men who remain are pallid and thin."[146]

As their economic base deteriorated, the Guaraní population in the thirty missions declined, dropping by nearly 50 percent, from 88,828 in 1768 to 45,720 in 1799.[147] Weakened by malnutrition, excessive work, and disease introduced by increased contact with the Hispanic world, Guaraníes died at a faster rate than they had under the Jesuits.[148] Many simply left, despite efforts to contain them. Some migrated to Portuguese territory, where they found employment. Others responded to a rising demand for labor in the Spanish towns and countryside, where the Bourbon reforms precipitated an economic upswing, particularly after the creation of the viceroyalty of the Río de la Plata in 1776. Some took refuge among unconquered Minuanes and Charrúas, but relatively few seem to have reverted to savagery, as imaginative writers once supposed. Rather, most of these highly acculturated people rebuilt their lives in the Hispanic world. Meanwhile, those Guaraníes who remained in the fading old mission towns found ways to accommodate to civil administrators, just as they had to Jesuits. Indeed, the most opportunistic of the old Guaraní elite made common cause with their new secular overseers.[149]

As the thirty Guaraní missions declined, the Franciscans, Dominicans, and Mercedarians who had assumed their spiritual direction stood by helplessly. "I established the new spiritual and temporal government," Governor Bucareli later explained to his successor, "putting the clergy in the position of absolutely limiting their duties and authority to serving the churches and caring for souls." For good measure he distributed members of the same religious order among the Guaraní towns in ways that would impede their communication with one another.[150] Reduced to the role of diocesan priests, the regular clergy could deliver tough sermons, but they lacked authority to halt pillaging and mismanagement or restore order and prosperity.[151]

High-ranking bureaucrats in distant centers of power also seemed powerless to arrest the missions' decline, as they vacillated between promoting individual freedom and initiative and protecting the Guaraníes and their property from exploitation and preserving stability in what came to be called the province of Misiones. Liberal critics, apparently unaware that communal life had worked well for the Guaraníes before the arrival of Spaniards,[152] criticized Bucareli for protecting a communal system that discouraged individual initiative. They, in the words of one of the most knowledgeable reformers, insisted that Indians be granted "complete liberty so that each might work for his own profit . . . and that they live and are treated in every way like the other vassals of the King."[153]

At century's end, the reformers found an ally in a new viceroy of the Río de La Plata, the marqués de Avilés (1799–1801), who began to privatize the missions, placing individual Indians in possession of mission communal lands.[154] Pleased with the results, in 1803 Carlos IV extended freedom to all of the Indians of the Guaraní missions—the thirty ex-Jesuit missions as well as seventeen Guaraní missions founded by other orders.[155] But even a royal decree from an enlightened despot did not bring freedom to the Guaraníes. Convinced by traditionalists that Indians "would return to the savage life in a few years" or let production languish, leaving the mission region vulnerable to Portuguese occupation,[156] the Council of the Indies killed the plan in 1806. When Napoleon invaded Iberia in 1808 and threw Spain into a crisis, the Guaraní question became one of many pieces of unfinished business.[157] Forty years after the expulsion of the Jesuits, Guaraníes continued to live under many of the same restrictions that Jesuits had placed on them.

On the western side of the Chaco, in the province of Tucumán, officials tried a different tack. They hoped to return to the old Jesuit system, without the Jesuits. Some 3,350 *chaqueños* (principally nonequestrian Lules and Vilelas but also equestrian Tobas) lived in seven Jesuit missions in 1767. After the Jesuits' expulsion, civil administrators had looted those missions, too. Their residents fled in droves. By 1771, their population had declined by 35 percent. That year Gov. Gerónimo Matorras of Tucumán moved quickly to revive the dying missions, which he saw as essential for controlling Indians and expanding Spanish ranching on this turbulent frontier. In 1771, Matorras removed the civil administrators, turned the missions over to Franciscans, and provided the friars with supplies, gifts for Indians, and annual stipends. With royal approval, he ignored Aranda's instructions for administering former Jesuit missions and gave the Franciscans temporal as well as spiritual authority. Matorras limited the Franciscans' independence by making them responsible to himself and the bishop of Tucumán but gave them substantial authority within individual missions. At the end of the century, as the missions' economies and populations continued to decline, the government reassigned civil administrators to some of these missions but made them responsible to Franciscans.[158]

In the remote tropical forests and savannas of modern-day eastern Bolivia, where Jesuits had built thriving missions in what they called the provinces of Moxos and Chiquitos, officials tried to maintain the Jesuit system with secular clergy rather than with Franciscans or civil administrators. At the time of the Jesuits' expulsion, some thirty thousand Indians lived in fifteen mission towns at Moxos; twenty-three thousand lived in ten missions in Chiquitos.[159] Fearful that radical change would cause Indians to desert the mission communities, officials put *curas* in charge of the missions' temporal and spiritual affairs.[160] Their plan violated Aranda's instructions but won crown approval. The secular priests, who lacked the training, zeal, and resources that sustained religious orders, proved as incompetent and corrupt as the civil administrators of the Guaraní missions. In 1790, the Audiencia of Charcas, which supervised Moxos and Chiquitos, stripped the *curas* of responsibility for the temporalities and transferred it to civil officers. This formula also achieved dismal results. Mission Indians, who once contributed to Spanish defenses of the region against the Portuguese, now found it increasingly difficult to defend themselves from the Guaycuruans of the Chaco. Indian leaders looked back to the Jesuit era as a time of "plenty of cloth, knives, scissors, religious medallions, beads, and all things." The new plan, Viedma complained in 1793, continued to rob Indians of their freedom and deprived the government of prosperous, tax-paying subjects.[161]

19. In 1831, the French explorer Alcide d'Orbigny visited Mission San José, the former headquarters of the mission province of Chiquitos, and found its Indian population diminished to fifteen hundred from a high of five thousand under the Jesuits. He admired the stone architecture and expressed surprise that Indians "who had hardly left the savage state" could have constructed the town. This lithograph is based on his sketch of the large mission plaza. The three-story Moorish tower served as an entryway to the school to the right of it. The mission chapel stands to the left of the tower, and a mortuary chapel to its left. Vue de la place de St. Jose. *Lithograph in Orbigny, 1835–47, vol. 3, ser. 1, no. 14. Courtesy, John Carter Brown Library at Brown University.*

As these cases suggest, local conditions rather than Bourbon policies shaped the future of former Jesuit missions: their strategic importance; their economic resources and proximity to markets; the temperaments, talents, and interests of local government officials, priests, and colonists; and the interests and strategies of mission Indians themselves. Missions on the upper Amazon and upper Orinoco decayed rapidly. Two missions to the Mocobíes in the eastern Chaco near Santa Fe died a slow death at the hands of civil administrators. More mature and strategic missions, like those of the Guaraníes, remained viable if much-diminished communities long after Spanish Americans won independence from Spain. Highly acculturated Yaquis in northwestern New Spain worked seasonally in the labor-starved mines of Nueva Vizcaya to maintain the integrity of their eight former mission towns in the face of repeated official efforts to privatize them. To the east of the Yaquis, in the Sierra Madre Occidental, many Tarahumaras abandoned their missions and turned to raiding Spanish livestock after civil administrators sold Tarahumara horses, cattle, mules, oxen, plows, and seed, and Apache raids made mission life untenable.[162]

Despite their efforts to direct change from the center, Bourbon officials had limited control over local institutions and individuals in their far-flung empire. Seventeen years after the Jesuits' expulsion, even the most determined of regalists, José de Gálvez, Spain's chief minister for American affairs (1776–87), had to ask bureaucrats in America how each of the former Jesuit missions functioned rather than dictate how they should function. Were secular or regular clergy in charge? Did they receive a salary? If so, from what branch of government? Did Indians participate in governing mission communities? What property and income did Indians own in common?[163]

Whatever the fate of individual missions, the Jesuits' expulsion dealt a blow to their plans to push deeper into the lands of unconverted Indians.[164] Their looted or mismanaged former missions could barely support themselves, much less provide surpluses to support the "spiritual advances" that the crown required of missionaries who took up where Jesuits left off.[165]

After ousting the Jesuits from their missions, the Bourbon reformers had made a gesture toward the so-called new method by attempting to limit the clergy to the spiritual care of Indians. In the former Jesuit missions, however, the Bourbon reformers stopped short of applying the new method as fully as Escandón had in Nuevo Santander. Like Escandón, the reformers limited preachers to preaching, but unlike Escandón they insisted on maintaining mission communal property and putting it, along with Indians themselves, under civilian administrators' direct control. In the Guaraní missions, officials maintained the separation between the spiritual and the temporal for the rest of the colonial period, with only a brief hiatus. The division of the two spheres broke down in Moxos and Chiquitos, however, where officials put *curas* in charge of both spiritual and temporal affairs, and in Tucumán, where Governor Matorras simply replaced Jesuits with Franciscans. In these former Jesuit missions, Bourbon administrators avoided the risky step of granting individual Indians freedom and turning communal property over to them. Nonetheless, some Bourbon officials would insist that missionaries moving into new mission fields abstain from controlling Indians or their communal property and convert Indians with nothing more than friendly persuasion.

Mendicants vs. the New Method

With Jesuits gone, the conversion of Indians fell to mendicant orders, so called because they refused worldly goods and lived on alms, or *limosnas*. Of those orders, which included Dominicans and Augustinians, Franciscans were by far the most numerous and operated more missions in Spanish America than any other religious order except the Jesuits. Like other mendicants, the followers of St. Francis had grown dispirited over the course of the 1600s, above all in areas like eastern Peru and New Mexico, where baptized Indians seemed mired in apostasy and heathens resisted conversion.[166]

In the late 1600s, however, the Franciscan friars, or brothers, as they called one another, began to energize their stalled missions by building a string of missionary colleges in Spanish America. Supported by Rome and modeled after European missionary colleges, these *colegios de propaganda fide* operated independently of the Franciscan provinces that had supported earlier missions. The colleges existed solely to train friars to reignite the faith among Christians, wherever they might be found, and to convert heathens in their own languages on new frontiers. New conversions, *conversiones vivas*, had become ever more challenging as preachers moved beyond the great Aztec and Inca empires into lands where bands and tribes spoke numerous mutually unintelligible languages or dialects. Missionaries found these languages barbarous as well as difficult to learn, but some colleges met the challenge of teaching them more readily than others.[167]

By the time of the Jesuits' expulsion, Franciscans had founded nine American missionary colleges: four in Mexico—Santa Cruz de Querétaro (1683), Nuestra Señora de Guadalupe de Zacatecas (1704), San Fernando de México (1732), and San Francisco de Pachuca (1732); two in New Granada—Nuestra Señora de las Gracias de Popayán (1753) and San Joaquín de Cali (1757); one in today's Bolivia—Nuestra Señora de los Angeles de Tarija (1755); one in Chile—San Ildefonso de Chillán (1756); and one in Peru—Santa Rosa de Ocopa (1758). Between 1784 and 1812, the friars founded another seven colleges: two in Mexico and one each in Panama, Venezuela, Peru, Bolivia, and Argentina, bringing the total to sixteen. Thus, even at a time when the Bourbon state moved to reduce the number of mature Indian parishes, or *curatos,* in control of missionaries, Franciscan missionary colleges proliferated.[168]

The colleges tried to respond to a chronic shortage of missionaries. Religious orders in Spain and America overflowed with members but, to the annoyance of enlightened Catholics and regalists like Campomanes, few chose to leave the comfort of cathedrals and monasteries to serve a ten-year tour of duty and privation in a remote mission. In 1789, for example, the Franciscan Province of Buenos Aires had 291 friars, but only 45 of them served in missions. A standard manual for missionaries, published in 1783, described the situation: "The missionaries now do not go to live in the plains or in the forests, but to their Provinces and their convents." Many of those who did volunteer to serve in missions balked at reenlisting for a second ten-year stint.[169]

The colleges also responded to Bourbon requests for missionaries trained in sciences, arts, and "things useful to society," rather than those educated for the contemplative life. "The work of the missionary is not learned in the schools of Latin, philosophy, and theology," the viceroy of New Granada, Pedro de Mendinueta, insisted in 1803.[170]

Although the Franciscan missionary colleges aimed to increase the number of Franciscans available for missionary work, the number of recruits declined in the last decades of the eighteenth century. Fewer young men entered religious orders on both sides of the Atlantic. In part this decline reflected financial difficulties that made the religious life increasingly unattractive and testified to the Bourbon's success at reducing the number of clergy.[171] Then, too, Spaniards' own intertribal rivalries had aggravated the situation. European-born Spaniards, convinced of their superiority over American-born clergy, had consistently dominated missionary work in America. As the Council of the Indies noted in 1778, *criollos* took the same religious vows as *peninsulares,* but they lacked the *peninsulares'* "robustness" and could not withstand "the variety of climates and other works that are carried out in the missions."[172] Bourbon officials like the conde de Florida-blanca believed that clergy born in America had become "notably lax" and insisted on keeping them under the control of clerics who came from Spain itself (much as those same officials believed that *peninsulares* made more efficient administrators than *criollos*).[173] By placing Spanish-born clergy in charge of the religious orders, Bourbon administrators added to the climate that discouraged American-born *criollos* from volunteering to serve in remote missions.

Convinced themselves of the superiority of Spanish-born clergy and dependent on Spanish-born recruits, the leaders of the Franciscan colleges in America found it difficult to fill quotas, particularly with the intensification of European wars in the 1790s and the upheavals of the wars of independence in the early nineteenth century.[174] In their insistence on relying on Europeans, the missionary colleges also deprived themselves of the priests who may have best understood American conditions. The *criollos*, Ambrosio O'Higgins argued, could understand Indians' "temperament" better than Europeans. He recommended that one Spanish-born missionary and one *criollo* be assigned to each mission.[175]

By the 1780s, few of the Franciscan colleges or provinces in America had sufficient clergy to staff each of their missions with two friars, as the rules of their order required (the same might also be said of Dominicans, who tried to increase their missionary activities to help fill the void left by Jesuits; *criollo-peninsular* tensions also blossomed among the Dominicans).[176] The shortage of mendicants was most acute in remote, difficult places such as the mountainous land of the Tarahumaras in the Sierra Madre Occidental of northern New Spain, where eighteen Franciscans attended to thirty-one towns, and the province of Mainas on the headwaters of the Amazon, which had thirty-two missions but no more than a dozen missionaries to serve them. Franciscans had set their sights on "great spiritual harvests . . . of savage nations." They hoped, for example, to build missions from Mainas north to the missionary province of Popayán and to link Popayán with their missions on the upper Orinoco.[177] Instead, as one friar noted in 1784, unconverted Indians remained "buried in the abyss of infidelity and barbarism for lack of ministers."[178] In some places, Indians who had already received instruction had to be abandoned because no missionaries could be found to serve them. "To return those Indians later to religious instruction and sociability required nearly as much work as when they were [first] taken from the woods," the Council of the Indies observed in 1802.[179]

As the supply of mendicants shrank in the late 1700s, demand for their services rose. Not only did they have to fill the vacuum at former Jesuit missions, but also minister to Spaniards in desolate places that secular priests avoided. A succession of thirty-two Franciscans and Mercedarians, for example, served soldiers and convicts assigned to the bleak Malvinas Islands (Falklands), three hundred miles east of the Strait of Magellan, between 1767, when Spain first occupied the islands, and 1793.[180] Then, too, the crown encouraged mendicants to further their "spiritual conquests" of independent Indians.

However hostile they might have been to Jesuits, many Bourbon officials continued to see missions as necessary for the conversion of Natives and the consolidation of the empire's endangered American borderlands. Spain could not hope to fortify its extensive coastlines, from Tierra del Fuego to California, but low-cost missionaries might be able to turn independent Indians into loyal subjects who would defend those regions. Missionaries themselves did not hesitate to make that point as they sought support from the crown.[181]

Immediately after the expulsion of the Jesuits, the crown feared that a single religious order might monopolize a large area, as Jesuits had done. To prevent that, the conde de Floridablanca had distributed the thirty Guaraní missions equally among Franciscans, Dominicans, and Mercedarians. In Guayana, Governor Centurión urged that the former Jesuit missions of the middle Orinoco be put in charge of one religious order but that missionaries be recruited from different religious provinces in Spain so they would compete with one another and thus improve the quality of their work.[182]

By and large, however, officials in the post-Jesuit years evinced greater concern about secularizing missions and moving missionaries to new frontiers than they did about religious orders controlling large regions. The mendicants' vows of poverty and their self-abnegation seemed to make them less dangerous than Jesuits. The conde de Campomanes, whose views probably reflected the conventional wisdom among high Bourbon officials, believed that Franciscans had no desire to control Indians' possessions, deny Indians the right to trade with Spaniards, or block Spaniards from entering Indian missions. He pronounced the friars free of the Jesuits' "ambition and despotism."[183]

The mendicants' manifest poverty also impressed some Indians, but lack of resources weakened the mendicants' missionary efforts more than it strengthened them.[184] In some areas, such as the western Chaco, where Franciscans took over Jesuit missions, shaky financing stood among the principal causes of their slow demise.[185] Franciscans did not possess the great revenue-producing estates that sustained Jesuit missions, colleges, and universities, and after the Jesuits' expulsion some declined to take direct control of Jesuit estates.[186] The Franciscan ethic required that they depend on the generosity of others. In the case of missionaries who worked among Indians, this usually meant alms in the form of supplies and *sínodos,* or annual allowances from the crown, amounting to some 300 to 350 pesos per friar per year in the late 1700s. Missionaries who presided over mature parishes could also expect to receive food and lodging from mission Indians, but friars who tried to make new converts found that Indians expected to receive gifts, not give them. Gifts, the crown had consistently asserted, constituted "the real means to bring about conversions," yet it granted such meager support to the friars that some dipped into their own stipends to buy gifts that, to hear them tell it, always seemed insufficient.[187] As Spain fell into ruinous wars with England and France after the death of Carlos III in 1788, government support for missions declined still further, to the point that even the friars' annual stipends stopped coming.[188]

If Franciscans did not have enough food and gifts to attract "heathen savages" to their

missions, they did have another alternative.[189] In theory, at least, friars could build enduring mission communities whose Indian workers produced surpluses to support further
spiritual conquests. In practice, however, this strategy collided with the views of those
enlightened Bourbons who believed that older missions should be secularized and that
missionaries engaged in *conversiones vivas* should utilize the new method, confining their
activities to the spiritual realm.

Mendicants, then, had strong economic reasons to oppose both secularization and
the new method. Profitable older missions could support new missionary endeavors,
and under optimal conditions, the temporalities at new missions would produce revenue
to sustain them and to permit still further expansion. Indeed, in some places, religious
orders had financial incentive to hold onto secularized Indian parishes because the tithes
paid by Indian parishioners provided income for the missionary and relieved his religious
order of that burden.[190]

Regular clergy defended their retention of decades-old missions, however, with more
altruistic arguments. First, missions buffered Indians from the Spanish world and prevented
them from slipping into apostasy. In sharp contrast to Bourbon reformers, who argued
that exposure to the workaday world of Spaniards represented the Indians' best path
toward acculturation and progress, missionaries often saw Indians' contacts with Spaniards
as the cause of the "destruction of the [Indian] towns and the complete backwardness of
the poor Indians."[191] Second, the transformation of Indians into Spanish Christians required decades, rather than the decade that the Bourbon officials came to think of as
optimal. As one Franciscan theologian explained in an influential primer for priests published in 1783, some Natives were "so rude and slow to learn the ineffable mysteries of
the Faith, and so slothful and lazy to work and farm, so that in this period [of ten years]
they have not been able to adjust to the laws and order of a civil society."[192]

Economics and theology combined, then, to stiffen Franciscan resistance to secularization and the new method. In the old highland mission province of Apolobamba in today's Bolivia, for example, a much-traveled royal tobacco inspector chided the Franciscans
in 1780 for keeping so-called Chunchos in ignorance of the fact that the crown had ordered their secularization. "Notwithstanding the antiquity of their missions," he said,
the Franciscans "have not permitted outsiders to establish relationships or trade, nor
have they permitted Indians to leave."[193]

Alta California and the Failure of the New Method

The conflict between the Franciscans' paternalism and the Bourbons' new method
came into stark relief when Spain moved to occupy the coast of Alta California, the first
great push for new territory in New Spain since Escandón's venture into Nuevo Santander and the last of the colonial era. Expansion up the Pacific coast to Monterey Bay
was the brainchild of José de Gálvez, whom Carlos III had sent to New Spain in 1765
as inspector general, or *visitador general,* with extraordinary powers to recommend sweep-

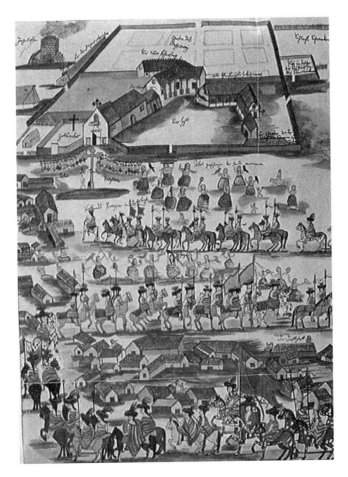

20. At the Mission of San Javier, established among the Mocobíes
on the eastern side of the Chaco in early 1743, Jesuits encouraged
Indians to pay elaborate homage to the Spanish monarch on the feast
day of San Javier, much as Spaniards did in nearby Santa Fe
on the day of their town's patron saint. While some mounted Indians
carried banners of damask cloth embroidered with threads of silver
and silk, Indian women who received them in front of the church
danced with gourd rattles and the heads of their enemies.
Detail from a watercolor by the Jesuit Florián Paucke, in Paucke,
1942–44, vol. 3, part 1, plate cxiii.

ing administrative and economic reforms. One of the most vigorous Bourbon administrators, Gálvez had personally overseen the expulsion of the Jesuits from New Spain
and had made it clear that he favored the dissolution of mission communities and the
rapid integration of Indians into Hispanic society.[194]

Gálvez learned quickly, however, that missions failed as economic enterprises if mendicants lacked control over their temporalities and their Indians. In 1768, he inspected Baja

California and found that military administrators had let the former Jesuit missions fall quickly to ruin. Gálvez replaced the soldier-administrators with Franciscans from the College of San Fernando in Mexico City, putting them in charge of the missions' properties and Indians.[195]

The next year, in 1769, when he launched the "Sacred Expedition" to take possession of the Alta California coast above San Diego to secure it against foreigners, Gálvez granted Franciscans from San Fernando similar authority.[196] He initially considered missionaries peripheral to the success of this venture, but he soon discovered that Alta California's isolation made them central. Unlike José de Escandón, who could move colonists into Nuevo Santander from neighboring provinces, Gálvez had the costly challenge of moving colonists to Alta California by sea over great distances and keeping them supplied until they could sustain themselves. Nuevo Santander could generate capital by sending livestock to nearby markets, but remote California promised to lose money. Little wonder, then, that Gálvez turned to missionaries who, in theory if not always in practice, could turn Indians into Spaniards at a fraction of the cost of importing and maintaining colonists.

Gálvez also tried to restore the traditional system at the Pimería missions in Sonora, which he regarded as a key to the development of Alta California. As elsewhere, civil administrators had looted or neglected these former Jesuit missions, many of which stood on the edge of Apache territory. Pimas had begun to leave and agricultural production had fallen to the point where Hispanic consumers of Indian-produced grains felt the shortages.[197] Convinced by the Franciscans' logic that whatever weakened the missions also weakened the fragile frontier provinces, Gálvez turned the temporalities of the Pimería Alta missions over to the Franciscans.[198] He also permitted Franciscans to administer sacraments to Pimas and non-Indians without obtaining permission from diocesan officials, as they previously had to do, and he ordered punishment for Pimas who declined to receive Christian instruction or work for their mission communities.[199] To the east of the Pimería, in Nueva Vizcaya, he took similar measures to restore the temporalities of the former Jesuit missions among the Tarahumaras, also looted by administrators and menaced by Apaches.[200]

Thus, in both Californias and in parts of Sonora and Nueva Vizcaya where foreigners or hostile Indians threatened and where the Spanish population and investment capital was sparse, Gálvez relied on traditional missions as instruments of Indian control. In contrast to Paraguay, where the crown divided former Jesuit missions among three religious orders to keep any one of them from obtaining a monopoly, Gálvez put the Californias and the Pimería Alta in the hands of a single order, the Franciscans. Gálvez, who opposed conventional missions in theory, had no choice but to give the regulars the kind of local authority Jesuits had enjoyed. Like other Bourbon reformers, however, he maneuvered behind the scenes to bring the missionary colleges under tighter royal and episcopal control.[201]

Bourbon officials who succeeded Gálvez in northwestern New Spain tried to revive the new method of operating missions, but they met staunch resistance from the friars.

In 1772, when officers in charge of Alta and Baja California tried to limit missionaries "only to say mass and preach," fray Francisco Palóu replied, "If it must be that way, better that we retire to the College."[202] Faced with that threat, Viceroy Antonio María Bucareli y Ursúa, a career officer whose brother had overseen the expulsion of the Jesuits from the Río de la Plata, lost interest in the new method. Alta California was not Nuevo Santander, where the withdrawal of the College of San Fernando did no economic harm to Escandón's enterprise.[203] Remote California needed productive missions to survive, and toward that end, Viceroy Bucareli noted in 1776, "I hope that the missionary fathers dedicate their zeal to farming and ranching."[204]

Subsequent California governors had little luck at weakening the friars' control over mission Indians or temporalities. None tried more enthusiastically than Gov. Felipe de Neve (1775–81)—or met more resounding defeat. Neve failed to force the friars to grant self-government to mission Indians, reduce the number of clergy at each mission from two to one, or convert missions into parishes. He could not even get them to report their assets.[205] Unsuccessful at limiting Franciscan control over Alta California's existing missions, Neve and his superior officer, Teodoro de Croix, decided to apply the new method to new missions. In 1782, Neve tried to limit Franciscans' efforts to convert Chumash Indians along the Santa Barbara Channel to preaching and good example. He ordered the friars to let Indians remain in their villages, "in their complete natural liberty" rather than force them into missions and turn them into "implacable enemies." The idea withered in the blistering heat of Franciscan opposition.[206]

Two years before Neve's failure, Croix had put a similar plan in motion, but it ended tragically. In 1780, Croix authorized the building of two settlements among the Yumas at a strategic crossing of the lower Colorado River, on the trail from Sonora to Alta California. Croix gave missionaries responsibility for converting the Yumas, but he prohibited the friars from using anything more than "sweetness and gentleness." He admonished the priests not to baptize Yumas until they achieved understanding of Christian doctrine through voluntary instruction. In this way, Croix said, the faith "will take root in them with greater strength."[207] Established in late 1780 and early 1781, the two walled towns lasted only half a year. Yumas destroyed them in July 1781 and killed many of the Spaniards, including four priests. The outsiders and their voracious livestock had strained the desert-dwelling Yumas' fragile resource base to the limit, but Franciscans found an alternative explanation for the disaster. By declining to give them authority over Indians, the friars said, Croix had gone "against the laws, against custom, against experience. . . . Thus the government discovered how important it was to take the advice of practical missionaries."[208]

In Alta California's coastal missions, Bourbon officials like Neve had to heed the missionaries' advice because Franciscans wielded considerable power in that isolated province. California's Spanish population consisted chiefly of a scattering of soldiers and their families, who lived in and around four humble presidios—San Diego (1769), Monterey (1770), San Francisco (1776), and Santa Barbara (1782). Until fourteen families founded San José in 1781, California had no municipality. Just two more sparsely populated towns followed: Los Angeles (1781) and Branciforte (1797). Missions, in contrast, grew rapidly. By 1800, they numbered eighteen, and the population of mission Indians, some 13,500, exceeded the Spanish population by a ration of seven to one. Since friars controlled mission Indians, who provided labor that built Spanish garrisons and produced the surpluses of grain that fed Hispanic California, government officials had a weak hand.[209] Gov. Diego de Borica, for example, expressed outrage at the high death rates, diet, punishments, and fugitivism at California missions and professed "pity and compassion" for "what those sad and unfortunate Indians have suffered."[210] Like other reform-minded officials, however, he could do no more than fulminate. The light population of Spanish settlers in California put no countervailing pressure on the padres to secularize missions and free up mission land. Powerful and independent, Franciscans in California built new missions that resembled the old Jesuit missions of Paraguay.[211]

Like Jesuits in Paraguay, Franciscans owed much of their success in California to Indians themselves. Isolated by desert and mountains, California's coastal peoples lacked horses, guns, and tactics to repel Spaniards and had little previous experience to make them wary of non-Indian visitors. At first, California Indians had offered Spaniards a friendly reception—as they did in so many places when they first encountered Europeans. Gaspar de Portolá, after two journeys up and down the coast between San Diego and Monterey in 1769 and 1770, reported that the Indians were "tractable" and "pleasant, with no fear of us, freely bestowing whatever their misfortune allowed."[212] In keeping with Gálvez's instructions to win Indians over with kindness, Portolá had done his part to maintain friendly relations. In this state-run enterprise in the Age of Enlightenment, Portolá's men did not kidnap, torture, or raid Indians or use them as beasts of burden —this in sharp contrast to Spanish behavior on the privately financed *entradas* of the sixteenth century under Francisco Vázquez de Coronado, Hernando de Soto, and others.[213]

Kindness and forbearance continued to be official Spanish policy in Alta California, but the actions of some soldiers and missionaries gave Indians ample reason to rebel.[214] The strictest of Franciscans ordered overseers to whip disobedient Indians or throw them into shackles and stocks, and they sent soldiers to hunt them down when they fled.[215] Indian women, sexually abused by soldiers outside of missions, found their sexuality scrutinized and restricted by priests when they took up residence inside in the patriarchal missions. Some missionaries confined unmarried women to fetid nighttime quarters, adding to already high mortality rates.[216] Such outrages might have provoked massive rebellion from better-armed or better-organized Indians, but Indian revolts in California tended to be local, as at San Diego in 1775 and San Gabriel in 1785. More commonly, Indians resisted missions by avoiding them or fleeing from them into the vast California interior. Or resistance expressed itself within mission settings, where some Indians professed Christianity yet found myriad ways to retain their religious traditions and subvert the missionary enterprise—including abortion and infanticide.[217] In fact, most Indians stayed away. Measured against the large numbers of Indians in California (some three

hundred thousand in 1769, the highest density of any area of North America), missionaries'
success at attracting Indians seems modest.[218]

Until the end of the colonial period, Franciscans sought to run the Alta California
missions in the classic manner. In theory but not always in practice, missionaries retained
full control of Indian property and of baptized Indians, who, in the main, were not to
leave their segregated communities without the priests' permission. That permission
might be given to an individual in the form of a safe conduct pass, or permission might
be granted to groups of Indians when missions could not produce sufficient food to support baptized Indians. That was the case at drought-ridden San Diego during its earliest
years and at the impoverished missions that Dominicans began to operate in northern
Baja California after Franciscans shifted their focus to Alta California. As they did
throughout Spanish America, California missionaries permitted baptized Indians to live
away from the mission when food ran short—"a lesser evil than permitting them to remain pagans," one friar said. By the end of the century, however, agriculture and livestock
production sustained most California missions, and there was no need to grant general
leaves.[219]

Mission Indians, however, did not thrive as well as crops and cattle. Many died or ran
away, and birthrates in the missions declined. The loss of Indians, however, did not create
a labor shortage or diminish mission production. Franciscans replenished their supply
by sending troops to recruit from California's high Native population or with Indians
from the interior, who continued to enter the missions willingly as their societies deteriorated. Overgrazing by Spanish livestock and other environmental changes set into motion by Spanish-introduced flora and fauna had threatened the subsistence of Indians
who lived beyond the missions, and diseases had also diminished their numbers. Impoverished and vulnerable to attack, some Indians sought refuge in missions, even as
others fled from them.[220]

As the mission economies of Alta California prospered and matured, some Bourbon
officials continued to pressure Franciscans to secularize the missions and to make new
conversions using the new method. In 1796, the *comandante* at Santa Barbara argued that
Chumash at the nearby village of Syuxtun refused baptism because they did not want
"to go to live at the mission." He urged the missionaries to take the sacraments to the
Indians and allow them to remain outside the mission.[221] The friars continued to resist.
They suspected, perhaps with good reason, that the reformers' motives had less to do
with the welfare of Indians than with gaining easy access to their land and labor. The
head of the Franciscan order in California, Fermín Francisco Lasuén, countered with
an economic argument: if Indians enjoyed freedom to come and go "missions would be
left with too much land and without people to use it." That could have dire consequences
for California's Hispanic population, which depended on mission production. Moreover,
the erasure of Natives' religious beliefs and practices and their adoption of Spanish ways
would not occur, he said, by "leaving them in freedom and in their *rancherías* after being
baptized." In 1803, the viceroy sided with the Franciscans.[222]

Bourbon reformers had argued vigorously that Indians were best acculturated by introducing them to colonists and commerce and limiting missionaries' prerogatives to the care of souls. The example of Alta California, however, suggests they had to compromise in a strategic area where Spanish colonial society was feeble and where Indians could be drawn or forced into traditional missions.

The Araucanía and the Failure of the Old Method

In places where independent Indians had horses, guns, or foreign allies mendicants seldom fared as well as they did in California. The Araucanía offers a prime example. Just as the Pacific Coast of North America took on strategic importance for Spain in the late eighteenth century, so did the Pacific Coast of South America. Foreigners—English and Dutch in particular—seemed poised to plant colonies in the Araucanian country, and, indeed, the English seemed a threat as far south as the Strait of Magellan and up the Atlantic coast of Patagonia.[223] In Chile as in California, officials turned to missionaries to help win the loyalty of Natives, and missionaries used foreigners as bogeymen to extract more aid from the crown.[224] Missionaries, however, had considerably less success among the Araucanians. The new method was not an issue in the Araucanía, perhaps because the old method had failed and the new method already operated there by default, to the satisfaction of Mapuches if not to missionaries.

Jesuits had tried since 1593 to convert Araucanians, and the Spanish crown had supported their work at a sizable cost. After a century and a half, the Jesuits had performed thousands of baptisms and helped foster dialogue between Spaniards and the most northerly Araucanians, the Mapuches, but they attracted few Indians to mission communities.[225] As an elderly Indian on the point of death told a priest who urged his last-minute conversion, "Padre, do not tire yourself, because it is an inviolable custom and law of my forefathers not to believe anything that Spaniards say."[226] The Mapuches, one official observed, knew that if they settled in communities "Spaniards would rule and enslave them, and they feared this oppression more than death."[227]

Unable to bring Mapuches to them, Jesuits went to the Mapuches. Wearing ponchos and spurs, Jesuits traveled on mule or horseback every spring or summer to the scattered Mapuche communities. In the words of one Jesuit, "They baptized the young, instructed the Indians in the things of God, confessed them, and married them."[228] Left to their own devices between these yearly visits, Mapuches remained, in the words of one officer, "in their old savagery, without abandoning the polygamy and superstitions in which they blindly live." In Chile, then, as in other places where the balance of military power lay with independent Indians, Jesuits had failed to carry out the official policy of congregating or reducing Indians. The few Jesuit missions among Mapuches served primarily as hubs from which priests annually toured an Indian world.[229]

In the mid-1700s, a group of young Jesuits lobbied to abandon these missionary circuits, or *misiones circulares,* and congregate Mapuches in towns. Inspired by the ideals of the

21. Jesuits crossing the Río Laja above its famous cataracts (today a well-known recreation area). The Laja continues westward some forty kilometers to merge with the Biobío. "Salto de la Laja," from Gay, 1854. Courtesy, John Carter Brown Library at Brown University.

Catholic Enlightenment, which emphasized a good Christian life over Christian ritual, they hoped to draw Indians into *reducciones* as their order had done so successfully in places like Paraguay. These young Jesuits believed that confining Araucanians in missions, from which they could neither hunt nor raid nor follow herds, would force them to end their use of intoxicants, their multiple marriages, and their traditional religious practices.[230] Against the advice of their more experienced elders, the Jesuit reformers made their case to Gov. Antonio de Guill y Gonzaga and in 1764 persuaded him to force Mapuches into towns. The experiment backfired. Guill provoked the second great Mapuche revolt of the eighteenth century. In 1766, the year before Spain expelled the Jesuits from its empire, Mapuches expelled them from the Araucanía. They profaned churches, attacked towns, burned houses, and drove Spaniards from their lands.[231]

In contrast to Guaraníes, Moxos, Chiquitos, and other peoples who traded life in missions for protection against Spanish slave hunters or other enemies, most independent Mapuches had no need to congregate in tight mission quarters where they would compromise traditional social, economic, religious, and family life and expose themselves to fatal European diseases.[232] By the mid-1600s, the Mapuches had achieved autonomy and security below the Biobío. Through trading and raiding networks, which reached to the

Argentine side of the Andes, they had easy access to horses, alcohol, and manufactured goods. Without surrendering independence they could enjoy yearly visits by priests who brought them gifts and the sacrament of baptism. Since priests presented them with gifts on the occasion of baptism, Mapuche parents found it advantageous to have their children baptized repeatedly and, with passage of time, Mapuches came to think of baptism as an *admapu*—an ancestral custom.[233]

In this, Mapuches were not unique. Peoples like the upper, or western, Tarahumaras also accepted baptism in large numbers and incorporated Christian elements into their rituals even as they continued to live in "distant places," as one Franciscan said, "subject to nothing but their own free will." The Tarahumaras' success at resisting missionary life owed much to the rugged terrain of their homeland on the western escarpment of the Sierra Madre, with its "almost inaccessible ravines." There they found sanctuary, and Spaniards could not readily find them. Their population, some twenty-five thousand, remained substantial in the late 1700s.[234]

Before the Araucanian revolt of 1766, Jesuits had seventeen missions in the Araucanía. After the revolt, only seven remained. Following the expulsion of the Jesuits in 1767, secular priests took over the four Jesuit missions closest to the Biobío, where a bishop of Concepción later described the Indians as "converted and no longer neophytes." Franciscans took charge of the remaining three missions, where Indians were "still undergoing conversion"—at the coastal mission of Arauco, below Concepción in Mapuche territory, and at Valdivia and nearby Mariquina in Huilliche country.[235]

Franciscans were not newcomers to the Araucanía. Together with Dominicans, they had first come in the 1550s, preceding the Jesuits' arrival in Chile by forty years. After the great Araucanian revolt of 1598–1603, however, Franciscans and Dominicans had abandoned the field to the Jesuits. The Dominicans turned their attention to running schools and parishes and never returned.[236] The Franciscans established a missionary college at Chillán in 1756 and looked again toward the Araucanía.

Like the Jesuits, Franciscans had a tradition of using a single mission community as a hub, or *cabecera*, from which they visited chapels in nearby satellite villages, which they termed *visitas*. Franciscans, however, performed mass and other sacraments in their nearby *visitas* with frequency, often weekly. Jesuits in the Araucanía, on the other hand, baptized Indians in a circuit so large they could only visit them once a year. Franciscans from Chillán deplored the fact that Jesuits abandoned baptized Araucanians for a year at a time. Without sustained instruction, one Franciscan said, baptized Indians remained "as fixed in the darkness of their errors, superstitions, and savage customs as the other heathen nations who never knew a missionary."[237]

To Franciscan critics from Chillán, the Jesuit circuits had done more harm than good. Heathens, by definition, could not commit sacrileges. By baptizing Indians and then leaving them without further instruction for long periods of time, however, Jesuits had given their neophytes both the capacity and the liberty to commit sacrileges. By way of example, a scandalized Franciscan claimed that one poorly instructed Mapuche had learned so little from the Jesuits that he asked if "it would suffice to baptize their penises, then all of their future children would be baptized and with this they [the Franciscans] would not have to tire themselves in traveling to Indian lands every year to baptize the little ones."[238]

Following the expulsion of the Jesuits, Franciscans had the Araucanía to themselves and the good fortune to work in a time of relative peace. In a rebuke to Governor Guill, who had advocated the extermination of Araucanians following their revolt in 1766, the crown rejected offensive warfare as a viable policy against the Araucanians. The crown, however, also rejected a plan of the bishop of Concepción, Pedro Angel Espiñeira, to increase the missionary presence and rely solely on "gentleness." Even after years of missionary labors, the crown noted, Araucanians continued to "live and die submerged in libertinage." In a shift of strategy the crown ordered the governor of Chile to establish a seminary to educate the children of Araucanian chiefs and train those youngsters to become missionaries who "will reduce their relatives to a rational and Christian life."[239] That idea, which followed the recommendation of the viceroy of Peru, Manuel de Amat y Juniet, a former governor and captain general of Chile, won the support of other enlightened officials. Who could better convert Araucanians than Araucanians?[240]

Educating Indian children or preparing them for the priesthood was not an innovation of the Enlightenment. Schools for the children of Indian nobility had existed in the sixteenth century, and missionaries had a long tradition of targeting Indian children when their parents proved resistant to conversion. The friars hoped, as Bishop Espiñeira explained in the case of the Araucanians, that the children "would little by little lose their natural and passionate love for their parents and turn all of their loving affection toward the missionaries."[241] Spanish military officers also saw Indian children as educable agents of change. In 1786, for example, the commander in chief of the Interior Provinces of New Spain recommended that children of Spain's Comanche allies be sent to Mexico City to be educated. Adult Comanches, he believed, were too old to learn "the Spanish language, our usage and method of government."[242] The Chilean attempt to train the children of independent Indians as missionaries and use them to convert their people, however, may have been unique.

The Franciscans' efforts to educate Araucanian children took its most sophisticated form at the Seminario de Naturales, a seminary for Indians run by the Franciscan missionary college of Chillán. With the moral support of the crown and funds generated by the Jesuits' confiscated properties, the school opened in 1775 in Santiago. Because it functioned poorly under secular clergy, however, in 1785 it moved to Chillán, where the padres sought to train Araucanian boys in isolation from other Araucanians. The boys, whose parents received gifts for sending them to Chillán, were not permitted to go home lest they be exposed to "the vices and licentiousness associated with their [people's] irreligious state and their complete lack of civil society."[243] Some of the boys fled, but others stayed to become what Gov. Ambrosio O'Higgins described as "Hispanicized through education." A small number became priests. In 1794, two became the first Indians ordained to the Catholic priesthood in Chile, and at least four more were ordained before the school closed in 1811.[244]

Meanwhile, Franciscans had not given up on building missions. They had modest successes among Huilliches south of the Río Toltén—first near Valdivia and finally at Osorno, when Spaniards reoccupied that long-abandoned town in 1796.[245] Like their Jesuit predecessors, however, Franciscans failed to congregate significant numbers of Indians in mission communities, and officials chaffed at their slow pace. In 1793, following an Araucanian uprising that set missionary efforts back still further, Governor O'Higgins grumbled about the padres' failures. Missions, he said, "annually spend many pesos without any result other than soothing the royal conscience." Like other enlightened officers, O'Higgins believed that missionaries should devote themselves solely to Indians' spiritual welfare. As to the task of congregating Indians into towns, O'Higgins believed that soldiers could do it better than clergy.[246]

O'Higgins, however, had a decidedly unspiritual task in mind for missionaries. He wanted them to help secure the coast from Concepción south to Osorno.[247] He called on the friars to spy on the Araucanians, reporting "any machinations or treachery," and to convince the Indians "of the beneficence of the Spaniards, instilling in them subordination, love, and respect for our government."[248] He encouraged the friars to revive the Jesuits' circuit-riding system.[249]

The college at Chillán rejected O'Higgin's proposal. Performing annual baptisms without true conversions, the head of the college protested, violated the rules of the Franciscan order and the instructions of Carlos III.[250] Not all Franciscans at the college agreed. Dissenters argued, as Jesuits had before them, that they needed to save the souls of innocent children through baptism and that there would never be enough priests to instruct all of the Araucanians. The dissenters, however, remained a minority.[251]

Franciscans from Chillán were not alone in preferring, as one missionary in Paraguay put it, to let Indian infants remain "in infidelity rather than baptize them and abandon them to the superstitions they see in their heathen parents." Félix de Azara had condemned the practice as an "imprudent prostitution of baptism."[252] Meanwhile, however, Franciscans from the distant but well-staffed College of Ocopa in the Peruvian highlands showed greater flexibility when they took over the former Jesuit missions on Chiloé and its surrounding islands and islets. In little boats powered by wind and Indian oarsmen, Jesuits had journeyed from island to island and port to port through cold and often turbulent waters making annual visits to chapels that numbered over seventy by 1767. Those chapels served over nine thousand native Chilotes—older converts like the descendants of the original Huilliche inhabitants of the island and new converts brought from farther south, including Chonos and Caucahues. Like their brethren from Chillán, Franciscans from the college at Ocopa hoped to consolidate these scattered little communities into more sizable missions, each with a resident priest who might deepen the Chilotes' faith; geography, settlement patterns, and the friars' own small numbers, however, worked against them. Thus, Franciscans from the college at Ocopa continued to use the Jesuit circuit system among the Chilotes, even as their brethren from the college at Chillán refused to make annual treks to baptize or marry Araucanians.[253]

On the mainland, nothing seemed to push or pull Mapuches into missions. Even a great smallpox epidemic in 1791 failed to drive Mapuches to seek solace from the padres, perhaps because they associated them with last rites and death.[254] In 1804, after years of frustrating failures to lure meaningful numbers of Mapuches into missions peacefully, the head of the Franciscan order in Chile asked civil officials to force baptized Indians —those who had "voluntarily submitted to the gentle yoke of the gospel"—to fulfill their "Christian duties."[255] His request made its way to the governor of Valdivia, the intendant of Concepción, and the *audiencia* of Santiago. All denied his request. Spanish law, they said, did not apply to Araucanians who had voluntarily given missionaries permission to enter their lands. No one, the *audiencia* ruled, had the right to force Araucanians to live Christian lives; friars could use no means other than "gentleness, prudence, and leniency" in their dealings with Araucanians.[256] It may also be that civil officials recalled the revolt of 1766, provoked by Jesuit efforts to force Mapuches into mission towns.

Thus, at the same time that Franciscans in Alta California received help from soldiers to forcibly keep Indians in mission compounds and retrieve those who ran away, Franciscans in Chile were denied official approval to exert authority by force. While Franciscans in California maintained control over mission properties in the face of official opposition, Franciscans in Chile had little mission property to defend.

In California in 1783, just fourteen years after they began work there, Franciscans had built nine missions over a 500-mile stretch between San Diego and San Francisco, with over 4,000 Indian residents (see map 6). That year, one of the Franciscans' staunchest critics, Felipe de Neve, praised them for their rapid economic progress—the abundance of harvests and the size of herds—and for their skill at attracting Indians and keeping the "pagans submissive and obedient."[257] In the Araucanía, where missionaries had worked for over two hundred years, Franciscans operated fifteen missions in 1789, from Arauco 350 miles south to Osorno (see map 4). These missions, however, had fewer than 2,000 Indians attached to them. The preponderance of baptized Araucanians (not to mention the even more numerous heathens) lived in what the friars called "a lamentable dispersion," "excessively averse to civility," and "enshrouded in the regrettable darkness of infidelity."[258] In Chile, Franciscans tried to draw Indians to missions with rations of bread and beef jerky furnished by the government; in the California missions, Indians themselves produced surplus grain and beef that the padres used to expand their operations.[259]

Clearly these differences owed as much to the nature of Indian societies and to Indians' circumstances and previous experience with Spaniards as to Franciscan efforts or Bourbon policies. California's more numerous coastal people spoke a variety of languages, making it difficult for them to unite. More important, California Indians might have been living in the sixteenth century, given their innocence of Spaniards, Spanish arms, and horses. Four soldiers with guns could frighten an entire village, one Franciscan said, even as he warned that Indians would become unconquerable as they learned the Spanish "style of fighting [and] the nature of our arms."[260] Araucanians, on the other hand, had become "unconquerable" after two centuries of experience with Spaniards. When Spaniards tried to force Mapuches to congregate in towns in the 1760s, they successfully blocked the attempt. By the 1780s, some thoughtful officials, ecclesiastical and civil alike, came to view the Franciscans' efforts among Araucanians as quixotic; it seemed impossible to convert or "domesticate" them either by persuasion or by force.[261]

But resistance to missionaries as exemplified by many Araucanians and reluctant co-operation as exemplified by some coastal California Indians did not represent the full range of Native-American responses to missions. The independent Karankawas along the Texas coast, for example, did not wait for seasonal visits from priests but instead visited missions every spring as part of their seasonal migration from the coast to the interior. Rather than adopting Spanish ways, they "integrated the Spanish mission into their own [migratory] culture," one anthropologist has explained.[262] Tobas in the Chaco integrated missions into broader cycles, coming to them in times of drought and leaving them when they no longer served their needs but always maintaining "daily communication," one official said, with Tobas who remained outside the missions.[263] On the middle Orinoco, some Indians lived at missions only in theory. In reality, they spent most of their days tending crops far from missions that lacked sufficient arable land to support them. Other Indians along the Orinoco left one mission to seek hospitality in another, taking advantage of rivalries that existed between several religious orders in that region.[264]

Indians and the New Method

The Bourbon reformers had made their intentions clear. They wanted to secularize mature missions, end Indians' enforced tutelage, and free missionaries to make new conversions. When missionaries advanced to new frontiers, the reformers sought to apply a new method, which would restrict missionaries' authority over Indians to the spiritual realm. Rather than rely on traditional missions to incorporate independent Indians into Spanish society, reformers preferred the marketplace and the labor market. This strategy, so reasonable from the vantage of Madrid or Mexico City, worked poorly on many edges of the empire, forcing some of the reformers to reconsider both secularization and the new method.

Secularization of missions had proceeded swiftly in the core regions of the empire following royal directives of the mid-1700s but faltered on the frontiers.[265] Until the end of the colonial era, Bourbon reformers complained about the slow pace of frontier conversions and the financial drain of maintaining long-lived missions. Missionaries' progress, Viceroy José de Ezpeleta of New Granada insisted in 1796, "should have been measured by the number of [Indian] towns that they should have delivered to the bishop, than by the number of Indians brought from the woods and reduced to a mission."[266] When regular clergy sought to deliver mature frontier missions to a bishop, however, they often found that dioceses often lacked sufficient priests to operate them. To a greater extent than the regular clergy, secular priests avoided service in "uncultured and distant places" throughout the empire.[267]

When Franciscans in Texas finally secularized the four declining San Antonio missions that Teodoro de Croix had excoriated in 1776, no secular priests came to relieve them. Franciscans had finished their work in San Antonio by the 1790s. As one friar explained, no "nation of pagans" remained nearby, and the residents of the mission could no longer "be called neophytes, or even Indians, since most of them, being children of marriages between Indians and white women, are mulattos or half-breeds."[268] In 1794, the friars turned their lands over to civil officials and parishioners and planned to begin *conversiones vivas* among new peoples, including Comanches. Secular priests, however, could not be found to replace them, perhaps because Texas seemed "worse than Siberia and Lapland," in the words of one governor, whose cook had quit rather than accompany him to San Antonio, where he feared "Indians would eat him." Friars, then, continued to serve Spaniards and Christian Indians in San Antonio until the end of the colonial era.[269]

When *curas* did assume control of secularized Indian parishes, some achieved such poor results that the crown occasionally reversed the process. In 1753, for example, the same year in which the crown issued firm orders to complete the secularization of mature missions throughout the empire, it also ordered the return of sixteen secularized missions in Cumaná to regular clergy.[270] This had nothing to do with philosophy, but everything to do with the political influence of religious orders and with Indians themselves. If secular priests proved less effective than regular clergy, "Indians will move," Viceroy Revillagigedo (the younger) of New Spain told Carlos IV in 1793.[271] It was a false economy, he argued, to secularize missions if secularization drove Indians from the Spanish sphere. He pointedly quoted royal instructions sent forty years earlier to his father, who had also served as viceroy of New Spain and who had favored the rapid dissolution of missions. "You will do a greater service to your King by promoting the conversion of souls," the orders said, "than by sending him all the treasure of the Indies."[272]

Some Bourbon officials also came to understand that the new method of integrating Indians through the marketplace and the labor market could succeed only in places where nearby Spaniards generated paying jobs for Indians. Among the Guaraníes in Paraguay and the Opatas and Pimas Bajos in northwestern New Spain, for example, the demand for workers in free wage labor markets absorbed former mission Indians as the Bourbon reformers hoped they would.[273]

On frontiers distant from Spanish labor markets, on the other hand, the new method failed. Remote, isolated places like the Californias and the lower Orinoco held little attraction for colonists, who were essential to making the new method work.[274] When officials refused to grant friars authority over temporalities on such frontiers, missions sometimes came to a violent end, as among the Yumas, or simply faded out of existence. These missions might have failed in any event, but friars argued that the new method assured their demise.

In many areas of the empire in the late colonial era, then, officials had little choice but to acknowledge the failure of the new method and to restore control of the temporalities to the friars. Gálvez had done this in Baja California, Sonora, and Nueva Vizcaya in 1768–70 and would do so a dozen years later in Cumaná, where he faulted civil administrators. They lacked "humanity," he said, and treated Indians "like individuals of another species . . . worse than slaves."[275] Beneath his expressions of concern for Indians, however, lay the more practical problem of Indians abandoning deteriorating mission communities. Only tradition, Gálvez apparently concluded, could halt the decline.

As the new method fell into disgrace, officials allowed missionaries to operate in traditional ways when they moved into new lands: in Alta California, the dry country of far northern New Spain, the tropical forests of Chiriquí in western Panama, the tropical plains of New Granada and Venezuela, the swampy delta of the Orinoco, the highland and lowland jungles of eastern Peru, in the Cordillera de los Chiriguanos, the scrub country of the western Chaco, and the frozen south Pacific, where friars sailed hundreds of miles through the Archipiélago de los Chonos and across the Golfo de Penas to lure or force Caucahues off of islands of Guayaneco and bring them back to missions on Chiloé. One critic's observation in 1788 that the Caucahues taken to Chiloé "were not conquered, but imprisoned" might have applied to other places as well, except that the prisoners could not as easily be contained. On the surface, it seemed as if the Bourbon reforms had never reached missions such as these.[276]

Where they were pressed to defend remote areas from foreigners, as in Alta California, authorities had a powerful reason to fall back on the tried and true Habsburg formula of forts and traditional missions. In the Chaco, defense against the Portuguese and the need for a direct route between Buenos Aires and Upper Peru, prompted some Bourbon officials in 1790 to revive the idea of building a chain of traditional missions along the Río Bermejo. In Chile, Bernardo O'Higgins projected a string of missions that would follow the coast from Concepción to Osorno and help secure it against foreigners.[277] In both plans, forts would anchor these places, but missionaries would play a key role in Hispanicizing Indians.

In most places where they used traditional missions, mendicants expanded their influence over Indians in fits and starts. They advanced slowly and incrementally into Indian territory, if they advanced at all. We lack sufficient studies to reconstruct missionary expansion in the late colonial era comprehensively, but it appears the Franciscans' rapid thrust up the Pacific coast to California was exceptional.[278] In the llanos of today's Colombia and Venezuela, for example, the Dominicans, Capuchins, Franciscans, and Augustinians (Recoletos) took up where Jesuits left off and expanded the mission field by the end of the century. Nonetheless, the number of missions on the llanos remained at thirty-one, where it had been before the Jesuits' expulsion. The number of mission Indians had increased by just 5 percent, and missionary operations remained precarious in the face of meager resources, few clergy, and soils and seasonal changes that favored nomadism over sedentary agriculture.[279] The missions on the llanos did not collapse as some chroniclers have suggested, but their advances were so modest that in 1803 Viceroy

Mendinueta discerned "little or no progress in those missions," a judgment he might have rendered about many other places.[280] In northern New Spain, one Franciscan lamented in 1795 that conversions had gone so slowly that even after two centuries of Christian preaching the number of "wandering savages" exceeded the number of mission-ized Indians by "a thousand to one."[281] Little wonder that some friars became disenchanted with the religious life, lost their enthusiasm for conversions, and broke their vows of poverty, chastity, and obedience.[282]

If missionaries using traditional methods did not expand at a rate that would have pleased Bourbon officials, part of the explanation could be found in contradictory Bourbon policies. Even when authorities allowed missionaries to take control of Indian property and Indian lives in traditional ways, reform-minded officials continued to chip away at missionaries' authority. Reformers urged missionaries to teach mission Indians Spanish, to grant mission Indians self-government, to cede control over Indian properties after ten years, to open mission towns to families of "civilized people" who would serve as role models, and, in the words of Viceroy Mendinueta of New Granada, "not to use any kind of force to introduce the religion of peace and gentleness." When missionaries failed to make rapid progress, Bourbon officials exhorted the religious orders to send better-trained and more zealous missionaries. At the same time, regalist officials who deplored the high numbers of clergy in Spain and its colonies often delayed or denied Franciscan requests to build new missions or recruit more missionaries in Iberia.[283]

Thus, although Bourbon strategists like Campomanes and Gálvez continued to advocate the use of missions to expand into new territory and to control Indians along strategic frontiers threatened by foreigners, they seldom succeeded. Hopes of checking English expansion in North America by converting Indians, by building chains of missions in North America connecting San Antonio to Santa Fe to San Francisco, and by pushing missions north into the Apache country of present Arizona failed to become realities.[284] In Central America, where missionaries could not compete with Miskitos and Englishmen, missionary progress stalled in the last decades of the eighteenth century.[285] In South America, too, missionaries met defeat on a number of fronts. They failed to win the hearts and minds of various Indians in the Amazon and the Chaco in order to prevent them from allying themselves with the Portuguese; they failed to Christianize Pampas and Patagonians who might have helped secure the exposed coastlines of southern Chile and southern Argentina.[286]

This is not to gainsay the valiant achievements of individual missionaries who blazed new trails into the lands of independent Indians, many of them previously unknown to Spaniards. Francisco Atanasio Domínguez and Silvestre Vélez de Escalante found their way from New Mexico into the Great Basin in 1776 looking for an overland route to the Pacific; Francisco Murillo journeyed down the Bermejo in 1780–81 in search of a navigable route across the Chaco; friars from the college at Ocopa opened new trails down the eastern slope of the Andes through tropical mountain gorges to the Huallaga and Ucayali rivers of the central Amazon basin in the 1780s and 1790s, where one of them discovered "twenty-two nations" of previously unknown "heathens"; Francisco Menéndez crossed the frozen Andes by way of Lake Nahuel Huapi in 1792 to link Franciscan missions in Chiloé with Patagonia.[287] These remarkable ecclesiastical explorers dispelled myths, brought back knowledge of Natives, and created a documentary base that emerging nations in Latin America would later use to buttress claims to territory, but none of these heroic treks resulted in the establishment of enduring missions in those isolated regions.

In the end, missionaries' methods, successes, and failures depended as much on Indian initiatives as they did on missionary zeal, Bourbon policies, or propinquity to Spanish colonists. As in the past, when Indians' resource bases diminished or new enemies appeared on the horizon or internal power struggles pitted band against band, some of the most implacable Natives welcomed missionaries. That was the case with *Motilones Perversos,* as they appeared on a Spanish map just south of Lake Maracaibo, who greeted a Franciscan in 1772 "with applause and imponderable rejoicing . . . as if we were of the same nation." On this, as on other such happy occasions, Spaniards praised their own "prudence and sagacity" and failed to understand that Indians had their own reasons for entering a mission and surrendering "the old liberty in which they have lived."[288]

When Indians took refuge in missions, they found ways to use them to their advantage. None did so more successfully than Chiriguanos, who entered mission towns in record numbers in the late eighteenth century. Earlier, they had spurned the Jesuits, who had insisted they perform communal labor. Between 1767 and 1810, however, some twenty-four thousand Chiriguanos, representing a fifth to a sixth of the total population, had gathered in twenty-one Franciscan missions on the periphery of Chiriguano territory.[289] The Chiriguano adults resisted communal labor and came to baptism slowly, but they expected the Franciscans to keep them supplied with tools, seeds, and other gifts. Desperate to keep the long-desired Chiriguano missions alive and to protect them from Bourbon reformers and land- and labor-hungry colonists alike, the Franciscans ran relaxed missions. In the words of one priest, the friars "tolerated" the Indians' "old customs, in order to avoid annoying them," refrained from administering "all punishment and violence, so that they do not escape to the savages," and gave Chiriguanos food and drink and paid them a "daily wage."[290] If priests ran the Chiriguano missions like a "closed prison, where no person whosoever could enter," as one official complained in 1788, it also appears that the inmates had taken control of them "from the inside."[291]

So long as Franciscans delivered the goods, Chiriguanos stayed. The Indians had no reason to flee or destroy the mission towns. While Franciscans deplored what they saw as Chiriguano sloth, Chiriguanos imagined the Franciscans as successful chiefs and shamans who had a responsibility to provide protection and material goods. Instead of serving as tribute-paying vassals of the Spanish crown, the Chiriguanos became collectors of tribute, paid and protected by missionaries. They, not the crown, had forced Franciscans to use the new method. They had inverted the colonial order, and they were not alone.[292]

Although some Indians had reasons to seek mission life and turn it to their advantage, Indians who had the means and the will to resist missionaries often continued to do so. Even as Chiriguanos who lived in regions bordering hostile Spaniards or hostile tribes opted for missions, most Chiriguanos rejected missions until the end of the colonial era. So, too, did equestrians like Apaches, Araucanians, Pampas, and Patagonians.[293] No Native people, however, rejected missionaries more effectively than those who enjoyed access to foreign trade goods and weapons. The Miskitos' close relationships with English traders, for example, drove one Franciscan to despair in 1754: "Until the English are driven from the coast, missionary work is hopeless, for the enemy perverts the Indians and turns them against us."[294] He might have said the same of many of the Native peoples of the circum-Caribbean who had access to European goods from non-Spanish sources: Payas and Jicaques of northern Honduras, Sumus and Chontales in the Nicaraguan interior, Talamancas in Costa Rica, Guaymíes and Cunas in eastern Panama, Guajiros and Caribs along the Caribbean coast of today's Colombia and Venezuela, Guaraúnos (Waraos) in the Delta of the Orinoco, and Creeks, Cherokees, and Chickasaws in what is today the southeastern United States. On the edges of Portuguese Brazil, Charrúas, Minuanes, Payaguás, and some Mbayás obtained European trade goods from Spain's Catholic rival and had little need for Spanish missionaries.[295] To bring such places under Spanish control in the late colonial period, Bourbons came to rely less on the friendly persuasion of missionaries than on force, trade, and diplomacy. Creating men had proved to be a difficult and inexact science.

4

A Good War or a Bad Peace?

The savage Indians daily flood these fields like a violent torrent, taking
away innumerable horses and cattle, pillaging the homes of the unhappy
residents who border on this capital, making the roads insecure, and
leaving many unfortunate victims of their fury, who die inhumanely
every day at their hands, in a horrible and frightening way.
Francisco de Viedma, Buenos Aires, May 1, 1784

A bad peace with all the [Indian] nations who may ask for it
will be more beneficial to us than the efforts of a good war.
Bernardo de Gálvez, Mexico, 1786

In 1800, Barcelona-born Francisco de Serra y Canals drew on
more than three decades of experience in the Argentine province
of Cuyo in telling the Spanish crown how to promote the growth
of his province and, by extension, of all southern South America.
Progress, he argued, required the forcible subjugation of the Pampas and the Araucanians. Serra y Canals spoke from firsthand experience. The Pampas, whom he characterized as savages and
murderous heathens, made transportation insecure along the route
between Buenos Aires and Mendoza, the capital of Cuyo. Their
depredations drove up the cost of doing business at silver and quick-
silver mines he operated in the nearby Andean valley of Uspallata.[1]

Rather than presume to offer advice directly to the crown, Serra
y Canals composed a fictional dialogue, following a literary convention of his day that allowed him to criticize the government indirectly and safely. His two characters, one an American-born

Spaniard, or *indiano,* and the other Spanish-born, an *español,* looked back nostalgically at the sixteenth century when, as the indiano put it, a few Spaniards "conquered the enormity of the New World." In the present day, the indiano complained, the situation had reversed itself. Spaniards had become victims of small numbers of Indians. "They rob us of our women, with whom they increase their numbers, and our frontiers become destitute and decay." The "rats" had put "the bell on the cat."[2]

The español and the indiano saw eye to eye on the need for an offensive war to rid Argentina and Chile of troublesome Pampas and Araucanians, as one might get rid of lice.[3] Powder and ball would succeed, they argued, where years of preaching had failed. Indians captured in their proposed war should be placed in missions or assigned to work in mines, where "with work and salaries they would learn rationality."[4] Indians who resisted should be put to the knife and their children distributed among Spanish families, who would raise them until age thirty, by which time they would know right from wrong.

Although both of Serra y Canals's characters were war hawks, they differed on strategy. The indiano urged a large-scale military campaign to push nomadic Indians south toward Cape Horn, from which "these wild people have no place to escape."[5] The español, whose words reflected the views of the Barcelona native Serra y Canals, objected that it would take too many men, horses, and supplies to cover such vast terrain. Troops would exhaust themselves chasing Indians who had no fixed residence and who would not stand still to fight. Rather than look to the army or the militia to conduct a campaign, the español suggested that frontiersmen themselves do the job. Spaniards raised on the Indian frontiers had become "similar to or worse than the Indian heathen."[6] These hardy men knew how to live and fight like Indians and required little government support. They could live on wild game and the booty they seized from Indians, of which their captain would receive a tenth. Outfitting them, the español argued, would cost the government less than it spent to maintain the forts and troops along the present frontier and produce better results. Operating east and west of the Andes, the frontiersmen would drive Pampas, Aucas, and Araucanians south to the Strait of Magellan. In effect, the español proposed a return to the sixteenth century, when semiautonomous bands of conquistadors swept through the Americas in pursuit of plunder, serving the interests of the crown even as they served themselves.

Serra y Canals knew his plan for an offensive war—a *guerra ofensiva*—ran counter to crown policy, so his fictional characters touched gingerly on that subject. The only reason Spaniards had not yet eliminated hostile Indians, Serra y Canals has his indiano say, was that "the love and piety of the Sovereign does not permit offensive war, only defensive." But the fictional español replies that he cannot believe the king would wish to protect savages who profess no religion and who fail to follow "the natural law as reason prescribes." The noble and pious intentions of the king had been thwarted by deceitful Indians and bad advice from some of his representatives.[7]

Offensive War and Economic Development

In that age of *proyectistas* (essayists who showered the government with plans for reforms), Serra y Canals was not alone in suggesting that the conquest of independent Indians would benefit the crown and the Indians themselves. Felipe de Haedo, a Spanish-born mineralogist and high-ranking military officer serving in Córdoba, explained to the viceroy in Buenos Aires in 1777 that the conquest of independent Indians would eliminate their potential for allying themselves with foreigners, raise the number of tax-paying vassals for the crown, and convert innumerable pagans. Indian captives, he argued, could be sentenced to ten years of servitude, where they would learn useful trades before being released and given land and animals. Distributing captives in Spanish households would also make them good Catholics because "you will hardly find a house in these provinces in which the rosary of our lady is not said daily and in which they do not perform other religious acts." Where missionaries had failed, Haedo believed, the piety of individual Spaniards would succeed.[8]

Along with their plans to conquer and redeem independent Indians, most of the *proyectistas* intended to benefit themselves—a point that did not elude Bourbon officials. In 1767, when a wealthy Spanish-born merchant who had relocated to Buenos Aires, Gerónimo Matorras, offered to conquer the Indians of the Chaco at his own expense, he asked for the governorship of the province of Tucumán in exchange. Known in Buenos Aires for his lack of scruples, he also may have intended to open a secure route to smuggle silver from Peru to Buenos Aires via the Río Bermejo.[9] In 1776, when a militia captain from the mining town of Huancavelica sent the crown a plan to drive Indians from the Río de la Plata to the Strait of Magellan at his own cost, he asked the king for the exclusive privilege of exporting hides, tallow, and salted meat from the conquered area.[10] In 1787, when Gov. Antonio López Carvajal of Santa Cruz de la Sierra in today's Bolivia recommended using two hundred men to conquer the Guaycurúes (including the riverine Payaguás) in the Chaco, he hoped to reap rewards by opening a road through the pacified country to Paraguay.[11]

Owners of mines and haciendas and other Spanish entrepreneurs had much to gain from offensive wars that provided cheap labor in the form of Indian captives, opened up Indian lands for development, and secured new routes for commerce. They also had little to lose. The poorest sectors of society, augmented by Indian allies, did the actual fighting. Prosperous citizens purchased substitutes to fight in their names or paid a fee to exempt themselves from duty—practices that the viceroy of the Río de la Plata, the marqués de Avilés, condemned as lamentable and illegal. Privileged men hired "the worst vagabonds" to take their places, one governor of New Mexico complained in 1794, and the surrogates caused campaigns to fail because they lacked equipment and provisions.[12]

Private citizens who advocated war found powerful allies among corrupt local military officers, who siphoned money from the military budget, and from hawkish high-ranking military officers, whose influence in American affairs had increased substantially by the

time of Carlos III. The Bourbons had filled the highest political offices with reliable professionals instead of selling them to the highest bidder as their Habsburg predecessors
had done. Many of those professionals were European-born career officers. With England
threatening Spain's American colonies from without and independent Indians chipping
away at it from within, it made sense for the crown to turn to men with military experience.
Moreover, officers who commanded armed forces might implement the Bourbons' political and economic reforms more effectively than bureaucrats, who relied on persuasion.[13]

The crown placed some of these officer-administrators close to areas threatened by
independent Indians or foreigners or both. In the eighteenth century, foreigners had begun to plant permanent colonies in territory that Spain claimed but had not occupied,
territory ranging from British Jamaica and Dutch Curaçao to French Louisiana; further,
they seemed poised to move into other areas that Spain had ignored. These remote lands
lay far from viceregal centers. Until the Bourbon ascendancy, just two viceroys governed
Spain's American empire. The two ensconced themselves, respectively, in Mexico City
and Lima, where silver from the mines of New Spain and Peru and taxes from sedentary
Indians could sustain the trappings of royalty and feed the appetites of bureaucrats.
From these two administrative centers, however, viceroys found it difficult to govern
distant frontiers. At best, as one viceroy lamented, they had to make decisions based on
"the variety of reports and opinions [that] obscure the truth."[14]

In the eighteenth century, Spain tried to extend its authority over previously neglected
areas, which one minister described as "lands devoid of gold or silver that remain completely abandoned" (Indian residents did not count).[15] First, Bourbon administrators
carved up the old viceroyalty of Peru. In 1739 (after a false start in 1717), they responded
to English and Dutch threats to the Caribbean by establishing a third viceroyalty in Bogotá—the viceroyalty of New Granada, with jurisdiction over northern South America.
In 1776, the crown created a fourth viceroyalty, that of the Río de la Plata, with headquarters in Buenos Aires, to check the loss of silver smuggled out through that port and
to counter the territorial threat posed by Portugal and Great Britain. The viceroyalty
of the Río de la Plata embraced most of present Argentina, Uruguay, Paraguay, and the
mineral-rich area of Charcas, or Upper Peru—today's Bolivia. At Bogotá and Buenos
Aires a military officer usually presided over the new viceroyalties, serving as both *virrey*
and *capitán general*. The Bourbons also elevated some endangered areas to the status of
captaincies general (*capitanías generales*)—Venezuela (1777) and Chile (1778)—and raised
all of northern New Spain to a commandancy general (*comandancia general*), known as
the Interior Provinces of New Spain (1776).[16]

Whether or not they favored offensive war, Bourbon officer-administrators in this expanding bureaucracy would have agreed with Serra y Canals that economic development
required the pacification of Indians. "Agriculture, cattle raising, mining, and commerce
cannot flourish" in areas that suffered from Indian attacks, the commander in chief of
the Interior Provinces of New Spain from 1783 to 1784, Brigadier Felipe de Neve, observed.[17] Then, too, independent Indians who allied themselves with Englishmen or

other foreigners facilitated smuggling, which hampered development by cutting Spain's share of the market in its own colonies.

Economic development, however, often *caused* conflict between Spaniards and independent Indians. In the Río de la Plata, for example, new markets for hides and tallow stimulated Spaniards to expand their ranching operations into the lands of the Pampas, to the south and west of Buenos Aires, and into Charrúan territory, north of the Río Negro in today's Uruguay. Indians fought to defend their resource base, turning peaceful frontiers into zones of raids and counterraids.[18] Similarly, an economic spurt in the last third of the eighteenth century sent ranchers into Chiriguano lands, ending a period of stability and inaugurating a new cycle of turmoil.[19] In North America, Spanish expansion into Navajo lands caused a peace agreement of 1786 to unravel.[20] In these and other cases, Spanish officials regarded Indian resistance as an obstacle to progress rather than acknowledging that alleged progress provoked Indian resistance.

Bourbon officer-administrators, who believed they needed to pacify Indians in order to develop frontier regions, recognized that they needed the loyalty of those Indians to defend the empire against foreigners. The danger seemed all too real that independent Indians might succumb to the blandishments of foreigners bent on conquering Spanish territory. Areas proximate to Dutch, English, and French bases in the Caribbean seemed especially menaced but so, too, did remote areas in southern South America. In what is today Bolivia, officials feared that Guaycuruans would join with the Portuguese to overrun the poorly built, weakly defended missionary province of Chiquitos.[21] In Argentina and Chile, officials worried that British invaders might establish themselves on an unguarded coast in Patagonia or Tierra del Fuego and ally themselves with Araucanians or Pampas.

These fears were well grounded. Spanish officials had read the boastful calculation of the British admiral George Anson, in a book published in England in 1748, that fifteen hundred Englishmen could drive Spaniards out of both Chile and Peru if Britain gained the support of the Araucanians. In published accounts, other British and French observers had offered similar assessments, arguing that Araucanians and Patagonians disliked Spaniards so intensely that they would turn against them. One of those accounts came from the pen of an English-born Jesuit, Thomas Falkner, who had lived amidst Pampas and Patagonians and thus spoke with disquieting authority. The foreigners' talk had also turned to action. Anson had attempted to establish a base on the Chilean coast in 1741, and England and France each established bases in the Falklands in the 1760s, a step away from Patagonia (though they turned out to be short-lived).[22]

Although foreign threats were clear, their implications for Spanish policy toward independent Indians remained murky. In Chile, Ambrosio O'Higgins argued that Spain could not defend its vast Pacific coast from foreigners without the good will of Indians, and Indians would not support Spaniards "while we may be at every moment irritating and striking at Indians along the frontiers, making them internal enemies."[23] Other high-ranking officers, however, favored force over diplomacy and urged the conquering of independent Indians to prevent them from allying with foreigners.

Many of the officer-administrators who governed Spain's colonial provinces in the late Bourbon era had seen action in Europe, won membership in military fraternities, and believed in the honor and efficacy of war. Conventional wisdom among these men, particularly during the reign of Carlos III (1759–88), held that Spain should use force to subdue America's savages once and for all. The Bourbons had steadily expanded and professionalized the army and militia in America, but Carlos III dramatically accelerated the buildup after Spain's disastrous showing in the Seven Years' War (1756–63) revealed the weakness of colonial defenses.[24] Some officers, emboldened by this military escalation, supposed they had sufficient firepower and manpower to win wars against independent Indians. Others, naively optimistic about their own prowess and contemptuous of Indians, imagined that even small numbers of Spanish forces would prevail. Gov. Antonio López Carvajal of Santa Cruz, for example, announced in 1787 that with two hundred well-armed men he could conquer the Guaycurús and Payaguás in six months and open a road across the Chaco to Paraguay.[25]

It would be too much to claim, as has one historian, that "where the Habsburgs used priests the Bourbons employed soldiers." Habsburgs and Bourbons alike relied on missionaries,[26] but the most aggressive Bourbon officers rejected their predecessors' faith that "Christian temples and the holy doctrine of the Gospel . . . are sufficient to pacify wild beasts."[27] War hawks in the military shared the pessimistic view of those clergy who judged aggressively resistant pagans as unredeemable and advocated their destruction or exile. "It is morally impossible to build a permanent mission while there are Caribs in the Orinoco," one Jesuit had written in 1743. Another Jesuit pronounced the Guaycurúes to be hopeless candidates for missions, urging in 1767 that they be captured and sent to Potosí to work in mines, refineries, and bakeries. They "have been born only to rob, kill, and destroy everything that is not Guaycurú."[28]

War on the Seris: Victims or Rebels?

The most prominent proponent of war in the era of Carlos III was José de Gálvez. A civilian, Gálvez gained firsthand experience with Indians when the king sent him to New Spain as inspector general in 1765, at the beginning of the military buildup.[29] Gálvez planned to develop northwestern New Spain, with its rich mineral resources, and use Sonora as a launching pad to occupy the Pacific coast of today's California. Before he left Spain, he worried that foreigners might try to establish a foothold in California, and he planned to preempt them.[30] Once in New Spain, however, he learned he could not develop northwestern Mexico without first dealing with hostile Indians. Apaches raided Sonora from the north and east, and Seris from the west. Together, they wrought havoc on Spanish ranching and mining. Spaniards had fled the region. By the mid-1700s, in the words of one contemporary, Sonora was left with "only the sad remembrance of its former prosperity."[31]

The Seris—fishers, hunters, and gatherers who occupied the arid coast of the Gulf of California from Guaymas north to Río de la Concepción—had fought successfully to maintain their territory and way of life (see map 6). Spain had never conquered the Seris, although some had entered Pima missions and then joined Pima neophytes in a general revolt in 1740. Spain's tactics against the so-called rebels, which included duplicity and deportation, had hardened Seri resistance. Transformed from "petty raiders into guerrilla fighters," in the words of one historian, Seris pushed back the Spanish frontier in Sonora.[32]

Convinced that he possessed sufficient resources to crush the Seris with a European-style offensive, Gálvez sent an army into Sonora in 1767. Numbering eleven hundred men, seven hundred of them professional soldiers, it was the largest military operation Spanish Sonora had seen or would see. Led by Col. Domingo Elizondo, Spanish forces tried on three occasions to invade the Seri stronghold in the Cerro Prieto, a rugged range between Guaymas and Pitic (today's Hermosillo), and engage the Seris in battle. The Seris, however, failed to "present themselves to fight face-to-face ... in convenient locations," as one officer complained.[33] Using the terrain to their advantage, Seris eluded the Spaniards and taunted them: "You are splendid in the open, but in the forests and the mountains we are."[34]

In the midst of Elizondo's fruitless campaign, Gálvez traveled to Sonora to oversee operations. Landing on the coast in May 1769, he offered Seris and Pimas a time-honored Spanish formulation: bread or the stick.[35] Spanish law gave officials permission to "pardon the crimes of rebellion," and Gálvez announced that rebels who surrendered would receive a pardon for the crime of "high treason against God and man." Those who failed to surrender within forty days would be "exterminated. No memory of them will remain except that they perished by blood and fire."[36] This was not an idle threat. Some years later, the commander in chief of the Interior Provinces of New Spain, Felipe de Neve, ordered that Tarahumara rebels be taken from prison, hung, drawn, and quartered, and their heads taken to their villages as a lesson to others. At least twenty-four Tarahumaras met this grisly fate before Neve's successor, José Antonio Rengel (1784–86), suspended the executions.[37] Gálvez's offer to forgive the supposed Seri rebels was fraught with meaning. Most Seris, however, had never submitted to Spanish rule, so the offer of a pardon for treason would have amazed them. If they knew of it, they and their Pima allies ignored it.

By labeling the Seris rebels instead of defining them as unconquered or independent Indians, Gálvez knew he could take action against them without seeking royal approval. Spanish law granted colonial officials the authority to act on their own initiative to punish Indian rebels who committed crimes or excesses against Spaniards or against "peaceful Indians."[38] Those same laws, whose antecedents reached back to sixteenth-century debates about the nature of just war, forbade colonials from launching an open, or offensive, war against Indians without cause or without the king's permission. Spaniards could take up arms in self-defense against unconquered Indians, but they had to limit themselves to necessary force, "and no more."[39]

Colonial officials appreciated the distinction between rebels and unpacified Indians. The *fiscal protector de indios* of the royal *audiencia* of New Granada, Francisco Moreno y Escandón, justified an invasion of the Guajira Peninsula in 1771 (see map 7) on the "fortunate" grounds that many of the Guajiro Indians were "apostates and rebels." Spaniards could use force against them, he said, "with less concern" than against unconquered Indians.[40] As his reference to "less concern" suggests, Spanish laws that permitted the use of arms to defend life and property from alleged rebels did not give colonial officials unqualified license. The crown also required that Indian rebels be brought back "to our royal service with gentleness and peace, without war, robbery, or deaths," and Bourbon monarchs and their high-ranking representatives in America often invoked that clause.[41]

Early in the campaign against the Seris, the king admonished the viceroy of New Spain, Carlos Francisco de Croix, marqués de Croix, to halt Elizondo's campaign. Gifts and offers of peace, Carlos III told the viceroy, would be more effective than war. Royal orders notwithstanding, the viceroy continued to back Gálvez's campaign, and as the war wore on, the crown continued to reproach him. "Forceful means," the king told Croix, "will not achieve the desired goal."[42]

In the short run, however, force prevailed. Elizondo changed strategies after he concluded that Seris would not stand and fight: "It is necessary to follow their trails to find them, as it is with wild animals."[43] Following the advice of veteran frontier commanders, he broke his forces into smaller units in the fall of 1769 and waged a war of attrition. A year of harassment wore the Seris down, as it did the Pimas who had joined them. Group by group, Indians surrendered in 1771.[44] Elizondo, whom the next generation of military commanders viewed as a model of "the art of fighting and defeating Indians,"[45] had mastered the lesson that "civilized soldiers" had to learn if they were to prevail over "primitive warriors." As the French and English also learned, Europeans could win only when they adopted Indians' tactics, using small mobile units, light arms, the element of surprise, and the destruction of food stores and livestock.[46]

Wars of attrition could devastate Indian communities. One Spanish officer has left us an unusually vivid description of the damage caused by a single expedition sent to destroy the resource base of one group of Chiriguanos in what is today Bolivia. Indians suffered heavy casualties, he said, as Spanish forces moved into the valleys of Abatir and Ingre in 1780. Most Chiriguanos fled before the invaders, carrying off their wounded and dead; the water in one arroyo ran with blood. Spaniards seized horses, salt, cotton, and one hundred tons of corn, burning the corn they could not haul away and reducing the Indians' settlements to ashes. The silence of the brush country, the officer said, was broken only by the "howls of women" who, he imagined, would remind their husbands of the trouble they had brought upon their people and "serve as a check so that from now on they would live with friendship and quiet." Friendship and quiet, however, were not to be. Rather than urging their men to seek peace, the Chiriguano women apparently encouraged them to seek revenge.[47]

Spanish sources grant only occasional glimpses of the roles Indian women played in stiffening male resolve to resist Spaniards. A Spanish observer in Nuevo Santander recorded the powerful harangue of an Indian woman who urged warriors to take the offensive. She began with the old days, when Indians ate well, suffered no fear, and traveled everywhere "like deer and never dying of a knife or ball." Those days had ended, "my husband and son dying; another of my husbands also dying; I saw it, so much blood, so much fear, so much weeping." She taunted the young warriors, telling them that now there was no one to kill Spanish soldiers: "The soldier is now brave like the wolf; the Indian is cowardly like a rabbit, fleeing."[48]

Elizondo's war of attrition over Seri men and women owed as much to his Indian allies as to his tactics. Since the days of Hernán Cortés, Spaniards had relied on the aid of what one scholar has called primitives in order to defeat primitives.[49] It could not have been otherwise. Spread throughout the margins of the empire, Spanish troops and militia generally found themselves outnumbered.

In Louisiana, for example, Gov. Luis de Unzaga observed in 1772 that "toleration" had failed to control the Osages. Only a policy of "extermination" would end Spanish troubles, "but we are not in a position to apply it because [we] lack people and supplies, and lastly because of the expense."[50] The balance of power never shifted. In the 1780s, Spain could bring just 350 men to bear against Osages, who had over a 1,000 armed men at their disposal. As elsewhere, Spaniards had to look to Indians for help in fighting other Indians—in this case, to Quapaws, Illinois, Delawares, Shawnees, and Miamis.[51] Divide and conquer remained a basic tenet of Spanish Indian policy; Spaniards either invited Indian allies to fight alongside them or fomented internal discord among tribes so that Indians fought Indians and Spaniards shed less blood.[52]

Elizondo had promised no quarter early in the campaign against the Seris, but he ended it all by granting pardons and refusing to disarm the Indians or take away their horses.[53] The Seris and Pimas, he said, "need to be treated with love and kindness and governed with prudence."[54] He blamed Spanish civilians for provoking the uprising by treating Indians like slaves. Pressured to deport the Seris, Elizondo refused. The crown supported his decision, ruling that Spain should honor the terms of the Seris' surrender, which assured them that they would retain possession of their lands.[55]

The war against the Seris reveals Spaniards divided over the best way to pacify Indians. The crown urged peace over war, and the king's representatives close to the scene urged war over peace. Those who favored war disagreed among themselves about the most effective tactics. Should they emphasize offensive or defensive war? If they took the offense, should they mass troops, as Elizondo did initially? or should they divide troops into smaller units that could move swiftly and enjoy the element of surprise, as Elizondo did in the later stages of the Seri campaign? Victory achieved, should Spaniards be magnanimous or punitive?

The crown usually argued for peaceful persuasion, as in the case of the Seris, but it made exceptions when Indians had a long history of failing to respond to peaceful overtures or when pressures from officials close to the scene became intense.[56] Viceroys and military officers showed less consistency. Where one might favor offensive war, another might urge defensive war, and still another call for peaceful negotiations.

Personal proclivities and material considerations shaped these competing viewpoints. From the crown's perspective, wars drained the royal treasury and cost more than peace. On the other hand, presidial commanders, local merchants, and hacienda owners, who were often closely related if not one and the same, regarded war, or the appearance of war, as profitable. Management of military payrolls offered opportunities for profits and graft, and soldiers constituted pools of free labor that local officers could exploit for personal gain. Some parties, then, worked to maintain what one historian has termed "the business of war"—a business that required an adversary, real or imagined. José Perfecto de Salas, a civilian attorney who traveled through parts of the Araucanía in 1749, concluded that soldiers along the Biobío maintained the "fiction" of a Mapuche threat in order to profit as Chile's protectors. If the Mapuche menace disappeared, so would military careers, salaries, and extra income. Soldiers who portrayed Mapuches as the enemy also welcomed those same Indians to their forts and crossed the Biobío to trade arms, wine, and livestock. They enjoyed a near monopoly in the Indian trade and larger profits than if the border had been open to civilian competition. Mapuches, whom the frontier military described as "so savage, wild, and inhuman," Salas reported to the king, "are tame, docile, and rational in my experience."[57]

Whether Spanish soldiers perceived Indians to be warlike or peaceful depended as much on Spaniards' designs on Indians as on Indians' behavior. Like philosophes who romanticized Indian society in order to reproach their fellow Europeans and like missionaries who portrayed Indians as eager for the gospel in order to justify their ministries, military strategists often drew the Indians they wished to see. When Gálvez planned to crush the Seris with military force, he described them as rebels and enemies. When Elizondo wanted to firm up a peace with Seris, he characterized them as victims of Spanish oppression who fought to defend their interests. Officers like Lieutenant Colonel Hugo O'Conor who were eager to make war on Apaches described them as perpetrators of "inhuman cruelties" who tore infants from their mothers' wombs.[58] Officers who wanted to make peace with Apaches described them as reasonable and peaceable, more sinned against than sinners.[59]

In 1784, a decade after the Seri war had ended, the commander in chief of the Interior Provinces, Felipe de Neve, sought royal approval for a surprise attack on the Seris who lived near Pitic. Neve, who believed in waging "incessant war" against Apaches, Comanches, and other seemingly irredeemable peoples, would exile the Seri men to places beyond Mexico, "where they would have no hope of ever returning to their lands," and ship the women and children to Baja California. He justified these harsh measures not just on the grounds that the Seris had continued to rob and murder, but also on their well-known character: "fickleness, treachery, arrogance, and other detestable vices." Speaking through José de Gálvez, who had returned to Spain to become the minister of the Indies (1776–87), the king granted approval.[60]

Authorizing Offensive War: Apaches

In northern New Spain, the military buildup that began in 1764, following the Seven Years' War, led some officers to believe they had sufficient resources to make war on Apaches and Seris at the same time. Since the mid-1700s, Apache raids had escalated to such a degree in Sonora, Nueva Vizcaya, New Mexico, and Texas that they jeopardized Spain's control.[61] The crown, which had urged peace with the Seris in the 1760s, supported a bellicose strategy against Apaches, persuaded by the report of an inspector sent to reconnoiter the Apachería, the marqués de Rubí.

One of four field marshals sent from Spain to beef up the defenses of New Spain, the marqués de Rubí toured the northern reaches of the viceroyalty between 1766 and 1768. Covering some seventy-six hundred miles, Rubí witnessed the destruction wrought by Apaches and listened to the laments of the Spanish residents. Among officers close to the scene, a consensus had developed. Apaches had to be exterminated because they were perfidious, inhumane, and "have been, are, and always will be enemies of the Spaniards and of every rational being."[62] "Only by not admitting them in any way, but shedding their blood by means of firearms—pardoning only the children or those who voluntarily surrender—will their pride be punished," one Spaniard in Monclova told Rubí.[63] Convinced by these arguments, Rubí concluded that Spain's only recourse against Apaches was "extermination, or at least their complete reduction." He defined Apaches not as rebels but as an untrustworthy "mob of savages." Defeating them would require what his military engineer, Nicolás de Lafora, described as "continuous offensive war in their own territory."[64] In Lafora's judgment, Spanish forces had no chance of winning a defensive war against Apaches. A frontier soldier, poorly trained, heavily equipped, and leading a string of fresh horses, "never can run as fast or for so long a time as an Indian." Lafora offered a simple solution: "Since it is impossible to surprise or overtake them in our territory, why do we not invade theirs[?]"[65]

In 1772, Carlos III issued military regulations for northern New Spain that adopted much of what Rubí and Lafora recommended. The *Regulation and Instruction for the Presidios . . . of New Spain* ordered a "vigorous and incessant war" against enemy Indians in general and Apaches in particular, "attacking them where possible in their own *rancherías* and lands." Thus, the regulations of 1772 made Apaches an exception to the crown's customary opposition to offensive war against unconquered Indians. Apaches ceased to fall under the protection of the Royal Orders for New Discoveries of 1573, which permitted only peaceful pacification.[66]

The regulations of 1772 also exempted Apaches from rules that required Spanish officers to offer peace to Indians prior to attacking them and took the power to enter into peace agreements from individual commanders and put it in the hands of the viceroy.[67] As they did with other royal directives meant to elevate or legitimize Spanish behavior, frontier commanders had often winked at the requirement that they offer Indians peace. One satirist told of a captain in Nueva Vizcaya who pretended to hear Indians ask for *pan,* or bread, when Indians asked for *paz,* or peace. In this way he ignored the Indians' request and still obeyed the "pious maxims of our kings, who repeatedly ordered that peace be granted to Indians who requested it."[68] Under the regulations of 1772, however, even the king's "pious maxims" ceased to apply to Apaches—in theory. In practice, just as some frontier commanders violated earlier instructions by denying Indians' requests for peace, some now violated the new regulations and accepted Apaches' pleas to surrender.[69]

In ordering frontier commanders to reject Apache overtures for peace, the regulations of 1772 represented a 180-degree turn from prior military rules for northern New Spain.[70] The regulations reflected a growing sentiment that it was counterproductive for a frontier commander to make a separate peace with the enemy in the midst of a general war. Officers who took this stance pointed out that Apaches who enjoyed peaceful relations at one presidio often raided neighboring areas then returned to that presidio to dispose of their loot.[71] Wherever Spaniards fought Indians, officers also worried that a truce gave Indians time to regroup before committing further depredations. Finally, officers recognized that even when Indian leaders wanted peace, they could not guarantee the conduct of all of their warriors. This, Viceroy Juan José de Vértiz y Salcedo of the Río de la Plata complained, put Spaniards at a disadvantage because they could not tell which Indians had agreed to peace and which had not. All looked alike "by their physiognomy, dress, and other external characteristics."[72]

To better prosecute war against Apaches, the regulations of 1772 also streamlined the administrative structure of the northern frontier of New Spain and called for the professionalization of frontier forces and a more rational use of presidios. Prior to Rubí's inspection, frontier garrisons patrolled and defended their immediate area. The regulations created the position of *comandante inspector,* or inspector in chief, to coordinate the maneuvers of frontier garrisons and take the war to the Indians. First to hold the office of *comandante inspector* was Lt. Col. Hugo O'Conor, one of the many Irish-born Catholics who fled English oppression in their homeland for a career in the Spanish army. O'Conor distinguished himself in fighting the British in Portugal during the Seven Years' War, was knighted in the honorary military Order of Calatrava, and sent to New Spain. Convinced of the perfidious nature of Apaches after a stint as governor of Texas, *Comandante Inspector* O'Conor embraced the new offensive war. He laid plans "to invade simultaneously all the land the treacherous Apaches occupy from east to west and from south to north."[73]

All-out war against Apaches would inevitably mean capturing some of these "declared enemies."[74] The regulations of 1772 supported Rubí's recommendation that Apaches taken in combat receive good treatment. Frontier officers, Rubí charged, commonly turned Indian prisoners over to Spanish colonists, who treated them like slaves and even sold them—"an occasion of abuse against all humanity and the rights of men."[75] The regulations prohibited this abuse and ordered that some captives be returned to their people in prisoner exchanges. The crown hoped that if Apaches had the opportunity to exchange captives, their "self-interest will destroy the cruelty that so many times has led them to murder their captives and awaken in them sentiments of humanity."[76] The regulations, however, limited frontier officials to exchanging Apache captives only under extraordinary circumstances. The crown still adhered to an older requirement that officials exile Apache captives rather than admit them to missions or to the protection of military garrisons or allow them to be enslaved by the locals. Apaches were to be sent far from their homeland, where women and children would receive religious instruction, usually in private households, and men would be assigned to forced labor. Under Spanish law in this era, however, prisoners of war were not slaves, and the crown ordered that they be well treated.[77]

Military administrators of the late Bourbon era may have banished Apache captives more efficiently than did their predecessors. By the late 1780s, authorities had begun to send Apaches as far away as Cuba to prevent them from returning home if they escaped. In 1790, the crown itself required that Cuba become the final destination for Apache prisoners. Despite the king's orders to treat Indian captives well, large numbers died before reaching Havana. Dislocation, disease, and the hardships of traveling in chains took a terrible toll.[78] So, too, did vengeful soldiers. If some troops killed captured Apaches "in cold blood in the jails of Durango and in Chihuahua's main square," as the bishop of Durango reported, other soldiers must have taken their revenge on Apache prisoners in less public places.[79]

Apaches, it would appear, suffered banishment to distant islands more than any other group of unyielding Indians. Officials talked of shipping Karankawas, Miskitos, and Guajiros to overseas locations but never followed through.[80] In the Río de la Plata, Viceroy Vértiz sent the Pampa cacique Licon Pagni to the Malvinas Islands, but this appears to have been an exceptional case. Licon Pagni had come to the fort at Luján in 1779 asking for a truce, but Vértiz regarded him as untrustworthy and so "surprised" him by taking him captive—a surprise that probably suggested to Licon Pagni that Vértiz himself was unworthy of trust. The crown approved of Licon Pagni's exile to the Malvinas, which it probably regarded as a routine matter, for Argentine officials also exiled Spanish deserters to the Malvinas. Licon Pagni never returned.[81] On at least one occasion, the idea of exiling independent Indians raised legal eyebrows. In rejecting a plan to banish Chimilas, the governor of Santa Marta in New Granada, Antonio de Narváez, doubted it was "proper and just to exile men who have never recognized vassalage."[82]

When Bourbon officers talked of exterminating or annihilating Apaches—or other Indians like Osages, Karankawas, Seris, and the equestrians of the Chaco—they did not necessarily mean that they wished to kill every one of them.[83] In 1780, the captain general of Venezuela ordered that Spaniards who engaged in rowdy nocturnal activities be pursued and punished "to their complete extermination," but it seems unlikely he intended to execute them for unruly behavior.[84] Similarly, in calling for the extermination of a group of Indians, officials like José de Gálvez engaged in hyperbole.[85] In a war to exterminate independent Indians, Spanish officers certainly tried to kill combatants, but they also took prisoners of war and exiled them to mines, plantations, and offshore islands. They often spared women, children, and noncombatants. Bourbon authorities, then, used the word *extermination* to mean total war against Indians, much as their Habsburg predecessors had used "war by blood and fire."[86] A policy of extermination was neither a Bourbon innovation, as one scholar has argued, nor the preferred way to end Indian resistance.[87]

Under both dynasties the crown consistently sought to turn Indians into Spaniards and erase their ethnic identities, but however vigorously it pursued ethnocide it did not endorse genocide. Where Spaniards needed Indian labor or had established lucrative trade with Indians, as on the pampa south and west of Buenos Aires, exterminating Indians made no sense to the locals.[88] To the contrary, officials often saw it in their interest to protect and strengthen certain Indian societies. If Pehuenches disappeared, for example, nothing would stand between Spanish Chile and the Huilliches, and so Bourbon authorities worked from the 1760s on to halt internecine wars among Pehuenches and ally themselves with them.[89]

Some Spaniards did, of course, support or promote the complete annihilation of Indian groups. The town council of Tarija, for example, favored a war that would eliminate the Chiriguanos rather than allow them to practice their scandalous polygamous relationships and, more important, occupy rich lands that Spaniards coveted.[90] Commenting on a smallpox epidemic in 1780, Gov. Domingo Cabello of Texas told Teodoro de Croix that "without offending decency one might hope that not a single Lipan Apache lives through it, for these Indians are pernicious—despite their apparent peacefulness and friendliness." Cabello, who as governor of Nicaragua had dealt with Miskito raiders before coming to Texas, may have had an especially low opinion of un-Hispanicized Indians.[91] Nonetheless, his hope that smallpox would accidentally eliminate Apaches pales next to the intentional use of smallpox by a governor of Paraguay. That governor's fear of savages ran so deep that when a group of missionized Mbayás came to Asunción with an offer to help defend the city against hostile Indians, he murdered the Mbayá volunteers by sending smallpox carriers into their camp.[92]

Individual Spaniards who wished to annihilate Indians by any means possible had counterparts among all colonial powers. The commander in chief of the British army in America infamously proposed in 1763 to infect Indians in the Ohio Valley with smallpox "as well as to try Every other method that can serve to Extirpate this Execrable Race."[93]

Rejecting Offensive War: Mapuches

Although it supported the marqués de Rubí's recommendation for an offensive war to exterminate Apaches, the crown continued to prohibit offensive war against unconquered Indians. Like their Habsburg predecessors, the Bourbons kept the principle but made exceptions on a case-by-case basis, and Apaches became an exception. Defensive war remained the rule, as is clear from events in the Araucanía, where the crown rejected a proposal for offensive war against Mapuches.

As we have seen, Mapuches had "revolted" in 1766 when the governor of Chile, Antonio de Guill y Gonzaga, tried to settle them in towns. Guill, a brigadier in the royal army who came to Chile in 1762 after a stint as governor of Panama, responded to Mapuches' defiance by calling for a large-scale offensive war. He urged war against Araucanians on both sides of the Andes, with forces converging on them from Buenos Aires as well as Concepción and Valdivia. His goal was "to subject [the Indians] to perpetual obedience, or to annihilate the rebels, removing all of them from their lands and distributing them throughout the kingdom [of Chile] . . . and distributing the women and children among the haciendas."[94]

Governor Guill's war plan reached Madrid at the same time that a recommendation for a more vigorous missionary program among the Araucanians arrived from the bishop of Concepción. Faced with proposals to support missionaries or launch a war, the crown sought an informed opinion. Carlos III turned to the viceroy of Peru, Field Marshal Manuel de Amat y Junient, who had served as governor and captain general of Chile (1755–61) before his promotion to viceroy (1761–76). Viceroy Amat dismissed the bishop's plan to expand missions as hopeless. Over two hundred years of experience, he said, had demonstrated the Araucanians' "hardheartedness and complete disdain" for religion.[95] He also rejected Guill's plan for a war.

Viceroy Amat argued that using military force to reduce the Araucanians "to obedience and vassalage" would never bring about lasting security. Like others before and after him, he pointed out that Spain had not been able to defeat the Araucanians when those Indians had fewer horses and less experience at fighting.[96] Even if the Spaniards achieved a costly victory over the northernmost Araucanians, those of the llanos, they would gain only "a few leagues of desert land." Indians would move farther south, where they would "merge with enormous and more savage nations." From there, they would "return to recover what they lost," touching off a "perpetual war." Amat acknowledged that the local militia, motivated by the prospect of female captives and plunder, could do great damage to the Araucanians, but he argued that they could not prevail.[97] The viceroy also invoked Spanish law. He accused those who championed military operations against Araucanians of forgetting that the law prohibits "open war" against Indians and "permits only punishment in the case of a crime or an uprising." He made that observation, however, only after assessing Araucanians' strengths. Had he found them weaker he, too, might have forgotten the law.

In 1774, Carlos III endorsed Viceroy Amat's position. He insisted on negotiations instead of war and reiterated his "pious intentions to attract the Indians by gentle and peaceful means rather than by force and rigor." This strategy would allow his vassals to enjoy the fruits of peace and also "free my Royal Treasury from enormous expenses that the restlessness of those Indians has occasioned."[98] If it was the right decision for the king's treasury, it was also the right one for Mapuche–Spanish relations. The year 1766 marked the last major Mapuche rebellion in the colonial era.

Carlos III, then, rejected offensive war against Araucanians in 1774, two years after approving all-out war against Apaches. No change of advisors explains the crown's contra-dictory decisions. The same person, Julián de Arriaga, served as minister of the Indies (1759–76) during those two years (and may have been more reluctant to authorize offen-sive war than his successor, Gálvez).[99] The explanation does have much to do with Span-iards' informed suppositions about Araucanians and Apaches, for pragmatism outweighed principle in Spanish dealings with independent Indians.

In New Spain, officials from frontier captains to the viceroy had convinced themselves by 1772 that Apaches were too savage, perfidious, cruel, and inhumane to win over through peaceful means. Spaniards and Christian Indians alike had suffered from years of ruinous Apache raids, which they remembered as beginning in the mid-1700s. Spain had to "smash their pride and teach them a lesson by force of arms," Viceroy Antonio María de Bucareli told Arriaga.[100]

In contrast, Spaniards in Chile could look back on decades of failed attempts to defeat various groups of Araucanians and recent decades of relatively peaceful and profitable relations with Mapuches. Along the Biobío frontier, commerce had replaced punitive expeditions, slavery, and forced labor.[101] Nonetheless, Araucanians remained independent, or in rebellion, as some Spaniards preferred to describe their status, and while Mapuches were at peace with Spaniards, Huilliches and Pehuenches raided on the eastern side of the Andes. Spanish officials knew, however, that they needed to maintain the Araucanians' good will in the event foreigners tried to establish themselves in the region and win In-dians to their side. An attempt to raise Spain's military profile south of the Biobío could turn Indians against Spaniards.[102] Conversely, officers in northern New Spain knew that Apaches had no potential European allies.

No one understood better than Amat that the Mapuche uprising in 1766 was an aber-ration in a time of peace. A field marshal with a brilliant service record in Africa and Italy, Amat had no qualms about using force. In 1772, he had ordered mutineers on a Spanish ship to hold a lottery in which the losers lost their lives. That same year he exe-cuted a ring of soldiers who had carried out a string of robberies in Lima and displayed their heads on pikes as an object lesson to others.[103] Amat did, however, understand the limits of force against Araucanians, and he knew they could be reasonable. He himself had negotiated a peace treaty with Pehuenches at Salto de Laja in 1755 and had traveled extensively in the Araucanía in 1760.[104] "The only and main way to maintain those Indians in peace," he told the king, "is to administer justice with impartiality, and without dis-tinction of color, listening to the complaints of the Indians and making amends for their injuries."[105]

Offense or Defense? War Against the Pampas

Although the crown continued to assert its principled opposition to offensive war against independent Indians, as in Chile, it sanctioned offensive war when the benefits seemed worth the cost. To arrive at these determinations, Madrid responded to the advice of well-informed officials close to the scene, as the cases of the marqués de Rubí and Viceroy Amat suggest. Even in the age of efficient bureaucrats and enlightened Spanish despots, policy did not flow solely from government to the governed or from the core to the periphery. Policymakers in Spain also responded pragmatically to pressures from colonial leaders. When it came to relations with *indios bárbaros,* local officials and oligarchs sometimes favored war, sometimes favored peace, and sometimes vacillated. When they wavered, the crown wavered with them.

The influence of colonial officials on policymakers in Madrid is nowhere clearer than in their schemes to drive Indians off the pampa south and west of the Río de la Plata. Within weeks of his arrival in Buenos Aires in the autumn of 1777, the first viceroy of the Río de la Plata, Pedro de Cevallos, urged the minister of the Indies, José de Gálvez, to approve a large-scale invasion, or *entrada general,* into the lands of the Pampas. In its extraordinary scope, the plan resembled the offensive that Governor Guill had proposed a decade before. One of Spain's most distinguished officers, the seventy-two-year-old Brigadier General Cevallos had just led a force that expelled the Portuguese from Colonia de Sacramento on the eastern shore of the Río de La Plata. He imagined a similar triumph over the nettlesome Indians of the pampa, one that would end with their "extinction." Efforts to subdue the Pampas rather than annihilate them, he explained to Minister Gálvez, had been "in vain, and there is no hope, not even the most remote, of converting them or reducing them to live in a fixed place."[106] Cevallos planned to bring together men from Córdoba, Mendoza, San Luis, and Buenos Aires and to invite Chile to send forces as well.[107] He predicted that ten to twelve thousand men could "destroy this mob of despicable Indians, detested even by the members of their own species who live in the [Andean] mountains."[108] The combined assault would occur in February, after the harvest, and would take three months. Spanish troops would be home before winter.[109]

No *proyectista* inspired this plan. Cevallos drew on his own experience. Two decades earlier he had served as governor of the province of Buenos Aires and in 1759 had proposed a similar scheme to conquer the Indians of the Chaco by invading it simultaneously from three provinces: Buenos Aires, Tucumán, and Paraguay. The crown had approved. The queen mother, Isabel Farnese, acting as regent for Carlos III, had urged Cevallos to "continue with the vigor necessary to extinguish them or reduce them to a civil and political life."[110] She justified these harsh measures as the only way to halt the "hostilities, robberies, and murders" that the Indians of the Chaco had carried out with "inhuman frequency." She went on to say, however, that punishing Indians would not bring about a lasting peace. She urged Cevallos to continue to apply force until Indians abandoned "their wild and untamed life, the immoral, awful root of their crimes." Cevallos proclaimed his *entrada* of 1759 a success, but it fell far short of the queen mother's objectives of reducing Indians to settlements and converting them to Catholicism. The conquest of the Chaco and the opening of trade routes across it continued to elude Spaniards.[111]

Nearly twenty years after his mother had approved Cevallos's coordinated assault into the Chaco, Carlos III approved his plan to sweep the pampa from several directions.

Cevallos left office and set sail for Spain, however, before royal approval, forwarded by Gálvez, arrived in Buenos Aires in mid-1778. It fell to Cevallos's successor, Juan José de Vértiz, also a career officer from a military family, to implement the plan.[112] Vértiz had served in Italy and Portugal and, since 1770, as governor of Buenos Aires province. He initially expressed support for Cevallos's *entrada general.* The "savages," he told Gálvez, required severe punishment or "they will become more insolent in their cruelties."[113] Since Gálvez had approved the *entrada,* Vértiz may have believed he had little choice except to support it. He surely knew that Cevallos would get credit if the *entrada* succeeded and that he would receive the blame if it failed. He may have had those unpleasant alternatives in mind when he summoned a *junta* of experienced frontier officers to discuss the feasibility of Cevallos's plan.

The officers rescued the new viceroy from his dilemma. They concluded that they could neither raise the ten to twelve thousand men Cevallos called for, nor provide sufficient logistical support. They calculated that the expedition would require staggering numbers of horses, cattle, and provisions, and that agriculture and manufacturing would suffer while the men were in Indian country. Moreover, the campaign seemed doomed to fail. Indian fighters would have to penetrate "wide uncharted lands for which we have no accurate maps or guides to give us even a moderate knowledge." Rather than kill Indians, the expeditionaries themselves would die in what the officers imagined to be a waterless desert. If "by fortune or accident" Spaniards encountered Indians, some would surely escape and alert other Indians. No good, then, could come from chasing Indians made up of "wandering groups, without community or fixed residence, who lack all worldly possessions . . . who do not need fire to eat, or other provisions for their operations." The Argentine *junta* declared the *entrada* impractical and recommended instead building a line of forts.[114] Argentine officers, then, rejected offensive war.

Viceroy Vértiz endorsed the *junta's* report and sent it to Gálvez, who, with the same alacrity with which he had previously approved it, agreed to suspend the war against the Pampas.[115] Questions of morality or consistency do not appear to have entered into his calculations, either when he authorized offensive war or when he suspended it. In this case, as in many others, Gálvez personified Bourbon pragmatism. When he expressed concern for the well-being of Spain's Indian vassals, for example, he did so on the grounds that treating "poor Indians" badly had economic consequences for Spaniards. Abused Indians tended to flee, and their departure meant lost tax revenue for the royal treasury.[116]

As his term as viceroy ended and defensive measures brought no relief against Indian raiders, Vértiz planned another, more limited offensive against the Indians of the pampa. He, too, left the execution of the campaign to his successor. In March 1784, the marqués de Loreto, a brigadier in the royal army who doubled as captain general and viceroy of the Río de la Plata, sent simultaneous expeditions into the pampa from Buenos Aires, Córdoba, and Mendoza. Totaling twenty-eight hundred men, the *entrada* was a quarter of the force Cevallos had envisioned, and its goal seemed to be to punish Indian raiders, offering them no quarter even if they asked for peace. Indians suffered some casualties, but, warned by spies of the Spaniards' approach, most melted away. Historians have interpreted this offensive as a military success, perhaps because they believed the rosy account the viceroy sent to Gálvez.

The campaign marked a turning point in Spanish–Indian relations on the southern frontiers of Buenos Aires and Cuyo, but the new era of amicable relations that followed the *entrada* of 1784 probably derived from its relatively meager results rather than from its success. It made clear to most key officials that Spain lacked the means to launch a large, definitive *entrada general*, and it sank the ambitious hopes of the war hawks. Thereafter, military force in the Río de la Plata would be applied locally rather than transregionally. The modest results of the campaign of 1784 also buoyed advocates of defensive war and diplomacy, whose strategy proved more affordable and effective than offensive war.[117] For his part, Gálvez continued to take his cues from the viceroy in Buenos Aires. He praised the marqués de Loreto for the successs of the *entrada* of 1784 and endorsed a policy of "continuous pursuit of the savages of the frontiers."[118]

War Against Apaches: Offense or Defense?

At the same time José de Gálvez did his about-faces in the La Plata, first authorizing, then suspending, then authorizing offensive operations against the Pampas, he also changed course in northern New Spain. In rapid succession, he urged defensive war, offensive war, peace, and offensive war. The unhappy recipient of these flip-flopping messages was the first governor and *comandante general* of the newly created Comandancia General of the Interior Provinces of New Spain, Teodoro de Croix, who served from 1776 to 1783.

In 1776, Carlos III had followed Gálvez's recommendation to separate northern New Spain from the immediate oversight of the viceroy and put it under an officer who combined the powers of a governor and a commander in chief and who reported directly to the king as well as to the viceroy. The *comandante inspector*, a position first held by O'Conor, became subservient to a *comandante general*, or commander in chief, charged with carrying out the regulations of 1772. With various permutations, this arrangement lasted until the end of the colonial period. When he received his appointment as *comandante general* in 1776, Croix brought thirty years of experience in the Spanish army, five of them in America. He had completed a tour of duty in New Spain when his uncle, the marqués de Croix, served as its viceroy (1766–71).

Gálvez initially instructed Croix to defend the interior provinces from Apaches in traditional ways—by promoting missions and settlements, shoring up the militia, and making alliances with friendly Indians. Gálvez also charged Croix with carrying out the regulations of 1772, with their call for reforms of military garrisons and a "vigorous and incessant war" against Apaches and other Indian enemies. In his instructions to Croix, however, Gálvez stopped short of urging all-out war. Instead, he urged Croix to "contain and punish the enemy Indians . . . [by] making frequent sorties against them."[119] In effect,

Gálvez recommended defensive war. Raids—*correrías* or *mariscadas*—against Indian miscreants were crown-approved tactics of defensive war.[120]

As he began to inspect his vast domain, which included the Californias, Sonora, Sinaloa, Nueva Vizcaya, New Mexico, Coahuila, and Texas, Croix decided he needed to do more than punish and contain Apaches. Meeting in a war council, he and his senior officers concluded, as had Rubí, O'Conor, and others before them, that Apaches were faithless. Gifts, entertainment, good treatment, and agreements were wasted on them.[121] Croix had a low opinion of all Indians. Even those who had submitted to Spanish rule could not be trusted, he told Gálvez, because they were drawn "to the absolute liberty of the savages," and like them would be inclined to "robbery and treachery." This was "the character of all Indians."[122]

Croix calculated he would need to double the two thousand troops he had at his disposal. He needed men to defend ranches, mines, and settlements while others went on campaign. His military advisors estimated that Apaches could field five thousand fighting men and "an equal number of women, who, if they do not make war in the same way as the men, aid it in whatever actions the Apaches undertake. . . . they form regularly a reserve corps [and] round up the horses while the men attack our troops."[123] (Spaniards believed that Comanche women played a similar role.)[124]

Croix recognized that Apaches would not engage his men directly, but he argued that a large-scale offensive war would lead nonetheless to the "extermination" of the Indians. His soldiers would "pursue them incessantly, obliging them to live without tranquility, to carry the heavy load of their children and women, and to die of hunger."[125] He had in mind a war of attrition such as Elizondo had waged against Seris.

Croix's request for additional troops met a chilly reception from Viceroy Bucareli. Croix's predecessor, O'Conor, had convinced the viceroy that he had made great progress against the Apaches, and Bucareli accused Croix of inflating his reports of Indian depredations. Moreover, the viceroy lacked two thousand extra men.[126] A good bureaucrat, Croix countered with a steady stream of memos, directing them at Gálvez as well as Bucareli. Croix recounted the damage done by Indian raiders and maintained that Apaches, Seris, and others of their ilk understood force and force alone. By the end of 1777, he had persuaded Gálvez to order the viceroy to send more troops.[127]

Before the promised troops arrived, Gálvez stunned Croix with orders to shift course. Strapped for resources as he prepared for war with Great Britain, Gálvez could not afford to spare men and supplies to fight Apaches. He explained to Croix, however, that his orders to abandon offensive war were "dictated by religion, natural reason, and true policy." In a royal order dated February 20, 1779, Gálvez told Croix that the king believed that "the kind of Indian who infests these regions cannot be exterminated or reduced with a decisive blow, or by that methodical series of wisely directed battles that make glorious campaigns in war between cultured nations." The numerous *indios bárbaros* had the advantage. They risked little in their raids and could flee into their harsh, vast, and impenetrable territories, where Spanish troops could not find subsistence. "Their land, their nakedness, their agility, their poverty, and even their disorder and cowardice" neutralized Spanish tactics and arms. The remedy, Gálvez said, was a defensive war, in which Spanish troops protect towns and haciendas and command Indians' respect so that "they might solicit our friendship sincerely." A strong defense, which presented Indians with proof of Spain's "power and resolve," would open the way to fulfill the "pious wishes of the king." Carlos III, Gálvez reported to Croix, would be better pleased by "conquests, however slow, . . . carried out with kindness, good treatment, and benevolence, than by large, showy, and rapid conquests that spilled human blood, even if it might be of the most savage enemy." The king preferred that Indians see the advantages of a Spanish life and come to it willingly rather than through force. The result would be "slower but surer conquests than those of the largest and most disciplined armies."[128]

Croix acquiesced to the royal wisdom of offering peace to enemies against whom the regulations of 1772 required him to make war. He turned his attention to preparing a good defense, taking steps to make more efficient use of resources and troops and improving military discipline and training, which he found deplorable. Echoing Gálvez, he declared that results of his reforms would be slow but sure.[129]

Nonetheless, even as he praised the sagacity of the crown's new policy of "pious, prudent, and gentle means," Croix could not conceal his impatience with it. Some Indians did not deserve kindness and would not respond to it. He singled out Lipan Apaches as "not worthy of the sovereign piety his royal Catholic spirit dispenses to them in the royal order of February 20 of '79."[130]

Croix's goal remained the forcible "settlement or extinction" of the Lipans and other eastern Apaches. He would make up for the shortage of Spanish manpower, he told Gálvez, by encouraging savages to fight one another. Yet he soon renewed his requests for more troops to gain and maintain the respect of Indian allies and to fall back on in the event that "kindness" proved insufficient.[131] The days when conquistadors could prevail over Indians who lacked guns and horses had long passed, he told Gálvez. Now, "the Indians have the advantage."[132] In October 1781, Croix began to criticize the royal orders of February 20, 1779, whose "wise and pious principles," he said, "prevented me from prudently using the troops of my command . . . which the method of warring upon the Indian demands."[133]

Soon thereafter Gálvez learned from Viceroy Bucareli that Indian hostilities in the Interior Provinces had begun to affect central New Spain. Apache raiders had curtailed commerce and slowed the mining of gold and silver in Chihuahua. Indians had killed so many ranch hands and robbed so much livestock that cities throughout New Spain, including Mexico City, suffered a shortage of beef. Wealthy landowners were on the verge of abandoning their haciendas.[134]

Initially, Croix's appeals and Bucareli's alarming reports of Apache destruction had little effect on Gálvez, who merely reiterated his instructions to "contain and punish the savages."[135] Gálvez changed his tune, however, when two wealthy residents of Mexico City complained directly to the king. In June 1782, a month after receiving the viceroy's account, Gálvez received a petition from Juan Lucas de Lasaga and the marqués de San Miguel de Aguayo. Both men lived in Mexico City but owned large cattle ranches near Parras, in Coahuila. Lasaga, a *caballero* in the new Royal Order of Carlos III, a title given to nobles for distinguished service to the crown, was New Spain's chief mining official. The marqués de Aguayo descended from one of Coahuila's wealthiest ranching families. The two painted a vivid picture of their calamitous loss of livestock and the suffering of their employees: "The insolence of the Indians has reached an extreme never seen before." Spaniards no longer protected the frontier. Instead, they and their wives and children "served as bait" for the savages.[136] They blamed Croix for deteriorating relations with Indians and praised O'Conor, citing O'Conor's self-promoting report of how he had achieved "an invincible superiority over the savages." They felt no obligation to explain that they would profit if the cost of frontier defense shifted away from private individuals, like themselves, to the state.[137]

When Aguayo and Lasaga's petition reached him, Gálvez changed course. In ordinary times, the opinion of powerful oligarchs would have concerned him, but in these precarious times he had more reason for concern. A trusted disciple Gálvez had sent to New Spain, Francisco de Saavedra, had concluded that the *criollo* elite was disillusioned with the government and might follow the example of the rebellious Anglo-American colonists. Gálvez, then, had political as well as economic reasons to placate Aguayo and Lasaga. He quickly forwarded a copy of their petition to Croix and ordered him in the name of the king to take immediate measures to halt the Indians' "invasions, horrors, deaths, and robberies."[138] Where earlier he had insisted on defensive war and claimed that Croix's offensive maneuvers provoked Apache belligerence, Gálvez now advised Croix that "repeated experience" had shown that defensive war would not contain enemy Indians. He ordered Croix "to seek them out and maintain a continuous little war against them, without observing the solemnities of the law." Other commanders had accomplished more with fewer troops.[139] Reprimanded for failing to take measures he had been prohibited from taking, Croix must have gnashed his teeth. But, knowing that the war with England was over, Croix had not waited for Gálvez to see things his way. Months before receiving Gálvez's new orders, Croix had already sent Gálvez a detailed plan for offensive war.[140]

The Limits of Offensive War

One historian has suggested that the royal orders of February 20, 1779, which had called a halt to offensive war in the Interior Provinces of New Spain, represented "a reassertion of and an enlargement on a consistent royal policy of conciliating the hostile Indians and treating them as human beings."[141] As José de Gálvez's vacillations suggest, however, consistency yielded to a cost-benefit analysis when Spanish officials weighed the principle of defensive war against the advantages of offensive war. Looming large in the equation was the question of whether Spanish forces would emerge victorious in an offensive war against independent Indians.

Some Spanish officers, like those who advised against war with the Pampas, believed they could not defeat Indians who lived off the land and lacked permanent towns.[142] They noted that nomads and seminomads handled horses with admirable dexterity, moved with remarkable speed, fought with endurance, discipline, courage, and savvy, and could endure extraordinary hardships. The Pehuenches, wrote an admiring Manuel Amat, seem to have been "raised among rocks."[143] Furthermore, Indians did not obey European rules of war. They traveled stealthily at night, attacked before dawn, and conducted ambushes. As one unimpressed observer in New Spain put it, "The Indians' war consists of trickery, treachery, and betrayal rather than boldness, courage, and strength."[144] Such people could and did fight indefinitely, setting the tempo and the venue for conflict. They put Spaniards on the defensive and sapped the morale of Spanish soldiers and militia, which was already low.

Despite increased government expenditures on the military and efforts to professionalize the army, many frontier garrisons remained understaffed, undersupplied, and riddled with ineffective soldiers and officers. Unable to attract first-rate men to dangerous frontier posts with low pay (which often failed to arrive) and hard, manual labor, officers who themselves were often not above reproach welcomed thieves, murderers, prisoners, and other social misfits into their ranks. No wonder the army displayed little enthusiasm for pursuing Indians. Unpaid militia, fighting on their own time with their own weapons, horses, and supplies, had even less incentive to pursue Indians—except the bonus of booty if they won an unexpected victory.[145]

On some occasions Spanish forces engaged their Indian opponents to devastating effect. The best of the frontiersmen fought like Indians, using horses and lances with a skill that, their officers said, European-trained soldiers lacked.[146] With the odds against them, however, Spanish forces usually returned home exhausted and empty-handed from fruitless pursuits of Indians who refused to show their faces. Rather than suffer the hardships of thirst, hunger, and exposure to the elements on predictably futile campaigns, some Spaniards simply deserted. When Gov. Gerónimo Matorras of Tucumán led an expedition into the Chaco in 1774, a fifth of his militia (130 men) had evaporated before it even set out. Desertions continued to plague the expedition. After a month out, Matorras left behind a group of 150 men "for their cowardice and unwillingness." They had remained fearful despite having a three-month supply of food and ammunition.[147] In 1779, Viceroy Vértiz issued regulations to improve the conditions and effectiveness of the militia in the Río de la Plata and to discourage chronic desertions by threatening the death penalty. Desertions continued nonetheless.[148]

Soldiers and militia who did not desert preferred the safety of numbers when they entered Indian country, and that played into their adversaries' hands. Officials like Gálvez understood that punitive expeditions consisting of large numbers of troops were ineffective "because Indians spot them and avoid them more easily."[149] In practice, however, as the governor of Paraguay observed, inexperienced Indian fighters entered Indian territory in large groups "out of an intense fear that they had developed of the force of the power of the savages." Thus, he said, they assured the failure of most of their campaigns.[150]

Indians, however, did not hold all the cards. With the elaborate delivery systems and technologies that only states possess, Spain could defeat tribal peoples if it could destroy their resource base. That, however, required special conditions. Spaniards needed to have sufficient men, material, and motivation. They also needed Indian adversaries whose homeland Spaniards and their Indian allies could surround. Initially, for example, Spanish forces could not subdue the Chimilas who lived in what is today northern Colombia (see map 7). Slash-and-burn farmers, Chimilas never built permanent settlements or population centers larger than the extended family. They seemed unconquerable. When Spanish ranchers and miners from Santa Marta moved into their territory in the early 1700s, Chimilas resisted. They attacked Spanish ranches and menaced travelers on the Río Magdalena, making transit insecure between the coast and the interior. They blocked the flow of grains and beef from the rich area around Valledupar from reaching the urban centers in the provinces of Cartagena and Santa Marta.[151] Slowly, however, Spanish settlements encircled the Chimilas' territory, leaving them little room to flee when Spaniards began a campaign in 1764 to burn their crops, hunt them down, and place captives in missions. The Spaniards and their Indian allies who fought this war of attrition were not poorly paid soldiers trying to defend the crown's honor, but locals eager to gain Chimila land and labor. Members of the local elite vied for the title of "captain of the conquest of the Chimilas" and the salary that went with it. After the 1770s, the Chimilas no longer constituted a serious obstacle to Spanish expansion, but they continued to harass Spaniards into the early 1800s, their dwindling numbers augmented by blacks and mestizos.[152]

Spaniards could defeat small groups like the Chimilas under the right circumstances, but they could not so easily break the resistance of peoples with vast hinterlands like Araucanians, Pampas, and Apaches through military means alone. To conquer any one of them by force of arms might have been a "certain impossibility," as one Chilean officer said of the Araucanians.[153] To attempt to conquer all of the independent peoples throughout the edges of the empire would have stretched Spanish resources beyond their limits. In the single province of Sonora, Spain lacked sufficient force to defeat both Seris and Apaches.[154]

Spain had other demands on its military resources in the late 1700s. From 1779 to 1783, Spain fought with England, emerging on the winning side. Between 1792 and 1795, Spain fought against France, and troops from the French Republic invaded Spain and forced it to sue for peace. From 1796 to 1808, England again became Spain's adversary and imposed a blockade that effectively cut Spain off from its empire, with only brief periods of respite, until 1808. During a lull in these European wars, the widespread Tupac Amaru rebellion of 1780–81 in the viceroyalty of Peru and the *comunero* revolt of 1781 in the viceroyalty of New Granada diverted military resources to the Andes. In Spain's American colonies alone, the cost of defense rose between 1700 and 1790 by at least a factor of seven. Badly overextended, the crown turned increasingly to private citizens for loans to finance military operations in its colonies.[155] Troops, always in short supply in the Americas, became scarcer during these European wars.[156] Little wonder that Gálvez could not meet the demands of officers like Croix for more men or that the crown often approved new military initiatives with the proviso that they be carried out "with the least possible burden to the royal treasury."[157] To supply all the troops, military supplies, and fortifications that Spain and its colonies seemed to require, Gálvez wrote in 1779, "would be an impossible enterprise, even if the king of Spain might have at his disposition all the treasure, the armies, and the storehouses of Europe."[158]

If Spaniards lacked sufficient force to win offensive wars against Araucanians, Pampas, Apaches, and other peoples who fought chiefly with traditional weapons, they had even less hope of defeating Indians who had foreign allies and a good stock of firearms and ammunition.[159] Such peoples included Comanches, armed early on by the French and then by the British, Anglo Americans, and various native intermediaries; Cherokees, Chickasaws, Creeks, and other nations in southeastern North America, armed first by the British and then by Anglo Americans; Miskitos and Cunas in Central America, supplied by British traders; Guajiros and Caribs along the north coast of South America armed by British and the Dutch; and Tobas and Mbayás supplied by the Portuguese.[160] Strengthened by their alliances with foreigners, most of those Indians had spurned Spanish missionaries. Bourbon attempts to beat these Indians into submission generally failed.

In 1771, the viceroy of New Granada, Pedro Messía de la Cerda, ordered the invasion of the hot, dry Guajira Peninsula, an area the size of Massachusetts that had strategic value although it had attracted few Spaniards. The Guajiros had allegedly rebelled two years earlier. They had burned a half dozen missions and driven Spaniards out of Guajiro territory. In fact, Spain never held effective dominion over the equestrian Guajiros. Some Guajiros had tolerated missionaries, but few had internalized Christianity or lived like Spanish Christians.[161] Most, as one officer said, "lived in complete liberty" as "absolute masters" of the peninsula and made no secret of their contempt for the Spanish military.[162] On one occasion a group of Guajiros captured and disarmed a detachment of fourteen soldiers, then returned the Spaniards' guns, saying they could obtain better weapons from the English.[163] Spaniards understood that the Guajiros obtained English firearms in exchange for stolen Spanish livestock and for Cocina captives, whom they sold into slavery. As early as the 1720s officials talked of cutting off the Guajiros' access to the English by deporting them to Cuba and Santo Domingo.[164] That impractical idea never progressed beyond the talking stage, but beginning in the 1760s Spanish officials took more aggressive action to seize control of the Guajira Peninsula. They hoped to halt contraband that flowed through the Guajiros to Spanish towns and to gain access to pearl fisheries controlled by Guajiros. Spanish raiders destroyed fields, burned houses, and took captives. The pastoral Guajiros defended their turf, and in 1769–70, as Guajiro resistance intensified, Spanish officials defined it as an uprising and planned the large-scale invasion of 1771.[165]

The Guajiros' thievery alone justified war against them, in the view of the *fiscal pro-*

tector de indios Francisco Moreno y Escandón. Throughout New Granada, he noted, every province was "infested to some degree by savage Indians,"[166] but he described the Guajiros as among the worst. They stole cattle and other property in the provinces of Riohacha, Santa Marta, and Maracaibo. They interrupted commerce and communication, hampered farming and timber harvesting, and impoverished the Spanish residents. As the official protector of Indians, Moreno y Escandón recognized he was obliged to uphold the laws that required gentle treatment of Indians, and he could not recommend the use of arms against them. Nonetheless, he argued, the wounds the savages left on the "body politic" could only be "cauterized with arms." Three hundred years of "warnings and gentleness" had only made the "savages more insolent."[167] The defense of the king's vassals and the conservation of his dominion against foreigners offered Spain no alternative other than war.

The invasion thus justified, over a thousand men assembled in 1771 at Riohacha to march into the Guajira Peninsula. Many of them lacked functioning firearms, ammunition, supplies, and shelter. When an epidemic swept through the ranks and depleted his force, the expedition's leader, Col. José Benito Encio, concluded he could not vanquish Guajiros in their own territory. The Guajiro nation, he estimated, could field six to seven thousand warriors with firearms and bows. In a stunning turnabout, he called off the invasion and stayed to answer charges of cowardice, ineptitude, and dereliction of duty. His superiors compared him unfavorably with Hernán Cortés, who, they observed, had defeated the Aztecs with fewer men.[168]

Bourbon officials also tried and failed to conquer the Miskitos, but only after taking extraordinary steps to win them over through "gentle means." Spanish–Miskito negotiations had borne fruit at least as early as 1769, when a three-man delegation representing the Tawira-Miskito leader, Adm. Trelawney Dilson, visited the governor of Costa Rica at its capital, Cartago.[169] A decade later, in 1778, a delegation led by Fara, the son of a Tawira-Miskito governor, Colville Briton, traveled to Panama with a convoy of canoes, crossed the isthmus to Panama City, and came to terms with its governor. Each visit resulted in peace treaties with similar provisions. In 1778, for example, Fara gained the right to hunt turtles in Spanish-patrolled waters of Bocas del Toro and access to "free trade in all the [Spanish] ports from the Rio de San Juan to the Chagres." Eager to drive English traders from the Mosquito Coast, Panama's governor won the Miskitos' promise to avoid trading with foreigners and to join Spaniards in fighting against the English— provided Spain furnish the military supplies. Missionaries did not figure into this agreement, but both parties agreed that Spain would send instructors to the Miskitos, "who would teach them to read and write, and other mechanical and liberal arts." Whether Tawira-Miskitos sought this or Spaniards urged it on them is not clear.[170]

The Tawira-Miskitos' interest in hunting hawksbill turtles unmolested by Spaniards might have drawn them toward this rapprochement; or they might have been pushed toward the Spaniards by their rivalry with the more numerous Zambo-Miskitos, who enjoyed close relations with Englishmen. Whatever their motive, their diplomatic initiative widened the fissure between Tawiras and Zambos. Admiral Dilson, who won Zambo opprobrium for aligning himself with Spaniards in Costa Rica, was murdered under circumstances that pointed to Zambos and their English partners. Violence also followed the treaty that Fara signed in Panama in June 1778. That autumn, Jeremiah Terry, a North American agent working for Spain, sailed into Caribbean waters with instructions from Gálvez to turn the Miskitos against the British. Terry's negotiations with Zambo-Miskitos began auspiciously, but within weeks Zambos attacked his frigate, took him prisoner, and sent him to Jamaica. The Zambos had operated under orders of their British patrons, whom they had kept informed of their dealings with Spain and its agents.[171]

By then Spain had gone to war with England and needed the Miskitos' neutrality. Instead of ordering reprisals against Miskito leaders for their insulting treatment of Terry, the governor of Costa Rica, José Perié, offered them gifts, flattery, and forgiveness. In a remarkable bit of dissimulation, Governor Perié said that his king "does not aspire to more dominions . . . he hates slavery and only wants to have free, rich, and happy vassals, even when they follow a different religion."[172]

In 1783 and again in 1784, after the war with England ended and freed up military resources, Gálvez ordered Viceroy Antonio Caballero y Góngora of New Granada to crush the rebel Miskitos "by blood and fire as a punishment to them and all the heathen of that region."[173] Gálvez's older brother, Matías, headed the operation in his capacity as captain general of Guatemala. Hearkening back to the age of Cortés, Matías de Gálvez asked for trained dogs to use against "savages" and "cruel Englishmen." Dogs, he said, inspired more fear "than 20 armed men."[174] If the dogs arrived, they were never used against Miskitos. José de Gálvez had to suspend the offensive within months of ordering it. He feared that a war against the Miskitos might upset his government's delicate negotiations with the Miskitos' ally, England.[175]

By the 1780s, supporters of offensive wars had little to boast about. Spaniards could not conquer Indians with large hinterlands, such as Apaches and Pampas, and could not easily defeat Indians armed by other Europeans, like Guajiros and Miskitos. As offensive actions fizzled and as Spain's European troubles reduced the number of men and material it could bring to bear on Indians, defensive war became the practice as well as the policy. Increasingly, enlightened Spanish officers came to believe it would be easier to contain Indians than to conquer them.

Critics of offensive war had the weight of Spanish law and tradition on their side, but, more important, they could point to lessons learned from observation. Experience suggested that large-scale invasions of Indian territories devoured men, animals, resources, and capital, yet rarely brought lasting peace.[176] The marqués de Rubí had erred in recommending offensive war against Apaches, Alejandro Malaspina charged, because he failed "to take into account the well founded belief of the Abbé Raynal, that it is much easier to conquer a populated country than one in control of a savage and wandering people."[177] If the goal of offensive war was to reduce Indians to a civil life in settled communities, then it would be impossible to hold Araucanians in towns, Ambrosio O'Higgins wryly

observed in 1793, "because for each [Araucanian] it would be necessary to have one soldier to contain him."[178] If the goal was to exterminate hostile Indians, O'Higgins said,
this seemed foolish if not immoral. Who would perform the manual labor of the Indies
if Spaniards annihilated Indians? To O'Higgins, the answer was clear: "To make offensive
war against the Indians . . . or to bring about their extinction would be the end of the
Americas."[179] O'Higgins had no objection to "some hard blows against Indians of bad
faith, the rebels and the incorrigible thieves, whose number is infinitely superior to that
of the honorable Indians," but throughout his long career he continued to believe that
offensive war was a mistake.[180]

In northern New Spain, the shift from offensive to defensive war became official in
1786, when the viceroy, Bernardo de Gálvez, issued new *Instructions for Governing the Interior Provinces of New Spain,* which remained in effect until the end of the colonial period.
The nephew of José de Gálvez, Bernardo had fought against Apaches as a young officer
and respected their fighting abilities. He described them as excellent horsemen and
strategists: "an enemy a thousand times more subtle than can be imagined." He had become convinced that Spain could not win a war against a people who had nothing to
defend but who occupied "an expanse equal to that from Madrid to Constantinople."[181]
He ordered Jacobo Ugarte, who took over as *comandante general* of the Interior Provinces
in 1786, to maintain military pressure on Indian adversaries but to also try less bellicose
measures to bring them to terms. "A bad peace with all the [Indian] nations who may
ask for it will be more beneficial to us than the efforts of a good war."[182]

Hardliners continued to extol the wisdom of offensive war in northern New Spain.
Félix Calleja, an officer recently arrived from Spain and with no experience on an Indian
frontier, challenged Gálvez directly in 1795, arguing that "a bad peace" with Indians was
"infinitely worse than war," for it left "the enemy inside the house itself."[183] He charged
that Gálvez's peace policy had paralyzed Spanish troops by making an Indian "a temple,
never to be touched." Responsible for maintaining peace under Gálvez's *Instructions,*
officers feared an actual encounter with Indians, Calleja said, lest war break out and the
blame fall on them.[184] Some war hawks wanted to combine bread and the stick, while
others believed that sticks alone would do the job. The bishop of Durango, Esteban
Lorenzo de Tristán, wrote mockingly of them, "Inflamed with their bravery and warrior
spirit (but not warriors), they believe that with the sword they can do it all." The bishop
himself did not shrink from offensive war but advocated covering the iron fist with a vel-
vet glove, as did the recipient of his missive, the viceroy of New Spain, Manuel Antonio
Flores (1787–89), who had previously served in New Granada and in Buenos Aires.[185]

Nonetheless, in theory, if not always in practice, offensive war as advocated by these
enthusiasts and by the regulations of 1772 had become a dead letter in the northern
provinces of New Spain. As Viceroy Revillagigedo (the younger) explained in 1791, it
was better to overlook the Apaches' minor transgressions "in order to avoid the greater
harm which they would do us in open war."[186] Or, as he put it a few years later, "War in
the [Interior Provinces] is of a different order than that to which civilized nations are

accustomed because it is necessary to accommodate to the character and manner of making war on savages, with whom, in general, peace is always preferable."[187]

In effect, Revillagigedo reiterated a central theme of Gálvez's *Instructions* of 1786, which also echoed down to the local level in the Interior Provinces. When officers at the Texas presidio of La Bahía recommended offensive war against the Karankawas in 1793, for example, the governor rejected the proposal. The Karankawas, he observed, have "given us cause to exterminate [them] many times, but the king's policy demands gentleness and encouragement that they should give up their heathen life."[188]

Spaniards who debated the merits and morality of offensive and defensive wars had definitions in mind. For example, Pedro de Nava, *comandante general* of the Interior Provinces in 1796, distinguished between Apaches' offensive war, or *guerra ofensiva*, and his own "vigorous war," or *guerra viva*, aimed at punishing or containing them.[189] From the point of view of Indian adversaries, however, it was a meaningless distinction. Spaniards' punitive expeditions could do horrifying damage, blurring any difference between offensive and defensive war in the eyes of Indians, if not in the minds of Spanish jurists. In 1792, Capt. Tomás Figueroa led Spanish troops and Indian allies out of Valdivia to the Río Bueno to put down a rebellion by some Mapuche caciques who had been friendly to Spaniards. Figueroa matched atrocity with atrocity. He burned homes and fields and sentenced rebel leaders to death. Before they died, the condemned men rejected his attempts to baptize them. Only one, Figueroa reported, "had the pleasure of dying a Christian."[190] Rather than fall into Spanish hands, some Indians drowned themselves, and one nursing mother killed her infant. Figueroa's men took some women and children alive. He sent them to Valdivia, along with livestock and the head of the cacique Cayumil.[191]

Forts and the Limits of Defensive War

Throughout the empire in the late 1700s, officials who disagreed with the crown's policy of gentleness and who continued to advocate and prosecute offensive war against Indians could still be found. When the governor of Paraguay expressed concern that Mbayás would attack Asunción in 1795, the viceroy of the Río de la Plata, Nicolás de Arredondo, assured him, "You do not have to be only on the defensive, but ready to set out on a sortie to annihilate them on the battlefield." Arredondo, who was also a brigadier general, took the view that "war against heathens is always just, even if it might not be specifically against those who did damage."[192]

In the last two decades of the eighteenth century, however, the ground had shifted. Officers with Arredondo's views were in the minority. Bourbon military strategists devoted more attention to traditional defensive measures. They increased the number of men on the payroll, improved their training and equipment, sent out punitive expeditions, courted Indian allies, and moved colonists into frontier zones. In short, they continued to use time-honored techniques of holding frontiers against Indians, but under Carlos III they did so more efficiently and professionally.

The Bourbons' construction and deployment of fortifications exemplify their rational approach to defense. Just as they streamlined public administration with an eye toward improving efficiency, Bourbon administrators tried to make forts more effective institutions for Indian control. Before the military buildup of the late eighteenth century, forts on the Indian frontiers had tended to be few, far between, and often shabby. Some amounted to little more than crude enclosures; one observer described the Chilean fort of Purén as unfit even as a "corral for cows." Some forts remained primitive until the end of the colonial period, but as the Bourbons turned their attention to the empire's defenses, frontier forts generally became more substantial as well as more numerous. Soldiers and Spain's Indian subjects built or rebuilt them, usually following plans developed by military engineers.[193]

When Carlos III endorsed the marqués de Rubí's plan to take the war to the Apaches in 1772, he also supported his proposal to realign or construct fifteen forts. These *presidios,* as forts were called in northern New Spain, were to stretch over a 1,800-mile line that approximated the 30th parallel, from Altar in Sonora to La Bahía, Texas (see map 6). The first two officials responsible for the newly created Interior Provinces of New Spain, Hugo O'Conor (1772–76) and Teodoro de Croix (1776–83), understood that the best offense is a good defense. They devoted much of their attention to overseeing the relocation and reconstruction of old presidios and the construction of new ones.[194]

At the same time, on the pampa south and west of Buenos Aires, Viceroy Vértiz (1778–84) began to build new forts and refurbish old ones after his advisors persuaded him of the impracticality of his predecessor's *entrada general.* Earlier plans to professionalize the frontier soldiery and construct new forts had amounted to little, but with the arrival of a viceroy who had the attention of the crown and with the growing importance of the Río de la Plata, talk translated into action. With Gálvez's approval, construction proceeded. By 1781, six principal forts (*fuertes* in Argentina) and five little forts (*fortines*) ran in a line from Melincué, on the edge of Tucumán province, over 250 miles to Chascomús, southeast of Buenos Aires (see map 4). Paid soldiers, called *blandengues* in Argentina, staffed the *fuertes,* and militia staffed the *fortines.*

Nowhere else in the empire did an Indian frontier come so close to a viceregal capital—just seventy miles separated Buenos Aires from the nearest forts at Chascomús, Ranchos, and Monte. That was not because Indians had advanced on Buenos Aires, but rather because the Bourbons had transformed Buenos Aires from a backwater town on the edge of Indian country into the political and economic center of Spanish activity in the South Atlantic. Commerce that once ran northward between the Argentine interior and Potosí now shifted toward the newly opened port of Buenos Aires. The city's population quadrupled, from twelve thousand in 1750 to fifty thousand by 1800. On other Indian frontiers, Spaniards built forts to protect small provincial towns, haciendas, and mining districts far from the metropolitan nerve centers of the empire.[195] On the *frontera de Buenos Aires* they built forts to protect the rapidly growing capital, its expanding hinterlands, and the road between Buenos Aires, Córdoba, and Mendoza, where escalating

22. *In this watercolor Florián Paucke, a German Jesuit who ministered to the Guaycurúes from 1749 to 1769, depicts a confrontation between a Spanish soldier and a Pampa Indian in 1749, which Paucke observed as he traveled west from Buenos Aires en route to Córdoba. The fort and corral in the background apparently represent Pergamino, which Paucke ridiculed. If the little compound, walled with upright poles, "deserved to be called a fort, then every farmer in our country who has enclosed his farm with walls has a much better and more defensible fort." Paucke, 1942–44, vol. 1, plate vii; quotation on p. 203.*

A generation later, in 1773, another traveler described the fort at Pergamino as having "a very good moat with a wooden drawbridge capable of lodging within it the 40 residents of the town and as many militiamen with their corresponding officers." Concolorcorvo, 1965, 71.

caravan traffic came under frequent assault by Indians. The line of forts remained until the end of the colonial period, although the Río Salado, just a dozen miles farther south at some points, became the official border between Spaniards and Indians in 1790.[196]

In the 1780s and 1790s, officials in the Río de la Plata also built or refurbished a dozen *fortines* to protect the rich *estancias* in the jurisdictions of Córdoba and San Luis and added to another line of forts that ran northward from Córdoba, along the western side of the Chaco, to the province of Tucumán (see map 5). Officials in Tucumán had abandoned offensive war in the early 1770s in response to royal directives, but Spanish missionaries and settlers continued to expand into the northwestern Chaco, accompanied by fortifications.[197] In 1778, a fort went up in the Zenta Valley, the first of several to the northeast of Jujuy, aimed to protect missionaries and settlers from Tobas, Chiriguanos, and Mocobíes and to secure that stretch of the king's highway, the *camino real,* to Peru. Farther north, the late 1700s saw still another spate of forts arise on the eastern edge of the Chiriguanía.[198]

On the eastern side of the Chaco, along the Río Paraguay, Spain built another line of forts to defend communities and commerce from the Abipones, Tobas, Mbayás, and Payaguás. Prior to the expulsion of the Jesuits in 1767, a string of forts ran down the Río Paraguay from Asunción to the Paraná. Each had a signal cannon to alert the troops to gather when Indians appeared. The Jesuits' expulsion in 1767, the end of their monopoly over the trade in yerba maté, and the opening of new markets in the Río de la Plata ushered in a Golden Age of river commerce that gave those forts additional importance. At the same time, the expansion of Spanish ranching into northern Paraguay led to the construction of new fortifications. In 1773, officials established the fortified villa of Concepción on the Río Paraguay some two hundred miles north of Asunción in Mbayá territory. After learning from Mbayás that the Portuguese had built Fort Nueva Coimbra in Mato Grosso in 1790, "in lands that manifestly belonged to Spaniards" according to the viceroy in Buenos Aires, Spain built Fort Borbón (today Fuerte Olimpo) still farther up the river in 1792 and Fort San Carlos del Río Apa in 1794, in the hope they would check Portuguese advances and help maintain the loyalty of the Mbayás in that contested territory.[199]

In Chile, where defensive war had been official policy off and on since the early 1600s, fortifications had a long pedigree. By the late 1700s, a series of small forts, modernized in the Bourbon era and known to Chileans as *plazas* or *fortines,* stood between the Spanish and Araucanian worlds along the Biobío and Laja rivers. Another line of forts ran south from Concepción to Valdivia, providing travelers on the coastal road with respite, fresh horses, and sanctuary. In the early 1790s, O'Higgins, then serving as captain general and governor of Chile, pushed the Spanish frontier south of Valdivia. He extended the line by building forts at Río Bueno, on the site of a Franciscan mission recently burned by Indians, and at Osorno. O'Higgins, who encouraged peaceful expansion over warfare, regarded the forts as purely defensive. Given the lengthy peace between Spaniards and Mapuches, however, one historian's observation seems especially astute: "The forts in the

23. Spaniards and Araucanians in front of the remains of the fort at Arauco, at the foot of the
Cerro de Colocolo, on the coast south of Concepción. Walls of cut stone were unusual for Spanish forts
on the Araucanian frontier. (Villalobos R., 1992, 336). From an engraving in Gay, 1854.
Courtesy, John Carter Brown Library at Brown University.

eighteenth century now had no clear offensive or defensive function, but rather [served
as points of] cultural contact, commercial penetration, and of demographic occupation."[200]

In the 1770s through the 1790s, then, new forts and refurbished or relocated forts became a key institution in many places where the Spanish frontier impinged on the lands
of independent Indians. At the same time, Bourbon officials also constructed forts far
from its colonial frontiers, in Indian-controlled territories where foreign powers seemed
likely to establish a foothold by building alliances with Indians. In 1778, for example,
Gálvez ordered the occupation of several key points on the Patagonian coast. He and
his advisors hoped the forts would serve as beachheads from which to expand into the
dimly understood interior, bring Patagonians into the Spanish orbit, and preempt English
attempts at making alliances with Native leaders. A decade earlier, Gálvez had succeeded
in building sustainable forts and missions on the coast of Alta California, but his thrust
into Patagonia failed. Missionaries, vital to Spanish success in California, played no
meaningful role in Patagonia. In contrast to the mature viceroyalty of New Spain, which
lent material assistance to Alta California, the young viceroyalty of the Río de la Plata
lacked the resources to support forts on the harsh, arid South Atlantic coast. Moreover,
Spain's entry into war against Britain in North America in 1779 and the rebellion of Tu-

24. Built on sand dunes on the north bank of the Río Negro, about thirty-five miles from its mouth, the fort at Carmen de Patagones sheltered a small farming and trading community. Spain maintained the fort to block access to the Río Negro, in the mistaken belief that the river was navigable to Chile. When the French explorer Alcides d'Orbigny sketched the fort and town in 1829, a recent war with the Portuguese and a blockade of the Rio de la Plata had transformed it into a thriving little commercial center. Lithograph from Orbigny, 1835–47, vol. 3, ser. 1, no. 4. Vue du village du Carmen. *Courtesy, John Carter Brown Library at Brown University.*

pac Amaru in the Andes in 1781 siphoned off metropolitan resources. After 1783, only Carmen de Patagones on the Río Negro remained. Fearing the Río Negro was navigable to Chile and hence of strategic value, Spaniards had built the fort on the north bank of the river about thirty-five miles from its mouth.[201]

If military planners had their way, forts would have continued to proliferate in the 1790s, both on Indian frontiers and beyond, but ruinous wars with France in 1792 and England in 1796 soaked up resources and building slowed. Some projects, such as stringing forts across the Chaco in order to shorten the route between upper Peru and Buenos Aires and "convert and civilize the Indians," never left the talking stage.[202]

The Bourbons' forts fulfilled one of their purposes. Many became nuclei of towns and haciendas, as their guns, walls, and military payroll attracted colonists as well as soldiers and their families.[203] In 1781, for example, Spaniards built new forts along the *frontera de Buenos Aires* in areas where, an official observed, "one does not usually see even a single Spanish resident." By 1797, the forts had attracted a population of 6,440, a fifth of the province's growing rural population of farmers and ranchers.[204] "Two kinds of men populate the present borders," an experienced militia captain from Mendoza told the crown in 1803: "soldiers . . . and *paisanos* who live under the cannon of the forts."[205] North of Buenos Aires on the Río Paraná, the elite that controlled Santa Fe consciously used forts more as potential townsites than as bastions against Indians. In the late 1700s the city fathers built or realigned a cluster of forts to the north and northwest of Santa Fe in order to control migrants, vagrants, and persons without title to land, whom they forcibly relocated to the forts.[206]

As civilian populations grew around forts, Spaniards' capacity for defense seemed to improve. It was an article of faith among Bourbon officials that towns and colonists held the key to security against Indian attacks. "The best defense of the frontier provinces against heathen and enemy Indians," Gálvez observed, "has always been the establishment of towns."[207] If Spaniards and Hispanicized Indians lived in towns instead of scattered in the countryside, the bishop of Sonora opined in 1784, then it would be "impossible" for Apaches, who came to rob cattle and horses, "to attack us and burn the houses."[208] "The truth is that there is no other means of dealing with the Indians except defensively, and by curtailing their numbers gradually by increasing our own," another Bourbon bureaucrat declared.[209]

Some officials argued that it would suffice to establish towns without building forts. "Settlements are living fortifications, self-sustaining bulwarks, and inexpensive presidios," one official asserted.[210] In lands of war, however, the building of forts or garrisons usually preceded the building of towns. Colonists had little desire to move to places like the Mosquito Coast, Darién, or the Chaco without military protection. Even Spanish soldiers served reluctantly in such places, and so many deserted that officers assigned convicted criminals to staff remote presidios, such as Fort Borbón in northern Paraguay.[211]

On some Spanish-Indian frontiers the construction and refurbishing of forts seemed to usher in long periods of peace, as in northern New Spain and along the southern and western edges of the Río de la Plata. Peace did not come, however, because forts intimidated Indians. Most forts served no purpose other than to protect their occupants and the nearby residents, and that mainly because Indians avoided attacking a fortified position and sustaining heavy casualties. Indians, as Spanish officers understood, only fought when "their victory is certain."[212] Otherwise, they "disappear like smoke," leaving the field to fight another day—a strategy some Spaniards described as cowardly rather than sensible.[213]

Aware that Indians seldom attacked a fixed position, Spaniards built forts to fit the circumstances. Where it had high stakes in protecting a site against its European rivals, as at Havana, Veracruz, and Cartagena, Spain built massive stone fortresses. These forts needed to be "state of the art," O'Higgins observed, but against Indians a fort "of any quality is sufficient."[214] His view, while overstated, represented the common sense of his fellow officers. Arguing against plans to build an elaborate bastion against Huilliches at what was then the confluence of the Diamante and Atuel rivers, the military engineer Félix de Azara noted that "the local style," a palisade and moat, would do. "It seems useless to begin to make other fortifications that will cost a great deal yet only be used against some mounted Indians who lack firearms."[215]

Although individual forts served by default as effective bastions against Indians, they functioned poorly as instruments in an ensemble. Spanish military planners imagined that captains of frontier forts would take actions in concert to maintain defensive lines.[216] Forts, however, stood far apart. On the Argentine pampa and in the Interior Provinces of New Spain—sites of the two lengthiest lines of fortifications—one hundred miles separated forts from one another. Undermanned garrisons, which were supposed to patrol the area between the forts at daily intervals, had little prospect of intercepting Indians, who rode between them with impunity.[217] This official's concise assessment of the cordon along the western Chaco might have applied to all of Spain's lines of fortifications: "They are sufficient to make the invasions of the enemy [Indians] difficult, but not to completely stop them, because the frontier is very vast and the distance between forts is great."[218] Lines of forts that guarded a waterway did no better. As one Jesuit explained, forts situated along the Río Paraguay did not so much deter Indian raids as provide early warnings of their approach by firing cannons so that nearby residents could "flee or, if the moment seemed right, take up arms."[219]

Hacienda owners were furious that Indians passed easily through presidial lines to raid their estates. The bishop of Durango, writing in support of *hacendados* in northern New Spain in 1788, observed that it was not a "prudent decision to guard the field and leave the house unprotected." Because the hacienda owners paid taxes to support a distant and ineffective presidial line, they suffered from "two pillagings," the bishop said, one in the form of taxes and the other at the Indians' hands.[220]

While Indians moved with ease between Spanish forts, Spaniards traveled with trepidation through territory they imagined was their own.[221] Along the post roads between Buenos Aires, Córdoba, and Mendoza, where fear of Indian attacks had discouraged cattle ranching and frightened some people into fleeing, Spanish travelers made their uneasy way between way stations, or *postas,* that were too lightly fortified for comfort.[222] By the late eighteenth century so many crosses marked spots along the roadways of northern New Spain where Spaniards had died at the hands of Indians that the ranking military officer in the region ordered the crosses removed. Although he claimed he wanted to prevent Indians from mistreating these sacred symbols, he seemed more concerned that the sight of the crosses demoralized travelers and increased the "audacity and pride" of the "savages," who "know what those crosses mean."[223] Following the indigenous revolts in the Andes of 1780 and 1781, Spaniards feared reprisals from tribute-paying Indians as well as attacks by independent Indians. As the anxiety over Indian attacks moved from the edges of the empire toward colonial centers, Gálvez ordered that cities and *villas* be enclosed by walls. In effect, he hoped to turn them into forts "to defend them from any *internal* invasion."[224]

Whatever their failings, forts protected their residents on the internal frontiers of the empire. On the strategic external frontiers, however, forts functioned less effectively wherever Indians had access to foreigners and foreign arms. The only times, it appears, that Spanish forts fell to direct Indian attack was when Indians acted in concert with

Europeans or under European influence. Fighting with Englishmen, Miskitos took Fort Inmaculada on the Río San Juan in Nicaragua in 1778. Fighting under British influence but apparently without direct British aid, Miskitos seized Fort Quepriva at Río Tinto in Honduras in 1800. Allied with the Portuguese and supplied with Portuguese guns, Mbayás overran Fort Borbón in northern Paraguay in 1812.[225]

Even when they did not attack Spanish forts directly, Indians with foreign allies and foreign arms, such as Cunas and Guajiros, made it difficult for Spain to maintain garrisons in their territories. In 1772, a year after the abortive attempt to invade the Guajira Peninsula with over a thousand men, a new viceroy of New Granada, Manuel Guirior, decided to subdue Guajiros slowly, using forts, colonists, and missionaries. By 1775, Spaniards had constructed forts at Pedraza and Sinamaica that together with the old fortified town of Riohacha formed a line along the base of the peninsula. They also built a new post at Bahía Honda, on the peninsula's northern edge, and colonists began to settle around these forts. The local comandante granted all Guajiros a "general pardon." He instructed his troops to treat the Indians with "affability, hospitality, and some little gifts" and warned them to punish Indian miscreants as individuals and take no action that would precipitate a war.[226] War erupted nonetheless when Spaniards tried to build a fortified town deep in Guajiro territory at Sabana del Valle. Guajiros destroyed the town, killed many of its soldier-settlers and a priest, and defeated Spanish troops in a battle at nearby Apiesi in 1775. Far from advancing beyond the presidial line, Spaniards had difficulty holding it. The governor of Riohacha noted in 1779 that if the Guajiros became provoked, Spaniards would have to abandon Riohacha, the oldest Spanish settlement on the peninsula.[227]

Some Spanish officials continued to urge a military expedition to crush the Guajiros, arguing that it would be less expensive than "the gentle method that has been followed up to now" and that Indians would respond only to "fear and power."[228] But limited resources made a new invasion impractical. Instead, Spain had to retreat. It abandoned and destroyed the fortified town of Pedraza in 1790. Sinamaica remained in Spanish hands but needed reinforcements from Maracaibo to resist Guajiro attacks in 1798 and 1800.[229] At the end of the colonial period the Guajira Peninsula remained firmly in the hands of Guajiros, who continued to trade with the British. "Not being subject to our laws," the governor of Riohacha lamented in 1801, the Guajiros "cannot be made to obey them." Moreover, any attempt to stop the Guajiros from trading with the British could have serious consequences for all of New Granada. "Who can calculate the length to which they [the Guajiros] would go to get revenge?"[230] The Guajiros remained independent until the end of the colonial era. Indeed, in the middle of the twentieth century one Franciscan described them as "savages" who "remain unsubjugated to the present day."[231]

In Darién, the eastern portion of the Isthmus of Panama, forts also failed. There, most Cunas had rebuffed missionaries and maintained their independence. They had not become mercenaries or slave hunters like the Miskitos, but they did trade freely with the English in Jamaica as well as with Dutch and French pirates and merchants. In 1783, as

Map 9. The Guajira Peninsula, 1775. Few streams flowed year round on the arid Guajira Peninsula, but the Alta Guajira, from Cabo de la Vela north, was especially arid and scantily populated; most Guajiros lived in the southern part of the peninsula. Spain had long claimed this Guajiro territory as the province of Riohacha, but it met Guajiro resistance when it tried to occupy the peninsula by establishing fortified towns. Adapted from Kuethe, 1978, 134.

Spain's latest war with England ended and freed up military resources, Gálvez decided to preempt Britain from establishing a beachhead in that strategic region where Spain had only a token force. He ordered the "reduction or extermination" of the Cunas.[232] Military leaders in New Granada disagreed about the best way to carry out Galvez's instructions. A majority wanted to sweep the isthmus with the help of Chocó Indian allies and kill or capture the Cunas. A minority favored a slower, more peaceful means of gaining control. That faction urged the construction of fortified towns to protect Spanish colonists who would gradually push the Cunas back or acculturate them. The minority won the ear of Viceroy Caballero y Góngora, who initially had supported the more aggressive course. In 1784, Caballero y Góngora moved his official residence from Bogotá to Cartagena to oversee the operation personally and strengthen coastal defenses. At considerable expense and with the help of black militia and Chocós, Spaniards built five fortified towns in Darién in 1785–86. When Cunas attacked one of the forts, Caballero y Góngora ordered the burning of Indian towns, the slaughter of their animals, and the destruction of their fields. He also invited Cuna leaders to his residence near Cartagena and plied them with gifts and generous conditions for trade if they would recognize Spanish sovereignty and permit Spanish colonists to settle among them.[233]

Missions apparently played no role in this venture. Like those in the Guajira Penin-sula, however, the fortified towns in Darién proved costly to maintain, and Spain had to abandon them as European problems mounted. A new viceroy, Francisco Gil y Lemos, met with Cuna leaders in Cartagena in 1789 and put a favorable gloss on Spain's departure. The king, he lied, had ordered the destruction of several of the forts as "proof of his sat-isfaction with them [the Cunas]." Soldiers razed the forts, colonists left, and Cunas re-mained permanently outside the Spanish sphere.[234]

A Bad Peace

Although forts grew more numerous and elaborate, soldiers who protected them more professionalized, and punitive expeditions against Indians more sophisticated, these al-legedly defensive measures were usually no more successful than offensive war in pacify-ing powerful groups of independent Indians for good. From several corners of the empire, Indians taught Bourbon officials a lesson their Habsburg predecessors had already learned in their failed attempts to conquer Chichimecas and Araucanians and what locals al-ready knew: a bad peace was less costly and more effective than either offensive or defen-sive war.[235] The killing of "twenty or thirty poor heathens perpetuates hatred against Span-iards," the viceroy of the Río de la Plata, the marqués de Avilés, noted in 1801 as he condemned punitive expeditions against Indians in the Chaco. A career soldier, Avilés was not averse to using force, but he preferred to achieve peace "not by means of blood and devastation but through negotiations and treaties."[236]

In advocating those more pacific measures at the century's end, Avilés represented the views of the most progressive Bourbon administrators and of his enlightened personal secretary and legal advisor, Miguel Lastarria.[237] Like many other Bourbon administrators who articulated progressive ideas, Viceroy Avilés responded to political pressure. When he became viceroy of the Río de la Plata in 1799, he inherited an escalating conflict with Charrúas, who spilled out of the no-man's-land beyond the Río Negro to raid Guaraní missions and Spanish ranches along the Río Uruguay in the Banda Oriental (today's Uruguay). Fifteen years earlier, Azara had encountered Charrúas in a Guaraní mission and reported that they were at peace. He described the Charrúas and their Guaraní hosts as playing in tournaments in which they imitated "skirmishes and battles between savages and Spaniards."[238]

In the late 1790s, however, aggrieved Charrúas played for keeps. Spanish ranchers, eager to supply the growing market for hides in Montevideo and Buenos Aires, had claimed Charrúa cattle, horses, and land and pushed the Indians north. Bands of Spanish ruffians had raided the Indians' camps, burning and sacking them "not once but many times," putting older people to the knife, and capturing the young. Their plight touched one sympathetic observer who noted that the Charrúas, "although savage, enjoy the pre-rogatives and rights of Nature and of Man."[239] A veteran officer, Agustín de Pinedo, con-vinced Avilés that the Charrúas had done nothing more than defend themselves against

Spaniards. He believed that their numbers did not exceed a thousand and that they could be brought to order "by the gentle methods" that Spanish law prescribed.[240]

When Charrúas struck back, Avilés responded with peace overtures. He sent diplomatic representatives and two Christian Charrúas from Buenos Aires to translate for them and put into motion a plan to bring permanent peace to the area by resettling reluctant colonists in a new town, Belén, high on the Río Uruguay. But diplomacy failed. When ranchers complained of continuing depredations of Charrúas and the bandits who lived among them, Avilés unleashed a substantial force of militia, Guaraní Indians, and professional soldiers (*blandengues*) to "punish the bandits and contain the savages." The Cuerpo de Blandengues de la Frontera de Montevideo had been formed in 1797, partly to mollify ranchers who demanded law and order in the countryside. In a series of attacks in 1801 Spanish forces broke Charrúa resistance. "Blood and devastation" trumped "negotiations and treaties." Many of the surviving Charrúas gravitated north to the Portuguese border only to be betrayed in 1806 by a Portuguese officer who captured them and traded them to Spaniards in exchange for livestock. Some Charrúas, however, emerged from Portuguese territory in the 1810s and joined insurgents fighting for independence from Spain.[241]

Officials like Avilés might exercise forbearance, advocate negotiations, and tout the advantages of a bad peace over a good war, but when they needed to impress local *hacendados* with their resolve or end a damaging stalemate with dispatch they still relied on war. Little wonder, then, that at century's end a *proyectista* like the Argentine mine owner Francisco de Serra y Canals would urge an offensive war against Araucanians and Pampas, even though he knew it violated royal policy. Serra y Canals had lived in the New World long enough to understand that savages invited exceptions from the Bourbon state. Bourbon officers who championed a bad peace could still find reasons to make a good war, and Bourbon officials at the highest level could be hawks or doves as the circumstances seemed to require.

5

Trading, Gifting, and Treating

The reduction of the savage nations can only be carried out by three means: the first is through commerce and friendly relations, the second is through force, and the third is through persuasion.
Félix de Azara, ca. 1790

To prefer dominion over the advantages and utilities of commerce and friendly trade with the savage nations caused past conquests to end badly and others . . . not to be carried out.
José del Campillo y Cosio, 1789

Through this commendable way of friendship and good faith, we will . . . dominate entirely those who are today our implacable enemies, without spilling blood.
José de Gálvez, 1779

In 1800, the governor of Cochabamba, Francisco de Viedma, ordered that a Chiriguano chief first be baptized and then executed by hanging. The chief, Sacuarao, had been among the leaders of a "rebellion" the previous autumn. In the worst Chiriguano uprising of the century, mission Indians and pagans had destroyed six recently founded mission towns. Although deeply devoted to justice for Indians, Governor Viedma would not countenance rebellion.[1] He turned Sacuarao over to a group of pro-Spanish Chiriguanos, who hung him, cut his body down, shot it full of arrows, and burned it.[2]

The brutality of Sacuarao's execution surprised and horrified Governor Viedma, but the death sentence he had issued incensed the crown's chief attorney for the region, Victorián de Villava.

Serving as protector of Indians as well as chief attorney, Villava described Sacuarao's execution as a "return to the times of Atahualpa," the Inca chief whom Francisco Pizarro's men had deceived, baptized, and executed by strangulation.[3] In sentencing Sacuarao to death for treason, Villava said, Spaniards had acted like savages. Governor Viedma had treated Sacuarao as a criminal without reflecting on the nature of crime. A crime, Villava asserted, can occur only when a member of a society breaks that society's social compact. Since Chiriguanos did not live in Spanish society they could not commit the crime of treason or rebellion. Chiriguanos had invaded Spanish territory and "the invasion of another nation," he said, "would be an offense against natural law that could be vindicated with arms, but not a crime that can be punished under civil law."[4]

Villava's belief that Chiriguanos had not rebelled because they had never recognized Spain's dominion over them contrasted sharply with the Spanish practice of assuming that Indians were Spanish subjects and making war on them when they resisted.[5] When José de Gálvez described the unconquered Seris as rebels in 1769, he invoked that legal fiction. Years later, Gálvez similarly suggested that the independent Miskitos "have always been rebels."[6] Villava, on the other hand, argued that Indians had to submit before they could rebel, and he prescribed using peaceful means to bring them into Spanish society. "It is better policy," he said, "not to punish them but attract them. By having punished them with whips, they have punished us with arrows, and by not knowing how to negotiate with them and civilize them, we are in continuous war with men who have no place, land, or fixed residence, which makes it impossible to defeat them or subject them."[7] Villava would draw Indians into the European sphere and transform them with trade goods and good example. "An Indian transplanted to London," he observed, "could become a loyal and eloquent member of the opposition," but force would not turn a savage into a member of Parliament.[8]

Trade and Civilization

A Spanish-born scholar who had taught at the University of Huesca for thirteen years before coming to America, Victorián de Villava represented a venerable school of thinkers who championed humane treatment of Indians. The most celebrated proponent of that view, the sixteenth-century Dominican Bartolomé de Las Casas, had argued that war against Indians was unjust and that missionaries should win Indians over through persuasion. The crown adopted Las Casas's position in the Royal Orders for New Discoveries of 1573. Bourbon officials like Villava, however, took another tack. Instead of relying on professional Christians to pacify and "civilize" Indians, they looked to the "indirect" influences of commerce to introduce savages to what they imagined to be "the necessities and comforts of a civilized life." For men like Villava, imbued with the sensibilities of what he called "the most enlightened century," trade and civilization went hand in hand.[9] "It is almost a general rule," Montesquieu had observed, "that wherever the ways of men are gentle there is commerce, [and] wherever there is commerce the ways of men are gentle."[10] Montesquieu's dictum echoed in Spanish thought in the late Bourbon era. "A people without communication or trade with other people can never be civilized," one of Alejandro Malaspina's officers observed.[11] "Men become smoother with trade, as river rocks do from continuous rubbing," the Argentine savant Gregorio Funes declared.[12] The stanzas of a lengthy "Ode to Commerce," which appeared in an Argentine newspaper in 1801, suggested that the "art" of commerce had already redeemed humankind from savagery. Certainly, then, it would rescue the savages who remained.[13]

The Bourbon's Habsburg predecessors had understood the value of commerce and required Spaniards entering new lands to bring gifts and trade goods for Indians. The Habsburgs, however, did not envision commerce itself as the principal agent of cultural change. Rather, they prescribed gifts and trade goods as inducements to draw Indians peacefully into missions, where missionaries, not merchants, would Hispanicize them. Well before the Habsburg era ended, however, it was apparent that missions had failed to bring some Indians into the Spanish fold.[14]

In the Bourbon era, some Spaniards opposed commerce with independent Indians. Cutting off all trade to Araucanians, one Jesuit argued, would leave them "hungry, naked, unarmed, and forced to receive the [Spanish] law"—a strategy one Franciscan dismissed with a rhetorical question: "Did they [Indians] not eat before they knew Spaniards?"[15] More worrisome, as an official in northern New Spain explained in 1750, trade would make Indians "more astute, sagacious, and informed" and thus more formidable adversaries.[16] Legal trade would also open the way for Indians to obtain knives, guns, ammunition, and alcohol from unscrupulous Spaniards, making Indians at once more dangerous and unpredictable. This was no idle concern. One foreigner, traveling in the Río de la Plata, observed that Spaniards in search of profits sold Indians weapons "that then could be used to cut their own throats." Responding to these dangers, war hawks like Gov. Antonio de Guill y Gonzaga in Chile and Viceroy Juan José de Vértiz of the Río de la Plata, not only prohibited trade with independent Indians but also threatened to punish Spanish violators with death.[17]

Other Spaniards of the Bourbon era thought that the strategy of trading with Indians would fail because Natives were so wedded to tradition that they would not buy Spanish goods.[18] Conversely, José Mariano Mozíño, a botanist on the Malaspina expedition, feared that trade would work too well. Mozíño, who romanticized Indians, thought European trade goods would corrupt the Nootkas and sully "the primitive simplicity of their customs."[19] Few Spaniards, however, thought well of Indians' "primitive simplicity." More typically they associated the primitive with vices, which trade would eradicate. Indians who acquired "certain comforts of life unknown to their elders," Gregorio Funes wrote, found that "gluttony and pure laziness were no longer the foundation of their happiness."[20]

Putting such reservations aside, most progressive Spanish officials in the last two decades of the eighteenth century would have agreed with Villava that it was better to trade with Indians than to make war on them. Spaniards, Alejandro Malaspina observed, needed to liberate themselves from the "frightening noise of the cannon and war, replacing them with the sweet ties of lucrative trade."[21] The swift, well-mounted Indians in the Chaco, Féliz de Azara concluded, could not be converted or defeated. The only solution, he told the viceroy in Buenos Aires in 1799, was "good treatment and commerce with those savages, so that they maintain peace out of self-interest."[22] These officials did not see missions as agencies for civilizing savages but instead assumed that missions would succeed as a consequence of the civilizing influence of trade. Speaking of independent Indians on the southern plains of North America, one officer stated the philosophy clearly. They "should not be invited nor obliged to enter the brotherhood of our religion until times of [their] greater enlightenment," which would come about, he said, when Spaniards exposed them to trade and kind treatment.[23]

To some extent, this late eighteenth-century emphasis on trade as the preferred instrument for controlling independent Indians represented a practical response to Spain's declining ability to fight Indians in America as wars in Europe siphoned off Spain's resources.[24] The situation had become so dire that one frontier commander in the Chaco, who saw his region as "peaceful only in appearance," warned that taking offensive action against Indians would only reveal Spanish weakness. If Indians discovered that Spain lacked troops "to do nothing more than poorly guard the house, what would they do?"[25] The new emphasis on trade also reflected the Bourbons' larger interest in making their American colonies more profitable. At the highest levels, policymakers took to heart Montesquieu's criticism that Spain had made the mistake of treating its American colonies as objects of conquest rather than as trading partners. The conde de Campomanes, who served as legal advisor (1762–83) to and then head (1783–91) of the Council of Castile, which governed Spain itself, made the argument succinctly. Dominion seemed hollow, he said, if it brought no profit to the crown.[26] Increasing the profitability of the empire meant trading even with independent Indians, who offered goods that made substantial impacts on primitive frontier economies.[27]

Nowhere in Spanish thought were arguments for trade with independent Indians articulated more clearly than in the well-known *Nuevo sistema de gobierno económico para la América,* a master plan to revive the economy of the empire. Scholars disagree about the authorship of the *Nuevo sistema,* which seems to have been written before 1743 but circulated widely as a manuscript. Part of it was apparently plagiarized and published in 1779 as the second half of a book entitled the *Proyecto económico,* by the Spanish economist and *ilustrado* Bernardo Ward. In 1789, when the *Nuevo sistema* first appeared in its entirety as a discrete title, the publisher identified its author as José del Campillo y Cosío, a former minister of the Indies who died in 1743. Some scholars accept this attribution of authorship; others doubt it. Scholars disagree, too, about the influence of the *Nuevo sistema* on Spanish policy, but if it was not, as one historian has argued, the "reformers' bible, the definitive text which inspired this Bourbon revolution in government," it did at the least reflect the views of some of the liberal policymakers who redesigned the administrative structure of Spain's American colonies under Carlos III.[28] Many Bourbon administrators referred explicitly to it, as did Viedma, when he noted in 1784 that the Indian threat on the pampa would diminish if Pampas were treated with friendship and trade as the French did "with similar savages, and as Mr. [Bernardo] Ward recommends with good reason in his *Proyecto económico.*"[29]

Ward, Campillo y Cosío, or whoever wrote the *Nuevo sistema* charged that Spain had wasted millions of pesos in making war against Indians who, "if treated with tact and friendship, would be of infinite use to us." In the early 1500s, Spain had no alternative to military force "for there were few Spaniards in America and millions of Indians to subject." But Spain made the mistake of "preserving the spirit of conquest beyond its time, and preferring dominion over the advantages and utility of commerce and friendly trade with the savage nations." Even as the wildest beast can be tamed by kind treatment, the *Nuevo sistema* analogized, "there is no savage who cannot be dominated by industry and made sociable by a ready supply of all the things he likes."[30]

Other Europeans traded advantageously with "wild Indians," but Spaniards had a special handicap. Over the years, they had earned "the hatred of neighboring Indian nations." But if Spanish missionaries could enter the lands of hostile Indians by treating them with kindness, the *Nuevo sistema* argued, so could merchants. In fact, traders would have an easier time of it. They make no demands on Indians and provide them with goods they need and "alcohol that they so esteem," whereas missionaries "threaten [Indians] with hell if they become drunk or take more than one woman."[31]

In the enlightened formulation of the *Nuevo sistema,* Indian consumers would become the foundation of Spain's commercial and economic revival in America. To cast Indians in that role, however, the *Nuevo sistema* had to portray them as capable of making what Europeans understood to be rational economic choices. If an earlier generation of Spaniards had expected Indians to adopt the Christian faith when missionaries revealed it to them, the *Nuevo sistema* expected Indians to behave like European consumers when merchants displayed their wares. If Spanish officers believed that Indians were warlike by nature and that only force would make them peaceable, the *Nuevo sistema* presented Indians as commercial by nature, ready to be pacified by gifts and trade goods.[32] If Spanish employers viewed Indians as so lazy that they had to be forced to work for their own good, the *Nuevo sistema* argued that Indians were as self-interested and ambitious as Europeans.[33] Once Indians profited from the fruits of their labor, the *Nuevo sistema* declared, they would voluntarily become producers and consumers.[34] In short, Indians would change if the system changed, giving them opportunities instead of oppressing them. The benefits for Spain would be enormous. Commerce would win the allegiance of Indians, while the costs of war and of maintaining formal political or institutional control over them would be avoided.[35]

In recommending an Indian policy built on trade, the author of the *Nuevo sistema* drew inspiration from French and English practices in North America, overlooking Spain's own colonial experience. In contrast to the English, who used guns and alcohol (and, in China, opium) as instruments of colonial control, Habsburg and early Bourbon Spain prohibited its subjects from providing weapons or alcohol to Indians. In Spanish Florida, however, local officials ignored the law and tried to counter the English by playing their game. As early as the 1710s, Spanish officials in Florida competed with Englishmen from the Carolinas for the loyalty of Yamasees and Creeks by offering them guns, rum, and other trade goods. They had mixed results. A chronic shortage of merchandise and money usually left Spaniards at a competitive disadvantage against the English.[36]

English and French example, rather than Spain's own colonial experience, continued to inspire Bourbon policy in North America. Campomanes had long admired the way English fur traders controlled Indians without the aid of missionaries. In 1784, from his post as head of the Council of Castile, he urged Minister of the Indies Gálvez, to adopt the English system as the best way to manage "wild Indians" along Spain's borderlands with the new United States. "This [English] method," Campomanes said, "can be advantageous to our present situation and an indirect way of keeping those [Indian] nations free from the dominion of the American Republic." Campomanes did not, of course, have the Indians' interest at heart. Indians allied with Spain, he thought, would stop Americans from moving closer to Spanish territory and settling along the banks of the Mississippi and Ohio rivers.[37]

For his part, Gálvez did not need Campomanes to tell him about the successful example of Spain's European rivals in North America. He had his own sources of intelligence, including his nephew and protégé, Bernardo de Gálvez, whom he had appointed acting governor of Louisiana in 1776. Drawing from his firsthand knowledge of French and English practices (in Louisiana he married the daughter of a prominent French fur trader) as well as from previous experience fighting Apaches, Bernardo de Gálvez had urged his uncle to rely on trade to control Indians rather than fight costly, ineffective wars. Through trade, he argued, "the King would keep [Indians] very contented for ten years with what he now spends in one year in making war upon them."[38]

Bernardo de Gálvez sent this message to his uncle in October 1778. Just a few months later, in February 1779, José de Gálvez ordered Teodoro de Croix to call off the offensive war against Apaches in the Interior Provinces of New Spain. In addition to telling Croix to take only defensive action, Gálvez urged Croix to make Indians dependent on Spaniards for merchandise, including luxury goods and guns, so that "they will not be able to live without our help."[39] As we have seen, a shortage of military resources, not the sagacity of his nephew's advice, had prompted Gálvez to order this defensive stance. Three years later, in 1782, Gálvez ordered Croix to return to offensive warfare when Apaches refused to substitute trading for raiding and when powerful oligarchs angrily demanded aggressive action to protect their dwindling herds from Indian predators.[40]

Unlike his uncle, Bernardo de Gálvez never wavered in advocating trade as the key to Indian control. In 1786, in his new position as viceroy of New Spain, he ordered officials in the Interior Provinces to return to José de Gálvez's conciliatory policy of 1779. Although he placed greater emphasis on keeping military pressure on Apaches than had his uncle, Bernardo de Gálvez still saw trade as the long-range solution. He would force Apaches to appeal for peace and then cement that peace with gifts and trade goods. "In time," he suggested in his influential *Instructions* of 1786, trade "may make them dependent on us."[41] Like the author of the *Nuevo sistema*, Bernardo de Gálvez believed that "commerce tightens and binds the interests of men." Introducing Apaches to Spanish foods, clothing, and weapons would make them "realize the advantages of rational life."[42] Gálvez and his fellow officers did not expect Indians to change behavior quickly. They did believe the new policy would lead to change within a few generations so that, as one military engineer put it, "the grandchildren of the savage, fierce, destructive, and bloody Indians would become useful subjects."[43]

By including guns and ammunition among the goods Spaniards might offer to Indians, Bernardo de Gálvez took a sharp turn away from Spain's long-standing but frequently violated strictures against providing independent Indians with firearms, or indeed any type of metal weapons.[44] Gálvez was not the first high-ranking official to advise Spain to arm "wild" Indians, but he had the authority to implement it.[45] In Louisiana he had permitted licensed traders to continue to furnish firearms and ammunition to Indians, as the French had done, and then extended the policy to northern New Spain when he became viceroy in 1786. In his *Instructions*, Gálvez urged officers to make ammunition available in generous quantities. The more Indians used powder and shot, the sooner they would "begin to lose their skill in handling the bow," which Gálvez regarded as deadlier than the gun.[46] He also ordered that guns destined for the Indian trade have long barrels and be made of poorly tempered metal. This would make them awkward to use and prone to breaking and force Natives to return to the Spaniards for repairs or replacements.

Gálvez's *Instructions* of 1786 also recommended that officers encourage Indians to acquire a taste for alcohol, "creating for them a new necessity that will oblige them to recognize their dependence upon us more directly."[47] A generation earlier, the governor of Chile had offered similar counsel. Noting that Mapuches had become prosperous by trading woven ponchos for Spanish manufactured goods, he suggested that Spanish traders also offer them wine. Wine would make them "more needy and dependent and less well armed and powerful" and increase Spain's chance of bringing about their "subjection."[48]

In contrast to England, both France and Spain traditionally opposed furnishing alcohol to Indians except on ceremonial occasions. At least as early as 1594, the crown had prohibited the sale of wine to Indians in order to prevent "the serious damage that results to the health and well-being of the Indians."[49] Colonial officials had continued to issue similar prohibitions, often because they feared alcohol would make Indians "violent and unmanageable," as one official said of the Miskitos.[50]

Where Spaniards competed with foreigners, as in Florida and on the Mosquito Coast, or where they enjoyed regular commercial relations with Indians, as they did with Mapuches in Chile through much of the eighteenth century, alcohol flowed nonetheless. In such places, the crown and its representatives tried to regulate its distribution rather than prohibit it entirely. If Spain controlled the quantity of alcohol available to Indians, Carlos III told the captain general of Chile in 1774, that "would imperceptibly oblige them to recognize their dependency without exasperating them."[51] Officials tried to put that policy into practice. Thus, the viceroys of the Río de la Plata sought to use measured quantities of alcohol to court Indian caciques, and Gov. Ambrosio O'Higgins prohibited its export into the Araucanía while allowing it to be sold to Indians who came to frontier forts. While authorities tried to regulate the flow of alcohol, however, private merchants made their own deals with Indians. Wine and ardent spirits, or *aguardiente,* were the most popular items they peddled to independent Indians in the Araucanía, the pampa, and Patagonia. Indians preferred alcohol over indigo, glass beads, or any other trade item. Wine for the Araucanians, one group of merchants explained, "is like the *real* gold coin for us."[52] Thus, like their British counterparts, who tried unsuccessfully in 1763 to restrict trade west of the Appalachians to licensed traders at specified posts, Spanish officials failed to keep Spaniards from trading alcohol, or anything else, in Indian territory.[53]

When Bernardo de Gálvez advocated that his officers in the Interior Provinces furnish Indians with alcohol, he may have simply legitimized what had already become a common practice, but the subject remains dimly understood in that region. There is no evidence that the Spanish military in the Provincias Internas distributed alcohol in the years following Gálvez's *Instructions,* either in treaty negotiations or in the supplies given to Apaches on reservations, or *establecimientos de paz,* that came into use at this time.[54] In New Mexico, Gov. Joaquín del Real Alencaster served wine to Comanches when he entertained them at his table, and that may have been the local custom. The Indians, one observer noted "do not guard against getting drunk" from what they called "crazy water."[55]

If we know little about their use of alcohol in their dealings with Indians after 1786, we do know that officers in northern New Spain made annual gifts of guns and ammunition to some Indian allies, including Comanches and the various peoples Spaniards knew as the Nations of the North.[56] These distributions of weapons were probably modest, since Spanish military forces on the frontier suffered from a chronic shortage of firearms and ammunition for their own use. Indeed, the shortage was so acute that on some occasions New Mexicans obtained firearms *from* Comanches, and residents of San Antonio traded them *from* Apaches and Wichitas in exchange for horses and "trifles."[57] In the short run, at least, firearms did not replace bows and arrows, as Gálvez hoped they would, and Spanish gunsmiths corrected defects in Indians' Spanish-made muskets. Gálvez's policy only added to the Indians' arsenal, one officer complained.[58]

However spotty its execution, Gálvez's *Instructions* had brought Indian policy in northern New Spain in line with practices in what he called "our new colonies"—Louisiana and the Floridas. In the "new colonies," Indians' expectations and the presence of British and Anglo-American traders had forced Spain to continue the French tradition of trading in guns and ammunition and of hiring gunsmiths to live in Indian villages.[59] Gálvez's *Instructions* merely recognized the futility of withholding firearms and ammunition from Indians, whose networks reached into neighboring Louisiana. The best that officials in the Interior Provinces could do was regulate the supply of guns and powder and try to stop private parties from offering them to Indians.[60]

In places where independent Indians did not have access to foreigners to supply them with firearms, officials continued to uphold traditional strictures. In 1786, the same year Bernardo de Gálvez advocated arming independent tribes, the president of Chile, Ambrosio de Benavides, warned the Franciscan college in Chillán not to teach Indian students how to make firearms. "Never," he said, should this knowledge be introduced "in the territory of the heathen."[61] Authorities found, however, that it was difficult to keep the door open to trade with independent Indians while closing it to guns and ammunition, and to profess trust in Indian allies yet not trust them with firearms.[62] Like Spain's efforts to regulate the behavior of its vassals on distant frontiers, attempts to limit trade in firearms met scant success. Those Indians who could not obtain firearms from foreigners could still get them from individual Spaniards, including poorly paid soldiers, renegades, and merchants who peddled arms as well as alcohol.[63]

Gifts and Entertainment

Since the days of Cortés and Pizarro, Spaniards had tried to win Indians' friendship with gifts and entertainment. "There are no children more fond of toys" than are Indians of gifts, one officer noted in 1599 as he urged the distribution of presents to cement peace accords throughout the empire.[64] In the Habsburg era, however, missionaries had been the primary dispensers of gifts on Indian frontiers. In the Bourbon era, army officers assumed that role. Like missionaries, they saw gifts and entertainment as essential to establishing and maintaining good relations with independent Indians. Thus, as Spanish interest in developing peaceful commercial relations with savages grew in the late 1700s, so did the budget for gifts and entertainment.

Independent Indians made it clear to Spaniards that peace had its price. Indians' expectations and tastes determined the nature and quality of gifts that Spanish officials gathered for distribution: food, drink, clothing (from shoes to hats), cloth, ribbons, banners, indigo, tobacco, glass beads, metal manufactures of all kinds (including hatchets, spurs, stirrups, bits, spoons, and earrings), and livestock.[65] If they failed to deliver the right stuff, Indians did not hesitate to complain,[66] and they forced Spaniards to be sure that the quality and quantity of gifts corresponded to the status of individual recipients. Leaders—or Indians whom Spaniards wished to anoint as leaders—received what the crown called "tangible signs of distinction."[67] These gifts, which incorporated Indians symbolically into the Spanish sphere, included elegant suits of clothes and staffs of office, or *bastones,* with gold or silver handles. At a single meeting, or *parlamento,* in 1771, Spanish authorities distributed two hundred silver-handled bastones to Araucanian *caciques gobernadores.* The *caciques'* women received the fabric du jour—Castilian baize in blue and pink.[68]

Late in the colonial period, Spain began to bestow specially minted medals on Indian leaders because those leaders were accustomed to receiving them from Spain's European rivals.[69] Unlike bastones, which enjoyed long use throughout the empire, medals of honor had apparently not come into use until after Spain acquired Louisiana and In-

25. This well-worn medal with the bust of Carlos III was presented to a Quapaw chief. Courtesy of Mr. and Mrs. Lawrence Supernaw, and Morris Arnold. See Arnold, 2000, 82.

dians demanded them. As Louisiana's first Spanish governor remarked in 1767, Spain needed to distribute medals "since the old tribes have them from the time of the French government."[70] By 1783, Spanish authorities were giving away so many expensive medals in Louisiana that Bernardo de Gálvez urged cutting back to one "medal chief" per village.[71] Officials closer to the scene recognized this economizing would irritate Indian leaders and never followed through.[72] Indian leaders also forced Spaniards to increase the size of their honorific medals. A Quapaw chief, Cazenonpoint, rejected a Spanish medal in 1771 because it was smaller than one given to him by the French and implied that his status had diminished.[73] José de Gálvez responded by ordering smaller medals melted down, the silver reused. He had done this by 1779, when he sent large silver and gold medals from a mint in Spain to Guatemala, explaining they were necessary to win

26. By the 1790s the awarding of medals to Indian leaders had become so routinized in Louisiana that
Spanish authorities had printed special citations to present to Indians along with medals. The printed
citation contained an illustration of a Spanish governor, perhaps the Baron de Carondelet himself, shaking
hands with a generic Indian leader. The printed form left room for officials to fill in the identity and
achievements of the specific Indian honoree. This citation, issued in New Orleans on May 16, 1794,
honored the Osage Petit Oiseau (Little Bird), naming him a Spanish captain and ordering Spanish
authorities to recognize his office. For the context, see Din and Nasatir, 1983, 260, and Rollings, 1992, 174.
With thanks to Dan Usner and permission of the Historic New Orleans Collection, accession no. 67–12-L.

the friendship of the Miskitos and other nations and urging that they be conferred on
their chiefs.[74]

If Spain's use of medals to recognize Indian leaders began in the late colonial era as
a way to meet a demand created by Spain's rivals, the practice seems to have spread to
areas of the empire where Indians apparently had no previous familiarity with medals.
In New Mexico they seem to have been used for the first time in 1786, when Gov. Juan
Bautista de Anza sealed peace agreements by presenting large medals to a Navajo leader,
"don Carlos," and a leader of the western Comanches, Ecueracapa. From their dealings
with Mississippi Valley tribes, Comanches were probably familiar with medals, but more
isolated Navajos were not. The medals served a dual purpose in Anza's view. As he told
Carlos III, he decorated Ecueracapa "with the medal of your royal bust" so that "with
this insignia he may be respected by his subjects and treated with honorable distinction
among the Spaniards."[75] The practice continued among Comanches. After Ecueracapa
died from wounds sustained in a battle with Pawnees in 1793, Anza's successor, Fernando

de la Concha, a Spanish-born career officer who governed New Mexico from 1787 to 1793, traveled into Comanche territory to witness, if not influence, the election of Ecuera-capa's successor, Encanaguané. Pleased with the outcome, Concha recognized the new leader by embracing him and presenting him with a bastón, a flag, an insignia, and a medal with a bust of Carlos IV.[76]

In southern South America, where the English and French had not socialized Indians to expect medals, officials seldom used them. In Chile, Gov. Agustín de Jáuregui gave silver medals to four Araucanian ambassadors who took up residence in Santiago in 1774.[77] After the uprising of Tupac Amaru, the president of upper Peru asked for and received permission to give specially minted medals to two caciques who had helped protect Plata (today the city of Sucre) from an attack by Indians from the Chaco in 1781.[78] These seem to be exceptional cases. More commonly, Spanish officials in South America used the traditional bastón to signify an Indian leader's special relationship to the crown.[79] On some occasions in the viceroyalty of the Río de la Plata, Spanish coins served as passports. At Mendoza in 1794, Maestro de Campo de las Milicias José Francisco de Amigorena, provided friendly Huilliche emissaries with silver pesos suspended by a cord that ran through a hole above the king's bust. The caciques were to wear these pesos outside their ponchos when they traveled so they would not be taken for enemies. Similarly, in an apparent reference to silver coins, a treaty of 1796 signed at Córdoba required friendly Ranqueles to show "signs of silver" when they visited Spanish forts.[80]

In the late 1700s gifts and hospitality to independent Indians represented a rising expense for Spain. No one in the centralized Bourbon bureaucracy, however, knew the total annual cost of gifting and entertaining Indians throughout the empire because local officials drew from a variety of funds.[81] In Chile the cost of gifts alone could represent nearly half of Spain's expenses for periodic high-level peace talks, or *parlamentos*, with Araucanians. Some of the money came from a special "Indian entertainment fund." In 1780, that fund contained 800 pesos, to be divided up among all of the commandants along the Chilean–Araucanian frontier. It could not meet the regular demands Araucanians made on it, much less purchase gifts and entertainment for parlamentos. One of the most lavish parlamentos of the colonial era, held at Negrete in 1793, cost 10,897 pesos —at a time when a frontier soldier's annual salary was less than 250 pesos. To support these events, officials had to cobble together funds from a variety of sources.[82]

On the other side of the Andes, commanders of frontier presidios also had a budget for entertaining Indians, a *fondo de agasajos de indios*. So, too, did officials in cities where Indians increasingly came to visit and trade. In the 1780s, the viceroy in Buenos Aires spent 500 to 600 pesos a year on delegations that came from as far away as Chile, using the municipal war fund to cover some of the expense. In the 1790s, skyrocketing costs of war in Europe pushed officials to economize. In response to orders from the intendant of Córboba, officials in Mendoza cut rations of meat and wine in half in 1797, although Indians who performed valuable services as spies continued to receive full measure.[83]

In northern New Spain, governors drew from a *fondo de aliados* or a *fondo de paz y guerra*,

27. *Conference at Negrete, 1793. While the dragoons and militia maintained formation, Mapuches on horseback put on a display around the ramada where official conversations took place. Soldiers' tents stand in the background. To the left, at a distance, were kitchens, a dining room, a henhouse, and storehouses containing gifts, merchandise, and provisions for soldiers and Indians. To the right, at a distance, a village of temporary ramadas housed the merchants, sutlers, musicians, and civilians. Of the 4,205 people who attended this* parlamento, *2,853 were Mapuches and Pehuenches. They set up their lodgings well beyond the Spanish campground depicted here. (Méndez Beltrán, 1982, 157–59, reproduces and analyzes the contemporary sketch on which this engraving is based.) "Parlamento de Presidente Ambrosio O'Higgins, Negrete, March 3, 1793." From Gay, 1854. Courtesy, John Carter Brown Library at Brown University.*

to supply independent Indians with gifts and entertainment. By 1790, if not before, most of the cash put into these funds came directly from the crown (4,000 pesos in the case of New Mexico), and the presidial supply master used it to purchase gifts, food, and drink. The amount actually spent on gifts, however, varied wildly from year to year. In addition to tapping the *fondo de aliados,* presidial officers entertained and regaled Indians from a catchall fund, the *fondo de gratificaciones,* attached to each presidio. The amounts varied from presidio to presidio and changed over time. In 1796, the royal treasury contributed 16,000 pesos to the *fondo de gratificaciones* for all of the presidios on this immense and dangerous frontier, but local funds might supplement royal funds, as in Texas, where the presidio at San Antonio received additional revenue from the sale of wild horses. Thus it seems unlikely that the crown knew exactly how much was spent on gifts and entertainment for Indians, since funds came from a variety of sources.[84]

Although the precise amount spent on gratifying Indians defies measurement, it was substantial, and there was a direct correlation between Indians' potential to aid Spaniards and the amount spent to mollify them. In New Mexico, for example, Comanche allies received the lion's share of gifts compared to the equally friendly but less numerous Jicarilla Apaches. In Louisiana and West Florida, where Spain had to compete with British and then American traders for Indian loyalties, the annual cost of purchasing gifts for Indians represented a large drain on the economy. It rose from 4,000 pesos in 1769 to 55,209 pesos, or 10 percent of the entire administrative budget, in 1794.[85] Had Spain followed the English practice of sending Indian delegations to Europe to impress them, the costs of entertainment would have been higher. Instead, Spanish officials settled for impressing Indians in viceregal capitals and other imperial cities—many of them more opulent and impressive architecturally than any city in the English colonies.[86]

Certainly not all of the money budgeted for gifts and hospitality found its way to Indians. It appears that some Spanish middlemen found illegal ways to siphon some of the funds to their own accounts.[87] Even the largest sums, however, seemed inadequate to supply Indians' demands. Officials in charge of distributing gifts seemed caught perpetually between the crown's demands for frugality and Indians' demands for generosity.

In the Habsburg era, missionaries obtained converts and workers in exchange for gifts and entertainment, and local officials acquired cheap Indian labor by gifting Indian caciques. In the late Bourbon era, however, gift-giving Spanish officers hoped for little more than security. As Teodoro de Croix baldly put it, Spaniards gave gifts to Indians so they would not need to steal.[88] Buying the "friendship" of potentially hostile tribes seemed like a good return on investment.[89] It was expensive to shower the Mbayás with gifts, the governor of Paraguay observed, but "it will be worse to have them as enemies."[90]

Although Spanish officials self-consciously bribed Indians with gifts, they knew that gifts and hospitality signified voluntary acts of generosity in Native worlds. To be efficacious, gifts had to be presented with magnanimity, equity, and respect. Form was as important as substance. Governor Concha explained to his successor that gifts to Comanches, Utes, Navajos, and Apaches who frequented Santa Fe had to be given by "the hand of the governor himself, in order that they may be more grateful."[91] The bestowing of gifts, which increased the status of the giver, often established an alliance or a familial relationship—a "fictive kinship," and the receipt of gifts came with the obligation of reciprocity, even among "kin." Repayment for gifts might take the form of "courtesies, entertainment, ritual, military assistance, women, children, dances, and feasts," in the words of one scholar.[92]

Native gift economies, in which individuals achieved status by giving away goods rather than accumulating them, did not conform to enlightened Spaniards' notions of Indians as rational consumers and producers. But Indians made their expectations of Spanish largesse clear in the most rational terms. Pehuenches de Malargüe, who had given Spaniards the generous gift of peace, expected generosity in return. Gifts, they had learned from Spanish officers, came in the name of the king, and a powerful cacique like the Spanish king would surely send a generous amount.[93] Adopting a more ingratiating

tone, the powerful Ranquel cacique Carripilún purportedly explained to a Spanish delegation in 1806 that "since we lack good things we have the life of a dog.... The dog loves
whoever gives it [things], and is also grateful and faithful to him." Carripilún observed
that he, too, was loyal and "rational."[94]

In effect, gifts and entertainment were obligatory gestures for maintaining alliances
and friendships between Native societies, yet Spaniards, like Indians, sought to maintain
the fiction that they gave voluntarily. Gifts, Croix told the governor of Texas, should be
given in such a way that Indians "not be given cause for conceit or arrogance nor acquire
our gifts as if we had been forced to give them."[95] Whatever the appearance, however,
the reality was that Spaniards, who *collected* tribute from incorporated Indians, *paid* tribute to independent Indians. Like nomads on the steppes of inner Asia, who built great
empires by extracting tribute from their Chinese neighbors, Apaches, Comanches, Araucanians, Chiriguanos, and others collected taxes from Spaniards who preferred to identify
those taxes as gifts and entertainment.[96] "That which in the name of your majesty are
called favors, they receive as tribute," Chilean Governor Guill y Gonzaga bluntly told
the king in 1766.[97] "Peace is enjoyed on this frontier," the bishop of Concepción wrote
in 1785, "but [is] advantageous only to the enemy," whom Spaniards had to pay and entertain.[98] Indians believe, Antonio de Ulloa wrote after a stint as governor of Louisiana,
that they are "more able, wise, and astute than those who ask them [for peace], fear them,
and give them gifts."[99]

Just as some war hawks opposed trading with Indians, so did they object to giving
them gifts, arguing that presents made Indians insolent rather than cooperative, greedy
rather than grateful.[100] In 1795, one Franciscan bemoaned the lack of Indian gratitude
in the Interior Provinces of New Spain. "Despite the enormous and even excessive kindness with which they are treated," he said, Indians continued their raids, "returning
death and destruction for the gifts and good treatment of their benefactors."[101]

He and other critics of gift giving overstated their case. Indians interpreted graciously
given gifts as signs of good faith, and Spaniards who understood that simple fact gained
and maintained influence with tribes or tribal factions. Gifts also had more influence
within Indian societies than Spaniards supposed. Spaniards certainly recognized the
symbolic power of the staffs of office, medals, flags, and uniforms they distributed to Indian leaders. They did not seem to understand, however, that some European goods acquired new power when they crossed cultural boundaries into Indian societies. Some
Indians believed that European merchandise like medals and flags had power to bring
good or evil and imbued beads and mirrors with such spiritual weight that their owners
took them to the grave.[102]

Building Peace on the Foundations of Commerce

Spanish trade goods and gifts, then, became powerful lubricants for smoothing relationships, and in some areas their use ushered in a period of relative peace that lasted

until the wars of independence in the 1810s. One of those areas was northern New Spain, where Gálvez's *Instrucción* of 1786 may have been less a prescription for change in policy than the reflection of a shift already under way. After 1786, authorities offered independent Indians access to trade, gifts, cooperation against mutual enemies, and equitable and consistent treatment—policies once urged by a handful of officials but now the conventional wisdom.[103] By offering Indians more than life in missions and the absence of war, Spanish authorities increased their chances of forging an enduring peace. They did so with Comanches, Navajos, and many Apache groups, ushering in an era of economic growth and demographic expansion for northern New Spain.[104]

In the case of the western Comanches, the peace pact they signed with Anza in 1786 gave them an entrée to the Spanish market and the promise of equitable treatment at the annual trade fair at Taos, where Comanches complained that New Mexican traders had cheated them in the past.[105] The agreement of 1786 endured into the 1810s, as much because of Comanches' interest in being at peace with Spaniards as because of Spaniards' interest in maintaining peace with them. Eastern and western Comanches alike needed new sources of firearms and ammunition. The French and English firearms that once flowed into the Comanchería from French Louisiana via Wichita and Kansas Indians began to diminish after Spanish officials took over Louisiana in 1766 and gradually restricted the trade. Western Comanches had suffered a rare military defeat in 1779, when Anza's forces (nearly half of them Pueblo Indians) destroyed a Comanche camp in southeastern Colorado and killed a prominent war chief, Cuerno Verde. In 1780–81, a continent-wide smallpox epidemic apparently took a terrible toll throughout the Comanchería. Comanches, then, had their own reasons for making peace in 1786 and maintaining it.[106]

Anza's successor, Fernando de la Concha continued to use gifts and trade to maintain alliances with both Comanches and Navajos (Anza had also signed a peace treaty with Navajos in 1786).[107] Concha described Comanches, whom Spaniards once dismissed as faithless, as especially trustworthy: "In this tribe one finds faith in the treaties that it acknowledges, manifest truth, good hospitality, and decent customs."[108] Under Concha's leadership, Comanches and Navajos joined with Spanish forces to increase military pressure on Gileños, Chiricahuas, Mimbreños, and other Apaches. Meanwhile, Spaniards and their Opata and Pima allies from Sonora and Nueva Vizcaya squeezed Apaches from the south. By the 1790s, many Apaches had sued for peace and its attendant benefits—not only in southern New Mexico, but also across the northern frontier.[109]

Spaniards and their Indian allies had pushed Apaches toward peace by fighting a pitiless war in which Spaniards offered rewards for pairs of Apache ears and sent Apache prisoners into permanent exile.[110] In the spirit of the *Instructions* of 1786, however, Spanish officers had offered the carrot along with the stick. They settled some Apaches on reserves near presidios, gave them weekly rations of corn, meat, tobacco, and sweets, and instructed them in the ways of Spaniards.

In these so-called peace establishments—*establecimientos de paz*—soldiers rather than missionaries tried to convert Apaches into town dwellers who farmed, ranched, practiced

European trades, and learned self-government. Officials in northern New Spain continued to rely on missions to Hispanicize Indians in places where they seemed docile, as in Alta California, but peace establishments became the preferred institution for effecting cultural change among Apaches, who had resisted missions. Pedro de Nava, serving as commander in chief of the Interior Provinces in 1791, expressly forbade missionary proselytizing in the *establecimientos de paz,* lest it annoy Apaches and cause them to flee. Nava supposed that soldiers, like missionaries, would control Apaches' movements; Indians who needed to travel over twenty-five miles from an *establecimiento* were to be issued passports. Nava also ordered the officers who presided over Apaches *de paz* to tolerate "the Indians' crude and gross ways," learn the Apaches' language and customs, dispense Apache justice on the reservations, designate Apache *capitancillos* as judges, and regale Apache chiefs with gifts. He had no illusions that Apache men, "accustomed only to war and hunting," would take up farming and ranching, "but the women and children may." On a personal level, officers were to form friendships with individual Apaches and encourage their own children to play with Apache youngsters.[111]

Peace with the Apache bands, whether they lived inside or outside of *establecimientos de paz,* was never as firm or as enduring as that with Comanches. Even after agreeing to peace, Governor Concha noted in 1790, Gileño Apaches continued to "distrust" Spaniards, "perhaps for good reasons."[112] Continued raids and occasional outbreaks of war notwithstanding, contemporary Spaniards perceived that they had entered a new era in relations with Apaches. With gifts, trade, and diplomacy they had turned former enemies into permanent allies and then used those new allies to control Apaches. "We would not have believed the benefit that has resulted to the province from this policy if we hadn't seen it with our own eyes," one New Mexican recalled in 1812.[113]

Spaniards also tried to convert Comanches and Navajos into town-dwelling farmers without using missionaries. They failed. The commander in chief of the Interior Provinces, Jacobo Ugarte, hoped to introduce both peoples to agricultural settlements following their pacification in 1786. As Ugarte explained, Comanches needed to understand that "the animals they hunt with such effort for sustenance are not at base inexhaustible, like agriculture." Ugarte ordered Anza to settle Spaniards and Pueblo Indians among the Comanches to teach them to farm by example. One Comanche band, the Jupes, agreed. Suffering from drought and eager to firm up their economic relations with New Mexico, which furnished them with trade goods, agricultural products, and a market for captives, meat, and horses, Jupes signed on to build a town on the Arkansas River northeast of Santa Fe. Together with Spanish laborers from Taos, Jupes built and occupied nineteen houses by the winter of 1787 and had more homes under construction. Then tragedy struck. The favorite wife of the band's leader, Paraunarimuco, died, and the Comanches abandoned San Carlos de los Jupes. The town site had become a painful reminder of a death.[114] Spanish efforts to turn Navajos into town dwellers also failed. As Spaniards pushed into Navajo lands in the 1790s, hostilities resumed, and the Spanish–Navajo détente of 1786 unraveled. Punitive expeditions and new peace agreements in 1805 and 1819 were not enough to mend it in the last decades of Spanish rule over New Mexico.[115]

Although Spaniards failed to settle Comanches and Navajos in farming villages, the enlightened ideas that informed their efforts lived on. Lt. Col. Antonio Cordero y Bustamante, a veteran frontier soldier, summarized the new conventional wisdom in 1796. In a discussion of Spanish policy toward Apaches in particular, he observed that the "wise measures" of the Spanish government were bringing the war with Apaches to a close. Spain did "not aspire to the destruction or slavery of these savages," he noted with pride. Rather, it sought "their happiness . . . leaving them in peaceful possession of their homes" while getting them to acknowledge "our justice and our power to sustain it."[116] Instead of dismissing all Apaches as untrustworthy and spurning those who wished to make peace as the crown had ordered in 1772, the current policy was to treat individual Apaches justly, rewarding good behavior and administering "punishments in proportion to the crimes which they commit."[117] Indians who asked for peace were to be granted it, and the Apaches' "crude and gross ways are to be tolerated and their impertinence overlooked."[118]

The pacific policy that Colonel Cordero applauded could not work, however, if it remained clothed in the old justifications for war. Officers intent on destroying Apaches had demonized them. They had portrayed Apaches as innately cruel, treacherous, indolent, and thieving, and they had displayed little interest in understanding Apaches' motives.[119] "Because the Indians' natural unreliability and malice is so well known," one officer noted in 1690, "it will not be necessary to ponder the matter."[120] It sufficed to explain Apache raiding as a consequence of Spaniards' failure to punish them, and there was no reason to negotiate with them since, as Croix observed in 1781, they were "savage Indians of perverse inclinations and customs."[121] If Apaches, Comanches, and other independent Indians were not "capable of responding to reason or persuasion" and "cannot live in peace and tranquility in their own country," as Felipe de Neve proclaimed in 1783, then it stood to reason that nothing less than war would bring peace.[122]

Frontier officers interested in controlling independent Indians through peaceful means needed a more hopeful view of Apaches, and they adopted one. By the end of the century, officers commonly depicted Apaches as fierce, courageous, and skilled warriors who fought to protect themselves from exploitation. In the spirit of the Enlightenment, these officers sought to explain Apaches' aggressive behavior as a response to external forces rather than as an innate characteristic. Apaches possessed "extraordinary robustness" because they lived outdoors and ate basic foods; they moved with great agility, speed, and endurance because of daily exercise and the conditioning of a nomadic life.[123] They waged "cruel and bloody war" against Spaniards because of Spaniards' own "trespasses, excesses and avarice," as Colonel Cordero put it.[124] They robbed because hunting alone would not support their "basic needs" and they would "die of hunger and poverty."[125] "If the Indian is no friend," Bernardo de Gálvez observed, "it is because he owes us no kindness, and . . . if he avenges himself it is for just satisfaction of his grievances." "The truth is," Gálvez wrote, "that they are as much grateful as vengeful, and that this latter [quality of vengeance] we ought to forgive in a nation that has not learned philosophy with which to master a natural feeling."[126] "If the Indians had a defender who could represent their rights on the basis of natural law," another officer wrote in 1799, "an impartial judge could soon see that every charge we might make against them would be offset by as many crimes committed by our side."[127] It was not the case, then, that "Spanish observers . . . failed to understand their own role in provoking or instigating Native American responses," as one historian has asserted without qualification.[128] It was the case that Spaniards usually found it convenient to overlook their own provocations.

On the southern and western frontiers of Buenos Aires, officials also entered into relatively peaceful relations with independent Pampas. There, as in northern New Spain, peace came about when Spaniards treated Indians as if they were reasonable and offered gifts and trade, and when Indians believed they would benefit more from trading than from raiding. Trade in itself had not brought peace with the peoples of the pampa. In the mid-1770s, the Pampas and others had intensified their raids on the estancias south of Buenos Aires even as their commerce with Spaniards accelerated. Indians had continued to run off Spanish livestock on the pampa while trading furs, hides, leatherwork, cloth, ostrich feathers, and salt in Spanish markets on the other side of the Andes. Dwindling herds of feral stock on the pampa and a growing market for livestock in Chile had pushed Indians to appropriate cattle and horses wherever they could be found. One historian has suggested, however, that by the late 1770s some of the Pampas had developed their own herds and wanted peace because they knew that ranching would be more profitable in the absence of war.[129] Perhaps, too, they saw peace with Spaniards in Buenos Aires as a prerequisite for gaining access to its burgeoning market for cattle hides. The creation of the viceroyalty in 1776 and the lifting of trade restrictions in Buenos Aires had sent exports of cattle hides soaring, from some 50,000 per year in midcentury to an average of 758,117 per year between 1792 and 1796. In 1785, Buenos Aires also began to ship salted beef to feed the growing slave population of Cuba.[130]

In the late 1770s, Pampas began to make peace overtures with Buenos Aires. Instead of welcoming them, Viceroy Vértiz duplicitously captured a Pampa ambassador, Licon Pagni, in 1779 and sent him into permanent exile in the Malvinas, some three hundred miles off the coast of southern Patagonia. He prohibited Spaniards from trading with Indians—even with *indios de paz*—and refused to grant a truce or negotiate.[131] In response, at least two Pampa caciques, Guchulep and Callfilqui (whom Spaniards also called Lorenzo), stepped up raiding. Perhaps, as one historian has argued, the two caciques raised the level of violence to force Spaniards to the bargaining table. One of Callfilqui's wounded and captured warriors, however, explained it somewhat differently: "If the Christian does not give peace to [Callfilqui] and send him the Indian men and women that are in Buenos Aires in exchange for the many Christian captives they have there, they will make continual war everywhere in order to get revenge."[132]

The next year, in September 1780, the threat of a British attack on Montevideo caused Viceroy Vértiz to make his own peace overture to the Pampas. Fearful that he would have to divert troops to Montevideo and leave the Indian frontier exposed, Vértiz reluctantly lifted the ban on the Indian trade and held out the olive branch. The Pampas did not reach for it, however, until a new viceroy, the marqués de Loreto, replaced the untrustworthy Vértiz in 1784. Loreto saw what his predecessor had overlooked: Pampa caciques would welcome "peace and legal trade."[133] After a period in which both sides exchanged visits and gave signs of their trustworthiness, Pampa leaders and Spanish officials in Buenos Aires signed a formal treaty in 1790.[134] By then, independent Indians frequented Buenos Aires in small groups at all seasons of the year. They checked in at a frontier military post, received a permit to enter the city, and traded, as another viceroy noted, without "offenses or robberies on their part."[135] After 1790, the roads across the pampa to Córdoba and into the Andes to Mendoza and Chile become safer for Spanish travelers, and the Spanish population in the countryside south of Buenos Aires grew dramatically. The peace that followed the signing of the treaty of 1790 was far from perfect, but it lasted until the end of the colonial period, notwithstanding Viceroy Vértiz's assertion that the "savages do not have sufficient principles to comprehend the power of these pacts."[136]

Spaniards credited commerce with achieving what force had not. Trade with Indians "changes their savage customs and makes them citizens useful to the state," one official reported from Buenos Aires in 1802. "It is well known that commerce performs these miracles, and there is no need to pause to praise it."[137] The following year, a generation after Viceroy Vértiz had prohibited trade with Pampas under pain of death, a Buenos Aires newspaper noted that hardly a day passed without Indians from the pampa entering the city with trade goods—hides, leather goods, feathers, woolen textiles, and other handicrafts. Initially the Indians bartered for yerba maté, tobacco, and liquor, but increasingly, the newspaper said, they traded for European textiles they had begun to use for their clothing. Soon "they will abandon ... their barbarous customs and we will be indebted to commerce for the permanent friendship of the savages, which earlier was believed impossible to maintain."[138]

By the 1790s, the viceroy in Buenos Aires could also boast that residents of Mendoza could ranch, farm, and trade without danger from Pehuenches, Ranqueles, or Huilliches who had plagued the city and its environs. Peace in that part of the Andes began when Spaniards won over a group of Pehuenches who had settled on the Río Malargüe, on the eastern slope of the Andes south of Mendoza (see map 4). The Pehuenches de Malargüe, as Spaniards knew them, had sided with Spaniards in Chile during a Mapuche rebellion in the 1760s and, as one of their caciques later put it, they were expelled by other Pehuenches and forced "to search for a life on the other side."[139] Before their exile, Pehuenches de Malargüe had made both sides of the Andes their home, crossing mountain passes at will and raiding estancias near Mendoza, San Luis, and other places in the province of Cuyo, which had been the weakest link in frontier defense between Buenos Aires and Concepción.[140] After moving to the eastern side of the Andes, the Pehuenches continued to raid. In 1770, when Spaniards tried to build a fort in Pehuenche

28. *At age twenty-four, E. E. Vidal arrived in Buenos Aires in 1816 with the British navy, served there for the next three years, and drew a number of sketches. This engraving, based on one of his sketches, first appeared in 1820 in his book* Picturesque illustrations of Buenos Ayres and Monte Video.
It portrayed Pampas in Buenos Aires, he noted, "at the door of a store in the Indian market . . . at which their manufactures are purchased wholesale, and retailed to the inhabitants" (p. 55). The Pampas brought ponchos, leather work, hides, boots, stirrups, and ostrich feather dusters and traded them for "brandy, Paraguay tea or matté, sugar, confectionery, figs, raisins, spurs, bits, knives, &c." (57). The Argentine, Vidal said, "is indebted to the savage Indian for the supply of many of his wants, and some of his luxuries" (p. 55). "Pampa Indians," reproduced from Vidal, 1943, a facsimile edition, following p. 52.

territory at San Carlos, some sixty miles south of Mendoza, the Pehuenches de Malargüe attacked it and wiped out the small guard. Continued Pehuenche attacks on the struggling garrison at Fort San Carlos brought Spanish retaliation. Between 1779 and 1781 the intrepid José Francisco de Amigorena sent punishing expeditions from Mendoza into the uncharted lands below the Río Diamante. Militia forces carried away women and children and left behind burned villages and scorched earth.

Military victories, Amigorena recognized, would not bring permanent peace and might even be counterproductive by stirring up the desire for revenge among his Indian adversaries. Offering to return captives, including the principal wife of one cacique, Amigorena drew the Pehuenches de Malargüe into conversations. He achieved remarkable results. Between 1783 and 1786, twenty-nine caciques signed individual treaties in which each side promised peace and mutual assistance. Some of the Pehuenches de Malargüe agreed to settle in the Valle de Uco, near Fort San Carlos, where they received regular rations and trading privileges both at the fort and in Mendoza. The arrangement resembled the *establecimientos de paz* that officers in northern New Spain had created for Apaches, although there is no evidence that Spaniards saw a need to turn the pastoral Pehuenche stockmen and merchants into farmers or to make them abandon their tents for more permanent structures.

With Pehuenches de Malargüe as his allies, Amigorena pressured a more southerly group of Pehuenches, those at Balbarco, to sue for peace in 1787. As Amigorena's alliances with Pehuenches grew stronger, Ranqueles felt more isolated and, after a multiyear courtship, their leading cacique, Carripilún, signed a pact in 1799, just months before Amigorena's death. These arrangements lasted into the 1820s.[141]

Amigorena built an enduring peace with the eastern Pehuenches and Ranqueles in much the same way Anza forged a détente with Comanches. Like Anza, he first won respect on the field of battle, then maintained that respect by developing personal relationships: he served as godfather to baptized Indian captives, delivered on his promises of military aid, and generously bestowed gifts in the manner of a successful cacique. Years later his widow recalled how he had given away his own clothes to "his loyal and obedient [Indian] allies."[142] When viceregal officials suggested it would be in Spain's interest if Amigorena allowed Huilliches and Pehuenches to destroy one another, Amigorena acknowledged the advantage but invoked "Natural Law," suggesting the immorality of this strategy, and made clear that he preferred the crown's policy of peace.[143]

Yet, to credit Amigorena with bringing about peace single-handedly, as Spanish officials and many historians after them have done, is to tell only half the story. Like the Comanches, Pehuenches and Ranqueles had their reasons for making peace and keeping peace. In the case of Pehuenches de Malargüe, wars with Huilliches and Ranqueles and a civil war with Pehuenches de Balbarco had diminished their numbers to perhaps eighteen hundred to two thousand by 1780. Turning Spaniards from enemies into allies, then, seemed a prudent alternative to captivity or death. Spaniards also offered manufactured goods and a granary. Exiled from the land of the *pehuenes*, the pine trees whose nuts—

harvested and stored for the winter—had been the staple of their diet, the Pehuenches de Malargüe adapted to Spanish wheat from Mendoza. For their part, residents of Mendoza welcomed the Pehuenches' military assistance and trade goods (salt and woolen ponchos and blankets), along with grazing lands that peace had made accessible. By 1788, enough Spaniards from Mendoza had settled near Fort San Carlos to form a *villa*, or town. Each side had economic reasons, then, to appreciate peace.[144]

Some contemporaries believed that force had played an insignificant role in pushing independent Indians toward accommodation. One informed observer, the Buenos Aires–born legal advisor to the cabildo of Buenos Aires, Feliciano Chiclana, noted that when the "wild nation" of Ranqueles that had settled on the pampa south of Córdoba in the 1770s came to terms with Spaniards in 1796, it "was not due to frontier forts, nor to the small number of soldiers." Rather, he said, it resulted from "the interests and utility that the Indians see in their trade in skins, feathers, and manufactured goods." Eight years later, Spanish settlers had moved their farms and ranches fifty to seventy-five miles beyond the protective cordon of fortifications and still Ranqueles had not disturbed them.[145] Chiclana may have been correct in this instance, but it would be naïve to underestimate the profound impact of force, or the threat of force, in pushing Indians and Spaniards alike to prefer peace.

Although the destructive effects of raiding and warfare often gave Spaniards and Indians incentives to take the first steps toward peace, peaceful relations endured only when leaders on both sides believed that peace served their economic interests. Pehuenches, Pampas, Comanches, Navajos, and other sizable Indian groups had come to share that view with Spanish neighbors in the late colonial period. Where that did not occur, as in much of the Chaco, Indians continued to raid and Spanish officials continued to build forts and plan military actions that might hold Indians at bay "for fear of our arms."[146]

The Failure of Commerce on Strategic Frontiers

Spaniards had their best chance of using gifts, trade, and diplomacy to come to accord with independent Indians on frontiers where they had a monopoly on European manufactures. On the strategic frontiers of the empire, where Indians could play one European power off against another, Spain often came out on the losing side. Spanish merchants simply could not offer merchandise at competitive prices, and Indians judged, often correctly, that the quality and quantity of Spanish goods and gifts compared unfavorably to those offered by other Europeans. Bourbon authorities had chipped away at trade restrictions, monopolies, and taxes that kept prices of manufactured goods high in the colonies, but they still remained so high that they encouraged Spain's own subjects to smuggle. Then, too, Spain's manufacturing capabilities and economic infrastructure continued to lag behind Britain's, leaving Spanish merchants at a disadvantage in obtaining goods and credit they needed for the Indian trade.[147] When Spain suffered a British blockade and lost control of the seas in the 1790s, its ability to ship goods to America diminished dramatically.[148] Thus, at the very time that the idea of using commerce to control independent Indians came into fashion in Spain, its ability to deliver goods declined. This had dire consequences in areas where Spain vied with foreigners for the loyalties of Indians, as in southeastern North America, the Mosquito Coast, Darién, and the northeastern Chaco.

In northern Paraguay, where they vied with the Portuguese for the affections of the Mbayás, frustrated Spanish authorities learned that the law of supply and demand outweighed gifts and diplomacy. In the 1770s and 1780s, Spanish ranchers pushed up the Río Paraguay beyond Asunción into Mbayá territory.[149] As Spaniards increased their herds of cattle and horses, Mbayás reduced them, trading the stolen livestock to the Portuguese in neighboring Mato Grosso for metal tools and gold. The Portuguese in Mato Grosso needed livestock. Spaniards in northern Paraguay had a surplus. The Portuguese had gold as well as metal tools. The Mbayás followed the market. In this respect, they resembled their Spanish neighbors in Concepción, whose proclivity for trading illegally with the Portuguese was well known.[150]

In 1791, the year after the Portuguese founded Nueva Coimbra on the edge of Spanish territory, several Mbayá caciques entered into a formal alliance with the Portuguese at the new fort. Spanish officials countered by making their own alliances with sixteen Mbayá caciques in 1792 and with twenty-seven more in 1793, giving them bastones with silver handles and other gifts.[151] Even as some Mbayá caciques came over to the Spanish side, others continued to appropriate Spanish stock for the Portuguese markets. Spanish–Mbayá relations deteriorated when enraged militia from Concepción massacred a group of unarmed Mbayás in 1796 (an act censured by the governor in Asunción).

Some officials toyed with an ill-considered scheme to capture all of the Mbayas' horses and turn these equestrians into pedestrians, but, in the main, Spanish officials continued to try to engage the Mbayás through trade and gifts. Too weak to fight the Mbayás, the commandant at Fort San Carlos was reduced, as he described it in 1797, to giving them gifts and treating them "with affection to keep their good friendship and peace."[152] Gov. Lázaro de Ribera declared in 1803 that Spanish forces "will not proceed against them offensively, except in cases of insults or resistance" and urged giving the Mbayás cattle and sheep so that "forgetting their savage and wandering life, they will change by necessity into herders and farmers." Although Ribera regarded the Mbayás as "perfidious and bloody thieves," he hoped his conciliatory plan "would civilize them little by little."[153] Miguel Lastarria, the legal advisor to Viceroy Avilés, also counseled Spaniards to turn the other cheek toward the Mbayás and other independent Indians who lived on Spain's strategic frontiers, but he carried the argument further. They "should not be characterized as thieves," he wrote in 1804, because of the "state of ignorance and savagery in which they find themselves."[154] Gifts, cattle, understanding, and "affection," however, failed to match Portuguese markets for return on investment. Mbayá raids on Spanish livestock continued, and most Mbayás remained in the Portuguese orbit.[155]

Spain's effort to entice the Cunas of Darién away from their British trading partners provides another example of Spain's relative weakness on its strategic frontiers. In 1787, Cuna leaders traveled to Turbaco, near Cartagena, where they met with the viceroy of New Granada, Antonio Caballero y Góngora, at his residence. They arrived at Cartagena on the *Amistad,* a vessel owned by one Henry Hooper, whom the viceroy had hired to persuade them to come. The Cunas trusted Hooper. They had traded with him for two decades, and he served as their translator, apparently speaking Spanish and "English, which many of the Indians spoke." Led by a "cacique general" known to Spaniards as Bernardo of Estola, the Cuna caciques (who included a Capt. William Hall and a Capt. Jack) signed a peace treaty in which they declared themselves vassals of the Spanish crown and subject to punishment as rebels if they violated the treaty's terms. They agreed to allow colonists to enter Darién and promised to stop trading with all foreigners except Spaniards. Bernardo also agreed to leave a son as a hostage, an acceptable practice under international law in treaties between nations; his fate is not known.[156]

The Cunas (and perhaps Hooper as well) seem to have entered into these discussions to promote trade at a time when a growing Spanish military presence in Darién was hindering their commerce with other Europeans. Spanish authorities, desperate to control Darién and aware that they lacked force to do it, offered Cunas more than they gave. The viceroy met the Cunas' demand that they be permitted to sell their products in Spanish markets—even in cities like Panama, Porto Bello, and Cartagena. If the Indians could not find a buyer or if Spaniards offered lower prices than English traders paid, the commanding officer of the nearest military post would purchase the Cunas' products on the king's account. Spaniards who tried to cheat Cunas would be punished. Two years later, in Cartagena on October 25, 1789, a new viceroy, Francisco Gil y Lemos, signed another pact with Cuna leaders that similarly obligated the Indians to avoid trade with foreigners and to remain "faithful friends of the Spaniards."[157] In that same agreement, however, Gil y Lemos announced that Spain would evacuate three forts in Darién. Spain could not afford to maintain them, much less have its commanders buy Cuna goods. Spain withdrew from Darién the next year, and Cunas resumed trading with the British.

Spanish attempts to lure Miskitos from the British sphere came to a similar end. An extraordinary opportunity for a Spanish–Miskito détente presented itself in 1786 when England agreed to surrender its claims to the Mosquito Coast and other points in the Caribbean to Spain in exchange for clear title to Belize. In making this transfer, England extracted a promise from Carlos III that he "will not exercise any act of severity against the Mosquitos . . . on account of the connections which may have subsisted between the said Indians and the English." In turn, King George III of Britain agreed to "strictly prohibit all his subjects from furnishing arms, or warlike stores, to the Indians . . . situated upon the frontiers of the Spanish possessions."[158] The next year, when over twenty-five hundred disgruntled English settlers and their slaves pulled out of the coast and moved to Belize, Spain tried to fill the vacuum. It sent more than a thousand colonists from poor regions of Spain—Asturias, Galicia, and the Canary Islands—along with soldiers and black slaves from the Caribbean, who Spanish authorities believed were better suited than whites to labor under the tropical sun. Tropical diseases, however, took the lives of the colonists, soldiers deserted, and many of the black slaves fled to live with Zambo-Miskitos, who had absorbed blacks for two centuries.[159]

At the same time Spain tried to occupy the Mosquito Coast with troops and colonists, it tried to buy the good will of the Miskitos with gifts, kind treatment, and trade goods. That plan, carried out "in imitation of the English," as one local official put it, became official policy at the highest level.[160] Speaking in the name of Carlos III, the secretary of state, the conde de Floridablanca, explained the strategy in 1787 in a private memo to the king's council. Spain, Floridablanca said, needed to win the Miskitos over with "favors, gifts, and all manner of good treatment" and take the same approach in all "the principal places where we border other nations."[161] In the case of the Miskitos, kind treatment would disabuse them of "the bad ideas and impressions of Spaniards that our enemies have given them." Spanish officials, he said, should make the Miskitos understand that the English operated in "bad faith" and intended to take over Miskito lands when they had sufficient strength. As evidence of the Englishmen's bad intentions, Floridablanca wanted Spanish officials to explain to Miskitos what the English "have done with the Indians of the North, where now exists the new United States of the American colonies."[162]

Again, Spanish resources could not match Spanish strategy. In Central America as elsewhere, administrative expenses exceeded income in the late colonial period, and Spain could not compete with the British in offering Indians manufactured goods of high quality.[163] Ironically, Spanish authorities had to turn to British traders to supply Spanish merchants with manufactured goods for the Miskito trade. They relied mainly on Colville Cairns, a disreputable Scotsman, and Robert Hodgson, Jr., an Englishman who had lived on the Mosquito Coast at Bluefields since 1750 and knew its politics better than anyone of his generation. Both had stayed on after England left the coast, and they continued to import British manufactures while living under the Spanish flag. But Spanish shopkeepers peddling British goods failed to win the loyalty of the Miskitos. Spanish merchants did not extend generous credit to Indians or sell them muskets, powder, and shot, as their British predecessors had.[164] It might be a mistake, however, to look solely at credit and trade goods to explain Spain's failure to win the loyalty of Miskitos from the British. One historian has argued that the British outflanked the Spanish in Darién because they had a deeper understanding of Cuna society and dealt more effectively with its leaders. The same might be said of British dealings with Miskitos, although British traders' lack of scruples about arming Indians must have added immeasurably to their influence.[165]

As Spain's growing troubles in Europe limited its access to manufactured goods, its plan to placate Miskito leaders with annual gifts and trade goods proved unworkable. In 1797, officials in Guatemala City offered Miskito leaders an annual salary instead of gifts. The Zambo-Miskitos, led by King George II (1777–1800), preferred the gifts. Unsuccessful at ending the impasse, a frustrated Spanish agent advocated eliminating King George II by poisoning him. That plan, condemned by the president of Guatemala as a "horrible project," never went forward, but King George II proceeded to eliminate Spaniards.[166] In 1800, he led an attack on Río Tinto, destroying the only Spanish settlement along the Mosquito Coast and freeing the remaining black slaves. Although England had withdrawn officially from the coast, British subjects drifted back. Spaniards continued to try to buy Miskito loyalty with gifts but never established a firm presence. Spain, Carlos IV lamented, was "unable to make a few miserable divided Indians respect it."[167]

In southeastern North America also, Spain's shortage of trade goods hindered its ability to keep Caddos and Wichitas in its orbit, but Spain had some success in winning over Indians menaced by the expanding United States: Cherokees, Chickasaws, Choctaws, Creeks, Alabamas, and Seminoles (see map 2).[168] Spain had given Florida and the coastal region east of the Mississippi to England at the end of the Seven Years' War in 1763, but twenty years later, when Spain won the Floridas back from Britain, it found itself face-to-face with the newly independent United States. Each country claimed ownership of territory that Indians actually controlled. As Carlos IV's council observed in 1792, "In the Floridas we occupy only the ports and forts of Mobile, Pensacola, and St. Augustine and their surrounding areas; the Indians occupy and utilize the interior of the country."[169]

Neither Spain nor the United States had sufficient military force to conquer the powerful Indian nations who controlled southeastern North America, but each tried to win their loyalty through trade, as the British had before them. The southeastern Indian tribes had less affection for the land-hungry Anglo Americans, however, than Miskitos or Cunas did for British traders. Indeed, some southeastern Indians found much to abhor in the black slave societies of the Carolinas and Georgia.[170]

As on the Mosquito Coast, Spanish authorities in Florida had to rely on British manufacturers and merchants to supply the Natives with the tools, clothing, and liquor they had become accustomed to receive as gifts and trade goods. The most successful of these British enterprises, the firm of Panton, Leslie, & Company, was owned by two Scots and had its beginnings in British Florida. When Spain reacquired Florida from Britain in 1783, the partners had stayed on. The crown made the rare exception of allowing the firm to import goods directly from England, since Spanish sources could not fill local demand for goods for the Indian trade from Spanish sources. Panton, Leslie took advantage of its privileged position to expand operations westward, establishing trading posts at San Marcos de Apalachee, Pensacola, Mobile, and finally, in 1795, at Fort San Fernando (present-day Memphis). Indian leaders were not shy about pressing their competing suitors for more gifts and better trading conditions. Although Spanish officials remained suspicious of the Scottish firm, fearing, as one put it, that the foreigners might "alienate the Indians from Spanish friendship," Panton, Leslie helped Spain maintain the ostensible loyalty of southeastern tribes. Florida Indians, a Spanish officer noted with satisfaction in 1787, were "abandoning the barbarousness of wandering without a fixed residence" and, with the help of black slaves, traded furs and livestock to Panton, Leslie representatives. Outsiders could enter their villages and be treated with "good faith" by Indians who had become dependent on "our commerce."[171]

In 1795, when Spain blundered toward a war with Britain, these ties unraveled. Hoping to win the neutrality of the United States, if not its friendship, Spain surrendered its claims to West Florida above the 31st parallel. Along with its claims, it lost its alliances with Creeks, Choctaws, and Chickasaws, whose lands now fell squarely in U.S. territory. Five years later, in 1800, France forced a weakened Spain to cede Louisiana in a secret treaty, and its hard-won alliances with Indians in that quarter vanished as well.[172]

The Limits of Dominion

From the example of their European rivals, Bourbon administrators learned they could exert influence on independent Indians without exercising dominion over them or paying the cost of governing them. Until their withdrawal from the Mosquito Coast in 1787, for example, English traders recognized Natives as legitimate rulers, and those rulers, in turn, remained fiercely loyal to Englishmen. Not only did Britain avoid the expenses of governance, but its citizens profited from the arrangement. A small number of Miskitos fishing turtles brought in more revenue for English traders in 1769 than fifty thousand tribute-paying Indians in Nicaragua provided for the Spanish crown in that same year.[173]

The thrifty example of England and France inspired Spanish critics and policymakers. The author of the *Nuevo sistema* put it succinctly: "To prefer dominion over the advantages and utilities of commerce and friendly trade with the savage nations caused past conquests to end badly and others . . . not to be carried out."[174] Few Spanish officials went as far as the conde de Aranda, who, in the belief that Spain would collect more from trade than from taxes, advised Carlos III that "your Majesty should rid himself of all his dominions on the continent of both Americas."[175] Bourbon officials did, however, come to see practical advantages to abandoning long-held claims to territory that Spaniards had not occupied and to recognizing the sovereignty of independent Indians. Indians themselves pushed Bourbon policymakers in this new direction.[176]

Initially Spain claimed much of the New World by right of discovery, the controversial papal donations of 1493, and the Spanish–Portuguese realignment in the Treaty of Tordesillas of 1494, which gave Spain all but the eastern portion of South America (see map 1). By the late eighteenth century, however, Spanish officials understood, as Malaspina vividly put it, that "an arbitrary [papal] decree that runs from one pole to the other" would not assure Spanish possession over most of the hemisphere, much less over its peoples. Spain could guarantee its borders only through "authentic treaties with other European powers."[177] Acting on that premise, Bourbons had surrendered claims to dominion in the heart of South America when they came under heavy pressure from the Portuguese. In the Treaty of Madrid, signed in 1750, Spain conceded the fact that the Portuguese had moved westward, far beyond the Tordesillas line. The Treaty of Madrid called for a new border, and Spanish and Portuguese surveyors set out to locate natural boundaries, rather than imaginary lines, to separate their possessions.[178]

Even as Spain retreated in the face of Portuguese expansion, however, it tried to expand where it seemed to serve its strategic interests. In 1762, Carlos III reluctantly acquired Louisiana, knowing that it had lost money for France but would buffer New Spain from the British Colonies. In 1788, he sent colonists to the Mosquito Coast to replace the British, who had left the year before. Under Carlos III, Spain also moved to firm up its claims to territory where neither Spaniards nor other Europeans lived: the Falklands, Patagonia, Easter Island, Tahiti, Alta California, and Vancouver Island. The Bourbons recognized that only occupancy buttressed territorial claims. They sent poor residents from the Canary Islands and Iberia to strategic frontiers, from Louisiana to Patagonia, and even permitted foreign Catholics to settle in some particularly vulnerable areas. Until the end of the colonial era, however, Spain had more places to colonize than it had colonists, and it lacked resources to sustain those it sent. At Carmen de Patagones, founded in 1779 at the mouth of the Río Negro in Patagonia, a handful of colonists lived in caves for a generation before the government fulfilled a promise to build housing. Unable to colonize effectively its far-flung pieces of real estate, the government sent soldiers and convicts to built forts. Some of those structures were so small and lightly garrisoned, however, as to be symbolic—mere "signs that the land is ours," one of the king's advisors acknowledged.[179]

Critics argued that constructing forts to hold sparsely populated lands drained the treasury and served little purpose. Malaspina observed that Spain lost money building military posts to establish the right of possession, while its rivals made money by building trading posts. He thought it foolhardy for Spain to build forts on the Pacific coast of North America to stop Russian expansion. He dismissed the cordon of forts that crossed New Spain's Interior Provinces as little more than "fodder" for the savages: "A border that consumes a million pesos to defend property worth 100,000 pesos should be avoided."[180] A generation earlier, the marqués de Rubí had recommended that Spain stop trying to expand in northern New Spain and withdraw instead to a more realistic position closer to the edges of Hispanic settlement. Spain, he said, should build a line of forts that would control only those regions that Spain could effectively occupy—"what should be called the dominion and true possessions of the King."[181] Malaspina, however, suggested that Rubí did not go far enough. Spain, he argued, should forgo costly forts altogether and let colonists develop the region by trading peacefully with Indians. Misinformed by Thomas Jefferson's *Notes on Virginia* (1787), Malaspina pointed to the United States as the model for peaceful, low-cost relations with Indians.[182]

Malaspina's advice went unheeded. Spain never withdrew its garrisons from the coast of Alta California or the Interior Provinces, although economic stringency forced it to abandon some of its symbolic garrisons. Forts at Nootka (1789–95) on Vancouver Island and on Neah Bay on the Strait of Juan de Fuca (1792–95), some one thousand miles by sea above San Francisco, much like their remote counterparts on the Patagonian coast, could not be sustained.[183]

Although Spain claimed dominion over American land, the exact nature of that dominion raised a number of questions that Spanish jurists continued to grapple with in

the eighteenth century. Did the papal donation give Spain permanent or temporary dominion over the lands of the New World? Did dominion include the inhabitants as well
as the land? If it included the inhabitants, did dominion extend to organized societies
with governmental structures or only to savages who seemed to lack government?[184]

Early on, these troubling questions had prompted the crown to seek additional legal
justification for its rule over Indians, and it did so in part by entering into contractual
arrangements with them. At first, it sanctioned the use of the notorious *requerimiento* of
1513, a legal document (from the Spanish point of view) that unilaterally required Indians
to recognize the Spanish crown as their sovereign or face destruction.[185] As the *requerimiento*, with its tortured logic, fell from favor in Spain (it never seems to have enjoyed
favor among Indians), Spaniards simply demanded the allegiance of Indians who occupied
Spanish-claimed land. When Indians resisted and succumbed to Spanish force, Spaniards
offered terms of peace. Few of these agreements appear to have been written, and so we
have only a hazy idea of their nature. What is known of the early accords suggests that
they were, in general, little more than terms of surrender—unilateral directives masquerading as bilateral agreements. Usually negotiating from a position of weakness, Indians
promised to keep peace, free captives, fight with Spaniards against other Indians, live in
assigned areas, accept missionaries, pay tribute, put themselves at the complete service
of the crown, and leave their leaders' sons as hostages or human surety bonds.[186] In advice
to Spanish caudillos published in 1599, Capt. Bernardo de Vargas Machuca spelled out
the ideal peace arrangement: Indians should surrender everything in exchange for Spanish
protection from enemies.[187]

When relations of power between Indians and Europeans were markedly unequal,
treaties served, in the words of one scholar, as "a weapon in the arsenal of the stronger
power." Indians in a relatively weak position signed agreements that made them "virtually
captive to the rules of a society that they still saw as alien."[188] This appears to have been
the case with a series of agreements Spaniards entered into with Lipan and Mescalero
Apaches between 1781 and 1799, in Texas, Coahuila, Nuevo Santander, and Nuevo León.
Weakened by struggles with the Spanish military, by Comanches, and by internal conflicts,
bands of these eastern Apaches began to seek peace with Spanish officers. In most of
these agreements, Spanish officers dispensed gifts and titles to Indian leaders and permitted them to trade in Spanish forts and towns under certain conditions, but Indians
made most of the concessions. They had to return captives (Spaniards agreed to return
only unbaptized captives), live in restricted areas (sometimes close to Spanish forts),
prevent crimes against Spaniards, and fight with Spaniards against common enemies.[189]
In 1787, for example, some Mescalero leaders entered into an agreement at Presidio del
Norte. The pact required the Mescaleros, whose population Spaniards estimated at
three thousand, to live near the fort and not to leave the area without a written permit.
Instead of receiving rations, they would support themselves by farming and stock raising
—supplemented by hunting, with special permission. Not surprisingly, Mescaleros failed
to meet the terms of the agreement, which some Spanish officers saw as unrealistic.[190]

Spanish officials referred to the Mescalero accord as a *capitulación*.[191] That word could serve as a synonym for a treaty, as scholars have pointed out, but it could also signify a contract between parties of unequal strength or a concession from the strong to the weak, that is, a capitulation. Terms such as *artículos de paz* ("articles of peace") and *tratado* ("treaty") generally implied greater equality between the parties, but those words, too, could also describe a document of surrender.[192] Each of these words may have held precise meaning for jurists, but legal distinctions blurred in practice as Spanish officials used them interchangeably.

When Spaniards had the upper hand, they saw no need to negotiate with Indians as if they were a sovereign people,[193] but Indians who successfully resisted Spanish aggression forced Spanish officials to regard them as appropriate subjects for negotiations and treaties that recognized their sovereignty. Mapuches may have been the first group to negotiate a written treaty of peace with Spaniards without surrendering their sovereignty. At Quillín in 1641, some Mapuche leaders agreed to a written treaty with the governor of Chile in which they purportedly recognized "their vassalage" to the Spanish crown, accepted "the Royal protection of his Majesty," and permitted missionaries to come among them. Much hinged on the meanings that "vassalage" and "protection" held for Mapuches, and one historian makes a convincing case that in this and subsequent treaties Araucanians and other Indians regarded these words as "signifying a relationship of brotherhood, a reciprocal military alliance, and a promise of assistance."[194] Whatever their thoughts, Araucanians' actions make it obvious that they did not see themselves as Spanish subjects. Neither, legal niceties aside, did Spaniards. The powerful Mapuches forced Spaniards to regard the Río Biobío as a permanent boundary. South of the river these *indios amigos,* as Spaniards in Chile called their new Mapuche allies, had no obligation to pay tribute to the king, as did other Indian vassals between the ages of eighteen and fifty-two, or to provide labor to the crown or to serve individual Spaniards. If Indians worked for Spaniards, it was to be voluntary, and they were to be paid.[195] Parlamentos, written treaties, and generous distributions of gifts became standard mechanisms through which Spaniards maintained peace with Mapuches. Nearly a century later, one embarrassed military officer lamented that his countrymen "make peace treaties with them as with a foreign power."[196]

The Treaty of Quillín of 1641, with its implicit recognition of the independence of the crown's Araucanian "vassals," represented an exception to the Habsburg policy of requiring Indians to surrender, settle in *reducciones,* become Catholics, and pay tribute. This treaty was also exceptional because it was written rather than oral, ratified in Spain, and the only treaty with Indians to appear in a twelve-volume published compendium of treaties that Spain signed with other nations through the mid-1700s.[197] Mapuches, then, had won an extraordinary acknowledgment of their sovereignty at that early date and enjoyed de facto independence until the end of the colonial era. When Capt. Tomás O'Higgins traveled through Araucanian lands south of the Bíobio in 1797, he met friendly caciques who swore loyalty to the crown, but he understood that he had traveled from "our lands" into "their lands." Told by O'Higgins that Mapuches had stolen livestock from a group of Spaniards traveling north toward Valdivia, the cacique Millapanhi assured O'Higgins that Spaniards themselves "were to blame because besides entertaining them very stingily, there were some [in the group] who did not even visit their houses to greet them."[198] Millapanhi had no doubt about whose territory the Spaniards had entered.

Written treaties between Spaniards and Indians became more frequent in the last half of the 1700s, as the Bourbons faced up to the reality that they needed to come to terms with Indians whom they could neither defeat nor convert.[199] By definition, nations make treaties with other nations, not with their own subjects, yet in many cases Spanish negotiators signed treaties with Indian peoples Spain chose to define as vassals, as it had Araucanians. This may seem anomalous, but European states engaged in such a practice among themselves and continued the practice in French America, Spanish America, English America, and the United States.[200] As one German jurist summarized a long-standing facet of European international law in 1788, "Mere alliances of protection, tribute or vassalage, which a state may contract with another, do not hinder it from continuing [to be] perfectly sovereign."[201] Even when they succeeded in requiring Indian nations to put themselves under the crown's protection, then, sophisticated Spanish negotiators did not necessarily believe that Indians had surrendered all sovereignty. Sovereignty was divisible under European international law. And of course, Indians who enjoyed sovereignty in fact did not imagine they had lost it. After the Treaty of Quillín, no Spanish treaties with independent Indian nations appear to have made their way into published compilations of Spanish international accords. Later treaties between Indians and Bourbons, however, reveal much about the way Indians wrung concessions from Spanish officials.[202]

Spaniards believed that written treaties had legal force and could be reviewed, so officers took as much care with their form as with their substance. They found it vexing, however, to deal with kin-based tribal societies that played by different rules. At the most basic level, Spanish officers understood that many Indian groups had no permanent single leader. An annoyed post commander in Arkansas complained of the difficulty in working out agreements with the Quapaws: "It is necessary to make all of them happy, since among these people every voice is equal—the great and the small." Teodoro de Croix similarly lamented the futility of negotiating with Apaches, "a crowd of savages, scattered and without a head, because each Indian is a free republic."[203] He did not mean that as a compliment. To enlightened Spaniards, societies that did not have a single leader seemed dysfunctional, if not freakish—"a monster with many heads," as one friar put it.[204]

On some occasions pragmatic Spanish officers understood that a group had two or more leaders and accepted the fact that they had no choice but to negotiate with them rather than with a single head of state. Eager to begin construction of a new fort, San Rafael, on the Río Diamante over 120 miles south of Mendoza, one militia captain signed a treaty with twenty-three Pehuenche caciques in 1805.[205] Spanish officers preferred, however, to identify a single individual who could be held responsible for enforcing a treaty's terms. Thus, if a kin-based society lacked a single head, Spaniards, like representatives of other colonial powers, often designated one. Anza apparently orchestrated the election of Ecueracapa as chief of the Comanche nation, then put him on the Spanish payroll with the title of captain general and a salary of two hundred pesos a year to be paid in goods.[206] Similarly, New Mexico officials insisted as a condition of peace with Navajos in 1819 that they name "a general of the Navajo nation so that this government of New Mexico might have someone to direct itself to," and the Navajo nation would have someone to "govern and direct it."[207]

The lengths to which Spaniards went to convince themselves that a single individual spoke for an entire people can be seen in dealings that Gov. Gerónimo de Matorras of Tucumán had with the Mocobí leader Paikín and his successor, Queyaveri. In 1773, Governor Matorras asked the king for permission to negotiate with the "famous elder" Paikín, characterizing him extravagantly as "the principal leader or chief of all the nations of Indians in the Gran Chaco."[208] The next year, when he traveled into the Chaco, however, Matorras learned that Paikín was just one of several Mocobí chiefs. Nonetheless, in his official correspondence Matorras continued to describe Paikín as the principal leader of all native peoples in the Chaco and to treat him as such.[209] Matorras had much to gain.

After years of hostility toward Spaniards, Paikín had initiated discussions with Matorras. He said he wanted baptism and peace, and Matorras soon learned he also wanted firearms and Spanish allies in a war against Abipones. He denied Paikín the firearms, but he had him baptized, drew up terms of peace and alliance, and showered him with gifts, including a gold-handled bastón and a suit of fancy clothing. He also promised to build a mission in Paikín's territory to teach religion, along with reading and writing in Spanish, to the young. In exchange, Matorras required Paikín to swear to become a vassal of the Spanish crown but guaranteed the Mocobíes possession of their lands and exemption from tribute. Like other officials who favored pacification over war, Matorras understood that there could be no peace if Spanish *hacendados* and self-serving officers pressed Indians into servitude or despoiled them of their lands. The treaty-signing ceremony, held in July 1774 on the Río Bermejo some 240 leagues from Salta and 60 leagues from Corrientes, represented a triumph for Matorras. It ended with Indians shouting three times, "Long live the King of Spain and the Indies, Carlos the Third"—or so the governor told the king.[210]

Paikín appears to have been one of several Mocobí leaders, but his connection with Matorras seemed to give him an edge over the others. After his death at the hands of Abipones in 1776, Mocobí and Toba caciques took the unhappy news to Salta, along with their wish to renew the treaty. Indian and Spanish leaders alike understood the intensely personal nature of these alliances and sought to renew treaties when original signatories died. On the frontiers of the empire, people made treaties with people, not with abstractions called nations.[211] The caciques also brought Paikín's gold-handled bastón. His widow, they explained, wished to return it to the governor because her children were not old enough to exercise authority. Matorras delegated a Franciscan to return to the Chaco with the caciques and award the bastón to another leader, Queyaveri, naming him the "principal cacique." Queyaveri received the bastón with great pleasure, the friar said, "asking me that I do the same thing the next day in the presence of the other caciques."[212]

Just as Spaniards preferred to negotiate with a single chief in order to legitimize treaties with so-called Indian nations, so did Indian leaders like Queyaveri appear to welcome the Spaniards' imprimatur in order to enhance their position as first among equals within their own societies. One well-informed New Mexican understood that Comanche leaders disdained "the titles they receive from their own government . . . unless they are confirmed by our officials in the name of the Great Captain [the king]."[213]

Precisely what an Indian leader's anointment by Europeans signified to other members of his tribe or band must have varied from one Indian society to another and may never be fully understood. It is certain, however, that Spanish authorities altered hierarchies and unintentionally sowed discord within tribal societies as they designated Indian leaders. It is also clear that some Indian leaders valued recognition as paramount chiefs because of the gifts, honors, and status that followed. Spaniards apparently gave those leaders the means to gain ascendancy over rivals and thus contributed to the amalgamation of kin-based peoples into larger social and political units. Just as war with Spaniards promoted the concentration of power in Indian societies, so did negotiations that resulted in gifts, peace, and trade.[214]

In the treaty of 1774 with Paikín, Governor Mattoras conceded the limits of Spanish dominion. Like Araucanians a century before, Mocobíes became vassals of the crown, but they paid no tribute and continued to govern themselves in their own territory. The treaty of 1774 drew no clear line between Spanish and Mocobí territory, perhaps because Paikín governed lands distant from Spanish settlements, and the region lacked a defined geographical border like the Bíobio.

The peace treaty signed in Buenos Aires in 1790 by a group of Pampa caciques, which also testified to the limits of Spanish dominion, did establish a boundary line. Led by Callfilqui (alias Lorenzo), several Pampa leaders agreed to stay south of the Río Salado "in order to avoid all disturbances between Indians and Christians." Indians would return any Christians who fled to their territory to live among them, and Spaniards promised to return Indian fugitives from their side. In a phrase that signatories on both sides must have known to be a juridical fiction, the treaty designated Callfilqui as the "principal cacique of all the Pampas and head of this new republic." In using the word *república,* Spanish officials did not mean to suggest a completely independent nation, but rather that Indians would govern themselves under the larger umbrella of the crown. Since the sixteenth century, Spaniards expected conquered Indians to live in their own political community, or *república,* and to become Christians and pay tribute.[215] The unconquered Callfilqui, however, agreed to a different set of obligations. He would report suspicious foreigners and ill-intentioned Indians to authorities in Buenos Aires and control the hunting of wild horses in his territory, licensing only parties of no more than a dozen Indian hunters so that Spaniards would not mistake them for a war party. If Spaniards

29. *In 1775 the artist Tomás Cabrera produced a 910 x 1250 mm oil painting of a Spanish camp on the Bermejo River in Salta de Tucumán in 1775. He followed a firsthand sketch drawn in 1774 by Julio Ramón de Cesar, a military engineer, and the instructions of Governor Matorras, who wrote the captions. Cabrera divided this composition in three parts. The upper part, not reproduced here, shows the Virgen de Nuestra Señora de las Mercedes with San Bernardo on her right and San Francisco de Paula on her left. Their intercession, the caption says, made possible the signing of a treaty with the Mocobí chief, Paikín. The Spanish camp, with its officers, tents, and cannons, dominates the rural setting in the center panel. The lower part, pictured here, shows the key moment when Paikín declares himself a vassal of Carlos III. Detail from "Campamento del Gobernador Matorras," courtesy, Museo Histórico Nacional de Buenos Aires.*

needed to cross Callfilqui's territory to transport men and war materials to Patagonia, his people would provide a convoy and the necessary animals, for which they would be paid. In the treaty of 1790, Spanish officials made it clear that Callfilqui governed the lands beyond the Salado. The treaty never mentions hostages, tribute, or evangelization in Callfilqui's lands, where missionaries had already met defeat.[216]

In effect, Spaniards recognized the Río Salado as the Río Biobío of Buenos Aires and Callfilqui's people as juridical equals. As new Indian and Spanish leaders came on the scene, they renewed the treaty. Negotiating differences took precedence over fighting about them. Individual Spaniards moved south of the Salado, and in the early 1800s the government studied various proposals to advance the line of forts. Yet, from the viceroy to the cabildo of Buenos Aires, officials made it clear that any expansion would occur peacefully, in consultation with Pampas. In the last decades of Spanish rule, the *indios*

bárbaros of the pampa became simply *indios* in official discourse. The cultural divide between Pampas and Spaniards blurred and would have blurred even more if the cabildo
of Buenos Aires had its way. In 1808, the cabildo invited Pampa caciques to send their
sons to Buenos Aires to be educated in Spanish ways, but only one accepted the invitation
before Spanish rule came to an abrupt end in the Río de la Plata.[217]

Six years after Spaniards in Buenos Aires signed a treaty with the Pampas, the Ranquel
cacique Cheglén signed a peace treaty at Córdoba, further securing the borderlands between the peoples of the pampa and the viceroyalty of the Río de La Plata. In that treaty,
Ranqueles seemed to accept more limits than the Pampas under Callfilqui had. Rather
than receive distinction as head of a republic, Cheglén purportedly recognized Carlos IV
as his "lord and sovereign," although we cannot be sure these words were his or, if so,
what meaning those words would have held for him.[218]

Elsewhere on the edges of empire in the era of Carlos III, other independent Indians
like Tawira-Miskitos and Cunas also entered into written agreements in which they apparently acknowledged Spanish authority but did not, in fact, surrender sovereignty. A
Tawira-Miskito negotiator, Fara, may have signed a peace treaty with Spain in 1778 and
agreed "to live under the flag of our Catholic Majesty," but his majesty's flag never flew
over the Miskito villages.[219] In North America, putative leaders of indomitable peoples
like Comanches and Navajos signed written agreements for the first time in the mid-
1780s, treaties which entitled them to gifts, trade advantages, and a Spanish ally, yet
caused them to suffer no loss of sovereignty.[220] In 1786, the principal leader of the western Comanches, Ecueracapa, submitted "his entire nation to the dominion of the king,"[221]
Governor Anza of New Mexico reported, and two Navajo leaders, a don Carlos and a
don Joseph Antonio, received Anza's assurances that he would seek for them the "protection of the king" if they offered their "subordination and fidelity."[222] Although they
spoke of subordination, these treaties of friendship and alliance did not obligate either
Comanches or Navajos to accept missionaries, pay tribute, leave hostages, or come under
direct Spanish governance or law. As late as 1819, Navajos who signed a treaty in Santa
Fe agreed to accept Spanish "protection," in exchange for which Spanish officials, "in
the name of the King … concede to the Navajo tribe the lands they have enjoyed up to
the present." The treaty specified that a boundary line, following local landmarks, would
separate Navajo and Spanish spheres.[223]

What treaty-signing Pampas, Mocobíes, Miskitos, Cunas, Comanches, and Navajos
had in common was strength relative to Spanish weakness and an interest in pursuing
peaceful trade with Spaniards.[224] When peace negotiations got under way, Spaniards'
and Indians' perceptions of their relative strengths and economic interests influenced
the type and range of concessions they demanded from one another. Even when Spanish
officers thought their position was too weak to force missionaries or tribute on Indians,
for example, they might still demand that Indians leave hostages, as in treaties with Cunas in 1787, Ranqueles in 1796, and Navajos in 1819.[225] Although concessions on both
sides varied with local circumstances, it is evident that these powerful Indian societies

had forced Spain to limit its own dominion by recognizing them as "interior nations" —societies that governed themselves within a larger nation's jurisdiction.[226] Their interior status, however, represented a Spanish legal fiction, recognized by Indians and Spaniards alike. Even when leaders of these Indian groups swore to be vassals, or subjects, of the crown, they were not subject to Spanish political authority. Possessed of real power, these putative Indian vassals continued to live beyond the control of the Spanish state. If they were subjects, they remained unsubjugated.

"Free and Independent Nations"

Indians who enjoyed the most power in relation to Spaniards lived on the strategic frontiers of the empire, where they had potential to build alliances with other state societies—England, France, Holland, and Portugal. Some used their accident of location to play one state off against the other and force Spaniards to acknowledge not just the limits of dominion, but the absence of dominion. None did so more successfully than the tribes in southeastern North America.

After Spain acquired Louisiana from France in 1762 and reacquired the Floridas from England in 1783, the southeastern tribes pushed Spaniards to enter into written agreements with them as if they were sovereign—an innovation for that part of the empire, which might have spread westward from there to Texas and New Mexico. Southeastern tribal leaders' recent dealings with the French and the English had taught them to expect written treaties from Europeans. More important, leaders of the southeastern tribes looked to an alliance with Spain as a counterweight against Anglo Americans who, as one delegation reported to a Spanish official, "thought of little more than usurping their lands."[227]

For its part, Spain was pleased to ally itself with independent Indians who might block the "torrent" of Anglo-American settlers streaming westward like a force of nature into territory claimed by both Spain and the United States.[228] Spanish officials understood that the United States sought to establish sovereignty over Indian lands and then force Indians to vacate them so the government could sell them to settlers and shore up its weak treasury. Spain recognized that in reality most of the Southeast remained, as the conde de Aranda put it, "the country of savages." Both Spain and the United States had an equal right to exert claims over lands possessed by Indians, Aranda told the American minister John Jay in 1782, and, he wryly added, "equal *injustice* in wanting to."[229]

Hoping to use independent Indians to contain the flood of Anglo Americans and eager to prevent those Indians from allying themselves with Anglo Americans, Spanish officials signed treaties that made unusual concessions. In 1784 alone, Spanish authorities in Mobile came to terms with representatives of Alabamas, Chickasaws, and Choctaws. That same year in Pensacola officials reaffirmed a treaty with the Creeks, first signed in 1781 after Spanish forces seized that city from the English.[230] These were treaties of peace, trade, and mutual assistance. Representatives of the Creeks and Choctaws purportedly recognized the king of Spain as "our sovereign," but in none of these cases did Indians declare themselves vassals of the king. Instead, these Indian nations, as in the case of the Creeks, agreed to peace and alliance *with* the king's "subjects and vassals." The Creeks promised to obey the laws of Spain, but only those laws "that are compatible with our character and circumstances."[231] This arrangement, one scholar has noted, inverted Spain's usual legal relationship to Indians, in which Spanish law, together with what Spaniards called divine and natural law, prevailed over Indian law.[232]

The treaties of 1784 with southeastern tribes did not mention missionaries or suggest that Indians leave hostages to ensure their compliance. Unlike Anglo Americans and the English before them, Spanish negotiators did not attempt to coerce Indians to cede or sell land (except for small parcels around Spanish forts). To the contrary, in a treaty signed at Natchez in 1792, the governor of Spanish Louisiana's Natchez district, Manuel Gayoso de Lemos, granted that a boundary existed between lands claimed by Spain and lands that "legitimately and indisputably belong to the Chickasaw and Choctaw nations."[233] There was, of course, nothing altruistic about his position. In contrast to the Anglo-American colonists who surged into the Ohio and Mississippi valleys, Spain's minuscule population in southeastern North America made no significant demands for Indian land.[234]

Although they had the strength to force concessions from Spaniards, leaders of the southeastern tribes portrayed themselves as children and Spaniards as their fathers. Characteristically, Creek representatives in 1781 told Spaniards at Pensacola that they came "as good children to the feet of their father and protector." Tribes elsewhere used the same metaphor. A Comanche leader whom Spaniards knew as Camisa de Hierro (Iron Shirt) referred repeatedly to the governor of Texas as "our father," in a speech that a Spanish interpreter recorded in 1785. Pehuenche leaders in 1787 referred to Spaniards as fathers, and a few years earlier some expressed pleasure that they had been treated as sons by the commandant of the Spanish fort at San Carlos.[235] Spaniards may well have put these words in Indians' mouths or, as the only keepers of written records, added this patriarchal trope to their script as they sought to claim paternity over Indians they regarded as childlike.[236] Certainly Spaniards treated incorporated Indians as children, too ignorant to commit heresy, too immature to own property as individuals, too naïve to appear in regular Spanish courts, and too defenseless to get along without a special protector.[237] It seems more likely, however, that Indians designated European leaders as fathers in an effort to establish family ties that invested Europeans with fatherly responsibilities.[238]

Whatever its source, the father-child metaphor probably held very different meanings for the many matrilineal peoples in the hemisphere than it did for patrilineal Spaniards. Choctaws, one scholar has observed, regarded fathers "as kind, indulgent nonrelatives who had no authority over them."[239] Love and kindness flowed from the father, to whom children owed no special obligation. Other Indians might have been more obedient to their fathers than were the Choctaws, but they, too, expected fatherly generosity. Told that the Spanish king loved him like a "powerful father," the Ranquel cacique Carripilún purportedly replied through an interpreter, "From now on I will be a faithful soldier of that great king . . . he being so powerful, like a father, solicitous of us in order to do us good."[240]

After readily claiming the role of fathers, Spaniards in southeastern North America inadvertently fulfilled Indians' expectations of fatherly generosity. Bourbon officials treated them as autonomous nations, gave deference to Indian leaders, and made no overt effort to change Indians' spiritual, political, or cultural lives. Rather than attempt to tax the southeastern Indians, Spaniards paid lavish tribute to them in the form of gifts and hospitality, as the French and English had done before. Under the articles of trade that accompanied these treaties, only traders licensed by Spain could enter Indian lands —and they did. Traders who understood Indian languages and customs, many of them mestizos with names like Brashears and Thompson, went on the Spanish payroll and lived among Indians. Although these traders performed the same function that *capitanes de amigos, or Indian agents,* did in Chile, Chilean antecedents had no apparent influence in Spain's North American policy. Rather, Spanish officials in Louisiana and the Floridas pointed to the example of their English and French predecessors.[241]

Spanish–Indian alliances in southeastern North America culminated in a final treaty of mutual assistance, signed in October 1793 at the Fort of Nogales between Spaniards and Alabamas, Cherokees, Chickasaws, Choctaws, and Creeks. Whereas on other frontiers Spaniards had used a strategy of divide and conquer—turning one tribe against another —in the gulf region they worked to unify warring tribes. On paper, Spain succeeded. The five Indian nations formed an alliance in 1793, defining themselves as "one single nation" under the "protection" of the Spanish crown. Spain promised to intercede with the United States on their behalf in order to put them in "peaceful possession of *their* lands" and to distribute gifts to them annually at places they designated. For its part, the five nations promised to defend Spain's dominion in the Floridas and Louisiana.[242] By recognizing Indian sovereignty and promising gifts and trade, Spain had gained Indian allies who would help it defend its own claims to territory in the region from the United States. Not that Spain had a choice. As the conde de Campomanes rightly observed in 1792, if Spain tried to assert direct control over the savage "Indians" along the Gulf of Mexico or build settlements among them, the Indians "will lose confidence [in us] and will call the Americans to their defense."[243]

The tribes of southeastern North America, then, used their strategic position to force Spaniards to treat them as if they were entirely sovereign. Governor Gayoso offered that view explicitly in regard to Creeks, Chickasaws, and Choctaws, when he wrote in 1792 that those Indians "are free and independent nations; although they are under His Majesty's protection, we cannot forcibly prevent them from signing a treaty with the United States."[244] Spaniards' actions spoke as loudly as Gayoso's words. When the Creeks signed a treaty with the United States in 1790 after signing a similar document with Spain, the governor of Spanish Louisiana, the barón de Carondelet, chose not to break relations with the Creeks over their breach of diplomatic etiquette. He simply negotiated a new treaty with them and gave them more gifts.[245]

In southeastern North America, Spanish officials who might ordinarily have threatened to use force to make Indians bend to their will were reduced to using persuasion. "Be faithful to your agreements with the Spaniards, and you will lack nothing, and you will be as happy as your fathers," the barón de Carondelet warned Choctaws and Chickasaws in 1793, "but . . . if you do not mark my words, you will be hounded from your lands one after another, and all your fires will be put out. You will see your wives and your children killed or dying from hunger, and you will have to abandon the bones of your fathers."[246] Carondelet did not mean to suggest that Spaniards would unleash this mayhem on Indians. Lacking force of his own, Carondolet tried to persuade them that Anglo Americans would put out their fires. Only with Spain as their ally, Carondelet suggested presciently, could Indians prevent Anglo Americans from driving them westward, across the Mississippi.

One scholar has suggested that Spanish policymakers believed that "the 'barbarism' of the Indians necessitated and justified their subjection, and their purported placelessness deprived them of any autonomous right to a frontier territory."[247] Another scholarly study represents Spanish policy as "integrating far-flung Indian peoples for the sake of dominion but not dispossessing them entirely."[248] The Spanish monarchs, it has been supposed, "*never* reduced their territorial or jurisdictional claims over the New World or its inhabitants."[249] Certainly Spanish officials sought to subject and integrate Indians from the earliest days of the conquest and continued to do so, but it is also clear that some Indians forced Bourbon authorities to recognize tribal sovereignty. Even as the benevolently despotic Bourbon monarchy tightened its grip over its own subjects— Spanish aristocrats, American *criollos,* and *indios domésticos*—it loosened its claims to dominion over powerful independent Indians.[250]

Ideas versus Opportunism and Avarice

Bourbon policymakers in the administrative centers of the empire had embraced a new strategy that emphasized control of independent Indians through commerce, gifts, and limited claims to dominion, and Bourbon thinkers had elaborated a theoretical and legal rationale for granting the autonomy of Indians (who were, of course, autonomous in fact). The new policy afforded ideological space for Spaniards to build relationships with independent Indians based on the law of nations, rather than to require Indians to submit or suffer the consequences of war.[251] It is tempting to see this as a victory of humane ideas in the Age of Reason. It appears, however, that those ideas often went down in defeat when confronted by opportunism and avarice.

Spanish treaties with tribes in southeastern North America in the late 1700s went farthest in acknowledging Indian sovereignty and assuring a steady supply of gifts and trade items, but they represented a response to local realities more than to the power of new ideas. Simply put, Indian nations on that edge of the empire demanded the kind of treatment they had received from the French and English, and they had the power to force Spain to accede to their demands.[252] Spanish officials had learned valuable lessons about the power of trade and treaties earlier in other parts of the hemisphere, but they did not apply them in North America—either in the Southeast or in the Southwest—until Indians forced them to. Then, policymakers looked to foreign practice rather than to their own precedents. Earlier South American triumphs, as among the Araucanians, seemed to have no direct influence on Spanish Indian policy in North America. If Bourbon officials ignored South American precedents, it may have been because of their tendency to look to the present and the future without deeply consulting their past. As one historian has explained, "Charles III and his ministers knew less of Spanish America than do modern historians. The records lay around them. . . . But they seem not to have read them, or if they read them, not to have understood their meaning. The past was ignored, indeed repudiated."[253]

Bourbons did, of course, invoke the ideas of the age. Foreign ideas, in particular, had cachet. When Ambrosio O'Higgins urged in 1793 that Spain abandon "ideas of conquest and substitute in its place measures that will provide these [Indian] nations with trade and friendly treatment,"[254] he urged the crown to adopt the English system of using Indian superintendents. O'Higgins argued that the system worked well with "the savage tribes" of North America because superintendents and their agents gained Indians' confidence and spied on them even as they regulated trade.[255] O'Higgins knew but did not trouble himself to mention that *capitanes de amigos* already served this function in the Araucanía, where it had also worked well with Araucanians.[256]

Malaspina, too, seems to have discerned that Bourbon policymakers tended to look abroad for solutions to Spanish problems. He had visited Chile in 1790 on his epic reconnaissance of the Pacific and learned that trade, treaties, and toleration had produced harmonious relations between Spaniards and Araucanians. Malaspina lamented the sharp contrast between the northern provinces of New Spain, where "the ground is uselessly darkened with Spanish blood," and Chile, where "our border with the *araucanos* is peaceful, under a system almost identical to that which the English colonies have followed." In recommending a more peaceable approach to Spain's Indian relations in northern New Spain, however, Malaspina emphasized the English system rather than the Chilean.[257]

Whatever their source, foreign or domestic, it was one thing to espouse ideas and another to believe them. This is evident in the question of trust. The new peaceable approach required trust, and Spaniards were aware that they needed to establish their own trustworthiness rather than simply rail against Indians' supposed duplicity. Spanish officials worried that shortages of gifts and trade goods might lead Indians to conclude they were "less than exact" in fulfilling their treaty obligations,[258] and the crown repeatedly instructed Spaniards to keep their word, treat Indians fairly, and give them no cause for complaint.[259] Such instructions would have been unnecessary had Spaniards been more trustworthy, but Spanish officials did not always practice what they preached. "No one can ignore the fickleness and bad faith of all the Indians," Bernardo de Gálvez observed, "but good faith has not always been encountered in our own actions."[260] Spain's policy toward Guajiros and Cunas, the viceroy of New Granada, Pedro Mendinueta y Múzquiz, noted in 1803, was to pretend to recognize the independence of those peoples—a "simulation of their independence." Conceding that Spain could neither defeat Guajiros and Cunas nor win them over with kindness, Mendinueta's strategy was to "temporize" without explicitly renouncing Spain's "uncontestable right of Sovereignty."[261] For Mendinueta, recognition of Indians' sovereignty was a tactic forced upon Spain by circumstances rather than wise policy guided by principles. If Spain had greater strength than Guajiros and Cunas, his remark implied, Spaniards would not have to dissimulate. Other officers surely shared his view but were more guarded in expressing it.

At bottom, Spanish officials remained distrustful of Indians even as they tried to appear trusting and trustworthy. At the Apache *establecimientos de paz,* Nava instructed officers to feign trust. "Indians at peace should never see mistrust," he said, yet officers should spy on Apaches on the reservation and remain "distrustful [and] ever vigilant."[262] In New Granada, Spaniards slowly reduced the number of Cocinas who remained outside their control by winning some Cocinas to their side and using them to fight others. One of these co-opted Cocina leaders, Sarara, helped Spanish troops ambush a band of some seventy or eighty "enemy" Cocinas, shooting and stabbing them to death. Having thus demonstrated his loyalty to the Spanish side, he turned to the Spanish leader, José Galluzo, and said "*Hombre,* now there are no more thieves." "Well, *hombre,*" Galluzo replied, "if they rob from me now, the thief will be you."[263]

Just as Spanish efforts to build trust were at odds with their profound distrust of Indians, so their commitment to control and gradually acculturate Indians through peaceful means was in conflict with their assumption that using force against savages was justifiable and wise. As to treatment of Indians who lacked foreign allies or relative strength, Spanish officials continued to emphasize force over diplomacy. Viceroy Antonio María de Bucareli was pleased to give gifts and the title of "General of his Nation" to the Lipan Apache leader Cabello Largo, but he made it clear that the Lipanes needed to maintain their friendship "if they do not want to see themselves subjugated and defeated by the strength of the king's arms."[264] When Indians repeatedly failed to come to terms, Spanish officials turned to war—as they did with the Osages in 1792–94.[265] Where Spaniards had greater strength than Indians and coveted Indian lands and labor, Spaniards resorted to naked force, their actions indistinguishable from those of the first generation of conquistadors.

One of those places was the Chiriguanía—the territory of the Chiriguanos, where the crown's chief attorney for Charcas, Victorián Villava, had protested the hanging of the supposed rebel leader Sacuarao in 1800 and urged negotiations instead of war as the only way to end conflict. There, one of the Chiriguanos' more conspicuous leaders, Cumbay, had also sought peaceful ways to reduce tensions. This leader of unconquered Indians had traveled to the city of Plata (today's Sucre) in April 1799 to file a formal complaint with the *audiencia* to stop Spaniards from encroaching on Chiriguano lands in the Ingre Valley, where he lived. Through an interpreter, Cumbay asked for protection in the name of the king, so that "we may plant and cultivate to have produce to feed ourselves and thus live in peace and quiet."[266]

The *audiencia* turned down Cumbay's petition. Five weeks later, in November 1799, the Chiriguano "rebellion" began at the missions of Parapiti. From there, violence against Spaniards spread and continued unabated until 1804, when it intensified in a year of drought and hunger. Some Spanish observers understood that the source of Chiriguano bitterness lay in their hunger and narrowing options as Spaniards encroached on their lands and Spanish cattle trampled their cornfields. Most, however, echoed the view of the president of the *audiencia* of Charcas, who attributed Chiriguano hostility to "the natural inconstancy of Indians, to their propensity to steal and, finally, to their brutal condition."[267] Rather than acknowledge Chiriguanos' rights to land, as Spanish policy required, the president of the *audiencia* of Charcas asserted Spaniards' rights: "All the unknown lands occupied by savages are called borders. Our possessions always continue growing with the population of new missions and ranches established beyond [those borders], because of interest in good pastures and fertile lands, as has always occurred since the pacification of this continent."[268]

Chiriguano resistance to Spanish expansion ended in "an offensive war of fire and blood," ordered by the viceroy in 1808.[269] Spanish forces launched a coordinated *entrada general* into the Chiriguanía in the dry autumn months when soggy terrain would not impede their travel. They burned houses, drove off livestock, leveled orchards and corn-fields, and hauled away stores of corn. In the Ingre Valley they captured one leader, Man-anday, and cut off his head as a trophy; they took the ears of another executed prisoner as evidence of their achievement. Scouring the canyons, they rounded up women and children, although one Chiriguano cheated them by throwing his two children to their deaths rather than let them be taken alive.[270]

Dependent on mountain valleys for farming, Chiriguanos had no large hinterland to which they could flee and regroup, as did Apaches, Pampas, and Araucanians. They lacked the foreign allies and firearms which strengthened the resistance of Comanches, Miskitos, Cunas, Guajiros, and the various tribes of southeastern North America.[271] Spaniards thus had no need to placate people like the Chiriguanos with treaties, gifts, and trade or to tolerate their independence or transgressions.

In the Age of Reason, then, the peaceful coexistence and slow integration of independent Indians which the crown generally favored and high-ranking Spanish officials often es-poused did not always prevail. In places where Spaniards coveted Indian land and had the means to take it, enlightened policies gave way to avarice, opportunism, and collective violence.[272]

6

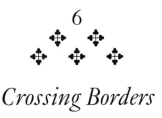

Crossing Borders

They told me . . . of a captive named Pedro Pablo,
who has been heard to say that he wanted more to be
among the Indians than to return to the Christians.
Comandante de Fronteras Francisco Balcarce, Luján, 1784

The borders between civilization and barbarism have become more
transparent, allowing us to catch a glimpse of "savage" Indians more
westernized than was thought, and subjects of the King whose lifestyle
was similar to that of the Indian peoples who surrounded them.
Salvador Bernabéu, historian, 1999

Making coherent stories out of the fragments we find lying about
is a natural human inclination, and socially a necessary one,
but when doing history it must be resisted.
Inga Clendinnen, historian, 2003

In the winter of 1790, the prominent Pampa cacique Callfilqui, known as Lorenzo to the Spaniards, journeyed to Buenos Aires to finalize a peace treaty with viceregal authorities. An interpreter, twenty-nine-year-old Blas de Pedrosa, went out from Buenos Aires to meet him at the frontier fort of Ranchos. Pedrosa brought gifts for Callfilqui from the viceroy—wine, yerba maté, and bread —and he escorted the cacique back to the viceregal capital. In Buenos Aires, Pedrosa translated as Callfilqui negotiated a nine-point treaty. The accord marked a turning point in Pampa–Spanish relations. It established the Río Salado as the boundary between the Pampa and Spanish worlds, but it allowed Callfilqui's people to enter Buenos Aires to trade. When Pampa merchants entered the city, Callfilqui agreed, they would make their first stop at Pedrosa's house so he could identify them. Callfilqui also agreed to use Pedrosa as the escort for any caciques or messengers whom he sent to confer with vice-regal authorities.[1]

Blas de Pedrosa, who acted as an intermediary for Callfilqui's Pampas in 1790, had escaped from Pampas just four years earlier. Indians had captured him near Córdoba in 1776, when he was a teenager traveling from Buenos Aires to Mendoza. They killed most of his party, which numbered some forty men, and took him prisoner. Wounded in the shoulder by a lance but healed by the Pampas, he became the servant of the cacique Ante-mán. The young Pedrosa slowly gained the confidence of his captors, becoming a trans-lator and scout. Ten years later, in November 1786, he fled captivity when he learned that a caravan of Spaniards had penetrated deep into Indian territory to harvest salt at the Salinas Grandes, some 450 miles southwest of Buenos Aires.[2] In Pedrosa's day, Span-iards visited these salt flats annually, guided by Indian interpreter-scouts who knew the way to vital waterholes along the route and who arranged payments of tribute to Indian leaders whose lands they crossed. The 1786 caravan, with some 400 soldiers accompany-ing 250 creaky oxcarts, was by far the largest to make the run.[3] When the oxcarts re-turned to Buenos Aires, laden with the salt that Spaniards needed to cure cowhides and preserve meat, the ex-captive entered the city with them.

In the viceregal capital, officials recognized that Pedrosa might serve them as a trans-lator and scout, just as he had served the Pampas. Buenos Aires suffered no shortage of people who spoke the language of the Pampas, but they tended to be poorly educated. As a result, Viceroy Nicolás de Arredondo claimed, they spoke Spanish too poorly to translate adequately, and the protector of Indians lamented that they lacked skill to deal with Indians, "with whom it is necessary to use a thousand precautions to perpetuate peace."[4] Pedrosa, born in Spain at La Coruña and the son of an army colonel, was liter-ate and apparently skillful. Beginning with the marqués de Loreto in the late 1780s, three successive viceroys tried to put Pedrosa on the payroll as an official translator. They probably knew that a precedent existed in Chile, where Spanish agents called *capitanes de amigos* served as official, salaried translators. All three viceroys failed to win the parsi-monious crown's approval. Pedrosa's services were not necessary, the crown declared: "For the cases in which there might be a need to have dealings with the Pampas there is never lacking a peon, mule driver, or soldier who understands their language."[5] Officials closer to the scene knew better. Although they could not put him on the payroll, viceroys did employ Pedrosa to guide annual expeditions to the salt beds, negotiate the freedom of captives, lay the groundwork for peace treaties, and translate, as he did for Callfilqui. Pedrosa skillfully played those roles into the early 1800s.

Between these special assignments, Pedrosa operated a trading post in Buenos Aires called the Esquina de los Pampas. It stood in the best neighborhood in the city. At this *corral* or *corralón,* as the locals uniquely termed their trading posts, Pedrosa provided Indian guests with lodging as well as cloth, yerba maté, tobacco, and alcohol in exchange for the horses, hides, salt, leather goods, feathers, woolen textiles, and other handicrafts the Indians brought to the city. Two competing *corraleros* ran rival establishments, and Pedrosa tried to put *them* out of business by asking the viceroy, the marqués de Loreto, for a monopoly. He alleged that he was the only trader who had sufficient knowledge of the Indians' languages to understand them when drink loosened their tongues and they talked carelessly about their plans to raid Spaniards. Viceroy Loreto declined to take customers away from Pedrosa's competitors, but when a new viceroy took office, Pedrosa renewed his request. In 1790, Viceroy Arredondo divided Indian clients between the two remaining *corraleros*. He assigned Ranqueles and Pehuenches to Pedrosa, and Pampas and other nations to a longtime trader to the Indians, Manuel Izquierdo. With his wife, María de las Nieves Estela, Izquierdo operated an establishment in Buenos Aires called La Pampa as well as a chain of trading posts at the forts of Monte, Luján, and Ranchos on the edge of the Indian country.[6] By the end of the century, however, Pedrosa seems to have become the most successful Indian trader in Buenos Aires. "Savage merchants," one observer noted in 1804, "came and went frequently with their women," selling Pedrosa their wares for cash and then spending it in other shops in the city.[7]

Pedrosa had made a career of his decade of captivity by Indians beyond the Río Salado. When he first entered the Indian world he had crossed a line that must have seemed to him, as it did to many of his compatriots, to separate "savagery" from "civilization." Pablo Zizur, for example, a one-legged naval pilot, found himself in chaotic, frightening surroundings when he visited a Pampa village near the Sierra de la Ventana in 1781. He had made the journey, thirteen days' travel from Buenos Aires, at the behest of the viceroy, to exchange captives, gather intelligence, and explore the possibility of peace with the cacique Calpisqui. Instead, he found himself amidst armed, painted Indians who made menacing gestures. They wanted to kill him, his translator explained, because Christians had killed many of their people. Spared, it would appear, by his interpreter's diplomatic skills, Zizur proceeded to the heart of Calpisqui's village, where Indians pressed him for tobacco, yerba maté, and *aguardiente,* and where the noise of their all-night revelries left him sleepless. The village of tents, crowded around a pond and surrounded by grazing livestock, appalled him. It did not appear to contain the homes of "rational people, but rat holes."[8] Zizur had no doubt he had entered a savage world. "The border with the Indians," one Argentine historian has noted, "was more than a dividing line between two enemies. It was an abyss that marked the boundary between two opposing ideas of life. Ephemeral sexual or commercial ties between heathens and Christians did not diminish their complete incompatibility [or] their mutual rejection."[9]

After years of residence on the Indian side of the line, however, Pedrosa had discovered that the Salado could be a crossing point as well as an abyss. A lightly fortified border followed the general course of the Salado, but that border was a "political-military fiction" intersecting a "symbiotic world," in the felicitous phrase of another Argentine scholar.[10] Goods moved back and forth, and people came and went. One Petronila Pérez, for example, had been captured by the Pampas and remained with them after she had children, but two former captives, both Spaniards, came to visit her every year.[11] In its permeability, the Salado resembled other borders between Spaniards and independent Indians. The Biobío, fabled as a dividing line between Araucanians and Chileans, was so porous that when a smallpox epidemic raged through the lands south of the river in 1791, Spaniards found it impossible to enforce a quarantine.[12]

Independent Indians, then, crossed borders designed to separate them from Spanish society, and Spaniards crossed lines intended to separate them from independent Indians. Some individuals crossed borders willingly, and others came unwillingly as captives. In either case, the effects could be the same. Voluntarily or involuntarily, independent Indians and Spaniards learned one another's ways, developed strong informal ties, and discovered compatibilities between societies that some of their compatriots, as well as historians, deemed incompatible.[13]

Spanish Captives

Bilingual and bicultural Spaniards had bridged the gulf between Spaniards and Indians since the days of Cortés and Pizarro.[14] Initially, these individuals were few and far between, but by the late eighteenth century they had become ubiquitous on the frontiers of the empire as more Spaniards lived among Indians, learning their languages and their ways. Cultural intermediaries also found their services increasingly in demand as Bourbon administrators sought to control or influence Indians through trade and diplomacy. In contrast to making war, establishing the conditions for peaceful trade required clear verbal communication.

Like Pedrosa, some Spaniards acquired knowledge of Indians quite unintentionally. The numbers of Spaniards taken captive are incalculable, but whenever Spaniards rescued or ransomed their countrymen from Indians, they invariably learned from them of others still being held.[15]

In southern South America, Araucanians took hundreds of Spanish captives during the long struggle that Spaniards knew as the War of Arauco, from its beginnings in the mid-1500s through the mid-1600s.[16] As peaceful relations developed between Spaniards and Mapuches along the Biobío and around Valdivia in the 1700s, captive taking diminished dramatically. Perhaps the most prominent of the Mapuches' captives in the 1700s was Bishop Francisco José de Marán, who traveled into their territory at an inopportune moment in 1778. Unable to agree on whether Bishop Marán should live or die, two competing groups of his captors proceeded to play a few rounds of a cricketlike ball game, *chueca,* to decide the outcome. Those who wished to kill him lost the game, and the bishop lived.[17]

In the eighteenth century, Mapuche raiding shifted to the provinces of Cuyo and Buenos Aires on the Argentine side of the Andes, which had become "Araucanized." In the most intense period of raiding, from the 1740s through the 1780s, Araucanians, Pehuenches, Pampas, and Ranqueles seized Spaniards along with their property. The Pampas

30. The game of chueca, *from Frézier, 1717, plate 9 facing p. 72.*
Courtesy, Huntington Library, San Marino, California.

"have infinite captives," Pedrosa reported.[18] Indeed, the Pampas had so many Spanish captives that one, María Concepción, taken by Indians as an infant in the province of Buenos Aires, reportedly learned Spanish while in captivity.[19] Indians on the pampa had an excess of captives, and they traded some to distant Huilliches. Exploring remote Lake Nahuel Huapi, high in the southern Andes in 1794, fray Francisco Menéndez met four women who belonged to a Huilliche cacique, Chulilaquin. Two spoke Spanish, and they identified five additional women from Buenos Aires whom Chulilaquin had just acquired. For a time, fray Francisco had no need of his translator because he met so many Huilliches who spoke Spanish, "although badly."[20]

Much of what is known about the ways Spaniards experienced captivity must be inferred from their actions, for they left few words in the historical record. Rescued and ransomed captives rarely wrote about their time among Indians. They did undergo interrogations by Spanish officials on release, but their interrogators hoped to gain intelligence from them about Indian adversaries and evinced little interest in the captives' lives among the Indians. Although many captives were illiterate, they might have told their story to a writer who would publish it as fact or fictionalize it, but that never came to pass.[21] This dearth of firsthand accounts of captivity in Spanish America contrasts sharply with English America, where Indian captivity narratives became a wildly popular genre.[22]

Some writers have explained this difference by pointing to a lower level of literacy and a more limited market for books in Spain and its colonies than in England and English America. That may be. By the late eighteenth century, however, there was no shortage of books published in Spain and Spanish America, ranging from religious tracts to satire. Moreover, Spanish Christians did publish accounts of captivity at the hands of Muslim pirates from North Africa. The explanation, then, probably goes deeper and may well be found in cultural differences, including the meaning of redemption in Protestant and Catholic thought. Puritans imagined the captives' plight as punishment for their sins and the captives' rescue as a sign of god's favor. Catholics—in French as well as in Spanish America—may have ignored the captivity narrative because for them, one scholar suggests, "suffering for one's faith led naturally to death, as it did for Christ and for martyred saints, and not to deliverance."[23]

If there were substantial numbers of captivity narratives for Spanish America, they would probably reveal, as they do in English-speaking America, that captives' experiences varied with the caprice of their individual captors, the customs of particular Indian societies, and captives' responses to their situations.[24] It also seems likely the narratives would reveal that former captives' motives for publishing their work distorted their story. Francisco Núñez de Pineda y Bascuñán's classic "Happy Captivity," an account of his life among Araucanians in 1629 (one of the rare captivity narratives from Spanish America) became happy only when he reconstructed it many years later in order to influence official opinion about Indians.[25]

One must also judge Indian captors more by what they did than by what they said, and their actions suggest that in South and North America alike, Indians captured Spaniards for similar reasons: to exact revenge, replenish their populations, add to their store of slaves or messengers, show them off as war trophies, or exchange them for trade goods, money, or their own people. As Spaniards understood, Indians valued Spanish children because they acculturated more easily than adults, and they valued women over men, whom they often killed.[26] Tobas in the Chaco, one rescued captive testified, raided haciendas to take "young captives . . . in order to raise them in their manner, and to kill the older ones."[27] Women, who did not try to flee as readily as men, had value as sexual partners and bearers of children. In those Native societies in which a bride's family demanded a generous gift from the groom, a captive woman represented a bargain.[28]

For some of the same reasons they captured Spaniards, Indians also captured Indians from other tribes and bands. The practice, of course, antedated the arrival of Europeans. Spanish captives, however, had additional value. Indians used them as pawns and signs of good faith in the early stages of negotiations with other Spaniards, to carry messages safely into Spanish territory, and to translate.[29] The historical record occasionally reveals a glimpse of these captives at work: a Spanish woman, captured from Asunción, kept by Mbayás as a reluctant translator; one Toribio Espinosa, taken by Miskitos to Panama City to translate during treaty negotiations in 1778.[30] As a commodity, captive Spaniards also had value to other Spaniards, who would ransom them by exchanging Indian prisoners, manufactured goods—spurs, stirrups, bits, sheets of brass, clothing, cloth, *aguardiente*, and yerba maté, or hard cash.[31] The prices that Indians charged to return Spaniards ranged wildly, from a silver peso that Chiriguanos customarily received for repatriating Christian captives at Santa Cruz de la Sierra, to one hundred pesos that the viceroy in Buenos Aires paid for a male captive in 1788 (he paid half that for a woman just two months later).[32] In 1779, officers at the Presidio del Norte at Junta de los Ríos in Nueva Vizcaya ransomed two Spanish boys and a girl from Apaches for about thirty pesos each —one-sixth of a soldier's annual salary in the Interior Provinces of New Spain.[33]

Prior to 1780, funds for ransoming Christians captured by heathens in northern New Spain came from their families or from budgets for the support of presidios. In 1780, however, officers in New Spain's Interior Provinces institutionalized the system and created a special fund that invited donations from private citizens.[34] The crown approved the creation of that fund in 1782, with the warning that it might give Indians incentive to seize more Christians and so escalate the cycle of captivity and redemption.[35] Royal concern proved unwarranted. Funds remained chronically insufficient there and throughout the empire. In Buenos Aires, the viceroy did not have enough cash to redeem captives from Callfilqui, as promised in the treaty of 1790. The viceroy could not find sufficient funds even in the face of threats that Pampas, "entirely possessed of vile avarice," would break the peace if they did not receive payment.[36]

Meanwhile, the crown also turned to a religious order as a source of funds to redeem Christian captives: the Real y Militar Orden de Nuestra Señora de la Merced, Redención de Cautivos, founded in Barcelona in 1218 to ransom Christians seized by Muslims. After the discovery of America, the Mercedarians expanded their operations to the New World, converting Indians and continuing to collect alms to redeem Christians from Muslims. Wealthy America soon eclipsed Europe as the major source of revenue that Mercedarians used to free Spaniards from Muslim captivity, but the crown forbade the use of American-raised funds to free Christians captured by Indians in America, arguing that it violated the Mercedarians' founding charter. On December 14, 1786, Carlos III reversed the order. He permitted the use of American monies to free Christians enslaved in the Philippines, northern New Spain, Chile, and in the viceroyalty of Buenos Aires—the four places that the crown apparently believed had the busiest traffic in Christian captives.[37]

Some Spanish captives confounded their would-be rescuers by resisting repatriation.[38] In particular, Spaniards taken captive as children became highly acculturated to Indian societies and reluctant to leave their captors. Marcelino, a mulatto captured before he was old enough to pray or know the surname of his mother, grew up to ride with Mescalero

Apaches who raided Spanish settlements in Coahuila and Nueva Vizcaya. He had become, one Spanish officer said, a murderer and a "perfect horse thief."[39] Well aware of children's integration into Indian societies, Spanish officers sometimes declined to retrieve them, as when they permitted Apaches who settled on reservations to keep those Christians they had captured "at a tender age."[40]

Some women also preferred to remain among Indians, especially after they had children by their captors. A Spanish trader in Texas described two Spanish women as unlikely to leave the Taovayas (a Wichita band) because, "having had union with the Indians, from which have issued children, whom their fathers would not give up, they would remain, not alone because of their natural mother-love, but also through the well-merited shame which they would suffer among Christians for their infamous unchastity."[41] His accusation of "well-merited shame" speaks volumes about why Spanish women captives declined to return to their own society. Among Indians, such women might become respected matriarchs; matrilineal Navajos trace the lineage of several of their clans back to captured Spanish women.[42] On the other hand, some women who reentered Spanish society probably had cause to regret their decision. That was apparently the case with Juana María Sánchez, captured by Pampas as a very young child. Years later she returned to Buenos Aires as an adult, with an Indian husband and four children. Within two years she rejoined the Pampas, but having revealed her Spanish identity to authorities in Buenos Aires, she could not go home again. Spanish officials "rescued" her and brought her back to the city.[43]

If female captives reentered Spanish society without shame, they probably came from the lower rungs of society, where women had less honor at stake than did upper strata women.[44] That appears to have been the case with Juana Hurtado de Salas and her half sister, Juana "la Coyota." After living in captivity among Navajos, both returned to New Mexico and married Spanish men, without apparent social stigma. From Spanish New Mexico, however, the two Juanas continued to maintain relations with Navajos. Here, too, borders that separated Spaniards from independent Indians were permeable.[45]

Spanish officials also understood that some adult captives, men as well as women, became so loyal to their captors that they became anti-Spanish.[46] Two years after Comanches seized Miguel Menchaca near San Antonio in 1781, for example, his former neighbors recognized him in Comanche garb, staking out the presidial horse herd.[47] Spaniards seized by Abipones, one Jesuit observed, refused to flee or, if ransomed, returned faithfully to the Indians. They joined the Abipones in war "and never feared to dirty their hands with Spanish blood, although it ran in their veins."[48] Luis de la Cruz observed in 1806 that Pehuenches "have many Spanish captives in their lands, some of whom conceal themselves and these are our worst enemies."[49] A group of high-ranking officers who met in Chihuahua in June 1778 to formulate a new policy for the Interior Provinces of New Spain voiced a similar sentiment: "The large number of captives" taken by Apaches "accommodated themselves happily to the lives of the Apache [and] are worse than the Apaches themselves at war since the captives serve as guides and do more wicked deeds than the barbarians."[50] Jacobo Ugarte, the commander in chief of the Interior Provinces, expressed relief at the rescue of fifteen Spanish captives in Sonora, Nueva Vizcaya, and New Mexico in 1786–87: "In time they would have become as dangerous to us as the [Apaches]."[51]

When Spaniards who had become assimilated into tribal societies were rescued, they had to be resocialized into a Hispanic community that often regarded them with suspicion. Spaniards born among Indians or who spent many years among them as captives, one Chilean officer noted in the late 1600s, "so love their vices, customs, and liberty that they are dangerous among us . . . they are worse than the wildest savages, because they are savages with the use of reason."[52] When male captives did return, Spanish authorities carefully interrogated them, suspicious that they might have become spies for the Indians who adopted them.[53]

Returned to the Spanish world, some former captives found occasional work as translators and guides, while others turned their previous misfortune into a career.[54] Freed from the Patagonians at Río Negro, a black slave whom Spaniards respectfully called doña Magdalena Guzmán was hired as a translator because "she spoke the language of those heathen perfectly." The crown authorized an expenditure of 250 pesos to compensate her master for his loss and gave her double rations and a wardrobe, but no pay.[55] Juan José de Acevedo, captured near Salta as a young boy and raised in the Chaco, served the crown on a number of key expeditions into the Chaco between 1774 and 1787, including Gov. Gerónimo de Matorras's successful negotiation of peace with the Mocobí chief Paikín. Unlike Guzmán and Pedrosa, Acevedo had the good fortune to go on the royal payroll, commanding a salary of 8 pesos a month by 1781.[56] Francisco Xavier Chaves, captured by Comanches near Albuquerque at the age of eight and traded to the Taovayas after the death of his adoptive Comanche mother, worked in Texas as a soldier-translator from 1784, when at the age of twenty-two he reemerged in Spanish society at San Antonio, until his retirement in 1832. Like other longtime captives, Chaves knew the culture as well as the language of his captors. When he and a companion, Pedro Vial, visited a Comanche camp in September 1785, the Indians expressed alarm that they brought smallpox with them. "We responded," they wrote in their joint diary, "that they could see for themselves that since we had entered that *ranchería*, the sun had not clouded and that it was always very clear and bright, which proved our coming healthy and well."[57] Chaves, whose eyelids were tattooed in the Taovaya manner, played a key role that autumn in bringing Eastern Comanches to the bargaining table in San Antonio and brokering an enduring peace.

Some former captives apparently urged a humane alternative to making war on independent Indians. Following his liberation, Pedrosa judged that Indians of the pampa could be pacified with "pure, faithful, humane, and very generous trade."[58] Chaves and Vial wrote from San Antonio in 1785 that peace with Comanches "could be lasting, as long as they are treated with kindness and love." The two recommended that Spaniards give presents annually to Comanche leaders, "without forgetting the young men." More cynically, Chaves and Vial added that Comanches, whose character disposed them to be "ambitious and greedy," are "friendly if they are given what is equivalent to the pillaging, thefts, and hostilities that they may make when at war."[59]

Through firsthand experience, Indianized Spaniards had come to the same view that enlightened Spaniards arrived at through study: an enduring peace could be built on a foundation of gifts, trade, and trust. Some captives, then, became intermediaries, clearing paths between two cultures. Others remained in the Indian sphere, serving the interests of Indians in their dealings with Spaniards. Still others returned to the Spanish world, where they facilitated Spaniards' communication with Indians. In the process of serving one side or the other, most of these cultural brokers also served themselves.[60]

Spanish Traders and Deserters

Along with captives, independent Indians harbored Spaniards who came to them by choice. Nearly always males, they included merchants, government agents, and fugitives from Spanish society. Like captives, they bridged the cultural divide that separated Spaniards and their savages.

Itinerant Spanish traders were fixtures in the camps and villages of independent Indians in places as disparate as the Araucanía, the Pampa, the Chaco, the Guajira Peninsula, the Apachería, the Comanchería, and the southeastern woodlands of North America. The numbers of Spaniards involved in the Indian trade probably grew in the late eighteenth century as the Bourbons brought new economic vitality to previously neglected areas and made trade their preferred mode of Indian control.[61] In the Araucanía, with its early history of conflict, Spanish–Indian trade had become so regularized by the mid–eighteenth century that a Spanish trader could leave goods on consignment with a cacique, confident that he would be paid on his next visit.[62]

Eager for trade goods, Indians often treated Spanish merchants hospitably during times of war as well as peace. The Guajiros, who remained unconquered until the end of the colonial era, would kill "whoever would take the liberty of intruding upon them," observed a Frenchman who lived in Venezuela between 1801 and 1804. "It is, nevertheless, a matter of fact," he added, "that Spanish smugglers, on paying a certain consideration, obtain a passport and escort to traverse the country of the Goahiros [Guajiros]."[63]

Spanish officials regarded Indian traders with ambivalence, often dismissing them as peddlers (*mercachifles*) rather than describing them with a more dignified word like merchants (*comerciantes*).[64] Authorities suspected, often quite rightly, that traders smuggled alcohol, arms, and other prohibited goods into the territory of hostile Indians, and they feared some were renegades who had "gone native."[65] In 1792, Ambrosio O'Higgins summarized the viewpoint of many officials when he characterized Spanish traders who entered or crossed the Andes to trade with Pehuenches and Pampas as "usually wicked, perfidious, and malevolent." They planted "diabolical ideas against the government among the Indians and on their return they rob those very Indians and commit a thousand other injustices against them."[66] He tried to limit traders to one or two expeditions per year, but to little effect. At a *parlamento* in 1796, O'Higgins declared "free trade" for Araucanians. He permitted Indians to trade at any frontier fort, apparently in the hope of undermining Spanish traders who planned to venture into Indian territory. This was not an innovation, but a reiteration of a failed policy. At least as early as 1726, Chilean authorities had tried without success to limit the Indian trade to frontier forts, where trade would be controlled by local *comandantes* and *capitanes de amigos*.[67]

In the Araucanía, the site of Spain's earliest innovative policies toward independent Indians, paid *capitanes de amigos* had lived in communities of friendly Mapuches (called *indios amigos* in Chile) since the mid-1600s. The capitanes occupied a precarious position. As the sole representatives of Spanish authority south of the Biobío, they were supposed to spy on Indians and influence them. Their power depended entirely on the degree to which Araucanians found them useful as advisors, intermediaries, and merchants. If it was true, as one Franciscan complained in 1783, that the Araucanians "obey only their *capitán* [de amigos] or lieutenant and no one else," then Araucanians found the capitanes useful indeed.[68]

In 1775, Bourbon administrators standardized salaries of *capitanes de amigos* and reduced their numbers, which had proliferated. They assigned a *capitán* to each of the four *butal-mapus* at salaries of 144 pesos a year, and they placed fifteen additional capitanes in Indian communities at annual salaries of 96 pesos. That was higher than an infantryman's annual salary of 80 pesos, but less than a translator's 216 pesos.[69] The number of capitanes remained at nineteen until the end of the colonial era. Two *comisarios de naciones,* one headquartered in Valdivia and another in Concepción, apparently had authority over the capitanes as well as over the forts and Indian towns south of the Biobío—"below the border" as one contemporary put it.[70]

Men who served as *capitanes de amigos* were usually mixed bloods, born on the frontier, able to read and write Spanish and to speak Araucanian. Colonial authorities valued them for their expertise on Indian affairs in the interior, the *tierra adentro*. To the dismay of authorities, however, *capitanes de amigos* also seemed to acquire the habits of Indians. Toward the end of the seventeenth century one officer claimed to have heard some Mapuches bragging that their way of life was superior to that of the Spaniards. As evidence the Indians pointed to the *capitán* who had come to live among them. After a few months, the Indians said, the *capitán* "forgets he is a Christian, learning to be a heathen, marrying in the Indian manner with some women, and drinking and gambling with the Indians." The same officer who told that story also purported to know an elderly *capitán de amigos* who had eleven Indian wives: "They cried among themselves because he could not put out the fire that burned in all of them."[71] Decades later, *capitanes de amigos* still had a reputation for going native. Manuel de Amat, who traveled extensively in the Araucanía, lumped the *capitanes de amigos* together with petty merchants and interpreters who frequented the Indian country and condemned them all as men "without religion, and with abundant vices, especially drunkenness." He accused them of providing Araucanians with "great quantities of wine, knives, iron, and other prohibited goods" in exchange for the Araucanians' woven ponchos.[72]

Like other Europeans who lived intimately with independent Indians—the French *coureurs de bois* and the Anglo-American "squaw man"—*capitanes de amigos* acquired unsavory reputations in their home cultures. Ironically, the sexual relations for which fellow Spaniards condemned them brought them into Native kinship networks and made them more effective cultural brokers. Outcasts from their own societies, they played critical roles in maintaining peace by mediating between Indian and non-Indian worlds.[73]

In the late 1700s, officials in Cuyo, on the Argentine side of the Andes, also began to employ *capitanes de amigos*. Pehuenches familiar with the institution in Chile had asked the comandante at Mendoza, José Francisco de Amigorena, to assign a *capitán* to them. They had come to the right official. Amigorena had a long-standing interest in this Chilean institution and had inquired about it years before.[74]

Elsewhere in the empire Spain had no paid agents living among independent Indian nations until it acquired Louisiana in 1762, along with the French system of placing paid trader-interpreters in Indian villages and setting fair prices.[75] From there, the system seems to have skipped across Texas to New Mexico, where interpreters, drawing the pay of soldiers, were assigned in the mid-1780s to live among Navajos and Comanches "to observe them and to give an account of their movements."[76] In contrast to Chile, New Mexico had no forts outside of the capital and no elaborate system of *capitanes de amigos*, but officials monitored the private parties of Spaniards and Pueblo Indians who traded in the strategic Comanchería in the years following the Comanche peace of 1786. The government required traders to obtain a license and take along "one of the interpreters or another trusted person," in the words of Gov. Fernando de la Concha. Serving as the eyes and ears of the government, these "trusted persons" were to see to it that the traders did not cheat or anger the Comanches; they and the traders they accompanied were to bring back intelligence so New Mexicans could wage war more effectively if Comanches broke the peace.[77]

Along with Spaniards who entered Indian territory in search of profits, others went to find sanctuary or make a fresh start. Some Spaniards fled their society to move in among Christian Indians, in violation of much-repeated laws that prohibited Spaniards from living in Indian towns.[78] Although these fugitives lived with Christian Indians and thus remained within Spain's political jurisdiction, José de Gálvez condemned them as "incorrigible, disobedient, and harmful." The most desperate, embittered, or impoverished Spaniards, however, moved beyond the pale and cast their lot with *indios bárbaros* who lived beyond Spain's jurisdiction. Criminals moved in with independent Indians to escape punishment; social deviants fled ridicule or harsh treatment; mestizos, mulattos, and blacks turned their backs on a racist, discriminatory Spanish society; slaves and peones sought relief from oppressive masters; conscripts ran away from harsh conditions of army or militia service; young people ran away from unhappy homes.[79] Socially or geographically marginalized Spaniards who fled their own society probably imagined that prospects were brighter in Indian country. "The poverty that is felt more and more every day in this bishopric," the bishop of Concepción observed, "is such that many of its people long to cross over and live in the lands of the Indians to find there the abundance they lack in their own lands."[80]

We cannot know how many Spaniards became renegades and apostates, as Spanish officials termed them. Certainly they were to be found wherever Spaniards lived in proximity to independent Indians, and the late eighteenth century may have seen an increase in their numbers.[81] As the Bourbons poured money into public works and built up local militias, they targeted vagrants and beggars. The Spanish crown had consistently deplored the unemployed, but under Carlos III administrators took energetic measures to force them into military service or to toil on public works. The Bourbons hoped to give manual labor respectability, which they believed it had previously lacked in Spanish society. They regarded manual labor as a form of rehabilitation rather than merely a means of punishment, but so-called idlers and vagabonds who resisted Bourbon therapy were to be sent to "the mines or presidios in the manner of condemned criminals." For Spanish nonconformists, whose government defined them as vagrants and rogues—*vagos* and *pícaros*—life with Indians may have seemed an attractive alternative to harsh and demeaning labor or to repression and poverty.[82]

Spaniards who defected to the Indians discomfited officials, who suspected renegades of betraying their fellow Spaniards by smuggling guns, teaching Indians how to repair firearms and make gunpowder, aiding Indians who raided Spanish settlements, spying, and inciting Indian resistance.[83] Christian apostates in the Araucanía, one Spanish scientist observed in 1782, "are usually . . . the major instigators of disturbances and uprisings and revolts, so they can maintain their independence and live in complete liberty."[84] The Pehuenches, Viceroy Avilés noted in 1799, were peaceful unless "some Spanish fugitive deceives them, pretending that we intend to do them some harm."[85] In 1800, when Viceroy Avilés launched a military campaign against Charrúas and Minuanes in what is today northern Uruguay, he hoped to bring an end to what he called "the frequent robberies, murders, smuggling, killing of livestock, and other serious crimes" caused not just by the Indians, but by the "vagrants, criminals, and fugitives" who "infest" the area.[86] Authorities in Buenos Aires had learned not only that the Charrúas and Minuanes harbored Spanish criminals, but that those Spaniards had become the Indians' leaders.[87]

Rescued captives confirmed the authorities' suspicions of renegades' perfidious behavior. Blas de Pedrosa testified that a Spaniard in his midtwenties, Juan de Dios, lived among the Pampas, had a Pampa wife, and served as a spy for the cacique Antemán. Blue-eyed, fair-skinned, and redheaded, Dios dressed in Spanish clothing to reenter Spanish society. He scouted out the best routes for Indian raiding parties, then returned to Antemán's village to direct bloody raids on his fellow Spaniards.[88] Little wonder, then, that in negotiating treaties with Indians, Spaniards insisted on the return of fugitives as well as captives living among the Indians.[89] Like redeemed and rescued captives, some of the renegades who rejoined Spanish society brought valuable information. Three fugitives who returned to San Antonio seemed so useful that authorities pardoned them for their unauthorized residence among Indians and employed them as interpreters.[90]

At the end of the colonial era, the number of Spaniards who lived willingly or unwillingly among independent Indians may have been relatively small, but their impact was large. Adopted into tribal societies, Spaniards helped rebuild Indian populations depleted by disease and warfare, and their mestizo children blurred racial distinctions. One visitor to southeastern North America described Indians' straight black hair, lack of beards, and copper-colored skin, but also reported that mixture with Europeans had produced "many exceptions to this general rule."[91] Some Spaniards brought new technologies and information that increased the capacity of unconquered Indians to resist or raid Spaniards. Other Indianized Spaniards facilitated accommodation between independent Indians and Spanish authorities. Where Indians forced Spanish officials to emphasize trade and diplomacy, these facilitators played a vital role. As translators they helped build the climate of trust and mutual understanding that allowed Indians and Spaniards to bridge their differences. Missionaries had often performed that function in the past, but many of the native peoples who remained independent of Spaniards had spurned missionaries. In their absence, it often fell to Spanish captives, merchants, renegades, and apostates to mediate between Spaniards and their savages.

Indian Captives

Like Spaniards captured by Indians, some Indians came into the Spanish world under duress. Some arrived as prisoners of war or as criminals. Others came as indentured servants, seized by Spaniards or captured by other Indians and ransomed to Spaniards. Many entered the Spanish world as slaves in fact, if not under the law.

With a few exceptions, which included Chichimecas and Araucanians at certain points in time, the Spanish crown prohibited its subjects from enslaving American Indians for any reason, even in a so-called just war. That prohibition, which responded to the Dantesque horrors of the Indian slave trade of the early 1500s, became codified in the master Compilation of the Laws of the Indies in 1680.[92] Thus, at the same time that Puritans captured Algonquians during King Philip's War and sold them into foreign slavery, the Laws of the Indies reaffirmed that Spaniards should treat Indians captured in combat as prisoners of war or as criminals, not as slaves. "In no case, place, or time" could American Indians be taken as slaves, the crown reaffirmed in 1756, an unqualified statement it proceeded to qualify by exempting Caribs from this protection.[93] With the exception of the fearsome Caribs, Spain's prohibition of Indian slavery in 1756 remained in force until the end of the colonial period. After Spain acquired Louisiana from France in 1762, for example, Spanish officials who justified enslaving blacks tried to stop the local practice of enslaving Indians.[94]

Official policy, as reiterated by the crown's officers, required that Indian captives be turned over to authorities and treated as prisoners of war.[95] As prisoners of war, adult

male captives were to be sentenced to work in mines or on haciendas for a specified period of time—usually ten years—rather than claimed as chattel for life. Authorities
took some interest in enforcing these sentences, requiring on occasion that the names
of punished individuals be recorded and preserved so they could be put at liberty after
ten years and not pressed into slavery.[96] Some of the captives did not live long enough
to appreciate the distinction between slavery and a ten-year sentence, however, and
many others became virtual slaves.[97]

Just as Indians found it economically advantageous to enslave Spaniards, Spaniards
found it profitable to enslave Indians and so found ways to circumvent the law.[98] Some
probably did so without any qualm of conscience. Unlike Christians, one theologian
noted in 1791, "savages" did not deserve "liberty or manumission," which came to them
"only due to the clemency of the Catholic king."[99] Paradoxically, Spaniards assuaged
their consciences by both baptizing Indian captives and by rhetorically dehumanizing
them; Spaniards commonly referred to Indian captives as *piezas*—the same word Spanish
hunters used for game animals.[100]

Spaniards not only captured Indians, but also bought or "ransomed" them from Indian
captors and purchased Indian children from their parents or family members, "like loose
change" as two critics charged.[101] In so doing, Spaniards violated a royal prohibition
against buying and selling pagan Indians. The Laws of the Indies, as the protector of Indians in Chile noted in 1777, "closed the door entirely to the purchase of Indian captives,
as well as their use, prohibiting buyers from using their services or having them in their
houses, farms, ranches, or towns, even if the Indians wish it."[102] Several treaties with Araucanians reiterated the illegality of the practice, and one Franciscan noted that a series
of popes had ordered the excommunication of Spaniards who bought and sold Indians.[103]

Ransoming Christians from pagans enjoyed royal approval because it saved baptized
souls from perdition, but the crown discouraged ransoming pagans from pagans because
it turned Indians into commodities. The bishop of Plata (today's Sucre) explained the
principle to Chiriguanos when he offered them gifts if they would surrender captives:
"Understand that this is not . . . formal ransom." The king, he told them, would not countenance traffic in "rational persons . . . buying and selling them, as if they were donkeys."[104]

But buy and sell rational persons they did, some Spaniards expressing the noblest of
reasons to justify their purchases. Spaniards who ransomed Indians argued that they
saved some of them from torture and death at the hands of their captors. Spain's Indian
allies would "kill their captives in cold blood," the legal advisor to the commander in
chief of the Interior Provinces noted in 1796, if they could not sell or ransom them.[105]
When they were not purporting to save captives from certain death, Spaniards claimed
that they freed Indian captives from "the slavery of the Devil" by saving their "souls"[106]
or that they freed them from a lifetime of enslavement by other Indians. In theory, purchased or ransomed Indians entered a period of tutelage leading to their conversion to
Christianity and freedom within Spanish society. One experienced Indian trader in
Texas suggested that missionaries should buy Apaches captured by Spain's Indian allies

and thus simultaneously rescue the captives and replenish the diminishing population of the Texas missions.[107] Ransomed or purchased Indians, however, seldom ended up in missions. Instead, private citizens took them into their homes and, if they followed the law, saw to their Christianization and acculturation. Ransomed Indians, a Franciscan in New Mexico noted, were, in effect, "emancipated to work out their account." He thought of them as indentured servants.[108]

In official reports, Spanish officers like Amigorena took pains to describe how they followed the king's wishes by treating captives "with humanity." Amigorena oversaw the distribution of women and children "for their care and education" in selected Spanish households.[109] Two of Alejandro Malaspina's officers noted approvingly that Spanish explorers in the Pacific Northwest purchased twenty-two boys and girls from the Nootkas and placed them in reputable homes in the Mexican port city of San Blas "with the knowledge of an absolute liberty once they become adults."[110] The commander in chief of the Interior Provinces of New Spain, Felipe de Neve in 1783, alluded to the "good fortune" of Indian children ransomed from Indians by Spaniards, who "raise them with the same love and affection as if they were their own children."[111] Spaniards' displays of Christian charity, he asserted, contrasted sharply with the cruel treatment Spanish captives received at the hands of Indians.

Less altruistically, Spaniards who favored ransoming captive Indians knew from experience that trade in captives helped keep peace. If Spaniards refused to purchase Indian captives, they might offend Indian allies. In Chile, Ambrosio O'Higgins recommended that Pehuenches be permitted to bring Huilliche captives "to our lands" and sell them to Spaniards, even though the sale of captives is "prohibited by the *parlamentos* and repeated royal orders." It would be difficult to deny the Pehuenches, he said, since they were fighting against enemy Huilliches and working to win the release of Christians captured by Huilliches.[112] Residents of Santa Fe, on the Río Paraná north of Buenos Aires, won decades of peace with Charrúas by offering them horses, cattle, arms, ammunition, clothes, liquor, and playing cards in exchange for captives—many of them Guaraníes whose labor the residents of Santa Fe needed.[113]

Beneath these altruistic and strategic reasons for ransoming heathens from heathens lay a fundamental economic truth: Indian laborers brought profits. In some urban areas, householders valued Indian women and children as servants and bought them in lieu of more expensive African slaves.[114] Frontier zones, characterized by chronic conflict with Indians, did not attract Spanish settlers and Spanish capital, and so local residents turned to Indian captives when they needed extra hands to work on haciendas, plantations, and mines.[115] It was also in these remote frontier areas where royal authority was weakest that laws could be violated with the greatest impunity. In much of northern New Spain, local officials traditionally sanctioned the ransoming of Indians, regardless of crown policy. Some authorities certainly invoked the law, but others caved into local demand and settled for regulating the ransom of Indians by setting prices rather than enforcing directives against it.[116] Indeed, some officials bought and sold Indians themselves, royal threats of fines and banishment notwithstanding.[117] Circumstantial evidence from New Mexico suggests that the worst official abuses occurred under the Habsburgs, and that Bourbon administrators behaved more professionally. Successful criminals, however, leave little trace for historians. One is left with bits and pieces of evidence, such as a Franciscan's characterization of ransomed Indians in New Mexico as the "gold and silver and richest treasure for the governors, who gorge themselves first with the largest mouthfuls from this table, while the rest eat the crumbs."[118]

The demand for ransomed or captive Indians varied with local circumstances. Hispanic residents of Alta California had little need for them because the thriving missions that dominated the local economy provided the coerced Indian laborers who did much of the work that supported the province's sparse Hispanic population. Hispanic residents of Buenos Aires made little use of forced Indian labor in the late colonial era because, as residents of a port city, they had ready access to black slaves. Unlike Indians, blacks could not flee to their homeland and thus constituted a more stable workforce. They could also be acquired legally. Although the crown prohibited the enslavement of Indians, it permitted enslaving of blacks. In Buenos Aires, blacks did the work that Indian captives did elsewhere: they were the artisans, domestic workers, ranch hands, and farmworkers. Without them, one historian has pointed out, economic life in the city and its environs "would have come to a standstill in a matter of hours."[119]

In many areas in which Spaniards and independent Indians forged new diplomatic and commercial relationships, however, the capturing and ransoming of Indians became a growth industry that further destabilized frontiers. Comanches, for example, who hunted captives to trade to their new allies in New Mexico after 1786, still needed to fill their own internal demand for captive Indian labor. They met the new demands by intensifying their raids on other tribes and by capturing Spaniards from other provinces.[120]

Like Indians who captured or purchased Spaniards, Spaniards who acquired Indians preferred to assimilate children rather than adults into their societies. Placed in Spanish households, little children were still malleable enough to become fictive kin and to acquire "rational customs."[121] Bourbon officials who sent Apache and Chichimeca prisoners of war into Cuban exile first culled out the children to stay behind, receive an education, and learn a trade at the crown's expense.[122] In 1786, the commander in chief of the Interior Provinces of New Spain, Jacobo Ugarte, made the Spanish preference for children plain. He offered to ransom Apache captives from Spain's new Comanche allies, but only those younger than fourteen years. Adults of both sexes, he said, were "excluded from this mercy, notwithstanding that it appears to us that everyone captured will be destined to suffer death [at the hands of Comanches]." By offering to buy Apache children from Comanches, Ugarte hoped to "stimulate our [Comanche] allies to search and capture because of interest in the ransom."[123] Ugarte's offer of ransom money to Comanches came just a year after officials at San Antonio got Comanches to agree to cease taking captives from other Indian nations.[124] As in other questions of Spanish Indian policy, consistency yielded to pragmatism.

By offering to buy Apache children and refusing to buy adults, Ugarte tacitly encouraged Comanches to kill Apache grownups in order to capture their youngsters. He
also spared himself the trouble and expense of dealing with adult prisoners. In 1787, he
had the costly task of disposing of over three hundred Apache adults of both sexes, whom
he had sent from Arizpe, in Sonora, to Guadalajara "in chain gangs, to be kept there
without risk of their escape, which was feasible here."[125] Difficult-to-control males were
especially troublesome and costly. Perhaps for that reason, the commander in chief of
the Interior Provinces Teodoro de Croix had offered one hundred pesos in 1780 to anyone in New Mexico who took a male Indian enemy, dead or alive.[126]

Spaniards, like Indians, preferred to acquire women rather than men. They paid a
higher ransom for women than for men and usually took more women captives.[127] In
1780, Maestre de Campo Amigorena returned to Mendoza from an expedition against
Pehuenches with 123 prisoners, all women and children. The men, he said, either escaped
or "preferred to die rather than surrender."[128] That, at least, was the official story from
an officer known for his severity as well as for his mercy.[129] Over and over again, Spaniards
returned from forays into Indian country with fewer male captives than women and
children, except in places where Spaniards had a market for live male captives.[130] Spaniards
on the western edge of the Chaco, for example, kept the women and children captives
as household servants but worked adult males in the sugar fields. Spaniards in far northern
New Spain sent adults to work in mining camps and on haciendas farther south, where
forced labor and paid labor coexisted amidst seasonal labor shortages.[131]

The placing of ransomed and captured Indian women and children in Spanish households had its origins with captive Muslims in Iberia.[132] Like Muslims, Indian captives
taken into Spanish homes became *criados,* a word that meant both "reared" and "domestic
servant." Both meanings of the word applied. First, *criados* were reared by Spaniards,
who fed and clothed them, baptized them, gave them religious instruction, and tried to
acculturate them. Second, *criados* served Spanish masters. Like Spaniards adopted by
Indians, some Indian *criados* apparently became closely attached to their new Spanish
families, deeming their guardians more akin to foster parents than masters, and their
guardians regarding them more as foster children than as servants.[133] It is difficult to tell,
however, where bonds of affection ended and self-interest began. What is one to make,
for example, of the motives of a doña María Marmól? In Buenos Aires, a former Jesuit
residence had been converted into the Residencia de las Chinas to receive captive Indian
women like the "gang of *chinas* [Indian women] and children of both sexes" taken in attacks on Charrúas and Minuanes in 1798. From the residencia, the captives were distributed to "wealthy people of good habits," who were to instruct them in "civil and
Christian life" under the watchful eye of the parish priest and the local alcalde.[134] Doña
María acquired one of those captive women but soon learned that the captive's infant
daughter had been given to someone else. Doña María appealed directly to the viceroy
to have the despondent woman's infant daughter reunited with her mother. This was

not only "right and proper" she insisted, but it was important "to have these people content that they might embrace our religion."[135]

Whether or not *criados* became "content," the law made clear that *criados* were not the slaves of their guardians and could not be bought and sold "as if they were Negros or trade goods."[136] The law defined Spanish guardianship as a temporary condition and required Spaniards to free *criados* from their indenture once they had become Hispanicized and had worked sufficiently to repay their master's expenses for ransoming and rearing them. The cost of this, one Franciscan in Chile observed, was very low, and *criados* could easily pay it from their wages. *Criados,* he insisted, were not slaves.[137]

In practice, some *criados* became slaves, bought and sold or disposed of as gifts or in wills. Aware that Spanish law prohibited Indian slavery, Spaniards who illegally enslaved Indians usually referred to them as *criados* or *indios de depósito,* rather than *esclavos.* In the province of Tucumán, however, and perhaps elsewhere, the enslavement of Indians was so common that Spaniards dropped the euphemism and spoke plainly in baptismal records, marriage registers, and wills. "I declare I have an Indian woman from the Mocobí nation, my slave; I declare her as such and order that she be delivered to my son Joseph as with all the other property," one María Mate de Luna declared in her will.[138] "María, a Mocobí Indian … has served me more than a slave, with all love, fidelity [and], honesty," a resident of Tucumán, Bernardino Pérez de Padilla, explained in granting her freedom in his will.[139] Spaniards with liberal inclinations had good reason, then, to fear that the "trustees" of ransomed Indian children "might under the cloak of religion try to justify a type of permanent dominion over these unfortunate beings."[140]

Like Indian men who captured Spanish women, some Spanish men abused criadas sexually and in every other way.[141] Ransomed or captured Indians, however, had rights under Spanish law, even when treated as de facto slaves, and some found ways to exercise those rights. Officials, some of whom bought and sold Indians or had *criados* in their homes, responded when *criados* or their defenders appealed to the law or when abuses became public. In Santa Fe, New Mexico, Gov. Tomás Vélez Cachupín moved two criadas to other households when they reported that their masters had failed to teach them to pray.[142] Similarly, in 1779 the governor of Valdivia responded to revelations of bad treatment of *criados* by issuing a strong warning against what he acknowledged was the long-standing abuse of enslaving Indians under the pretext of ransoming them. Residents had to notify officials that they had ransomed Indians in their custody, pay them for their work, feed, educate, and clothe them, and teach them to pray. Once baptized, he noted, ransomed Indians could not "return to the heathen way of life, even if their relatives want them."[143]

As in all theological matters, the fate of baptized, ransomed Indians was not always clear-cut. In 1779, for example, jurists divided over the morality of trading a captive Indian girl who wished to be baptized for a baptized Spanish girl captured by Indians. In general, though, Spaniards refused to send Christianized Indians back into heathendom, even stipulating in treaties that they would not return baptized Indians to their people.[144] In this sense, however free ransomed Indians might be under Spanish law or within Spanish society, they suffered a confinement that must have seemed indistinguishable from enslavement. How individuals responded to their confinement, however, varied from person to person and family to family. In New Mexico, one writer has held, "Indian slaves . . . were simultaneously exploited and cherished, even within the same household." That seems to have been the case wherever Spaniards acquired *indios bravos* and "reared" them as *criados*.[145]

Once freed from servitude, some captive or ransomed Indians apparently blended into Spanish society but remained at its lowest strata along with other Hispanicized Indians and mestizos.[146] Like lower-class Hispanics, detribalized and Hispanicized Indians found it difficult to find a marriage partner outside of their class or to afford the cost of marriage (those still in indenture had the additional burden of obtaining the consent of their guardians to contract marriage). Freed Indian captives, then, had a high rate of illegitimate births, and the stain of illegitimacy, coupled with their Indian origins, impeded their children's quest for a marriage partner. Those children, then, might become part of the floating frontier population of men and women without spouses and without fixed residences—their tribal origins lost to memory.[147]

The degree to which detribalized Indians assimilated, however, depended on circumstances in the locale where they lived. In New Mexico, where they apparently constituted over 10 percent of the population by 1750, ransomed and captive Indians retained their individual and communal identity well beyond the end of the colonial era.[148] There, liberated *criados* and other detribalized Indians were numerous enough to define themselves, and be defined by others, as a distinctive people living within the Spanish world. One group of former captives living in Santa Fe, for example, sent a delegation through dangerous Apache territory to Arizpe, in Sonora, to present a grievance to the commander in chief of the Interior Provinces. The delegation's leader, Ventura Bustamante, told Teodoro de Croix that if the government failed to meet the group's demands, he and his people would "go in search of relief to our lands and our Nation."[149]

Bustamante identified himself to Croix as the "lieutenant of the *genízaro* Indians of the Villa of Santa Fe," appropriating the name his Spanish neighbors applied to him. In eighteenth-century Spain, *genízaro* simply meant a Spanish-born son of a foreigner; New Mexicans, and New Mexicans alone, used the word to describe detribalized Indians.[150] Although individual *genízaros* surely blended into New Mexico society, New Mexico's *genízaros* maintained their identity partly because many of them lived in distinctive *genízaro* communities. Working as farmers and tradesmen, they replicated the economic dimensions of Spanish village life, but many also maintained ties with independent Indians.[151] Along with other poor, rural New Mexicans, they traded with Comanches on the Great Plains after the autumn harvest and journeyed into the remote Great Basin to trade with Utes. New Mexico's *genízaros* also maintained their sense of identity because their Spanish neighbors regarded them as distinctive, potentially seditious, and socially inferior.[152] Paradoxically, New Mexicans suspected *genízaros* of maintaining ties to independent Indians, yet also used them as soldiers, scouts, and interpreters in fighting and trading with independent Indians. In 1808, New Mexico's governor deployed a special military unit to fight Indians, the *tropa de genízaros,* and put it under the command of a *genízaro* corporal. New Mexico governors also rewarded the *genízaros* with grants of land to settle in new communities on the edge of the Indian frontier and so built a cordon of *genízaro* towns around the province to defend it from Navajos, Utes, Comanches, and Apaches. Detribalized descendants of *indios bárbaros,* then, served to defend New Mexico from *indios bárbaros*—that is, from their own relatives.[153] The military role of detribalized Indians in New Mexico has suggested to some scholars that they acquired their name from *Janissaries,* another meaning of the word *genízaros.* The elite guard in the army of the Ottoman Turks, Janissaries consisted of slaves, prisoners of war, and male children who had been taken as tribute from conquered Christians and become Muslims.[154]

Residents of the neighboring province of Sonora employed the word *nixora* to encompass Indians from a variety of tribes who had entered the Hispanic world.[155] Elsewhere, however, detribalized Indians seem to have retained their identity, at least for the first generation, as members of their individual tribes rather than falling under some umbrella term.[156]

Much as some Spaniards became Indianized and served the interests of their captors, so some Indians became Hispanicized and served Spaniards as cultural brokers. An eight-year-old Tonkawa boy captured by Lipan Apaches and sold to a Spanish soldier in San Antonio grew up to become an acculturated adult named Miguel Peres. When he learned of the whereabouts of his natural father and brother, however, he frequently left San Antonio to visit them. Although he evinced no desire to return to tribal life, he served as a human link between Spaniards and Tonkawas; on one critical occasion he helped preserve an alliance between the two communities.[157] In Venezuela a young Motilón captive, baptized as Sebastián José and raised in the house of the treasurer of Maracaibo, served as translator and diplomat to pave the way for a major rapprochement between Spaniards and Motilones to the south of Maricaibo in 1772. Sebastián José put Motilones at ease when a Spanish expedition entered the Motilón refuge in the Andean piedmont of Venezuela. He may also have been responsible for helping his Spanish master gain an appreciation of Motilones as hardworking, clean, abstemious, truthful, and peaceful people. Indians like Sebastián José and Miguel Peres, who grew up in Spanish society, were more likely, of course, to enjoy the trust of Spaniards than Indians who entered Spanish society as adults.[158]

Indians in Spanish Worlds, Willingly

Just as some Spaniards went willingly to trade or live in the lands of independent Indians, some Indians willingly entered Spanish domains. Once over the threshold, some never turned back. Others came and went. Some Indians lived in Spanish society undetected by church or civil authorities. Others appeared so conspicuously that we know their names and much about their motives.

Among the most conspicuous visitors were Indian leaders who went into the Spanish world as dignitaries. In the autumn of 1776, for example, Juan Bautista de Anza took a Yuma leader, whom he called Salvador Palma, to Mexico City. The Yumas controlled a strategic crossing place on the Colorado River along the most practical overland route between Mexico City and California. As the Spanish officer in charge of opening that route, Anza had assiduously courted Salvador Palma, mistakenly assuming that the impressive Palma was the principal chief of the Yumas. In reality he was one of many chiefs, but Palma played along. In the capital, he asserted that he was the head of his people and asked for baptism, missions, and guns. He got two of three. Convinced of the importance of winning the Yumas' loyalty, Viceroy Antonio María de Bucareli received Palma and three companions at a celebration of the king's birthday in the royal palace on November 4. He provided them with resplendent Spanish-style clothing and religious instruction. The four Yumas received baptism in the main cathedral on the Zócalo on February 13, 1777; Anza served as Palma's godfather. After Palma returned to the Colorado River, Franciscans followed, building two missions near the Yuma crossing in 1780. The missionaries and the colonists who joined them arrived with more demands than gifts and quickly become liabilities rather than assets. Disillusioned Yumas, Palma among them, destroyed the missions the next year. Spain never regained influence in the region.[159]

Palma's visit to Mexico City demonstrates the lengths to which Spanish authorities might go to impress Indian dignitaries with Spain's power and largesse. Giving Indian leaders a firsthand picture of life in a Spanish-American metropolis seemed worth a thousand words.[160] In 1787, when the viceroy of New Granada, Antonio Caballero y Góngora, tried to impress Cuna leaders, he not only entertained them in the city of Cartagena, but set them up in a house in the nearby village of Turbaco, where he resided. "I wanted them to see how happy and content the Indians of this town are under the gentle yoke of your majesty," he told the crown, "that they might observe . . . their good houses, sown fields, and comforts." The viceroy also wanted the Cunas to see that he himself lived among Indians, "without luxury, without troops, and with complete confidence."[161]

The next year, when he entertained Gov. Colville Briton of Tuapí Lagoon, recognized by British and Spaniards alike as the governor of the strategically important Tawira-Miskitos, Caballero y Góngora took even more extraordinary steps to make a good impression. The viceroy was eager to build a constructive relationship with Governor Briton so that Spain might fill the void the British had left when they withdrew from the Mosquito Coast in 1787. The task of courting Governor Briton was made easier for Spanish authorities by the fact that he was wooing a young Spanish girl, María Manuela Rodríguez. Miskitos had captured the girl in an attack on the Nicaraguan village of Juigalpa in 1782, when she was ten years old. When she became fifteen, Governor Briton wanted to marry her. She apparently insisted that he receive the Christian sacrament of baptism, and he obliged. Twice. First, he was baptized close to home, then sailed to

Cartagena in 1788, where he expressed interest in learning more about the Spaniards' faith and in receiving baptism again. Spanish authorities, delighted at the prospect of a former enemy turning friend, pulled out all the stops to impress him. At his second christening, in the cathedral at Cartagena, Briton took on two new names: Carlos, for the king, and Antonio, for the viceroy. Now called Carlos Antonio de Castilla, Briton received the sacrament of confirmation immediately after being baptized. The viceroy, who also served as archbishop, performed the ceremony; Field Marshal Antonio de Arévalo acted as godfather. Apparently pleased with his new faith and the gala celebrations that followed, Briton permitted one of his sons to be baptized and to travel to Spain for an education.[162]

Before leaving the Mosquito Coast for Cartagena, Governor Briton had freed María Manuela and sent her to León, the Spanish capital of Nicaragua, to arrange their marriage. Her escort party included one of his wives and a daughter, both of whom were baptized by the bishop in the cathedral of León on July 6, 1788, the same day Briton was baptized in Cartagena. Freed from captivity, María Manuela expressed reluctance to marry a considerably older man (Briton was between fifty and sixty) who already had four wives.[163] A Franciscan persuaded her to sacrifice herself in the interest of converting the Miskitos to Christianity, and the legal advisor to the intendant of Nicaragua erased Briton's previous marriages with convenient erudition. Citing the seventeenth-century Spanish jurist Juan de Solórzano, the legal advisor noted that heathens fell into three categories. Miskitos, he said, belonged to the lowest group—those who lived "uncultivated and like wild animals ... without law [and] without king." Thus, Briton had no wives because Miskitos were ignorant of the laws of marriage. In his new Christian incarnation, however, Briton had sufficient knowledge to marry María Manuela Rodríguez.[164]

Returning to the Mosquito Coast from Cartagena, Briton traveled to León, receiving honors along the way at the Spanish Fort of San Carlos and the City of Granada. He married María Manuela in León on December 20, 1788, and Spanish officials celebrated with bullfights, parades, and rocket fire. After lingering in the city for over a month after the wedding, don Carlos Antonio and doña María Manuela returned to Tuapí Lagoon. They did not live happily ever after. Fearful that he would move the Tawira-Miskitos into the Spanish orbit, British agents worked to discredit him, as did his intensely pro-British Zambo-Miskito rival, King George II (1777–1800). In the end, Briton's supporters, apparently alienated by his rapprochement with Spain and his efforts to convert them to a religion that permitted only one wife, assassinated him in 1790. Two missionaries, discouraged by their lack of progress amidst the intensely anti-Catholic Miskitos, had fled before his death. With Briton's consent, one of them had spirited the pregnant doña María Manuela away and returned her to her family. She gave birth to a son on whom she bestowed the Christian name of his father—Carlos Antonio de Castilla.[165]

Indian leaders like Salvador Palma and Governor Briton entered the Spanish world as objects of curiosity, not of respect—pomp and circumstance notwithstanding. In 1774, Chilean governor Agustín de Jáuregui invited representatives of the four Araucanian *butalmapus* to send "ambassadors" to represent them in Santiago. Araucanians might have taken this as recognition of their sovereignty, but Governor Jáuregui intended to hold Araucanian leaders as hostages "with the specious title of ambassador."[166] By dealing directly with Araucanian representatives in Santiago he could also cut back on the expense of holding *parlamentos.* The four ambassadors arrived on April 4, greeted by ceremonies and outward signs of respect, but officials could not control popular displays of derision. Just two days after the ambassadors' arrival, Jáuregui found it necessary to threaten three hundred lashes and ten years of exile on the island of Juan Fernández to anyone who ridiculed the Indian leaders.[167] The governor made much of their visit, reporting to the crown that they "swore to be faithful vassals of the king our lord, and prostrated themselves before a portrait of his royal person."[168] Others took a less rosy view. One officer complained, "They do not represent their nation because it does not have any kind of government." The ambassadors, he said, spend their time visiting the "principal gentlemen of the city, with no other purpose than asking them for a couple of coins [*reales*] in order to drink."[169]

Even when Spanish officials expressed respect for Indian leaders, they did not imagine Indians as their equals. Ambrosio O'Higgins, who prided himself on his excellent relations with Araucanians, offered this revealing advice to his nephew: "Use all the prudence, gentleness, sweetness, and sagacity that is necessary when you deal with this kind of people, who despite their savagery and idiocy know how to give their esteem and confidence to those who treat them in that way."[170]

While some Indian leaders entered the Spanish domain with fanfare, other Indians crossed unheralded into the Spanish world to visit Spanish missions, forts, towns, haciendas, and farms. The détente that characterized Spanish–Indian relations in many peripheral areas of the empire in the late 1700s, and the economic growth that followed, opened the way for independent Indians to come into Spanish settlements to trade, work, or receive gifts—yet still remain independent of Spanish political control.

The Bourbon reforms sparked economic and demographic growth in many frontier regions. New Mexico's economy and Hispanic population rebounded dramatically in the 1780s and 1790s, following a period of drought and a devastating smallpox epidemic in 1780–81.[171] Along the north side of the Biobío, on what Spaniards called the Isla de Laja, the single town of Los Angeles grew from thirty-five people in 1746 to three thousand in 1780 and stimulated growth even as it reflected it.[172] These and other expanding Spanish markets, such as the frontera of Buenos Aires and the province of Tucumán on the western side of the Chaco,[173] seem to have attracted independent Indian traders as never before. Pehuenches, for example, some of whom had become Spanish allies in the 1760s, controlled vital Andean passes and brought salt from the central pampa to be traded in Chilean communities as far north as the town of Talca, 160 miles from Santiago.[174]

As visits by independent Indians increased, Spanish communities created special facilities to receive them. The Indian inns that Blas de Pedrosa and his competitors operated in Buenos Aires were not unique. In San Antonio, Texas, Gov. Domingo Cabello anticipated an increased number of visits following the peace of 1785 with Comanches and ordered the construction of a special lodging for Indians. A local interpreter with whom visiting Indians usually stayed provided land next to his house on the banks of the San Antonio River. The building, 144 feet long and 15 feet wide, contained four rooms to house visitors from different tribes. In the waters of the river Indians could indulge their habit of daily bathing—an exotic indulgence from the point of view of Spaniards, who, like other Europeans, bathed infrequently.[175] As New Mexico entered a period of peaceful relations with Indians in the late colonial period, Santa Fe also received visits from Comanches, Utes, Navajos, and Apaches. They came with such frequency that representatives of two or more groups sometimes arrived simultaneously. When that occurred, Governor Concha specified that they be lodged separately, although where they stayed is not clear.[176] In all cases, however, the demand for government-funded gifts, food, and drink for visiting Indians stimulated local economies.[177]

"Wild" Indians entered the Spanish world to work as well as to trade. Where peaceful relations obtained and labor shortages existed, independent Indians moved in and out of Spanish society as short-term salaried workers on a seasonal and even daily basis.[178] Scholars once assumed that the shortages of labor in peripheral areas of the empire favored systems of forced labor, but a closer look has revealed that conditions were mixed. Employers in need of seasonal workers found it less trouble to hire workers than to coerce them. By the late eighteenth century, forced labor had given way in many areas of the empire to free, salaried employment.[179] In California it cost less to hire heathens than to employ Christian Indians from the missions, so some presidial commanders hired pagans for construction projects.[180] Mapuches regularly crossed the Biobío in the spring to spend the summer as agricultural or ranch workers or to strengthen Spanish forts and fortified plazas.[181] Groups of Guanás, or Chanés, men, agriculturalists from the Chaco, whom one observer described as semicivilized but not Christian, annually crossed the Río Paraguay to do seasonal farmwork in Paraguay; they left their women and children behind.[182] Chiriguanos traveled to haciendas near Santa Cruz to harvest sugarcane, and groups of Matacos, Guanás, and Guaycuruans emerged from the Chaco to work in the cane fields near Jujuy and Salta—a pattern they continued well into the next century. The shortage of labor in Salta, one official noted in 1806, "obliged its residents to contract with the heathen for all work on foot or on horseback, in the countryside as well as the city."[183] Authorities could comfort themselves that independent Indians who temporarily entered Spanish society had begun a journey toward civilization, and *hacendados* and others who needed seasonal labor could avoid the expense of keeping employees on the payroll year-round.[184]

Like certain Spaniards, some Indians apparently crossed borders to escape the conventions of their society, but we know little about the forces that pushed individual Indians to live amidst aliens. One historian conjectures, for example, that Santa Fe and San Antonio served as places of refuge for Comanche adulterers fleeing "the harsh penalties that adultery evoked under Comanche law."[185] An Indian from the pampa, taken prisoner

near a Spanish fort in 1779, explained that he was headed "to the land of the Christians."
Asked why he, "being from an opposite nation, would come to live voluntarily with the
Christians," the Indian purportedly offered several unrelated explanations. He was poor,
he had poor eyesight, he was bored with his countrymen, and they intended to kill him.[186]

Some Indians who took up permanent or temporary residence in Spanish territory
probably melded into the floating populations of *mestizos* and baptized *indios domésticos,*
their origins unrecognized. In Chile, where Araucanians had captured large numbers of
Spaniards, observers reported there were "many Indian men and women in those nations
as white and blonde as the Spaniards of that country [Chile]." During times of peace,
these Indians found it particularly easy to work on Spanish haciendas and spend their
wages in Spanish establishments. Some returned to the Araucanía; others remained.[187]

Indians who chose to leave their lands to trade or work in Spanish territory seemed
to confirm progressive Bourbon officials' faith that the Spanish economy was the key to
Indians' ultimate assimilation. It stretches the point, however, to suppose that Indians'
interest in acquiring material possessions was, as one scholar claimed, "identical to that
of the Spaniards and mestizos."[188] Whatever the proclivities of some individual Indians,
not all Native societies shared Europeans' enthusiasm for the market economy and accumulation of goods. Matacos who collected their pay and then rode back into the Chaco,
pausing to steal horses and kill settlers along the way, had a value system that made them
undependable harvesters of sugarcane in a monetary economy.[189] Nomads, in particular, enjoyed a way of life that worked against acculturation, for it demanded that they
acquire no more property than they could transport conveniently.[190]

If some "savages" remained among Spaniards and blended into the lower strata of
Spanish society, others could not disguise their tribal origins. New Mexico officials who
arrested four men for sedition at the village of San Miguel del Vado on the edge of the
buffalo plains in 1805 readily identified three of them as members of specific independent tribes: Francisco the Comanche, Francisco Xavier of the Pawnee nation, José María
Gurulé of the Kiowa nation.[191] At Asunción there could be no mistaking the branch of
the Payaguás who lived peacefully in and around the city. Like other Guaycuruans, the
women had tattooed faces and the men wore body paint and scanty clothing. Félix de
Azara, who had ample opportunity to observe these Payaguás in the 1790s, when they
numbered about a thousand at Asunción, reported that they "fish and work to the benefit
of this city, and although they are not Catholics they may be considered useful partners."[192]
Payaguás, whose name Spaniards appropriated in somewhat altered form for the river
and province of Paraguay, had long been regarded as ferocious, but some had made
peace with Asunción in 1740. After fifty years of day-to-day living and working amidst
Spaniards, however, they had retained their customs "without changing absolutely anything." They were not baptized, Azara said, and "they absolutely do not want to be Christians, and if they are required to they would start another war."[193] It scandalized priests
to have heathens working and living in Spanish society, but Spanish laypersons justified
hiring them by suggesting that employment would lead to the Indians' civilization and

conversion.[194] Eager to have cheap Indian labor and to fill labor shortages, *hacendados* and small farmers tolerated heathens among them.[195]

Indians who returned to tribal societies after living among Spaniards carried with them knowledge of Spanish culture and the Spanish language. As that knowledge spread, the cultural divide that separated Spaniards and their savages seemed to narrow.[196] By the late 1700s, Spanish-speaking Indians could be found in the most remote places, facilitating communication between Spaniards and independent Indians. As he floated down the Río Bermejo in 1780 in search of a navigable route across the Chaco, fray Francisco Morillo encountered groups of Indians who gathered on the river's bank to ask for gifts. *Ladinos,* that is, Indians who spoke Spanish as well as their own language, translated for them. Among the Mataguayos and Matacos, a *ladino* named Luis spoke for the "mob," as Morillo described the Natives. The missionary recognized him from the convent in Salta, where he had once worked, and through him could exhort the Indians to heed "the truths of Jesus Christ" and avoid "the lies of Satan."[197] On the pampa and in the Araucanía some of the Indian women who marketed their textiles to Spaniards became bilingual and served as translators.[198] "Savage Indians" in southern Yucatán who traded with Spaniards to the north and Englishmen to the south became "commercial brokers between both parties" and spoke both English and Spanish, an official in Yucatán reported in 1804.[199] Contact between Spaniards and independent Jicarilla Apaches in New Mexico was so intense that Governor Concha noted in 1794 that the Jicarillas had no translator assigned to them because "it is very unusual to find among them anyone who cannot speak some Castilian."[200]

Neither Savage nor Spaniard

In the late Bourbon era, frontier zones throughout the empire contained numerous independent Indians who had fallen under Spanish influence but were not fully Christianized or Hispanicized.[201] Some of these Spanish-speaking Indians moved between the worlds of Spaniards and savages in ways that frustrated Spanish officials and defied conventional categories.

Spaniards in New Granada, for example, regarded one Guajiro leader, Cecilio López Sierra of the town of Boronata, as the *cacique mayor de la nación guajira*—the principal chief of the Guajiros. Twice married in the Catholic Church, cacique Cecilio had relatives in the Spanish community and once visited Spain. He also had relatives among Guajiro bands who continued to resist Spanish domination. López Sierra, as his biographer noted, served as a "point of contact between Spanish authorities and 'rebel' Indians."[202] Spaniards valued him for his influence with Guajiros; Guajiros valued him for his influence with Spaniards. Spaniards used him as a guide and intermediary for activities in Guajiro territory, and they expected him to report the activities of foreigners among his people. Behind the scenes, López Sierra smuggled black slaves into New Granada, obtaining them from foreigners and using his influence with Spanish authorities to legalize their presence. Franciscans regarded him as a Catholic and depended on him to smooth the way for missionaries, but he also protected the religious beliefs of his people. López Sierra, then, was an independent Indian who appeared to have become a Spanish subject and a Spanish subject who retained his ties to independent Indians.

There were others like him—Hispanicized Indians who maintained close relationships with Indians Spaniards regarded as savages. In New Granada, a Chimila captive testified that some of his people who lived in Spanish missions slipped away on occasion to reintegrate themselves into bands of still-independent Chimilas. While drinking and feasting, the mission Indians, or *indios reducidos,* helped their independent brethren to plan raids on Spaniards. After a successful attack, the *reducidos* and the independent Chimilas gathered "to celebrate the robberies and murders they had carried out."[203] In Sonora, Teodoro de Croix concluded that auxiliary units of Christian Yaquis and Lower Pimas who refused to fight alongside Spanish troops against Seris and Upper Pimas remained enthralled by the independent Indians: "The example of absolute liberty of the savages incites them to seek their own [liberty]. The family ties that some have with the savages compels them toward infidelity."[204] In Nueva Vizcaya the governor and captain general bemoaned the fact that Christian Indians had become "friendly with and mixed with" heathens, conspiring with them to rob Spanish settlers and *hacendados.* In 1755, he required Christian Indians to carry a passport when they left their community and threatened those who disobeyed with arrest. Indians who resisted arrest would be executed as rebels. In 1772, another governor of Nueva Vizcaya issued similar orders, adding that any Spaniard who failed to enforce them would be punished as a "traitor to the King."[205]

If Spaniards had difficulty telling "good" Indians from "bad" Indians, independent Indians masquerading as Spanish soldiers or as Spanish country folk compounded the problem of recognition. Spain's Pima allies learned of this ruse when Apaches wearing the leather jackets and hats of Spanish soldiers and carrying guns attacked them by surprise in 1780.[206] It seems likely that those Apaches had among them a figure like Josecillo el Manco, an Indian taken from a Spanish mission by Lipan Apaches as a young boy. Josecillo grew up with an Apache band and became its captain and go-between with the Spanish world—he was one of the empire's many "domestic enemies."[207]

Conversely, some Spanish criminals and Christian Indians disguised themselves as wild Indians to raid Spanish settlements. For Spanish Christians, dressing like Indians showed sinful indifference to Catholicism.[208] That, however, was probably the least of the miscreants' sins in the eyes of their church. Felipe de Neve described gangs of "villains and evildoers" who roamed the countryside in northern New Spain. Joined by Indians who had fled Spanish towns and missions, they robbed and murdered, but "it is not easy to determine the true perpetrators [of these deeds] because they carry them out disguised in the clothing of Apaches." In Spanish society, where all races mingled, race itself did not signify friend or foe. Clothing was a more useful social marker, but since that could be changed readily, Spanish authorities turned to paper. Like officials before and after him, Neve hoped to tell who was who by requiring Indians and mixed bloods in the northern provinces of New Spain to carry documentation when they traveled. They were to obtain a travel permit from local officials or priests, who would specify their destination and the duration of their journey. In the hope of stopping spies from entering Spanish communities, Neve also instructed owners of haciendas not to let undocumented persons work for them.[209]

The gangs of masquerading "villains and evildoers" about whom Neve complained were composed of individuals who had fled the constraints of both the Spanish and Indian worlds and who had augmented their numbers by raiding Spanish haciendas and capturing women and children. Multiethnic and multiracial, these bands included former mission Indians, lower-class Spaniards, renegades from the societies of independent Indians, and blacks brought to America as slaves.[210]

Black slaves toiled principally on the plantations of the Caribbean, where Spaniards found them to be more suitable laborers than Indians, but black slaves also lived in temperate zones far from plantations. They worked on the haciendas and in the mines of Nueva Vizcaya and lived in towns like Saltillo and San Antonio in northern New Spain[211] and in Buenos Aires, where the slave trade kept pace with the city's burgeoning population growth. Between 1778 and 1810, Africans, African Americans, and mulattos constituted 30 percent of the population of the city of Buenos Aires.[212] Some of those blacks became Indianized when they fled into Indian country or when Indians captured them or purchased them. Peoples as various as Chiriguanos, Chimilas, Comanches, Creeks, Cherokees, Miskitos, and Caribs absorbed black captives into their societies as readily as they absorbed whites, and some blacks found their way into renegade bands that operated in the interstices between Spaniards and "savages."[213]

The best documented of these groups operated out of a base camp in the dry, rugged Sierra del Rosario, about 250 miles south of Chihuahua in Nueva Vizcaya. In 1773, Spanish officials interrogated several men who had been in the camp and learned that it had a sizable population. Estimates ranged from one thousand to seventeen hundred people, including women and children. Even the more conservative number was significant at a time when the capital of Nueva Vizcaya, Durango, scarcely contained sixty-five hundred people.[214] The outlaw community's leaders, a father and son both named Calaxtrin, were Apaches, but most Indians in the group were Tarahumaras. Some of its members lived undercover in Spanish settlements, permanently or temporarily, where they gathered intelligence. The outlaws supported themselves by rustling livestock from Spanish haciendas, which they consumed or traded. Apaches were an especially important market. Apaches offered arrows, lances, and leatherwork for stolen horses and mules, which they drove to northern markets. Spaniards had trouble distinguishing between Apaches rustlers and members of the Calaxtrins' band—or similar bands of outlaws who came from Spanish towns and missions. The outlaws' tactics, which included raids by the light of a full moon, resembled those of Apaches, and they used Apache arrows. At the same time, Indians and non-Indians who rode together in the Calaxtrins' small raiding parties often dressed like Spaniards and rode with Spanish saddles. Some women, dressed like

Spanish men, joined them. When in doubt, though, Spaniards in Nueva Vizcaya blamed Apaches.

Perhaps the Calaxtrins' group was a den of thieves, as Spanish officials believed. Or perhaps, as one scholar has supposed, these were revolutionaries intent on destroying a repressive Spanish colonial society and redistributing the wealth of its elite. In either case, members of the band had adopted elements from both Spanish and savage societies, even as they belonged to neither. The outlaws reportedly drew on the spiritual power of an indigenous drug, peyote, to incorporate new members into the group, yet devoted themselves to a Spanish patron saint in the form of a statue of Nuestra Señora de los Dolores.[215]

Through multiple forms of contact with Spaniards, then, independent Indians acquired substantial knowledge of Spaniards. The ways they used that knowledge, however, ranged across the spectrum. Some "savages" entered the Spanish world to become law-abiding Christians, others learned enough of the Spanish world to reject its religion and its laws and become dangerous renegades—joining renegades from Spanish towns and missions.

Spaniards as Savages?

Independent Indians who became Hispanicized had Spanish counterparts who became Indianized. Spanish frontiersmen often found it in their interest to make their own peace with Indian neighbors, whose economies often articulated with theirs. By definition, frontiersmen lived in regions where Spanish institutions were weak—areas "without law, without faith, and without king," *sin ley, sin fe, sin rey,* in the popular phrase of the day. Spanish frontiersmen who gravitated toward Indians, then, felt a weak institutional pull from the opposite direction.

In contrast to Spaniards from the upper echelons of society, Spaniards who lived in poverty in scattered homesteads on the frontiers of the empire did not have to cross an abyss to enter the societies of independent Indians, either in physical distance or in social space. If urban Spaniards found themselves disoriented in Indian territory, poor Spaniards from rural areas found much that was familiar.

In Argentina's southern frontier, the lowest strata of Spanish society shared poverty, geography, and an equestrian culture with Indians of the pampa.[216] Dispersed over a vast countryside, many rural Spaniards lived far from representatives of the church and state. "They hardly have, or recognize, anyone to obey or fear," one sophisticated observer noted, "and as a result they differ little from the savage Indians."[217] Similarly, an officer from Buenos Aires who visited isolated Spanish settlements on the edge of Indian territory in 1810, thought it unavoidable that the residents "would acquire some savage customs, and . . . feel the bad effects of the indolence and ignorance of their savage neighbors." These Spaniards, who traded with Indians or made clandestine visits to Indian camps to sell alcohol and other items, had become "only slightly less ferocious and uncivil than the Indians themselves."[218] Gauchos, rootless poor rural Spaniards who killed cattle on

31. A Chilean huaso, *1830. Lithograph entitled* Un guazo *from Orbigny, 1835–47, vol. 3, ser. 3, no. 3. Courtesy, John Carter Brown Library at Brown University.*

the pampa and marketed their hides without a license, also fit his description. Gauchos hunted cattle with an Indian weapon (*boleadoras* or *bolas*), drank Indian tea (yerba maté) to the point of addiction, used Indians to assist them in hunting, traded with Indians for hides, and adopted Indian words into their vocabularies.[219] Other frontiers of the empire had counterparts to the gauchos, men who also adopted some of the clothing, diet, and strategies of their Indian neighbors: *llaneros* in what is today Colombia and Venezuela, *huasos* in Chile, and *vaqueros* in Mexico.[220]

Urbane Spaniards saw these Indianized rural people as living proof of the baneful effects of living side by side with wild Indians. In Buenos Aires, Viceroy Juan José de Vértiz concluded that Spaniards on the pampa had "continuous dealings with the heathens, by which the heathens know our movements . . . and they are the heathens' guides or scouts." He described the rural poor as a people "of abominable customs, dedicated to injuring and killing people, robbing horses and women."[221] One Franciscan denounced Spaniards who lived in the basins of the upper Pilcomayo and Bermejo rivers on the northwestern edge of the Chaco and in remote valleys in the foothills of the Andes as "apostates" who possessed "worse habits than the savages themselves." They stirred up the savages with their "thievery and wickedness."[222] In Chile, another Franciscan complained that Spaniards who lived "scattered in the countryside" on the north side of the

Biobío had no appreciation for "civil life" and "live and die less well than the Indians."[223] Spaniards, who along with blacks made up the majority of the Indian village of Boronata on the Guajira Peninsula, lived "naked like the Indians in their liberty."[224] Officials suspected that these poor Spanish villagers, many of them fugitives, warned Guajiros of impending military operations. Although they shared much with Guajiros, the local Spaniards robbed livestock from Guajiros, just as Guajiros robbed livestock from them. "I do not know," the governor of Riohacha wrote, "who are the most savage and the least religious."[225]

In some areas, Spaniards had practical reasons to live outside of towns, in homesteads on the edge of Indian territory. Officials like Governor de la Concha of New Mexico probably confused cause with effect when they supposed that Spaniards lived outside of towns in order to emulate "the liberty and slovenliness they see and take note of in their neighbors the savage Indians." In arid New Mexico, farmers and herders needed to live in homesteads strung out along watercourses, so they could tend to their fields and orchards and keep watch over their herds and flocks.[226] In Spanish provinces, where small numbers of families monopolized land closest to markets, Hispanics who moved into Indian country also gained access to land.[227] Settling in remote areas might also offer relief from taxes and tithes, freedom from the social constraints of urban or village life, and the opportunity to trade illegally with independent Indians.[228]

In frontier regions, trade showed no respect for the lines that seemed to separate savagery and civilization, or friend and foe. Underpaid or unpaid soldiers and militia continued a long tradition of trading illegally with supposedly hostile Indians, furnishing them with weapons and ammunition, and it appears that an unscrupulous ranch foreman traded livestock to Indians and then reported it stolen by what he called enemy Indians.[229] In southern Chile, some country people stole horses from their well-to-do neighbors and traded them to Indians south of the Biobío. The most adventurous Spaniards journeyed into the Andes to exchange stolen livestock for salt and ponchos from Pehuenches or even crossed the Andes to the source of salt in the province of Cuyo. Chilean officials' prohibitions against trading in Indian territory (one governor threatened the death penalty in 1770) had little impact. Even government-paid *capitanes de amigos* often aided the smugglers rather than apprehending them.[230] Spaniards who lived in remote areas along the edges of the Chaco also profited from illegal trade with Indians.[231] Spanish residents of Santa Fe, on the eastern edge of the Chaco, one Franciscan complained, "do not wish for any other thing than that the Indians remain calm so that they can trade with them in peace . . . they do not care if they are pagans or Christians."[232]

Where the Spanish population was thin and social boundaries were weak, Indian influence was particularly strong.[233] Along the Araucanian frontier, one Chilean-born Jesuit observed disapprovingly, the mostly Spanish rural population spoke Araucanian and dressed "in the Araucanian manner."[234] On the remote island of Chiloé, Huilliches influenced Spaniards' dress, foods, medicines, farming techniques, work patterns, and recreation. In 1784, the governor suspended the town council at Castro, the island's capital, accusing its members and other islanders of enjoying Indian-inspired orgies that featured the consumption of immoderate amounts of hard cider (*chicha de manzana*) and sex.[235] Another governor of Chiloé noted that the Spaniards of all social levels used two languages, "Castillian, very badly spoken, and Huilliche ... very well [spoken]." Spanish remained the language for official matters on the island, but Huilliche served for everyday conversation.[236]

Racial as well as cultural borders blurred in rural areas, where most Hispanics had high percentages of Indian blood. Racial blending, which had begun with the first generation of Spanish conquistadors, continued throughout the colonial era as Spaniards entered into relationships with *indios domésticos* as well as with the most obdurate of independent Indians. Along the Araucanian frontier in Chile, for example, the process of mestizaje began well before peace came. By the late eighteenth century, mixed bloods made up much of the populations on both sides of the Biobío.[237]

Miscegenation was a feature of life wherever Spaniards and their savages found common ground. Even when Indians were at war with the Spanish, individual Spaniards and Indians fashioned or maintained amicable personal relationships. As Spanish ranchers expanded their holdings toward the upper Pilcomayo and into the Chiriguanía, for example, they met strong resistance from Chiriguanos. Some Chiriguanos joined Spaniards, however, even as others fought them, and out of unions between Spanish men and Chiriguano women there emerged mestizos tied by blood to both communities.[238]

In English America, whites worried that they were becoming "too like unto the Indians," in the words of one Puritan leader, yet a deep racial divide separated Englishmen and Indians.[239] In Spanish America, blurred racial boundaries left culture as the only clear sign of whether one was an Indian or a Spaniard. Thus, it was possible in Spain's colonies for *indios domésticos* to avoid paying tribute by dressing like Spaniards and thus concealing themselves from the tax collector—in plain sight. Despite the ubiquity of racially mixed people throughout the Spanish empire, light-skinned, upper-class Spaniards commonly believed that race determined human worth. In New Spain, Viceroy Revillagigedo (the younger) expressed the conventional wisdom of the elite when he noted in 1793 that the "mulattos and other infected castes" in the scattered settlements of Nuevo Santander were poor role models for Indians. Because they were "naturally inclined to laziness and all kinds of vices, they needed the good example of families or people of better habits to correct them."[240]

Although elite Spaniards took a dim view of mixed-blood frontiersmen, they praised their prowess at fighting Indians. They portrayed frontiersmen as being as tough as Indians: skilled horsemen, able to fight without firearms, and accustomed to travel for days with little food, clothing, or shelter. When officials in Montevideo tried to raise a force to fight Charrúas in 1797, they looked for men who were "cut from the same cloth" as the Indians.[241] They found them in the frontier army itself. One officer described the frontier soldiers, or *blandengues,* from the Banda Oriental as "killers, thieves, bandits, criminals, [and] loafers who live permanently without religion, residence, or law."[242] If some officers worried that such men lacked military training, others dismissed the problem because "to fight Indians you do not need military maneuvers."[243]

When it came to fighting Indians, then, Hispanic frontiersmens' vices were also their virtues. Life on the edge of Indian country had made frontiersmen "specialists in violence," in the phrase of one scholar, and they could be as brutal to one another as to Indians.[244] The leader of the *blandengues'* campaign against the Charrúas, Capt. Jorge Pacheco, enjoyed a reputation for his brutal punishment of Spanish bandits. He wrapped them in raw leather then left them where the sun would shrink the leather and slowly crush them to death.[245] Like many military men of his era, however, Pacheco also had a gentler side. Why not use "civilization and preaching" to subdue the Charrúas, he suggested to the viceroy in 1808, "instead of the devastation of arms that do not serve the progress of Religion."[246]

Spaniards preferred to see themselves as merciful and Indians as cruel. When Pehuenche allies presented the severed head of a powerful Ranquel chief, Llanquetruz, to the comandante of a Spanish fort in Chile in 1789, one officer described the gesture as the "custom among nations of these heathens." Yet Amigorena, the Spanish commander of the Frontera de Mendoza, had offered five hundred mares for Llanquetruz's head on orders from Viceroy Loreto. The Indians had merely delivered it, encouraged by Spaniards who had their own custom of severing the heads and ears of their Indian victims throughout the hemisphere.[247] Carlos III, for example, had expressed satisfaction in learning that Spanish forces had killed a rebel cacique in Chile, Ayullapan, and presented "his head to our comandante, Ambrosio Higgins."[248] When it came to severing heads, however, Bourbon officials did not single out Indians for special treatment. They also ordered that the heads of Spanish rebels and criminals be displayed in public places as object lessons.[249] If Spanish frontiersmen had become "specialists in violence," it appears their leaders in the empire's administrative centers did not lag far behind.

On the edge of Indian country, the poor, illiterate Spaniards who lived like Indians, looked like Indians, and fought like Indians were also, paradoxically, the Spaniards most likely to take the brunt of Indian attacks.[250] On the northwest edge of the Chaco, for example, Indians raided the livestock of poor Hispanics because they were easier targets than the rich, well-armed *hacendados*. At the same time, paradox on paradox, Spanish authorities accused rural settlers of inciting Indians to violence.[251]

Erasing the "People without Reason"

As in other frontier regions around the globe, the impulse for crossing borders came from local people. Their lives shaped by the dualities of conflict and interdependence, friction and exchange, peoples who face one another across frontiers often find common ground.[252] High-ranking Bourbon officials, however, saw frontier Spaniards' accommodations to independent Indians as a lamentable but temporary expediency. The most pro-

gressive Bourbon officials believed that in the long run Indians could and would acculturate when exposed to Spaniards and Spanish culture. One scholar has suggested that
Spanish policymakers saw independent Indians as "an enemy to be exterminated or segregated in enclaves rather than incorporated into colonial society," but Bourbon authorities favored peaceful coexistence and incorporation over extermination. Segregation in
separate *repúblicas* for Indians and Spaniards had become a distant memory.[253]

Bourbon logic suggested that acculturation could run in only one direction, away
from barbarism and toward civilization. Indians might temporarily influence the manners
and customs of frontier Spaniards, but over time Native cultures would succumb to
Spanish example. Pedro Mendinueta, who served on the Indian frontier as governor of
New Mexico before becoming viceroy of New Granada, maintained that Spanish colonists
offered Indians an opportunity to communicate with civilized people. The Indians "will
observe the colonists' behavior and customs. They will see that the colonists enjoy certain
conveniences under an established order. Once the powerful incentive of the Indians'
own comfort or the spirit of imitation works on them, there will be progress."[254] Or, as
another enlightened officer put it, through association with "people of reason," the
"people without reason," would acquire the technology and arts and that would make
them "men" and "vassals useful to the Monarchy." By the second or third generation,
racial and cultural blending would turn Indians into Spaniards. It would produce individuals "who scarcely maintain the nonessential quality of being Indians. Raised among
Spaniards, their language, practices, and customs will not differ from ours."[255]

At the highest levels, Bourbon policymakers advocated interracial marriages as a way
to bring Spaniards and savages together. "I have expedited the marriages of thirty-five
Spanish men with the principal Indian women of the Carib, Guaica, and Guaraúna nations," the governor of Guayana reported in 1771. He predicted that these marital alliances would unite Spain with the Indian nations.[256] A few years later, Carlos III expressed
"much satisfaction" that some Araucanians had sought religious instruction in order to
marry Christians and that one of the four Araucanian ambassadors who came to live in
Santiago in 1774 was going to marry a Christian.[257]

Ferdinand and Isabel had encouraged the assimilation of American Indians a decade
after Columbus's discovery, and Frenchmen had practiced it in New France and Louisiana
(in contrast to Englishmen in America, who tended to keep their distance from Indians).[258]
Some enlightened Spanish bureaucrats, however, justified assimilation as good science.
Pedro Fermín de Vargas, a consummate *ilustrado* from New Granada, drew an analogy
in 1791 to the benefits that came from cross-breeding animals, and José María Aurrecoechea, a royal official who served in Venezuela in the early 1800s, compared Indians to
trees that bore poor crops. Such trees were "better for grafting than to hope for good
and abundant fruit from them in their natural state." Grafting whites and blacks onto
Indian stock, he confidently predicted, would produce a more robust "new species."[259]
For racist-but-optimistic Bourbon officials like Aurrecoechea, racial and cultural mixture

produced benefits and was to be encouraged—a position that the Positivists who came to power in late nineteenth-century Latin America would reject. Rather than incorporate the "people without reason" into their societies, the Positivists would exclude them. Although poles apart, neither the inclusionary Bourbons nor the exclusionary Positivists imagined leaving a permanent space within their civilized societies for the uncivilized —or for the peoples in between.

Insurgents and Savages, from Inclusion to Exclusion

I had the honor of finishing off a horde of savage and ferocious nomads [the Charrúas]. . . . I did what others before me had been unable to do.
Fructuoso Rivera, president of Uruguay, ca. 1831

The extermination of that new "free man" was quickly completed. The work of three centuries of "slavery" was lost in fifty years of "liberty."
Jorge Comadrán Ruiz, historian, 1955

Faithful Brothers

In late June 1806, British forces seized Buenos Aires and forced the viceroy to flee. Several Pampas who were in the city on business slipped away and carried the stunning news to their people. Weeks later a Pampa envoy, known to Spaniards as Felipe, returned to Buenos Aires and made two appearances before the city council. Speaking through an interpreter, Felipe reported that he spoke for sixteen Pampa caciques who stood ready with horses and hundreds of men "to protect the Christians from the *colorados*," as he called the red-coated English soldiers. The Pampas had declared a truce in their war against the Ranqueles, who promised to patrol the area to the west of Buenos Aires while the Pampas themselves guarded the coast south to Patagonia.[1]

Before the Pampas had a chance to act, the residents of Buenos Aires retook their city from the *colorados*, but a British squadron remained in the Río de La Plata, and the Spaniards braced for another assault. During the tense months that followed, two delegations of Pampa caciques visited the city council to offer help. Addressing the city leaders through an interpreter as Children of the Sun and the Fathers of the Country, the caciques congratulated the Spaniards for evicting the *colorados*. They offered to meet any new British threat with twenty thousand well-armed, leather-jacketed warriors, each accompanied by five horses. The city council thanked the Pampas for their "fidelity, affection, and patriotism" and gave them cash awards and silver medals engraved with the coat of arms of the city and inscribed, "to the Pampa and Araucano Caciques." The council accepted the Pampas' offer to patrol the unguarded coast, although it stopped short of inviting them to join in the city's defense. Large numbers of armed Indians could become uncontrollable, even if the city council had proclaimed them "faithful brothers."[2]

Among the "faithful brothers" who pledged their support against the *colorados* were Chulilaquín, a Huilliche cacique from the region of the Río Negro, and Carripilún, a powerful Ranquel cacique. A generation earlier these leaders had found Spaniards to be useful allies in power struggles with rival caciques. In 1780, a Spanish officer had rewarded Chulilaquín for his loyalty with a suit of luxurious clothing and a silver-handled *bastón*, and the impressively tall Chulilaquín remained a staunch Spanish ally thereafter. The wealthy Carripilún, who had made peace overtures with the city of Mendoza in 1793, also carried a Spanish *bastón* and wore Spanish clothing, given to him by the viceroy.[3]

The city of Buenos Aires had reaped the harvest of years of cultivating peaceful relations with such Indian leaders. By 1806, relations with independent Indians on the pampa had become routine, and Spaniards in Buenos Aires did not have to fight the British and the Pampas at the same time.[4] The "savage nations" received lavish praise in the local press for their offer to help retake the city for Carlos IV, and official newspapers in Peru and Mexico reproduced the story.[5] The Pampas' fidelity, one Buenos Aires paper observed, gave the lie to those foreigners who accused Spaniards of mistreating America's "nomadic races."[6]

Spanish officials of that era still had much to fear from independent Indians who had remained outside of Spain's orbit. They worried, for good reason, that Guajiros would facilitate a British invasion and that Miskitos would help Britain conquer Panama.[7] Where Spaniards had friendly relations with independent Indians, however, Indian loyalty seemed assured. When the English explorer George Vancouver visited Chile in 1795, he learned from its governor, Ambrosio O'Higgins, that Indians below the Biobío "now cease to be regarded with any apprehension by the Spaniards." O'Higgins "did not entertain the least doubt of their co-operating with the forces of his Catholic Majesty, should it be necessary to call them forth against the invasion of a foreign enemy."[8] British *colorados* never landed in Chile, so O'Higgins's assertion went untested. Nonetheless, even taking into account O'Higgins's interest in impressing his British guest (he boasted that ten thousand Indian warriors would join Spaniards in Chile's defense), there is no gainsaying the fact of a strong Spanish–Mapuche accord at the end of the colonial era.

In Texas, too, an Indian–Spanish alliance held when foreigners threatened. In early 1806, forces from the United States stood poised on the edge of Texas to support an inflated American claim that the Louisiana Purchase extended as far as the Río Grande. Spain had sent troops to the eastern border of Texas to defend it, and war seemed imminent. Apprised of the impending conflict, thirty-three Comanche chiefs accompanied by some two hundred warriors visited Gov. Antonio Cordero in San Antonio to offer to support their Spanish allies against the Anglo Americans. Spanish officials in Texas also believed they would receive assistance from Tonkawas, Orcoquisas, Coushattas, Alabamas, Choctaws, and Karankawas in a war against the United States. That war never came, but Spain's investment in a conciliatory Indian policy in Texas had paid dividends when danger threatened the region—just as it would in Florida, where independent Seminoles, longtime allies of Spaniards in St. Augustine, helped to repel Anglo-American invaders in 1812.[9]

Spain's alliances with independent Indians would pay off again, when a new wave of trouble washed across its American colonies in the 1810s. This time, the threat came from within, as Spain's own subjects sought to overthrow Spanish rule. By the mid-1820s they had succeeded nearly everywhere, but many independent Indians had fought against the insurgents or remained neutral, refusing to oppose a system from which they had benefited or to turn against the Spanish officials who represented the old order.

"Friends, Compatriots, and Brothers"

The British invasions of Buenos Aires in 1806 and 1807 marked the beginning of the end of Spanish rule in the Río de la Plata and in America. No fleet sailed from Spain to save Buenos Aires from the English invasion. England, at war with Spain since 1796, had crippled the Spanish navy, most spectacularly at Trafalgar in 1805, and blocked Spanish shipping to America. Then matters went from bad to worse. Napoleon's forces invaded the Iberian Peninsula in 1808. In the midst of the crisis the hapless Carlos IV abdicated the throne to his ambitious son, Ferdinand VII, but Napoleon forced both father and son to relinquish power. In their place Napoleon installed his brother Joseph on the Spanish throne, throwing Spain and its colonies into chaos.

In Spain, a Junta Central formed in 1808 to rule in defiance of Napoleon and in the name of the deposed Ferdinand, whose father had died that year. By 1810 the junta had given way to a parliament, or cortes, which established itself in one of the few places free of danger from French attack, the port city of Cádiz in southern Spain.

In Spanish America, Spain's loss of a legitimate ruler sparked a series of rebellions against Spanish rule. The course and duration of those rebellions varied from place to place, but they began as early as 1810 with demands for greater local autonomy, accelerated into open wars for independence, and lasted until 1826, when Peru, the last of Spain's mainland colonies, won independence. During those years Spanish-American rebels, led mainly by *criollos,* fought against Spanish-led forces and against those *criollos* who remained loyal to Spain. Internecine struggles between Hispanics continued even after the coming of independence as victorious insurgents, as the crown labeled them, or patriots, as they defined themselves, continued to jockey for power. Throughout these civil wars, contending parties appealed to Indians for support, looking for military assistance from independent Indians as well as from Indians who lived under Spanish rule.

Criollo leaders in Buenos Aires, emboldened by their victory over the British in 1806, had led the way toward self-government in Spain's American colonies. On May 25, 1810, they unseated a viceroy appointed by the Junta Central in Spain, on the grounds that he did not represent a legitimate Spanish monarch. In his place, they formed a government that professed to rule in the name of the deposed Ferdinand VII. The new *criollo* leaders quickly sent a delegation into the pampa to maintain good relations with friendly caciques, and they welcomed Indian emissaries who came to Buenos Aires. When a Tehuelche cacique, Quintelau, and his entourage visited the city in 1811, Feliciano Chiclana, head of the ruling triumvirate, assured them that "we are shoots from the same trunk . . . Friends, compatriots, and brothers."[10]

By 1816, *criollos* had abandoned the pretext of ruling Buenos Aires in the name of Ferdinand VII and declared the United Provinces of the Río de la Plata independent from Spain. They published their declaration of independence in bilingual editions—in Spanish and Guaraní and Spanish and Aymará—as part of an ongoing attempt to court Indians.[11] Far from being united, many of the neighboring provinces resisted the new government in Buenos Aires. As competing factions fought to control pieces of the former viceroyalty, each tried to enlist Indians to fight on its side. In the Banda Oriental (the future Uruguay), José Gervasio Artigas showed himself a master at rallying small bands of what he called wild Indians, or *indios bravos*—mainly Charrúas and Minuanes, mounted, armed with pikes and bows and arrows. Long alienated from Spaniards, these remaining "wild Indians" fought with Artigas to dislodge Spanish loyalists from Montevideo between 1811 and 1814, then continued to fight with him as he tried both to resist the Banda Oriental's incorporation into the United Provinces and to check a Portuguese invasion. Artigas imagined a postcolonial society that would include Indians as equals, and he offered nomads land, tools, and livestock if they would settle in the Banda Oriental.[12] Instead, his forces crumbled, and he went into exile in 1820.

Their internal problems notwithstanding, the United Provinces quickly became the launching site for Gen. José de San Martín's bold scheme to cross the Andes and liberate Chile from Spanish rule. He had to pass through the lands of the Pehuenches, and he needed their permission. In his capacity as governor of the province of Cuyo, with his headquarters at Mendoza, San Martín summoned Pehuenches to meet him at Fort San Carlos on the Río Diamante in 1816. Speaking through his translator, fray Francisco Inalican, one of the few Araucanian youths ordained to the priesthood at the Franciscan College of Chillán, San Martín reportedly told the Pehuenches, "I, too, am an Indian."[13] He described Spaniards as the foreign enemies of American Indians and as people who would steal Indians' land, livestock, women, and children. He asked the caciques to allow him to cross their territory and to help care for his army's livestock. He also misinformed them about his intended route, believing the Pehuenches would relay the information to their Spanish allies in Chile. They did. San Martín took a different route, caught royalist forces by surprise, and seized Santiago early in 1817.[14]

In Chile, some Araucanians fought for the insurgents, but most who took up arms sided with the royalists. Mapuche, Pehuenche, and even some Huilliche leaders, like the corpulent and prosperous Calfucurá, had little to gain from overthrowing a regime that had served their economic interests.[15] To the contrary, siding with insurgents could shatter their trans-Andean trade networks, the source of their livelihood. Although Mapuches and Pehuenches had shown little enthusiasm for their cause, victorious Chilean insurgents tried to woo Araucanians once the fighting ended. "We know no enemy but the Spaniard; . . . we are all descended from the same fathers," Bernardo O'Higgins, the supreme director of independent Chile and son of Ambrosio O'Higgins, assured Araucanian leaders in 1819.[16] In a reply dripping with sarcasm, one Mapuche cacique, Francisco Mariluán, proclaimed his innocence in siding with the royalists. The fault, he said, was with "my parents, who never warned me that the Spaniards were our tyrants and that they had taken our liberty."[17]

Throughout Spanish America, insurgents and royalists alike tried to enlist Indians to fight on their side.[18] Far from the frontiers, in the settled highlands of Peru and New Spain, the contending parties appealed to Indians who lived under Spanish rule, simultaneously flattering them and fearing them.[19] Sometimes those Hispanicized Indians fought for the insurgents, most famously in Mexico in 1810–11 when large numbers joined Father Miguel Hidalgo to bring an end to "bad government" in the name of Ferdinand VII and the Virgin of Guadalupe.[20] On other occasions they fought on the side of royalists, as some did in New Granada; or they fought on one side and then switched to another.[21]

Indian leaders, it would appear, supported those Spaniards who had treated them well in the past and who seemed likely to treat them well in the future. That was as true of *indios bravos* as it was of *indios domésticos*. Comanches, who had been staunch allies of Spaniards in New Mexico and Texas since the mid-1780s, offered to fight for the crown when they learned of Hidalgo's revolt in 1810; some joined royalist forces in an engagement against rebels in Coahuila in 1811.[22] In Bolivia, on the other hand, the Chiriguano leader Cumbay traveled to Potosí with a small retinue to offer his services to an insurgent general, Manuel Belgrano. Before the outbreak of war against Spain, Cumbay had tried to protect his peoples' lands from encroachment by Spanish ranchers, but Spanish officials had spurned him. Their rejection apparently pushed him to the insurgent side. Eager to gain Cumbay's support, Belgrano treated him lavishly and put several battalions through maneuvers to impress him. Cumbay seemed equally eager to impress Belgrano. When the general asked him what he thought of the troops, one witness said, Cumbay boasted that "with his Indians he could destroy all of that in a moment."[23]

Indians had symbolic as well as military value for the Spanish-American insurgents.

In need of authentic icons to rally support for their new nations, revolutionary propagandists and *criollo* intellectuals often turned to indigenous figures—much as their English-American counterparts appropriated a generic Indian princess to represent the fledgling United States.[24] In the Spanish era, Indian motifs in the graphic arts had often symbolized the American continent's inferiority to Europe, but insurgents replaced the symbols of subservient Natives with Indians breaking the chains of colonialism. They represented Indians as paragons of liberty and rationality whose glorious civilizations brutal conquistadors had destroyed. The *criollo* insurgents then identified themselves as oppressed descendants of those great Native civilizations, and as indigenous freedom fighters struggling to liberate their long-occupied lands from the Spanish usurpers. Spanish troops became the new conquistadors; Gen. Pablo Morillo, sent to crush the insurgency in New Granada, became the "new Pizarro."[25] In their selective use of the past, *criollos* conveniently ignored their own roles as oppressors of Indians in the long interval between the age of Cortés and Pizarro and the wars of independence.

In the main, *criollo* rebels invoked the Indians' glorious past. Living, tribute-paying Indians seemed to have become enervated by centuries of harsh Spanish rule and thus were of little symbolic value to the insurgents, except as examples of the effects of oppression.[26] Independent Indians like Apaches and Mbayás, whom *criollos* saw as thieves and murderers, also lacked symbolic power. Indians who remained independent but peaceful in the early 1800s, however, had a useful symbolic resonance—none more than Araucanians. Enjoying a long history of harmonious economic relations with their Spanish neighbors, Araucanians also had literary cachet. Throughout the Spanish-speaking world, Alonso de Ercilla's epic poem *La Araucana* had kept alive the memory of their heroic deeds in liberating themselves from Spanish control.

Chilean insurgents quickly adopted Araucanians as a symbol of successful resistance against Spanish tyranny and of national identity. Rebels used the word *Araucanian* as a synonym for Chilean, newspapers appeared with names like *Insurgente Araucano,* and the *criollos'* war against Spain became metaphorically "the war of Araucanian independence."[27] On September 18, 1811, the first anniversary of the formation of a junta to rule in the name of the deposed Ferdinand VII, elite women attended a ball at the government palace in Santiago dressed as Indians.[28] The fact that many Araucanians actually fought with the royalists or viewed the insurgent cause with indifference did little to tarnish their luster as icons of freedom.

Rebels beyond Chile also appropriated Araucanian symbols. In Cádiz and Buenos Aires, as in Santiago, advocates of independence founded secret Masonic lodges named for the sixteenth-century Araucanian leader Lautaro, who had fought courageously against Spanish domination. The leader of independence forces in New Granada, Simón Bolívar, found inspiration in the Araucanians, whom he described in 1815 as "proud republicans," "free and indomitable": "Their sublime example is proof to those fighting in Chile that a people who love independence will eventually achieve it."[29]

Royalists dismissed this rebel rhetoric as nonsense. Royalists praised Indians who had remained loyal to the monarchy and denigrated the rest. They wrote off the precontact Native societies as illegitimate regimes headed by lawless barbarians, lauded the advantages for Indians of Spanish colonial rule, and mocked the rebels' image of virtuous Indians. "Observed up close and examined in the light of impartiality," one Spanish official who had spent time in Venezuela noted, Indians were not the superior people portrayed in Ercilla's *La Araucana*. Rather they were "like a species of automatons, or in the first stage of civilization."[30]

Contradictions, then, abounded. Some royalists portrayed Indians as both loyal and degraded. Some rebels exalted past Indian resistance even as they deplored the behavior of living Indians. Idealization and condemnation of Indians coexisted within the discourses of rebels and royalists alike, as each side tried to fashion useful symbols from a people whom, deep down, they deplored as slothful, barbarous, and untrustworthy.[31]

Nor did the contradictions end when Spain left the scene. In the decades immediately after new nations emerged out of the old empire and divided into political parties, liberals continued the insurgent tradition of representing themselves as descendants of Aztecs, Incas, and Araucanians; even the long-defeated Chichimecas became an occasional point of reference in Mexico. In the newly independent regimes, conservatives took on the role of the royalists, portraying themselves as the children of Spain. Over the course of the nineteenth century, however, liberals gradually abandoned what one writer has termed the "indianesque" and, by century's end, joined conservatives in celebrating their *Hispanidad*.[32]

Indians as Equals

Insurgents went beyond using Indians as symbols and wooing them to join their cause. Some insurgent governments also declared Indians equal before the law. In 1811, when Venezuela became the first province in Spanish America to announce its complete independence from Spain, the framers of its constitution granted Indians juridical equality, liberated them from paying tribute, and permitted them to privatize their communal lands. The constitution of 1811 charged local governments with educating those "citizens who up to today have been called Indians" and promised to lift Indians "from the abjection and rusticity in which the old state of things has kept them." The constitution explicitly revoked all of the protections and privileges that Spain had granted the Natives. By treating Indians as legal minors, the constitution said, the old laws "had damaged them beyond measure, as experience has shown."[33] In truth, experience had taught more ambivalent lessons. If the paternalistic Spanish crown had reduced Indians to the status of minors before the law, it had also protected their communal lands, exempted them from military service, the Inquisition, and the payment of tithes. In some respects the crown's Indian subjects had been better off than lower-class Spaniards—although the latter had regarded themselves as superior to Indians.[34]

The idea of political equality for Indians, which many of the new republics of Spanish

America put into effect, reflected a rising liberal tide that engulfed Spain and its colonies alike. The Cortes of Cádiz, which replaced Spain's governing Junta Central in 1810, included delegates from the American colonies as well as from the Iberian Peninsula. In 1810, even before all of the American delegates had arrived, the cortes defined as Spaniards *all* free people born in Spain or its dominions.[35] Spain's first written constitution, which the cortes drafted in 1812, made it clear that free, employed Indian men who lived in towns were the equal of Spaniards.[36] Along with granting town-dwelling Indians legal equality, the cortes ordered the abolition of Indian tribute, an end to compulsory work levies for Indians, secularization of missions over ten years old, the distribution of mission lands to individual Indians, and the elimination of towns governed exclusively by Indians. The delegates voted to maintain protections that Spanish law afforded Indian communal lands but opened the way for the sale of surplus Indian lands. In all other ways, Indians' special protections fell by the wayside as they took on a new juridical identity as Spaniards rather than Indians.[37]

Some delegates to the Cortes of Cádiz questioned Indians' capacity to participate as equals in government. The delegate from Seville, for example, who had ample experience in America, argued that Indians suffered from a "shortage of wit" and a "propensity to laziness."[38] Most of the delegates, however—those from Spain as well as America—defended the rationality of Indians and pointed to their social environment as the breeding ground of their poverty. If Isaac Newton or Gottfried Wilhelm Leibniz had lived in such unfortunate conditions, the delegate from the Mexican province of Tlaxcala observed, "they would have remained rustics."[39] The majority of delegates wanted to rehabilitate Indians by turning them into Spaniards—changing their indigenous language, dress, and customs and gradually privatizing their communal lands. The delegates believed, as one student of the cortes has explained, that Indians had "natural aptitudes that would allow them to 'de-Indianize' themselves in order to better serve the interests of the projected modern and dynamic society."[40]

The prescriptions for Indians contained in the Venezuelan Constitution of 1811 and the Spanish Constitution of 1812 represented the momentary triumph of classical liberalism, an ideology that sought to limit the power of the state and promote the liberty of the individual. Like other aspects of the liberal program, the idea that Indians should no longer have the legal status of minors had immediate antecedents in Enlightenment thought. Under the Bourbons, a generation of enlightened thinkers had argued that Indians were fully capable of integration into mainstream society and that the material progress of Spanish America required it. Vested interests, however, combined with the crown's traditional paternalism and a large body of Spanish law, had prevented the progressives' reforms from becoming fully realized. It took the French invasion of Iberia to break the power of old institutions and open political space for reforms to move forward.[41]

In Spain, the work of the Cortes of Cádiz came undone with the defeat of Napoleon. Ferdinand VII returned to the Spanish throne in 1814 and annulled all the acts of the cortes, including the Constitution of 1812. Restored Spanish colonial laws brought

American Indians back under the protection of the crown and required that they pay tribute.

In America, however, *criollo* insurgents continued their struggle for independence following Ferdinand's return, and where they took the reins of power they initially adopted liberal legislation aimed at incorporating Indians into their new republics. They declared Indians equal before the law, abolished all forms of slavery and personal service, and authorized the privatization of lands that belonged to Indian communities and mission Indians.[42] Special courts that under Spain had provided legal recourse solely for Indians disappeared everywhere as Indians lost their status as persons in need of special protection.[43] Years of humiliating paternalism, which liberal *criollos* and outside observers like Alexander von Humboldt judged to have enfeebled Indians, came to an end.[44]

In practice, these liberal measures left Indian communities vulnerable to rapacious non-Indian neighbors. Stripped of their special legal status, Indians gradually lost control of their communal governments and communal resources, including mission lands. The losses came in fits and starts as governments rose and fell, but in areas where land had commercial value non-Indians expanded their landholdings at the expense of Indian communities, and Indians quickly became landless laborers.[45] As one historian succinctly put it, "The Indians were losers from independence."[46]

Under the Bourbons, local officials and oligarchs had also ousted Indians from their lands in the name of making them more productive, but in so doing they knowingly violated or circumvented laws intended to protect those lands.[47] In the new republics, Indians lost their lands legally. Some tribute-paying Indians who once rejoiced at the departure of Spanish officials looked back with nostalgia at the old regime.[48] Leaders of one Indian town in New Granada, appalled at their inability to halt the encroachment of non-Indians on their lands, claimed in 1812 that under Spain "we have been the lowest of slaves," but "we were protected and now there is no one to shelter us."[49] Or, as Chilotes complained to Charles Darwin in 1834, Chileans treated them badly "because we are poor Indians and know nothing; but it was not so when we had a king."[50]

Just as they declared the political equality of Spain's former Indian subjects, some newly independent countries also extended it to Indians whom Spain had never conquered and to territory Spain had never held. Chile's Constitution of 1822 identified the nation's borders as extending to the Strait of Magellan and declared that all persons born within these borders were Chileans. With the stroke of a pen, Araucanians became Chileans, their status as a separate people erased along with their historic boundary at the Biobío. This was an exercise in writing fiction. Even a casual visitor could see, as one did in 1825, that the Araucanians remained "unconquered" and that they "will probably continue to view with unfriendly feelings any increase of Chileno inhabitants and strength in their vicinity."[51] Some Chilean leaders wondered if it would not be more logical to think of different Araucanian groups as nations within the nation, but most apparently adhered to the wishful view expressed by Bernardo O'Higgins in 1830: "I regard the Pehuenches, Puelches, and Patagonians as much our countrymen as the others."[52]

Chilean leaders were not alone in trying to accomplish with the pen what Spain had failed to achieve either with the sword or with treaties and trade. In Bogotá, the Congress of Gran Colombia declared in 1826 that all of the "uncivilized Indians who live in the territory of the Republic," including those in the Guajira Peninsula, Darién, and the Mosquito Coast, "will be protected and treated like Colombians."[53] Mexico's declaration of independence proclaimed that "all residents of Mexico, without any other distinction than their merits and virtues, are citizens." Mexico's first government decreed in 1822 that no one be classified according to racial origin in either private or public documents. All Indians, then, from long-subjugated Aztecs to independent Apaches, became Mexicans. The Mexican Constitution of 1824 implicitly reaffirmed the equality of all Mexicans, although it did not mention Indians specifically.[54] One of the earliest proponents of Mexican independence, fray Servando Teresa de Mier, had criticized Spaniards for assuming themselves "legitimate owners of the New World" on the strength of the "laughable" papal donation of 1493, and for making war on Lipan Apaches and Comanches who were the legitimate if "unhappy owners of the country."[55] Yet, independent Mexico did no better than Spain. It, too, claimed sovereignty over independent people, basing its claim on a document of its own creation.

Even as new nations embraced independent Indians as brothers, however, they made it clear that some siblings enjoyed greater privileges than others. The Chilean Constitution of 1822, for example, separated Chileans into citizens and noncitizens. Citizens—men alone in this patriarchal world—had to meet certain social norms, such as knowing how to read and write and possessing a fixed address. Another Chilean Constitution, adopted in 1823, specified further requisites for citizenship, limiting it, for example, to Roman Catholics who possessed real estate worth at least two hundred pesos. Independent Araucanians might be Chileans under the law, but they would not meet the requirements for citizenship. Neither would independent Indians in other Spanish-American nations, where Hispanics continued to purchase Indian women and children and use them as indentured household servants, if not as slaves.[56]

Then there was the problem of brothers who refused to recognize these distinctions or the right of the state to govern them. What to do with Indians who did not recognize the nation, the Chilean minister of war wondered in 1835? Responding to his own rhetorical question, he sanctimoniously noted that the government preferred "gentleness and prudence to reduce these rustic people, as much as possible, to a social life." Should that approach fail, however, he would make war on Araucanians with the help of other, friendly Araucanians.[57] That same year, the comandante general in Chihuahua similarly asked the Mexican secretary of war if "tribes in rebellion," such as Apaches, "should be considered as children of the great Mexican family, or as enemies to be driven beyond the boundaries of this state?" President Antonio López de Santa Anna replied personally. Rebellious tribes, he said, "are Mexicans, because they were born and live in the Republic.... The state of barbarity in which they are raised prevents them from knowing their universal obligations, and those that belong to them as Mexicans." Santa Anna preferred that "kindness and consideration" be used to bring these "unfortunates" to live peacefully in settlements under legal authorities. Only if that failed would he authorize the use of force.[58] Several years later, Santa Anna made the same point when he approved of a treaty that authorities in Coahuila had signed with a group of Comanches. He objected, however, to a clause that called them a *nación,* since they lived inside Mexican boundaries.[59]

"War and Extermination"

Notwithstanding official rhetoric that declared Indians the juridical equals of non-Indians in the new republics and that lumped independent Indians together with Spain's former Indian subjects, most government officials recognized that independent Indians lived in worlds apart—worlds that continued to collide with their own. During the wars of independence, Spanish gifts, hospitality, and markets had begun to shrink. Troops garrisoned on Indian frontiers were transferred to other areas, and royalist and rebel military forces intent on destroying one another had neither time nor resources to deter Indian raiders. In some areas, once-amicable relationships with independent Indians began to unravel even before insurgents had gained independence. As the last Spanish governor of New Mexico observed of the heathen near Santa Fe in 1821, "lacking the gifts to which they are accustomed, they begin to threaten the province."[60]

With the disappearance of Spanish personnel and the breakdown of institutions and mechanisms that had maintained peace, the frontiers of the new Spanish-American republics came under stepped-up assaults from independent Indians. In the absence of the moderating influence of the Spanish crown, Indians also suffered increased attacks from their non-Indian neighbors, and cycles of raid and counterraid resumed on the northern frontier of Mexico, in the Chaco, and on the pampa.[61] One English visitor to Argentina in the mid-1820s, J. A. B. Beaumont, observed that the pampa had been the scene of "peace and amity . . . for a long course of years, but since the revolution these have changed to war and extermination."[62] Some "wild Indians" continued to trade in the towns, but war, "inglorious and cruel," had become the new leitmotif. "On the part of the Indians, it has consisted in driving away the cattle from the farms on the frontier; killing all the men they could find, and carrying off the women and children." On the part of the Argentines, it "has consisted in hunting them [the Indians] over the plains, and in like manner putting all the men to death; and bringing in the women and children to Buenos Ayres, where they are made slaves." Beaumont claimed to have witnessed two hundred Indian prisoners brought into Buenos Aires on one occasion, all of them women. "The men," he said, "had been put to death."[63]

As difficulties mounted, some Spanish-American governments tried to control Indians in the old ways, as if nothing had changed. Initially, most officials experimented with some combination of the carrot and the stick. Whether they emphasized peaceful means —missions, gifts, trade, and treaties—or relied more heavily on physical force depended as it always had on several independent variables. How badly did non-Indians want

Indian trade or Indian lands? Did a government have sufficient resources to purchase peace or conduct war? What values prevailed among government officials? As in the Bourbon era, authorities also weighed the costs of war against the benefits of peace. Would Indians fall into line or put up fierce resistance? Would they operate as a political unit or was their leadership fragmented?

In remote areas where missionary activity had been intense in the late Bourbon era and where populations of non-Indians were weak republican governments tried to revive missions that had fallen apart during the wars for independence. Simón Bolívar and his contemporaries, for example, recognized that the government in Caracas had little prospect of moving troops or colonists into the sparsely populated llanos of Venezuela and eastern Colombia but hoped that low-cost missionaries might succeed at forming stable Indian communities, as they appeared to have done in the past.[64] In Mexico in the 1820s, liberals viewed missions as antiquated institutions and shut them down, but their conservative successors tried to restore them. With all of northern Mexico reeling under attacks from Comanches and Apaches, Santa Anna invited Jesuits back in 1843 to reestablish missions and use them to control Indians, as he supposed they had done prior to their expulsion in 1767.[65] In fact, missionaries had little success historically with Apaches or Comanches, and subsequent administrations ignored Santa Anna's quixotic idea. As one historian succinctly explained, in nineteenth-century Mexico the method of putting an end to savages changed "from reducing them by means of evangelization to annihilating them through war."[66] Indeed, throughout the new republics governments evinced little interest in using missionaries to alter the cultures of powerful, independent peoples such as Araucanians and Pampas. On occasions when they did, as in the Chaco after midcentury, results were meager.[67]

Although many of the new republics had declared the juridical equality of Indians and non-Indians, those same governments continued to sign treaties of peace and commerce with unconquered Indians as if they possessed their own legal identity. Chilean authorities held periodic *parlamentos* with Mapuches and Pehuenches, even though those Natives had become Chileans under the law.[68] In the fragmented provinces that would become the single Argentine nation in midcentury, individual provinces and cities made their own peace with Indian leaders. Buenos Aires, Córdoba, and Santa Fe signed treaties with Pampas and Ranqueles; Mendoza with Pehuenches; Corrientes with Abipones.[69] In Mexico, too, individual provinces continued to sign treaties with Indians, as did the central government. Agustín de Iturbide's regime had erased legal distinctions between Indians and non-Indians after declaring independence from Spain in 1821, yet it exempted Indian nations residing within Mexico from paying sales tax or duties. In effect, it treated Indians like independent entities, as the Spanish government had done before. Iturbide's representatives signed treaties with Caddos in 1821 and with Lipan Apaches and Comanches in 1822. Lipan and Comanche delegates received military escorts to Mexico City for the signing ceremonies, and just before Iturbide's downfall in March 1823 a delegation of Cherokees had arrived in Mexico City to confirm a treaty signed with the Mexican governor of Texas. The Cherokees, newcomers to Texas, had received a promise that "they shall be considered Hispano Americans, and entitled to all the rights and privileges granted to such."[70]

Officials in the new republics continued to negotiate peace accords with Indians well into the nineteenth century. In entering into these arrangements, however, authorities seemed less interested in ending wars than in bringing momentary peace to their immediate area or in buying time to regroup for battle.[71] (The same might have been said of some Bourbon officers, but in general Bourbon treaty makers worked toward harmonious long-range solutions.) Indian nations who entered into treaties with the Spanish-American republics also lost the legal identity they had enjoyed under Spain (or, for that matter, possessed in the United States). As one legal historian noted in the case of Argentina, the republic pursued a contradictory policy in signing treaties with Indians: "On the one hand it did not recognize that the indigenes formed juridical communities at the level of a nation (not sovereign states), and, on the other hand, it had signed treaties of peace with them that implied this recognition."[72]

Treaties alone, whatever their signers' intentions, required more than legal constructs to assure peace. The new republics needed funds to buy peace, as the Bourbons had done, and the willingness to spend those funds on peace rather than war. More often than not, funds were not forthcoming. In northern Mexico, budgets earmarked for gifts and hospitality for Indians shriveled during the wars of independence and were never fully restored by the cash-strapped nation. Neither was the military budget. At the same time resources shrank, the cost of buying peace with Indians rose. Anglo-American traders, who once operated largely to the east of the Mississippi, entered Mexican territory in the 1820s and 1830s. They provided Apaches, Comanches, and Utes with a new source of weapons, ammunition, and alcohol, along with a motive to raid Mexican ranches for horses they could trade to Anglo Americans for that merchandise. From California to Texas, Mexico's northern border with independent Indians became a far more violent place than it had been in the late Spanish era.[73] In the decade of the 1840s, the Mexican press reported almost four hundred accounts of Indian incursions into Sonora, Chihuahua, Durango, Coahuila, and Zacatecas. Apaches and Comanches carried out most of these raids, striking sedentary Indians such as Yaquis, Opatas, and Tarahumaras as well as Mexicans and ranging as far south as Sinaloa and San Luis Potosí. After the United States conquered northern Mexico at midcentury, Indians living on the American side conducted raids in Mexico, then recrossed the border with little fear of pursuit from Mexican forces. Not until 1882 did the United States and Mexico come to an agreement that allowed troops from either side to cross the border in pursuit of Indians.[74]

While Mexico lost ground to independent Indians in the decades following independence, Argentines expanded into Indian territory south of Buenos Aires. Residents of the pampa had enjoyed years of peace since 1790, when the Pampa leader Callfilqui agreed that the Río Salado would form the border between the province of Buenos Aires and the *república* of the Pampas. Pressure to appropriate more Indian land had grown, however, as stock raising increased on the pampa north of the Salado and as non-Indians, in violation of the treaty, began to settle to the south of it.[75] Indian raiding increased with the political turmoil of the independence era and the contradictory policies of the first republican governments. By the early 1820s, the late colonial peace seemed to have collapsed.

Relative peace resumed again, however, during the regime of Gov. Juan Manuel Rosas, who revived the time-tested Indian policy that had proved so effective for the Bourbons. A stockman, or *estanciero*, Rosas received an appointment in 1825 to head the government's Comisión Pacificadora de Indios. Four years later, in 1829, he became governor of Buenos Aires, defeating his political enemies with the military assistance of Indian friends from the pampa. He remained in power until 1852 as the first among equals in the thirteen independently governed provinces that made up the Confederation of the United Provinces of the Río de la Plata. Rosas knew the Pampas well. He compiled a Pampa grammar and dictionary and introduced smallpox vaccine to the Pampas. He also valued living Indians over dead ones. He believed Indians could be attracted to Argentine society and turned into workers who would "make up for the present scarcity of laborers." On his *estancias*, he boasted, "I have some Pampa peones who are faithful to me and are the best."[76] As for Indians who did not find it in their interest to live in harmony with non-Indians, he said, "It is necessary to destroy them," and he did. Like the Bourbons, however, Rosas preferred peaceful expansion and the use of force for defense, but he opposed offensive war.[77]

Initially, in the 1820s, *estancieros* like Rosas bought the friendship of Indians. Indians whom Argentines termed *indios amigos* received promises of protection against enemy Indians, safe conduct passes, and large annuity payments of rations, clothing, livestock, and the *vicios* of alcohol and tobacco. In exchange, they agreed to settle in strategic locations, defend the country against hostile Indians, and abandon claims to land. Other Indians, termed *indios aliados*, maintained their lands and lifeways but accepted gifts in exchange for spying on hostile Indians and fighting on the side of Argentine forces. Like Bourbon officials, then, Rosas made agreements with Indians, but his treaties tended to be verbal rather than written. He seems to have placed greater trust in personal bonds than in words on paper. His vigorously executed policies allowed Buenos Aires to expand its ranching frontier southward to the Sierra de la Ventana and the Sierras de Tandil in the early 1820s and then, with his fabled military campaign of 1833–34, to the Río Negro and the edge of Patagonia. Indians who resisted found themselves fighting the Argentines' Indian friends and Indian allies as well as Argentines.

The Rosas regime did not develop commercial relations with Indians or treat them as juridical equals. It did continue the Bourbon practice of expanding into Indian territory, incorporating Indians as laborers and as military allies, rewarding Indians who cooperated, and punishing Indians who resisted. By pushing the frontier to the Río Negro, Rosas fulfilled the dream of several *proyectistas* of the early 1800s, whose plans to extend Spain's authority over the pampa in a relatively peaceful fashion had been interrupted by the British invasion of 1806 and the struggle for independence.[78] In contrast to Mexico, the province of Buenos Aires under Rosas had sufficient resources to buy peace and finance war. The prosperous region produced most of Argentina's exports in the first decades after independence, so stockmen themselves could afford to support Indian clients. After he gained political power, however, Rosas shifted the costs to the state. As dictator he enjoyed sufficient authority to extract funds and livestock from the citizenry and shift it to Indian friends and allies. The western provinces of Mendoza, Córdoba, and San Luis enjoyed neither the strong hand of a Rosas nor the burgeoning economy of Buenos Aires. Indian raids, particularly by Ranqueles, continued unabated in those provinces, which also happened to be in control of Rosas's political enemies and hence received no assistance from Buenos Aires.[79] Thus, it was on the pampa west of Buenos Aires where travelers like Beaumont found the going rough in the Rosas era.

When independent Indians were weak and the demand for Indian lands was great, leaders of the new republics had little motive to mix diplomacy with force, as Rosas had done. In Paraguay, the enduring supreme dictator of the new nation, Dr. José Gaspar Rodríguez de Francia, authorized the destruction of Mbayás and Guanás north of Concepción in 1815. He ordered the militia not to return "until it exterminated them and ruined them completely."[80] In Uruguay, the state moved quickly to make the country secure for ranchers by eradicating the last independent Charrúas, who could not have numbered more than five hundred. The president himself, Gen. Fructuoso Rivera, personally led a campaign into the sparsely populated center of the country in search of the Indians. When he located them near Uruguay's Río Negro in April 1831 at a place aptly named Salsipuedes (Leave-If-You-Can), he feigned interest in a peace agreement and plied them with gifts and firewater—*aguardiente*. Then, his men fell upon the inebriated Indians. Leaving at least forty dead Indians behind, Rivera set out to return to Montevideo with some three hundred captives. Along the way he distributed nearly half of them to Hispanic householders. The remaining prisoners made the full 150-mile march to the capital—eighty-five women, sixty-eight children, and thirteen men. There, a Swedish mariner watched as the scantily clothed prisoners, the men with their hands tied behind their backs, were marched through the street and "put in a corral like animals .... given meat from an ox that had been quartered and a little firewood and a hot coal."[81] Eventually the women and children were distributed in Uruguayan households, under guidelines for their physical and spiritual well-being that echoed those issued earlier by Spain. Meanwhile, the government allowed four men and a woman to be taken to France to be studied and exhibited like animals. Two of the men died within months of arrival and the third man's fate is unknown, but the woman, Guyunusa, lived for over a year before dying of tuberculosis. During that time she gave birth to a daughter in France, and then had a brief career with a traveling circus, whose owner had purchased her and her infant.[82]

Uruguay had solved its "Indian problem" quickly and violently. Other countries would carry out similar military actions when, as in Uruguay in 1831, national development

32. Colored lithograph by Delaunois from a pamphlet, Arrivée en France de quatre sauvages
Charruas, par le brick français Phaéton, de Saint-Malo, *attributed to François de Curel
(Paris, 1833). The four Charrúa captives appear with accoutrements and dress that the
French public would find exotic and pay to see. On the left are Senaqué and Vaimaca-Perú,
close friends in their midfifties. They died within months of arrival. Seated to the right,
twenty-six-year-old Guyunusa and her twenty-three-year-old husband, Tacuabé,
both baptized as infants. Vaimaca's remains were repatriated to Uruguay in 2002.
Reproduced from Curel, 1959, a facsimile edition, plate I.*

reached the point where independent Indians seemed to stand in the way of progress
and when the state possessed sufficient resources and political stability to move against
them. In some economically marginal areas, such as the Guajira Peninsula and the Delta
of the Orinoco, Indians remained beyond government control into the twentieth century.[83]
Where vigorous export economies provided incentives to bring more land under production at an earlier date, however, authorities found ways to seize Indian lands and exclude
Indians from national life when they had the means to do so.

In Argentina that moment did not come until the 1870s. After Rosas's fall from power
in 1852, the state had reduced its financial support for *indios amigos* and *indios aliados.* In
the absence of rewards for good behavior, some of Rosas's Indian clients had cut their
ties with Buenos Aires, resumed raiding, and seized what they had previously been given.
Emulating the *indios enemigos* against whom they had fought as Spanish allies, they drained
the haciendas of cattle, captives, and goods. While the Argentine provinces fought one
another in a civil war and then waged war on Paraguay, Indians regained control of much

of the pampa that Rosas had seized. Ironically, years of receiving and redistributing Argentine rations and supplies had strengthened the authority of the once-friendly caciques, who now led larger and better-equipped forces than ever before.[84]

In the 1870s, war with Paraguay over, the consolidated Argentine state might have returned to Rosas's policy of accommodation and expansion. Instead, it yielded to the interests of powerful ranching families who sought to convert Indian lands into their private preserves by ridding them of Indians altogether. Their private interests became a national project, culminating in a massive military campaign in 1879, the so-called Conquest of the Desert. Five columns of Argentine forces, their fighting skills honed in the recent war against Paraguay, carried out the *entrada general* that Viceroy Pedro de Cevallos had imagined but failed to execute a century before. Armed with repeating rifles, the well-provisioned military columns moved south from the provinces of Buenos Aires, Córdoba, San Luis, and Mendoza. Subduing and killing Indians, they "cleansed" the southern and western pampa to Patagonia. The survivors endured a program of forced acculturation, euphemistically called regeneration, which included the dissolution of tribal governments, prohibition of native languages, and forced labor at menial work or obligatory service in the national guard or the navy. Indian land became, first, public land and then a source of revenue for the government, which sold it to private parties. In the next few years, Argentine forces repeated these operations in Patagonia and in the Chaco, completing their last sweeps through each of these regions in 1884.[85]

In the Chaco, where operators of sugar refineries and lumber mills had no ready source of labor except Indians, the military campaigns of the early 1880s were less lethal. Dead Indians cannot work. Where practical, military forces merely dispossessed hunters and gatherers of their lands and concentrated them in settlements in an effort to remake them into proletarians. As in the past, Argentines continued to look to the countryside as a source of pagan Indian women and children to serve them in exchange for "civilizing" them. "I hope you will not forget to send me a pair of Indian girls, six to eight years old. I will pay the shipping charges," one resident of Santa Fe wrote to an officer in charge of the northern Chaco in 1879. In 1885, a Buenos Aires newspaper reported the arrival of a steamship from the north bearing 154 Indian women, "to be distributed" among families in the capital. Without the moderating power of the crown, pressing Indian women and children into household service apparently met even less opposition than it had in the colonial period.[86]

Less swiftly but no less inexorably or cruelly than in the pampa and in Patagonia, Chileans completed the military conquest of the Araucanians between 1867 and 1883, combining forces with Argentina in the last years of the campaign. The Chileans' final assault on the Araucanians had awaited the conclusion of the War of the Pacific, in 1881. Then, an army raised to fight Peruvians and Bolivians was sent southward to fight Indians.[87]

The economic vigor of Buenos Aires and Santiago had provided sufficient revenue for government officials to buy peaceful relations with Indians in the early nineteenth century and win wars against them toward the century's end. Mexico, broke and politically

unstable during its first decades of independence, had found its efforts to maintain peace
undermined by Anglo-American traders. After midcentury, however, as it slowly recovered
from the devastating loss of half its territory to the United States, Mexico also turned
its military force against nomads. In some cases individual states launched their own offensives, as in 1850 when the State of Coahuila contracted with Kickapoos and Seminoles
to make war on Comanches, Kiowas, and Lipan and Mescalero Apaches.[88] After Mexico's
army gained experience in expelling the French in the 1860s and its central government
achieved stability, federal troops entered the fray. In 1880–81, for example, two expeditions
set out to clear the desert between Coahuila and Chihuahua of Lipan and Mescalero
Apaches. By then, Mexico had cooperated with officials from the United States to move
Apaches, Comanches, and Kickapoos onto reservations in the United States, and few
independent Apaches remained in northern Mexico. Even in small numbers, however,
nomads and seminomads instilled fear among non-Indians, who believed that such people
stood in the way of progress and had to be eliminated. The expeditions of 1880–81 succeeded, but their commander opined that perfect peace would not come about until
every savage was gone from the border region, plucked out "like a noxious plant."[89]

Like Bourbon officials before them, leaders of the new republics did not agree on Indian policy, but the growing economic and political power of national governments and
their interest in developing new lands had put those who favored eliminating independent Indians in the ascendancy. Even public figures sympathetic to Indians found it hard
to imagine that "savages" could coexist with non-Indians within a single nation. As independent Chile's first president, Bernardo O'Higgins had ordered that all Chilean Indians
be called thereafter "free Chilean citizens like the other inhabitants of the nation."[90] A
generation later, he came to champion separate spheres for Indians and non-Indians.
Ousted from power in 1823, O'Higgins had closely watched American affairs from his
exile in Peru. In 1837, a few years before his death, he recalled that "my first playmates
were Araucanians" and that the first school he ever attended was one that his father, Ambrosio, had founded for the sons of Araucanian caciques at Chillán. He respected Indians
and yet he had come to the conclusion that the "red & white races cannot increase &
prosper in the same territory." Indians would be overwhelmed by whites. O'Higgins suggested the formation of a separate Aboriginal Empire in northernmost Mexico, between
the Rocky Mountains and the Pacific. It would stretch from Baja California to British
Columbia; the Rocky Mountains would shield Indians from westward moving Anglo
Americans. O'Higgins supposed that Mexico, which still owned this remote region in
1837, would gladly surrender it and the United States (already embarked on its own program of Indian removal) and Canada would pay to transport Indians to the new state
beyond their borders and help launch it "in the glorious Cause of Humanity." It is not
clear if O'Higgins had in mind transporting Araucanians and other independent Indians
to this zone from Spanish America. It is apparent, however, that he advocated a separate
land base for autonomous Indians, such as Araucanians, Pampas, and others had enjoyed
in their treaty arrangements with Bourbon Spain. In such places, he said, missionaries

could bring them "Christianity & Civilization" and Indians would "have an Opportunity of proving that in all respects they are not inferior to any other race which inhabits this Globe."[91]

Civilization over Barbarism

Some Spanish-American leaders justified their annihilation of Indians and seizure of Indians' lands by reimagining independent Indians as savages. Voices that represented independent Indians as reasonable and capable of evolving toward a civilized life had lived on in the nineteenth century and could still be heard, but the rising chorus of those who vilified Indians drowned them out.[92] As a new generation rewrote national charters and national laws, guarantees of equal rights to "Indian brothers" fell by the wayside. Thus, the prosperous Araucanians, a source of republican inspiration to Bolívar's generation, came to be seen as "savage hordes," incapable of civilization or progress. Victory over the Araucanians, one commentator noted in a Valparaíso newspaper, would represent "the triumph of civilization over barbarism, or humanity over bestiality."[93] "Who would not prefer a thousand times over that his sister or daughter marry an English shoemaker rather than an Araucanian nobleman?" the Argentine statesman Juan Bautista Alberdi asked in 1852. "In America everything that is not European is barbaric. There is no division other than this one: 1st the Indian, which is to say the savage, and 2nd the European, which means us—we who were born in America, speak Spanish, and believe in Jesus Christ."[94] Had anyone been listening, an Araucanian reply might have been found in a message that a group of Araucanian caciques sent to the Chilean president in 1861: "Although they call us savages, we know what is just."[95]

In Argentina, Indians on the pampas underwent a similar transformation. Although they had come to terms with Spaniards in the late eighteenth century, traded their produce and handiwork in Buenos Aires, and proffered aid against British invaders in 1806, the Pampas were reduced to bands of wandering thieves by rhetoric that justified their dispossession. For Domingo Sarmiento, the journalist, historian, president of Argentina (1868–74), and author of the famous and polemical *Civilization and Barbarism* (1845), the Argentine countryside was a place of "savages ever on the watch, who take advantage of moonlit nights to descend like a swarm of hyenas upon the herds in their pastures, and upon the defenseless settlers."[96] Argentine officials, like their counterparts throughout the hemisphere, came to regard the civilizing of Indians as an impossible task. As the author of *El Gaucho, Martín Fierro,* the most celebrated Argentine poem of the nineteenth century, wrote in the 1870s, the Indian of the pampa "clings to his savagery.... The savage only knows how to get drunk and fight."[97]

If savage Indians were mired hopelessly in their barbarism and backwardness, then the new logic suggested that they deserved annihilation and dispossession. As the authors of a plan to defend Coahuila from *indios bárbaros* put it in 1849, "This enemy does not deserve pardon, and it is useless to offer it. He is a rabid animal, incapable of domestication.

33. Argentine artists also reimagined Indians in the darkest terms. In this scene, Pampa horsemen flee from a successful raid with golden objects and the whitest of women. Return from the raid/"La vuelta del malón." *Oil on cloth by Angel Della Valle, 1892. Courtesy, Museo Nacional de Bellas Artes, Buenos Aires.*

To try to reduce him to a mission is a delirious dream, a quixotic manner of thinking. There is no room here for the noble voice of humanity and clemency, because severity is absolutely necessary."[98] At the least, irredeemable savages had no right to land in the new nations. By definition, savages would not use land wisely. Indians of the pampa, Sarmiento wrote, "show themselves incapable, even under compulsion, of hard and pro-tracted labor." Thus he described them paradoxically as occupants of "uninhabited" land.[99] Bolivians similarly imagined the Chiriguanía as a place of unappropriated and uncultivated lands, even though it took them three and a half decades of nearly uninter-rupted warfare, between 1840 and 1875, to overrun the Chiriguanos who farmed and defended it and to reduce the Chiriguano population from its late eighteenth-century high point of some two hundred thousand to fewer than fifty thousand.[100] Even accultur-ated Indians might be redefined as savages and their dispossession justified if they resisted the domination of the state. In the midst of a series of violent revolts of Indian peasants that swept across southern Mexico between 1842 and 1846, for example, Gen. Nicolás Bravo termed the rebels "miserable Indians, incapable of understanding the benefits of civilization, returned to a barbarous state worse than that of savage tribes."[101]

As leaders of nineteenth-century liberal states portrayed Indians as irredeemable sav-ages, they found it convenient to forget Spain's successful eighteenth-century détentes with societies of independent Indians and looked instead to Spain's sixteenth-century conquests as useful models. Sarmiento, who admired U.S. Indian policy, described the Spanish conquest as necessary and beneficial, even if unjust. "Thanks to this injustice," he wrote in 1844, "America, instead of remaining abandoned to savages incapable of progress, is occupied today by the Caucasian race, the most perfect, the most intelligent, the most beautiful, and the most progressive of the races that populate the earth." Sarmiento explicitly repudiated the generation of Spanish-American insurgents who claimed an affinity with oppressed Indians as they sought to free themselves from colonial domination. Savages like the Araucanians, Sarmiento believed, had nothing in common with the descendants of Spaniards. "We must be fair with the Spaniards; by exterminating a savage people whose territory they were going to occupy, they merely did what all civilized peoples have done with savages . . . absorb, destroy, [and] exterminate."[102] Although Sarmiento recognized Spain's great achievement of absorbing Indians, he concluded nonetheless, "There is no possible amalgam between a savage and a civilized people."[103]

In this intellectual milieu, Spanish-American oligarchs tended to look toward Europe as a source of workers and citizens, rather than try to redeem seemingly irredeemable savages. As early as 1828, an Englishman who had come to Argentina as a colonist noted the irony: "It is much to be regretted that the rulers of Buenos Ayres, who profess so strong a desire to increase the population of their country, and *offer to pay largely* for the transport of Europeans into it, should entertain the design of driving from the lands of their inheritance, or to exterminate the aboriginal inhabitants. These natives have given ample evidence of the docility of their nature, and of their aptitude to become excellent artisans and faithful troops."[104]

In thought and in deed, then, the new conquistadors of the nineteenth-century Spanish-American republics seemed to turn their backs on Bourbon Spain's peaceful policy of trade, treaties, and toleration. Bourbon policymakers had been flexible enough to recognize the existence of tribal lands and autonomous tribal governments, to negotiate the terms of sovereignty with those governments, and to honor reciprocity even as they maintained the long-range goal of incorporating independent Indians into a racially mixed Spanish society.[105] When local officials lost sight of that goal and urged offensive war, the crown often (but not always) reminded them of its preference to proceed gently. The rhetoric of the Bourbons' nineteenth-century successors, which built an insurmountable wall between savagery and civilization, implicitly rejected Spain's frequently reiterated goal of gradually acculturating and incorporating Indians. In this, leaders of the Spanish-American republics were not alone. Throughout western Europe and the Americas in the nineteenth century, as one scholar has explained, the "lively optimism" of the Enlightenment, with its sense that all of humankind might grow in rationality and progress toward becoming more like Europeans, gave way to "the dour and oppressive Social Darwinism that saw progress in terms of winners and losers."[106]

Yet, there was more continuity between imperial and republican policies than meets the eye. The Bourbons had their own share of war hawks who advocated the destruction of resistant societies of independent Indians, but doves usually prevailed because wars with powerful Indian groups often seemed beyond winning and because the crown generally favored gentle means of bringing Indians into the body politic. In the Bourbon era, then, pragmatism often combined with principle to recommend peaceful means as the best way to achieve security and economic growth. Nonetheless, the Bourbons did permit war when gentle means failed to pacify the enemy, and when Spanish officers reported that they had sufficient strength to win. In those cases, principle gave way to pragmatism. It was power, then, more than the power of ideas, that had determined how enlightened Spaniards would treat "savages"—and it is in this sense that the Indian campaigns of the last half of the nineteenth century represented a continuation of Spanish policy rather than a repudiation of it. Ideas may have the power to shape policy, but power also shapes ideas.

Notes

Abbreviations

AF =   Archivo Franciscano, Biblioteca Nacional
            de Mexico, Universidad Nacional Autó-
            noma de México, Mexico, D.F. Negative
            photostats of selective documents, cata-
            logued as Archivo de San Francisco el
            Grande, Center for American History, Uni-
            versity of Texas at Austin.
AGB =   Archivo General de Bolivia, Sucre, Bolivia
AGI =   Archivo General de Indias, Sevilla
AGN =   Archivo General de la Nación (AGN,
            Buenos Aires; AGN, Caracas, and AGN,
            Mexico)
AHN =   Archivo Histórico Nacional, Madrid
AMS, PM =   Archivo Municipal de Saltillo, Mexico,
            Presidencia Municipal
ANSC =   Archivo Nacional de Santiago de Chile
FF =   Fondo Franciscano, Archivo Histórico del
            Instituto Nacional de Antropología e His-
            toria, Mexico, D.F.
MM =   Colección de Manuscritos de José Toribio
            Medina, Biblioteca Nacional de Chile
SANM =   Spanish Archives of New Mexico, Santa Fe,
            New Mexico (references are to the reel and
            frame of the microfilm edition and to
            Twitchell numbers)

Introduction

The epigraph is from Barbara Kingsolver, *High Tide in Tucson: Essays from the Now or Never* (New York: Harper Collins, 1995), 154.

1. Knox to Washington, Dec. 29, 1794, *American State Papers: Indian Affairs* (Washington: Gales and Seaton, 1832–61), 1:544. Called to my attention by Prucha, 1984, 1:70. See, too, p. 337, for Knox's policy of benevolence, and Berkhofer, 1978, 142–45.

2. Sheehan, 1973, 5; Callahan, 1958, 314–37.
3. Knox to Washington, June 15, 1789, quoted in Prucha, 1984, 1:62.
4. Knox to Anthony Wayne, Jan. 5, 1793, quoted in Prucha, 1984, 1:66.
5. Jefferys, 1762, xx. See, too, Kagan, 1996, 423–46, Powell, 1971, Lepore, 1998, 8–11.
6. Lynch, 1989, 253; García Pérez, 1998, 139–53.
7. Llombart, 1992, 29–95, 295–306, 325–35, Castro, 1996, 29–48, 419–44.
8. Solano, 1981, 1–100, analyzes the contents of Gálvez's library at the time of his death, compares it to other libraries of his day, and provides a complete listing. For Robertson, see p. 20.
9. Villava, 1946, cxix ("en siglo más ilustrado"; "la filosofía de este siglo y de sus escritos luminosos").
10. Francisco Javier Eugenio de Santa Cruz y Espejo, *El Nuevo Luciano de Quito . . .* 1779, quoted in Johnson, 1993, 145 ("la e poca del idiotismo y . . . el siglo de ignorancia"), who ably analyzes his intellectual life.
11. Navarro García, 1997a, 3, whose suggestive article explores these differences in depth.
12. I am aware that a close scholarly look at any aspect of the Enlightenment reveals a category in crisis. It is useful, nonetheless, to understand this as an Age of Reason, as did literate contemporaries. I discuss the Enlightenment in Spain and its colonies in chap. 1, but for introductions to the subject in English, see Lynch, 1989, 247–61, and Aldridge, 1971, 4–9. For an introduction to the contradictions inherent in Spanish enlightened despotism, see the classic essay by Palacio Atard, 1966, 31–35. For enlightened Spanish ministers jockeying for political influence, see Lynch, 1989, 291–98, and Stein and Stein, 2003.
13. Keen, 1971, 217; Mörner, 1970, 337–47; Walker, 1996, 89–112. For power over principle, and the employment of similar data to reach separate conclusions on slavery, see Davis, 1975, 49, 164–84, 195, 258.

14. Villava, 1946, cxix ("igualdad y confraternidad").

15. Lastarria, "Declaraciones y expresas resoluciones soberanas que sumisamente se desean en beneficio de los Indios de las Provincias de la banda oriental del Río Paraguay, y de las márgenes del Paraná y Uruguay . . . ," Madrid, Aug. 31, 1804, in Lastarria, 1914, 114–15 ("imponer respeto con la fuerza, tampoco se atinaba con el medio"; "Solo con la dulzura, desinterés, y buena fé, podemos lograr paz, y comercio con los más fieros, y esforzados, quales son los Araucanos de Chile entre todos los Indios; y que un proceder contrario convertirá en fieras a los más lánguidos y tímidos cuales son los del Perú").

16. Chiokoyhikoy, 1997, 113. Zavala, 1983, 14, 282.

17. Azara, 1923, 2:142 ("tiempos atrasados"; "un voluminoso Código de leyes, de las que cada frase y cada palabra respiran una humanidad admirable y la protección completa a los indios"). Some modern scholars would agree with Azara. See, for example, Osterhammel, 1997, 42. Zaragoza and García Cárcel, 1979, 273–79, briefly but elegantly introduces Bourbon suppression of critics of the conquest.

18. Campomanes, 1988, 238–39, 265. For a similar comparison, see Lázaro de Ribera, Asunción, 1800, quoted in Acevedo, 1997, 144. To a large extent he was right. More than most European states, Spain had consistently sought to refashion Indians, by placing them in an idealized Spanish society of orderly urban spaces where the state could control them, conscript them, and tax them. See Scott, 1998, for this state policy in comparative perspective.

19. Elliott, 1994, 4, whose rough estimate puts the Indian population of Spanish America at over 50 percent in 1789, and the Indian population east of the Mississippi at 6 percent in 1770. His estimate appears to include independent as well as incorporated Indians east of the Mississippi.

20. Service, 1955, 412–13, argues that Indian societies determined European practices. Elliott, 1994, 3–23, makes a convincing case that attitudes Europeans brought to the New World explain as much about their tendency to incorporate Indians as did the nature of the Indian peoples and local circumstances. Oberg, 1999, explores the tension between metropolitan and local interests in English America.

21. Burkholder, 1976, 404–423; García Pérez, 1998, 127–36. Among historians a minority hold that Carlo III's achievements were no less remarkable than those of his Bourbon predecessors, and his American reforms were forced upon him by circumstances. See Barbier, 1990, 2–18.

22. Adelman and Aron, 1999, 815–81, draw a useful distinction between frontier and borderland. "By frontier, we understand a meeting place of peoples in which geographic and cultural borders were not clearly defined. . . . We reserve the designation of borderlands for the contested boundaries between colonial domains" (p. 815). I have followed their usage for borderland but also used a more descriptive term, "strategic frontier," for space contested by colonial powers. I've borrowed this term from Bushnell, 2002, 19–21, and modified it for my own purposes. "External" frontiers would seem to represent a synonym for a "strategic" frontier, but Latin American scholars do not use it that way (Schröter, 2001, 374 n. 87), nor does Bushnell.

23. For the revolution and reconquest, see Brading, 1984, 397, 400; for "second conquest" see Lynch, 1973, 7. Many scholars have doubted the effectiveness of this revolution in the heartlands. See, for example, Coatsworth, 1982, 25–51.

24. Bougainville and Diderot, 1966, 69, 70 ("qu'ils nomment Indios bravos; ces Indiens sont courageux, aguerris, et le temps n'est plus où un Espagnol faisait fuir mille Américains").

25. MacLeod, 1998, 130. See, too, pp. 131 and 142, where MacLeod reaffirms this argument.

26. Spicer, 1962, 332, a sophisticated anthropologist who did recognize that "adjustments of program" followed the expulsion of the Jesuits, including Bernardo de Gálvez's 1786 *Instrucción,* which he misread as a pessimistic document built on the assumption that "Apaches could never be civilized."

27. Slatta, 1998, 93, 96.

28. Lemann, 1992, 151–52.

29. Alonso, 1995, 63.

30. Gibson, 1978, 13, who offers this statement but concludes his essay by noting two exceptions from North America.

31. Seed, 1995, 97–98. Emphasis added. Seed's study encompasses the years 1492–1640, yet she suggests a timeless quality for Spanish practice and policy.

32. Levaggi, 1997, 103 ("reafirmación de la política de conquista pacífica"); see, too, Levaggi, 2002, 35.

33. The sensibilities and policies of the Enlightenment that affected Spanish perceptions of and policies toward savages had a Portuguese counterpart. For a fine introduction to the changes launched by the marqués de Pombal, see Sweet, 1992b, 49–80.

34. The *visitador* Padre Tomás Torrico, Lagos, 1908, 420 ("porque el Consejo de Indias no ha de determinar nada sin pedir informe al Gobierno de Chile, que ha de tirar a defender sus determinaciones ¿y que saldrá de este? Más daño que provecho. Teniendo paciencia; que lo que no se puede en un año se puede en otro, y lo que no se puede en un gobierno se puede en otro"). I assume that Padre Torrico was a royal inspector, but he may have been an ecclesiastical inspector. Whatever the case, I have translated his title, *visitador,* as inspector. See, too, Taylor, 1985, 172.

35. The historian Jack Greene has observed that authority did not merely flow "by imposition from the top down or from the center out but through an elabo-

rate process of negotiation among the parties in-volved"—even in situations in which relationships of power were unequal. Greene, 1994, 4, applies this model to Spain "at least down to the Bourbon re-forms" (p. 18) but clearly continues into the Bourbon era. As Kuethe and Inglis, 1985, 119, 137, rightly ob-serve, the Bourbons as well as the Habsburgs took into account "the realities and needs of the indi-vidual colonies" and did not abandon "the Spanish habit of advancing change piecemeal, proceeding by trial and error." See, too, Kuethe, 1991, 288, Stein, 1981, 2–28, Lockhart and Schwartz, 1983, 315, and Castro Gutiérrez, 1994, 32. Pietschmann, 1998, 278, argues that in New Spain power shifted from penin-sula to the viceroy in the early 1790s. On the inter-play between the periphery and the core in the shap-ing of policy, also see Patch, 1993, 167, who argues that "the Bourbon Reforms in Yucatan, in short, were possible only because of social and economic changes that were fundamentally internal in origin." For interest groups comprising the state, see Perry, 1996. For the U.S. failure to implement Indian policy, see Hinderaker, 1997. The idea that frontier peoples helped shape policy may seem self-evident, yet it bears noting since Wallerstein's influential world-systems theory focused heavily on the core and slighted the ways that peripheral nonstate societies prevented the core from unilaterally imposing poli-cies on them. See, for example, the critiques by Duna-way, 1996, 455–70, and Hall, 1989, and the model proposed by Baud and van Schendel, 1997, 219.

36. Saavedra, 1989, 184, diary entry, Pensacola, May 11, 1781. A royal inspector, Saavedra was privy to the views of Spanish officials at the highest levels.

37. Quoted in Weber, 1992, 284. I discuss this further in chap. 6.

38. Jedidiah Morse, *American Universal Geography* (1793), quoted in Fitzgerald, 1980, 49. For North American knowledge of Spanish America, see Bernstein, 1961, 32. For the continuation of such views into the 1820s, see Johnson, 1990, 44–53.

39. As Nancy Farriss wrote in 1984, "Historians have made much of the effect of the Bourbon reforms on the creoles . . . the effect on the Indians has largely been overlooked." Farriss, 1984, 355. Exceptions among North American scholars include Gibson, 1964, Farriss, 1984, Patch, 1993, Smith, 1990, Taylor, 1996, and Wortman, 1982, all of whom focus on *in-dios domésticos*. Scholars of the institutions and society of the most Hispanicized parts of the empire in the late eighteenth century generally find Indians of in-terest when they rebel or join in rebellions, which are often seen as precursors to the wars for indepen-dence, as in O'Phelan Godoy, 1991, 395–440. See especially pp. 426–27, where she explicitly makes that link. Overviews of the late eighteenth century also focus on the impact of the Bourbon reforms

and the coming of independence, but they leave un-conquered Indians out of the story. For an admirable yet characteristic treatment see Bakewell, 1997, chap. 12. Lockhart and Schwartz, 1983, chaps. 8, 9, pay more attention to the peripheries of the empire than do other writers.

40. For example: MacLeod, 1973, Stern, 1982, Korth, 1968, Kellogg, 1995, Calero, 1997. Studies that look comparatively at policies or attitudes toward Indians tend to include sixteenth-century Spain, then aban-don Iberia to move on to the English or the French in the seventeenth and eighteenth centuries, as does Williams, 1990, and Berkhofer, 1978, as if Spanish thought had become congealed. The Columbus Quin-centenary gave further impetus to the study of the sixteenth and seventeenth centuries. For an over-view of that literature, see Altman and Butler, 1994, 478–503.

41. Until recently, relatively few scholars in Spain or Latin America treated Spanish relations with inde-pendent Indians at the end of the colonial era. For evidence of that lack in Spain, see "Indigenísmo y culturas indígenas en América Latina, siglos XVI–XVIII," *Cuadernos Rayuela: Bibliografías sobre América Latina*, no. 4 (1994), a bibliography of 404 items pub-lished in Spain between 1980 and 1994, mainly jour-nal articles, and Tovar Zambrano, 1994, 1:21–134. As my endnotes and bibliography attest, the last two decades have seen a rise in interest in Latin Amer-ica, particularly in Chile and Argentina. For the re-cent florescence of literature on the frontiers of Span-ish America, much of it concerned with "Indian frontiers," see Schröter, 2001, 353, 374.

42. An idea suggested by Cerda-Hegerl, 1990, 5.

43. Esteva-Fabregat, 1995, 232, calculates that indepen-dent Indians controlled 3.9 million square miles. Figures for continental Latin America include Mex-ico (761,601), Central America (188,708), and South America (6,875,000), for a total of 7,825,309 square miles. The actual area under control by independent Indians was much larger; Esteva-Fabregat did not factor in Spain's possessions in what is now the United States. Castillero Calvo, 1995, 26, estimates that 30 percent of the area of Central America re-mained in Indian hands at the end of the colonial period.

44. Wallace and Hoebel, 1952, 12.

45. "Living independently" is, of course, a relative term. In using it I do not mean to deny that incorporated Indians maintained degrees of autonomy, whether in the religious sphere, where they blended their own cosmologies with Christian belief, or in the world of work, where they made space for them-selves through "noncompliance, foot dragging, [and] deception." Scott, 1985, xvi; 29–30. *Indios domésticos* earned their measures of independence *within* the Spanish political system—a system that not only

facilitated their exploitation but also offered them institutional and noninstitutional ways to retain prerogatives. *Indios domésticos,* for example, enjoyed legal status, the protection of certain laws, and access to the Spanish judiciary. *Indios domésticos* also discovered that the system of Spanish governance tolerated limited local rebellions and used them as an extralegal means of removing especially abusive authorities. See, for example, Borah, 1983, and Taylor, 1979.

46. These crude estimates come from Esteva-Fabregat, 1995, 227, 231–34, who calculates a total mainland population of 12,252,808 in the late eighteenth century, of whom 2,680,000 were considered savages. For current understandings of "innate" and "adaptive" immunities and its implications for colonial period Indians, see Jones, 2003, 703–42.

47. Knox estimated that Indian "warriors" north of the Ohio River numbered between 2,000 and 3,000; south of the Ohio he thought the United States faced some 14,000 Indian adversaries.

48. López de Vargas Machuca, [1758], 97 ("la extención de este Govierno no se conoce actualmente, por que confina con varios paises no descubiertos, y habitado de Indios bravos"), 21 ("salvajes"; "indios bravos"; "naciones feroces e indómitas").

49. Lemann, 1992, 150–51. Ironically, Lemann was reviewing my book, *The Spanish Frontier in North America,* in which I failed to put North America in sufficient context to persuade Lemman to judge Spanish endeavors more sympathetically. On this last point, he quotes me out of context.

50. As scholars of the subject will understand, *Bárbaros* departs from Herbert Eugene Bolton's classic Borderlands model, with its very useful but explicitly limited purpose of understanding Spain's role in the area that would become the United States, to examine one important theme of borderlands history on an empirewide level and to respond to the need for more comparative and contextualized studies of borderlands. For a recent critique of the borderlands paradigm, see Light T. Cummins, "Getting Beyond Bolton," *New Mexico Historical Review* 70 (1995):201–215.

51. Quoted in the introduction to Requena, 1991, 7 ("Los países no conquistados son unas selvas y montañas de difícil tránsito y los llanos muy húmedos, cenagosos y ardientes, por lo que no pueden mantenerse los españoles").

52. Ecological explanations for low man–land densities in drylands and in tropical forests have come under attack. Evidence of great cultural diversity and large-scale settlements of sedentary Indians in the Amazon, including perhaps chiefdoms, has undermined the once widely accepted thesis of Meggers, 1996, 25–27, 100–01, 162–67, that plants had low nutritional value in rain forests and so discouraged Indians from settling in permanent villages. For an exchange between Meggers and some of her critics, see *Latin American Antiquity* 12 (Sept. 2001): 304–33, and Cleary, 2001, 72–81. Places with inhospitable environments and little attraction for Spaniards did become regions of refuge, however, where Indians maintained independence the longest. For a fine case study of Nueva Vizcaya which emphasizes the role of human and natural geography in ethnic persistence, see Deeds, 2003, 190–93.

53. Quoted in Requena, 1991, 7–8 ("no cuiden de cubrir su desnudez y sus casas son tan pobres que nada pierden aunque se los quiten.... Reducirlos por armas se ha tenido siempre por imposible").

54. Jiménez Núñez, 1967, 86 ("cuando más simple y pobre es el sistema sociocultural indígena, más difícil puede resultar su dominio efectivo sin llegar a la exterminación"). See, too, Zavala, 1979, 179–99, and the classic essay by Service, 1955, 411–25, who draws a finer distinction than I do between "marginal hunters, the lowland horticulturalists, and the highland intensive agriculturalists" (421).

55. Except for *bozales,* these usages were commonplace. For *bozales,* often used to describe blacks rather than Indians, see Cramaussel, 1990–91, 79.

56. Early in the colonial period, Spaniards used the words *bárbaro* and *indio* synonymously. The words encompassed Indians who lived in sedentary non-Christian societies with recognizable heads of state, governmental structures, and religion. Spaniards did, however, recognize different levels of barbarism, putting the most wild or savage barbarians at the bottom. See, for example, José de Acosta's thought, described by Pagden, 1982, 164–65, and Navarro Floria, 1994b, 120. Montesquieu regarded "barbarians" as a step beyond "savages." His "barbarians" occupied a low level of society, rather than living in dispersed groups. Pagden, 1994b, "The 'Defence of Civilization,'" 36. Navarro Floria, 1994b, correctly notes that degrees of barbarism or savagism continued to be recognized in the eighteenth century, including by the Scottish philosopher Adam Ferguson (p. 120), but I do not find eighteenth-century Spanish observers consistently using *salvajes* as a synonym for "bad Indians" and *bárbaros* for "noble savages," as Navarro Floria suggests (p. 134), and again in Navarro Floria, 1996, 101. Rather, *salvaje* and *bárbaro* were synonyms in general parlance. Navarro Floria asserts that Alejandro Malaspina drew this distinction, but see Malaspina's definition of "savage," which I quote below in this introduction.

57. Lastarria, "Declaraciones y expresas resoluciones soberanas que sumisamente se desean en beneficio de los Indios de las Provincias de la banda oriental del Río Paraguay, y de las márgenes del Paraná y Uruguay . . . ," Madrid, Aug. 31, 1804, in Lastarria, 1914, 119–25 ("estado adulto de civilización"; "Salvajes de los paises que no hemos conquistado"; "el

ínfimo grado de racionalidad"; "salvajes comerciantes"; "no ha progresado hasta el punto de mani-
festar en público su reconocimiento a la Divina
Providencia").

58. Malaspina, 1995, "Reflexiones políticas sobre las
Costas Occidentales de la América," 155, 163 n. 55,
discussing "comercio con los salvajes" ("esta voz
sacada del idioma francés, les sauvages, parece la
más oportuna para distinguir todas las tribus no su-
jetas a la Monarquía"). In the eighteenth century,
Spaniards used the word *bárbaro* more commonly
than they did *salvaje* (see, for example, Laserna
Gaitán, 1994, 33 n.34), but learned officials who read
the works of their enlightened French counterparts,
such as Malaspina and Francisco de Viedma (Viedma,
1969c–72c), 3:683, also employed the word *salvaje*.
Although *salvaje* gained currency in the late Bourbon
era, Spaniards had described some Indians as *salvajes*
in the sixteenth century. See, for example, Román
Gutiérrez, 1993, 323, and José de Acosta, quoted in
Navarro Floria, 1994b, 120. See, too n.56, above.

59. Although some anthropologists would strike "tribe"
from our lexicon, others argue the need for a term
to describe the organization of peoples between the
small units we think of as bands and larger units
that anthropologists know as "chiefdoms." "Bands"
are usually thought of as small, egalitarian, autonomous groups composed of relatives whose leaders
are temporary. "Chiefdoms," by definition, have formal hierarchical structures and centralized political
and economic institutions, often with a hereditary
leader or leaders. Located between band and chiefdom, the category of tribe suggests a network of
communities who share language, ideology, and material culture but who are governed by informal coun-
cils rather than a formal central political organization. Leaders of these groups win obedience through
persuasion rather than through coercion. Neither
the tribe nor the chiefdom are as complex as the
state, which has a central government with a professional bureaucracy and the power to coerce—to
collect taxes, draft labor, and enforce laws. See also
chap. 2 below.

60. Beckerman, 1979, 8–9, 14–18. For Comanches and
Aucas, see chap. 2 below.

61. Forbes, 1994, xvi, xx. For a classic statement on the
vagaries of tribal names, see Fried, 1975, 32–38. For
an elegant case study of "imposed identities," see
Nacuzzi, 1998. Cramaussel, 2000, 277–92, argues that
Spanish classifications do not correspond to modern
anthropologists' notions of ethnic groups, bands, or
tribes and that to impose them on the past is anachronistic. In chap. 2, I identify some of the indigenous
groups who term themselves "the people"—Araucanians, Chiriguanos, Comanches, and Apaches—but
there are many more, such as the Asháninka and Cam-
pas, of the central Peruvian jungle. Varese, 2002, 5.

62. Castro, 1971, 10–11, explains that the word *español*
was introduced from Provence in the thirteenth century; before that time Spaniards knew themselves
collectively as *cristianos*. Called to my attention by
Sahlins, 1989, 272–73.

63. Leutenegger, 1976, 31 ("cuando digo español se en-
tiende no indio, que así es lo corriente en este país").
For the analog in Portuguese Brazil, see Barickman,
1995, 328.

64. For a critique of oppositional models, see O'Brien
and Roseberry, 1991; for a need to study accommodation as well as resistance, see Brown, 1996, 729–35,
Weber, 1997, 1–32.

65. Alonso Espinoza, 1764, quoted in Radding, 1995, 101
("rancherías errantes"). This was commonplace. See,
for example, Cruz, 2001, 155–56. See chap. 3 below
for other examples.

66. Sanz, 1977, 81 ("los más civilizados"; "barbarie"; "sus
antiguas costumbres, trajes, e idioma").

67. Moreno y Escandón, 1936, 573–74 ("disfrazados con
plumas y colores"). Moreno y Escandón was the *protector de indios* of the audiencia of New Granada.

68. The problem led the anthropologist Edward Spicer
to a dramatic overstatement: "For the most part there
is really no history of the Indians, only a history of
the Spaniards in their contacts with the Indians."
Quoted in Sheridan and Naylor, 1979, 6.

69. A long literature testifies to this. Recent examples
include Basso, 1996, Descola, 1996, Deloria, 1997,
and the essays in Fixico, 1997, particularly those by
James Axtell and Richard White, for recent thinking about the limitations and opportunities of ethnohistory. See, too, the essays in Shoemaker, 2002, especially Patricia Albers's suggestions for a balance
between cultural and materialist approaches. I should
also be clear that my book makes no contribution
to subaltern studies because the independent Indians with whom I am concerned had not become
subordinate to Spaniards. For an introduction, see
Mallon, 1994, 1491–1515.

70. Elliott, 1995, 399.

71. Axtell, 1995, 679. Indian voices do, of course, emerge
from Spanish documents, but always mediated by
Spaniards; published Indian oral traditions shed
little light on this era. See, for example, Fernández,
1995. For an introduction to some of the theoretical
problems, see Salomon, 1999, pt. 1:19–95, and for a
generously inclusive definition of "Indian history,"
see Fixico, 1998, 84–99, who offers the possibility
that non-Indians can write some form of Indian
history.

Chapter 1. Savants, Savages, and New Sensibilities

The epigraphs are from Malaspina, "Descripción física
y costumbres de la California," in Malaspina, 1885, 445

("Dichosos ellos si contentos con la situación en que los colocó la Naturaleza, sin enemistades con los vecinos, sin disputas por la propiedad y libres de la ambición que atormenta a la culta Europa, subsisten largo tiempo en aquel apacible estado que les ofreció la madre bienhechora de los mortales"), translated in Cutter, 1960, 65, and the anonymous report, translated from the manuscript by Cutter, 1990, 131.

1. The "plan de un viaje científico y político," dated at Isla de León, Sept. 10, 1788, and directed to Antonio Valdés, is in Malaspina, 1885, 1–2. Malaspina explicitly rejected the idea that his voyage would be "una imitación servil de los viajes ingleses." Malaspina, "Estudio Preliminar," in Malaspina, 1984, 31. For Malaspina's first voyage around the world, see Manfredi, 1987, 69–95, which contains much fresh information. Outram, 1995, 48–49, asserts that it is anachronistic to apply the word "scientist," as we understand it today, to Enlightenment thinkers because the word was "not invented until the 1830s in England." It existed well before then in French, Italian, and Spanish, although in French, she tells us, "science" signified knowledge in general rather than the study of the natural world. Malaspina's plan, however, clearly distinguishes between scientific and political knowledge, for they did work we would regard today as scientific—trying to understand the natural world in a systematic way. Pimentel, 1998, makes this clear. Donald C. Cutter, "Introduction," in Malaspina, 2001, xxxii, suggests that "scientific motivation" represented the public face of the expedition, but that "inspection of the empire" was its "primary aim."

2. *Investigación malaspiniana* has become a minor industry. See Sáiz, 1992, and n. 6, below. Manfredi, 1994, 52, discusses the naming of the ships. For a recent introduction to the expedition, see Cerezo Martínez, 1987. Kendrick, 1999, 36, suggests that the well-connected Malaspina had approval for the voyage even before he formally sought authorization.

3. As Malaspina noted in his physical description of the northwest coast of America, the "number, customs, and reciprocal relations [of the Natives] will be examined little by little, with a philosophic inquiry, in order that the progress of the human species ... not seem to occupy a secondary place in our attention." Quoted in Pino Díaz, 1982, 402.

4. Malaspina, 1991b, 158 ("naciones ... cuyas arengas, pensamientos y costumbres denotan sus principios civiles"). This volume contains ten "political axioms concerning America," statements of self-evident truths that would inform him on his journey. Malaspina may have drafted them in the winter before he set sail, although the possibility remains that he wrote them afterward. See Kendrick, 1999, 100–107.

5. Pino Díaz, 1982, 422, argues that the expedition's

greatest contributions to ethnography came from his study of independent rather than dependent Indians.

6. Malaspina, "Estudio Preliminar," in Malaspina, 1984, 42 ("este libro será ... una redacción de obras ajenas, más bien que un trabajo original"). Lieutenants Viana and Tova kept the main diaries, and their entries at many points are nearly identical, suggesting collaboration. To demonstrate the point, in the notes below I have indicated some of the places where accounts resemble one another (including those of other officers). Lieutenant Viana's work exists in an authoritative edition (Viana, 1958); Tova's diary has also appeared in print (Tova, 1943), but Sáiz, 1992, 318, believes the edition contains a carelessly transcribed manuscript. Reliable extracts from Tova's diary are in Higueras Rodríguez and Pimentel Igea, 1993, 34–40, 127–46. Malaspina appears to have based his final report on his own diary (some of it published in Malaspina, 1885, but published definitively as Malaspina, 1990 and translated into English in Malaspina, 2001), the Viana and Tova diaries, and reports by other participants, including Espinosa y Tello, Pineda, Ciriaco Cevallos, and Felipe Bauzá. Malaspina, 1984, v. The reports of the expedition's participants, some in several drafts, variations, and handwriting, became so scattered and mingled that scholars have found it difficult to discern the authorship of individual documents (see my n. 1, for example). Higueras Rodríguez and Pimentel Igea, 1993 ("Apéndice documental"), 243–71, sorts them out. For other sources Malaspina relied upon, see Higueras, 1988a, "Cuestionarios científicos y noticias geográficas," cvii–cxxix. Malaspina's final report was never published under his direction, and his notes were scattered. Some were retrieved and published in the nineteenth century, most completely in Malaspina, 1885. Mercedes Palau, Aránzazu Zabala, and Blanca Sáiz reprinted the heart of that work (Malaspina, 1984) and added some new material but omitted many reports, making it essential to still consult the 1885 edition. The scattered sources were finally brought together in the definitive multivolume *La expedición Malaspina, 1789–1794,* published in Madrid in 1987–99.

7. For the varied interests of intellectuals of the Enlightenment, see Gay, 1966–69, 321–22. For biographical sketches of Malaspina's officers and scientists, see Malaspina, 1984, 605–11.

8. Malaspina to Gian Francesco Ala Ponze, Feb. 6, 1789 ("del Creador, del hombre y de la superficie por él habitada"), quoted in Manfredi, 1994, 41. I have drawn from Manfredi, 1994, 19–41, and Kendrick, 1999, chaps. 2 and 3, for Malaspina's early life.

9. For another notable example of the naval officer as scientist, see Rubin de Celis, 1788, 37–42.

10. Galera Gómez, 1988, 5–14, 241–43.

11. Viana, 1958, 1:2; Street, 1959, 47, 66–73 and *passim*. Viana's father, José Joaquín de Viana, had served as governor of Montevideo.

12. "Mapa geográfico que comprehende todos los modernos descubrimientos de la costa patagónica…," 1786, prepared at the request of the viceroy, the marqués de Loreto, by a Portuguese officer named José Custodio Saa Faría who was captured by Spanish forces in the Río de la Plata. Reproduced in Martínez Sierra, 1975, 1:239, illus. no. xxxviii ("terreno habitado por varias naciones de india barbara [i.e., indios bárbaros] e ignorado de los españoles"). For Spain's jurisdictional claims to Patagonia in the late 1700s, see Zorraquín Becú, 1959, 119–23, 223, who places it firmly in the viceroyalty of Buenos Aires. Some Chilean scholars take a different view. See Eyzaguirre, 1997, 40–45, and Villalobos R., 1993, 553, who argues that Chilean claims to Patagonia are overlooked in European scholarship. Amidst these competing claims, the fact remains that Indians, not Spaniards, held most of Patagonia.

13. Malaspina, "Suelo de las costas de la tierra patagónica e islas Malvinas, …" in Higueras Rodríguez and Pimentel Igea, 1993, 30. For Spanish settlements in northern Patagonia, see map 4 and chap. 4 below. Only one of those settlements, Carmen de Patagones, remained at the time of Malaspina's visit.

14. The first quotation is in Malaspina, 1991 ("los patagones errantes y no obstante civilizados"), 158; see, too, Pino Díaz, 1982, 418. The second quotation, "todo corrobora que sus costumbres no les hacen acreedores a la más remota denominación de salvajes," is in "Suelo de las costas de la tierra patagónica," in Higueras Rodríguez and Pimentel Igea, 1993, 32. Malaspina had not visited the Argentine coast on his first voyage around the world, but had read much about it at that time. See Manfredi, 1987, 82. See, too, González Montero de Espinosa, 1992, 79–80.

15. Malaspina, 1990, 80 ("sentados ya, en cerco, y deshechada por una, y otra parte toda desconfianza empezó a esplayarse el deseo, inato en el hombre, de querer conocer más de cerca a su semejante").

16. Lerner, 2000, 287–89; Tanck de Estrada, 1999, 168–89. For Spanish as the lingua franca, see, for example, the *real cédula* of May 10, 1770, in Solano, 1991, 257–61. For word collecting as a project of the Enlightenment, see Gray, 1999, chaps. 4 and 5.

17. See, especially, Gerbi, 1973, 82–86, and Smith, 1985, 34–38.

18. Malaspina to Antonio de Ulloa, Cádiz, Jan. 31, 1789, in Malaspina, 1885, 7 ("un objeto de mucha entidad para la historia de la propagación de la especie humana").

19. Malaspina, "Suelo de las costas de la tierra patagónica e islas Malvinas," in Higueras Rodríguez and Pimentel Igea, 1993, 29 ("daremos ahora una noticia,

si no tan individual, como desearamos, a lo menos tan verídica, como debe exigirla el actual estado de las ciéncias filosóficas en Europa").

20. Galera Gómez, 1988, 57–58, 207–08; González Montero, 1992, 78. The oil portrait of a Patagonian man, attributed to Pozo and referred to by Manfredi, 1994, 54, is apparently my figure 10. Junchar is also spelled Junchan.

21. Viana, 1958, 1:140–41 ("guerrera por necesidad"; "una nación libre, independiente y feliz"; "el destrozo, la desolación y la muerte").

22. Viana, 1958, 1:125–29. The quotations are on p. 129 ("la indigente incultura"; "como aprisionados en su propio país"). In describing Chilotes, Viana may also be talking about mixed bloods and Spaniards, who numbered 15,601 according to a Franciscan census of 1791, which put the Christian Indian population at 11,794. In addition to Huilliches (Veliches), the Christian Indian population consisted of Chonos and Caucahues, brought from the southern mainland. Urbina Burgos, 1990, 23, 38–40. Natives apparently numbered 50,000–60,000 at the time of conquest, a figure that had dropped to 3,000 by 1602. Vázquez de Acuña, 1991–92, 419, 426. González Montero, 1992, 110–33, provides a detailed portrait drawn from manuscript sources. See, too, Pino Díaz, 1982, 422.

23. López de Vargas Machuca, [1758], 20 ("habitantes no guardan leyes ni religión, no tienen ninguna población; y es un país poco conocido").

24. Viana, 1958, 2:63 ("Los tejuneses, según la práctica ordinaria de todos los salvajes, se pintan"); Suría, 1980, 35–36. The English mariner George Dixon, who stopped over in 1787, appears to be the first European encountered by the Tlingits.

25. Viana, 1958, 2:50 ("su música, aunque la empleaban para pedir o denotar la paz, se resiente del carácter salvaje, y es más propia para avivar las pasiones marciales, que para excitar los sentimientos dulces y tiernos"); Gutiérrez de la Concha, 1993, 160, uses the same language.

26. Kendrick, 1991, 129, 133. The use of song or dance to smooth initial encounters was not unusual, but Europeans often seem to have initiated it. See Clendinnen, 2003, 6–10, 291–92.

27. Viana, 1958, 2:65. Modern anthropologists have found war an endemic feature of native societies on the Pacific northwest coast, a result of conflict over resources in the well-considered view of Ferguson, 1984, 267–328.

28. For a good account of Spanish–Tlingit relations, see Cutter, 1991, 44–63.

29. For Malaspina's statement on his intellectual rivalry with Cook and others, see Pino Díaz, 1982, 434. For the question of names, see Arima and others, 1991, 6–12.

30. Malaspina, "Descripción física de las costas del

Noroeste de la América," in Malaspina, 1885, 354 (this report can be found, too, in Monge and Olmo, 1991, 163–235, and in Higueras Rodríguez and Pimentel Igea, 1993, 91–126. See, too, Viana, 2:95; Pino Díaz, 1982, 440–45).

31. Malaspina, "Descripción física de las costas del Noroeste de la América," in Malaspina, 1885, 353 ("en un grado más provecto de civilización").

32. Malaspina, "Descripción física y costumbres de la California," in Malaspina, 1885, 443 ("aquella prodigiosa flojedad y languidez con que, dice el redactor de esta historia, pasan en perpétua inacción y ociosidad su vida, con horror a cualquier trabajo y afán"). The 1885 publication of Malaspina's "Descripción física y costumbres de la California," is based on MS 425 in the Museo Naval, Madrid, and this has appeared in a modern version in Malaspina, 1991a, 163–235. A different manuscript version of the "Descripción física . . . de California" appears in Mathes, 1987, 1:129–227, who attributes it to Felipe de Bauzá y Cañas. Mathes transcribed MS 621 from the Museo Naval de Madrid; Dolores Higueras, "Apéndice Documental," in Higueras Rodríguez and Pimentel Igea, 1993, 258, identifies the author of MS 621 as Francisco Viana, not Bauzá y Caña, but the text bears great similarities to Malaspina's MS 425. Venegas wrote his "Noticia de la California," in 1739, although it was not published until 1757.

33. Malaspina, "Descripción física y costumbres de la California," in Malaspina, 1885, 445 ("libres de la ambición que atormenta a la culta Europa"), trans. in Cutter, 1960, 65. The translation of this same document in Galbraith, 1924, 215–37, is incomplete.

34. Malaspina, "Descripción física y costumbres de la California," in Malaspina, 1885, 447 ("la venida de los españoles ha traído a estos naturales, sin la más leve efusión de sangre, la cesación de mil guerras intestinas que los destruían, los principios sociales, una religión pura y santa, unos alimentos sanos y seguros"). See, too, Cutter, 1960, 53ff., and Rawls, 1984, 25–43, for comparisons of Malaspina's views with those of his contemporaries.

35. Viana on leaving Port Mulgrave, Viana, 1958, 2:62 ("abandonamos estos lugares rústicos, con la dulce complacencia de no haber procurado el perjuicio más leve a sus moradores"). Lieutenant Ciriaco Cevallos, quoted in Cutter, 1991, 63; Tova, 1943, 150, and Gutiérrez, 1993, 162, repeat these very words.

36. Malaspina, 1990, 345 ("nuestro roce pacífico con los naturales había a la sazón echado raíces mucho más solidas, si bien a costa de varios regalos . . . [y] una continua contribución de galletas").

37. For continuity in Spanish thought of this era, see Pérez, 1988, 267–79. For the long history of the "wild man" in European thought, see Bartra, 1994.

38. Grafton, 1992, 252.

39. Azara, 1943a, 99 ("el indio por más bárbaro que sea,

es la parte principal y más interestante de América"; "indios silvestres"). See, too, Azara, 1923, 2:1.

40. Malaspina, "Descripción física de las costas del Noroeste de la América," in Malaspina, 1885, 343 ("que últimamente puedan guiarnos a otras indagaciones más importantes para la historia de la sociedad"). See, too, p. 345.

41. Ibid., 344 ("Es preciso fijar nuestra atención en las cualidades morales: allí es donde el filósofo mira con una curiosa admiración los vicios y las virtudes naturales en el hombre, las inclinaciones innatas . . . los principios informes de la Sociedad").

42. Ibid., 349 ("las leyes melodiosas de la Naturaleza relativamente al respeto y cuidado paterno y al amor conyugal y filial").

43. Malaspina, "Estudio Preliminar," in Malaspina, 1984, 35 ("ya no pretenderemos violentar la naturaleza, para que destruya las leyes que ella misma se ha prescripto, sino más bien sujetaremos las medidas sociales al recto equilibrio que debe siempre conservar con el instinto inconstante del hombre").

44. For these ideas in Spain, see, for example, Sarrailh, 1957, esp. 39–74 (on the search for knowledge) and 580–600 (on the powers of the monarch). See, too, Gay, 1966–69, 2:320.

45. Pombal, 1742, quoted in Maxwell, 1995, 7. Cañizares-Esguerra, 2001, 134, 158–60.

46. Lafuente, 1988, 13–18. For the questionnaires, see, for example, Solano, 1988. The publication in Spain of forty-three volumes of travel literature between 1795 and 1801 (Estala, 1795–1801) testifies to the growing market for travel accounts. Laserna Gaitán, 1994, 18. See, too, Cañizares-Esguerra, 2001, 11–22, 49–51, for the new skepticism as it applied to Native Americans.

47. For an overview of these and other expeditions, see Pino Díaz and Guirao de Vierna, 1988, 19–69; for Ruiz and Pavón, see Steele, 1964; for New Spain, see Arias Divito, 1968, and Engstrand, 1981. Pérez Ayala, 1951, 181–84, notes that Mutis collected manuscript copies of Chibcha and Sáliva grammars and an Achuagua dictionary. The crown sent the order to collect these grammars and dictionaries in 1787, but only the viceroy of New Granada, Antonio Caballero y Góngora, who appointed Mutis, took action.

48. Steele, 1964, 46–49. For the use of "useful knowledge," see Burke, 1977, 5.

49. Verde Casanova, 1980, 82.

50. Malaspina, "Descripción física de las costas del Noroeste de la América," in Malaspina, 1885, 342 ("un examen filosófico, para que los progresos de la especie humana . . . no parezcan haber ocupado un lugar secundario en la atención nuestra a estos objetos"). Few Spanish scientists displayed Malaspina's interest in the natural or societal forces that shaped Indians' lives. As one example, see the journal of the

Spanish-born naturalist José Longinos, 1994. For Spaniards doing scientific work, independent Indians were more often the object of fear than a subject of study. See, for example, fray Diego García to José Celestino Mutis, Ciudad de Hacha, Sept. 24, 1787, in Mutis, 1968-75, 3:377.

51. Saavedra, 1989, 175, writing in his diary from Pensacola on May 11, 1781 (a diary that has only appeared in English); Alcedo, 1967, 2:234, under the heading "Indios" ("una pintura vivísima de la más remota antigüedad").

52. Burke to William Robertson, June 9, 1777, quoted in the epigraph to Marshall and Williams, 1982, a work devoted entirely to the English perceptions.

53. *Discourse on the Origin of Inequality,* quoted in Lévi-Strauss, 1963, 10.

54. "Plan para escribir su viaje, dado por Malaspina al P. Gil," Madrid, Oct. 3, 1795, in Malaspina, 1885, xxv ("las costumbres de los salvajes"). For Rousseau's influence, see Pimentel Igea, 1989, 97-100.

55. The quotations are from Jean-Jacques Rousseau's *Discourse on the Origin of Inequality,* in Rousseau, 1967, 248, 201. For the Spaniards' explanations, see above.

56. Lieutenant Tova quoted in Cutter, 1991, 54. The identical quotation is in Viana, 1958, 2:64 ("entre unos hombres cuyas necesidades son tan limitadas, y los medios de satisfacerlas igualmente fáciles"). The theory was subscribed to by Adam Ferguson, among others, with whom Malaspina was acquainted. My reference is to Rousseau's fourth stage, when private property ends the idyll. Symcox, 1972, 242; Rousseau, 1967, 220 ff. (*Discourse on the Origin of Inequality*).

57. Malaspina, "Descripción física de las costas del Noroeste de la América," in Malaspina, 1885, 344. Pino Díaz, 1982, 431, misreads this.

58. Malaspina, "Descripción física de las costas del Noroeste de la América," in Malaspina, 1885, 347 ("no podemos dejar de envidiar este rudo estado de las naciones, en el cual la misma falta de propiedad hace que el hombre trabaje para todos y sea útil a todos").

59. Pino Díaz, 1982, 460, notes those thinkers mentioned by name. Malaspina may have had copies of their books with him or notes from them—or perhaps consulted them on his return. In his "Descripción física de las costas del Noroeste," he cites Ferguson by section and part and quotes Saint-Pierre (in Malaspina, 1885, 344). For Malaspina's intellectual formation, especially Adam Smith, see Palau, 1992, 129. In my use of the French word "philosophe" I am here following Gay, 1966-69, 1:10. For Locke, see the naval officer Ciriaco Cevallos, quoted in Cutter, 1991, 99. Cevallos does not indicate who propounded the theory that criminal law was supposed to follow civil law, but it appears to reflect Locke's influence, and late eighteenth-century Spaniards

did have acquaintance with Locke. *Two Treatises of Government* (1690), in *Philosophers Speak for Themselves: From Descarte to Locke,* Marjorie Grene and T. V. Smith, eds. (Chicago: University of Chicago Press, 1940), 772-73.

60. Manfredi, 1994, 47-48.

61. Manfredi, 1994, 42-44, 49-50, 52; Malaspina, "Estudio Preliminar," in Malaspina, 1984, 43.

62. Pagden, 1994d. In the rest of Europe, it appears that the Enlightenment was less antireligious than scholars once thought. Sheehan, 2003, 1061-80.

63. For the beginnings of Enlightenment thought in Spain in the late 1600s and early 1700s (earlier than most of the traditional historiography suggested), see Sánchez-Blanco, 1999, and Pérez Magallón, 2002. McClelland, 1991, illuminates the "ideological confusion" among Spanish intellectuals in the first half of the century. Soto Arango, Puig-Samper, and Arboleda, 1995. See, too, Stolley, 1996, 345, and Cañizares-Esguerra, 2001, 146.

64. Both quotations are in Sarrailh, 1957, 496-97 ("El autor de esta obra no habla como matemático . . . sino como hombre que escribe en España, es decir, en un país donde existe Inquisición"; "¿No será ultrajar éstas el pretender que se opongan a las más delicadas demostraciones de geometría y de mecánica?").

65. For Spain itself, see especially Sarrailh, 1957, Herr, 1958, 35-85, and López, 1995, 63-124; for Spanish American, see Roland D. Hussey, "Traces of French Enlightenment in Colonial Hispanic America," and John Tate Lanning, "The Reception of the Enlightenment in Latin America," in Whitaker et al., 1961, 23-51, 71-93. Whitaker, 1970, 256-71, is a dated but still valuable introduction to the literature, much of it concerned with the impact of Enlightenment thought on the Spanish-American wars of independence, a subject beyond the scope of this book. Whitaker's essay appears, too, in Aldridge, 1971, a collection of essays that look at aspects of enlightened thought in Iberia and its diffusion in the Americas. Adelman, 1999, chap. 3, offers a more recent look at the circulation of enlightened thought regarding economic development in the Río de la Plata. On English influence, particularly Locke, Adam Smith, and Adam Ferguson, see Polt, 1964, and Smith, 1968.

66. Spell, 1938, 27, whose work informs this paragraph.

67. José Clavijo y Fajardo ("Todo es bueno, dice un autor famoso, cuando sale de manos de la naturaleza; todo es malo, después, que pasa por la de los hombres"), in Spell, 1938, 30, citing *El Pensador* 16 (Dec. 1762). Jean-Jacques Rousseau, *Émile or On Education,* Alan Bloom, ed. and trans. (New York: Basic Books, 1979), 37.

68. Spell, 1938, 72; Álvarez Barrientos, 1991, 234-42.

69. Herr, 1958, 63.

70. Álvarez Barrientos, 1991, 216-17.

71. Lanning, 1956, 115, 348. For the variety of ways the Enlightenment was received, see Whitaker, 1970, 163.

72. An undated document, "De la América en general," written perhaps after his term as a special commissioner in 1780–82 but perhaps after his term as intendant of Caracas ended in 1788. Found in Saavedra's papers and quoted in Morales Padrón, 1969, 357 ("la nueva filosofía va haciendo allí muchos más rápidos progresos que en España"; "nuevas ideas sobre los derechos de los hombres y los soberanos"; "libros franceses"; "filósofos modernos"; "entusiasmo"; "revolución"). In his diary, Saavedra, 1989, 247–48, 250–51, 255, 259–60, notes discontent with Spanish rule in Mexico in 1781.

73. Cañizares, 2001, 9, and see his chap. 5. Eyzaguirre, 1959, for the arrival of prohibited books in Chile. Chiaramonte, 1989, 98–116, offers a modulated discussion of the Enlightenment's reception in the Río de la Plata.

74. One Pérez y López, *Principios de Orden* (Madrid, 1785), quoted in Sánchez Agesta, 1979, 93 ("meros sueños de un hombre despierto").

75. Quoted in Arciniegas, 1967, 251. Noel, 1973, finds greater resistance to the Enlightenment in Spain under Carlos III than has been supposed and takes issue in particular with Herr, 1958.

76. Gay, 1966–69, offers a magisterial overview of the crosscurrents of the age. The Age of Reason was not, however, the uniformly self-confident, rational era that studies of the philosophes might suggest. See, for example, Terry Castle, *The Female Thermometer: 18th-Century Culture and the Invention of the Uncanny* (New York: Oxford University Press, 1995). For the divergent views of enlightened thinkers, see also Schmidt, 1996. For an engaging introduction to the seventeenth-century origins of a growing belief in "the pastness of the past," see Grafton, 1992, 197–252 (the quote is on p. 205).

77. Payne, 1973, 2:371.

78. Ezquerra, 1962, provides a systematic review of ideas regarding America by peninsular thinkers, drawn largely but not entirely from the published literature.

79. Las Casas presented these judgments in a manuscript, "Apologética historia" (ca. 1551), that, in the words of one historian, offered "the first detailed comparative analysis of Amerindian culture" (Pagden, 1982, 146, 156). Las Casas's manuscript was not published until the twentieth century. Acosta moved closer yet to modern formulations in his *Historia natural y moral de las Indias* (1590), with its description and classification of unique cultural traits. There is a large literature on this subject, which is admirably summarized and expanded upon in Pagden, 1982, 119–45, 146–97. For stylish clarity, brevity, and insight, the summation in Elliott, 1970, 43–63, remains unsurpassed in English.

80. Elliott, 1970, 31; Sánchez-Blanco Parody, 1985, 189; Pagden, 1982, 175–79; Pagden, 1990, 99; Meek, 1976, 42–49; Rozat, 1996, 77–94, 183. Cervantes, 1994, chaps. 1 and 5, ends his study in 1767, at which time he argues Mexican intellectuals had not yet embraced the European shift to a Newtonian, mechanistic world.

81. Pagden, 1982, 155. For a more appreciative view of Acosta, see Pino Díaz, 1992, who argues that Acosta employed references to the devil in order to avoid censure, and that he explained even Aztec human sacrifice with cold, scientific detachment. Cañizares, 2001, chap. 2, offers a fascinating account of the way in which eighteenth-century Spanish scholars dismissed the same indigenous sources that Renaissance scholars found so valuable.

82. Lipsett-Rivera, 2002, 205–08. Hodgen, 1964, 484, gives insufficient weight to this distinction between the thought of the Renaissance and the Enlightenment, noting that the latter merely substituted "the idea of progress for that of providence."

83. Viana, 1958, 1:140 ("les ha hecho adoptar por su criador un principio malo"; "El desorden aparente del universo"). Pino Díaz, 1982, 422. For the context of Viana's observation, see Manuel, 1959, 140–41, and Marshall and Williams, 1982, 218. For changing Spanish attitudes toward the causes of insanity, see Huertas, 1998, 155–64.

84. Not all enlightened thinkers would have made that argument, of course, or taken such a positive view of human nature. See, for example, Gay, 1966–69, 2:99–102, 168–74, 187–94, 322.

85. Then, too, if Nature itself was simple and noble, as some philosophes believed, then the savage, as a child of nature, personified those virtues. Smith, 1985, 42.

86. Malaspina, 1984, 97 ("un pueblo casi desnudo y bárbaro"; "el filósofo moral"; "menos viciosos y propensos naturalmente a la vida brutal").

87. Viana, 1958, 1:77 ("una nación abandonada a sí misma en el fondo remoto y estéril de la América meridional, sepultada en la ignorancia más lastimosa"; "la buena fe, el candor y la probidad"). Manfredi, 1987, 75.

88. Viana, 1958, 1:78 ("naciones artificiosas, pérfidas, sanguinarias en quienes el robo, la embriaguez y el engaño, ocupan el lugar de todas las virtudes").

89. Malaspina, "Descripción física de las costas del Noroeste de la América," in Malaspina, 1885, 347.

90. Malaspina, 1991, 156 ("El indio, o por el clima que habita o por su transpiración demasiado rápida, origen luego de cierta indolencia tanta en la edad más adulta"), perhaps reflecting the influence of Montesquieu's *De l'esprit des lois* (see Pagden, 1990, 113, and Montesquieu, 1949, 1:221–24).

91. Malaspina, "Descripción física de las costas del Noroeste de la América," in Malaspina, 1885, 356

("admitir una verdad tan ignominiosa a nuestra especie"). See, too, Cutter, 1991, 100–103.

92. Requena, 1991, 112–13 ("la mala costumbre en alimentarse de sus prisioneros, vicio que deben frecuentarlo tal vez más por necesidad que por gula, vista la falta de carne que tienen en estas partes").

93. Keen, 1971, 218, 222, 286; Berkhofer, 1978, 38–44.

94. The last quotation is from the Jesuit Sánchez Labrador, 1936, 103 ("natural inquieto"), and the two prior quotations are from the English Jesuit Falkner, 1935, 109, both of whom completed their writing following their expulsion from Buenos Aires with other Jesuits in 1768. Sánchez Labrador also saw alcohol as a cause of nomadism. Viana, 1958, 1:80; Malaspina, "Suelo de las costas de la tierra patagónica e islas Malvinas," in Higueras Rodríguez and Pimentel Igea, 1993, 29, and González Montero, 1992, 73. For the theory of functionalism, see Pino Díaz, 1982, 419.

95. Dickason, 1984, 273.

96. Viana, 1958, 1:81 ("el carácter indolente del americano").

97. Malaspina, quoted in González Montero, 1992, 90–91 ("parecen subsistir allí contra los dictados de la misma Naturaleza; todo denota, que ese Suelo les es estraño, que han realmente degenerado de los Caracteres Indicativos de la Clase de Hombre pasando a una estupidez que no le es natural"). Navarro Floria, 1994b, 116, 125–27, sees no inconsistency here, but rather that some Patagonians were more primitive than others.

98. Malaspina, "Descripción física y costumbres de la California," in Malaspina, 1885, 442 ("La vida errante de sus moradores, origen siempre de la despoblación y de las discordias").

99. The idea of social evolution, at the core of Condillac's Essai sur l'origine des connaissances humaines (1746) and Montesquieu's De l'esprit des lois (1748), and repeated in the work of Buffon and others, replaced the theory that political society developed suddenly by means of a social contract. Symcox, 1972, 231. See, too, Berkhofer, 1978, 44–49.

100. Ferguson's Essay on the History of Civil Society first appeared in 1767. Malaspina's reference to Ferguson is in his "Descripción física de las costas del Noroeste de la América," in Malaspina, 1885, 344, and he cites section II, part II. Another of Malaspina's contemporaries, Gaspar Melchor de Jovellanos, reportedly had read Ferguson's Essay on Civil Society three times (Polt, 1964, 9). For discussions of Ferguson's work, see Meek, 1976, 150–55; and Gay, 1966–69, 2:175, 336–43. Meek concerns himself with how this theory dominated "socio-economic thought in Europe in the latter half of the eighteenth century," but Meek ignores Spain in that era. Stage theory was not incompatible with environmental explanations; those who believed in stages of development allowed for local variations.

101. Malaspina, "Estudio Preliminar," in Malaspina, 1984, 35 ("los primeros grados de la sociedad").

102. Malaspina, "Estudio Preliminar," in Malaspina, 1984, 42 ("civilizados, unidos, amantes del orden y del gobierno").

103. Ferguson, An Essay on Civil Society, excerpted in Peter Gay, ed., The Enlightenment: A Comprehensive Anthology (New York: Simon and Schuster, 1973), 550.

104. Malaspina, "Estudio Preliminar," in Malaspina, 1984, 42; Symcox, 1972, 238–39; Rousseau, 1967, 189–92 (Discourse on the Origin of Inequality).

105. Ferguson, "An Essay on Civil Society," 552.

106. See, for example, Hodgen, 1964, Rowe, 1965, 1–20, and Pagden, 1982. Pagden suggests sixteenth-century origins for modern anthropology.

107. E. E. Evans-Pritchard, Social Anthropology and Other Essays (New York: Free Press, 1962), 21, 25. Harris, 1968, 8–52; Gay, 1966–69, 2:319–96. For a weighty defense of this idea, questioned by Michel Foucault and others, see Keith Michael Baker, Condorcet: From Natural Philosophy to Social Mathematics (Chicago: University of Chicago Press, 1975).

108. Pino Díaz, 1982, argues this point convincingly. So, too, Herda, 1997, 74. Carretero Collado, 1995, 148, notes the rigor and modernity of the botanist José Moziño's work on Nootka peoples. Gay, 1966–69, 2:319, suggests the emergence of cultural relativism among Europeans in the late eighteenth century; for the thinness of that relativism, see Douthwaite, 1992, 20.

109. Viana, 1958, 2:64 ("tan distintas son las opiniones de los hombres sobre lo hermoso como justa la opinión de Mr. Buffon, en que el gusto es pura convención"). Tova is quoted in Cutter, 1991, 54. But see, too, Peter Martyr's comment inspired by the same phenomenon, quoted in Rowe, 1965, 13.

110. Monge, 1989, 51–59, who implicitly addresses and rejects Pino Díaz's argument that the work of the Malaspina expedition could be termed anthropology. The quotation is on p. 57 ("para estructurar y sistematizar rigurosamente el cuerpo de información recogida"). Monge, 2002, elaborates on this theme.

111. Clastres, 1987, 168, put it well: "Primitive societies are not overdue embryos of subsequent societies."

112. Harris, 1968, 13. Wilde, 2003, 105–35, contrasts the discourse of description, classification, and comparison of enlightened Bourbons with fluid relations and ambiguous identities of Indians and rural people.

113. This literature is substantial. See, for example, Clifford, 1986, wherein several writers address the "historical predicament of ethnography ... caught up in the invention, not the representation, of cultures" (p. 2); Comaroff, 1992; Obeyesekere, 1992, with its critique of Marshall Sahlins's acceptance of the idea of James Cook's apotheosis and Sahlins's reply, How "Natives" Think About Captain Cook, For Example

(Chicago: University of Chicago Press, 1995); Lévi-Strauss, 1966; Todorov, 1984, 15–22.

114. Shweder, 1982, offers a fine example; see also Torgovnick, 1990, 11: "For Euro-Americans ... to study the primitive brings us always back to ourselves, which we reveal in the act of defining the Other."

115. The *Brevísima relación de la destrucción de las Indias* is available in many editions. I have taken this quotation from *The Devastation of the Indies: A Brief Account*, Herma [*sic*] Briffault, trans. (Baltimore: Johns Hopkins University Press, 1992), 28. For the putative influence of these writers on the development of the myth of the noble savage, see Abellán, 1976, and Cro, 1990, 13–51 (who ignored Abellán).

116. The first quotation is from "Of Cannibals" (1578–80) in *The Complete Essays of Montaigne*, Donald M. Frame, trans. (Stanford: Stanford University Press, 1965), 156, where Montaigne famously observed that "each man calls barbarism whatever is not his own practice" (ibid., 152). The second quotation is from "Of Coaches" (1585–88) in ibid., 694. Bartra, 1994, 171–74, notes that Montaigne borrows from the long European "wild man" tradition. For Montaigne's influence, see Berkhofer, 1978, 75, and Fairchild, 1928, 128. See, too, Smith, 1985, 5, 37–38, who offers a useful distinction between hard and soft primitives, and Pagden, 1994b.

117. That Rousseau did not take an unqualified sentimental view of savage life, either in his *Discourse on Inequality* or in *Émile*, has been well known. See Fairchild, 1928, 120–39, and Symcox, 1972, 223–47. Ellingson, 2001, 81, notes that Rousseau never used the term "noble savage." Ellingson has found its modern source in the mid–nineteenth century, thus disproving Hayden White's assertion that "the theme of the Noble Savage may be one of the few historical topics about which there is nothing more to say." White, 1976, 1:121.

118. Álvarez Barrientos, 1991, 302–07, describes several novels published in Spain that employ the trope of *les bons sauvages*, but these were written by Frenchmen and translated into Spanish. I am grateful to him for assuring me that the good Indian as a protagonist in literature in eighteenth-century Spain "no tuvo tanto eco ni utilidad como en otras culturas." Personal communication, Nov. 26, 2002. Although one cannot prove a negative, works like Urruela V. de Quezada, 1992, 91–108, also suggest that savages, noble or otherwise, were not tropes in eighteenth-century Spanish literature. Vargas, 1944, 87, 99, provides an example of a highly enlightened essayist from New Granada, and other examples follow in notes below.

119. "Tratado teórico-práctico de enseñanza," 1802, in Jovellanos, 1956, 1:254, called to my attention by Polt, 1971, 109 ("su barbarie primitiva"; "en un caos de absurdos y blasfemias"). For deism, Christianity,

and the noble savage, see Smith, 1985, 5, 147. Berkhofer, 1978, 75, observes that the cult of the noble savage was primarily a French construct.

120. Tova, "Ocurrencias en Pto. Deseado [1789]," in Higueras Rodríguez and Pimentel Igea, 1993, 36 ("El amor recíproco de padre a hijos, hermanos, etc., y una honestidad cual se ha notado particularmente en las mujeres, pueden servir de modelo a los pueblos más civilizados").

121. Malaspina, 1991, 158–59 ("jamás han sido atraídos a desear nuestro método sociable, aunque no puedan percibir sino su agradable aspecto externo, ocultándoseles por consiguiente cuánto han de perturbar la felicidad interna las excesivas desigualdades en las clases y en las riquezas, las ideas perniciosas de la comodidad y la indolencia, todas las discordias procedidas de aquellas causas y el verse envueltos en todas la [*sic*: las] guerras de Europa"). See, too, the comments of Seville-born Saavedra, 1989, 184, based on a brief visit to Pensacola.

122. Malaspina, 1991, 156 ("tranquilo el indio, no conocía el valor de la plata y del oro, ni necesitaba para su cómoda subsistencia de un trabajo asiduo y penoso").

123. Malaspina, "Estudio Preliminar," in Malaspina, 1984, 35 ("el vicio social que triunfa hoy en día").

124. Moziño, 1970, 42; Mociño y Losada, 1998, 69, for the original Spanish ("como los vicios crecen con las necesidades y éstas con el lujo de las naciones viciadas, nadie dirá que exagero si afirmo que son pocos los de estos salvajes, comparados con los nuestros. No se ve allí la ambición de la hacienda ajena, porque los artículos de primera necesidad son muy reducidos y comunes todos. A nadie obliga el hambre a saltear en los caminos ni hacer en las costas la piratería.... El tráfico con los europeos les ha hecho conocer varias cosas de que les hubiera sido mejor haber carecido siempre"). Engstrand, in Moziño, 1970, 42, translates "viciadas" as "sophisticated," but "vitiated" or "spoiled" seem more likely.

125. Moziño, 1970, 58; Mociño y Losada, 1998, 82, for the original Spanish ("¿Qué no tienen Dios ni los españoles ni los ingleses que sólo celebran la fornicación y la embriaguez?").

126. Suria, 1991, 132 ("En ella se les da una idea sublime, tan distinta de lo que ven los ojos"). See, too, Suría, 1980, 51 (Suria's name appears with an accent in some works). "The work of Suria's fellow artist, the apparently untrained José Cardero, on the other hand, ennobled California Indians." See Perry, 1999, 12.

127. "Descripción física y costumbres de la California," in Malaspina, 1885, 442 ("entregando al hombre a sus propias pasiones y al único cuidado de su conservación animal, le degradan, le entorpecen y casi convierten su vida en una viva representación de la de los seres irracionales"). For Rousseau on this point, see especially Fairchild, 1928, 131.

128. Malaspina, 1984, 97 ("vida brutal"). See n. 86, above.

129. Viana, 1958, 1:129 ("un pueblo sin comunicación ni tráfico con otras gentes, jamás puede civilizarse"); Caamaño, 1938, 208. Indians might be happy, one of Malaspina's contemporaries suggested, but it was only because they were ignorant of civilization. Navarro Floria, 1994b, 125.

130. Anonymous report of the *Sutil* and *Mexicana*, translated from the manuscript, in Cutter, 1990, 131.

131. Espinosa y Tello, 1885, 574–75 ("como almáciga y criadero de los bárbaros"; "rey de la Naturaleza"; "son estos indios toscos, incontinentes, vagamundos, flojos, groseros en sus conceptos, y grandes guerreros"), who traveled with the cartographer Felipe Bauzá y Cañas. Their account of their journey has been mistakenly attributed to Tadeo Haenke. Cutter and Destefani, 1966, 101–02, 106.

132. Azara, 1923, 2:112 ("salvajes de América"; "sin preámbulos ni ceremonias"; "Todas estas cualidades parecen aproximarlos a los cuadrúpedos y parecen tener aún alguna relación con las aves por la fuerza y finura de su vista"). Azara raised the question of Indians' animal-like nature as he wrestled with the old question of monogenesis vs. polygenesis and the American Indian.

133. Fray Juan de la Fuente, quoted in Lavallé, 1990, 337 ("sospecho que el suelo y el cielo de la América no es tan bueno para hombres como para yerba y metales").

134. Pagden, 1990, 106; for English-American intellectuals, see Kornfeld, 1995, 299.

135. Lavallé, 1990, 342.

136. García, 1969a-72a, 357 ("incapaces de razón . . . sino que también en las ciudades capitales de América se encuentran hombres de casi iguales sentimientos"; "una pública ignorancia"; "sagacidad").

137. De Pauw's *Recherches philosophiques sur les Américains* (Berlin, 1768), quoted in Gerbi, 1973, 58. Gerbi summarizes and analyzes de Pauw's work on pp. 52–79. Robertson explained American Indians' apparent apathy as partly a result of climate and the ease by which Indians could support themselves, but for Robinson that apathy, Gerbi says, "is a quality that is by now innate and indelible" (Gerbi, 1973, 168). For the remarkable story of a momentary Spanish interest in translating Robertson's work because of its supposed impartiality, see Cañizares, 2001, 54, 134, 171–82. See, too, Marshall and Williams, 1982, 219–20.

138. Gerbi, 1973, 233–39.

139. Alzate, 1993, 75–83. In the late eighteenth century, de Pauw's theory of American decline had few supporters among enlightened Spaniards, and in Spanish America, in the words of one historian, it provoked "more mirth than admiration." Lanning, 1956, 307. See, too, Gerbi, 1973, 289–324, and Cañizares, 2001, 284–85.

140. Pagden, 1994a, 76–77.

141. Alcedo, 1967, 2:465–66 ("Mixteca") ("celebre jurista"; "varón de tanta virtud y ciencia, que destruyó la opinión de que los indios no eran capaces de los conocimientos de los europeos"), called to my attention by Lerner, 1971, 85.

142. Pagden, 1994a, 66–69. See, too, Phelan, 1960, 760–70. I explore this question further in chap. 7.

143. Bustamante, 1981 ("el indio mexicano"). Cañizares, 2001, chap. 4, adds a class dimension to this analysis, arguing that the *criollo* clerics who wrote about Indians identified themselves with the Indian nobility and presented Indians in general as "degenerate" (p. 265).

144. I do not see place of residence—America vs. the metropolis—as an important indicator of the views of Spanish observers, as does Navarro Floria, 1996–97, 115–43.

145. Malaspina, 1991, 156–60, quotation on 157 ("la vida ociosa y casi errante a la vida laboriosa de una sociedad bien ordenada").

146. The quotations are in Malaspina, 1991, 156 ("en continua acción chocando unos contra otros y causan con una constante reacción la verdadera debilitación del todo"), and Malaspina, "Estudio Preliminar," in Malaspina, 1984, 33 ("la esclavitud política y la mercantil"). For his elaboration, see p. 38.

147. Locke spelled out his value theory of labor in his *Two Treatises on Government* (1690). Jovellanos's famous *Report on Agrarian Law* (1795) summarized Locke's ideas, which circulated in Spain well before 1795. Polt, 1971, 101.

148. Sarrailh, 1957, 513, who notes that "a fines de este siglo hay un espíritu nuevo de moderación y de justicia que inspira las doctrinas de los españoles sobre la manera de proceder con los indios."

149. Keen, 1971, 217. For this ambivalence and the question of race, see Mosse, 1978, 16.

150. Pimentel Igea, 1989, 101, and Pimentel Igea, 1993, 16–17, also notes Malaspina's contradictions. See, too, Wallace, 1999, for a Jefferson who both lamented the decline of Indians yet insisted that they must become civilized.

151. Revillagigedo's secret instructions to Lieutenant Mourelle, Sept. 9, 1791 (who did not sail—see Cutter, 1991), quoted at length in Cook, 1973, 328–30. See, too, the instructions from Revillagigedo to Alcalá Galiano and Cayetano Valdés, Jan. 31, 1792, in Kendrick, 1991, 53, and González Montero, 1992, 29–30, for Juan and Ulloa.

152. Juan Francisco de Bodega y Cuadra, quoted in Cook, 1973, 340. Gay, 1966–69, 2:29–45.

153. Kendrick, 1991, 79. For benevolence and its effects in North America, see Sheehan, 1973.

154. Carbia, 1944, 237, cites the list of 1790, noting that it repeated a prohibition made over a half century earlier.

155. Juderías, 1960, 305, maintained that in Spain "la leyenda negra no influye hasta muy entrado el siglo XVIII: hasta fines de aquel siglo." See, too, 249–56, 260–71.

156. Arthur P. Whitaker, "The Dual Role of Latin America in the Enlightenment," in Whitaker, 1961, 7–9.

157. Crusoe, quoted at length in Cro, 1990, 102. Solano, 1981, 56, notes that Gálvez possessed a French translation. For a spirited account of the spread of the Black Legend, see Powell, 1971.

158. Martínez Torrón, 1992, 27, quoting from book IV, discurso décimo, pp. 289–92, of the 1773 edition of Feijóo's *Teatro Crítico* ("desdichados aquellos que, oprimiendo con sus violencias al Indio, hacen padecer a toda la Nación. ¿Quién os parece que arde en más voraces llamas en el Infierno, el Indio Idólatra, ciego, o el Español, cruel y sanguinario?").

159. Viana, 1958, 1:135 ("heroicos bárbaros").

160. See, for example, the analysis of Clavigero's thought in Pagden, 1990, 104, and Juan A. Ortega y Medina, "La crítica a la ideología colonizadora de España," in Ortega y Medina, 1993, 123.

161. Haenke, 1942, 203 ("opresiones, tiranías y violencias cometidas por los españoles son patrañas que no merecen la fé y crédito público"). This is apparently the work of José de Espinosa y Tello, incorrectly attributed to Haenke. See, too, Cañizares, 2001, 131–33, 182–85, who explains Pedro de la Estala's and Juan Nuix's interests in seeing America as a nearly empty continent in the context of Spanish patriotism.

162. Carbia, 1944, 214–38, summarizes reaction to the Black Legend during the Age of Enlightenment. See, too, Viedma, 1969a-72a, 702–03, and the writings of fray Fernando de Ceballos and Juan de Escoiquiz, summarized in Ezquerra, 1962, 235–37. The debate has not advanced since then. See Gibson, 1971.

163. An anonymous but contemporary annotation of a 1791 MS by an *ilustrado* from New Granada, in Vargas, 1944, 88 n.1 ("cometen crueldades increíbles, no en un siglo de ignorancia como e l en que se hizo la conquista, sino en este ilustrado"). The annotator believed that Vargas had been too harsh in his assessment of the conquest and had adopted the point of view of Spain's foreign enemies.

164. Azara, 1923, 1:142.

165. Alcedo, 1967, 2:406 ("blasonen con este borrón de humanidad los ingleses y declamen contra las pretendidas crueldades de los españoles en la América, que aunque fuesen ciertas, no llegan a esta barbarie"). Called to my attention by Lerner, 1971, 90. Alcedo was Ecuadorian born, but worked on his encyclopedia in Spain.

166. Lieutenant Viana, for example, described the 1553 rebellion of the Araucanians in Chile as having been caused by "la tiranía de Valdivia y otros conquistadores, que exigiendo excesivas contribuciones ex-

asperaron los ánimos de aquellos belicosos naturales." Viana, 1958, 1:134–35.

167. Viana, 1958, 2:62 ("conforme al carácter benéfico, y humano de los españoles, confundirán algún día a cierta clase de escritores, que han tenido por oficio el denigrar a una nación ilustre y respetable, y que a pesar de sus ridículas y extravagantes declaraciones ocupará siempre un lugar distinguido en los fastos del universo"). Lieutenant Ciriaco Cevallos quoted in Cutter, 1991, 63; Tova, 1943, 150, and Gutiérrez, 1993, 162, repeat these sentiments in nearly identical language.

168. Viana, 1958, 1:79 ("mandadas por hombres brutales, sin educación ni sentimientos, y en cuyas operaciones suelen tener más parte el ponche y la cerveza que los movimientos del corazón").

169. Moziño, 1970, 71; Mociño y Losada, 1998, 93, for the original Spanish ("la perversa idea de enseñar a los salvajes el manejo de las armas de fuego, doctrina que puede ser perniciosa a toda la humanidad").

170. "Apuntes . . . de los salvajes habitantes del Estrecho de Fuca," Secundino Salamanca, 1792, MS, quoted in Archer, 1987, 60. Archer would agree with the invidious comparisons, at least in the Pacific Northwest, where, he concludes, Indians on the northwest coast in Malaspina's time "suffered less from the presence of Spain than they did from any of the other nations there to make profits from the fur trade." Archer, 1973b, 23. See, too, Christon I. Archer's Review of Frederic W. Howay, *Voyages of the 'Columbia' to the Northwest Coast, 1787–1790 and 1790–1793*, in *BC Studies* no. 93 (Spring 1992), 74–75.

171. Moziño, 1970, 84; Mociño y Losada, 1998, 103, for the original Spanish ("los marineros o en fuerza de su educación casi brutal o envidiosos del trato humano que el comandante y demás oficiales daban siempre a los naturales, los insultaron varias veces, estropearon a unos e hirieron a otros y no dejaron de matar a algunos. La humanidad es el mejor carácter de la civilización. Todas las ciencias y artes valen nada si sólo sirven para hacernos crueles y orgullosos"). See, too, Kendrick, 1991, 185, and Inglis, 1992. At least one officer contemplated attacking an Indian village to gain revenge but decided against it for fear he would hurt innocent Indians and lose some of his own men as well. Caamaño, 1938, 273, 281–82.

172. Payne, 1973, 2:369.

173. Ulloa, 1992, xxxvi–xl, 305–34.

174. Ruiz López, 1952, 221 ("naturalmente tétricos y belicosos"); 223 ("con la benignidad y tolerancia . . . que está mandada por los soberanos españoles").

175. Requena, 1991, 121 ("tal vez el demonio indujo a estos miserables la deserción para estorbarles el fruto que esperábamos sacasen catequizándolos y reduciéndolos a nuestra religión").

176. Kupperman, 2000, 10–11 and *passim*.

177. Both quotations are from letters to his brother Gia-

cinto, the first, Sept. 8, 1795, and the second an undated letter of ca. May 1795, quoted in Hendrick,
1999, 138 and 129, respectively. Malaspina's fate was
shared by other Spanish scholars. Cañizares, 2001,
135, points out that "the record of publication in
Spain [of histories of America] was dismal," as their
authors fell victim to "rivalries among different cor-
porations and groups of courtiers."

Chapter 2. Savages and Spaniards

The epigraph is from Clifford, 1986, 10.

1. José de Vargas Ponce, "Relación del último viage al
   Estrecho de Magallanes . . . 1785 y 1786," in Bitlloch,
   1994, 11–12. I translated *aguardiente* as "brandy," but
   Spaniards used this word to designate various ardent
   spirits. For *bolas* in the Chaco, see Saeger, 2000, 57.
2. Falkner, 1935, 112, reported that a Tehuelche cacique,
   whom he did not identify, used this phrase in describing his own visit to a European vessel. An English-born Jesuit, Falkner lived in the region in the
   mid-1700s.
3. Cultures, of course, exist in a constant state of change,
   antedating the arrival of Europeans. My attempt to
   discuss cultural changes in this chapter may seem
   like a fool's errand to anthropologists who recognize that we have neither a good baseline from which
   to measure change, nor adequate theory for explaining why changes occur. See especially Ramenofsky, 1991, 3:437–52. Then, too, some anthropologists have questioned the ability of scholars to
   describe cultures objectively. As James Clifford has
   noted, "Culture is contested, temporal, and emer-
   gent. Representation and explanation—both by in-
   siders and outsiders—is implicated in this emergence." Clifford, 1986, 19.
4. According to Vargas Ponce's report, Spaniards on
   the *Santa María* heard Francisco Xavier refer by
   name to Capitán Antonio Viedma and a pilot, Bernardo Tafor. Antonio Viedma had brought colonists
   to the short-lived colony at Puerto Deseado in 1780,
   and so it may have been there, or at the contempo-
   raneous settlements at San Julián and Carmen de
   Patagones, that Francisco Xavier had encountered
   Spaniards. For Antonio Viedma, see Luiz, 1997, 50.
   The case of Francisco Xavier was not unique. See
   Tova, "Ocurrencias en Pto. Deseado [1789]," in Higueras Rodríguez and Pimentel Igea, 1993, 36, 38.
5. La Pérouse, 1994, 1:49. For an early (1602) example
   of this process in English North America, see Kupperman, 2000, 5–6.
6. Of course, some areas of the hemisphere, such as
   parts of the Amazon basin and Tierra del Fuego,
   remained unvisited by Europeans or their allies.
   Sweet, 1992a, 1:266, and Darwin, 1989, 172–73. But
   even the most remote areas experienced indirect
   European influences. See Reeve, 1994, 106–38, and

Binnema, 2001, 86–106. For a fine case study of the
transformation of ethnic boundaries, see Whitehead, 1994, 33–53, who criticizes the use of "linguistically based models of contemporary Amerindian
society and culture [which] are uncritically projected
back into the past" (p. 34).

7. As one distinguished anthropologist has noted,
   "There was no single, uniform pattern in the way
   the cultures changed or the way the people preserved their identities." Spicer, 1962, 15. For a masterful overview of such transformations in South America and guidance to the literature, see Schwartz and
   Salomon, 1999, 468–74, 482–499. Polo Acuña, 1999a,
   7–29, and Barrera Monroy, 2000, 31–34, 174–75,
   strikingly contrast Guajiros, who survived by adopting foreign livestock and foreigners themselves, with
   Cocinas, who inhabited the same peninsula but who
   resisted cultural change and died out as a people.
   See, too, Powers, 1995, 3, and Deeds, 2003, who seeks
   to explain ethnic persistence (and, by implication,
   loss) among nonsedentary people in Nueva Vizcaya
   and offers a splendid introduction to theoretical approaches (pp. 1–11).
8. Beckerman, 1979, 20–21; Rausch, 1984, 231; Reff,
   1991, 281; Sheridan, 1999, 9. For current knowledge
   about Indian resistance to disease and the importance of contingency, see Jones, 2003, 740–42.
9. Aldunate del Solar, 1982, 73. For the disparaging
   terms, see Casanueva, 1988, 246.
10. Ercilla y Zúñiga, 1945, 35, 37. The poem was pub-
    lished in three parts, in 1569, 1578, and 1589.
11. Casanueva, 1992a, 2.
12. Korth, 1968, viii, argues that the main reason for
    Araucanian resistance was "the harsh treatment that
    the Indians experienced at the hands of whites," but
    this does not explain the success of Araucanian
    resistance.
13. Villalobos R., 1991, 305–13, emphasizes these ex-
    ternal circumstances. Although evidence points to
    a dense population, numbers remain highly conjec-
    tural. Cooper, 1946, "The Araucanians," 2:694. Jara,
    1990, chap. 4, elaborates on the private nature of
    Spanish forces.
14. Some scholars have translated this word simply as
    "enemy" or "rebel" (Villalobos R., 1989b, 202), but
    I am following the more precise usage, "savages,"
    of the ethnolinguist Adalberto Salas, quoted in Boc-
    cara, 1996b, 668.
15. Foerster G., 1991, 188–89.
16. For the parallel case of the Chichimecas, see Powell,
    1952, 47.
17. Casanueva, 1984, 5.
18. These weapons fell into Araucanian hands early.
    Sors, 1921–23, no. 46, 336, a Franciscan writing in
    1780 admired Araucanians' fighting techniques; he
    makes clear that they continued to acquire metal
    weapons. Writing in 1810, García, 1969a-72a, 359,

noted that Araucanians made machetes and lance heads with "perfección."

19. Jiménez, 1998, 59, quoting Esquivel Aldao to José Francisco de Amigorena, May 19, 1792 ("no hay que temerles pues no ofenden mas, sino con la primera descarga, que al dar esta se les atropella y quedan vencidos"). Most Spanish sources agree that Araucanian speakers in Chile—Huilliches, Mapuches, and Pehuenches—made little use of firearms even in the late eighteenth century. See Zapater, 1982, 86, and the report of Francisco Joseph Maran, Concepción, Aug. 28, 1784, quoted in Boccara, 1999b, 446. For an exception, see Figueroa, 1884, 21, 65–66, writing in 1792, who suggests that they were well armed by the end of the colonial period. For an example of short supply of ammunition, see Menéndez, 1896–1900, 2:309.

20. The prohibition of the sale or trading of offensive or defensive weapons to Indians is in the *Recopilación*, 1973, Libro 6, tit. 1, ley 24 and ley 33, but the evidence does not support the notion that "Spanish settlers rarely sold iron weapons or guns to Native Americans." Seed, 2001, 89. For Spanish law and practice, see Demaría, 1972, 131–39; Secoy, 1992, 4–5, 78–85; Schilz and Worcester, 1987, 1–10, and my discussion in chap. 5. See Ferguson and Whitehead, 1992a, 20, and Jiménez, 1998, 49–77, for the inferiority of European weapons. The more reliable flintlock came into use slowly in the seventeenth century. For a good discussion of the different ignitions, see Malone, 1991, 37–45. For Spaniards who regarded Indian weapons as superior in some respects, see Bernardo de Gálvez discussed in Weber, 1992, 230–34, and Santa María, 1930, 423–24.

21. Hernando de Machado, 1621, quoted in Gascón, 2003, 1 ("los indios de Chile se mueren de risa"). Since Araucanian culture prior to the arrival of Spaniards remains dimly understood, the extent to which Araucanian institutions, culture, and identity changed in opposition to Spaniards remains somewhat conjectural, but de Armond, 1954, Padden, 1957, Jara, 1990 (who focuses on the sixteenth century), Aldunate del Solar, 1982, and Casanueva, 1984, draw from many of the same sources to emphasize what Jara called "substantial transformations" (p. 68). This discussion is informed by these writers. With the exception of Casanueva, the later historians have not read the earlier ones. Padden sees the Araucanians' ability to adapt as the key to their survival. Jara takes a broader view, insisting that an explanation of Araucanian success must include an understanding of Spanish weakness.

22. Casanueva, 1984, 14, 17; Jara, 1990, 68. For a consideration of theoretical issues, see Salzman, 1979, 429–46. In this, of course, Araucanians were not unique. For the similar behavior of Comanche males, see Brooks, 2002, 174–78.

23. Villar and Jiménez, 2000, 698–99, offer a suggestive interpretation of the importance of this symbolism in the rise to power of the Huilliche cacique Llanketruz.

24. Fray José Antonio de Jerez to José Solano, Caracas, Feb. 8, 1766, in Carrocera, 1972, 3:118, reporting the question of one Cucuvi, a "capitán" on the upper Orinoco whose tribe he does not identify ("dirigiéndose a saber cuántas mujeres tenía nuestro rey").

25. Guarda, 1968. Whether these "indios toltenes" were Mapuches or Huillilches is not clear. For other examples, see Foerster G., 1991, 195–99.

26. For the configuration of *butalmapus* (also rendered *butan-mapus* or *vutalmapus*) in the mid-1700s, see Méndez Beltrán, 1982, 114, and the map in Méndez Beltrán, 1994, 19; for a close study of the appearance of the word *butalmapu* in historical sources, see Méndez Beltrán, 1994, 9–18. For pre-Hispanic leadership, see Casanova Guarda, 1989a, 31–46; for the new societal structure, see Casanueva, 1984, 4, Silva Galdames, 1995, and Boccara, 1999b, 427–34.

27. Araucanian speakers became, in the words of one scholar who has described the process, "encapsulated in European notions of nationhood and ethnicity and were increasingly affected by their own perception of themselves under that name." Galloway, 1995, 360, speaking of Choctaws.

28. By the mid–eighteenth century some Spaniards understood all Araucanian speakers to be Mapuches, the name by which most Araucanians identify themselves today, including Huilliches and Cuncos, a subset of Huilliches (Alcamán, 1997, 30, uses the term *mapuche-huilliche*). Falkner, 1935, 98, a keen observer who lived among the Pampas, noted that "the Moluches [Mapuches] are known among the Spaniards by the names of Aucaes and Araucanos" and described Mapuches as "divided into . . . Picunches, Pehuenches, and Huillilches." For an assessment of Falkner's utility to ethnology, see Mandrini's introduction to Falkner, 2003, 32–53. To avoid confusion, I use the more specific names of these subgroups and restrict the use of Mapuche to those Araucanians who lived between the Biobío and the Río Toltén. Cooper, 1946, 2:690–91, provides definitions for Araucanian words. For the muddied meaning of "Araucanian," used by anthropologists in the broad sense of a language group and more narrowly by historians as a synonym for Mapuche, see Villalobos R., 1991, 289–90, and for the contradictory views of scholars who see Mapuches as a subgroup of Araucanians vs. those who see Araucanians as a subgroup of Mapuches, see Boccara, 1996b, 663–69, who quotes the valuable insights of the ethnolinguist Adalberto Salas. Boccara offers the insight that the word "Mapuche" does not appear in Spanish documents until the last half of the eighteenth

century (p. 672). See, too, Boccara, 1999b, 425–61. For Mapuche cultural diversity, see Dillehay, 1990, 121–41.

29. Whitehead, 1990, 360–61. This transformation, termed tribalization by some anthropologists, represents a common response of kin-based peoples living at the edges of expanding states. Ferguson and Whitehead, 1992b, summarize the substantial literature on this subject and advance our understanding of it by suggesting patterns across time and space. *Precolonial* conflict may also have created tribes and certainly led to the aggregation of populations into larger communities and the formation of alliances. See Haas, 1990, 171–89, and LeBlanc, 2000, 50–51. This chapter makes the point with stories of well-known Native peoples, but Spaniards also provoked the formation of tribes and confederacies among lesser-known peoples in areas we understand dimly, such as Arawaks on the upper Orinoco and Negro rivers. See Vidal, 1999, 113–20, and Vidal, 2000, 653–54. See, too n.116, below.

30. Amat y Junient, 1924–28, no. 56, 371–72. For women's work among Pehuenches, see Varela and Font, 1998, 93–94, 100, 104–08, who offer some evidence from a later period.

31. For the ethnic diversity of Pehuenches, see Silva Galdames and Téllez Lúgaro, 1993, 7–53. As late as the mid-1600s, Pehuenches may have been in a state of transition, moving toward "Araucanization," according to Villalobos R., 1989b, 35; by the eighteenth century, when they become a concern of this study, they were clearly Araucanized. León Solís, 2001b, 18–28, examines competing theories. For the amalgamation of Pehuenches on the eastern side of the Andes, primarily the Pehuenches de Malargüe, in the late 1700s, see Roulet, 2002, 88.

32. Azara, 1923, 2:1, 3 ("libres o salvajes"; "se consideren ellos mismos como formando una sola y misma nación y que tienen el mismo espíritu, las mismas formas, las mismas costumbres y la misma lengua"). Álvarez de Miranda, 1992, 217, suggests the importance of context in determining the meaning of *nación* in this era, when it was used interchangeably with words like *patria, país, estado,* and *reino.* For *nación* as "group" into the early 1700s, see Cramaussel, 2000, 277, 288. For "nation" as synonymous with "nation-state," see the Jesuit Juan Nuix, who believed that European nations had the right to sovereignty over Indians since Indians lacked nations. See, too, Chiaramonte, 1997, 143–49, who sees "nation" and "state" as becoming synonymous by the early 1800s, and Cañizares-Esguerra, 2001, 184.

33. Boccara, 1996b, 671.

34. Alcamán, 1997, 50–62. Sors, 1921–23, no. 42, 40, suggests the existence of a *butalmapu* among some Huilliches in the late eighteenth century. León Solís has written extensively on the influence of intertribal

war on Huilliches and Pehuenches, but see in particular León Solís, 2001b, 29–37.

35. Espiñeira, 1988, 244, writing of his meeting with a Pehuenche cacique, Neicumancu, in 1758 in the region of Dagüegue and Neuquén ("vestido todo a lo español").

36. Sors, 1921–23, no. 42, 43 ("no reconocen a nuestro Soberano").

37. The population estimates come from Méndez Beltrán, 1994, 26, who bases them in large part on an Indian census of 1796 and a 1791 census of the Spanish population. See, too, Téllez Lúgaro, 1987, 204–07, whom Méndez overlooks.

38. Hernández, 1992, 51–52 and Corregido, 1984, 125–52, for pre-Columbian migrations.

39. González Montero de Espinosa, 1992, 75. The quotation is from Sánchez Labrador, 1936, 33 ("están las campañas inundadas de tales caballos, como si fuera una hacienda, o estancia").

40. Mandrini, 1994, 12. Frézier, 1717, 75, noted the source of the cattle but assumed they came from the "Plains of Paraguay." Pinto Rodríguez, 2000, 19–34, offers an especially cogent analysis of this trans-Andean trade.

41. Ras, 1994, 438–39. That same year, Spain signed the Treaty of Utrecht, which allowed an English company to supply black slaves to South America and made it easier yet to smuggle beef, hides, and tallow to external markets.

42. Ras, 1994, 388–92.

43. Azara, 1943a, 119 ("una división o parcialidad de los famosos Araucanos de Chile"). See, too, Azara, 1923, 1:28. Nacuzzi, 1998, 243–44. See above n.14.

44. There is a large literature on this subject. León Solís, 1990, 21–63, upon whom I have depended, summarizes and augments it. The chronology in Tapson, 1962, 10–13, remains sound.

45. Acuerdo de la junta de Guerra de Concepción, Jan. 6, 1765, quoted in León Solís, 1990, 93 ("la Nación más rebelde y obstinada que habita la otra parte de la Cordillera Nevada haciendo continuas hostilidades muertes y robos, a los Españoles que viajan desde Chile para Buenos Ayres"). Ibid., 69–70. For similar quotations from midcentury, see León Solís, 2001b, 33–34. Villalobos R., 1989b, 73–78.

46. Ras, 1994, 123; Mandrini, 1992a, 71, who notes that earlier scholars mistook the seasonal migrations of the Pampas for nomadism.

47. "Tehuelches" derives from "Chehuelches," with "cheuel," meaning "wild," as its root. Martínez Sarasola, 1992, 64. Sánchez Labrador, 1936, 30, on the other hand, used "Tehuelches" as a synonym for Patagonians alone. My use of the names Pampas and Patagonians represents an attempt to avoid more cumbersome designations. Spanish chroniclers and scholars have classified Argentine Indian groups with a bewildering variety of names, as Martínez

Sarasola, 1992, 44–46, and Nacuzzi, 1998 (in an elegant case study), point out, and the ethnic identity of these people has been the subject of heated debate. Martínez Sarasola adopts the view that all of the peoples of the pampa and Patagonia spoke Tehuelche, and he divides them into "tehuelches septentrionales" and "tehuelches meridionales" (pp. 64–70). Ras, 1994, agrees and separates them into "patagones tehuelches" and "Pampas pristinos tehuelches," the latter becoming "Pampas araucanizados" in the 1700s. Another school of thought, however, suggests that Pampas were a distinctive people with their own language. Mandrini, 1992a, 64–65, 69. Palermo, 1991, 156, suggests that the northernmost peoples of the pampa who lived near the Río de la Plata, and whom Spaniards first knew as "Querandíes" before terming them Pampas, may have been ethnically closer to peoples of the Chaco than to Tehuelche speakers. Whether or not the Pampas spoke a language different from Tehuelche, Spaniards identified them as Pampas into the nineteenth century, making that designator essential to any historical discussion. To some Spaniards of the eighteenth century, everything below the province of Buenos Aires to the Strait of Magellan was Patagonia. Furlong, 1992, 11. Today some scholars draw the line between Patagonia and the pampa at the Río Colorado (Hernández, 1992, 38), but most prefer the Río Negro.

48. Nacuzzi, 1996, 51–62; Zapater, 1982, 93–94. Jones, 1984, 13, who argues that "a shifting preference from guanaco and avestruz [ostrich] to horse meat among Tehuelche-speaking Indians meant concomitant changes in the yearly transhumant cycle, as it became less important to follow the native game through the seasons."

49. Palermo, 1986, 157–77, and Palermo, 1991, 153–92, contain nuanced discussions of the transformations of Pampas and Patagonians. Sánchez Labrador, 1936, 30, a Jesuit, describes the southernmost Patagonians in the mid-1700s as pedestrians and the northerly group as mounted.

50. For Huarpes as a subgroup of Pampas: Villalobos R., 1989b, 177, 197–98, and Martínez Sarasola, 1992, 60–62, 110. Experts disagree about the ethnic origins of Puelches (see Ras, 1994, 97, 102, who appears to disagree with himself!). Martínez Sarasola, 1992, 64, identifies them as a Tehuelche-speaking people, and Canals Frau, 1973, 538, finds that they spoke Araucanian by the mid-1700s. Menéndez, 1896–1900, 2:319, who visited Pehuenches at Lake Nahuelhuapi in 1792, noted that they spoke the same language as Indians of Chiloé, and another he did not understand.

51. Spaniards described themselves as güincas in dealing with the Pampas. See the treaty signed on Sept. 5, 1790, at Buenos Aires, in Levaggi, 2000, 13, arts. 4, 7.

52. Recent interpretations of this well-known phenomenon include a broad overview in Ras, 1994, 369–80; and the more sophisticated work of Mandrini and Ortelli, 1995, 135–50; Ortelli, 1996, 203–25 (who sees the diffusion of cultural traits preceding large-scale Araucanian migration), and Mandrini, 1997, 23–34, and Villalobos R., 1989b, 178.

53. Ras, 1994, 273; Mandrini, 1992a, 69.

54. Ortelli, 1996, 205.

55. Canals Frau, 1973, 540, for example, concluded that by the end of the eighteenth century "all [was] now *araucano* on the pampa." This classic study of the process of Araucanization has been modified by scholars who see the process as occurring more slowly and who point to the area around Buenos Aires as still the home of un-Araucanized Pampas in the late eighteenth century. See Mayo and Latrubesse, 1993, 15–17, and Villalobos R., 1989b, 176–79, who offers a nuanced discussion of geographically specific places of persistence.

56. Mandrini, 1993a, 45–74. Leonis Mazzanti, 1993, 75–89. Palermo, 1986, 157, 163; Mandrini, 1994, 15–16. For farming as women's work, see Mandrini, 1986, 30. This in opposition to the view represented by Tapson, 1962, 6, that all Araucanians who settled on the eastern side of the Andes abandoned agriculture to become predatory nomads. See Palermo, 1994, 63–90, for the impact of weaving.

57. Raúl Mandrini has explored these and similar transformations in a number of articles, but see especially Mandrini, 1991b, and his summation of recent scholarship in Mandrini, 2000, 693–706. Araucanians were not alone in this, of course. For the Guajiros, see Polo Acuña, 1999a, 13–14, and for Comanches, who raised horses and whose lifestyle marked them as pastoralists, see Hämäläinen, 2001, 167–71, who also provides guidance to the literature.

58. Mandrini, 1992a, 61.

59. Azara, 1943a, 117 ("en ninguna otra nación silvestre he notado esta desigualdad en riquezas, ni semejante lujo en vestidos y adornos"). See, too, Azara, 1923, 2:25–26, and De la Cruz, 1969a–72a, 444, for the horses' halters.

60. De la Cruz, 1969b–72b, 214–15 ("yo sé que Carripilún es el governador de estas tierras ... y que sería imprudente entrarme a su casa, sin primero anunciarle mi llegada a sus tierras"), called to my attention by Ortelli, 1996, 211, who discusses these socioeconomic transformations. For Ranqueles as Pehuenche group, see Fernández C., 1998.

61. García, 1969a–72a, 338–39 ("el señor, el virrey y el rey de todos los pampas"; "yo no iba a disputarle su virreinato, ni la legitimidad de sus propiedades"). Other caciques, however, did dispute Carripilún's ownership of the Salinas Grandes, which they said belonged to all (ibid., 347).

62. Falkner, 1935, 123.

63. Falkner, 1935, 104–08. Ras, 443–44, provides the date but confuses Cacapol with his son, Cangapol, on this occasion. Falkner identified Cacapol as a Tehuelhet, the southernmost of Puelches. I am using the generic identification, Pampas.

64. Mandrini, 1993b, 31, and Martínez Martín, 1994, 157. The quotation is from Juan Manuel Ruíz, Comandante at Mendoza, 1771, in Círculo Militar, 1973, 188.

65. Bucareli y Ursúa, 1880, 292 ("en el mayor desconsuelo, llorando muchos la pérdida de sus familias, el cautiverio de otras, y los más la destrucción y robo de sus haciendas").

66. The Chaco is 251,501 sq. km; Spain is 195,313 sq. mi. (505,992 sq. km); Wyoming is 97,105 sq. mi. (251,502 sq. km).

67. Dobrizhoffer, 1967–70, 1:221 ("su Palestina, su Eliseo"; "refugio de la libertad y el valladar contra servidumbre"; "Los cerros más altos les sirvieron de atalayas, los bosques intransitables en vez de una muralla, los rios y pantanos a guisa de fosas, los campos repletos de fieras y árboles frutales como almacenes"). Dobrizhoffer, 1822, 1:124, for the flawed English translation, which I have not used. The Chaco has substantially more variation and more distinctive ecological niches than I am able to delineate here.

68. By the late eighteenth century, Spaniards used the name Guaycurú specifically for the Mbayá-Guaycurúes, rather than for all Guaycuruan speakers, as ethnologists do today. That is, "Mbayás" and "Guaycurúes" became synonyms in the late eighteenth century (Vangelista, 1993, 52, n.2). To avoid confusion with the larger language group, I have used Mbayá even when the sources say Guaycurú. Not all of the residents of the Chaco were Guaycuruan speakers. Exceptions included Matacos, a linguistic group that did not adopt what some scholars commonly describe as the "warrior ethos" of the Guaycuruans. Matacos included a number of subgroups such as the Mataguayos. Súsnik, 1972, 12, 24–25, offers a synthesis of the fision, fusion, and movement of different peoples in the Chaco.

69. Dobrizhoffer, 1967, 2:417 ("Comenzaban a considerar inofensivos y poco peligrosos aquellos caños fulminantes de los fusiles, pues sabían que con frecuencia no sonaban, y si acaso disparaban, producían un ruido inofensivo"). For the Chaco's abundance, see Paz, 2002, 382–84.

70. Santamaría, 1994b, 273–300, provides an ecologically based explanation for Tobas' appropriation of livestock, which probably applies to other Guaycuruan speakers. See, too, Vitar, 1997, 73–80. Métraux, 1946, 1:197.

71. Lozano, 1941, 73, writing ca. 1730 ("grandes soldados que ciertamente a su modo compiten con los de Flandes"). Sánchez Labrador, 1910–17, 1:314, writing ca. 1769, repeats these words without acknowl-

edging Lozano as their source. Whereas Lozano, however, described them as a highly disciplined group (ibid.), Sánchez Labrador found them to be without "la menor disciplina militar" (ibid., 307). For Guaycuruans as societies of bands rather than tribes, see Saeger, 2000, 5, 9, 13, 113.

72. Vitar, 1997, 116–21.

73. Hemming, 1987, 116–27; the quotation is on p. 126. Hemming identifies these people as "Guaikurú." He is speaking of the Guaycuruans known as Mbayás.

74. Saeger, 2000, 3–25, 59–62, offers a masterful overview (the population estimate is on p. 6; like figures for other independent Indians, demographic information for the Chaco contains as much poetry as prose).

75. Some contemporaries thought of Chiriguanos as residents of the Chaco (Furlong, 1955, 117), but most saw them as inhabiting lands just beyond the Chaco.

76. Dobrizhoffer, 1967, 1:223–24 ("son hoy día los más decididos enemigos de los Españoles y son temidos en la región entera en todas partes").

77. Saignes, 1989, 15–16; 20, explains that the name Chiriguano derived from the Tupí-Guaraní word "chiri," meaning "expatriate," and an Arawak word, "guana," meaning "numerous," but was altered into the Quechua insult by the change of a single letter —from Chiriguana to Chiriguano. See, too, Saignes, 1990, 24, 219–22. For other interpretations of the origin of the word "Chiriguano," see Calzavarini, 1980, 54, and the standard sources cited below.

78. The classic account in English is Métraux, 1948, 3:465–506. Pifarré, 1989, summarized the large literature. The population figures are on pp. 40, 139; the Guaranís' absorption of other peoples is on pp. 35–36.

79. For the boundaries I am following Saignes, 1985, 106, the leading authority on the Chiriguanos, who places their southern border farther south than did Métraux, who put it at the Pilcomayo. Viedma, 1969, 239, describes the war paint.

80. As, for example, in Villaseñor y Sánchez, 1746, 2:294.

81. Wallace and Hoebel, 1952, 3–11. Spellings vary, including *numunuu*.

82. Hämäläinen, 2001, 28–45, 147–59; Anderson, 1999, 226–28; Weber, 1992, 189–91.

83. I take the population figures from Hämäläinen, 2001, 198. See, too, Hämäläinen, 2001, 127, 161–63, 226–36. Anderson, 1999, discusses the absorption of other peoples in the context of "Comanche Ethnogenesis." See esp. 20–26, 239. I take the two divisions from a 1785 account, in John and Benavides Jr., 1994, 50. For subdivisions, see Concha, 1949, 237; John, 1991b, 169; Kavanagh, 1996, 121–24.

84. Instrucción, Col. Fernando de la Concha to his successor, Lt. Col. Fernando Chacón, Chihuahua, June 28, 1794, in AGN, Mexico, Historia, 41:327R–52, facsimile courtesy Ross Frank ("se aman entre sí perfectamente . . . los intereses son comunes, y corren

en ellos una igual suerte"); translation in Concha, 1949, 238. Hämäläinen, 2001, 204–14, who also provides guidance to scholarly debates on this question.

85. Forbes, "Introduction to the Second Edition," in Forbes, 1994, vii–xxiii, places Apaches in the Southwest as early as 1,000 AD, earlier than most scholars do. For a summary of competing theories, see Opler, 1983, 381–84, and Perry, 1991, 110–54.

86. Worcester, 1979a, 7, who offers a lucid synthesis.

87. The quotation is from Cordero y Bustamante, 1864, 369, writing in 1796, who identified nine "tribus principales," which he described individually ("no componen estos en el día una nación uniforme en sus costumbres, usos y gustos"). See, too, Lafora, 1958, 79. For new tactics, see Mirafuentes Galván, 1987, 24–26. For the simultaneous processes of centralization and decentralization, see below, n.133.

88. West, 1998, 86–88. Secoy, 1992, 30–31, 81–85, makes the case that Apaches' spring and fall horticulture proved a handicap against the nomadic Comanches. Buffalo had also disappeared from the southern plains following a lengthy drought of the early 1700s that lasted until 1720. Anderson, 1999, 60–63, 70. For the size of Comanche populations relative to Plains Apaches, see Hämäläinen, 2001, 62–66.

89. Tomás Vélez Cachupin to the viceroy, Santa Fe, Nov. 27, 1751, in Thomas, 1940, 75, called to my attention by Hämäläinen, 2001, 196. Hugo O'Conor to Viceroy Bucareli, Chihuahua, Dec. 20, 1771, in Rubio Mañé, 1959a, 381, is among the many sources that note that Apaches had few firearms.

90. Teodoro de Croix to José de Gálvez, Jan. 23, 1780, Arizpe, oficio #458, AGI, Guadalajara, leg. 522 ("Los antiguos conquistadores pelearon con gentes que no habian visto caballos ni armas de fuego, pero los Apaches, los Comanches, y los demás Indios del Norte, manejan aquellos con destreza"). See, too, Weber, 1992, 191.

91. Cramaussel, 1992, 25 ("Creemos que más que una súbita y sorpresiva expansión de un grupo de nómadas, esta profusión de apaches se debe a un cambio semántico de la palabra apache; poco a poco, más y más grupos fueron llamados con el mismo nombre, y la voz apache adquirió un sentido genérico"). Conversely, Jack Forbes has argued that some of these groups were not absorbed by Apaches but were Apaches. I am following Griffen, 1969, 70–74, for eastern Nueva Vizcaya, Anderson, 1999, 105–27, 132–36, for Lipanes and Mescaleros, and Schroeder, 1974, 4:55. For the Apache political economy and long-distance trade, see Merrill, 2000, 644–48, 654. Ortelli, 2002, 461–79, and Ortelli, 2003b, 146–52, 182–83, 279, and passim, suggests that Apaches traded for stolen livestock in Nueva Vizcaya, but that the thieves themselves were Indian apostates and professional rustlers.

92. Spicer, 1962, 232; Moorhead, 1968, 3.

93. Nentvig, 1980, 81.

94. Antonio María Bucareli to Julián de Arriaga, Mexico, Oct. 27, 1772, in Velasco Ceballos, 1936, 1:69 ("Bajo el nombre de apache, son infinitas las naciones que se cuentan, con ninguna tienen verdadera amistad, y no hay paraje libre de sus irrupciones").

95. Spicer, 1962, 236; Gunnerson, 1974, 233. The quotations are from Rodríguez Gallardo, 1975, 3, and the one of four figures from Viveros's introduction to ibid., p. xxx.

96. The last few decades have seen rapid advances in our understanding of the postcontact transformation of southeastern peoples. For an introduction to this literature, see Usner, 1998, 1–13, and the anthology edited by Ethridge and Hudson, 2002. For the study of the impact of disease on the realignments or groups in one region, see Usner, 1998, 33–55.

97. Braund, 1993, 9, 181–83. For the importance of horses, see Wright, 1981, 224–25, and Braund, 1983, 76–77.

98. Braund, 1993, 5–6. Wood, 1989, 59, offers population estimates for Indians throughout the South. Saunt, 1999, 11–37, 90–110, describes the late eighteenth-century emergence of what he calls a new "social compact," arguing that it was a later phenomenon than scholars who "upstreamed" had supposed, and his fine study goes on to describe the civil war.

99. The Choctaws have been the subject of one of perhaps the most detailed, sophisticated, and multidisciplinary examinations of the process of ethnogenesis in any language. See Galloway, 1995, esp. 53–60. The quotation (p. 326) is from a Kasihta tradition recorded in 1735. Galloway's work ends in 1700. For later years and population, see White, 1983, 5, 107, and Carson, 1999, 26–50, who explores the differing interests of the polities that made up the confederation and would not cohere into a single "nation" until the early nineteenth century.

100. Lázaro Ávila, 1997, 34–50 and passim.

101. Clastres, 1996, 181–216, 217–55, who draws some of his evidence from Dobrizhoffer's account of the Abipones in the Chaco. The quotation is on p. 219 ("el hombre primitivo es, en tanto hombre, un guerrero"). See, too, Keeley, 1996, 39, and the academic warfare waged by Tierney, 2000, against Chagnon, 1968. Keegan, 1994, 12, asserts that war is "always an expression of culture."

102. Brian Ferguson offers some of the most compelling arguments that Western contact generated Native warfare. See, for example, Ferguson, 1990b, 237–57, and Ferguson, 1995, where he makes a case that Yanomamis (Chagnon's "fierce people" who inhabit a remote mountainous country between Brazil and Venezuela), were not fierce or warlike until European manufactured goods altered their trading relationships with neighboring peoples. On the supposedly limited nature of Indian warfare, see Ma-

lone, 1991, 9, 29, and Casanueva, 1984, 11–12. Scholars draw a useful distinction between raiding and warfare; raiding can be a tactic of warfare but can also exist independently of war. Ferguson defines war as "organized, purposeful group action, directed against another group . . . involving the actual or potential application of lethal force." Ferguson, 1990a, 26.

103. Keeley, 1996, summarizes the arguments and reviews the literature. For cases, see Ewers, 1997, 167–68; Haas and Creamer, 1997, 235–61; LeBlanc, 1999, and LeBlanc, 2000; Saeger, 2000, 120.

104. Calzavarini, 1980, 71, is eloquent on this point. See also Santamaría, 1992, 121–48, and Santamaría and Peire, 1993, 115.

105. José de Gálvez to Comandante General Teodoro de Croix, El Pardo, Feb. 20, 1779. Photocopy in the University of Texas Library, Archivo de San Francisco el Grande, vol. 33, XI, 1779, 33–39 ("de ladrones rateros, que eran en los principios, los vemos convertidos en astutos guerreros y a proporción de lo que dure nuestro empeño de hacerles la guerra"). Groups like the Utes, far removed from Spaniards, were pulled into the vortex of raid and counterraid as their Apache and Navajo neighbors gained access to Spanish horses and metal weapons and increased pressure on them. Blackhawk, 1999, 12–36, is a fine case study of this phenomenon.

106. Ferguson, 1990, 26–55, makes a persuasive case for this materialist argument.

107. Álvarez, 2000, 305–54 ("indios de guerra").

108. Santamaría and Peire, 1993, 103–04, discusses this problem lucidly for the Chaco. See, too, Ricklis, 1996, 148–50. Reff, 1991, 259, notes that cultures ravaged by disease would more readily accept domesticated stock. For the Apache and Navajo shift from trading to raiding in the 1670s, see Brooks, 2002, 52.

109. Dobrizhoffer, 1967, 2:138 ("les pertenecían"; "sin ningún derecho") (English translation: Dobrizhoffer, 1822, 2:140–41). Santamaría, 1998b, 189–91. Barrera Monroy, 2000, 176–80. See, too, Braund, 1993, 77.

110. McCauley, 1990, 7.

111. Respectively, the quotations are from Griffen, 1969, 147; Merrill, 2000, 655; La Vere, 1993, 324–25, 332, invoking Marshall Sahlins.

112. Saignes, 1985, 119; McCauley, 1990, 9–13; Lázaro Ávila, 1992, 597–98; León Solís, 1994a, 92.

113. Lázaro Ávila, 1992, 607–8. Rollings, 1992, 179–80, for example, describes what he calls "mitosis" among Osages because "single bands were unable to integrate all of the demands for position."

114. Ruíz, 1972, 15–16, lived among Comanches from 1813 to 1821 ("paraíso"; "hijo del sol y que va a gozarle para siempre lleno de felicidad").

115. Castillero Calvo, 1995, 28 ("Era el equivalente indígena a las misas que los católicos pagaban a la Iglesia por el sufragio de sus almas para gozar de felicidad eterna").

116. Barfield, 1989, 5–8, argues that state formation among the Mongols occurred not as a result of borrowing or cultural diffusion, but rather as a response to sedentary neighbors. For manifestations of this phenomenon among nomads, see Irons, 1979, 221–34, and Burnham, 1979, 361–74. Examples from Spanish-Indian borderlands are abundant. See, for example, Lázaro Ávila, 1992, 594. For more on tribalization, see above n.29.

117. Casanueva, 1984, 4; Mandrini, 1992b, 63–66; Wallace and Hoebel, 1952, 211. For Mocobíes, see the story of Paikín in chap. 5 below, and for leadership among Guaycuruans in general, see Saeger, 2000, 113–18. For bands, tribes, and chiefdoms, see my introduction.

118. O'Crouley, 1972, 52. O'Crouley never visited Apache country, but I quote him because he distilled what I take to be a conventional view of his day. For a similar reading of Comanches, see Ruíz, 1972, 11–12, who did live among Comanches, and the "hotly contested" scholarly debate about Comanche political organization summarized in Brooks, 2002, 168 n.10.

119. For the qualities that gave a chief authority throughout the American lowlands, see Lowrie, 1948, 15–17, a classic discussion, and Clastres, 1987, who augments Lowrie. For continued acceptance of the argument, see Saignes, 1985, 108. For examples from recent North American scholarship, see Braund, 1993, 21–22, for Creeks; Galloway, 1995, 2, for Choctaws; Sheridan, 1999, 2–3, for Seris.

120. De la Cruz, 1969b–72b, 2:264 ("no tengo por qué ser soberbio, pues ni poseo más bienes que mis vasallos, ni tengo otro caudal ni defensa que ellos; razón que me precisa a consultarlos para proceder con firmeza en cualquiera materia de estado").

121. Redmond, 1994, 129.

122. Cuello, 1989, 19. There is a substantial literature on tribes and chiefdoms. See Carneiro, 1981, for the debate over whether economic or political forces give rise to chiefdoms and his argument that war was the principal "mechanism that brought about chiefdoms" (p. 63). He defines a chiefdom as an "autonomous political unit comprising a number of villages or communities under the permanent control of a paramount chief" (p. 45). Carneiro also called for more research, a wish that scholars have fulfilled without challenging his definition, which emphasizes the permanency of chiefdoms versus the temporary nature of chieftaincies. Scholars, including Carneiro, continue to see "war and military leadership . . . at the very root of the chiefdom," although "the precise mechanism by which military leadership gave rise to chiefdoms still needs to be worked out." Carneiro, 1998, 21. See, too, my introduction n.59.

123. This is the central argument in Saignes, 1985. See also Calzavarini, 1980, 69–75, and Saeger, 1985, 496. White, 1983, 64, makes a similar observation about the Choctaws vis-à-vis the French and English.

124. Viceroy Vértiz to José de Gálvez, Buenos Aires, Nov. 30, 1778, quoted in Beverina, 1992, 371 ("los indios forman unos cuerpos errantes, sin población ni habitación determinada"). Hall, 1991, 48, and Lindner, 1981, 4.

125. León Solís, 1994a, 91–110, brilliantly analyzes these struggles among Araucanians and credits the description of horizontal and vertical wars to Jorge Pinto. He sees the last decades of the eighteenth century, when Spaniards had ceased to be the common enemy, as a time of especially bloody intratribal warfare.

126. Hämäläinen, 2001, 212 n.15.

127. In suggesting that the horse pushed Indians to coalesce into large political units, I am mindful that some, such as the Comanches, divided into ever smaller social units because the foraging requirements of their vast horse herds did not allow them to stay together for extended periods of time. Nonetheless, those smaller units developed mechanisms for coming together to make political decisions when the need arose—as Comanches did in 1785 and 1786, when they signed treaties with Spaniards in Texas and New Mexico. See my discussion of Comanches earlier in this chapter. For Indian fear of horses, see, for example, Jacobo Sedelmayr, report to His Majesty's Minister of Doctrine . . . , Tubatama, 1750, in Sedelmayr, 1996, 30. For the diffusion of the horse in North America, see Roe, 1955, 56–71, and Forbes, 1959, 189–212. Dobrizhoffer, 1967–70, 2:267–68 (English translation: Dobrizhoffer, 1822, 2:269), tells of Abipone horse burials. For North American burials, see Roe, 1955, 273–74. Among the many Indian societies for whom the horse acquired symbolic, if not religious, significance were the Guarijos. Polo Acuña, 1999a, 14, 17–19.

128. Gov. Urízar to the king, Salta, Nov. 23, 1708, quoted in Vitar, 1995, 56.

129. The Austrian-born Jesuit Dobrizhoffer, 1967, 2:416–17 ("Pizarro y Cortés . . . sometieron a innumerables indios, los mataron o pusieron en fuga; pero se trataba de indios pedestres. Si hoy volvieran esos mismos héroes a enfrentarse con los abipones, mocobíes, tobas, guaycurúes, serranos, chiquitos y otros pueblos ecuestres de Paracuaria, no me atrevería a asegurarles la misma gloria"). (Dobrizhoffer, 1822, 2:405, for a variant translation). *Recopilación*, 1973, Libro 6, tit. 1, ley 33, for a 1568 law. Seed, 2001, 74.

130. Hämäläinen, 2001, makes this point about Comanches.

131. The quotation is to West, 1998, 56, who provides a vivid explanation of the way horses converted grass into energy and transformed peoples on the Great Plains.

132. Fowler, 1996, 6–12, and Carlson, 1998, 43–48, provide a good overview of the impact of the horse on North American plains peoples. For the horse as provoking intertribal conflict, southeastern America alone offers abundant examples. See Smith, 1995, 15–16, Braund, 1993, 67, 76, and Axtell, 1997, 68–69. See, too, sources cited herein for specific Native peoples. Some scholars believe that the horse did not increase Indian warfare, but rather that Indians adopted the horse because they were warlike. See Santamaría and Peire, 1993, 115–16, for the Chaco. For Comanche raiding and warfare, see Wallace and Hoebel, 1952, 36, 245–84, and Kavanagh, 1996, 1–15, who reviews the literature about Comanche leaderships and concludes that Comanche leaders were more than temporary intermediaries with limited authority. For trenchant observations on Apache raiding and leadership, see Spicer, 1962, 229, 243, and Perry, 1991, 167–68. There is a large literature on Apache raiding and warfare, but as with Comanches, many of the sources derive from the nineteenth century.

133. Forces pushing Indians to both disperse and centralize their political structures are discussed in Anderson and LaCombe, 1999, 116–17, and Hall, 1989, 72, 107.

134. Anthropologists long ago rejected Clark Wissler's idea of a uniform Plains culture in North America. For a refutation of Wissler in southern South America, see Palermo, 1986, 157–77, and Champagne, 1994.

135. Anderson and LaCombe, 1999, 118. Palermo, 1986, 159, 167–68. For ecological niches, see Armillas, 1983, 295–300.

136. Hämäläinen, 2003, 836–37, who analyzes the different ways horses impacted Indians on the North American plains.

137. Braund, 1993, 67. Perdue, 1998, points out that Cherokee women continued to work as farmers, adding animal husbandry to their tasks, and men continued to hunt livestock as if it was still wild.

138. Worcester, 1951, 117; Spicer, 1962, 213–14, 244; Perry, 1991, 159; Lyon, 2003, 66–70. Fernando Chacón to Pedro de Nava, July 19, 1795, SANM, no. 1335, roll 13, frames 735–37, called to my attention by Flagler, 1990, 56 ("trabajan sus lanas con más delicadeza y gusto que los Espanoles"; "hombres como mujeres andan decentemente vestidos").

139. Hämäläinen, 2003, 834.

140. Palermo, 1991, 166; Palermo, 1988, 84–85.

141. Silva Galdames, 1990, 83–95. O'Brien, 2002, 70–97.

142. Ferguson, 1990a, 51–52.

143. For rich examples from the pampa, see Mandrini, 1994, 5–24; for North America, see Fowler, 1996, 9. For a number of sources on Comanches' trading of surplus horses to New Mexicans, see Merrill, 2000, 639.

144. See, for example, Paz, 2003, 111–44, on this phenomenon in the Chaco.

145. Salas, "Informe Sobre el Reino de Chile," Santiago, March 5, 1750, in Donoso, 1963, 1:119. Other contemporaries understood that war had ended in the mid-1600s. Haenke, 1942, 203. For more on the "business of war," see chap. 4, below.

146. For these and other advantages of imaginary war, see Ortelli, 2003b, chap. 6.

147. Pinto Rodríguez, 2000, 19–27. Villalobos R., 1989a, 17, suggests a long period of *relative* peace from 1683 to 1861. Mandrini, 1991a, 140, notes that scholars, too, have tended to see frontier zones exclusively as lands of war. Villalobos R., 1992, 259–64, explains the origins of the myth of a permanent state of war. Villalobos R., 1993, 553–66, describes the literature and castigates European historians for overlooking the new Chilean historiography. Casanova Guarda, 1989b, explicates the two rebellions and makes a further case for the 1700s as a time of peace. Villalobos also has critics. Bocarra criticizes Villalobos's "frontier school" for speaking of peace, since Spaniards had merely changed strategies for achieving control. Bocarra refers to those other strategies, which included trade, missions, and economic and political agreements worked out through *parlamentos*, as "una prolongación de la guerra por otros medios." Boccara, 1999a, 67. See, too, Boccara, 1996b, 667, and Boccara, 1996a, 29–41. Foerster G. and Vergara, 1996, 9–33, similarly push the boundaries of our shared understanding of language. They accuse Villalobos of misunderstanding that "peace" was "latent war," of defining "frontier" more narrowly than he actually does, and of not writing the book they would have written. Villalobos R., 1997, 5–20, offers a spirited reply. For the continuance of war and raiding in the interior, on both sides of the Andes, see especially Villar and Jiménez, 2002, 130–41.

148. Brooks, 2002, 80–116; 208–16.

149. Villaseñor y Sánchez, 1746–48, 2:413 ("todas [las naciones] piden la paz cuando les tiene cuenta, y rompen la guerra al tiempo, que hallan la ocasión de conveniencia, todos los años por cierto tiempo"). Alternating war and peace was widespread. See, for example, New Mexico governor Fermín de Mendinueta to the viceroy, May 11, 1771, complaining about Comanches, quoted in Kessell, 1979, 393; Morfi, 1935, 316, commenting on Apaches while visiting the presidio of San Juan Bautista del Río Grande in 1777; Depons, 1970, 220, for Guajiros.

150. Dobrizhoffer, 1967–70, 3:22 ("utensilios necesarios para la guerra"); Dobrizhoffer, 1822, 3:16–17.

151. Albers, 1993, 108, explains Plains Indians' raids on their own Indian trading partners "as a mechanism for resolving short-term imbalances in the distribution of goods" and argues that they acted with restraint during raids. Charges of Indian faithlessness abound.

152. Nentvig, 1980, 81; Saeger, 1985, 497.

153. Powell, 1952, 188, 197–98, 202; Powell, 1977, 107–15; Villalobos R., 1992, 266, 279–85 (Madrid had authorized the enslavement of Araucanians in 1608).

154. I discuss this in some detail in chaps. 4 and 6.

155. Fray Juan Díaz, Nov. 8, 1780, quoted in Forbes, 1965, 78, who has a fine analysis of this question. See also Kroeber, 1986, 148–74, who found warfare endemic among Yumans. See, too, Knack, 2001, 35–36, for Utes venturing into the remote lands of the Piutes in search of slaves.

156. Paucke, 1942–44, 2:9 ("pero los Españoles han engañado en demasía [*sic*] a nuestros antepasados; su amabilidad era una traición y una amistad simulada, pues sólo trataron de hacernos esclavos y matarnos a azotes y, como si nosotros no fuéramos seres humanos como ellos y no tuviéramos entendimiento, nos emplearon como bestias de carga"). It is unlikely, of course, that Father Paucke or his source recorded Ariacaiquin's exact words. Missionaries had their own reasons for having Indian leaders express such sentiments. See also Furlong, 1955, 124.

157. De la Cruz, 1969b–72b, 269 ("Siempre los indios fuimos desconfiados de los españoles, porque muchas veces nos engañan, y como un solo engaño es bastante para engendrar desconfianza, no es mucho se conserve en nuestros ánimos el recelo. No podéis, amigo, negarme esta verdad").

158. Villaseñor y Sánchez, 1746–48, 2:294 ("reducidas a el suave yugo evangélico"), whose summary of the conventional wisdom about the northern frontier at midcentury informs this paragraph. An extensive literature treats the peoples of northern New Spain, but Spicer, 1962, remains the best overview.

159. Villaseñor y Sánchez, 1746–48, 2:349 ("apostatas, y fugitivos"), writing about the area around Parras. *Ladino* has multiple meanings, one of which is *mestizo*. Mota Padilla, 1973, 462, writing in 1742, referred to Indians who knew Spanish ways but returned to their own people as "enemigos caseros." Authorities came to think of renegade Spaniards and Indian apostates alike as "domestic enemies." They are central to the study of Nueva Vizcaya by Ortelli, 2003b. See esp. 41–206, 277–79, 406–08.

160. Métraux, 1946, 203. Saeger, 1989, 59, 72–77; Saeger, 2000, 5, 29, 53–54, 59–60. For another example, see Vidal, 1999, 120–21.

161. For Mbayás in this context, see chap. 5 below.

162. The Caddos have been the subject of several fine books. The most recent provides an overview: La Vere, 1998 (see esp. 106–26). A case study by Areces, López, and Regis, 1992, 155–68, explores the Charrúas.

163. Weber, 1992, 145, 166; Saunt, 1999, 29; Hemming, 1987, 107–08.

164. For Caribs, see Whitehead, 1990, 146–70; for Creeks, Miskitos, and Guajiros, see elsewhere in this chap., and for Cunas see chap. 4.

165. Lt. Juan Rosa Amaya, 1769, quoted in Polo Acuña, 1999a, 19 ("sacan de la cartuchera dos cartuchos y que con una cargan la escopeta y el otro se quedan con e l en la boca, y que tan pronto como han disparado y tienen cargado otra vez"). See, too, Barrera Monroy, 2000, 200.

166. English visitors were also attracted by logwood (a source of blue, black, and purple dyes for textiles), but Offen, 2000, 113–35, makes the case it did not grow south of Belize and that no contemporary sources refer to it on the Mosquito Coast. In a personal communication, Feb. 24, 2003, he explained to me that safe harbors to careen ships and obtain fresh food initially drew them to the coast.

167. Helms, 1971, 16 n.5, who suggests they might have been of the Bawihka linguistic group. There is little solid evidence to describe these people in the precontact or protohistorical periods, and contradictory interpretations of that evidence abound. Lack of a baseline from the early contact period limits our ability to describe cultural changes. Helms, 1971, 25, for example, asks whether the society was matrilocal or if "demands of trade with Europeans actually may have produced matriolocality." Romero Vargas, 1995, 124–26, argues that "Mosquito" derived from a toponym, but Offen, 2002, 333, observes that the toponym might have acquired their name from the people.

168. The estimate is from Romero Vargas, 1995, 290; see, too, Floyd, 1967, 64–66. For the Miskitos' expansion to Costa Rica and Panama, see Castillero Calvo, 1995, 369–82. Each of these sizable groups has its own literature. For the Tol-speaking Jicaques, for example, see Davidson, 1985, 58–90; who offers evidence that independent Jicaques (a Nahuatl word meaning "rustics") numbered well over ten thousand at the end of the 1700s.

169. Dawson, 1983, 696–93.

170. Romero Vargas, 1995, 91; Dawson, 1983, 697.

171. Offen, 2002, 319–72, explores differences between these groups as no one has before, superseding much earlier literature on many points, including his discussion of turtles, and I follow his lead in employing the word "Tawira" (see his pp. 320, 337–38). The traditional view that Miskitos thought of themselves as a single people because they shared a common language, as articulated, for example, by García, 2002, 451, obscures deep divisions.

172. Romero Vargas, 1995, 163–217, describes the holders of these offices, their roles, and their rivalries. For leaders in 1780, see p. 186. Olien, 1998, 277–318, who did not make use of Romero Vargas, traces officeholders based on information he has drawn from published sources. Helms, 1971, 20, terms the kingdom a "paper protectorate" and the king a mere "figurehead," but the king and the other offices wielded power. Helms, 1969, 76–84, seems closer to the mark.

173. Floyd, 1967, 63, reporting an estimate made in 1759. Romero Vargas, 1995, 304, estimates that this was its apogee. In 1780, Spanish authorities put the Zambo-Miskito population at six thousand and the "pure" Miskitos at three thousand. García, 2002, 455.

174. On smuggling, see Dawson, 1983, 697, using a report prepared by James Lawrie in 1774. For Englishmen's understanding of the role Miskitos played as a buffer, see Edward Long, *The History of Jamaica* (3 vols., London, 1774) 1:320, quoted in Floyd 1967, 67. Floyd, 1967, 189, 99, 111–12; Castillero Calvo, 1995, 378–82.

175. La Vere, 1998, 91–105; Whitehead, 1990, 359; Rausch, 1984, 70–71, 109, 230. As throughout this work, I oversimplify by amalgamating different Carib-speaking groups into the group Caribs. For the names Caribs gave themselves, see Civrieux, 1976, 875.

176. Hämäläinen, 2001, 93; Albers, 1993, 100–102. As Albers makes clear in a fine analysis, these symbiotic relationships did not end intertribal raiding, which coexisted with trade.

Chapter 3. The Science of Creating Men

The epigraphs are from Marqués de Castelfuerte to his successor, quoted in Tibesar, 1983, 149 ("El arte de hacer cristianos es la ciencia de criar hombres"), and Rousseau, 1967 (*Discourse on the Origin of Inequality*), 257.

1. Carlos III and José de Gálvez to Croix, San Ildefonso, Aug. 22, 1776, in Velázquez, 1982, 134 ("el motivo principalísimo que he tenido para el nuevo establecimiento del empleo que os he conferido, es el de procurar la conversión de las numerosas naciones de indios gentiles que habitan al norte de la América Septentrional"; "los suaves y eficaces medios que previenen las Leyes de Indias, del halago, buen trato, persuación de los misioneros, dádivas y seguras ofertas de mi soberana protección").

2. Croix to Gálvez, Chihuahua, Sept. 23, 1778 (*oficio* #282), AGI, Guadalajara 270 ("Este infeliz no tiene ya a qué aspirar en el resto de su vida; un trabajo continuo, la desnudez, la hambre, la falta de libertad, y el mal trato son su suerte").

3. For a consideration of differences between *pagano* and *gentil* and the problem of translation, see Guest, 1996, 334–37.

4. Ibid. ("poco a poco se les va instruyendo en el catecismo que aprenden en Español, que no entienden, hasta que preguntados por los interpretes si quieren bautizarse, lo que jamás recusan, se les administra este Sacramento; se les repiten las penas de la Apostasia, y ya se califica neófito").

5. Ibid. ("Entran en las chozas de los neófitos, ven su

miseria, y la limitación de sus raciones, que solos los padres hacen los cambalaches: compararon el trabajo de aquellos con sus propias fatigas, aquella pobreza con su abundancia, y concluyen con evidencia, que es la mayor desdicha reducirse.")

6. Bushnell, 2004, 163.

7. Alcocer, 1958, 175 ("es la ocupación casi continua de P. Misionero andar, como los cazadores en busca de las fieras, buscando a los indios con inmensos trabajos por aquellos distantísimos desiertos, más espantosos que los de Siberia"). Fray José Mariano Reyes to the Viceroy, Mission Rosario, May 1, 1790, in Leutenegger, 1968, 594.

8. Caballero y Góngora, 1910, 1:227-28 ("fuerza y el temor"; "sociedad y religión"; "a repetir en su preciso orden un número infinito de palabras en que les dan a entender que aprenden la doctrina"), and ibid., 228 ("y prescindiendo de la legitimidad de estos medios, son ciertamente más proporcionados para hacer simulados e hipócritas, que fieles súbditos del Estado y de la Religión"). For Caballero as an enlightened figure, see Kuethe, 1978, 92. See, too, Croix himself complaining to José Rubio, Chihuahua, April 3, 1778, about Mescalero Apaches in Levaggi, 2002, 257 ("voluntariamente, sin que se les aflija con azotes ni otros castigos semejantes"), Weber, 1992, 186, and my discussion of missionaries and Mapuches, below, this chap. For a tortured defense of using force like strong medicine to make Indians "rational," so they might receive the "gift" of Christianity (an "obsequio racional"), see Miguel Lastarria, "Descripción topográfica y física: Noticias económicas y políticas de las referidas colonias hasta su estado actual … [y] plan para su nueva vigoroza organización y economía interior," Madrid, Dec. 31, 1804, in Lastarria, 1914, 273.

9. For a more nuanced picture of the San Antonio missions than Croix presented, see Hinojosa, 1991, Teja, 1998, 112-13, and the missionary guidelines in Leutenegger, 1976, 19-31, 47-49. For Indians regrouping and reinventing themselves in the San Antonio missions, see Anderson, 1999, chap. 4. Scholars suggest that this was the case elsewhere, too: Sweet, 1995, 1-48; Radding, 1998, 116-17; Saeger, 2000, 192-93. For Indian acculturation at the San Antonio missions, see Schuetz, 1980, chaps. 5-6. For remarkable scientific evidence that most Indians stayed fewer than ten years at one of the San Antonio missions, see Cargill and Hard, 1999, 199-213. A modern critic would say that mestizaje, rather than missions, Hispanicized Indians. Castillero Calvo, 1995, 362. Sweet, 1995, 31, sees missions as a catastrophe for Indians. For a direct rebuttal to Sweet and a call to examine local variations, see Saeger, 2000, chap. 8. In repeated legislation and orders, the crown tried to stop missionaries from abusing Indians and required them to teach Indians in their own languages.

See, for example, the royal instructions to viceroys Croix in 1765 and Bucareli in 1772 in Villegas, 1987, 23-25, 55-56.

10. Muldoon, 1994, 55. This was not Spain's only justification for legal title to the Indies. See Bushnell, 2001, 290, 297.

11. Reff, 1991, 249-64, 278-79, and Reff, 1998, 201 n. 3, emphasize the attraction of missions for the remnants of disease-wracked societies in the seventeenth century and argues that material benefits played little role. Saignes, 1990, 87-89, makes a similar argument, although he points out that access to material goods helped keep Chiriguanos in missions. Sources explaining the forces that pushed or pulled Indians into missions are abundant. See, for example, Larson, Johnson, and Michaelsen, 1994, 265, who emphasize environmental stresses in the case of the Chumash.

12. There is a large literature on this subject. For baptism of the uninstructed, different levels of instruction, and debates over them, see Ricard, 1966, 83-95; Oviedo Cavada, 1982, 305, 326; Gómez Canedo, 1988, 169-80; Borges, 1992e, 597-99; Saranyana, 1992, 549-68; and Saignes, 1990, 98-99, who looks specifically at Chiriguanos. The California baptism cum marriage was reported by a participant, Martínez, 2002, 90. Sandos, 2004, 15, suggests that California Franciscans erroneously equated baptism with full conversion. Some Franciscans from the College at Chillán in Chile, on the other hand, opposed baptisms that would not be followed up by ongoing instruction. See below, this chap. The quotation is from Tamajuncosa, 1969-72, 7:154-55 ("bárbaros, idiotas, incultos, y que necesitaban hacerles primero hombres racionales que cristianos"). Borges, 1992f, 521-22, lists the variations on this refrain, heard commonly in the colonial period; see also Trias Mercant, 1995, 97-115. Axtell, 1985, 131-33, quotes Rev. Charles Ingles in 1770 to the same effect "in order to make them Christians, they must first be made Men" (p. 133). For a deep comparison of the cultural, theological, and political differences that shaped English and Spanish mission programs, see Ortega y Medina, 1976, and Elliott, 1994, 18-19. There was, of course, no single English or Spanish program. In Spanish America missionary colleges and individual missionaries disagreed among themselves, so that any generalizations must be qualified.

13. Mena, 1916, 392 ("vagamundos"; "una vida licenciosa, y brutal, sin observar, ni un rastro de policía").

14. *Recopilación*, 1973, Libro 6, tit. 3, ley 1 ("olvidando los errores de sus antiguos ritos, y ceremonias"). Pagden, 1995, 23, and Kagan, 2000, 24-28. Spaniards settled nonsedentary people in *reducciónes*. Spaniards also resettled sedentary people from small, remote villages into larger units, called *congregaciones*.

15. I am not concerned in this study with the dynamics of mission life. Until recently, much of the voluminous

historical literature on this subject might as well have been written by missionaries themselves, for it eurocentrically extols missionaries as agents of civilization. A new approach (new to historians, but not to anthropologists) looks at the ways Indians responded to colonialism, rebuilding their societies within the mission context. For an introduction, see the essays in Langer and Jackson, 1995, and Griffiths and Cervantes, 1998. For the spread of Mediterranean culture in Europe, see Fletcher, 1998. Much has been written about the depth and trajectory of conversions, which responded to numerous independent variables, but for an especially penetrating analysis, see Merrill, 1993.

16. For the classic assessment of missions as agents of the Spanish state, see Bolton, 1979, 49–66. The quotations are from Sánchez Labrador, 1936, 142, 149, referring to the Pampas ("para Dios, y para el Rey"; "haciendoles hijos de Dios, y vasallos de España"). The state expected this kind of service from clerics in general. See García Belsunce, 1994, 17–42.

17. Borges, 1992a, 1:433, measures this at some 14½ million square kilometers (Spain is 505,992 sq. km), with no more than 20,000 missionaries working between 1493 and 1824. A closer look at the failures of English missionaries would also reveal differences between New England and Virginia, or between Puritans, Quakers, and others. For a classic introduction to this subject, see Pearce, 1965, 26–41, and more recently Sayre, 1997, 15–17, who compares English and French missionary strategies.

18. Bushnell, 2001, 297. "Ordenanzas de su Magestad hechas para los nuevos descubrimientos, conquistas y pacificaciones," July 13, 1573, in Colección, 1864–84, 16:149–54; Recopilación, Libro 4, tit. 4, leyes 5 and 8. See, too, Gómez Canedo, 1988, 49–51, 74–82. For examples of the crown's ongoing invocation of the law of 1573, see Korth, 1968, 123–24; Gálvez, 1873, 579 (no. 28); and Pérez de Uriondo, 1969–72, 630. For an example of ongoing violations, see Martínez Ferrer, 1996, 163–77.

19. Emphasis added. Real cédula to the audiencia of Guatemala, San Lorenzo, Nov. 19, 1787, in Peralta, 1898, 285 ("el Evangelio podia extenderse sin la fueza armada"; "muchas veces la Iglesia habia recurrido a las armas de los principes católicos para obligar a los infieles a oir la palabra de Dios"). On the use of soldiers in missions, see the fine piece by Del Rey Fajardo, 1995, and Hausberger, 1993, 37–39.

20. For the more difficult circumstances of the later era, see Gómez Canedo, 1983, 20–22, who argues against the conventional wisdom that missionaries of the 1600s and 1700s were less zealous than their predecessors. See Reff, 1991, 242, for the demographic recovery in northwestern New Spain; Newson, 1986, 309–10, 321, 333–34, for eastern Honduras; and Mer-

rill, 1993, 149, for a case study. Morey and Morey, 1980–88, 254–55, suggest that Sálivas, apparently seeking safety from Caribs by entering missions in the 1730s, may have lost more lives than they saved as epidemics swept through the missions. Saeger, 2000, 180–81, notes that the degree to which smallpox and other European illnesses affected mission residents depended on their premission experience with those diseases and on the degree of immunity they acquired before entering. Ill Guaycuruans, he observes, were shunned by their own people and more likely to be nursed back to health in a mission.

21. Sheridan, 1999, 133–34.

22. Dobrizhoffer, 1967–70, 3:9 ("no permitieron que se los venciera ni con las armas ni por medio de regalos"); Dobrizhoffer, 1822, 3:1. Along with other Guaycuruans, some Tobas, however, did find reasons to enter missions. Maeder, 1996, and Saeger, 2000, provide valuable overviews. For the failed Apache missions in Texas, see Wade, 2003, 183–203.

23. Pedro Anselmo Sánchez de Tagle to the king, Durango, May 2, 1754, quoted in Porras Muñoz, 1980, 202 ("He estado oyendo, y oigo mucho de alzamiento de indios y muy poco de nuevas conversiones"). Many studies chronicle the impoverishing effect of Spanish demands for labor and tribute. See, for example, Calero, 1997, 76, 130.

24. Fray Antonio Comajuncosa, writing ca. 1810 about the beginnings of missionary work in Tarija, in Corrado and Comajuncosa, 1990, 1:95 ("todo el horizonte estaba cubierto de infidelidad y barbarismo"). The second quotation is Villareal, 1741, 1 ("reducir a vida sociable la bravura de los Araucanos"), a Jesuit who saw Spanish bad behavior as the sole reason for Araucanian resistance. This, too, is the leitmotif in Juan Sanz de Lezaún, "An account of the lamentable happenings in New Mexico ... 1760," in Hackett, 1923–37, 3:468–79. See, too, Dobrizhoffer, 1822, 3:401–02.

25. Sánchez Labrador, 1936, 92 ("yo quiero vivir, y morir como buen Pampa, no como mal christiano [sic]"). See, too, ibid., 110. See San Alberto, 1788, 26, for an effort to convince Chiriguanos that every flock has a few bad sheep.

26. Rodríguez Gallardo, 1975, 30 ("la sombra del español mata al indio").

27. Floridablanca, 1867, 218 (art. XXXVI: "hacer aborrecible el nombre español entre los indios, africanos, asiáticos y demás a quienes intentamos reducir a nuestra santa fe"). Floridablanca often represented the predominate views of the regime of Carlos III. Ezquerra, 1962, 216. Some officials during the Habsburg era came to a similar conclusion (Martínez Ferrer, 1996, 171–75).

28. Bishop Carranza to the king, Buenos Aires, May 1, 1627, quoted in González Rissotto and Rodríguez Varese, 1991, 237 ("los charrúas son tan bárbaros

que no han podido sustentar un sacerdote que los doctrine").

29. Pedro Lozano, quoted in Furlong, 1938, 35 ("Tal vez a gentes tan viciadas, como eran los Pampas, les pareció excesiva la moral cristiana e inasequible para ellos").

30. Fernández, 1994, 25, writing in 1726 ("son de genio inconstante, más de lo que se puede creer, mudables a todo viento, no guardan la palabra que dan, hoy parecen hombres y cristianos y mañana apóstatas y animales").

31. Domingo de la Cruz, ca. 1765, writing of the Amages, east of Huánuco, and quoted in Lehnertz, 1974, 175 ("es el indio monstruo de la naturaleza"; "el vivir en sociedad común es para ellos vida infernal"). See, too, ibid., 44–48, 84. See, too, Tibesar, 1983, 156, and Román Gutiérrez, 1993, 314–24. For irrationality, see Nentvig, 1980, 55, quoting approvingly Joseph Gumilla's *Orinoco Ilustrado*.

32. Dobrizhoffer, 1967–70, the quotations are, respectively, from 2:144 ("puertas, llaves, trancas, arcas y guardias con que los europ[e]os guardaban sus cosas contra los ladrones"); 3:10 ("nos ocurre pensar que los abipones y sus aliados los mocobíes y los tobas habían sido reservados por la Justicia divina para castigar los delitos de los cristianos)." See, too, 2:137–44. These passages can be found in the English translation, which I have not used, in Dobrizhoffer, 1822, 2:148–49 and 3:2. Glimpses of virtuous and even heroic Indians appear especially in the work of Jesuits like Dobrizhoffer, who wrote nostalgically from exile after their expulsion in 1767. Sáinz Ollero, 1995, 94–95, drawing from José Sánchez Labrador and José Cardiel, points out that the noblest of Indians in Jesuit prose are those who are still independent rather than the "degraded" conquered Indians.

33. Girbal y Barceló, 1791, 80 ("bárbaros"; "perniciosos, y perversos Deistas de nuestro Siglo"; "fingidos Padres de la Filosofía").

34. Morelli, 1911, 3:219 ("la morada de Pan que ha vivido allí varios siglos sin verse perturbado por los crímenes de los crueles hijos de Europa"). The passage in the encyclopedia is, "C'est le siege de Pan qui est demeuré plusieurs siècles sans etre troublé par les crimes des cruels enfans de l'Europe." Diderot, 1751–1965, v. 12. For Franciscan views, see Gómez Canedo, 1988, 63–68.

35. Morelli, 1911, 219 ("sean estas consideraciones sinceras o irónicas, quien las hace ignora completamente la naturaleza de los sitios"). Muriel may be using *naturaleza* to suggest a primitive quality of place, too.

36. Santa María, 1930, writing in the mid-1790s, with quotations, respectively, on pp. 412, 430, 412 ("filósofos de nuestro siglo"; "la vergüenza de la especie humana"; "una verdadera anarquía"). Santa María saw Aztecs and Incas as exceptions, but he believed

they represented a tiny percentage of the mass of Indians (432).

37. Sors, 1921–23, no. 45, 278 ("Hombres son como los españoles y demás vasallos y en nada se distinguen de ellos, ni aún en el color de los españoles que trabajan a la inclemencia del cielo en el pastoreo del ganado y en la labor de las tierras"). Sors, writing in 1780, has copied much of this language from a Jesuit predecessor, Villareal, 1741, n.p., whose point of view he echoes. Leutenegger, 1976, 54 ("hay bueno, y hay malo, como en todo el mundo"). See, too, Alcocer, 1958, 155.

38. Fray Juan Rafael Verger, head of the college of San Fernando in Mexico City, writing about California Indians at San Diego just months apart, on Aug. 3, 1771, and Oct. 11, 1771, in Ponç i Fullano, 1990, 246, 265, called to my attention by Trias Mercant, 1995, 111 ("toscos, broncos, audaces e inclinados al latrocinio . . . ninguno daba esperanzas de su reducción"; "mansos y afavilísimos").

39. Taylor, 1989, 19, and Reff's splendid introduction and guidance to sources in Pérez de Ribas, 1999, 11–46, for Jesuit thought of the seventeenth century, which I see as little changed. Even the iconography of the late colonial Franciscan mission of San Xavier del Bac, near present Tucson, with their representations of mystics, ascetics, indulgences, and the devil at the Last Supper, suggests that the Enlightenment had not penetrated that far. Personal communication, Bernard Fontana, May 2, 2000.

40. Casanueva, 1992a, 7, 13–14; Urbina Burgos, 1990, 59, quoting the bishop of Concepción ("docilidad"); Benavides, 1945, 100, describing the initial Pueblo response.

41. Fray Juan José Granados, bishop of Sonora, to Viceroy Revillagigedo, Arizpe, April 16, 1791, in Gómez Canedo, 1971, 108 ("viciándose en el juego, embriagués y otras maldades"). For a classic statement of Indians as childlike, see "Leyes municipales de esta conversión de Puzuzu," probably written between 1758 and 1783 by a Franciscan from Ocopa, in Tibesar, 1983, 154–59, and Bringas in Matson and Fontana, 1977, 57–58. For a series of examples from California, and the status of ward, see Guest, 1996, 261–62. For the depth of this tradition, see Clendinnen, 1982; Bakewell, 1997, 143, 149; Borges, 1992d, 505.

42. J. J. Ortiz to the governor, Aug. 20, 1806, quoted in Santamaría and Peire, 1993, 120.

43. Fray Francisco Antonio Barbastro to Viceroy Revillagigedo, Dec. 1, 1793, in Gómez Canedo, 1971, 73 ("Experiencia ha enseñado esta ciencia, que parece está repugnando al discurso natural"), who penned a ringing defense of traditional missions, what he called *el método*. For similar sentiments, see Alcocer, 1958, 156–57.

44. For the image of Indians as beastlike, see Santamaría,

1994a, 69–70, who sees no change in missionary attitudes between the sixteenth and the eighteenth centuries. For a pithy discussion of Franciscan attitudes in the 1500s, see Román Gutiérrez, 1993, 315–17, and Gómez Canedo, "¿Hombres o bestias? Nuevo examen de un viejo infundio: el pretendido debate en torno a la racionalidad de los indígenas de América," in Gómez Canedo, 1993, 77–94, who argues that contrary to conventional wisdom, Spaniards did not generally view Indians as animals in the early sixteenth century, but rather that Las Casas and other Dominican defenders of Indians falsely accused exploiters of Indians of harboring this belief. For missionary discourse toward Italian peasants, see Selwyn, 1997, 11, and D'Agostino, 2003, 707–08.

45. San Alberto, 1788, 2–3 ("sois hermanos nuestros, y os reconocemos por tales, por lo mismo que todos somos obras, y criaturas de Dios, y que todos descendemos de un mismo hombre, aquel primero, que Dios en el principio del Mundo crió de la nada, y le puso por nombre Adán").

46. Hu-DeHart, 1981, 3–4, 24, and Saeger, 1985, 501–03, make the point that Jesuits intended to build permanent missions, and the same might be said of some eighteenth-century Franciscans. Hinojosa, 1991, 68–73, 82.

47. See Taylor, 1989, 5–68, for the disparate views of the clergy in New Spain; and for the disparate views of the church hierarchy in 1771, see Zahino Peñafort, 1990, 5–31, particularly her discussion of the enlightened archbishop of Mexico, Francisco Antonio Lorenzana (p. 9), and a *criollo* educator, Cayetano de Torres (p. 10). See also n. 44, above.

48. Pastoral letter of the bishop of Panama, Remigio de la Santa y Ortega, Santiago de Veraguas, Oct. 19, 1795, in Arcila Robledo, 1953, 244 ("el príncipe de las tinieblas y del error"; "garras"). For a fine analysis of the work of the devil in the thought of fray Antonio Caulín, the Franciscan chronicler of eastern Venezuela (1779), see García Gavidia, 1995, 218–26. See also Sánchez Labrador, 1936, 107–08; Trinchero, 2000, 81–86; and Serra in Tibesar, 1983, 2:114. In a case study of Baja California, Bernabéu Albert, 2000, 170–76, finds that Jesuits writing after their expulsion seldom invoked the devil and argues that they reflected a changing European mind—one that was perhaps slower to reach remote mission fields, although Casanova Guarda, 1996b, 75, finds Franciscans in Chile less likely to blame the devil for Indian behavior than did their Jesuit predecessors. See, too, my discussion of the devil in chap. 1, and Taylor, 1989, 9, 49–50. Lipsett-Rivera, 2002, 205–19, explains how the devil lingered on in late eighteenth- and early nineteenth-century culture as a metaphor or as a shorthand for "lust" or "passion," but missionaries seem to have seen the devil as an actual force.

49. Jossef [*sic*] Gregorio Salvatierra to Gov. Melchor Rodríguez, San Pablo de Guaicurús, May 3, 1799 (anticipating the revolt), and Salvatierra to M.P.S., San Xavier de Chiquitos, June 16, 1799, in AGB, 31, III (1795–1808).

50. Sors, 1921–23, no. 46, 340 ("impenetrables corazones totalmente poseídos del espíritu de Satanás").

51. Cortés de Madariaga, 1964, 506, referring to Guahibos ("los vicios de la poligamia y otros excesos inherentes a la naturaleza del hombre corrompido y brutal"). One doctor of "sagradas canones y leyes," Miguel Lastarria, argued that it required strong medicine to make Indians' rational, so they might receive the gift of Christianity ("racional"; "obsequio"). Miguel Lastarria, "Descripción topográfica y física: Noticias económicas y políticas de las referidas colonias hasta su estado actual . . . [y] plan para su nueva vigoroza organización y economía interior," Madrid, Dec. 31, 1804, in Lastarria, 1914, 273.

52. Santa María, 1930, 2:448, n.42. ("todo hombre nace para vivir en sociedad"; "todos los medios imaginables, sin esceptuar los castigos más rigurosos").

53. The quotation is from the "Refutation of Charges," by Fermín Francisco de Lasuén, Mission San Carlos, June 19, 1801, in Archibald, 1978b, 176. The entire document, a vigorous defense of the use of force, is in Lasuén, 1965, 2:194–234. The argument had a long pedigree and was applied in other times and places, as in the Colombian Chocó in the 1600s (Williams, 1999, 401, 410–12). Newson, 1986, 248–49, describes both the use of force and criticism of it.

54. Emphasis added. The Catholic position on conversion is unequivocal: "Force, violence, or fraud may not be employed to bring about the conversion of an unbeliever. Such means would be sinful. The natural law, the law of Christ, the nature of faith, the teaching and practice of the Church forbid such means." *The Catholic Encyclopedia*, vol. 4 (1st ed., 1908; Online Edition, Copyright 2003).

55. Whitehead, 1988, 104–22, 130; Whitehead, 1999, 399, estimates the 80 percent reduction, to twenty thousand in 1780. Capuchins assigned to the Guajira peninsula also favored the use of military force against Guajiros as the only way to missionize them. Barrera Monroy, 2000, 75.

56. San Alberto, 1788, 16 ("eternamente padecerán en compañía de Demonios"), warning the Chiriguanos of the consequences of failing to accept Christianity.

57. Guest, 1985, 84, who examined what the friars read as well as what they wrote, producing perhaps the finest examination of the *mentalité* of Spanish friars in North America. See his collected essays in Guest, 1996, and Borges, 1992d, 504–05, on methods of persuasion. For contemporaries, see Trias Mercant, 1995, 111–12, Bishop Juan José Granados to Viceroy Revillagigedo, April 16, 1791, in Gómez Canedo 1971, 108.

58. Rafael Verger to Viceroy Antonio Bucareli, "Primer

informe y método nuevo de misiones para su gobierno espiritual y temporal, Mexico," Nov. 15, 1772,
FF, 122:41v. ("pastores de indios civilizados"; "infelices, y bárbaros gentiles"). Copy courtesy of Ignacio
del Río. Head of the Franciscan College of San Fernando, Verger pointed to Libro 8, tit. 13, ley 6 of the
Recopilación but seems to have made an error. He
may have had in mind Libro 6, tit. 10, leyes 6 and 8.
He offered a spirited defense of whipping Indians
("con moderación"), citing scripture to suggest that
the Christians' god willed it. For an example of a
late colonial stricture against priests treating mission
Indians harshly, see Gálvez, 1873, 585 (no. 40).

59. Antonio Tamajuncosa [Comajuncosa], 1969–72, 155
("el Papa como el Rey les han conferido toda la autoridad y poderío que sea menester, para hacer de
sus indios unos hombres cristianos, económicos y
políticos"). He also describes the missionaries' temporal responsibilities, 157–60, and notes that the
most recent missions functioned "bajo un mismo
método" as the old (164).

60. Hausberger, 1993, 40–52, who discusses Jesuits, but
Franciscans also ordered the application of the lash
(missionaries delegated the task). We have many examples of missionaries advocating physical punishment, among them the bishop of Santa Cruz de la
Sierra, ca. 1788, quoted in Parejas Moreno, 1976a,
957, who urged the use of the whip at the missions
at Moxos to force Indians to comply with their duties
("sus deberes"). Similarly, see the padre comisario
de las misiones de Coahuila, 1780, quoted in Sheridan, 2000, 271. Viceroy Ezpeleta's *ordenanza* for the
good government of the Andaquíes mission of San
Javier de Ceja, July 2, 1790, exemplifies a high-
ranking Bourbon official's qualified approval of whipping, summarized in Mantilla R., 2000, 2:58–61.

61. Saeger, 2000, 184. The Indian death occurred at San
Javier de Ceja in 1770, prompting an inconclusive
investigation into the cause of death. Mantilla R.,
2000, 2:33–34.

62. Pike, 1983, 50–51, 152–55; "Real ordenanza para el
establecimiento e instrucción de intendentes de
ejército y provincia en el virreinato de Buenos Aires
[1782]," 1914, art. 56, p. 41; Martin, 1996, 62–63, 194–
95. The Spanish cortes abolished the use of the whip
throughout Spain and its dominions in a decree of
Sept. 8, 1813 (Guest, 1996, 276–77).

63. On written passes, see n. 219, below, and Boccara,
1996a, 34–36.

64. Saeger, 2000, 187–90, describes this situation in the
Chaco, where missionaries had little military force
and mounted Guaycuruans could flee. Acevedo,
1996, 292, quotes a Spanish complaint of 1808 about
Mbayás using misssions as a base for raiding. See,
too, the Chimilas described in chap. 6 below.

65. See fray Juan Antonio del Rosario Gutiérrez's plain-
tive statement, in 1784, of how missionaries oper-

ating alone could not succeed, in Mantilla R., 2000,
2:157.

66. Sweet, 1995, 36; Williams, 1999, 407–08; Hackel,
1998, 121–28; Deeds, 2003, 197–200.

67. Taylor, 1989, 15–16, 49–52, sees this shift from fear
to love as a phenomenon of the late eighteenth-
century parishes. For an example of the shift to peaceful persuasion when force no longer worked among
independent Indians, see the 1798 plan to convert
Jicaques in eastern Honduras in Newson, 1986, 250.
The question of whether missionaries should use
force or kindness had long been debated. See, for
example, the contrasting views of the Jesuits Sánchez
Labrador and Cardiel, described in Sáinz Ollero,
1995.

68. San Alberto, 1788. Quotations are on pp. 5, 33, and
8, respectively ("de paz, y de mansedumbre"; "armas
no son más que la verdad, la persuasión, y la dulzura"; "condenados eternamente al Infierno").

69. Merrill, 1993, 138, 149–50; Martin, 1996, 41–42;
Teruel, 1994, 236–40.

70. Sweet, 1995, 1–48, provides a masterful overview
of Indian perceptions of constraints and benefits of
mission life. For the maleness of Christianity, see
Grahn, 1998, 266–67. Hunters and gatherers in particular enjoyed a less nutritious diet in missions.
Bushnell, 2004, 147–48.

71. Saeger, 2000, 65–72, suggests that women's roles
changed less than men's in the Guaycuruan missions.
Vitar, 2001, 223–44, might dispute Saeger's assertion,
but she does not address him directly. Vitar argues
that the Chaqueñas had to learn new tasks—spin-
ning, weaving, and caring for livestock and leave an
equalitarian society to enter a patriarchal society.

72. As, for example, among the Araucanians. See Casanova Guarda, 1988, 139. Chiriguanos and other tribes
who valued war might also have chaffed against
Christian strictures regarding war and revenge.
Saignes, 1990, 90–91. Even patriarchal Guaycuruan
societies became more patriarchal in missions.
Saeger, 2000, 108.

73. Chindica, quoted in Saignes, 1990, 91 ("de ninguna
manera querais ser cristiano porque eso es un engaño para ponernos después curas y vivir nosotros
la amarga vida de opresiones que sabemos y vemos
en los cristianos. . . . ser muchacho de los españoles").

74. Capitán Orapene, quoted or paraphrased by Eugenio de Alvarado, 1754, in Ramos Pérez, 1976a, 617
("hombre de adelantada razón que abiertamente ha
respondido no quiere dexar de ser Rey para pasar
una infelicidad en la Misión donde no puede tener
mando, guarichas [mujeres] libertad para hacer Poí-
tos ni comerciar con sus Amigos los Olandeses"; "la
vida animal").

75. Fray Pedro de Altea, quoted in Grahn, 1998, 270,
who explains how missions heightened Guajiros'
"aversion for anything Spanish" (p. 271). We have

many other examples, such as Varese, 2002, 87–96, for the Campa revolts of 1737 and 1742; Weber, 1992, 135–36, for sources for the religious impulse behind Pueblo Revolt; Radding, 1998, 116–35, for religious symbols and rituals as points of appropriation and contestation.

76. See, too, Mota Padilla, 1973, 462, and Newson, 1986, 242, 246–48.

77. To Julián de Arriaga, Mexico, Sept. 26, 1772, in Velasco Ceballos, 1936, 1:68 ("el piadoso fin"; "al suave yugo de nuestra Religión Santa"). For examples of the use of war funds, see Bolton, 1979, 55, 57, Bushnell, 1994, 43, 53, and the cabildo of Asunción to Gov. Agustín Fernando de Pinedo, July 4, 1776, AGI, BA 48, which mentions a new mission at Remolinos, forty leagues (a league is 2.6 miles) south of Asunción, to be established at the request of the Mocobíes, with the expense of providing them with livestock to be paid for from the Ramo de Guerra (called to my attention by James Saeger). Examples of official insistence on religious priorities abound, even in the economically driven era of Carlos III. See the Ordenanza de Intendentes for New Spain, 1786, in Fisher, 1929, 253, art. 204, Floridablanca, 1867, 218, art. XXXV, and Borges, 1992a, 424–27.

78. Hugo Oconor to Barón de Ripperdá, governor of Texas, May 6, 1773, in Velasco Ceballos, 1936, 1:124 ("se prefieran [sic] las causas de éstos [infieles y neófitos] a las de los demás vasallos en estos reinos").

79. For the Bourbon program of acculturation and its failures, see Gruzinski, 1985, 175–201. The quotation, which is translated fully in the epigraph to this chapter, is from Marqués de Castelfuerte to his successor, quoted in Tibesar, 1983, 149 ("El arte de hacer cristianos es la ciencia de criar hombres").

80. Brading, 1971, 27–28. For a case in point, see Viceroy Antonio María Bucareli to Juan Bautista de Anza, Mexico, Jan. 9, 1775, in Garate, 1995, 39.

81. Elliott, 1994, 20, succinctly describes the *repúblicas* and their fate. For the porosity of some missions, see above n.66.

82. Lt. Col. Manuel Centurión (the governor and comandante general of Guayana and a military engineer), to the minister of the Indies, Julián Arriaga, Angostura, April 22, 1774, quoted in Lucena Giraldo, 1992b, 71 ("casi tan desnudos, bárbaros e inútiles al Estado como eran cuando vivían en las selvas antes de su reducción"). Centurión, who had overseen the expulsion of Jesuits from Guayana, continued to rely on missionaries but favored opening mission towns to Hispanics. See González del Campo, 1984, 129–30, 189–96. His province would become part of the Capitanía General of Venezuela in 1777.

83. Vicente de Emparán to the king, Cumaná, May 16–17, 1795, in Carrocera, 1968, 3:539 ("estupidez y barbarie"; "prefiriendo su comodidad, en la facilidad de gobernarlos idiotas, a los progresos que los indios

hicieran con la compañía y mayor actividad y conocimiento de los españoles").

84. Caballero y Góngora, 1910, 1:228 ("salgan de ser brutos, y empiecen a ser hombres, y elévense después a ser cristianos"; "Aquellas almas embrutecidas no se hallen en estado de conocer las sublimes verdades del Cristianismo"; "Dios libre a un Obispo de la Iglesia Católica de preferir alguna cosa a la propagación del Evangelio; pero el interés mismo de la Religión pide que no se arrojen las margaritas a los puercos"). One of his successors in 1796 repeated the first quotation in nearly identical language. Ezpeleta, 1910, 311.

85. Viedma, 1969a-72a, 6:696 ("nada es más precioso al hombre que la libertad con que Dios le ha criado"). See, too, ibid., 711–12. Dussel, 1983, 1:675.

86. Azara, 1969–72, 6:418 ("inútil"; "no ha tenido ni tendrá jamás un buen e xito"). Chiaramonte, 1982, 56–57, notes that Azara's enlightened anticlerical brother, Nicolás, might have influenced his views on missions. See, too, Azara, 1943b, 224–25.

87. Azara, 1923, 1:138–39 ("a ejercer su talento ni su razón, porque ni el más hábil, ni el más virtuoso, ni el más activo estaba mejor alimentado ni mejor vestido que los otros").

88. Azara, 1990, 150. See, too, Azara, 1943c, 245–46 ("Jamás habrá civilización, ciencias, ni artes mientras exista el gobierno de comunidad").

89. "Natural libertad" comes from Pedro de Nava to Revillagigedo, Chihuahua, Jan. 27, 1792, in Gómez Canedo, 1971, 111. "Su falsa libertad, y la licencia de sus brutales costumbres" comes from a Franciscan missionary manual, Parras, 1783, 2:126, and "haciéndose incorregibles por la libertad" is from Granados to Viceroy Revillagigedo, Arizpe, April 16, 1791, in Gómez Canedo, 1971, 108. The wings analogy is San Alberto, 1788, 20–21 ("Las alas son peso para el Pajarito; y sin embargo ellas mismas lo aligeran para que vuele, y ande por el ayre").

90. Bishop Esteban Lorenzo de Tristán to Viceroy Revillagigedo, Durango Nov. 16, 1791, quoted in Porras Muñoz, 1980, 204 ("Religión a la francesa").

91. Espinosa y Tello, 1885, 576 ("un hombre con un breviario, un crucifijo, una pequeña escolta y un asistencia de 300 pesos ánuos [anuales], que por regla general señala Su Majestad para su manutención, penetra por los inmensos paises, entre la multitud de los bárbaros"). Malaspina also looked favorably on missions (Malaspina, 1991b, 153–55), and see above, chap. 1.

92. Manuel Centurión to the viceroy, Guayana, Nov. 3, 1770, in González del Campo, 1984, 364, speaking of his interest in subduing Caribs in the lower Orinoco ("reduciendo ahora a sociedad civil y cristiana la multitud de indios salvajes").

93. Anza to Viceroy Antonio María Bucareli, Tubac, Dec. 15, 1772, in Kessell, 1972, 59.

94. Manuel Centurión to Julián de Arriaga, Angostura, April 22, 1774, in Lucena Giraldo, 1992b, 71 ("entre imperio y sacerdocio"); Barnadas, 1984, 535.

95. The "nuevo método de gobierno espiritual," inspired by a report of fray Antonio de los Reyes on the missions of Pimería Alta, July 6, 1772, was formulated with great subtlety by the *fiscal,* José de Areche, July 13, 1772 (who hearkened back, ironically, to the sixteenth-century segregated Indian communities of Vasco de Quiroga). A copy of Areche's *dictamen* is in Viceroy Bucareli to the Provincial del Santo Evangelio, Sept. 2, 1772, FF, MS 2/11. Sara Ortelli kindly made a copy for me. The quotation comes from the more graphic albeit scornful description by fray Francisco Antonio Barbastro to Viceroy Revillagigedo, Dec. 1, 1793, in Gómez Canedo, 1971, 74 ("que se pongan en libertad; que ya es tiempo que se gobiernen sin tutor; que comercien, que anden, que trafiquen, pues sólo así adelantarían").

96. The quotations are, respectively, from Anza to Viceroy Antonio María Bucareli, Tubac, Dec. 15, 1772, Kessell, 1972, 58, 59, Viedma, 1969c-72c, 683–84 ("hacer hombres, y hombres cristianos a este gran número de salvajes"), and the "Informe de don Miguel Constansó [Costansó] al Virrey," Mexico, Oct. 17, 1794, in Moncada Maya, 1994, 313 ("jamás podrán ser hombres ni vasallos útiles"). See, too, Anonymous, 1964, 421; Marmión, 1964, 451; Azara, 1943b, 225. See, too, León y Pizarro, 1795, 210. The severest critics of missions, like their later U.S. counterparts, also charged that Indians cynically used missions as safe bases from which to launch raids on Spaniards, knowing that pagans would get the blame. See, for example, Mota Padilla, 1973, 471, who condemns missions, called to my attention by Velázquez, 1981, 79–98, and Vitar, 1997, 301.

97. See, for example, Phelan, 1970, 87–88, and instructions from Carlos III to viceroys Croix in 1765 and Bucareli in 1772 in Villegas, 1987, 23, 55, and the *real cédula* of Carlos IV to Gov. Joaquín del Real Alencaster of New Mexico, San Lorenzo, Oct. 3, 1803, in Konetzke, 1953–62, vol. 3, tomo 1, 796. The longstanding interest of the monarchy in making Spanish the language of the empire caught fire among Bourbon officials, from Carlos III to his regalist bishops. For an introduction to the politics of this contentious issue, see Tanck de Estrada, 1999, 168–89, and for a rich collection of documents, see Solano, 1991.

98. Azara, 1990, 115 ("útil vasallo y hombre sociable"; "civilización"; "yo creo lo contrario") and 119 ("el gobierno es quien debe civilizar a estos bárbaros y no los eclesiásticos").

99. Some writers have mistaken the Bourbons' interest in reforming missions for a decline in interest in conversion. See, for example, Difrieri, 1980, 13–14. For the crown's perennial intention to liberate Indian subjects from oppressive demands, see Anes y Álvarez de Castrillón, 1994, 80–92, which is weak for the end of the colonial era and should be supplemented with García Bernal, 1997, 8–16.

100. So, too, did the Bourbon reforms weaken the Church's ability to function as an instrument of the state among Indians who lived within the empire. Gruzinski, 1985, 198.

101. Acuerdo de la junta general de guerra y hacienda sobre la conquista, pacificación y población de la colonia del Nuevo Santander con las providencias conducentes a ella, Mexico, May 13, 1748, in Lejarza, 1947, 17 ("bárbaras naciones de enemigos indios chichimecos, gentiles y apóstatas"; "con incendios, muertes, robos, y todo género de inhumanas atrocidades"; "pervirtiendo").

102. The opinion of the *auditor de guerra,* the marqués de Altamira, "Sobre la colonización de la Sierra Gorda," Aug. 27, 1746, in Velázquez, 1976, 43 ("irreconciliables enemigos . . . contra sus antiguos dueños"; "capitaneaban a dichos apóstatas a los demás indios gentiles en las invasiones de robos, muertes, incendios y todo [tipo?] de atrocidades"). Phillips, 1993, studies the powerful role played by refugees from California missions. I have used 2.6 miles to the league to convert the usual measure of 60 to 80 leagues wide and 100 leagues long to miles.

103. Velázquez, 1979, 88–91; Osante, 1997a, 116–17. For geopolitical reasons, see the dated work of Hill, 1926, 19–23. In the late 1700s, some officials began to refer to the American empire as "colonias," using the English cognate, but that was not the official name for any of the other Spanish American provinces.

104. Hill, 1926, 8, gives twenty-three towns by 1755, but see the fine short biography in Chipman and Joseph, 1999, 135, 141, for clarification.

105. Osante, 1997a, 146–51; the quotations are from Escandón to Viceroy Revillagigedo, Dolores, Feb. 8, 1753, both in ibid., 228 ("en peones de perpetua esclavitud a cuenta del rey"; "los enseñen a rezar, y todos los domingos vayan a misa y reconozcan a su misionero").

106. Osante, 1997a, 129, 224–27. For contemporary praise for Escandón's conversion policy, see Rodríguez Gallardo, 1975, 28.

107. Escandón to Viceroy Revillagigedo, Padilla, Sept. 21, 1750, quoted in Osante, 1997a, 151 ("inutilidad de la pacificación"). Dictamen del auditor de Guerra y Hacienda, sobre el estado general del Nuevo Santander, Mexico, Sept. 4, 1750, quoted in Osante, 1997a, 231 ("a fuego y sangre"; "uno solo que quedase, bastaría para perturbarlo todo"). Altamira also approved of Escandón's plan to integrate Indians without traditional missions. The population estimates are in Frye, 2000, 118.

108. The *Recopilación,* Libro 6, tit. 3, leyes 21–23, for example, prohibited Spaniards from living in Indian towns.

109. Acuerdo de la junta general de guerra y hacienda sobre la conquista, pacificación y población de la colonia del Nuevo Santander con las providencias conducentes a ella, Mexico, May 13, 1748, in Lejarza, 1947, 18 ("como que los indios, aun menos bárbaros, sólo se impresionan de lo que les entra por la vista, y por su natural inconstancia y desordenado apetito a su bárbara vida, necesitan de inmediatas poblaciones de españoles, que con su respeto los contengan, dociliten y . . . protejan"). See, too, Osante, 1997a, 147, who quotes from a different version of this document. The Junta's reference was to failures in the nearby provinces of Nuevo León and Coahuila and in the Sierra Gorda among the Chichimecas, but this language, almost certainly the work of the marqués de Altamira, was applied by Altamira to Indians in Sinaloa and Nueva Vizcaya as well. Río, 1995, 53–54; Velázquez, 1976, 116–17. For Escandón's economic influence, see Osante, 1997b, 127–28. For the *congrega*, which represented a continuation of the outlawed *encomienda*, see Cavazos Garza, 1994, 56.

110. Fray Bartolomé Ximeno to his superior, March 5, 1773, Tumacácori, in Kessell, 1964, 309, who also notes the burdensome nature of managing the temporalities. See, too, Engelhardt, 1908–15, 1:35–36. In San Antonio, fray José Rafael Olivas made a powerful argument for surrendering the temporalities in 1788, but he clearly had no intention of expanding the spent San Antonio missions. Leutenegger, 1978, 19–34.

111. Report of José Tienda de Cuervo, Oct. 13, 1757, in López, 1929–30, 2:153–56. I read Tienda de Cuervo differently than did the editor of this report, Rafael López. See ibid., 1:viii–x.

112. Fray José Joaquín García del Santísimo Rosario to the fiscal, Mexico, Oct. 8, 1765, in López, 1929, 2:261–68, and González Salas, 1998, 385–86. Four of their missions went to the Franciscan *custodia* of Tampico. See ibid., 74–92. Missionaries did continue to serve in Nuevo Santander, but as Viceroy Revillagigedo (the younger) noted in 1793, they had no missions because, with few exceptions, they had no Indians. Revillagigedo, 1966a, 86.

113. Chipman and Joseph, 1999, 145–48.

114. Viceroy of New Granada, José de Ezpeleta, 1910, 312 ("haciendo cristianos y vasallos Del Rey a los que antes eran bárbaros ó infieles, enemigos y salvajes").

115. In the eighteenth century, *misión, conversión,* and *reducción* were generally used as synonyms, although the words suggested different stages in the missionary process to some contemporaries. Parras, 1783, 2:73, 2:142, and Diego Bringas, 1796–97, in Matson and Fontana, 1977, 13–16, 43, 47.

116. Fermín Francisco de Lasuén, "Refutation of Charges," Mission San Carlos, California, June 19, 1801, in Lasuén, 1965, 2:202. For a contemporary expression of the philosophy of freeing regulars to begin new mis-

sions, see fray Juan José Granados, bishop of Sonora, to Viceroy Revillagigedo, Arizpe, April 16, 1791, in Gómez Canedo, 1971, 109.

117. *Real cédula,* Jan. 30, 1607, in the *Recopilación,* Libro 6, tit. 5, ley 3 ("se reduceren de su voluntad a nuestra Santa Fé"), a *cédula* which Franciscans of the late eighteenth century continued to see as the foundation of royal policy. Parras, 1783, 2:73; Bringas, in Matson and Fontana, 1977, 15.

118. Felipe V, *real cédula,* San Ildefonso, Oct. 5, 1737, in 3:202, refers to the laws "que disponen pasen a doctrina los indios de misión, luego que hayan cumplido los diez años asignados." No such laws appear to have existed, but the Crown, officials in America, and subsequent historians did come to believe that the law required missions to be secularized within ten years. See, for example, 2:832; the "Informe del excmo. sr. d. Pedro Felipe, obispo de la Concepción, sobre los curatos de la diócesis." Concepción, March 30, 1744 to the presidente [of the audiencia of Chile]," in Gay, 1846–52, 1:524–25. Geary, 1934, 27–30, discusses the mistaken belief in a law but incorrectly assumes that it originated in 1749. The sources above point to earlier origins.

119. For an example of Indians' loss of land as a result of secularization, see Garrido, 1993, 242–48. Among many examples of Spaniards' interest in the labor of mission Indians see Torre Curiel, 2001, 304, for Coahuila in New Spain.

120. Revillagigedo, 1991, 2:832–33 ("dominio despótico"; "en breves años se habrían extinguido las misiones, gozando los indios de libertad, del producto de sus labores y propio trabajo, y el rey de la contribución de los tributos)." For outstanding case studies, see Río, 1995, 33–58, Sheridan, 1999, 109–21, and Deeds, 2003, 131–89.

121. Some writers have suggested incorrectly that the crown ordered the secularization of all missions (for example, Geary, 1934, 26), but the crown had no intention of secularizing missions that still needed the services of regular clergy. The 1749 decree, in its various iterations and as interpreted by contemporaries, makes clear that the crown intended to secularize Indian parishes (*curatos*) and missions en route to becoming parishes (*doctrinas,* or what William Taylor has called protoparishes). The royal order of Feb. 1, 1753, appears in Gómez Canedo, 1974–75, 3:77–80, and refers only to "curatos." Nonetheless, the bishop of Caracas interpreted this to mean "todos los curatos y doctrinas de esta Diócesis" (ibid., 3:86), thus conflating *doctrinas* and *curatos.* See, too Ventura Beleña, 1981, 1:165 (CCLXII). For the context, see Taylor, 1996, 15, 84, 565 n.48, who cites a series of royal *cédulas.* Revillagigedo, 1867, 41, summarized the two decrees and the crown's philosophy. Brading, 1991, 492–93, suggests that the decree of 1753 applied only to mendicants, which would

have excluded Jesuits, but its language was broader. It applied to "regulares," meaning members of all religious orders. Morales, 1993, 465–96, argues that regulars brought secularization on themselves. In the late eighteenth century, some understood *doctrina* and *curato* as "una misma cosa" (Parras, 1783, 2:69), although some Franciscans and officials far from the scene continued to hearken back to an older, sixteenth-century meaning of *doctrina* in which it served as a synonym for a mission. See, for example, the Report of fray Francisco Sanz, Padre Guardian of the Colegio de la Purísima Concepción, Nueva Barcelona, Jan. 10, 1791, in Gómez Canedo, 1967, 2:217. One Franciscan authority on missions, Parras, 1783, 2:68–76, 142–45, notes that ongoing confusion notwithstanding, a *real cédula* of 1654 drew the distinction clearly. By the late colonial period, however, Franciscans who worked closely with missions knew that defining a mission as a *doctrina* signified that it was ready for secularization, and they resisted the state's efforts to define missions as *doctrinas*. See, for example, Bringas, in Matson and Fontana, 1977, 47, and Trias Mercant, 1995, 112. See Borges, 1992a, 431–32, for the evolution of these terms and their often contradictory uses. I have chosen to use the term "mature missions" for eighteenth-century *doctrinas*.

122. Francisco Hurtado, the intendant of Chiloé, ca. 1788, quoted in Urbina Burgos, 1990, 102 ("quieren ser deidades absolutas, imperando en lo civil, político y militar"; "por vivir entre ellos en la poligamia más desenfrenada, libres de sujeción").

123. Sarrailh, 1957, 612–60, Herr, 1958, 11–36, and Lynch, 1989, 269–80, provide fine overviews. Brading, 1991, 502–13, offers a rich reading of the thought of Campomanes and Jovellanos on this subject. See, too, Farriss, 1968, 88–92, and Taylor, 1996, 13–17. I use the word "justified" advisedly; see Góngora's analysis of the pragmatism of Campomanes, regalism's "most brilliant explicator" (ibid., p. 196).

124. For good introductions to the complexities and nuances of the "Catholic Enlightenment" in English, see Góngora, 1975, 194–205, and González Rodríguez, 1992b, with its useful guide to sources.

125. Callahan, 1975, 160–64, who sees the reform movement in stages: a period of pastoral reforms in the 1760s and 1770s and program of structural change in the 1780s and 1790s. See also Whitaker, 1970, 260–63, and Dussel, 1983, 1:673–74, 699–700, who analyzes "catolicismo ilustrado" in terms of class struggle.

126. José Antonio de San Alberto, *Catecismo real* (1786), quoted in Dussel, 1983, 1:702 ("En su reino son unas imágenes visibles de Dios." "El Rey está sujeto al pueblo?" "No, pues que esto sería estar sujeta la cabeza a los pies").

127. An unusually high percentage of Spain's male population of productive age was in the religious orders. For various calculations, see Mercader Riba and

Domínguez Ortiz, 1972, 9–10; Herr, 1958, 29–30, Lynch, 1989, 269. The clearest iteration of the Bourbons' position toward the regular clergy was the Instrucción of Oct. 17, 1769, written by Campomanes. Góngora, 1969, 47, and Góngora, 1975, 201.

128. The felicitous comparison of Farriss, 1968, 92, who examines this for New Spain.

129. The literature on this subject is vast. For good introductions in English, see especially, Lynch, 1989, 280–82, and Brading, 1991, 499, who notes the role of Franciscans in bringing about the Jesuits' demise. Mörner, 1965, remains a fine introduction to the subject.

130. José de Gálvez to Viceroy Antonio María Bucareli, Mexico, Jan. 30, 1772, in Rico González, 1949, 14 ("la frontera de los Indios Bravos"), speaking of New Spain.

131. Merino and Newson, 1995, 135, provides a valuable table; the three hundred thousand figure is from Mörner, 1970, 314.

132. Mörner, 1965, 15; Campomanes, 1977, 128–38, focused his critique on the Guaraní missions, but he makes clear his generalizations apply to Jesuit missions throughout America (p. 138). Campomanes did not, however, oppose missionization. Campomanes, 1988, 239, 251.

133. Ibid., 132 ("como monarca independiente y absoluto"). Ironically, the best-known of the Jesuit missions, those of Paraguay, abolished by Spain's most enlightened monarch, were one of the few Spanish institutions admired by enlightened French philosophes from Montesquieu to Raynal. Góngora 1975, 233–36.

134. "Temporalidades o bienes comunes de los indios." Pedro de Nava to Revillagigedo, Chihuahua, Jan. 27, 1792, in Gómez Canedo, 1971, 112.

135. Aranda, "Adición a la instrucción sobre el estrañamiento de los Jesuitas," Madrid, March 1, 1767, published in several sources, including Brabo, 1872, 42–45. Aranda (p. 44) uses the term "clérigos o religiosos sueltos," meaning he would accept either secular clergy or members of religious orders who will follow the directives of diocesan authorities.

136. Campomanes, 1977, 136 ("escandalosa usurpación de los bienes del indio").

137. San Alberto, 1788, 1–2 ("el Grande sobre todos los Grandes, el Rey Católico de las Españas don Carlos III . . . poder, y de la autoridad, que Dios, y las Leyes han depositado en su Real Mano").

138. Quoted in Block, 1994, 129. For the Guaraní missions, see Doblas, 1969–72, 5:85–87, and Ganson, 2003, 142.

139. Bucareli, "Instrucción a que se deberán arreglar los Gobernadores interinos que dejo nombrados en los pueblos de indios guaranís del Uruguay y Paraná," Candelaria, Aug. 23, 1768, in Brabo, 1872, 208 ("aplicar todos los medios conducentes a que se extinga la

odiosa separación que hasta ahora se ha conservado entre los indios y blancos"). These orders, both from Aranda and Bucareli, represented a departure from laws that prohibited Spaniards from living in Indian towns (*Recopilación,* Libro 6, tit. 3, leyes 21–23). Wilde, 1999, 619–44, analyzes Bucareli's departure from tradition and sees it as a forerunner of the assimilationist policies pursued after independence.

140. For efforts to enforce this law, see Lynch, 1958, 189, who also offers a good description of the missions' decline. In 1802, the protector of the Indians in Buenos Aires ruled that the law applied only to Indians "que no se hallen establecidos ventajosamente en alguna población y que por sí solos puedan atender a la subsistencia de sus familias." Opinion of the Fiscal de la Real Audiencia de Buenos Aires y Protector de Naturales, Manuel Genaro de Villota, ca. 1802, in Mariluz Urquijo 1953, 329. The law is in the *Recopilación,* Libro 6, tit. 3, ley 18.

141. Bucareli, "Instrucción a que se deberán arreglar los Gobernadores interinos que dejo nombrados en los pueblos de indios guaranís del Uruguay y Paraná," Candelaria, Aug. 23, 1768, in Brabo, 1872, 209–10 ("la conservación y aumento de los intereses de estos indios"). See also, ibid., 200.

142. For those orders, see Bucareli, "Adición . . . ," Buenos Aires, Jan. 15, 1770, in Brabo, 1872, 304–05. For the poor training and difficult circumstances of the administrators see Maeder, 1992, 100–104, and Poenitz and Poenitz, 1993, 22–23.

143. The marqués de Avilés to the king, Buenos Aires, March 8, 1800, in Lastarria, 1914, 43 ("cada uno de dichos vampiros quisiera ser solo para chupar la sangre a los desvalidos"). See, too Avilés, 1945, 506–13, for the viceroy's harsh appraisal. Súsnik and Chase-Sardi, 1995, 155–64, believe that Guaraní factionalism also intensified as Indians took sides with or against their new administrators.

144. David Block has noted that the Moxos missions, for example, received support from Jesuit estates in Peru: "In opposition to the usual pattern of capital flow, the center supported the periphery." Block, 1994, 175. White, 1975, 417–33, argues that the missions failed when they were incorporated into Paraguay's monocultural economy, which the metropolis bled.

145. Maeder and Bolsi 1981, 134, 136–37; Maeder, 1992, chap. 4; Maeder, 1990, 55–106. The pace and conditions of decline varied with local circumstances, of course. Whigham, 1995, 167–69, notes a difference between the missions north and south of the Paraná.

146. Quoted in Poenitz and Poenitz, 1993, 29 ("en el más deplorable estado que se pueda imaginar de necesidad, con un hambre que los hombres que han quedado están pálidos y flacos").

147. Maeder and Bolsi, 1981, 143.

148. Maeder, 1992, 57–58.

149. The viceroy in 1790 noted that he had sent troops to bring "deserters" back from living with heathen tribes. Loreto, 1945, 274 ("infieles Minuanes y Charrúas"). Mariluz Urquijo, 1953, 323–30, first challenged the widespread notion that Jesuits had prepared Indians so badly that they reverted en masse to savagery after their tutors were banished. Vives Azancot, 1982, 469–543, finds Guaraníes merging into the regional labor market and weakening the missions even before the expulsion of the Jesuits. For an example of the new economic growth, see Cooney, 1998, 139, who also notes the appalling working conditions. Wilde, 2001, 69–106, and Ganson, 2003, 125–36, offer rich analyses of the wide range of responses of Guaraníes who left the mission; Ganson also explores the responses of those who stayed (pp. 137–55).

150. Bucareli y Ursúa, 1880, 306 ("Establecí el nuevo gobierno espiritual y temporal, poniendo a los curas en el concepto de quedar absolutamente limitadas sus funciones y facultades al servicio de las iglesias y cuidado de las almas"). In his use of the word *cura* here, Bucareli is using shorthand for *curas regulares,* or regular priests, as opposed to *curas seculares.* Wilde, 2001, 88.

151. Wilde, 2001, 90–91. Members of the three orders divided the thirty missions evenly among them, but these regular clergy came under the direct supervision of either the bishop of Buenos Aires or the bishop of Paraguay, among whom the former Jesuit missions were divided. Vértiz y Salcedo, 1945, 111. Maeder, 1995, 71–84, comparing Jesuit and Franciscan missions among the Guaraní, concluded that more than anything else the Guaraníes' isolation from the labor demands of Hispanic society accounts for the Jesuits' relative success.

152. Poenitz and Poenitz, 85.

153. Doblas, 1969, 3:131 ("plena libertad para que cada uno trabaje para su propia utilidad, comercie con los frutos y efectos de su trabajo e industria, y que en un todo vivan y sean tratados como los demás vasallos del Rey"). The Spanish-born Doblas had been lieutenant governor of Concepción with eight former Jesuit missions in his jurisdiction.

154. Mariluz Urquijo, 1987, 303–23. See, too, Acevedo, 1997, 129–53, for Lázaro de Ribera's stinging criticism.

155. A royal cédula of May 17, 1803, noted in Poenitz and Poenitz, 1993, 81.

156. Santiago de Liniers to the king, Candelaria, June 28, 1804, quoted in Maeder, 1992, 224 ("en pocos años se habrán vuelto sus habitantes a la vida bárbara").

157. A revolutionary junta that seized power in Buenos Aires in 1810 tried to complete the work by granting the "derechos de libertad, propiedad y seguridad de que habéis estado privados por generaciones, sirviendo de esclavos a los que han tratado únicamente de enriquercerse a costa de vuestros sudores

y aun de vuestra propia sangre" (quoted in Maeder, 1994, 202). But the rebels failed, too. The final liberation of the Guaraníes fell to the three independent nations that inherited parts of the old Guaraní territory, Argentina, Paraguay, and Uruguay. See, too, Maeder, 1992, 222–31, and Lynch, 1989, 185–95 for an overview.

158. Gullón Abao, 1993, 162–65; Vitar, 1997, 299–302. Vitar's figures exaggerate the decline because she mistakenly places the number of Indians in the seven missions in 1767 at 3,946 instead of 3,346, but a decline from 3,346 to 2,148 four years later, in 1771, represented a 35 percent decline. Santamaría, 1986, 227, notes that on June 10, 1805, Carlos IV granted freedom to Indians of Moxos and Chiquitos, as he had done two years before for the Guaraníes. Santamaría, 1999, 9–12, reproduces a key document in his appendix (pp. 22–28).

159. Parejas Moreno, 1976a, 953, 954, 961, and Parejas Moreno and Suárez Salas, 1992, 309.

160. This plan seemed so promising that it inspired the first viceroy of the Río de La Plata to use it for the Guaraní missions. Cevallos, 1945, 12, called to my attention by Maeder, 1992, 194.

161. Viedma, 1969a–72a, 6:695–735. Maeder, 1988, 160, offers shrewd comparisons between the Guaraní and Bolivian missions. Block, 1994, 99–100, 126–48. Dependency on Spaniards for defense is clear from AGB, Chiquitos, vol. 25, IX (1780), and from vol. 26, III and V (1780–82). The quotation is from the "Indian justices of San Xavier (Chiquitos), to fray Thomas de Valencia," 1771, in Radding, 2001, 68.

162. Merino and Newson, 1995, 139–42, summarizes the fates of various Jesuit missions, utilizing a typology of overlapping categories. For the Mocobí missions, see Primo y Medina, 1986, 885–900, and Saeger, 2000, 38–40, who looks at the various fates of Guaycuruan missions; for the Yaquis, see Spicer, 1980, 126–36, and Hu-DeHart, 1981, 98–103; for Tarahumaras, see Benedict, 1972, 33, Deeds, 1998, 33–36, and Deeds, 2003, 187–88.

163. José de Gálvez, royal order of Jan. 31, 1784, quoted in Revillagigedo, 1966a, 17–19.

164. In Paraguay, for example, Jesuits had begun to build a chain of missions to connect Asunción with Chiquitos and Moxos; José Sánchez de Labrador had established Nuestra Señora de Belén among the Mbayás on the shores of the Río Ipane-Guazú, one hundred leagues or so from the most southeasterly Chiquitos missions in 1760. Meanwhile, Jesuits from Moxos and Chiquitos had moved to the edge of the Portuguese territory of Mato Grosso, where they blocked Portuguese advances and began to move in the direction of Asunción by converting Guaycuruans and trying without success to convert Payaguas. Parejas Moreno and Suárez Salas, 1992, 290, 297, 306–07. Maldi, 1996, 46–48. James Saeger found

no conversions of Payaguas in the colonial era. Personal communication, Dec. 29, 2003.

165. For a recent summary of the way in which old missions supported new, see Radding, 1997, 76. Radding and Torre Curiel, 2001, 319–20, observe also that not all surplus from Jesuit missions went directly toward that purpose, however. Much went to supply Hispanic communities. While coping with the rapid declines of two former Jesuit missions among the Mocobíes, San Javier (1743) and San Pedro (1765), for example, friars tried and failed to build additional Mocobí missions, Primo y Medina, 1986, 885–900; in the province of Moxos, for example, not until 1794 could officials boast of having established the first new mission since the days of the Jesuits. Gov. Miguel de Zamora to the Audiencia of Charcas, Pueblo de Nuestra Señora del Carmen de Guarayos, Nov. 13, 1794, in Parejas Moreno, 1976b, 137. The quotation ("adelantamientos espirituales") is from a printed royal decree, el Pardo, March 21, 1787, sent to governors throughout the empire and requiring frequent accounting of missionary activity. Capitanía general, vol. 736, no. 10651, ANSC.

166. Heras, 1983, 271–72; González de la Vara, 1991, 269–70, 283–86. Morales, 1993, 490, describes a decline in Franciscan zeal in the 1600s as missionaries shifted from spreading the faith to conserving the faith of Indians, and the same appears to have occurred with Dominicans. Medina, 1992, 146, 188–94, 298–300, 307–14, and elsewhere, who makes clear that the Dominicans' greatest evangelical activity occurred in the 1500s. In many areas, the decline of Franciscan zeal remained evident well into the 1700s, as seen in Porras Muñoz, 1980, 202–03. For a contrary view, see Gómez Canedo, "Misiones Franciscanas en el siglo XVII: ¿Decadencia o nuevos rumbos?" in Gómez Canedo, 1993, 42–44.

167. For missionaries' views of the elegance of the languages of the Aztecs and Incas and the barbarity of the languages of hunters and gatherers, see Vitar, 1996, 147–50. On the importance of Indian languages for missionaries, see Guest, 1996, 339. Revillagigedo, 1966a, 49, for example, believed the College of Zacatecas more adept than others.

168. I am not counting the college of Santo Cristo, established in Guatemala in 1694, which failed within six years. Saiz Díez, 1969, the best overview, provides a capsule history and guidance to sources on each of the American colleges (pp. 36–44). On learning Indian languages, see ibid., 101–02; for the colegios' two functions, *misiones populares* and *conversiones vivas,* ibid., 127–31. Abad Pérez, 1993, 86–88, 119–28, 237–84, lists them, gives their founding dates, and provides brief descriptions and guidance to sources. He gives the date of 1739 for the founding of Purísima Concepción de Píritu in Venezuela (p. 87); I follow Saiz Diez, 1969, 41, who with reason puts it at

1787; Gómez Canedo, 1967, 1:lvi, elaborates. Most of the colleges have their historians; Mantilla R., 2000, 1:553–660, is especially rich for the two colegios in New Granada, and their internal politics.

169. Córdoba, 1934, 276–78; Parras, 1783, 1:158–59 ("los Religiosos ya no iban a vivir en las campañas y bosques, sino a sus Provincias y respectivos conventos" [p. 159]); Campomanes, 1988, 251, 265–66; Borges Morán, 1977, 44–52.

170. Centurión to the Consejo de Indias, Sept. 17, 1771, in González del Campo, 1984, 208, 668. Gov. Vicente de Emparán to the king, Cumaná, May 16–17, 1795, in Carrocera, 1968, 3:538–39 ("las cosas útiles a la sociedad"); Mendinueta, 1910, 442 ("el ejercicio de misionero no se aprende en las escuelas de latinidad, filosofía y teología").

171. Borges Morán, 1977, 246–60; Herr, 1958, 31–33; Payne, 1973, 2:377. For an example from a single American province, see Gómez Canedo, 1974–75, 1:62–63, who provides statistics that show a sharp decline in the last quarter of the century. Complaints of shortages came not only from clerics, but from civil officials: for New Spain in 1793, see Revillagigedo, 1966a, 115; for New Granada, see Mendinueta, 1910, 436, 443–44. Wright, 1998, 221–30, seems to blame Bourbon officials for failing to allot more stipends to support friars. For the fiscal woes of one Franciscan province, see Torre Curiel, 2001, chap. 5.

172. Consejo pleno, Dec. 10, 1778, in Maas, 1917–18, 18 (March 1917), 212–13 ("no tienen aquella robustez y resistencia que concurren en los españoles para sufrir la variedad de temperamentos y otros trabajos que se experimentan en las misiones; pues los españoles, como criados en un clima donde cada una de las estaciones del año se hace bastante sensible, connaturalizados con todas ellas"). Called to my attention by Borges Moran, 1977, 56, who notes subsequent reaffirmations of this argument by the Consejo.

173. Floridablanca, 1876, 226 (art. XC: "relajado notablemente").

174. In general, the colleges' leadership continued a long tradition of favoring Spaniards whom they believed to be more zealous than American-born clergy. Borges Morán, 1977, 44–57, provides an overview. Luna Moreno, 1993, 358–68, explains that Spanish-born clergy were in special demand to fill political offices in the provinces and colleges and so were kept from working in the missions. For another college that relied almost entirely on peninsulares and that had unusual success in recruiting in Spain, see Gómez Canedo, 1967, 1:lii–lv; for more typical cases of unfulfilled quotas, see Hernández Aparicio, 1997, 579–92; Lagos, 1908, 393–95, and the Report of the contaduria general, El conde de Casa Valencia, on the shortage of missionaries in Charcas and in the audiencia of Buenos Aires, Madrid, April 18, 1804, AGI, BA 610.

175. O'Higgins, "Descripción del Reyno de Chile," Madrid, Sept. 2, 1767, in Donoso, 1941, 442 ("genio").

176. Medina, 1992, 84–85, 92–93, 95, 146–49, 196, 242. See, too, Córdoba, 1934, 274–78, for the shortages in the Province of Buenos Aires in 1777 and 1789.

177. Razón de las doctrinas y pueblos de misiones fronterizas a la gentilidad que hay en todas las Indias . . . , 1780, in Maas, 1917–18, 19 (July 1917):43–44, 48 ("grandísimas cosechas espirituales de naciones bárbaras").

178. Francisco Xavier Ramírez to Ambrosio Benavides, Chillán, Dec. 24, 1785, quoted in Ramírez, 1994, 28 ("sepultados en el abismo de infidelidad y barbarie por falta de ministros"). Casanova Guarda, 1988, 168, notes Chillán's shortage at the end of the century.

179. Informe de Consejo de Indias sobre la situación de la misión de Cumaná, Madrid, July 2, 1802, in Carrocera, 1968, 3:550 ("para volverlos después a doctrina y a sociabilidad, cuesta poco menos trabajo que cuando se sacaron del monte"), commenting on some neglected Guaraúnas in the Venezuelan province of Cumaná.

180. Brunet, 1969, 209–40.

181. For an example of that line of argument, see fray Pedro González de Agüeros to the crown, Madrid, July 1, 1792, in Medina, 1963, 3:163–67. The friars could not be stretched that far, however. When officials called on the College of San Fernando to staff the Jesuit missions of Baja California, the college cut the number of friars in its Sierra Gorda missions and then secularized them in order to free up enough friars. Gómez Canedo, "Un lustro de administración franciscana en Baja California (1768–1773)," in Gómez Canedo, 1993, 619, and Gómez Canedo, 1976, 107–11. For the shortage of secular priests, see, for example, Río 1995, 144. Aranda had anticipated the use of regular clergy to operate Jesuit missions. See above n.135.

182. Floridablanca, 1867, 226–27 (art. XCII).

183. Campomanes, 1977, 135 ("ambición y despotismo"). See also Bishop Esteban Tristán of Durango to Charles IV, March 8, 1793, quoted in Gómez Canedo, 1983, 24.

184. For examples from Chile and New Spain, see Casanova Guarda, 1988, 131; Torre Curiel, 2001, 318.

185. Gullón Abao, 1993, 185, 189–92.

186. See the two cases noted in Cano, 1983, 121, and Torre Curiel, 2001, 168. This question needs more study. Córdoba, 1934, 269, notes Franciscan efforts to obtain control of the Jesuit Estancia San Miguel, which succeeded in 1780, but the economic arrangements are not clear. Franciscans did not object to receiving money controlled by others, however, as was the case with their use of the so-called Pious Fund, originally set up to fund Jesuit missions, to support new Franciscan missions in California (Archibald, 1978a, 3–4), and with ranches or plantations that in

theory belonged to Indians but whose revenue supported missions. González del Campo, 1984, 130. Some Franciscans, on the other hand, competed vigorously for former Jesuit estates. See Urbina Burgos, 1990, 15–24, who also describes friars receiving obventions (called *camaricos* in Chile) from "old Christian" Veliches (Huilliches) at the *misiones circulares* of Chiloé but giving gifts to Chonos and Caucahues. He finds Franciscans poorer than their Jesuit predecessors but adequately financed. For the Jesuits' own moral qualms, see Cushner, 1983, 154, 169–78.

187. For the amount of stipends, see Alcocer, 1958, 159, for example. For friars who turned down *sínodos*, see Gómez Canedo, 1967, 1:xxxviii. The quotation is from a *real cédula* to the viceroy of the La Plata, Sept. 6, 1777, in Alumni, 1951, 264 ("los verdaderos medios para conseguir sus conversiones"). For friars using their own funds, see Jossef [*sic*] Gregorio Salvatierra to M.P.S, San Xavier de Chiquitos, June 16, 1799, in AGB, 31, III (1795–1808), who makes this point ("mis propios bienes y sínodos"). Lynch, 1999, 10–11, contains a marvelous account of an individual friar's search for funds. For the inadequate funding for gifts, see the report of the head of the order, Madrid, 1788, quoted in Maas, 1915, 205. Crown financing often came from the expropriated Jesuit properties, from the sale of former mission lands, from tithes, and from special excise taxes. See, for example, Gullón Abao, 1993, 187, 190.

188. Gullón Abao, 1993, 316–17.

189. Fray José García in the Sierra Gorda missions, 1759, quoted in Gómez Canedo, 1976, 93–94 ("infieles bárbaros").

190. Torre Curiel, 2001, 168–69, provides one example of maintaining *doctrinas* for financial reasons.

191. Prefecto Manuel de la Mata, Hospicio de Altagracia y pueblo de Santa María de los Angeles, Nov. 25, 1763, quoted in Carrocera, 1968, 1:337 ("el primero y total origen de la destrucción de los pueblos y atraso universal de los miserables indios"). Prefecto Manuel articulated a venerable argument. See Phelan, 1970, 89.

192. Parras, 1783, 2:75 ("tan ruda y tarda para imponerse en los inefables misterios de la Fé: tan floja y desidiosa para el trabajo y cultivo, que en ese tiempo [de diez años] no haya podido amoldarse a las leyes y policía de una sociedad civil"). For ten years as an ideal, see above n.118. Bringas, 1796–97, in Matson and Fontana, 1977, 49–50, appears to have consulted Parras on this point, or each consulted a common source.

193. Sanz, 1977, 74 ("no obstante la antiguedad de sus reducciones, no han permitido entrar gentes de afuera para tratar, ni comerciar ni salir a los indios"). For the shifting meaning of "Chuncho," see Varese, 2002, 40–43.

194. Castro Gutiérrez, 1994, 29.

195. Archibald, 1978a, 2–3; Weber, 1992, 242; Brandes, 1992, 2:156.

196. There is deep misunderstanding of this in California historiography. Jackson, 1998, 92, for example, suggests that the friars did not gain control over the temporalities until 1773. He states that in 1773 Serra "signed an agreement with the viceregal government in Mexico City. Under the terms of the agreement, the government granted the Franciscans control over the mission temporalities." Jackson cites himself (Jackson, 1991, 387–439), but his trail leads back to the historian Zephyrin Engelhardt, who did *not* make that point. Serra *did* tell Viceroy Bucareli that Gálvez had given the Franciscans control over the "training, governance, punishment and education of baptized Indians, or those who are being prepared for Baptism," and asked the viceroy to notify officers and soldiers not to violate the friars' authority by punishing Indians without priests' permission. Serra to Bucareli, March 13, 1773, Mexico, in Tibesar, 1955–66, 1:307. The viceroy granted that request on May 6, 1773. Palóu, 1926, 3:41, 50, 55. Like Jackson, Guest, 1996, 260, incorrectly assumed this was a new arrangement rather than the affirmation of an existing one.

197. Castro Gutiérrez, 1994, 29.

198. Gálvez, decreto, Alamos, June 3, 1769, cited in McCarty, 1981, 101, and Río, 1995, 143. See, too, Escandón, 1993, 277–91, for a fine overview. Escandón gives the date of May 17, 1769, for Gálvez's order. McCarty and Río put it at June 3, 1769. Gálvez's orders obtained in the Pimería Baja until 1776 and in the Pimería Alta until the end of the colonial era. Escandón, 1993, 288.

199. Decree given at Ures, Sept. 29, 1769, summarized in McCarty, 1981, 102.

200. Alcocer, 1958, 160, credits Gálvez with doing this in 1770.

201. To bring the regulars under the control of the secular church, Gálvez used a friend and surrogate, fray Antonio de los Reyes, to propose the creation of an archbishopric for the interior provinces of New Spain and tighter control from Spain over Franciscan activities. Much has been written about the regalistic Reyes, but Río, 1995, 142–52, is especially insightful on Reyes as the puppet of Gálvez. Although Reyes became bishop of Sonora, the crown required that any reforms be made in the mission system be approved by a junta dominated by civil officials. Gómez Canedo, 1971, 38–39. In 1769, when Dominicans petitioned for a share of California, Gálvez initially recommended against it, but he succumbed to political pressure that paved the way for Dominicans to take charge of Baja California's missions and mission temporalities in 1772. For Gálvez's initial opposition to Dominicans in Baja California and the crown's response, see Meigs, 1935, 3. For a critical introduction to the literature on Dominicans in Baja California,

see Bernabéu Albert, 1999b, 91–133, and for the question of temporalities and limits on missionaries' authority at one Dominican mission, see Magaña-Mancillas, 1999, 199–201.

202. Francisco Palóu, then Baja California, quoted in Rafael Verger to Viceroy Bucareli, Primer informe y método nuevo de misiones para su gobierno espiritual y temporal, Mexico, Nov. 15, 1772, FF, 122:40 ("si ha de ser así, más vale que nos retiremos al Colegio y que el Rey no haga gastos superfluos, sin esperanza de adelantar la fe católica, ni sus Dominios"), copy courtesy of Ignacio del Río. Viceroy Antonio Bucareli, Mexico, Sept. 2, 1772, had asked Verger, the head of the College of San Fernando, his opinion about the "nuevo método espiritual y temporal." Ponç i Fullano, 1990, 267. For Verger's response, see also ibid., 99–101, and Gómez Canedo, 1962, 572, who called this document to my attention. Pressure for mission land would not build up until the 1820s.

203. See above n.196.

204. Antonio Bucareli to Junípero Serra, Jan. 20, 1776, in Palóu, 1970, 120 ("es preciso que esas reducciones puedan subsistir por sí en lo correspondiente a víveres, y a eso espero que se dedique el celo de los padres misioneros fomentando las siembras y la cría de ganados").

205. Neve, 1994, 36–37, for the facsimile of the 1784 imprint of Neve's *Reglamento*. Beilharz, 1971, 64–65. For Neve's efforts to redefine missions as doctrinas, see Geiger, 1959, 2:159–63. Archibald, 1978a, 10, and Guest, 1990, 40, incorrectly state that Neve's *Reglamento* ordered the friars to surrender the mission temporalities.

206. Beilharz, 1971, 119–20; Servín, 1965, 138–39. The quotations are from Neve to José Francisco Ortega, Oct. 1, 1782, in Jackman, 1993, 6.

207. Croix's instructions, March 7, 1780, appear in full in Matson and Fontana, 1977, 97–105. The quotations are on p. 105. Santiago, 1998, 76–81.

208. Fray Diego Bringas, 1796–97, in Matson and Fontana, 1977, 86–87; see, too, 96, 105–12; the head of the Franciscan order in Madrid offered the same diagnosis. Maas, 1915, 206. For the context, see Weber, 1992, 258–60, and Forbes, 1965, 175–220, who also mentions Neve's failed plan.

209. Hornbeck, 1989, 426–28; Hackel, 1998, 116, 121–28. Hackel provides figures for nonmission Indians in the coastal area; mission and Hispanic population figures are in Weber, 1992, 258–59, 263–65 (in 1800: 13,500 to 1,800).

210. Gov. Diego de Borica to fray José María Fernández, Sept. 15, 1796, and Borica to Lasuén, Sept. 15, 1796, and the comments of Lasuén in Beebe and Senkewicz, 1996, 10, 11, 42–44.

211. For a good discussion of the use of Guaraní labor in the La Plata and Asunción, see d'Aquino Fonseca Gadelha, 1996, 16–22.

212. Letter of June 15, 1770, to the marqués de Croix, in Boneu Companys, 1983, 400. His companions agreed. See, for example, Miguel de Costansó's journal in ibid., 181, 182, 187, 188–89, 193, 200, 224–25.

213. Piqueras Céspedes, 1992–93, 115–19.

214. For the ongoing commitment to kindness and forbearance, see, for example, Gov. Felipe de Neve's Instructions to Pedro Fages, his successor, Saucillo, Sept. 7, 1782, in Beilharz, 1971, 157. Weber, 1992, 246–47.

215. Felipe de Goicoechea to Diego de Borica, Dec. 1798, in Jackman, 1993, 25, describes these corporal punishments. There is a substantial secondary literature on these punishments in California, which Franciscans defended. See in particular Guest, 1996, who offers guidance to the critics, whom he also refutes.

216. Gov. Diego de Borrica, 1797 and 1799, in Florescano and Gil Sánchez, 1976, 47, 54–55. Weber, 1992, 247.

217. Jackson and Castillo, 1995, chap. 4; Sandos, 1998, 203–210, whose essay also suggests the current state of historiography on the California missions, and Sandos, 2004, 55–68, 154–73; Castañeda, 1998, 235–38, and Hackel, 2003, 643–69, for a revisionist view of the 1785 revolt. Phillips, 1993, chap. 4, looks at resistance beyond the coastal missions, where mission refugees interacted with independent Indians.

218. Weber, 1992, 263.

219. For Indians in need of a pass to travel, see Sandos, 1998, 206. See Duggan, 2000, chap. 2, for San Diego; Magaña, 1998, 59–61, for Baja California. For both, see Fermín Francisco de Lasuén, annual report, San Diego, May 10, 1783, in Lasuén, 1965, 2:363, and Lasuén to José Gasol, Santa Clara, June 16, 1802, in ibid., 2:277–78. Quotation (ibid., 2:277), and a Spanish transcript courtesy of Marie Duggan ("menos malo que el dejarlos permanecer gentiles"). For baptized Indians living away from California missions in general, see Kelsey, 1985, 505, and Hackel, 2003, 646, who suggests that California missions may have been "more porous than scholars have realized." Deviation from the ideal may have been the norm. See above n.66.

220. Milliken, 1995, 220–23. No one has written more about the impact of disease on California Indians than Robert H. Jackson. See, for example, Jackson and Castillo, 1995, chap. 3.

221. Felipe de Goicoechea to Gov. Diego de Borica, Santa Barbara, March 12, 1796, in California State Papers, Missions, 2:92–98, Bancroft Library, Berkeley, California. Reference courtesy of John R. Johnson, Santa Barbara Museum of Natural History, who describes the effort to revive the new method and finds that the viceroy support of tradition coming in 1803. Johnson, 1986, 27–28. See, too, Jackman, 1993, 26. For ongoing pressure to secularize, see Servín, 1965, 133–49, and Weber, 1982, 60–67.

222. Both quotations are from Fermín Francisco de Lasuén to José Gasol, Santa Clara, June 16, 1802, Santa

Barbara Mission Archives, sect. 2, no. 399, photocopy courtesy of Doyce B. Nunis ("quedarían estas misiones con sobradas tierras, y sin gente que las utilizase"; "dejándolos en su libertad y en sus rancherías después de bautizados"). This letter is translated in Lasuén, 1965, 2:277 and 288, but these translations are my own. Duggan, 2004, 9.

223. Casanueva, 1982, 22, quoting from a plan enunciated by the president of Chile in 1767.

224. Sors, 1921–23, no. 45, 277, and no. 46, 326.

225. Foerster, G., 1996, argues against a historiography that posits a Jesuit failure in Chile. He points to Araucanian acceptance of baptism and priests to perform it. He also credits Jesuits with beginning the system of *parlamentos.*

226. Carvallo Goyeneche, writing in the 1790s, quoted in Zapater, 1998, 158 ("Padre, no te canses, porque es costumbre y ley inviolable de mis antepasados no creer cosa alguna de lo que digan los españoles").

227. Anonymous, "Memorial por via de informe a los señores de la real Junta, que mandó hacer el Rey N.S. para el mayor progreso de las misiones del reino de Chile, Santiago, Sept. 24, 1708," in Gay, 1846–52, 1:283 ("juzgan que estando en pueblos los han de dominar y avasallar los españoles, y temen más este yugo que la muerte").

228. Father André Febres, 1765, quoted in Foerster G., 1996, 337 ("bautizan a los chiquillos, enseñan a los indios las cosas de Dios, los confiesan, casan, y asi andan uno, dos o tres meses"). Such annual visits were not unique to Chile. Augustinians did the same in the Sierra Gorda. Gómez Canedo, 1976, 77.

229. The quotation is from Amat y Juniént, 1924–28, no. 56, 397–98 ("en su antiguo barbarismo, sin dejar la poligamia [y] supersticiones en que ciegamente viven envueltos"). Jesuits in New France used a circuit system among Hurons in the last half of the seventeenth century. Bushnell, 2004, 161.

230. Foerster G., 1996, 347–55, who sees this as a plan for a "utopia borbónica" in which Jesuits could bring about progress in arts and agriculture (p. 348). Pinto Rodríguez, 1988, 73, suggests that Jesuits were prodded by criticism and competition from the new Jesuit college at Chillán (1756), but Foerster G. makes it clear that the idea of congregating Indians into towns had deeper roots.

231. Oses, 1961, 43–45; Casanova Guarda, 1989b, 53–83, who also puts these efforts in the larger context of Bourbon efforts to consolidate Hispanic rural populations in towns.

232. Mission life often proved as hard, if not harder, on Indians as staying in their communities and facing their enemies. Driven from their scattered islands to missions on the great island of Chiloé by Alacalufes from the south, for example, many Chono fishermen deserted or died, unable to adjust to the sedentary life of farmers. Casanueva, 1982, 21–23.

233. Pinto Rodríguez, 1988, 61–62, makes this argument cogently, adding that Jesuits, for their part, recognized that mission production in the Araucanía would not articulate with the Chilean economy and that they could not, therefore, produce enough to support mission towns. But might not Jesuit enterprises elsewhere have supported Araucanian missions on the periphery, as was the case with Moxos and Baja California, if the Araucanians had been more receptive? For multiple baptisms, see Amat y Juniént, 1924–28, no. 57, 400, called to my attention by Zapater, 1998, 158, and for baptism in exchange for gifts or commercial advantage, see Espiñeira, 1988, 239, and Pedro Angel Espiñeira, Obispo de Concepción, to the crown, Aug. 19, 1767, MM, vol. 193, no. 4573.

234. The first quotation is from fray Francisco Rauzet de Jesús, 1786, in Sheridan and Naylor, 1979, 118, the second from Salcedo y Salcedo, 1990, 62 ("barrancas casi inaccesibles"). See, too, Alcocer, 1958, 161–62. For the Jesuit era, see Father Juan Isidro Fernández de Abee, 1744, in ibid., 80–83; Deeds, 1995, 97; Deeds, 2003, 104, 118–20, 185–88, 191, for the population estimate; Merrill, 1993, 141–43, 147, 151, who also notes that even today Tarahumara "converts" do not identify themselves as Catholics or Christians, but as "baptized Tarahumaras" (p. 156).

235. The quotations come from the report of Bishop Francisco José Marán to José de Gálvez, Concepción, Aug. 28, 1784, in Hanisch, 1990, 129 ("convertidos y fuera de la clase de neófitos"; "indios de conversión"). Casanova Guarda, 1988, 163–64, 163 n.42. Lagos, 1908, 173–84, recounts in detail the transition from Jesuit to Franciscan. For an analogous case, see Merrill, 1988, 40–49.

236. Medina, 1992, 276, 299, 309–12.

237. Ascasubi, 1846, 1:321–22 ("tan asiento en las tinieblas de sus errores, supersticiones y bárbaras costumbres, como las demás naciones de gentiles que jamás conocieron misionero"). For the *cabecera-visita* system, see Weber, 1992, 107, and Bushnell, 1994, 64–65. See above n.12.

238. Sors, 1921–23, no. 43, 194 ("que bastaría les bautizasen sus miembros viriles, con lo cual saldrían todos sus hijos bautizados y con esto excusaban cansarse en ir a sus tierras todos los años a bautizarles sus chiquillos"), writing in 1780.

239. For Guill y Gonzaga's bellicose policy, see Oses, 1961, 45, and Casanova Guarda, 1989b, 93. *Real cédula* to Agustín de Jáuregui, Gobernador y Capitán General del Reyno de Chile y Presidente de mi Audiencia de la Ciudad de Santiago. El Pardo, Feb. 6, 1774, ANSC, Fondos Varios, vol. 300, pieza 3 ("suavidad"; "libertinaje en que viven y mueren sumergidos"; "reducirían a sus parientes a una vida racional y cristiana"). Lagos, 1908, 312–13, quotes and contextualizes this *real cédula*, and a paraphrase appears in

Ayala, 1988–96, 7:351–53. The emphasis on peaceful persuasion continued. See the audiencia of Santiago to the King, June 28, 1781, quoted in Sors, 1921–23, no. 42, 15.

240. "Ningunos mejores misioneros podrán presentarse que influyan con eficacia en los corazones de los infieles para reducirse al suave yugo de nuestra religión." Gov. Ambrosio Benavides to José de Gálvez, Santiago, May 1, 1786, quoted in Casanueva, 1982, 24. Amat's informe, Dec. 6, 1769, is quoted in Barros Arana, 1884–1902, 6:240.

241. Bishop Pedro Angel Espiñeira, August 1767, to the missionaries of Chillán, quoted in Foerster G., 1992, 22 ("irían perdiendo poco a poco aquel natural y apasionado amor a sus padres y convirtiendo todo su afectuoso cariño a los misioneros"). See, too, pp. 23–24, and Sors, 1921–23, no. 43, 178, 197–98 ("de esta suerte solamente pueden conocer que el fruto va bien fundado"). For an introduction to the literature on Spain's efforts to train Indian clergy, see Olaechea Labayen, 1992, and Olaechea Labayen, 1976, 176–79, for the late eighteenth century, when Bourbons established a seminary in New Spain to train children of tribute-paying Indians for the priesthood.

242. Jacobo Ugarte to Juan Bautista de Anza, Oct. 5, 1786, in Thomas, 1932, 336–37. Some children of independent Indians were, indeed, sent to be educated by Spaniards. The Comanche chief Ecueracapa sent a son, Tahuchimpia, to Santa Fe to be raised by Anza Kavanagh, 1996, 119; and a Pampa, Cabeza de Buey, turned a ten-year-old boy over to the cabildo of Buenos Aires in 1808, which adopted him and paid for his education. Martínez Sierra, 1975, 1:268–69.

243. The quotation is from Ambrosio Benavides to José de Gálvez, Santiago, May 1, 1786, MM, vol. 197, no. 4792, p. 293 ("los vicios y libertinaje propio de su irreligión y entera falta de gobierno político"); for the use of Jesuit property, see Benavides to Gálvez, Feb. 1, 1787, in ibid., #4808, 350–53. For gifts and fugitives, see Rector del Colegio de Naturales sobre gastos del vestuario de los colegiales, 1783, Archivo de la Capitanía General, #7718 and #7789, sobre fuga de dos colegiales del Colegio de Naturales, both in ANSC.

244. Gov. Ambrosio O'Higgins to Pedro de Acuña, Santiago, April 12, 1794, quoted in Casanueva, 1982, 24 ("españolizados por la educación"). The two were ordained in 1794 as secular priests; at least four more Araucanians became Franciscans. See Lagos, 312–28, 470–84; Gunckel L., 1961, 146–47; Casanueva, 1988, 241.

245. Prior to the expulsion of the Jesuits, Franciscans built several missions among the Pehuenches, beginning in 1758 with Santa Barbara on the north side of the Biobío at the entrance to the mountainous Pehuenche territory, but the revolt of 1766 left them

only Santa Barbara. See Villalobos R., 1989b, 81–109, for a synthesis and guide to sources. For overviews of their modest achievements among Mapuches, Pehuenches, and Huilliches, see Casanova Guarda, 1988, 149–68, 237–38; Casanueva, 1988, 237–38; Noggler, 1972, 83–92, and Pinto Rodríguez, 1988, 74–87, who offers an insightful view of the Franciscan *mentalité* in Chile and beyond. For the new climate, see also Foerster G., 1992, 17–18.

246. O'Higgins to the conde de Aranda, Plaza de Los Angeles, Jan. 7, 1793, MM, vol. 201, no. 4963 ("las misiones que gastan anualmente muchos pesos sin otro fruto que el de cubrir la real conciencia").

247. Casanova Guarda, 1988, 167–68, notes O'Higgins's interest in 1793; Osorno would be reestablished in 1796.

248. Gov. O'Higgins to fray Benito Delgado, padre guardián del Colegio de Chillán, Santiago, Dec. 2, 1793, quoted in Pinto Rodríguez, 1988, 85 ("cualquier maquinación o perfidia de los indios"; "de la beneficiencia de los españoles, infundiéndoles subordinación, amor y respeto a nuestro gobierno."). For Franciscans' own view of their progress, see Ascasubi, 1846, 1:388–89.

249. Pinto Rodríguez, 1988, 85; Noggler, 1972, 89, 142.

250. Pinto Rodríguez, 1988, 86–87, summarizing Padre Delgado's reply to O'Higgins, Chillán, Dec. 30, 1793.

251. Foerster G., 1992, 26–28.

252. Padre Inocencio Cañete to the Ministerio de Estado, [Asunción?], Dec. 19, 1795, speaking of Payaguás infants in Paraguay. Gondra Collection, Calendar no. 2108 [MG 826], University of Texas, Austin ("es menos incombeniente dejarlos en la infidelidad, que bautizarlos, y abandonarlos, a las supersticiones, que ven en sus padres infieles"). Azara, 1969–72, 6:418 ("imprudente prostitución del bautismo").

253. Casanueva, 1992a, 27–28. Chillán, an offshoot of the Ocopa college, had been given the Chiloé mission field in 1768, after the bishop failed to staff it with secular clergy. Chillán did briefly utilize the circuit system in Chiloé, but it gave that mission field up in 1771, partly because it lacked enough missionaries for each town, and the crown put it in the care of Ocopa. Urbina Burgos, 1990, 6, 8, 11, 14, 49–77. The bishop of Concepción ordered Ocopa to maintain the Jesuit system (ibid., p. 159). For the friars in little boats (*piraguas*), see González de Agüeros, 1988, 41, 66–69.

254. Casanueva, 1992b, 201–10 ("al suave yugo de la ley de Jesucristo").

255. Francisco Javier Alday, Santiago, Jan. 24, 1804, quoted in Lagos, 1908, 406–15. The quotations are on p. 408 ("que voluntariamente se sometieron al suave yugo del Evangelio"; "deberes cristianos"). Called to my attention by Foerster G., 1992, 24–25. See, too, Foerster G., 1992, 56 n.57, Bishop Francisco José Marán to José de Gálvez, Concepción, Aug. 28, 1784, in

Hanisch, 1990, 110–45, and Ascasubi, 1846, 1:300–400, for the Franciscans' modest progress.

256. President of the real audiencia, Muñoz de Guzmán, n.d., quoted in Lagos, 1908, 419 ("suavidad, prudencia y lenidad"). The opinions of the governor and the intendant are on pp. 415–17. Only the *fiscal* disagreed.

257. Neve to Bishop Reyes, Dec. 29, 1783, in Geiger, 1959, 2:368–69. The figures are in Weber, 1992, 262–63.

258. The first two quotations come from the report of Bishop Francisco José Marán to José de Gálvez, Concepción, Aug. 28, 1784, in Hanisch, 1990, 122, a detailed look at the missions in response to a query from Gálvez ("en una lamentable dispersión," "sobradamente repugnante a la civilidad"); the third is from Ascasubi, 1846, 1:388 ("envueltos en las funestras tinieblas de la infidelidad"), whose figures I rely upon (pp. 397–400). Missionaries enjoyed most success at places like Niebla near Valdivia, where years of contact with Spaniards seem to have had an acculturating effect and where disease reduced the native population. Lagos, 1908, 274–77.

259. From 1773 to 1790, friars who worked out of the plaza of Valdivia in Chile received a daily ration of bread and beef jerky for their neophytes, in addition to the *sínodos*. Lagos, 1908, 375–86. I do not mean to overdraw the picture. Chile's sparse missions did produce some surpluses for its presidios by the 1760s, if not before. León Solís, 1990, 106. Although California mission production in general was high, neophytes themselves often received inadequate nourishment, and production varied among missions. Brandes, 1992, 2:165–66; Costello, 1989, 435–49. There is a large literature on the quality of the mission diets, which often represented a decline in diversity of foods. See, for example, Larsen, Schoeninger, Hutchinson, Russell, and Ruff, 1990.

260. Rafael Verger, guardian of the College of San Fernando, to Viceroy Bucareli, Mexico, Dec. 25, 1772, in Ponç i Fullano, 1990, 271 ("inconquistable"; "el modo de pelear, la calidad de nuestras armas").

261. Report of Bishop Francisco José Marán to José de Gálvez, Concepción, Aug. 28, 1784, and Ambrosio Benavides to José de Gálvez, Santiago, July 5, 1785, both in Hanisch, 1990, 144–45, 157–59.

262. Ricklis, 1996, 158.

263. Santamaría, 1994b, 285, quoting Marcos Ignacio Baldovinos, 1797. The historian Saeger, 2000, 31, tells us that the populations of Guaycuruan missions in general "were constantly changing as mounted Guaycuruans arrived and left."

264. Ramos Pérez, 1976b, 522–24, 526–30.

265. In the archbishopric of Mexico, 24 percent of the parishes were in hands of regular clergy in 1756; by 1765 the figure had fallen to 14 percent; none remained by the late 1770s. Gruzinski, 1985, 183. Taylor, 1996, 564 n.39, points to the relative swiftness of secularization in the dioceses of Mexico, Guadala-

jara, and Michoacán compared to Yucatán and Oaxaca. See, too, Guerra Moscoso, 1996. The diocese of Caracas, with no active missions among the *infieles* and just six mature but poor Indian parishes administered by Franciscans, secularized all six within a year (although they later tried to get two back). Gómez Canedo, 1974–75, 1:117–20, 162, 249–84.

266. Ezpeleta, 1910, 309 ("los progresos de los regulares en las reducciones que tienen a su cargo debían medirse más bien por el número de los pueblos que hubiesen entregado al Ordinario Eclesiástico, que por el de indios extraídos de los bosques y reducidos a población"). For New Granada alone, there was consistent criticism from the viceroys. See, for example, Messía de la Zerda [Cerda], 1910, 98, and Caballero y Góngora, 1910, 1:229, Mendinueta, 1910, 418–23. For New Spain, see Felipe de Neve (who succeeded Teodoro de Croix as commander), "Relación concisa y exacta del estado en que ha encontrado las Provincias Internas," Arizpe, Dec. 1, 1783, AGI, Guadalajara 268, 43. Copy, courtesy of Charles Cutter.

267. Floridablanca, 1876, 226 (art. XCL: "parajes incultos y distantes"), makes this point. The shortage of *curas* was evident throughout frontier zones. It affected all of northern New Spain, for example, hindering efforts at secularization. As late as 1791, only ten of the fifty-two Indian parishes in the bishopric of Durango had secular priests—Franciscans staffed the remainder, including sixteen in New Mexico, where friars also continued to serve in lieu of *curas* until the end of the colonial era. Porras Muñoz, 1980, 202; Weber, 1982, 59. For shortages elsewhere, see Block, 1994, 133–34, Ganuza, 1921, 1:226, González del Campo, 1984, 210, Urbina Burgos, 1990, 7–8, 11, 103–08.

268. López, 1974, 490. See, too, Leutenegger and Habig, 1978, and Schuetz, 1980, 183–98, who confirms the mixed-blood population of the missions.

269. De la Teja, 1998, 114, quoting Governor Cabello in 1779. A fifth mission, San Antonio de Valero, which had the largest income, was secularized entirely. Weber, 1982, 53–56. Leutenegger and Habig, 1978, 8, notes the annual payment of *sínodos* to the friars until 1816. For interest in converting Comanches, see Alcocer, 1958, 178. Officials faced shortages of *curas* in frontier areas everywhere. For northeastern Mexico ably summarized, see Morales Valerio, 1992, 189–91, Urbina Burgos, 1990, 38, for Franciscans serving Spaniards as well as Indian parishes of Chiloé until the end of the colonial era, and Carrocera 1968, 1:402–03, for the crown's 1805 suspension of an 1803 order to secularize missions in Cumaná because of the shortage of *curas*. The bishop of Durango had planned to send missionaries to the Comanches as early as 1788. Tristán, 1788, 24–25.

270. In 1753, against the advice of the governor of

Cumaná and the bishop of Puerto Rico, the crown
ordered that sixteen secularized Capuchino missions
(ten secularized in 1713 and six in 1739), be returned
to the Capuchinos as the secular priests in charge
died or resigned, and the order was carried out. Carrocera, 1968, 1:318–20; fray Silvestre de Zaragoza sobre
el estado de doctrinas y misiones, San Angel de
Caripe, Jan. 17, 1771, ibid., 3:335–52. Laserna Gaitán,
1989, 136. See, too, Mantilla, 2000, 2:40–44, for
the secularization of the Andaquíes mission of San
Javier de Ceja in 1773 and its return to Franciscans
in 1777.

271. Revillagigedo, 1966a, 114–15 ("no estoy muy conforme con las misiones que se han secularizado";
"los curas clérigos no pueden hacer más que los religiosos; y si éstos no alcanzan al desempeño de sus
pueblos de misión, resultará precisa consecuencia
que los indios mudarán"). See, too, Viedma, 1969a–
72a, 6:712–16, who urged giving power back to *curas*
rather than to administrators at Moxos and Chiquitos
in 1793. Bravo Guerreira, 1995, 46, cites Viedma on
this point, but Viedma wrote this in 1793, not 1788,
as she says.

272. Revillagigedo, 1966a, 116, quoting the marqués de
Ensenada to Revillagigedo, the elder, in 1753 ("Más
servicio hará a Su Majestad en adelantar la conversion de las almas, en evitar escándalos y administrar
justicia que enviarle todos los tesoros de las Indias").
Marchena Fernández, 1993, 526, taking this document out of context, mistakenly assumes that royal
officials in general wished to turn northern New
Spain into a "frontera misional."

273. Radding, 1997, 38, 113–15, 158–65. Radding, 2001,
83–84, contrasts the Sonora missions, with their
proximity to markets, to the less favored missions
of Chiquitos. Indeed, with or without Bourbon encouragement, there was a "high degree of integration" between Spanish towns and haciendas and
missions located near them. Cramaussel, 2000, 299–
300.

274. Marmión, 1964, 451.

275. Gálvez to the Governor of Cumaná, Nov. 18, 1782,
quoted at length in Laserna Gaitán, 1989, 144 ("humanidad"; "como a individuos de otra especie"; "los
tratan peor que a esclavos"). Administrators of mission Indian property in Cumaná were "capitanes
conservadores" and "corregidores."

276. The quotation is from an anonymous critic of 1788,
in Urbina Burgos, 1990, 88 ("no fueron conquistados,
sino aprisionados"). González Rodríguez, 1992a,
540, suggests that "de las pocas misiones vivas que
quedaban a comienzos del XIX, parece que sólo las
de los capuchines de Guayana permanecían cer-
radas a los foráneos," but additional study may reveal
that the number is much larger. Several sources provide comprehensive overviews of missions in the
colonial era (the most recent example being essays

in Borges, 1992c, vol. 2), but they fail to discuss the
actual impact of the Bourbon reforms on specific
missions. More research needs to be done, but some
idea of the widespread continuance of traditional
missions in the face of the Bourbon reforms can be
found in the following: fray Francisco Rauzet de
Jesús, 1786, in Sheridan and Naylor, 1979; pastoral
letter of the bishop of Panama, Remigio de la Santa
y Ortega, Santiago de Veraguas, Oct. 19, 1795, in Arcila Robledo, 1953, 243–45 (for missions among
Guaymíes, Gualacas, and others in Chiriquí beginning in the 1780s); Castillero, 1995, 391–427 (a devastating critique of the continuance of traditional
missions in Panama); Gómez Canedo, 1967, 1:xxxiv–
xxxv; lxii–lviii; 2:195, 297; Alcácer, 1962, chap. 8, for
the Motilones in the mountainous region south of
the Maracaibo basin; Martínez Cuesta, 1995, 661–
62, for the Meta River; Amich, 1988, 239–51; Carrocera, 1968, 1:354–55, 364–65, 368–75, 403, for
Guaraúnos in the Orinoco delta; Meigs, 1935, for
Baja California; Gullón Abao, 1993, 168, 172, for the
western Chaco; Saignes, 1990, 85–126, and Calzavarini, 1980, 210–12, for Chiriguanos; Urbina Burgos,
1990, 85–88, 99–108, for Chiloé and the attempted
reforms of Francisco Hurtado (1786–89). Bourbon
efforts to exert indirect control over frontier missions
failed in some areas, as exemplified in Sonora, where
in 1793 the *comandante general* abolished the *custodia*
established by Bishop Reyes, and governance returned to the status quo ante. Gómez Canedo, 1971,
33–41.

277. Acevedo, 1964–65, 46–47, describing responses to
a viceregal plan. The intendant of Salta, Andrés
Mestre, imagined traditional missions (p. 55), while
the intendant of Paraguay, Joaquín de Alós, thought
missions were "useless and unnecessary" ("inútil y
supervacáneo"), and it would be better to build towns
of Spaniards to civilize Indians (p. 49). In any event,
funds to construct missions and forts along the Bermejo were not forthcoming. Acevedo, 1965, 387–92.
See Casanova Guarda, 1988, 167, for O'Higgins's
plan of 1793.

278. Borges, 1992b, 487, 491, who also sees Chiloé and
the Río Negro of Venezuela as exceptions. For the
limited nature of the published data, see ibid., 491–
93.

279. The most dramatic expansion occurred on the Meta
River, where between 1773 and 1805 Augustinians
established six new missions among Achaguas, Sálivas, and even long-resistant Guahibos. Rausch, 1984,
107–22, provides a fine overview (and for Guahibos'
resistance 19, 38, 141, 206, and Morey and Metzger,
1974, 14). Rausch argues against a historiography
that sees missions in the llanos in decline after 1767
and distinguishes between the achievements of each
of these religious orders. She puts the number of
mission Indians at 15,679 in 1800 (p. 121). Jesuits op-

erated a third of these missions in 1767, but they were among the largest, including nearly half of the mission Indian population. Ibid., 62–63. See, too, Martínez Cuesta, 1995, 634, 660–74.

280. Mendinueta, 1910, 420 ("se notan pocos o ningunos adelantamientos en ellas").

281. Santa María, 1930, 426 n.27 ("errantes salvajes aún y bárbaros"; "mil a uno").

282. Norris, 2000, 150–53, paints a vivid picture of the moral lapses of friars in New Mexico in the late colonial period.

283. Mendinueta, 1910, 435–47; the quotations are on pp. 445 ("gentes civilizadas") and 435 ("no usar de género alguno de violencia para introducir la religión de paz y suavidad"). See, too, Revillagigedo, 1966a, 114, who otherwise defended traditional missions; Pedro de Nava to Revillagigedo, Chihuahua, Jan. 27, 1792, in Gómez Canedo 1971, 110, and Nava to the Governor of Texas, Chihuahua, April 10, 1794, in Habig, 1978–90, 2:94–95, for self-government and the ten-year rule. See, too, the failed efforts of Francisco Hurtado to challenge the hold Franciscans had over Chiloé, in Urbina Burgos, 1990, 101–08.

284. Campomanes, 1988, 265, for checking the English. Matson and Fontana, 1977, 39, 65, 81; Weber, 1992, 186–91, 253–56.

285. Floyd, 1967, 186, sees missions in 1800 as being where they were in 1760.

286. For the pampa, see Hernández Asensio, 2003, 77–108; for Argentine Patagonia, see Círculo Militar, 1973, 1:263–65; for Tierra del Fuego and the Strait of Magellan, see Urbina Burgos, 1990, 14, 32, 84–90.

287. Weber, 1992, 256; Cuesta Domingo, 1993, 293–342, who includes Murillo's diary (pp. 330–42); Arbesmann, 1945, 398, 411–16; Dueñas, 1792, 165 ("22 naciones de Gentiles"); Urbina Burgos, 1990, 90–97.

288. The quotations are from the diary of the treasurer of Maracaibo, Sebastián José Guillén, Maracaibo, Dec. 4, 1772, who set out with a Franciscan to convert Motilones peacefully. In Alcácer, 1962, 151–52 and 169, respectively ("Con aplauso y regocijo imponderable . . . como si fuésemos de su propia nación"; "Con la mayor prudencia y sagacidad, para que no lleguen a comprender (los indios) que instantemente se les oprime, privándoles de la antigua libertad en que han vivido"). Juan de la Cruz Cano y Olmedilla, *Mapa geográfica de América Meridional* (1775), in González Oropeza, 1987, 146 (lamina LXVI). See, too, the examples of the Mbayás, in chap. 2 above, and Tobas in Santamaría, 1994b, 284–87.

289. Saignes, 1990, 98–100.

290. Fray Antonio Comajuncosa, writing ca. 1810 (Corrado and Comajuncosa, 1990, 1:128) and discussing the mission of Salinas, some thirty leagues south of Tarija in a valley, where the neophytes were both Chiriguanos and Mataguayos ("ha sido preciso toler-

arlos algunos años en sus antiguas costumbres, para no exasperarlos; a abstenerse de todo castigo y violencia, para que no se escaparan a los bárbaros"; "dándoles bien de comer y beber, o pagándoles su jornal como a otro cualquiera").

291. Viedma, 1969b–72b, 6:763 ("presidio cerrado donde no entre persona alguna"), objecting to the missionaries' control over the temporal affairs of the Chiriguano missions (ibid., 760). Saignes, 1990, 124 ("control desde el interior"). For context, see Pifarré, 1989, 221–23. See, too, McCarty, 1981, 12, and Radding, 1997, 193.

292. Saignes, 1990, 98–100, 103, 119–26, whose argument contains subtleties that I lack space to develop. For a narrative of events and a view of Chiriguanos as more oppressed by missions, see Calzavarini, 1980, 181–205. Pifarré, 1989, 182–223, offers an orderly chronicle and analysis. For other examples of friars forced to tolerate "unacceptable" Indian behaviors lest Indians flee, see González González, 1977, 144, and Laserna Gaitán, 1993, 312–16, 334. Guaycuruans, whose demand for missions exceeded the supply in the late eighteenth century (ten of eighteen Guaycuruan missions were founded after the Jesuit expulsion), also appear to have used them as way stations, receiving more than they gave. Saeger, 2000, 29, 31, 41, 48, 64–65, 72–76, 180–94, and Appendix A on p. 195.

293. For failure among the Pampas south and west of Buenos Aires, see Aguirre, 1980, 1:55–66; for a case study of a short-lived Franciscan mission among Pampas near Córdova (1751–83), see Peña, 1997, 305–13. Bruno, 1992, 25–38, summarizes the failures in Patagonia.

294. Report of the Franciscan visitador Ortiz, quoted in Floyd, 1967, 100–101. See, too, the *real cédula* to the *capitán general* of Guatemala, San Lorenzo, Nov. 19, 1787, in Peralta, 1898, 262.

295. For Central America in general, see Newson, 1986, 246, 249, and García Añoveras, 1992, 251. For Talamancas, Guaymíes, and Cunas, see Castillero, 1995, 25, 367, 391–427; for Cunas and Guajiros, see Grahn, 1998, 259–70, and Kuethe, 1978, 130–50; for Cunas alone, see Mantilla R., 2000, 1:745–49; for Guajiros, see also Silvestre, 1950, 97–98; Grahn, 1995, 144–51, and Barrera Monroy, 2000, 52–68; for Caribs, see Ramos Pérez, 1976, 597–650, Gómez Parente, 1978, 473–974 [*sic*], Whitehead, 1988, 104–50, and Whitehead, 1999, 429 (who sees Caribs in Guayana as succumbing to Spanish force and missions by the 1770s partly because their trade relationship with the Dutch had ended); for Guaraúnos, residents of the Orinoco Delta estimated at five to six thousand, who obtained trade goods from the Dutch, see Heinen, 1980–88, 603; for Charrúas and Minuanes, see González Rissotto and Rodríguez Varese, 1991, 229–51, and Villegas, 1995, 97–111; for the Payaguás toward

the end of the century, see Vangelista, 1992, 160–63; for the Mbayás, see chap. 5 below.

Chapter 4. A Good War or a Bad Peace?

The epigraphs are from Viedma, 1969c–72c, 3:683–84 ("los indios salvajes, que a manera de un torrente impetuoso cada día inundan estos campos, llevándose tras sí innumerable ganado caballar y vacuno, asolando las tristes habitaciones de los vecinos fronterizos a esta capital, haciendo que los caminos no sean seguros, y víctimas de su furor a muchos desgraciados, que perecen inhumanamente cada día a sus manos, de un modo horrible y espantoso"), and Gálvez, 1951, art. 29 ("nos será más fructuosa una mala paz con todas la Naciones que la soliciten, que los esfuerzos de una buena guerra").

1. Serra y Canals, 1979, 45 ("infieles parricidas").
2. Ibid., 42–43 ("todo la inmensidad de este Nuevo Mundo"; "Ellos se nos roban nuestras mujeres, con las que se aumentan, y nuestras fronteras se destituyen y aniquilan"; "ha llegado al extremo de poner los ratones el cascabel al gato"). Concolorcorvo, 1965, 242, expresses similar sentiments in his well-known dialogic satire, which he published anonymously. Johnson, 1993, 109, provides a fine analysis.
3. Ibid., 48 ("sabandijas").
4. Ibid., 56, 53 ("Pólvora y bala"; "con el trabajo y sus salarios aprendiesen de racionalidad").
5. Ibid., 45 ("estos indómitos no tienen por donde escapar").
6. Ibid., 48 ("tales o peores que los indios infieles").
7. Serra y Canals, 1979, 44 ("el amor y piedad del Soberano no permite el que se les haga la guerra ofensiva y si solo defensiva"; "la ley natural que les prescribe la razón").
8. Haedo, 1872, 460 ("casi no se hallará casa alguna en las nominadas provincias en que diariamente no se reza el rosario de nuestra señora y que no se ejerciten otros actos de religión"). His plan of 1777 anticipates Serra y Canals. A biographical sketch is in Furlong, 1948, 400. Haedo lived en Córdoba as early as 1759, where he served as a *maestre de campo*. See, too, the economist Fernando Echeverz, who in 1742 recommended the formation of a private company that would expel the English from the Mosquito Coast and conquer the Zambos at its own expense. Echeverz, 1742, pt. 1, par. 50, reproduced in its entirety in Saenz de Santa María, 1982 (see p. 168). On *proyectismo*, see Muñoz Pérez, 1955.
9. Gullón Abao, 1993, 80–81. Gullón Abao offered the smuggling hypothesis to me in a personal conversation, Sevilla, February 1999. For Viceroy Bucareli on Matorra's reputation, see Brizuela, 1969–72, 250.
10. Capitán del voluntarios de Huancavelica, Josef Antonio del Castillo to the king, Madrid, March 22, 1776, AGI, Charcas 574. Castillo apparently submitted an earlier version of this plan. See the report

by Tomás Ortiz de Landazuri, [Madrid?], Oct. 26, 1775, which summarizes Castillo's project and the opinion of the viceroy of Peru, March 9, 1772. AGI, BA 21, transcript in the Museum of Ethnology, Buenos Aires (Palermo, 1992, J24).

11. A general *informe* by Carvajal, March 27, 1787, in AGB, Chiquitos, vol. 28 (1787). Azara, 1969–72, 6:424, lambasted still other *proyectistas* for their high-sounding rhetoric and their self-interested motives. In 1801, Viceroy Avilés similarly condemned a private plan to fortify and colonize the Bermejo in the Chaco as self-serving. Avilés, 1945, 505.
12. Fray Pedro Serrano to Viceroy Cruillas, 1761, quoting fray Andrés Varo, in Hackett, 1923–37, 3:490–91; Garavaglia, 1984, 24–26; Garavaglia, 1987, 228–30; Santamaría, 1999, 17–21; Avilés, 1945, 533; Concha, 1949, 244–45.
13. Marchena Fernández, 1992, 138–40; Brading, 1971, 25–35. On the trade in Indian captives, which motivated common soldiers as well as officers, see Doucet, 1988, 87, 106–07, and 109–14.
14. Viceroy Antonio María Bucareli to Julián de Arriaga, Mexico, Dec. 27, 1772, in Velasco Ceballos, 1936, 1:73 ("la variedad de informes y dictámenes obscurecen la verdad"). See, too, Bucareli to Arriaga, Mexico, Oct. 27, 1772, and Bucareli to Teodoro de Croix, Aug. 27, 1777, in ibid., 1:70, 369.
15. Campomanes, 1988, 22 ("terrenos desproveídos de oro o plata quedaron totalmente abandonados"), writing in 1762.
16. These dates can be found in standard reference works, except for the change in Chile, which I take from Navarro García, 1991, 229. Historians often assume that Chile was a *capitanía general* prior to 1778, confused by the fact that governors who had the proper military rank might be called captains-general, although the area over which they presided were not *capitanías*. Haring, 1947, 77–78. For example, on Feb. 6, 1774, the crown addressed Agustín de Jáuregui, as Gobernador y Capitán General del Reyno de Chile y Presidente de mi Audiencia de la Ciudad de Santiago (see below n.97). I am simplifying these administrative changes in Venezuela, which occurred in stages and which has remained a subject of controversy. See González Oropeza and Donis Ríos, 1989, 112–26. See Del Rey Fajardo, 1995, 62–65, for eastern Venezuela. Navarro García, 1991, 160, has called the Interior Provinces of New Spain a "frustrated viceroyalty" since they remained financially dependent upon the viceroy in Mexico City ("un virreinato frustrado").
17. Felipe de Neve, "Relación concisa y exacta del estado en que ha encontrado las Provincias Internas," Arizpe, Dec. 1, 1783, AGI, Guadalajara 268, copy, courtesy of Charles Cutter ("a facilitar y conseguir la paz"; "durante la hostilidad no pueden florecer la agricultura, y cría de ganados, ni la minería, y

comercio que tienen entre sí íntima relación"). See, too, Neve to Gálvez, Arispe, Jan. 26, 1784, and Neve to Gálvez, Arispe, March 8, 1784, AGI, Guadalajara 519. For a contrary view, see K. Jones, 1998, 102, who argues that "while raiding economies clearly impeded the development of colonial settlements, raiding was not intrinsically detrimental. This process simultaneously opened up tremendous new opportunities for trade for all parties involved."

18. I discuss Pampas in chap. 2, and Charrúas late in this chapter.

19. Saignes, 1990, 160.

20. Flagler, 1997, 193–215; Brooks, 1999, 26.

21. "Razón de la gente y petrechos que se necesitan para resguardo de esta Provincia de Chiquitos en el caso de Guerra," March 1, 1801, in AGB, MyCh XXXIII EC.1801 no. 94.

22. Campomanes, 1988, 92 n.33, who had consulted a French translation published in Geneva in 1750 of Anson, 1748. See, too, 27–32, 53, for Campomanes's concerns about North and Central America, based on reports from overseas officials. For Anson's base in 1741, see O'Donnell, 1992, 239. For concerns expressed from Chile, see the pioneering article by Couyoudmjian Bergamali, 1971, 57–176, and two deeply researched articles, León Solís, 1994b, 313–22, and León Solís, 2001a, 117–51. In the latter he elaborates on the long history of non-Spanish navigation and intelligence gathering in the region. Falkner's book, published in London in 1774, was immediately translated into Spanish, although it was not published in Spanish until 1910. Many writers have noted Falkner's influence on Spanish policy, but see especially Navarro Floria, 1994a, 31–34, 45–46. He errs, however, in asserting that the work was not translated until 1910 (p. 31). For a Spanish manuscript translation of 1774, see Paz, Olaran, and Jalón, 1992, 329, no. 1102. The 1774 edition is reprinted in facsimile in Falkner, 1935. See, too, Furlong, 1938, 14.

23. O'Higgins, "Descripción del Reyno de Chile," Madrid, Sept. 2, 1767, in Donoso, 1941, 439–40 ("mientras estemos a cada instante irritando y golpeando a los indios de las Fronteras haciéndose de enemigos intestinos").

24. Marchena Fernández, 1992, 91–210, provides an overview of the causes, nature, and consequences of Spain's military buildup and guidance to sources, including his own earlier work, Marchena Fernández, 1983, which explores some aspects of this buildup in greater depth.

25. Report of March 27, 1787, Santa Cruz, AGB, Chiquitos, vol. 28 (1787). Don Antonio López Carvajal, *capitán de infantería y teniente del regimiento de Saboya*, was named *gobernador interino* de Chiquitos July 3, 1786. René-Moreno, 1973, 357, reference courtesy of Cynthia Radding.

26. Brading, 1971, 27.

27. Pérez de Ribas, 1999, 700, speaking in 1645 of the way to conquer Chichimecas. Kuethe, 1970, 471, 481, is one of several authors who sees a "hardening imperial policy" in the Bourbon era and a decline in missionary influence. See, too, Weber, 1992, 145–46, 214.

28. The Jesuit Bernardo Rotell to the governor and *capitán general* in Caracas, 1743, quoted in Del Rey Fajardo, 1995, 52 ("es moralmente imposible hacer misión permanente mientras haya caribes en Orinoco"); Joseph Rodríguez to Gov. Luis Alvarez de Naba, July 27, 1767, Misiones de Chiquitos, AGB, Chiquitos, vol. 23, XXXIV (1767) ("solo han nacido para robar, matar, y destruir a todo no Guaicurús"). Also see the "Informe del excmo. sr. d. Pedro Felipe, obispo de la Concepción, sobre los curatos de la diócesis," Concepción, March 30, 1744, to the presidente [of the audiencia of Chile]" in Gay, 1846–52, 1:523, and the remarkable statement of Bishop Abad Illana of Tucumán, 1771, in Vitar, 1997, 301.

29. Gálvez's instructions appear in Priestley, 1916, 404–17. On the military buildup in New Spain, see Velázquez, 1950, and Archer, 1977. Both works focus on central New Spain, mentioning the northern frontier only in passing. As Velázquez points out, fighting Indians required troops who fought by different rules in a different way than the regular army or the militia (p. 92).

30. This is evident in Gálvez's "Discurso y reflexiones de un vasallo sobre la decadencia de nuestras Indias españolas [ca. 1760]," Ayala, MS 2816, Biblioteca del Palacio Real, Madrid (published in Navarro García, 1998), which he wrote prior coming to America. In that document only Miskitos, who harbored Englishmen, concerned him.

31. Pfefferkorn, 1989, 43. A Jesuit who served in Sonora in 1756–67, Pfefferkorn described the destruction vividly.

32. Sheridan, 1999, 19–20, 139–42; quotation, p. 141. Mirafuentes Galván, 2000, 591–612.

33. "Relación" of the expedition to Sonora, Mexico City, Sept. 1, 1771, unsigned but clearly written by Elizondo or by his commanders under his oversight, translated into English in Sheridan, 1999, 278; reproduced in Spanish, p. 345 ("si se presentaran a pelear cara a cara en parajes regulares con la tropa que había en los presidios y algunos auxiliares"). I have used my own translation.

34. Mirafuentes Galván, 1987, 24, quoted the testimony of a soldier who fought Seris in 1757 "vosotros sois guapos en el llano, pero en los bosques y las montañas nosotros").

35. Rodríguez Gallardo, 1975 ("No hay adagio más verdadero que los del pan y el palo para tener al indio sujeto").

36. Gálvez, edict, May 8, 1769, Bay of Santa Barbara [at the mouth of the Rio Mayo], in Spanish and in

English in Sheridan, 1999, 311–12, 373 ("reos de la Lesa Majestad divina y humana"; "extinguirlos, y que no quede más memoria de ellos que la de haber perecido a sangre y fuego"). I have used my own translation rather than Sheridan's. *Recopilación*, 1973, Libro 3, tit. 4, ley 8 ("perdonar los delitos de rebelión, que huvieren cometido, aunque sean contra Nos, y nuestro servicio"). See, too, Libro 4, tit. 4, ley 8; Libro 4, tit. 7, ley 23. Moreno y Escandón, 1936, 575, cited the Laws of the Indies in pardoning Indians. Levaggi, 1997, 106–07 n.4, provides numerous examples of official clemency.

37. Merrill, 2000, 636, who quotes at length Neve to José de Gálvez, Arizpe, March 8, 1784, and an anonymous letter writer, Chihuahua, May 29, 1784, published in the *Gazeta de México* 14 (July 14, 1784): 116. The viceregal approved of Rengel's decision. My thanks to William Merrill.

38. *Recopilación*, 1973, Libro 3, tit. 4, leyes 10, 11.

39. Ibid., leyes 9, 10 ("guerra abierta y formada"; "y no más"). There is a large literature on just war, but see Tanzi, 1974, 119, and Hanke, 1949. For an example of the continued invocation of the Royal Orders for New Discoveries of 1573, which specified only peaceful expansion, see José de Gálvez's instructions to the viceroy of the Río de la Plata, the marqués de Loreto, in 1784. Gálvez, 1873, 579 (no. 28). Velázquez, 1979, 66, argues that the Royal Regulations of 1772 for the Interior Provinces of New Spain signaled the crown's abandonment of the 1573 policy of "penetración pacífica," but it appears more likely that the crown made an exception specific to time and place.

40. Moreno y Escandón, 1936, 575 ("de suerte"; "apóstatas y rebeldes"; "con menos recelo").

41. *Recopilación*, 1973, Libro 3, tit. 4, ley 8 ("a nuestro real servicio con suavidad y paz, sin guerra, robos, ni muertes").

42. The Minister of the Indies, Julián de Arriaga, speaking for the king to the Marqués de Croix, April 25, 1770, quoted in Navarro García, 1964, 186 ("por vía de fuerza no se lograría el fin deseado"). Priestley, 1916, 271, notes the king's earlier opposition to war in Nov. and Dec. 1768, a matter not treated by Navarro García, who notes that the crown also objected through Arriaga on July 26, 1769 (pp. 185–86).

43. See above, n. 33 ("es preciso buscarlos por sus rastros como a las fieras"). I have used my own translation.

44. This paragraph is drawn from the introduction to documents in Sheridan, 1999, and Navarro García, 1964, 165–66, 170–87.

45. Tristán, 1788, 14 ("el arte de pelear y vencer los indios").

46. Malone, 1991, 128, and Taylor, 2001, 429.

47. Saignes, 1990, 131–32, quotes this officer without identifying him. For his analysis of women's roles in warfare, see 132–33.

48. Recorded ca. 1795 in Nuevo Santander by a Franciscan; he uses infinitives possibly in an attempt to convey Indians' use of Spanish. Santa María, 1930, 415–16 ("como venado y nunca morir con cuchillo ni con balazo. Mi marido y mi hijo, morir; otro mi marido también morir; yo lo vi, tanta sangre, tanto susto, tanto llorar y yo no poder sanar"; "soldado ahora valiente como lobo; indio cobarde como conejo, huyendo").

49. Keeley, 1996, 74. Radding, 1995, 92, suggests that Spain's dependence on auxiliary Indian troops to subject the indigenous peoples of Sonora to the power of the state represented a "fundamental contradiction." Such a contradiction was endemic to the colonial enterprise.

50. Unzaga to Piernas, New Orleans, Aug. 21, 1772, quoted in Din and Nasatir, 1983, 82.

51. Rollings, 1992, 169, 185–87.

52. León Solís, 1982, 35, argues that writers have given Spaniards too much credit for sowing internal discord among Indians, without realizing that Indians had ample reasons of their own for wanting discord. Spaniards, he says, preferred to end internal Indian wars rather than encourage them. That happened on occasion—as with the Treaty of Nogales that I discuss in chap. 5—but they seem like the exception.

53. Navarro García, 1964, 184–85.

54. "Relación of the expedition to Sonora," Mexico City, Sept. 1, 1771, unsigned but clearly written by Elizondo or by his commanders under his oversight. Translated into English in Sheridan, 1999, 343, which also contains the Spanish text, p. 402 ("tratarlos con amor, y dulzura, gobernándolos con prudencia y desterrando aquel trato de esclavitud con que han sido manejados, motivo por el que se exasperaron muchos y causaron las sublevaciones").

55. Navarro García, 1964, 184–85.

56. Along with cases described in this chapter, see Sheridan, 2000, 230–36.

57. José Perfecto de Salas, "Informe Sobre el Reino de Chile," Santiago, March 5, 1750, in Donoso, 1963, 1:119 ("ficción"), 120 ("tan bárbaros, fieros e inhumanos, ha hallado mi experiencia mansos, dóciles y racionales"), called to my attention by Villalobos R., 1992, 263 ("el negocio de guerra"). For Chile also see Cerda-Hegerl, 1990, 19–36, 89–92, who sees as too simple the argument that the military artificially extended the war and suggests that the military profited from slave raids into Araucanian territory and so maintained conflict (p. 30). By the 1700s, though, the market for Indian slaves had declined, by her own account (p. 88). Ortelli, 2003b, chaps. 1, 2, finds an analogous "war as a business" on the Apache frontier of Nueva Vizcaya in the mid-1700s and argues that Apaches were scapegoats (p. 442); Teruel, 1994, 230–31, 336, describes the same phenomenon in the Chaco.

58. O'Conor to Viceroy Bucareli, Chihuahua, Dec. 20, 1771, in Rubio Mañé, 1959a, 376, 374, called to my attention by Santiago, 1994, 35.

59. Cortés, 1989, 28–30, and see below, chap. 5. For a sixteenth-century example of the same dichotomous views, see Powell, 1952, 43–54, 189.

60. Neve to Gálvez, Arispe, March 8, 1784, AGI, Guadalajara 519 ("ultramarino"; "a donde no les quede esperanza de volver jamás a su país"; "inconstancia, perfidia, soberbia, y demás detestables vicios de los indios Seris"). The crown's approval, dated July 29, 1784, is noted on Neve's letter. For Neve's general philosophy, see Felipe de Neve, "Relación concisa y exacta del estado en que ha encontrado las Provincias Internas," Arizpe, Dec. 1, 1783, AGI, Guadalajara 268. Earlier, he made an exception in the case of California Indians. See Beilharz, 1971, 3, 116, 157–58.

61. See O'Conor, 1994, 35–45.

62. These were the conclusions of Antonio de Bonilla, who never saw the Apache frontier but who in 1772 summarized officers' reports from archival sources. West, 1904, 39, 60.

63. The rancher–Indian fighter Joseph de Castillo y Terán to Rubí, Monclova, June 27, 1767, in Jackson and Foster, 1995, 168.

64. Rubí made his recommendations as he went along but summarized some of them in Rubí, 1982 (the first two quotations are on pp. 56 and 49, respectively). Here he refers to the Lipan Apaches specifically but by extension to all of them ("como necesario el total exterminio de los Lipanes, o, por lo menos, su entera reducción"; "chusma de bárbaros"). Lafora, 1958, 216–17; Lafora, 1939, 280 ("la guerra ofensiva, continuada, en su propia casa"). For Rubí's tour, see Weber, 1992, 204–20.

65. Lafora, 1958, 216; Lafora, 1939, 278–79 ("jamás correrá tanto y tan largo tiempo como un indio"; "¿siendo como imposible sorprenderles o alcarzarles en las [tierras] nuestras, porque no iremos a las suyas?").

66. *Reglamento e instrucción para los presidios que se han de formar en la línea de frontera de la Nueva España* (Madrid, 1772) ("viva e incesante guerra, y en cuanto sea posible atacarlos en sus mismas rancherías y terrenos"). Facsimile and translation in Brinckerhoff and Faulk, 1965, 30–32.

67. For the law requiring peace offers before battle, see *Recopilación*, 1973, Libro 3, tit. 4, ley 9. The regulations of 1772, art. 10, tit. 2 (Brinckerhoff and Faulk, 1965, 30–33) prohibited frontier officers from granting Apaches anything more than a truce and empowered only the viceroy to set the terms of a peace. Moorhead, 1968, 118–19.

68. In Mills and Taylor, 1998, 287, whose translation is superior to Concolorcorvo, 1965. Carrió probably heard this story when, as a young man, he spent a decade, 1735–45, in Mexico, traveling as a merchant as far north as Chihuahua. Bataillon, 1960, 199; Concolorcorvo [Alonso Carrió de la Vandera], 1959, 247.

69. O'Conor, 1994, 73, writing in 1777, noted that "last year, 1773," Lipan Apaches made peace. See, too, Bonilla, 1776, art. 23, who noted that Lipan Apaches had been "admitted" to the presidios of San Juan Bautista, Monclova, and Santa Rosa. The question of when to accept a surrender was never satisfactorily resolved. In 1788, Viceroy Manuel Antonio Flores ordered that Apaches who surrendered during battle should be treated as prisoners of war; those who surrendered without military coercion, on the other hand, might be put into peace settlements. Moorhead, 1968, 193.

70. Its predecessor, the Reglamento of 1729, condensed and translated in Naylor and Polzer, 1988, 235–80, articles 41–43 and 190–95 (see in particular 193). See, too, Hadley, Naylor, and Schuetz-Miller, 1997, 191.

71. Fray José Ignacio María Alegre y Capetillo described the dangerous results of a separate peace by the commander at El Paso in 1771 and noted that a viceregal order dating to 1749 had prohibited such arrangements. Rubio Mañé, 1959b, 411–12, 421–24.

72. Vértiz y Salcedo, 1945, 150 ("por su fisonomía, vestuario, o otros accidentes exteriores"). See, too, Saeger, 2000, 41.

73. O'Conor, 1994, 81, and facsimile p. 82 ("abrazar a un mismo tiempo todo el terreno que ocupan los pérfidos apaches de oriente a poniente, y de sur a norte"). See, too, for example, O'Conor to Riperdá, Nuestra Señora del Carmen, May 6, 1773, in Velasco Ceballos, 1936, 1:124, and Santiago, 1994, 26, 29, 35–73.

74. Brinckerhoff and Faulk, 1965, title 10, article 1, p. 30 ("declaradamente enemigos").

75. Rubí, 1982, 80 ("una ocasión de abuso contra toda humanidad y derecho de las gentes"; "los vecinos que los tratan como esclavos, llegando hasta el extremo de venderlos").

76. Brinckerhoff and Faulk, 1965, title 10, article 3, pp. 32–33 ("muy posible que desterrada por el interés la crueldad con que tantas veces los han asesinado [los prisioneros], vayan despertándose en esos indios los sentimientos de humanidad").

77. With royal authorization, officials in Nueva Vizcaya deported Tobosos and Coahuiltecos in 1723 and 1726. Griffen, 1969, 63–70. Article 190 of the Regulations of 1729 required sending prisoners of war to the "outskirts of Mexico City." Translated in Naylor and Polzer, 1988, 279. See, too, Zavala, 1981, 286–88, 295, 300–07, who makes the point that these Indian captives of the late colonial period were not legally slaves (p. 300). See chap. 6, below, for more on the enslavement of Indians and the earlier rationalization of "just war."

78. Archer, 1973a, 376–85, and Moorhead, 1975b, 205–22,

explore the evolution of the policy and the practice. Moorhead wrote in apparent ignorance of Archer's earlier work.

79. Tristán, 1788, 12 ("a sangre fría en las cárceles de Durango y Plaza de Chihuahua").

80. Teodoro de Croix to Gov. Ripperdá, Chihuahua, Sept. 15, 1778, in John, 2001, 564 (and p. 570) for the Karankawas; Peralta, 1898, 126, for a recommendation of 1742 to send Miskitos to the Windward Islands. For Guajiros, see below, this chap.

81. Vértiz y Salcedo, 1945, 150–52; quotation, 151 ("me pareció justo sorprenderle"), and Crivelli Montero, 1991, 17–18, for the context (spellings vary, including "Linco Pangui").

82. Santa Marta, Aug. 31, 1787, quoted in González Luna, 1978, 117 ("aún prescindiendo de que fuese lícito y justo expatriar así a unos hombres que jamás han reconocido el vasallaje"). For sending Hispanic deserters to the Malvinas, see Operé, 2001, 125.

83. Sources for Apaches and Seris are above. For Osages, see Luis de Unzaga in Din and Nasatir, 1983, 82; for Karankawas, see Teodoro de Croix in John, 2001, 570. Gullón Abao, 1993, 79, notes increased use of the word "extermination" in the Chaco; Ramon de Castro, the comandante of the eastern Interior Provinces of New Spain, advocated the extermination of Chichimecas, as quoted in Revillagigedo, 1966a, 88.

84. Draft of a letter from Capt. General Unzaga to Juan Antonio Rodríguez, Caracas, Sept. 13, 1780, sobre la creación de un nuevo tenientazgo del otro lado del Rio Apure, AGN, Caracas, Gobernación y Capitanía General, Tomo 24 (1780), folio 18 ("hasta su total exterminio"). See, too, Thomas, 1941, 93.

85. See, for example, Lafora, 1958, 216–17, and the application of the regulations of 1772, discussed above, and Antonio de Bonilla, Mexico, Nov. 10, 1772, who had not fought Apaches but, basing his views on reports of fellow officers, wished that "this detestable nation be exterminated." West, 1904, 60.

86. Powell, 1952, part 3, suggests that "the viceregal government had held back from this type of 'total war'" (p. 275 n.8) in the sixteenth-century war against the Chichimecas. His own evidence seems to contradict this. In effect, officials did fight a "guerra a fuego y a sangre" against the Chichimecas, although they professed "to punish" rather than "to exterminate" ("castigar" instead of "exterminar"). See Powell, 1952, 109; Powell and Powell, 1971, 202, 210, 262; and Poole and Madrid, 1965, 115–37, for Mexican bishops' condemnation of the war. See, too, Gullón Abao, 1993, 179.

87. Riekenberg, 1996, 67, basing his argument on slender evidence, argues that extermination became an option "for the first time" in the second half of the 1700s (p. 67) and suggests that metropolitan officials favored extermination of Indians while local elites

did not. He bases much of his argument from the colonial period on the plan of Pedro de Cevallos, which I discuss below. The broader reality is more complicated and less schematic. Indeed, tendencies toward slaughtering Indians seem more likely to originate with local officials than with the crown, which usually condemned excesses, as in Roulet, 2002, 81–83. I see the use of the word "exterminate" as a rhetorical flourish rather than a change of policy, as I suggest below.

88. For the pampa, see Riekenberg, 1996, 71. Slatta, 1998, 93–94, argues that "the Spanish sought to exterminate and subjugate, not to incorporate, pampas nomads."

89. León Solís, 1982, 48; León Solís, 2001b, 37–40.

90. The cabildo of Tarija to the Real Audiencia, 1776, quoted in Súsnik, 1968, 217. Humboldt, 1822, 4:271, speaking of the Internal Provinces of New Spain: "We frequently hear at Mexico, that . . . the tribes of savages . . . ought not to be repulsed but exterminated. Fortunately, however, this barbarous counsel has never yet been listened to by the government."

91. Béxar, Oct. 20, 1780, quoted in Fenn, 2001, 212. For Cabello in Nicaragua, see his biography in Chipman and Joseph, 1999, 203.

92. Saeger, 2000, 37.

93. Sir Jeffrey Amherst, quoted in Fenn, 2000, 1556–57. Some of Amherst's subordinates apparently beat him to the punch.

94. Guill to the crown, May 1, 1767, quoted in Barros Arana, 1884–1902, 6:237–38 ("hacerles [a los indios] guerra hasta sujetarlos a perpetua obediencia, o aniquilar a los rebeldes, sacándolos a todos de sus tierras y distribuyéndolos por el reino . . . y distribuyendo a las mujeres y párvulos por las haciendas del reino"). Oses, 1961, 45, provides context in brief; Casanova Guarda, 1989b, 45–105, explores the 1766 revolt in depth (Guill's biography is on p. 59). León Solís, Silva Galdames, and Téllez Lúgaro, 1997, 17, for the multipronged approach.

95. Amat's informe of Dec. 6, 1769, parts of which are quoted in Barros Arana, 1884, 6:240 "insensibilidad y total desprecio"). See, too, León Solís, Silva Galdames, and Téllez Lúgaro, 1997, 17–26.

96. As one Jesuit similarly noted, even when they were "armed with those destructive weapons before which the most extensive empires of that [American] continent had fallen," Spanish soldiers could not defeat Araucanians. Molina, 1809, 2:307. Sors, 1921–23, no. 46, 329–40.

97. Amat's *informe*, summarized and quoted in the *real cédula* to Agustín de Jáuregui, Gobernador y Capitán General del Reyno de Chile y Presidente de mi Audiencia de la Ciudad de Santiago. El Pardo, Feb. 6, 1774, ANSC, Fondos Varios, vol. 300, pieza 3 ("iba a adelantar algunas leguas de territorio desiertas"; "se incorporasen con las inmensas Naciones más

bárbaras"; "volviesen a recuperar lo perdido: que es lo mismo que renovar, o introducir una guerra perpetua"; "olvidándose del punto político y cristiano, y de la defensa que hacen nuestras leyes de promover [prohibir] guerra abierta; permitiendo solo el castigo en casos de delito o alboroto"; "Propuso como único y principal medio para mantener en paz dichos Indios, el de la administración de Justicia con imparcialidad, y sin distinción de colores, oyendo las quejas de los Indios y reparando sus agravios").

98. *Real cédula* to Agustín de Jáuregui, Gobernador y Capitán General del Reyno de Chile y Presidente de mi Audiencia de la Ciudad de Santiago. El Pardo. Feb. 6, 1774. ANSC, Fondos Varios, vol. 300, pieza 3 ("mis piadosas intenciones de atraerlos por medios suaves, y pacíficos, con preferencia a los de la fuerza y del rigor"; "libertar mi Real Erario de inmensos gastos que ocasionaban las inquietudes de los referidos indios").

99. When José de Gálvez launched a campaign against the Seris, it was Arriaga, speaking in the name of the king, who described war as bad policy (Arriaga to the Marqués de Croix, April 25, 1770, quoted in Navarro García, 1964, 186), and when Gerónimo Matorras proposed a "conquista" of the Indians of the Chaco at his own expense, the Council of the Indies, with Arriaga presiding, approved only "missionization and colonization." (El Consejo de Indias sobre el proyecto presentado por un vecino de Buenos Aires, Gerónimo de Matorras, para la reducción y población de los indios del Chaco . . . Madrid, June 30, 1767, AGI, BA 18, called to my attention by Gullón Abao, 1993, 80 ("reducción y población").

100. Antonio María de Bucareli to Julián de Arriaga, Mexico, July 26, 1777, in Velasco Ceballos, 1936, 1:65 ("abatir su orgullo y escarmentarlos con el rigor de las armas"). See, too, Bucareli to Arriaga, Mexico, Oct. 27, 1772, in ibid., 1:64. For the fiction of Apaches wars beginning in 1748, see Ortelli, 2003b, chap. 1.

101. The thesis of Villalobos R., 1992, and Villalobos R., 1995. The latter reprints the Araucanian portion of the former. His viewpoint is widely accepted. See, for example, Boccara, 1996a, 27–39, who restates it in the language of Michel Foucault.

102. Sors, 1921–23, makes this point repeatedly in his prolix "Historia," written in 1780, and comes down on the side of defense as the only viable strategy. See especially vol. 42, no. 46, 337–39.

103. Campbell, 1978, 58.

104. Villalobos R., 1992, 339; Amat y Junient, 1924–28.

105. Amat's *informe*, summarized and quoted in the *real cédula* to Agustín de Jáuregui, Gobernador y Capitán General del Reyno de Chile y Presidente de mi Audiencia de la Ciudad de Santiago. El Pardo, Feb. 6, 1774, ANSC, Fondos Varios, vol. 300, pieza 3.

106. Pedro de Cevallos to Gálvez, Buenos Aires, Nov. 27, 1777, quoted in Torre Revello, 1970, 69 ("hasta

su extinción"; "en vano, y no hay esperanza alguna ni la más remota de convertirlos, ni que se reduzcan a vivir a puesto fijo"). I have translated *entrada* as an invasion—one of its many meanings in Spanish, although others might prefer to see this as an "expedition." Círculo Militar, 1973, 1:172.

107. Pedro de Cevallos to Gálvez, Buenos Aires, Nov. 27, 1777, quoted in Beverina, 1992, 68. He elaborated on it in his Memoria to his successor. Cevallos, 1945, 8–10. On these and other events, Ras, 1994, does not represent an advance over earlier studies, and his sources are often unclear.

108. Cevallos, 1945, 10 ("arruinar esa canalla de indios despreciables, y abominados aún de los propios de su especie que pueblan las serranías"), where he elaborates on his plan.

109. Pedro de Cevallos to Gálvez, Buenos Aires, Nov. 27, 1777, in Beverina, 1992, 68. Cevallos's biographer does not explore his ideas about combating Indians. Gammalsson, 1976.

110. Pedro de Cevallos to the crown, San Borja, Feb. 15, 1758, and unsigned copy of a reply to Cevallos by a member of the Council of the Indies (Julián Arriaga then served as secretary of the navy and the Indies) speaking in the name of the queen mother, [Madrid?], Oct. 4, 1759 ("se continue con el vigor que se requiere hasta consequir extinguidos, o reducidos a vida civil y política"). AGI, BA 18. Cevallos served as governor from 1757 to 1766; María Farnesse served as regent that autumn while her son, Carlos III, made his way to Spain from Italy to assume the throne. Martínez Sierra, 1975, 1:140, suggests that Cevallos was influenced by a plan of Felipe de Haedo, but Haedo's plan was dated Dec. 7, 1777, after Cevallos had drafted his own recommendation to the crown. Haedo expected the operations to take three years instead of three months and naively expected to turn Indian captives into Spaniards with ease. Haedo, 1872, 436–66.

111. Draft of a letter to Gov. of Buenos Aires, Pedro de Cevallos, with copies to the governors of Tucumán and Paraguay [Madrid], Oct. 6, 1759, AGI, BA 18. Cardozo, 1934, 65–66, summarizes events and quotes extensively from this document ("hostilidades, robos, homicidios"; "repetición inhumana"; "vida montaráz y silvestre la causa viciosa y malvada de sus delitos").

112. Cevallos's plan received approval in a *real orden* of March 5, 1778, which Vértiz, its recipient, mentions. Beverina, 1992, 69. I have been unable to locate this in the Archivo General in Buenos Aires, but León Solís, Silva Galdames, and Téllez Lúgaro, 1997, 30, quote from a copy in the Academia de la Historia, Colección Mata Linares, tomo 108.

113. Vértiz to Gálvez, July 16, 1778, quoted in Beverina, 1992, 69–70 ("bárbaros"; "se insolentarán más en sus crueldades").

114. The *acta* of the second of two meetings of the junta

(Sept. 10, 1778), in Beverina, 1992. The quotations are from 371–72 ("carecemos del conocimiento de sus grandes y ocultos territorios, por no tener planos verdaderos, ni sujetos que nos den aún siquiera una moderada luz de estos desiertos"), 375 ("por dicha o casualidad"), 317 ("cuerpos errantes, sin población ni habitación determinada; que carecen de todos los bienes de fortuna; ... que no necesitan fuego para comer, ni otras provisiones para sus marchas"), 376 ("impracticable"). My interpretation is informed by Juan Francisco Jiménez of Bahía Blanca, who generously shared with me an advance look at sections of his doctoral thesis.

115. Vértiz to Gálvez, Nov. 30, 1778, cited in Beverina, 1992, 370, and Gálvez to the viceroy [Vértiz], Pardo, March 15, 1779, in AGN [Buenos Aires], Reales Ordenes, 1779, [vol. no. 25–1–2] ("ha aprobado el Rey, que suspendiéndose la entrada general meditada por ser impracticable"). In his Memoria to his successor (Vértiz, 1945, 144–45), Vértiz also adopted the views and the language of the junta that recommended against offensive war in 1778.

116. Navarro García, 1997b, 400 ("miserables indios"). García Bernal, 1997, 8, 10, sees ethical and religious motivations behind Gálvez's policies but acknowledges the primacy of economic motives.

117. Marqués de Loreto to José de Gálvez, Buenos Aires, June 3, 1784, AGI, BA, transcript in the Museo Etnográfico, Buenos Aires (see Palermo, 1992, J29). In a doctoral dissertation still in progress at the Universidad del Sur in Bahía Blanca, Juan Francisco Jiménez analyzed this *entrada* and corrected the rosy picture presented by military historians such as Roberto Marfany and Juan Carlos Walther. I am also drawing from León Solís, Silva Galdames, and Téllez Lúgaro, 1997, 50–67, who similarly see this as a turning point, with only Mendoza dreaming of another multipronged offensive. Vértiz himself may have seen this as a punitive expedition rather than an offensive war. In his instructions to his successor, he predicts that offensives into Indian territory will fail, but he did continue to authorize punitive expeditions. Vértiz y Salcedo, 1945, 144–45. Levaggi, 2000, 125, sees him as a "partidario de guerra ofensiva," and the marqués de Loreto, in ordering no quarter in 1784, took a hard line. León Solís, Silva Galdames, and Téllez Lúgaro, 1997, 53.

118. Gálvez, *real orden* to the marqués de Loreto, San Lorenzo, Oct. 2, 1784, responding to the viceroy's letter of June 3, 1784. Gálvez's short reply appears in the *Revista de la Biblioteca Nacional* 2, no. 7 (July–Sept., 1938), 623 ("se ha servido aprobar que se persiga continuamente a los Bárbaros de las fronteras"). Reference courtesy of Juan Francisco Jiménez.

119. Gálvez to Croix, San Ildefonso, August 22, 1776, in Velázquez, 1982, 138 ("contener y escarmentar los indios enemigos que las [provincias internas] hos-tilizan, haciendo a este fin frecuentes salidas contra ellos").

120. The dehumanizing term *mariscada*, meaning literally a hunt for shellfish, seems not to have been used in South America as a synonym for a foray against Indians but was used commonly in the Mexican north. See, for example, Velázquez, 1976, 55, and Sheridan, 2000, 257–58.

121. Croix to Gálvez, Chihuahua, June 29, 1778, conveying the conclusions of a council of war, in Thomas, 1940, 199–200.

122. Teodoro de Croix to José de Gálvez, Jan. 23, 1780, Arizpe, *oficio* #458, AGI, Guadalajara 522 ("absoluta libertad de los bárbaros, les incita a buscar la propia"; "el carácter de todo indio, al robo y a la alevosía").

123. Croix to Gálvez, Chihuahua, June 29, 1778, conveying the conclusions of a council of war, in Thomas, 1940, 198, 193. Croix had asked Viceroy Bucareli for two thousand additional men as early as August 22, 1777. Velasco Ceballos, 1936, 1:367.

124. Ruíz, 1972, 14.

125. Croix to Viceroy Bucareli, Chihuahua, Jan. 31, 1779, quoted in Croix to Gálvez, Feb. 22, 1779, AGI, Guadalajara 270 ("la guerra ofensiva es la que puede reducir y acabar a los indios aún sin llegar a las manos, pues basta, para su exterminio y confusión que se les persiga incesantemente obligándoles a vivir sin sosiego a arrastrar la penosa carga de sus hijos y mujeres y a perecer de hambre").

126. Bucareli to Croix, Mexico, Aug. 27, 1777, in Velasco Ceballos, 1936, 1:369–70. Moore and Beene, 1971, 265–82. O'Conor, 1994.

127. Bucareli to Gálvez, Mexico, April 26, 1778, in Velasco Ceballos, 1936, 1:396.

128. José de Gálvez to Comandante General Teodoro de Croix, El Pardo, Feb. 22, 1779. Photocopy in the University of Texas Library, Archivo de San Francisco el Grande, vol. 33, XI, 1779, 33–39 ("dictado por la religión, por la razón natural, y por la verdadera política"; "la clase de enemigo que infestan estas regiones no puede exterminarse, ni reducircse con un golpe decisivo, ni por medio de aquella serie metódica de acciones sabiamente dirijidas, que hace gloriosas las campañas en la guerra entre naciones cultas"; "su terreno, su desnudez, su agilidad, su pobreza misma, y aún su desorden, y cobardía"; "soliciten sinceramente nuestra amistad"; "poder y firmeza,"; "piadosos deseos del Rey"; "serán a s.m. infinitamente más gratas las conquistas aunque lentas, y sin aparatos, que se [h]agan con la dulzura, el buen trato, y la beneficencia, que las más grandes, ruidosas, rápidas, que se consigan derramando sangre humana, aunque sea de los más bárbaros enemigos"; "haran más lentas, pero más seguras conquistas, que los ejercitos más numerosos, y bien ordenados"). This copy of Gálvez's orders called to my attention by Thomas, 1941, 43. Levaggi, 1997, 108–09, quotes

from the orders at length to suggest the continuity of a peaceful policy from Habsburgs to Bourbons —what he calls "la doctrina oficial"—but he does not note that in the case of the Apaches this represented a change of policy by Gálvez and the crown.

129. As in Croix to Gálvez, Jan. 23, 1780, a covering letter for a lengthy *informe* (*oficio* 458) of the same date. AGI, Guadalajara 522.

130. Croix's report of Oct. 30, 1781, in Thomas, 1941, 84, 82.

131. Croix to Gálvez, Arispe, May 23, 1780, *oficio* 519, AGI, Guadalajara 522 ("reducción o exterminio"; "medios del rigor, si no fueron suficientes los de la dulzura"). Croix's report of Oct. 30, 1781, in Thomas, 1941, 94.

132. Teodoro de Croix to José de Gálvez, Jan. 23, 1780, Arizpe, *oficio* #458, AGI, Guadalajara 522 ("sin gente y dinero"; "las ventajas estan de parte de los Indios").

133. Croix's report of Oct. 30, 1781, in Thomas, 1941, 93.

134. Viceroy Bucareli to Gálvez, Mexico, Jan. 17, 1782, AGI, Guadalajara 522.

135. Gálvez to Croix, Aranjuez, May, 1782, AGI, Guadalajara 522 ("contener, y castigar a los bárbaros").

136. Lucas de Lassaga [the modern spelling is Lazaga or Lasaga], who was *administrador general de minería*, and the marqués de San Miguel de Aguayo, Mexico, Feb. 20, 1782, AGI, Guadalajara 519 ("calamidades"; "la insolencia de los indios ha llegado al estremo nunca visto"; ("sirviéndolas de cebo"). For Lasaga, see the *Diccionario Porrúa*, 1971, 1:1165; for the new Order, see Anes, 1994, 22–24.

137. The quotation is from O'Conor, 1994, 94 and facsimile, p. 103 ("una superioridad invencible sobre los bárbaros"). South of the presidial line the burden of defense fell on frontier militia. See, for example, Adams, 2000, 325–46. Lassaga and the marqués also had a specific financial interest in blocking Croix's plan to levy local taxes to support militia and wanted the royal treasury to increase its support of regular troops. Vargas-Lobsinger, 1992, 148–52 (reference, courtesy of Sarah Ortelli). See, too, Cuello, 1988a, 308, 312–13, 316.

138. Gálvez to Croix, San Ildefonso, June 27, 1782, AGI Guadalajara 519 ("invasiones, horrores, muertes, y robos"). Saavedra's warnings, based on his visit to Mexico in 1781, are quoted at length in Morales Padrón, 1969, 354–58, and in Saavedra, 1989, 247–48, 250–51, 255, 259–60. See, too, Navarro García, 1997a, 6.

139. Gálvez to Croix, San Ildefonso, June 27, 1782, AGI Guadalajara 519 ("está vista por repetidas experiencias lastimosas que no basta mantenerse sobre la defensiva, y que el medio de contenerlos es buscarlos, y hacerles una continuada guerrilla sin estrépito"). Gálvez singled out José Berrotarán and Bernardo de Gálvez as models. The expressions "sin estrépito" is short for "sin estrépito y figura del justicio."

140. Moorhead, 1975a, 93.

141. Moorhead, 1968, 120.

142. Vértiz, 1945, 144, 55–56. For other examples see Mirafuentes Galván, 1987, 21–23; O'Conor, 1994, 72; Juan and Ulloa, 1978, 2:358.

143. Amat y Junient, 1924–28, no. 56, 371 ("criados entre rocas").

144. José Rafael Rodríguez Gallardo to the [*auditor de guerra?*], Mexico, July 11, 1765, in López, 1929–30, 1:249 ("la guerra de los indios más bien consiste en ardid, alevosía y traición, que en el arrojo, valor y fuerza"). For his experience with Apaches and Seris, see Rodríguez Gallardo, 1975. Officers' expressions of admiration mixed with opprobrium abound. For Apaches, see O'Crouley, 1972, 52, and Lafora, 1958, 216; Cortés, 1989, 71–76; for Comanches, Ruíz, 1972, 9–11; for Charrúas, Azara, 1923, 2:11–12, 22.

145. Gov. Lázaro de Ribera of Paraguay, 1798, in Cardozo, 1934, 56–57, and Dobrizhoffer, 1967–70, 1:211, on the militia. For the regular army, see Marchena Fernández, 1992, 181, 188–89, 244–72, and studies of the harsh conditions under which regular troops and militia labored, such as Moorhead, 1975a, 196–98, Mayo and Latrubesse, 1993, 65–75, León Solís, Silva Galdames, and Téllez Lúgaro, 1997, 38–40, 61, and Cruz, 2001, 140–53, who looked closely at the social composition of several military posts in the western Chaco. Despite efforts at reform, some local officers continued to skim the payroll before their men received their salaries or had soldiers work on their personal business. Acevedo, 1965, 393–94. Moorhead, 1975a, 269–70.

146. *Real cédula* to Agustín de Jáuregui, Gobernador y Capitán General del Reyno de Chile y Presidente de mi Audiencia de la Ciudad de Santiago. El Pardo, Feb. 6, 1774, ANSC, Fondos Varios, vol. 300, pieza 3, reflecting the views of Manuel de Amat, an experienced frontier officer.

147. Brizuela, 1969–72, 261, 270–73; quotations on 272 and 273 ("por su cobardía y mala voluntad"; "llenos de temores"). See Garavaglia, 1984, 26, for another case of desertion, and Mayo, 1991, 776. For a similar indictment of militia in Nuevo León, in New Spain, see Adams, 2000, 339, 342.

148. Juan José de Vértiz, "Instrucción que debe observar el Comandante de la frontera, subinspector de las Milicias del Campo . . . [May 5, 1779]," in Círculo Militar, 1973, 1:189–97. For continuing desertions, see the 1801 campaign against the Charrúas, in Mariluz Urquijo, 1987, 385–86. See, too, Acevedo, 1965, 62–63, and the excellent discussion of deserters' motives in Mayo and Latrubesse, 1993, 45–53. Substantial numbers of poorly paid soldiers deserted long before the 1700s. Cerda-Hegerl, 1990, 44–47.

149. Gálvez to Teodoro de Croix, Aranjuez, April 30, 1779, AGI, Guadalajara, 270 ("porque los indios las descubren y evitan más fácilmente").

150. Gov. Joaquín Alós to Viceroy Arredondo, April 24,

1790, quoted in Cardozo, 1934, 54 ("por el terror pánico que tenían concebido de la fuerza de los bárbaros, se malograban la más de las acciones").

151. Uribe, 1977, 116, 123. See, too, Fals Borda, 1979, 1:103A–113B and 107B. When the British laid siege to Cartagena in 1741, the necessity of getting foodstuffs from the interior became especially acute.

152. Uribe, 1977, 128–44; González Luna, 1978, 116–18 ("capitán de la conquista de los indios Chimila"). Many died in a smallpox epidemic of 1790. Chimilas occupied a triangular swath of tropical plains, bounded by the Magdalena River on the west and south, the César River to the east, and the Sierra Nevada de Santa Marta to the north.

153. Ambrosio de Benavides to José de Gálvez, Santiago, July 5, 1785, in Hanisch, 1990, 158 ("moral imposibilidad, por ahora, de conquistarlas por armas").

154. Mirafuentes, Galván, 1987, 29, makes this point about Sonora.

155. Gómez Pérez, 1992, 235. Serrano Álvarez, 2002, 32–38, suggests that historians have underestimated military expenses.

156. González del Campo, 1984, 92; Arredondo, 1945, 415. Spain also had to rely on American-born Spaniards to fill positions in the army and on its colonial militia, as it became difficult and then impossible to station troops from Iberia in America. Arming Americans posed a dilemma. Spain could not furnish enough peninsulares, yet putting arms in the hands of Americans gave some administrators pause. Marchena Fernández, 1992, 134–49, 187–88.

157. Conde del Campo de Alange to the Capitán General y Presidente de Chile [Ambrosio O'Higgins], San Lorenzo, Oct. 1, 1793, ANSC, *capitanía general*, vol. 747, no. 11526 ("con el menor gravamen posible del Real erario, mayor utilidad de la corona, beneficio y alivio de los vasallos de S. M.").

158. Gálvez to Viceroy Manuel Antonio Flores of New Granada, Aranjuez, May 15, 1779, in Gómez Pérez, 1992, 233, and in Marchena Fernández, 1992, 143 ("sería una empresa imposible aún cuando el Rey de España tuviese a su disposición todos los tesoros, los ejércitos y los almacenes de Europa").

159. For the advantages and disadvantages of firearms, see my discussion in chaps. 2 and 4.

160. I discuss the relations of these Indians with foreigners elsewhere in chaps. 4 and 5, but for the Tobas, see Santamaría, 1998a, 19–20.

161. Grahn, 1995, 144, 146, 151; Barrera Monroy, 2000, 52–68.

162. Col. Antonio de Arévalo to Viceroy Guirior, Cartagena, March 3, 1774, in Oliveros de Castro, 1975, 161 ("con entera libertad, echos dueños absolutos de ella"). La Guajira is 7,761.5 sq. mi. (20,180 sq. km), and Massachusetts is 7,838 sq. mi (20,378 sq. km).

163. Grahn, 1995, 134–35, describing an incident in the mid-1730s.

164. Ojer, 1983, 500; the unsigned proposal to deport them is reproduced in Moreno and Tarazona, 1984, 31–33. See, too, Narváez y la Torre, 1965, 39. For the sale of Cocinas, reportedly sent to Jamaica and to Philadelphia in the 1770s, see Polo Acuña, 1999a, 22–23.

165. Barrera Monroy, 2000, 173–97, which is especially revealing about Guajiro points of view.

166. Moreno y Escandón, 1936, 572 ("infestada por alguna parte de indios bárbaros").

167. Ibid., 574–75 ("cuerpo político del reino, no admite otra curación que el cauterio de las armas"; "las amonestaciones y la suavidad"; "sirven de insolencia a estos bárbaros"; "de suerte"; "con menos recelo").

168. Kuethe, 1970, 472–73, treats this at greater length than he does in Kuethe, 1978, 133; Barrera Monroy, 2000, 202–04, provides additional detail. I have drawn from the self-serving answers that Encio gave to a list of questions posed by Viceroy Guirior after the debacle. Encio's statement, Oct. 12, 1772, Riohacha, in Moreno and Tarazona, 1984, 177–84, which also includes other contemporary documents. The comparison with Cortés is in Gregorio de la Sierra to the viceroy, Cartagena, April 11, 1772, in ibid., 174.

169. Título de gobernador de la nación Mosquita, Dec. 29, 1769, in Fernández Guardia, 1881–1907, 10:23 ("medios suaves"). I have not seen the text of the 1769 agreement, made with Gov. José Joaquín de Nava and described in Offen, 2002, 348–49, and Olien, 1998, 305–06.

170. Pedro Carbonell y Pinto, Gov. of Panama, to José de Gálvez, Aug. 4, 1778 (reservado no. 4), AGI, Estado, Audiencia de Guatemala, contains a description of the "tratados de paz" ("comercio libre en todos los puertos desde el Río de San Juan hasta Chagres"; "maestros que lo enseñan a leer y escribir, y demás artes mecánicas y liberales"). The historian Romero Vargas, 1995, 196, speculates that the British superintendent, Colville Cairns, might have been behind this, hoping to gain Miskitos the right to fish for hawksbill turtles, or *tortuga de carey,* without Spanish interference. Romero Vargas, 1995, 182–83, and Floyd, 1967, 121–30, provide context but neither historian mentions Fara's visit to Panama. The treaty of "alliance and friendship" was signed in Panama City, June 16, 1778, and approved by Carlos III. Floridablanca to Gálvez, Jan. 4, 1779, AGI, Estado, Audiencia de Guatemala.

171. The attack on Terry was preceded by a peace treaty, signed on Terry's frigate in the mouth of the San Juan River on September 5, 1778, by the Zambo-Miskito king George II (recently returned from London), his brother Duke Isaac, Gov. Colville Briton (a Tawira!), and other Miskito leaders. It is in Fernández Guardia, 1881–1907, 10:78, and promised "paces permanentes, fijas y duraderas." For conflict-

ing accounts of this episode, which needs further study, see Floyd, 1967, 126–28, Preston, 1987, 17–22, and Romero Vargas, 1995, 184–85, 196–97. Floyd says that Miskitos killed Terry rather than shipping him to Jamaica. Salvatierra, 1939–42, 1:454–69, chronicles these events based on archival sources but generally does not cite specific documents and makes errors that render the work unreliable.

172. Perié to King George, Cartago, Aug. 5, 1779 ("no aspira a más Dominios . . . abomina la escalvitud y sólo quiere tener vasallos libres, ricos y gustosos, aún cuando sigan diversa religión"), in Fernández Guardia, 1881–1907, 10:79–81.

173. Gálvez to the Viceroy of New Granada, San Ildefonso, Aug. 4, 1784, in Peralta, 1898, 228–29 ("deben ser perseguidos y debelados a sangre y fuego para su escarmiento y el de todos los infieles de esa región"), called to my attention by Floyd, 1967, 164–65. Gálvez first ordered the "exterminio" of the Miskitos on Aug. 25, 1783, in a *real orden* to the viceroy of New Granada. See the reference to this in the viceroy to Gálvez, New Granada, March 21, 1784, in Peralta, 1898, 224. For Miskitos as rebels, see the *real orden* to the president of Guatemala, San Ildefonso, of Aug. 25, 1783. Ibid., 216. Gálvez may have had in mind agreements of 1769 and 1778 with the Tawira-Miskito leaders, in which they promised vassalage and could thus be branded as rebels.

174. Gálvez to Gálvez, Guatemala, Oct. 17, 1782, quoted in full in Calderón Quijano, 1945, 783–84, called to my attention by Floyd, 1967, 161, who misquotes and misinterprets the letter ("Salvajes"; "los crueles Ingleses"; "más se teme a un perro que a viente hombres armados"). Gálvez had asked for one hundred Cuban-trained dogs to catch runaway black slaves.

175. The correspondence regarding this episode is in Peralta, 1898, 242–48.

176. See, for example, Garavaglia, 1984, 22–23, describing the costs of *entradas* into the Chaco from Tucumán.

177. Malaspina, 1995, 145 ("no tuvo presente la reflexión bien fundada del Abate Raynal: que es mucho más fácil conquistar un país poblado que otro poseído de gentes bárbaras y errantes").

178. O'Higgins to Pedro de Acuña, Plaza de Los Angeles, March 17, 1793, in Levaggi, 1997, 116 ("porque para cada uno sería preciso un soldado que le contuviese").

179. Descripción del Reyno de Chile, Madrid, Sept. 2, 1767, in Donoso, 1941, 440 ("hacerles guerra ofensiva a los indios, según la opinión de algunos, o procurar su extinción, sería acabar con las Américas"). Writing in 1767, O'Higgins was ahead of his time.

180. O'Higgins to Gálvez, Concepción, April 23, 1785, MM, vol. 202, no. 5004 ("algunos golpes rudos, sobre los indios de mala fé los revoltosos y ladrones incorregibles, cuyo número es infinitamente superior a el de los indios honrados"). See O'Higgins to Pe-

dro de Acuña, Plaza de Los Angeles, March 17, 1793, in Levaggi, 1997, 117.

181. Bernardo to José de Gálvez, New Orleans, Oct. 24, 1778, in Hernández Sánchez-Barba, 1957, 122 ("un enemigo mil veces más sutil de lo que una imaginación viva puede pensar"; "un espacio igual al que hay desde Madrid a Constantinople"). This confidential letter appears to be the same as that quoted at length by West, "Indian Policy," 100–01, but Sánchez-Barba quotes a portion that West omitted.

182. Gálvez, 1951, art. 29 ("nos será más fructuosa una mala paz con todas la Naciones que la soliciten, que los esfuerzos de una buena guerra"). The extent to which Gálvez's *Instrucción* represented a new plan, as suggested by Faulk, 1979, 74, and Moorhead, 1975a, 100–101, needs clarification. In an earlier work, Moorhead more accurately characterized it as a synthesis that "did not introduce drastic changes" but was "revolutionary in some few details." Moorhead, 1968, 123.

183. Calleja, 1949, fols. xxxvii–xxxix ("mala paz"; "infinitamente peor que la guerra"; "Un enemigo dentro de la misma casa"). Calleja, who arrived in New Spain with Viceroy Revillagigedo in 1789, judiciously praised Gálvez's judgment before disagreeing with him.

184. Ibid., fol. xxvi, xxxviii ("un santuario, al que jamás se toca").

185. Carta reservada to Viceroy Manuel Antonio Flores, Sept. 16, 1788, in Tristán, 1788 ("inflamados de su valor y espíritu guerrero (pero no aguerrido), juzgan que con su espada lo pueden todo sin necesitar de otra para adquirir el glorisoso nombre de conquistador"). For additional examples of hard-liners who continued to advocate extermination, see Moorhead, 1968, 72–73, 227–28, 270–78, and *passim*, on Viceroy Manuel and Antonio Flores and Juan de Ugalde and Enrique de Grimarest to the viceroy, Alamos, July 31, 1792, quoted in Escandón, 1996, 292. For Ugalde, who professed affection for Lipan Apaches even as he sought to exterminate Mescaleros, also see Wade, 2003, 207–14.

186. Revillagigedo to Miró, March 2, 1791, translated in Kinnaird, 1946–49, vol. 3, pt. 2, 404–06.

187. Revillagigedo, 1966b, 254 ("La guerra que en ellas [las provincias internas] se hace, es por un orden distinto que los que se acostumbra en las naciones cultas, porque es preciso acomodarse al carácter y modo de hacerla a los salvajes, con quienes por regla general, siempre es preferible la paz, debiendo sólo hacerles la guerra para castigarlos y escarmentarlos; por la falta a las paces que hubieren tratado, y volvérselas a conceder de nuevo").

188. Gov. Manuel Muñoz to Capt. Juan Cortes of La Bahía, Dec. 13, 1793, in Ricklis, 1996, 152 (his translation). The crown had not approved (and perhaps rejected) an earlier proposal in the 1770s to exterminate the Karankawas. Morfi, 1967, 2:439.

189. Pedro de Nava to Miguel Joseph de Azanza, Quartel de la Primera Compañía Volante en Guajoquilla, Aug. 3, 1796 (*oficio* 297), AGI, Guadalajara, 293.

190. Figueroa, 1884, 29 ("tuvo la felicidad de morir cristiano"). Many works treat this, but Urbina Burgos, 1987, 247–29, provides particularly rich context.

191. Figueroa, 1884, 41, 43, 45.

192. Viceroy Nicolás Arredondo to Gov. Joaquín Alós, Buenos Aires, Dec. 28, 1795, quoted in Cardozo, 1934, 61 ("la guerra contra infieles, siempre es justa, aunque no fuese contra expresos damnificadores, y así no sólo ha de estar V.S. sobre la defensiva, sino dispuesto a emprender una salida hasta aniquilarlos en el campo").

193. The quotation is from Manual de Amat, 1763, in Cerda-Hegerl, 1990, 59 ("corral de vacas"). For other primitive forts, see José Perfecto de Salas, "Informe Sobre el Reino de Chile," Santiago, March 5, 1750, in Donoso, 1963, 1:117, and Beverina, 1992, 98. For the reforms, see Tapson, 1962, 19–20; Círculo Militar, 1973, 1:218–32; Guarda, 1990, 199; Moorhead, 1975, 161–77; and Fireman, 1977, 111–13, 147, 152. For an example of a fort that remained primitive even after the reforms, see Gillespie, 1818, 169, an Englishman incarcerated at Areco in 1807.

194. Details of this realignment were spelled out in the "Instrucción para la nueva colocación de presidios," which forms part of the Regulations of 1772, in Brinckerhoff and Faulk, 1965, 49–67. Weber, 1992, 220–27, and Moorhead, 1975a, 64–94. Although O'Conor was clearly a hawk, he appreciated the importance of defense. See O'Conor, 1994, 73–87, and Hugo O'Conor to Viceroy Bucareli, Chihuahua, Dec. 20, 1771, in Rubio Mañé, 1959a, 387.

195. Guy and Sheridan, 1998, 6, make this point in comparing Buenos Aires with the towns in northern New Spain, but it has broad applicability.

196. Much admirable work has been done on military operations in this period, but it does not significantly alter the picture presented in Marfany, 1940, 307–33, on which I have depended. See Beverina, 1992, 71–76, 216–20; Tapson, 1962, 18–20; and Barba, 1997, 8, who makes the case for the line of forts protecting the Buenos Aires–Mendoza route. Jones, 1984, 45–46, argues (incorrectly I think) that stopping criollos from smuggling was of greater concern to officials than Indian raids. I am grateful to Raúl Mandrini for informing me about the distances (110 kilometers from Buenos Aires to San Miguel del Monte, and 20 kilometers more to the Salado).

197. Gullón Abao, 1993, 83–109.

198. Robinson and Thomas, 1974, 21–22, and Gullón Abao, 1993, 271–85, and Viñuales, 1996, 207–31. Vitar, 1995, 59, counts a dozen forts along the western edge of the Chaco by 1750. As in other areas, some remained and others, no longer needed, were abandoned. Saeger, 2000, 41, notes that forts paired with

missions became "increasingly typical in the late eighteenth century" in the Chaco. For the Chiriguanía, see Pifarré, 1989, 168–69.

199. Arredondo, 1945, 406 ("en tierras que notoriamente pertenecen a los españoles"). In 1790, the system below Asunción gained a central command with the appointment of a "captain of the port," who made his headquarters in Asunción. Cardozo, 1934, 53 ("capitán del puerto"). The forts south of Asunción were called *puestos*, but the terms *presidio, castillo,* and *fuerte* were also used. James Saeger, personal communication, Dec. 29, 2003. Some areas were guarded by garrisons ("destacamientos") which apparently lacked a physical structure. Williams, 1976, 1–3; Cooney, 1998, 135–46. Cooney and Whigham, 1994, 215, describe this as a Golden Age. Cardozo, 1934, 78, 112, 129–61, who notes that Spaniards first learned of the Portuguese forts in 1784 (p. 101). I am following Areces, 1992, 54, and Cardozo for the founding of these northern forts, whose dates vary wildly in the literature.

200. Méndez Beltán, 1987, 249 ("Los fuertes en el siglo XVIII ya no tenían una función ofensiva ni defensiva muy precisa, sino más bien de contacto cultural, penetración comercial y de ocupación demográfica"). Guarda, 1990, 199–229; Cerda-Hegerl, 1990, 55–61, 89–92. Chileans used the words *plazas* and *fortines* for forts on the Indian frontier; they termed the larger coastal fortifications *fuertes*. O'Higgins advocated peaceful expansion on a number of occasions, as when he rejected the recommendation of the governor of Chiloé that he reestablish Osorno by force. Urbina Burgos, 1987, 234–37.

201. For the reasons for preemptive action, see above at n. 22. Spain constructed forts in Alta California between 1769 and 1782 at San Diego, Santa Barbara, Monterery, and San Francisco (Weber, 1992, 258–59), and in Patagonia between 1779 and 1780—on the Valdés Peninsula (San José), on the Río Negro (then the Fuerte de Carmen and today Carmen de Patagones), and farther south at Puerto Deseado and the Bahía de San Julián. An epidemic forced quick abandonment of Puerto Deseado (1780–81), and on Aug. 1, 1783, José de Gálvez ordered the abandonment of all but Carmen de Patagones. The most penetrating explanation of the erection and abandonment of these posts is Zusman, 2001, 37–59, and for other accounts, each with its own details, see Walther, 1976, 108–11; Gorla, 1984, 10–21; Navarro Floria, 1994a, 34–53; Luiz, 1997, 50–51, 344–45 (which reproduces Gálvez's 1783 orders). Other strategic areas included southeastern North America as late as 1794 and 1795 (Weber, 1992, 285), and Guayana (Whitehead, 1988, 129). The llanos of eastern New Granada and the Orinoco basin, regarded as impenetrable barriers against foreigners, were not among them. Rausch, 1984, 125.

202. The quotation is from Viceroy Arredondo to Gov. Joaquín Alós, Feb. 13, 1790, in Cardozo, 1934, 73 ("convertir y civilizar"). For overviews, see Acevedo, 1964–65, 46–49, and Maeder, 1996, 66–69. The long-discussed plan would have fortified the Bermejo River. So, too, war with Britain delayed the construction of forts along the Spanish-Portuguese border between what is today Uruguay and Brazil. Arredondo, 1945, 412.

203. Moorhead, 1975a, 222–42, 270. For forts to haciendas, see Cruz, 2001, 137–38. It would be difficult to exaggerate the importance of the additional military spending on local economies. See Mayo and Latrubesse, 1993, 18–20, for the relationship between military preparedness and salaries on the Argentine pampa.

204. Torre Revello, 1970, 69, quoting Juan José Sardeu, comandante general de frontera y subinspector de las milicias ("no se suele encontrar, ni un vecino"). Jones, 1984, 47; Barba, 1997, 52–55. For the same phenomenon in Chile, see León Solís, 1990, 133; for northern New Spain, see Weber, 1992, 325; Sheridan, 2000, 255.

205. Undiano y Gastelú, 1969–72, 2:510 ("dos clases de hombres son los que pueblan las fronteras actuales," "soldados . . . y paisanos que viven bajo el cañón de los fuertes").

206. Suárez and Tornay, 2003, 537–54, who offer a richer argument than my brief characterization suggests.

207. Gálvez to Croix, San Ildefonso, August 22, 1776, in Velázquez, 1982, 135 ("El mejor resguardo de las provincias fronterizas a los indios gentiles y enemigos, ha sido siempre el establecimiento de poblaciones"). See, too, Aboites Aguilar, 1995, 23, 33–40; Whitehead, 1988, 125; Azara, 1990, 120; Concolorcorvo, 1965, 243–44; Malaspina, 1995, 146; Viceroy Juan José Vértiz, in Marfany, 1940, 315–16; Schiaffino, 1983, 43–47, who describes the support for frontier settlements in Chile by Amat and O'Higgins, among others.

208. Reyes, 2002, 78 ("imposible"; "atacarnos, e encendiar las casas").

209. Alonso Carrió de la Vandera, in his famous satire published in 1773. Concolorcorvo, 1965, 245.

210. Rodríguez Gallardo, 1975, 7 ("vecindarios, que son fortalezas vivas, antemurales subsistentes y nada costosos presidios"). See, too, Gov. Joaquín Alós, Asunción, April 8, 1790, quoted in Cardozo, 1934, 73, and the marqués de Altamira in Hill, 1926, 88; Mota Padilla, 1973, 466.

211. Spain hoped to settle Canary Islanders, Panamanians, and North Americans at forts built at Darién in 1785–86 but failed to implement the plan (Castillero Calvo, 1995, 331, 333–34). Spain did send poor Canary Islanders, Galicians, Asturians, and blacks to the Mosquito Coast, but few survived. There were a number of reasons for the failure, but

as a leading student of this subject pointed out, "above all was the lack of support by government, and the shortage of troops" (Sorsby, 1972, 148–49). For the Chaco, see Vitar, 1997, 307, and Cardozo, 1934, 157–58, 163–75.

212. O'Conor, 1994, 72 ("cierta su victoria"). See, too, De la Cruz, 1969a–72a, 440, on Pehuenches, and Amigorena, 1988, 25, on Indians in general. Among secondary writers, Faulk, 1979, 67–78, and Moorhead, 1975, 177, make the point that Indians seldom attacked fortified positions; Tapson, 1962, 7, 19, seems to contradict himself.

213. Col. Antonio de Arévalo to Viceroy Guirior, Cartagena, March 3, 1774, in Oliveros de Castro, 1975, 166 ("desaparecen como humo"), speaking of Guajiros, who he said had little courage ("poco valor"). Allegations of the cowardice of Indians are abundant. See, for example, Concolorcorvo [Alonso Carrió de la Vandera], 1959, 296; Santiago, 1994, 37, quoting O'Conor, and Dobrizhoffer, 1822, 2:350, who says of Abipones in the Chaco and of Indians in general, "Though you may object to their cowardice, yet that method of warfare is surely admirable."

214. Descripción del Reyno de Chile, Madrid, Sept. 2, 1767, in Donoso, 1941, 438 ("construir los Fuertes según arte"; "cualesquiera calidad contra Indios, es suficiente").

215. Azara, 1943b, 222, speaking from Madrid as head of the Committee on Fortifications and Defense of the Indies ("al estilo del pais"; "le parece ocioso el empeñarse en hacer otras fortificaciones, que costarían infinito, y sólo servirían contra unos indios de a caballo sin armas de fuego"). On today's map there is no confluence of the Diamante and Atuel rivers because the Diamante changed course in the early nineteenth century. This fort, San Rafael del Diamante, was erected in 1805 in the territory of Pehuenches de Malargüe, allies of Spaniards in Mendoza since 1783. Clarification courtesy of Juan Francisco Jiménez of Bahía Blanca, personal communication, Oct. 30, 2000.

216. See, for example, Vértiz, 1945, 155–56, who concluded that punitive expeditions worked best when carried out from several directions, and Weber, 1992, 220.

217. Faulk, 1979, 67–68; Moorhead, 1975a, 196, notes the requirement of daily patrols. Juan Francisco Jiménez (see above n.117) points to Indian adaptability in responding to Vértiz's fortifications on the pampa in the 1780s. See, too, Marfany, 1940, 313, 318; Gullón Abao, 1993, 234–35; and Serra y Canals, 1979, 47. The Memoria of Juan José de Vértiz y Salcedo to his successor, Buenos Aires, March 12, 1784, in Radaelli, 1945, 155, mentions nighttime patrols. This was an old problem. González de Nájera, drawing from his experience in the early 1600s, criticized Chile's forts because they were too dispersed to

form a true barrier against Indians. They lacked offensive and strategic value, he argued, and "inútil-mente se consumen los principales gastos de aquella guerra." Quoted in Jara, 1990, 82.

218. The intendant of Salta, Feb. 3, 1803, quoted in Acevedo, 1965, 395 ("son suficientes para dificultar las invasions de los enemigos, pero no lo son para impedirlas absolutamente, porque la frontera es muy dilatada y la distancia, de unos fuertes a otros, mucha").

219. Dobrizhoffer, 1967–70, 1:211 ("para huir a tiempo o, si lo creen oportuno, tomar las armas"). In 1774, the governor of Darién described the same use for his one working cannon. Ariza, 1971, 107.

220. Tristán, 1788, 27 ("no es prudente acuerdo guardar el campo y desamparar la casa") 7 ("dos saqueos"). See, too, pp. 10, 15–16. For use of the same house metaphor by a frontier commander in the Chaco, see Cruz, 2001, 159. See, too n.136.

221. See, too, a Spanish botanist's fear of entering the Araucanian lands with an escort, in Ruiz López, 1952, 1:209.

222. Amigorena, 1988, 15, describing the region around Fraile Muerto in 1787 and the entire road system.

223. Copy of a communication from Felipe de Sarto, Durango, Feb. 19, 1784, to the alcaldes mayores y demás ministros de justicia de la cordillera del margen, conveying an order from the Comandante General de estas Provincias [Felipe de Neve], Dec. 22, 1783, Archivo Municipal de Saltillo, PM, c36, e 74, 1f ("precaver las irreverencias y vilipendios, a que están expuestas, como por lo que conduce a intimidar a los pasajeros de las infelices que en aquellos parajes han sido víctima de dichos enemigos, cuyo pensamiento los desanima para defenderse si los asaltan contribuyendo el pavor a que triunfen más facilmente los bárbaros al mismo tiempo que les aumentan su osidia y orgullo pues saben lo que denotan dichas cruces"). This custom dates at least to the early 1600s on the Chichimec frontier. Pérez de Ribas, 1999, 698.

224. Gálvez, 1873, 593 (no. 58) ("defenderlas de cualquiera invasion interior"). Emphasis added.

225. Floyd, 1967, 143–46; Sorsby, 1972, 152; Williams, 1976, 1–4; Vangelista, 1993, 67–68, who notes that Spanish forces had been withdrawn from the Paraguayan frontier.

226. Col. Antonio de Arévalo to Viceroy Guirior, Cartagena, March 3, 1774, in Oliveros de Castro, 1975, 161 ("perdón general"; "afabilidad, agasajo, y algunos regalillos").

227. [The governor of Riohacha] to the Gov. of Santa Marta, Antonio de Narváez y la Torre and to the viceroy, Manuel Antonio Flores, Riohacha, July 12, 1779, in Moreno and Tarazona, 1984, 248–54; Kuethe, 1978, 136; Barrera Monroy, 2000, 205–12.

228. Col. Antonio de Arévalo to Viceroy Guirior, Rio-

hacha, July 26, 1776, in Oliveros de Castro, 1975, 188 ("el método suave que se ha seguido hasta ahora"); Silvestre, 1950, 97–98 ("el miedo y el rigor").

229. On Pedraza, see the unsigned draft of a letter [Capt. Gen. Manuel González] to the Intendant [Francisco de Saavedra], Caracas, Feb. 27, 1784, and the reply of Francisco de Saavedra [the intendant] to Manuel Gonzalez, Caracas, Feb. 28, 1784, AGN, Caracas, Gobernación y Capitanía General, tomo 29, folio 101; unsigned draft of a letter from the Captain General of Venezuela to the governor of Maracaibo, Caracas, June 27, 1800, AGN, Caracas, Gobernación y Capitanía General, tomo 87, folio 265. González Oropeza and Donis Ríos, 1989, 26.

230. Informe reservado del governador de Riohacha, Oct. 14, 1801, in Moreno and Tarazona, 1984, 290 ("no estando sujetos a nuestras leyes, no se les puede obligar a su observancia"; "¿quién podrá calcular hasta donde extenderían su venganza?").

231. The Franciscan historian Arcila Robledo, 1950, 168 ("son salvajes, y hasta la fecha de hoy, permanecen irreductibles"). "Irreductible," in the sense of "not subject to obedience," translates poorly into English.

232. Viceroy Antonio Caballero y Góngora, 1910, 1:754, paraphrasing, if not quoting, royal orders of Aug. 15, 1783 ("la reducción o extinción de los indios, porque de todos modos debía ocuparse la Costa"). Kuethe, 1970, 474–81. Kuethe, 1978, 150. Howe, 1998, 12, for the distinction between Cunas and Miskitos. For its governor's description of the province a decade earlier, see Ariza, 1971, 83–115.

233. For the viceroy's move to the coast, where he remained until 1789, and the text of this treaty, signed at the viceroy's residence at Turbaco, twenty-four kilometers from Cartagena, on July 21, 1787, see Pérez Ayala, 1951, 157–58, 167–72. See chap. 5, below.

234. The quote is from Gil y Lemos, 1977, 157, which includes a facsimile reproduction of the terms of Spain's face-saving withdrawal, signed in Cartagena, Oct. 25, 1789 ("una prueba de la satisfacción que tiene de ellos"). Kuethe, 1978, 138–41; Luengo Muñoz, 1961, 375 (who tells only half the story); Castillero Calvo, 1995, 330–32, 334–35. The abandonment of these forts and the hope of replacing them with a less costly coast guard were discussed after the fact by the king's council on May 28, June 4, and Aug. 17, 1792. Actas del Consejo de Estado, 1792, in AHN, Estado, libro 5.

235. Powell, 1952, 181–223.

236. Avilés, 1945, 534 ("viente o treinta miserables gentiles, resulta perpetuar el odio contra los españoles"). Avilés to Amigorena, Buenos Aires, Oct. 14, 1799, instructing him on what to tell Pehuenches and Ranqueles, quoted in Levaggi, 2000, 160 ("no ya por medio de la sangre y la devastación sino por el de las negociaciones y tratados"). For his vacilation and then approval of war against Charrúas, see Mariluz

Urquijo, 1987, 365–70, 377–80. Remnants of the Minuanes, who once enjoyed peaceful relations with Spaniards, also raided with Charrúas.

237. Lastarria believed that the degradation of savages was contrary to the laws of nature, but it resembled a sickness. In theory, one might take strong measures to cure it, as one did a "raging mania," but, he asked, "Who will apply this medicine with charity?" It was beyond man's capacity to do so, he concluded, and hence "there is no other means than patience, tolerance, sufferance, and diligent beneficence." "Descripción topográfica y física: Noticias económicas y políticas de las referidas colonias hasta su estado actual . . . [y] plan para su nueva vigoroza organización y economía interior," Madrid, Dec. 31, 1804, in Lastarria, 1914, 273 ("salvaje"; "enfermedad"; "manía furiosa"; "¿Quién aplicará esta medicina con caridad . . . ?"; "no hay otro medio que el de la paciencia, disímulo, sufrimiento, y beneficencia diligente").

238. At Mission San Miguel, Sept. 29, 1784, quoted in Acosta y Lara, 1961, 162 ("escaramuzas y batallas de los bárbaros con los españoles").

239. This occurred under Avilés's predecessor. Bernardo Suárez to Viceroy Antonio Olaguer Feliú, Dec. 27, 1797, quoted in Acosta y Lara, 1961, 135 ("pueblos que aunque Salvaje goza[n] de las prerrogativas y derechos de la Naturaleza y de Gentes: Sus Pueblos o tolderías no una sino muchas veces fueron dados al fuego y saco, asesinados sus ocupantes como las reses en el matadero"). Street, 1959, 43, notes the expansion of *estancias* in the region between the Yí and Negro rivers.

240. Agustín de Pinedo to the marqués de Avilés, 1799, quoted in Mariluz Urquijo, 1987, 368 ("por los suaves medios que meditó el legislador en la Ley de Indias"). Miguel Lastarria, personal secretary and legal advisor to Avilés, also insisted on the need to reduce the Charrúas with gentle means—although he would exterminate the bandits who lived among them. "Descripción topográfica y física: Noticias económicas y políticas de las referidas colonias hasta su estado actual . . . [y] plan para su nueva vigoroza organización y economía interior," Madrid, Dec. 31, 1804, in Lastarria, 1914, 240, 252, 259, 274.

241. Mariluz Urquijo, 1987, 368–401, outlines the war through the end of 1801. The dénouement of 1806 is in Acosta y Lara, 1961, 221–22, who also reproduces some of the documents. See, too, Kleinpenning, 1995, 83–86, 100–101, who overlooked Mariluz Urquijo's fine work but who provides an unparalleled view of the expansion of Spanish ranching. He notes that Charrúas had been pushed beyond the Río Negro by 1750 and that hostilities did not resume until toward the end of the century, when ranchers began to claim lands north of the river. See the epilogue below for the demise of the last free Charrúas in 1831.

Chapter 5. Trading, Gifting, and Treating

The epigraphs are from Azara, 1990, 115 ("La reducción de las naciones bárbaras sólo puede verificarse por tres medios: el primero es por el comercio y trato, el segundo por la fuerza, y el tercero por la persuasión"); Campillo y Cosío, 1789, 14 ("preferir el dominio a las ventajas y utilidades del comercio, y trato amigable con las Naciones bárbaras, fue causa de malograr las conquistas hechas y de no hacer otras no menos importantes"); José de Gálvez to Comandante General Teodoro de Croix, El Pardo, Feb. 22, 1779, AF ("Por este recomendable modo de la amistad, y buena fe conseguiremos, no sólo las indicadas ventajas, sino también dominaremos enteramente sin efusión de sangre a los que hoy son nuestros implacables enemigos").

1. For Viedma's views on justice for Indians, see Viedma, 1969a–72a, 6:675–35. The missions were between the Parapiti and Guaypay rivers.

2. Mariluz Urquijo, 1966, 327. For a chronicle of events leading up to this war, see Pifarré, 1989, 244–59, and for a more interpretive work, see Saignes, 1990, 127–39.

3. The opinion of Villava, Plata [today's Sucre, Bolivia], June 29, 1800, in the "Expediente obrado a representación del señor Gobernador Intendente de Cochabamba sobre haber mandado ahorcar al indio rebelde Sacuarao." AGN, Buenos Aires, IX, Guerra y marina, 1800, leg. 24.3.6. Transcript courtesy of Sylvia Ratto. Villava was the attorney for the *audiencia* of Charcas, with its seat in Upper Peru.

4. "Así la invasión de otra Nación podría ser un atentado contra el derecho de gentes que podrá vindicarse con las armas pero no un delito que pueda castigarse con las leyes." Viedma and his supporters did not dispute the argument that the rebels were not part of the social compact. Viedma to the Viceroy of Buenos Aires, Oct. 15, 1800, in ibid. For an able analysis of this episode, see Mariluz Urquijo, 1966, 309–30, and for the slippery meaning of "nation" in this era, see chap. 2 above.

5. Olaechea Labayen, 1981, 114.

6. Gálvez's orders to the president of Guatemala, San Ildefonso, Aug. 25, 1783, in Peralta, 1898, 216 ("rebeldes que siempre han sido"). For the Seris, see above, chap. 4.

7. The opinion of Villava, Plata, June 29, 1800 ("Es mejor política no escarmentarlos sino atraerlos: por haberlos escarmentado con azotes, nos han escarmentado ellos a flechazos y por no saber tratarlos y reducirlos estamos en continua guerra con unos hombres sun no teniendo lugar, tierra ni domicilio fijo, es imposible vencerlos ni sujetarlos").

8. Discurso sobre la Mita de Potosí [1793], in Villava, 1946, xxxvi–xxxvii ("un indio trasplantado a Londres podría ser un constante, y elocuente miembro del partido de la oposición").

9. Discurso sobre la Mita de Potosí [1793], in Villava, 1946, xxxvi–xxxvii ("indirectos"; "las necesidades y comodidades de una vida culta"). Vista del fiscal Victorián de Villava, sobre la servidumbre de los indios, March 12, 1795, in Villava, 1946, cxix ("siglo más ilustrado").

10. Quoted in Pagden, 1990, 115; see, too, Pagden, 1994c, 1–22, for the larger context of Spanish thought about the transformative effects of commerce on society.

11. Viana, 1958, 1:125 ("un pueblo sin comunicación ni tráfico con otras gentes, jamás puede civilizarse").

12. Funes, 1856, 2:286 ("Los hombres se docilizan con el trato, como piedras de los ríos con el roce continuo"), writing about the Pampas' commercial relations with Buenos Aires in the 1780s. Other examples are cited below, but see also the diary of Francisco Saavedra, Nov. 27, 1781, a disciple of Bernardo and José de Gálvez, in Saavedra, 1989, 257, and Juan Ignacio de Madariaga on the need to win Indian allegiance with trade goods in Guayana, an undated document from the 1750s, quoted in Lucena Giraldo, 1992a, 291.

13. Much of this "Oda al Comercio," by an anonymous author, appears in Chiaramonte, 1989, 223–26. See, too, 261–75.

14. "Ordenanzas de su Magestad hechas para los nuevos descubrimientos, conquistas y pacificaciones," July 13, 1573, in Colección, 1864–1884, 16:144–45, 153–87, for the larger purpose trade goods would serve. See, for example, TePaske, 1971, 21, 23, 24, for comparisons with English and French policy in southeastern North America in the Habsburg and early Bourbon eras. Among the exceptions was the Araucanía.

15. Sors, 1921–23, no. 45, 285 and 42, no. 46, 335, presenting and critiquing the Jesuit plan ("hambrientos, desnudos, desarmados y precisados a recibir la ley"; "¿que no comían antes que conociesen españoles?"). In North America, New Mexico officials prohibited trade with the Utes in 1778. Hafen and Hafen, 1954, 262.

16. Rodríguez Gallardo, 1975, 41 ("más astutos, sagaces y avisados"). Some modern scholars agree. Keeley, 1996, 131, speaking of frontiers, notes that in the long run "exchange is an inducement to or source of war and not a bulwark against it. Precisely because frontiers display things that people need or want (such as land, labor, spouses, and various commodities) just beyond the limits of their own social unit and beyond easy acquisition by the methods normal within their own society (such as sharing, balanced reciprocity, and redistribution by leaders), the temptation to gain them by warfare is especially strong in these regions." In Argentina, scholars have noted that the commerce that began in the 1780s and extended through the Rosas years gave Indian societies advantages when they resumed warfare. See the epilogue below.

17. Anónimo, 1980, 364 ("que pueden servir luego para cortar sus propias gargantas"). The author of this account, a Scotsman, otherwise writes positively about Spaniards and was more than a casual observer. He lived contentedly in the region from 1752 to 1756, traveling overland from Buenos Aires to Santiago and Córdoba. Oviedo Cavada, 1982, 353 n.211, notes Guill's bando, or order, of Jan. 10, 1767. See, too, León Solís, 1990, 90. Juan José de Vértiz to José de Gálvez, Buenos Aires, Oct. 24, 1780, AGI, transcript in Buenos Aires Museo Etnográfico, J26, called to my attention by Palermo, 1992.

18. The satirist Alonso Carrió de la Vandera, who disdained Indians. Concolorcorvo, 1965, 246; Concolorcorvo [Alonso Carrió de la Vandera], 1959, 377.

19. Moziño, 1970, 42. Dionisio Alcalá Galeano, quoted in Kendrick, 1991, 79, expressed similar sentiments. Pedro Andrés García, while not opposing trade with Indians, worried that traders exposed Indians to the vices of Spanish society. Pampas and Ranqueles who lived closest to the Río de la Plata seemed less virtuous than the more distant Huilliches. Navarro Floria, 1999, 257–58.

20. Funes, 1856, 2:286 ("ciertas comodidades de la vida, que desconocieron sus mayores. La glotonería, y el puro ocio no eran ya las únicas bases de su felicidad").

21. Malaspina, 1885, 367 ("ruido espantoso del cañón y de la guerra, sustituyendo los dulces lazos de un cambio lucroso"). It seems to me too simple to argue that Spain had a single ideology, as some historians suggest. See, for example, Slatta, 1998, 96.

22. Azara, 1969–72, 6:423 [to the viceroy in 1799] ("lo que encuentro mejor y único en el día es, entablar buen trato y comercio con dichos bárbaros, para que por su propio interés conserven la paz"). For the context, see Maeder, 1996, 68.

23. Plan para la pacificación de las provincias internas de Texas, Coahuila, y Nuevo México, presentado por Juan Gasiot, al comandante de las dichas provincias, D. Felipe de Neve, Arispe, Oct. 9, 1783, AF. Copy courtesy of Frank de la Teja ("por ahora y hasta tiempos de mayor ilustracíon no se les convide ni obligue a entrar en el gremio de nuestra Religión"). McCarty, 1990, 316–20, purports to translate all of this remarkable document, but only included Gasiot's warning against American expansion. Gasiot saw an enlightened Indian policy as the key to halting American expansion.

24. Drawing from Michel Foucault, Boccara, 1996a, 38–39, notes that the goal of trade was not peace but rather to "discipline" Indians and to make war on them in a new form, "a silent war: the political." Boccara gives new meaning to the word "war."

25. Capt. Carlos Sevilla, comandante de fronteras with jurisdiction over the forts of Ledesma, Santa Barbara, and San Bernardo in the western Chaco, quoted in

Cruz, 2001, 159, who does not provide the date but it is between 1780 and 1800 ("sosegada sóla en apariencia"; "¿ . . . que no tenemos gente para nada más que guardar mal la casa, que harían?").

26. Campomanes, 1988, 360, 355, citing *De l'esprit des lois*. Campomanes initially served as *fiscal*. See, too, Pagden, 1995, 118–25.

27. González de la Vara, 2002, 107–34, makes this case for New Mexico, and it would seem to apply in many other places where Spaniards took risks for profits in the Indian trade.

28. The quotation is from Brading, 1971, 25. Brading adheres to the view that José del Campillo y Cosío wrote the manuscript version of the *Nuevo sistema* in 1743, the year of his death, when he served as minister of finance, of the navy, war, and the Indies, and of the state (early in his career Campillo had spent six years in Mexico and the Caribbean), and that the work was highly influential because it circulated in manuscript among Bourbon ministers even though it was not published as a discrete work until 1789 (Campillo y Cosío, 1789). Brading, 1991, 469–70, 486–87, continued to take that position, and he has been in good scholarly company. See, for example, Artola, 1952, 692, 711–14; Tiryakian, 1978, 234–35, 254–57; and Pagden, 1995, 121–22. For Campillo's years in America, see Campillo y Cossío [*sic*], 1993, ix–xxi. The *Nuevo sistema* first appeared in print as part 2 of the *Proyecto económico,* which the Spanish *ilustrado* and economist Bernardo Ward wrote in 1762, but which was not published until 1779 after his death. Ward has been accused of plagiarizing the *Nuevo sistema* and does indeed make only modest changes in it (part 2 of his work, "Sobre la América," included the passages on winning the loyalty of independent Indians through trade), but since the manuscript was found among Ward's papers and then published, it may be that it was mistakenly attributed to Ward by his publisher. See Sarrailh, 1957, 18 n.3, and Ward, 1982, 324–30. Other scholars, however, point to internal inconsistencies and errors that suggest to them that Campillo could not have written the *Nuevo sistema* and that the document did not so much influence as reflect the views of some Bourbon thinkers. For the arguments and citations to other critical works, see Navarro García, 1983, 22–29, and Navarro García, 1995, 5–14, who argues that it did not influence the administration of Carlos III. I am persuaded of its influence by Brading, cited above, and by García Bernal, 1997, 8–16. The editor of the most recent edition of the *Nuevo sistema,* Manuel Ballesteros Gaibrois, ignores the question of the work's clouded authorship (Campillo y Cosío, 1993, 30).

29. Viedma, 1969c–72c, 3:678 ("con semejantes bárbaros, y con cuanta razón nos lo recomienda el señor Ward en su proyecto económico"). See, too, Viedma, 1969b–72b, 6:785–86, for similar sentiments about controlling Chiriguanos, following Ward.

30. Campillo y Cosío, 1789, 16 ("tratadas con maña y amistad, nos darian infinitas utilidades"), 14 ("pues siendo pocos los Españoles en América, y teniendo que sujetar millones de Indios"; "conservar intempestivamente el espíritu de conquistas, y preferir el dominio a las ventajas y utilidades del comercio, y trato amigable con las Naciones bárbaras"), 211 ("no hay hombre salvaje que no pueda dominar la industria, y hacerlo tratable la pronta concurrencia a todo quanto sea a su gusto").

31. Ibid., 210 ("indios bravos"), 212 ("el odio que tienen a los Españoles las Naciones confinantes"), 212–13 ("que les amenaza con el infierno, si se emborrachan ó toman más de una muger"; "aguardiente que tanto estiman").

32. Two visions have remained contested in the anthropological literature. See Clastres, 1996, 209, on his differences with Lévi-Strauss, the former believing in primitive man as warrior and the latter as trader.

33. An idea still held by some enlightened Spaniards, such as Antonio de Ulloa. Ulloa, 1992, 305–34.

34. Tiryakian, 1978, 243. See, too, Nash, 1986, 41.

35. This vision of an informal empire held considerable appeal; American expansionists, for example, would champion it in the last decades of the nineteenth century. See Walter LaFeber, *The New Empire: An Interpretation of American Expansion, 1860–1898* (Ithaca: Cornell University Press, 1963).

36. TePaske, 1964, 193–226; TePaske, 1971, 30–36.

37. Campomanes to José de Gálvez, reservado, Madrid, Sept. 14, 1784, AHN, Estado, leg. 3.885, exped. 17, no. 4 ("indios bravos"; "Este método puede ser conducente a nuestra situación actual y un modo indirecto de mantener aquellas naciones libres del dominio de la República Americana"). Campomanes's missive to Gálvez was inspired by his receipt of a report from an agent in North America, but he had extolled the French and English models of controlling Indians through trade in 1762. Campomanes, 1988, 29–30, 106, 121–22. For his view that English did not rely on missions, see p. 239. Ezquerra, 1962, 219, reminds us that "las ideas de Campomanes no han sido meramente teóricas, ya que ha sido un estadista y uno de los miembros más activos del equipo reformador de Carlos III."

38. Bernardo to José de Gálvez, [New Orleans], Oct. 24, 1778, quoted in West, 1914–15, 100–101. Gálvez married the daughter of Gilbert Antoine de St. Maxent, María Felicitas, in 1777.

39. José de Gálvez to Comandante General Teodoro de Croix, El Pardo, Feb. 20, 1779, AF ("Conseguido esto no podrán vivir sin nuestros auxilios").

40. See above, chap. 4.

41. Gálvez, 1951, art. 24 ("con el tiempo los ponga bajo de nuestra dependencia"). Worcester includes the

Spanish-language version, too. I have cited articles rather than pages, for ready reference to the text in either language.

42. The quotations are, respectively, in ibid., art. 47 ("el interés del comercio enlaza y estrecha las voluntades de los hombres"), and art. 52 ("conocer las ventajas de una vida racional").

43. Cortés, 1989, 31, writing in 1799.

44. As Spanish officials armed Hispanicized Indians like the Pueblos, the prohibition came to be understood as applying only to non-Christian Indians. See, for example, Croix's orders of Jan. 24, 1778, in Moorhead, 1975, 82. For Spanish law and practice, see Demaría, 1972, 131–39; Secoy, 1992, 4–5, 78–85; Schilz and Worcester, 1987, 1–10, and my discussion of firearms in chap. 2. Violations included Florida, mentioned above, and Anza's gifts of a small number of *carabinas* to Comanches and Utes in 1786, before Bernardo de Gálvez issued his well-known *Instrucción* of 1786. Jones, 1966, 158.

45. Gov. Barón de Ripperdá of Texas had a similar vision. Ripperdá to the viceroy, San Antonio, April 28, 1772, in Bolton, 1914, 1:269–70, and Smith, 2000, 52–53, 57, 59, 68–69, for the contretemps that followed.

46. Gálvez, 1951, art. 78 ("vayan olvidando su diestro manejo").

47. Ibid., art. 67 ("constituirlos en una nueva necesidad que estrechamente les obligue a reconocer nuestra forzosa dependencia").

48. Manuel de Amat to the king, Santiago, March 16, 1759, quoted in Boccara, 1999b, 447 ("más necesitados y dependientes y menos armados y poderosos, con más fundada esperanza de la sujeción, a que se aspira").

49. *Recopilación*, 1973, Libro 6, tit. 1, ley 36 ("el grave daño que resulta contra la salud, y conservación de los Indios"). For the French and Spanish balancing act in Louisiana, see Holmes, 1974, 160–64, and Arnold, 1985, 66–71. For English policy and practice, see Mancall, 1995, 170–74, and Dawson, 1983, 692, as examples.

50. Alonso Fernández de Heredia, recommending against making alcohol available to Miskitos in 1769, as quoted in Floyd, 1967, 124. See, too, Levaggi, 2002, 303.

51. *Real cédula* to Agustín de Jáuregui, Gobernador y Capitán General del Reyno de Chile y Presidente de mi Audiencia de la Ciudad de Santiago. El Pardo, Feb. 6, 1774, in ANSC, Fondos Varios, vol. 300, pieza 3 ("poner alguna cuota, que minorándose insensiblemente les obligue a reconocer la dependencia, sin exasperarlos"). For the Miskitos and Caribs, see Levaggi, 2002, 303. For Florida, see the "Puntos que deben observar los vasallos de S.M. C, que se empleen en el trato con los indios Talapuches," in Gómez del Campillo, 1944–45, 1944, 1:420 (art. 5),

which permitted licensed traders to sell alcohol but only with official approval. See, too, TePaske, 1971, 30–36, and Finegan, 1993, who reports *aguardiente de caña* being given to Indians by Spanish officials at St. Augustine between 1785 and 1788.

52. A group of soldier-merchants at the Chilean fort of Arauco petitioning in 1729 for exemption from the prohibition of trading wine to Indians, quoted in Cerda-Hegerl, 1990, 89 ("siendo vino para ellos como la moneda real de oro para nostros"). León Solís, 1990, 116–17; Villalobos R., 1992, 303–07, who also explains why Araucanians preferred it to their native apple-based *chicha*. For the Pampas, see Martínez Sierra, 1975, 1:222–23, and the example of Viceroy Vértiz in Levaggi, 2000, 128. By the 1790s, Pampas regularly traded for *aguardiente* in Buenos Aires. Arredondo, 1945, 398. For its use as a trade item in Patagonia, see Jones, 1984, 52.

53. Hurt, 2002, 10–11.

54. See, for example, Pedro de Nava, Instructions for Dealing with Apaches at Peace in Nueva Vizcaya, Chihuahua, Oct. 14, 1791, in Hendricks and Timmons, 1998, 102–09, and fray Diego Bringas in Matson and Fontana, 1977, 119, who was a critic of these reservations and would have mentioned alcohol as another of their failings had it been in use. Officers concerned with Indian policy note the distribution of guns and other gifts but do not mention alcohol. See Cortés, 1989, writing in 1799, and Manuel Merino's report of 1804 in John, 1991b. Prior to the *Instrucción* of 1786, alcohol does not appear to have been used even in delicate negotiations with Indians on the northern frontier. See John and Benavides Jr., 1994, 29–30 n.7.

55. Pino, 1995, 51 and 43 n.8 of facsimile ("no se preserven de emborracharse"; "agua loco").

56. There is scholarly confusion on this point. Anderson, 1999, 141, apparently unaware of Gálvez's 1786 *Instrucción*, believes that New Mexico officials illegally furnished Comanches with guns in 1791. He also notes the distribution of powder and ball in San Antonio (p. 177). Moorhead, 1968, 128, does not find any significant distribution of firearms during the time of Ugarte (1786–91). Schilz and Worcester, 1987, 8, say, "The recommendations of Gálvez and others regarding an open gun trade were largely ignored by Spanish policymakers." For firearm distribution, see Cortés, 1989, 70, writing in 1799, and Manuel Merino's report of 1804 in John, 1991b, 171, 173. Kavanagh, 1996, 185, suggests that San Antonio rather than Santa Fe was the distribution center for guns and ammunition. If so, that may not have been the case at the end of the colonial era. Salcedo y Salcedo, 1990, 46–47, notes in 1813 that Comanches annually visited Santa Fe for firearms and ammunition. Officials also permitted some Apaches *de paz* to possess firearms, and they apparently received

ammunition from Spanish officials. Matson and Fontana, 1977, 119.

57. Kenner, 1969, 33; Merrill, 2000, 639. Croix to José de Gálvez, Chihuahua, Sept. 23, 1778, in Bolton, 1914, 2:223, who identifies Nations of the North, which included Wichitas, as the purveyors of guns, and who mentions the trifles. Smith, 2000, 72–93, points out that Wichitas themselves, however, also suffered from a shortage of firearms and other trade goods, which they obtained mainly from non-Spanish sources. Gunpowder itself was scarce in the Interior Provinces, partly because Spanish protective legislation prohibited its local manufacture. See Pino, 1995, 57. Unable to supply its own military with sufficient weapons in the last years of empire, frontier officials had to look to the United States as a source of supply. See the episode of 1800 in Kavanagh, 1996, 185, and Salcedo y Salcedo, 1990, 34, for Nemesio Salcedo's complaint in 1813.

58. Calleja, 1949, fol. xxvii, xxxi.

59. Gálvez, 1951, art. 66 ("nuestras nuevas Colonias"). See Arnold, 2000, 87, for gunsmiths. After Spain reacquired Florida from the British in 1783, Spanish officials there granted a similar concession. Finegan, 1993, analyzed lists of gifts to Indians between 1785 and 1788 in the East Florida Papers (roll 167, *legajo* 360) and found *escopetas,* powder, ball, and flint among the gifts that came from the *real almacén* in St. Augustine. For trading in firearms by the Spanish-licensed, private firm of Panton, Leslie in Florida, see Coker and Watson, 1986, 33, 188.

60. Teodoro de Croix to José de Gálvez, Informe General, Arizpe, Jan. 23, 1780, Guadalajara 522, AGI, observes that Spain's Indian enemies in Interior Provinces were well armed, and a generation later Lt. Cortés suggested the same. Cortés, 1989, 69–70. Cortés also distinguished between the official dispensation of guns and the policy of prohibition. For limiting ammunition in the Southeast in the hope that Indians would use it only for hunting, see the instructions to Alejandro MacGillivray, *comisario* for the Creeks, New Orleans, July 20, 1784, in Gómez del Campillo, 1944–45, 1944, 1:438 (art. 9).

61. Ambrosio de Benavides to the governor, May 1, 1786, quoted in Ramírez, 1994, 25 ("en la tierra de los infieles"). See, too, Villalobos, 1992, 307.

62. As in Chile (León Solis, 1990, 17–18), where the church recommended this balancing act (Oviedo Cavada, 1982, 310–16, 325, 350) and the crown preferred it as well (*Real cédula* to Agustín de Jáuregui, Gobernador y Capitán General del Reyno de Chile y Presidente de mi Audiencia de la Ciudad de Santiago. El Pardo, Feb. 6, 1774, in ANSC, Fondos Varios, vol. 300, pieza 3). In a famous treaty signed with Paikín and other Mocobí leaders in the Chaco in 1774, Spanish officials explicitly denied the Indians' requests for guns and ammunition to defend

themselves from Abipones. Levaggi, 2000, 84, art. 11.

63. See, for example, García, 1969a–72a, 303, 358–59, who even saw the latest styles of military uniforms in Indian villages. Called to my attention by Navarro Floria, 1999, 257.

64. Vargas Machuca, 1892, 2:13 ("no hay niños más amigos de juguetes"). In the late 1500s, Spaniards in northern New Spain had ended a bloody war with the Chichimecas by buying them off with gifts. Powell, 1952, 189–93, 217–20.

65. For Spaniards responding to Indians, see Moorhead, 1968, 157–58, Méndez Beltrán, 1982, 168, and Bernardo de Gálvez to Gilberto Antonio Maxent, Havana, July 7, 1783, quoted in Levaggi, 1996b, 374.

66. As occurred in the Chaco, where Mocobíes complained about *bastones* that had handles of tin rather than silver, and in Spanish Louisiana, where Quapaws complained of shoddy guns and chintzy entertainment. Fray Antonio de López to the governor [of Tucumán?], Gran Chaco, June 22, 1776, AGI, Audiencia de Buenos Aires, 244, reference courtesy of James Saeger. Arnold, 2000, 97–99; DuVal, 2001, 10–11.

67. *Real orden,* Nov. 11, 1776, to the president of Chile, in Ayala, 1988–96, 7:353 ("señales de distinción"). This practice occurred throughout the empire, with royal approval. See, for example, the *real cédula* to the viceroy of the La Plata, Sept. 6, 1777, in Alumni, 1951, 264.

68. I have drawn these items from Méndez Beltrán, 1982, 162–70, who lists and analyzes gifts presented at *parlamentos* of 1716, 1782, 1784, 1793, and 1803. For Spaniards annointing these *caciques gobernadores,* see León Solís, 1982, 41.

69. My examination of Medina, 1900, suggests that medals for the Indian trade did not come into their own until the era of Carlos III. Spaniards had used medals earlier, but for different purposes, as in 1735 when the governor of Cumaná asked the Council of the Indies for gold and silver medals to present to the most distinguished chiefs because they had inquired about the physical appearance of the king. The medals were specially minted that year. Carlos de Sucre to the Council of the Indies, April 1, 1735, discussed in Medina, 1900, 13.

70. Gov. Antonio de Ulloa to Capt. D. Francisco Riú, March 14, 1767, quoted in Ewers, 1974, 273. See, too, Usner, 1992, 131. In 1777, Bernardo de Gálvez had no medals to replace the British medals that a group of caciques had surrendered to him as a sign of loyalty to Spain, but he promised he would have some soon and Indians kept up the pressure. Levaggi, 1996a, 237–38. Prucha, 1971, 11, surveys the use of medals in the area of the Louisiana Purchase under Spain, but despite his broad title ignores Spanish use of medals in southwestern North America. Levaggi,

1996a, 229, citing TePaske, 1964, reports that the governor of Florida gave a medal to an Apalachicola delegation in 1717, but TePaske does not claim that medals were among gifts presented to Indians in Florida prior to 1763 (pp. 193–226). Levaggi, 2000, 265, also claims that a Spanish governor reported seeing a Comanche leader wearing a medal with an image of the king in 1762, but the document he cites says a cross, not a medal. Courtesy of Matt Babcock.

71. Bernardo de Gálvez to Gilberto Antonio Maxent, Havana, July 7, 1783, quoted in Levaggi, 1996b, 376 ("jefe de medalla"). During the recent conflict with Britain, officials had apparently tried to compensate for the shortage of goods for the Indian trade by distributing even more medals.

72. See, for example, Din and Nasatir, 1983, 268, 273, and O'Brien, 2002, 96.

73. DuVal, 2001, 1, 9–10.

74. José de Gálvez to Matias Gálvez, El Pardo, March 17, 1779, quoted in Ramos, 1990, 246. I have drawn other details from Miguel Múzquiz to José de Gálvez, Madrid, March 6, 1779, in AGI, Estado, Audiencia de Guatemala, 665.

75. Anza, *Relación de los Sucesos occuridos en la Provincia del Nuevo-Mexico con motivo de la Paz concedida a la Nación Comanche... desde 17 de noviembre de 1785 hasta 15 de julio de 86,* AGN, Provincias Internas, tomo 65, exped. 7 ("con la medalla de su Real Busto ... para que con esta insignia fuese respetado de sus súbditos, y tratado con honrosa distinción entre los Españoles"). Thomas, 1932, 302, 319–20 (July 15, 1786), and Pedro Garrido Durán's summary of Anza's negotiations with the Navajos in 1785–86, Chihuahua, Dec. 21, 1786, in Thomas, 1932, 347. In editing Anza's diary of an earlier expedition to California, Bolton, 1930, mistakenly assumed that Anza decorated the Yuma chief Salvador Palma with a red ribbon bearing a medal with the king's image (2:39–40; entry of Feb. 7, 1774), but Anza says he used a coin, or *moneda,* not a *medalla* (1:99; 2:163). The Spanish language version of Anza's complete diary is at http://anza.uoregon.edu.

76. Copy of a letter from Concha to Nava, Santa Fe, Dec. 4, 1793, AGI, Guadalajara, 290. Concha found some forty-five hundred Comanches in eight hundred tents gathered northeast of Santa Fe on the Canadian River. For the death of Ecueracapa, see John, 1975, 762.

77. Jáuregui to the minister of the Indies, Julián de Arriaga, Santiago, June 3, 1774, in Barros Arana, 1884–1902, 6:346, reporting that he gave each a silver medal on a silver chain.

78. Medina, 1900, 25–30, reproduces the documents. The medals, minted in Potosí, said, "EN PREMIO DE LA FIDELIDAD."

79. See, for example, my account of the aftermath of the treaty of 1774 with Paikín in the Chaco, where

his successors returned a *bastón* but not a medal, and treaties of 1805 and 1806 with the Ranquel chief Carripilún, in Levaggi, 2000, 161, 166. The expenses for *parlamentos* in Chile include *bastones,* but not medals.

80. For Amigorena, see León Solís, 1998, 173, 178, and Levaggi, 2000, 152; for the treaty of 1796 with Ranqueles, signed at Córdoba, see ibid., 159 (art. 6).

81. K. Jones, 1998, 103–06, suggests that the cost of supporting "indios amigos" in Buenos Aires, and of supporting Apaches *de paz* in northern New Spain with what she calls rations, represented a tiny percentage of the budget for the defense of these areas. The costs of the treaty system, she concludes, were minuscule compared to its financial benefits. Yet, as I suggest below, funds for entertaining and gifting Indian allies (which went beyond rations) also came out of parts of the budget that supported presidios. The expenses of buying a peace, then, were higher than her figures suggest.

82. Méndez Beltrán, 1982, 139–41, 167–68, 171 ("ramo de agasajo de indios"), who finds that gifts constituted nearly half of the costs of the 1793 *parlamento.* Moorhead, 1975a, 219, finds that a soldier's annual salary in northern New Spain was 240 pesos in 1787. Cruz, 2001, 147, finds soldiers earning 90 pesos a year, plus rations, tobacco, and uniform, in late eighteenth-century forts on the western edge of the Chaco.

83. The marqués de Loreto drew from Buenos Aires's municipal war fund in 1785. Levaggi, 2000, 131. Diego de Gardoqui to the viceroy of the La Plata, Aranjuez, Dec. 21, 1795, in Gardoqui, 1930, 355–56. Torre Revello, 1937, 126–30, reproduces the report of the junta in Mendoza. In Córdoba, too, there were pressures in 1805 to cut expenses for entertaining Indians, which amounted to ½ *real* per Indian in 1804. AGN [Buenos Aires], Hacienda, leg. 119, exped. 3033, and leg. 128, exped. 3230.

84. Teodoro de Croix to José de Gálvez, Arispe, May 23, 1780, AGI, Guadalajara, 271, complains that the *fondo de gratificaciones* at each presidio is inadequate. For that fund, see Moorhead, 1975a, 209–10. The viceroy of New Spain, the marqués de Branciforte, to Eugenio de Llaguno, Mexico, June 30, 1797, AGI, Guadalajara, 390. Simmons, 1968, 141–47, for the difference between the *fondo de aliados* and the *fondo de gratificaciones* in New Mexico, and, Frank, 2000, 132–35. For the great annual variation in New Mexico, and for income from wild horses in Texas, see Kavanagh, 1996, 182–183.

85. Holmes, 1965, 154. In Louisiana by 1794, the peso was equivalent to a dollar and so Holmes expresses this in dollars (p. 44 n.32). I have put it in pesos. Gullón Abao, 1993, 105–07, notes the rising costs of gifts in the Chaco in the last half of the 1700s. For the high percentage of expenditures on Comanches,

see Simmons, 1968, 146, and Kavanagh, 1996, 183, table 4.3.

86. Ramos, 1990, 144, finds no evidence of sending Indian delegations to Spain, although in the early Habsburg era, Indian children were sent to Spain to be educated. Olaechea Labayen, 1969, 103–14. See my discussion of the visits of the Yuma Salvador Palma to Mexico City, and the Miskito Colville Briton to León and Cartagena, in chap. 6.

87. Loreto, 1945, 277, notes the "punible codicia de los manipulates." DuVal, 2001, 17–22, is a fine case study of a local officer caught in the middle.

88. Croix to Gálvez, April 23, 1782, AGI, Guadalajara, 253.

89. Gov. Barón de Riperdá to Viceroy Antonio María Bucareli, San Antonio, April 27, 1772, in Velasco Ceballos, 1936, 1:58, on a peace with Comanches ("dádivas que les hizo para asegurar su amistad"). Similarly, Dr. Pérez de Uriondo, the *fiscal* of the *audiencia* of Santiago, to Gov. O'Higgins, Sept. 27, 1791, quoted in Casanueva, 1992b, 197.

90. Gov. Alós to Viceroy Arredondo, Asunción, Nov. 19, 1792, quoted in Cardozo, 1934, 142 ("Peor será tenerlos enemigos").

91. Instrucción, Col. Fernando de la Concha to his successor, Lt. Col. Fernando Chacón, Chihuahua, June 28, 1794, in AGN, Mexico, Historia, vol. 41, 327R–52, facsimile courtesy of Ross Frank ("Este expendio debe hacerse por la misma mano del gobernador, para que les sea más grato"). Translation in Concha, 1949, 242. White, 1983, 73, notes that Choctaws "resented the English perception of presents as mere bribes." This may have been the case with many Native peoples.

92. Mauss, 1967, 3 and *passim*; Godelier, 1999, summarizes Mauss's critics and takes his work in a new direction. Native societies throughout the hemisphere seem to use gifts as metaphors for relations of trust. La Vere, 1993, 322–37, is a fine case study.

93. José Francisco de Amigorena to the Real Hacienda, May 6, 1794, quoted and astutely analyzed by Roulet, 1999–2001, 225.

94. De la Cruz, 1969b–72b, 263–64 ("Nuestra rusticidad sólo se vence con la franqueza, pues como carecemos de cosas buenas, tenemos una vida de perro, y sus propiedades. El perro ama a quien le da, y le es también grato y fiel"; "yo soy racional"). Villalobos R., 1989b, 205, incorrectly identifies him as a Huilliche. For a brief biography, see Hux, 1991b, 25–29.

95. Croix quoting his own orders to the governor of Texas in Report of 1781 to José de Gálvez, in Thomas, 1941, 97.

96. See Barfield, 1989, 7–8, with its interesting parallels.

97. Guill to the crown, May 1, 1767, quoted in Barros Arana, 1884–1902, 6:238 ("esto que de parte de V.M. se llama agasajos, ellos lo reciben como tributo"), arguing that war against Araucanians would be cheaper than peace. See, too, Foerster G., 1991, 200–201, and Hall, 1991, 49. Chiriguanos, too, one Jesuit complained in 1756, saw gifts "como un tributo que les era debido" (quoted in Saignes, 1990, 125). For gifts as a sign of weakness, see also Haedo, 1872, 457.

98. Report of Francisco Joseph Maran, Concepción, Aug. 28, 1784, quoted in Boccara, 1999b, 446 ("Se goza en esta frontera de paz, pero solo ventajosa a los enemigos").

99. Ulloa, 1992, 333 ("forman ellos el concepto de ser más hábiles, sabios, y astutos que los que los solicitan, los temen, y los obsequian"). Called to my attention by Levaggi, 1996a, 235, who also quotes extensively from Ulloa's private correspondence antedating his Louisiana experience.

100. John, 1975, 638, summarizing the view of Texas governor Domingo Cabello in 1783; Silvestre, 1789, 97–98, criticizing Viceroy Guiror's treatment of Cunas and Guajiros "with caresses and gifts" ("con las caricias y regalos"); Calleja, 1949, fol. xxxvii.

101. Santa María, 1930, 2:426 ("Estos, no obstante la suma dulzura y hasta excesiva con que se les trata, no dejan de multiplicar sus incursiones haciendo frecuentes males, y volviendo muertes y destrozos por gratificaciones y buen trato de sus bienhechores").

102. Hämäläinen, 1998, 497; Ewers, 1974, 279–82. White, 1991, 94–95, offers an eloquent critique of those who see all exchange as economic—the so-called formalists. O'Brien, 2002, 75–76, and others remind us that in some times and places Indians attributed spiritual power to the people who had the ability to manufacture remarkable products like firearms.

103. For example, Tomás Vélez Cachupín, a two-term governor of New Mexico and practitioner of personal diplomacy. See Vélez Cachupín to his successor, Santa Fe, New Mexico, Aug. 12, 1754, in Thomas, 1940, 129–43, his brief biography in Ebright, Escudero, and Hendricks, 2003, 285–321, and Weber, 1992, 227, where I describe him as anticipating the new emphasis on trade, treaties, and toleration. Levaggi, 2002, 265–66, chides me for calling the new policy new and argues that it goes back at least to Vélez Cachupín in New Mexico. I agree, yet still maintain that it was new in the sense that it became the policy of choice after the mid-1780s instead of exceptional, as it was under Vélez Cachupín.

104. For an introduction to the relative peace of the late colonial era in northern New Spain and its literature, see Weber, 1992, 230–35, and Aboites Aguilar, 1995, 41–43.

105. See the Account of the Events Concerning Peace Conceded to the Comanche Nation, by Pedro Garrido y Durán, Chihuahua. Dec. 21, 1786, in Thomas, 1932, 305–06; Moorhead, 1968, 152.

106. Hämäläinen, 1998, 502–03, offers a brilliant synthesis and analysis. Anza's force of 600 included 259 Pueblos according to Jones, 1966, 155. For the smallpox

epidemic among the eastern Comanches, see John
and Benavides Jr., 1994, 37–38, 49, and Fenn, 2001,
211–15, 261–62. Even as Comanches maintained
peace in Texas and New Mexico, they continued
to raid in Nuevo León. Adams, 2000, 343. For more
on the 1786 treaty, see below.

107. For the Navajo treaty, see Thomas, 1932, 347–48,
Moorhead, 1968, 177, Weber, 1992, 231, and the Spanish version in Levaggi, 2002, 275–76.

108. Instrucción, Col. Fernando de la Concha to his successor, Lt. Col. Fernando Chacón, Chihuahua, June
28, 1794, in AGN, Mexico, Historia, vol. 41, 327R-
52, facsimile courtesy Ross Frank ("En esta nación
se encuentra fé en los tratados que estipulan, verdad
constante, buena hospitalidad, y costumbres modes-
tas"). Translation in Concha, 1949, 238. Benes, 1965,
63–76, concentrates almost entirely on Concha's
administration. August, 1981, 141–60, adds little more
to the subject.

109. Moorhead, 1968, 170–99, 200–269. See my brief
discussion of treaties with Apaches, below.

110. Weber, 1992, 231–32.

111. The details of governing the Apache peace establishments were spelled out by Pedro de Nava in Instructions of Oct. 14, 1791. These are translated in
Hendricks and Timmons, 1998, 102–09 (quotations
from par. nos. 3 and 33), and summarized in Moorhead, 1975, 261–65. For a contemporary view see
Cortés, 1989, 34. Stockel, 2003, 60–61, describes regular religious ceremonies at the *establecimiento* at the
presidio of Janos, but this seems entirely conjectural.
See Griffen, 1988, 109–10, a fine case study. See, too,
the lament of Diego Bringas in Matson and Fontana,
1977, 119. *Establecimientos de paz* had informal beginnings earlier in the century. See Juan Bautista de
Anza the elder to Manuel Bernal de Huidobro, Ures,
Aug. 13, 1735, in Polzer and Sheridan, 1997, 305–06.
Nava's policy represented a change from Croix's.

112. Rough draft of a letter from Concha to Jacobo
Ugarte, July 13, 1790, SANM, roll 12, frames 289–
91, called to my attention by Deloria and DeMallie,
1999, 1:136, who have confused sender and recipient ("desconfianza"; "tal vez por estos antecedentes").

113. Pino, 1995, 51–52 and 42 of the facsimile ("Jamás
hubieramos creído, a no haberlos visto, el beneficio
que ha resultado a la provincia de este rasgo de
política").

114. Jacobo Ugarte to Juan Bautista de Anza, Oct. 5, 1786,
in Thomas, 1932, 340. See, too, Moorhead, 1968, 154,
and John, 1975, 712, 732–33, who explains that Comanches abandoned the town because it was a reminder of the death, not out of fear of the dead.
Brooks, 2002, 162–64, explains Comanche strategy.
Hämäläinen, 2001, 219 n.31, notes the drought. The
crown continued to ignore the question of missions
and to exert pressure on Navajos to farm until the
end of the colonial era. See the "Convenio de paz

con la nación Navajó," Santa Fe, Aug. 21, 1819, art.
5, *Gaceta Extraordinaria del Gobierno de Mexico*, vol.
10, no. 144, Oct. 27, 1819.

115. Reeve, 1971, 101–32, 223–52; Flagler, 1997, 193–201.

116. Cordero y Bustamante, 1864, 379 ("En el día, las
sábias providencias de un gobierno justo, activo y
piadoso, la van haciendo terminar, debiéndose ad-
vertir que no solo no aspira su sistema a la destrucción ó esclavitud de estos salvajes, sino que solicita
por los medios más eficaces su felicidad, dejándolos
poseer sus hogares en el seno de la paz, con la precisa
circunstancia de que bien impuestos de nuestra justicia y poder para sostenerla"). For a translation, see
Matson and Schroeder, 1957, 350. Merino's 1804 report, in John, 1991b, largely plagiarizes Cordero's
report on Apaches and adds material on other tribes.

117. Cortés, 1989, 31.

118. Pedro de Nava, Instructions for Dealing with
Apaches at Peace in Nueva Vizcaya, Chihuahua,
Oct. 14, 1791, in Hendricks and Timmons, 1998, 102.

119. See chap. 4 above. For an introduction to the large
literature on the discourse of rationalization and its
application to an earlier era in northern Mexico,
see Gradie, 1994, 67–88.

120. Chapa, 1997, 48.

121. Nentvig, 1980, 82; Croix to Lt. Col. Manuel Muñoz,
Arispe, July 26, 1781, quoted in Levaggi, 2002, 249
("indios bárbaros de perversas inclinaciones, y costumbres"). See, too, Levaggi, 2002, 256, for Croix's
lack of confidence in Apaches.

122. Felipe de Neve, "Relación concisa y exacta del estado en que ha encontrado las Provincias Internas,"
Arizpe, Dec. 1, 1783, AGI, Guadalajara 268, 43, copy,
courtesy of Charles Cutter ("ni capaces de admitir
la razón, y la persuasión"; "no pueden vivir con
sosiego, y tranquilidad en su propio pais").

123. Cordero, 1864, 370 ("robustez extraordinario"). Similarly, see Bernardo de Gálvez in John, 1984a, 303–04.

124. Cordero, 1864, 379 ("cruel y sangrienta guerra"; "in-
fracciones, excesos y avaricia"). Merino, who copied
nearly all of Cordero's report on Apaches, did not
share this sentiment. John, Oct. 1991, 157 n.35.

125. Gálvez, 1951, art. 37 ("primeras necesidades"; "perecen de hambre y miseria").

126. Gálvez, 1925, 539 ("si el Indio no es amigo es por
que no nos debe beneficios, y que si se venga es por
justa satisfacción de sus agravios"; "lo cierto es que
son tan agradecidos como vengativos, y que esto último debiamos perdonarlo a una nación que no ha
aprendido filosofía con que domar un natural senti-
miento"). Translated in John, 1984, 304.

127. Cortés, 1989, 30. Spaniards interested in commerce
over war expressed similar sentiments about other
Indians as well. See, for example, Saavedra, 1989,
183–84, who holds that the vices of Indians of southeastern North America were a consequence of their
exposure to hostile Europeans. War hawks contin-

ued the old discourse, of course. See, for example, Calleja, 1949, fol. xxx, xxxv.

128. Seed, 2001, 108.

129. I am following the suggestive interpretation of Mandrini, 1993b, 31–34. For his explanation of the unraveling of this modus vivendi, see Mandrini, 1997, 23–34.

130. Adelman, 1999, 31 (and 37 for exports from the Banda Oriental); Garavaglia, 1994, 65–66, points out that many of the hides in the later years came from Indians on the pampa. See, too, Brown, 1979, 30.

131. The closure, dated Aug. 19, 1779, is quoted in Crivelli Montero, 1991, 17 ("los indios de paz"). Vértiz y Salcedo, 1945, 151–52, tells of sending Licon Pagni (whose name is spelled in many variations, including Lincon Pangui, Lincopán, and Lincón) to the Malvinas. Hux, 1993, 38, says he was sent to the prison at Martín García. The Malvinas had been placed under the jurisdiction of the new viceroyalty of the La Plata in 1776. Hoffman and Hoffman, 1984, 61.

132. Apparently from testimony taken from Alcaluán in 1780, quoted in Crivelli, 1991, 22 ("si el cristiano no le da la paz y le envían las indias e indios que están en Buenos Aires, para canjearlos por los muchos cautivos cristianos que tienen allá, harán guerra continua por todas partes a fin de vengarse"). It is Crivelli who suggests the raids were aimed to force negotiations.

133. The marqués de Loreto to Antonio Valdés, March 1, 1788, quoted in Torre Revello, 1970, 71 ("la paz y el trato lícito"). See, too, Loreto, 1945, 266.

134. For Indian motives I am following Crivelli, 1991, 6–32. For Spanish motives, see especially Levaggi, 2000, 125–37, who describes how the government of Buenos Aires and the Pampas (represented by a confederation headed by Callfilqui) groped their way toward a peace treaty on Sept. 5, 1790. I describe the treaty more fully below.

135. The marqués de Loreto's successor, Nicolás de Arredondo. Arredondo, 1945, 398 ("nada hemos tenido de insultos, ni de robos por parte de ellos"). Ortelli, 2003a, 71–110, details this trade.

136. Vértiz to José de Gálvez, Buenos Aires, Oct. 24, 1780, AGI, AB, leg. 60, transcript in the Museo Etnográfico, Universidad de Buenos Aires, carpeta J25 ("que no teniendo estos bárbaros principios bastantes para discernir la fuerza de estos pactos"). Barba, 1997, 59–60. As elsewhere, peace was relative. Avilés, 1945, 502, reported, for example, Pampa depredations at Chascomús in 1801, and Pedro Andrés García, one of the most astute observers of the Pampas, criticized it in 1811 as a time of robberies, which authorities failed to halt in the interest of an "amistad aparente." Quoted in Navarro Floria, 1999, 256.

137. Comadrán Ruíz, 1955, 73–74, quoting and paraphrasing an economic report of May 1802, June 23, 1802,

written perhaps by Manuel Belgrano ("irá reformando sus bárbaras costumbres y haciendo ciudadanos útiles al estado"; "es cosa sabida que el comercio hace estos milagros, y no hay para qué detenernos en elogiarlo"). See, too, José García Martínez de Cáceres, 1802, quoted in Torre Revello, 1970, 73, for the role of "agrado y dádiva." For examples from other areas, see Ebright, 1996, 227–29, on the successful Indian policy of New Mexico's Gov. Tomás Vélez Cachupín in the 1750s and 1760s, and Azara, 1969–72, 6:423, on Payaguás and Guanás in Paraguay and with Pampas in the province of Buenos Aires.

138. Torre Revello, 1970, 74, quoting the *Seminario de Agricultura, Industria y Comercio*, Feb. 16, 1803 ("Breve dejarán el Quillapi, y con sus bárbaras costumbres, y seremos deudores al comercio de la permanente amistad de unos salvajes, que antes se tuvo por imposible el conservarla"). See, too, the similar observation of Pedro Antonio Cerviño in the same newspaper (Dec. 22, 1802), quoted in Martínez Sierra, 1975, 1:257. For the barter in tobacco and drink, see the marqués de Loreto to Antonio Valdés, March 1, 1788, quoted in Torre Revello, 1970, 71.

139. Ancán Amún, whose father and uncle had joined the Spaniards, speaking after the event in 1781, and quoted in Jiménez, 1997, 48, whose work on the Pehuenches de Malargüe informs this discussion ("fueron espulsados luego de las tierras que poseian en las faldas de las cordilleras del lado de Chile y buscar la vida por la otra parte").

140. For the weakness of Cuyo and the damage inflicted, see León Solís, Silva Galdames, and Téllez Lúgaro, 1997, 33–37.

141. Amigorena was appointed Comandante de Frontera y Armas de Mendoza in 1781 and held that position until his death. A number of historians open windows on this time and place: Marfany, 1940, 326–31; Villalobos R., 1989, 204–06; Comadrán Ruíz, 1955, 54–57, 65; Levaggi, 2000, 144–48, 162–64. León Solís, 2001b, is the most detailed account, placing Pehuenche–Mendoza relations in the larger geopolitical sphere. Two major articles, Roulet, 1999–2001, 199–239, and Roulet, 2002, 77–78, 82–93, contain the richest analysis of Amigorena's modus operandi.

142. Quoted in Torre Revello, 1958–59, 30 ("sus leales y obedientes aliados"), which remains valuable for its reproduction of Amigorena's widow's rich description of his achievement and generosity (pp. 27–31). Roulet, 2002, 93–98, who points out how close Amigorena came to losing trust (pp. 78, 87). For context, see also León Solís, 1982, 31–67, Villalobos R., 1992, 338–40, and Casanova Guarda, 1996a, 72–92. For what is known about some of Amigorena's Huilliche–Ranquel adversaries, including Llanquetruz, see Hux, 1991b, 7–15.

143. Amigorena to the oficiales reales, Mendoza, May 6,

1794, quoted in León Solís, 1998, 174–75, and León Solís, 2001b, 251 ("Derecho de Gentes").

144. The population estimate is from Roulet, 1999–2001, 211. After allying themselves with Spaniards, Pehuenches saw more of their population swept away by epidemics. A census of 1796 counted 1,380, of whom 200 were men. Jiménez, 1997, 46–49. See, too, Villalobos R., 1989b, 64–65, for the importance of *pehuenes* to their diet.

145. Lic. Feliciano Antonio Chiclana to Carlos IV, Buenos Aires, Dec. 29, 1804, in Chiclana, 1945, 34 ("Brava Nación de Indios Ranqueles"; "al interes, y utilidad, que sienten los Indios en su comercio de pieles, plumages, y manufacturas"; "no se debe a las guardias fronterizas, ni al corto número de soldados blandengues"). He says twenty to thirty leagues, which I have converted to miles at 2.6 miles per league. For more on Chiclana, see Cutolo, 1968–85, 2:451–52, and Martínez Sierra, 1975, 1:259–60, 2:53–54. For the recent relocation of those Ranqueles, see Fernández C., 1998, 48–57, and for the treaty to which Chiclana refers, signed at Córdova in 1796, see Levaggi, 2000, 157–59—a commercial treaty which placed more restrictions on Ranqueles than Spaniards had on Pampas.

146. Arredondo, 1945, 400 ("se alejen por miedo de nuestras armas").

147. Esteban Miró to the conde de Campo Alange, New Orleans, March 4, 1788, quoted in Armillas Vicente, 1975, 4.

148. D. A. Brading, "Bourbon Spain and its American Empire," in Bethell, 1984, 1:434–35. Illegal trade represented two-thirds of all commerce in the empire in the late seventeenth century, and the percentage probably increased rather than decreased. MacLachlan, 1988, 160 n.29.

149. By then the Mbayás and their vassals, the Guanés, controlled the northern reaches of the Chaco from northern Paraguay westward to the missions at Chiquitos.

150. Arredondo, 1945, 428–30. Santamaría, 1992, 120–48, offers a fine analysis of Mbayá resistance in this period.

151. Gov. Alós to Viceroy Arredondo, Asunción, Nov. 19, 1792, quoted in Cardozo, 1934, 142, 152. Campomanes, 1988, 108, noted the Mbayás' affinity for the Portuguese as early as 1762.

152. Ca. 1797, quoted in Areces, 1992, 56 ("tratarlos con amor para conservar la buena amistad y paz").

153. Quoted in Areces, 1992, 57 ("ni se procederá contra ellos ofensivamente sino en los casos de insultos y resistencia"; "se les dejará todo el ganado vacuno y lanar para que olvidando su vida bárbara y errante se conviertan por necesidad en Pastores y Labradores"; "ladrones pérfidos y sanguinarios"; "se civilizaron poco a poco"). I owe much to the brilliant ethnohistorical analysis of Vangelista, 1993, 64–69, 75, to

which I cannot do justice in this brief discussion, and also to the overview in Súsnik and Chase-Sardi, 1995, 71–76.

154. Lastarria, "Descripción topográfica y física: Noticias económicas y políticas de las referidas colonias hasta su estado actual … [y] plan para su nueva vigoroza organización y economía interior," Madrid, Dec. 31, 1804, in Lastarria, 1914, 271 ("no deben caracterizarse de Ladrones"; "estado de ignorancia y barbaridad en que se hallan").

155. This is not to say that Spaniards did not have some success in winning over caciques from the highly segmented Mbayá society. See the treaty signed at Pueblo Atirá, Jan. 31, 1798, by Gov. Lázaro de Ribera and the Mbayá ambassador, Etiganuite, alias Luis Zavala, and the leader of the Guanás, Francisco Chupé Etelanoé, who represented nine caciques. Gondra Collection, Calendar no. 2118 [MG 1760c], University of Texas, Austin.

156. Levaggi, 2002, 304, summarizes Caballero y Góngora's instructions to Hooper and reproduces the 1787 treaty but omits both the opening paragraph that identifies the signatories and the final signatures. Caballero y Góngora, 1920, 197–202, lacks the final signatures. The complete version, termed a "convención" by the viceroy, is in Pérez Ayala, 1951, 168–72. The quotations are in article 1 ("tratará como a vasallos rebeldes") and among the signatures at the end ("inglés, que hablan muchos de los indios"). Góngora to [José de Gálvez], Turbaco, July 26, 1787, in Pérez Ayala, 1951, 172–75, discusses Hooper's role and describes the Cunas' demands. For context, see Kuethe, 1978, 137–48. This was not the first time Spanish officials made written concessions to Cunas. In 1738 and 1741, worried that the Cunas would take the side of the English in a war in the Caribbean, the crown signed treaties with two Cuna leaders, offering gifts and the promise that they would not be coerced into becoming Christians if they allied themselves with Spain. Gallup-Díaz, 2002, 286–88. On the rules regarding hostages, see Vattel, 1759, 1:210–11 (bk. 2, chap. 16, pp. 245–61).

157. The 1789 treaty is reproduced in facsimile in Gil y Lemos, 1977, 165–72, quotation, p. 157 ("fieles amigos de los españoles").

158. Convention between his Britannic Majesty and the King of Spain, London, July 14, 1786, in *The Annual Register, or a View of the History, Politics, and Literature for the Year 1786* (London: J. Dodsley, 1788), 264.

159. García, 2002, 460–62.

160. A report from an unnamed local official, quoted in García, 1999, 104. See, too, Peralta, 1898, 254–59.

161. Floridablanca, 1867, 230 [to the Junta de Estado] ("agasajos, regalos y todo género de buen trato"; "los puntos principales por donde confinamos con otras naciones"). For Floridablanca's power and influence, see Ezquerra, 1962, 216, and Lynch, 1989, 252–53, 297.

162. Ibid. ("las malas ideas e impresiones que les han dado nuestros enemigos contra los españoles"; "la mala fe"; "lo que han hecho con los indios septentrionales, en que ahora existen los nuevos Estados Unidos de las colonias americanas").

163. That expenditures exceeded income had become painfully clear by 1792, all the way to the king and his council. Session of May 14, 1792, Actas del Consejo de Estado, 1792, in AHN, Estado, Libro 5. Wortman, 1982, 154–55, characterizes the Central American economy.

164. Dawson, 1998, 68–78, 86–87; Dawson, 1983, 704. Romero Vargas, 1995, 104–13, 197–98, for Hodgson and his remarkable collaboration with Spanish officials. If British reports can be believed, Miskitos maintained a residual hatred of Spaniards, and there may be some material as well as historical basis for this animosity, which the British clearly encouraged.

165. Grahn, 97, 19–20, who kindly made his manuscript available to me.

166. González Mollindo to the Secretario de Estado y del Despacho Universal de la Guerra, Aug. 3, 1803 [Guatemala?], quoted in Salvatierra, 1939–42, 1:530, and describing a scheme of several years earlier proposed by one Miguel Sánchez Pareja ("el horrible proyecto de envenenar al primer jefe de los indios, y tuvo la demencia de proponerlo como un medio aprobado en política"). He does not name King George II, but he appears to have been the target, for he was the *primer jefe* until his death in late 1800. Romero Vargas, 1995, 181. For Mollindo, see Wortman, 1982, 199–203.

167. Sorsby, 1972, 145–53. The quotation, dated Dec. 18, 1798, is on p. 151. Wortman, 1982, 154–55; Romero Vargas, 1995, 297; García, 2002, 461–62.

168. Smith, 1995, 63–83; Smith, 2000, 72–91.

169. Session of Nov. 3, 1792, Actas del Consejo de Estado, 1792, in AHN, Estado, Libro 5 ("Nosotros en las Floridas solamente ocupamos los puertos y plazas de la Movila, Panzacola, y San Agustín con el territorio cercano: lo interior del pais lo ocupan y disfrutan los Indios").

170. Creeks, in particular. Saunt, 2002, 47–75.

171. Río Cossa, 1935, 13 ("abandonando la barbarie de andar errantes y sin domicilio seguro"; "alejar . . . a los indios de la amistad de los españoles"; "buena fe"; "nuestro comercio"). He appears to be speaking about the Creeks and Seminoles.

172. Watson, 1976, 9–17, describes the crown's interest in bringing French goods for Indians into Louisiana and West Florida. Coker and Watson, 1986, tell the story of Panton, Leslie. The crown's approval of direct importation from England is noted in the Sept. 22, 1788, session of the Junta de Estado, Actas de la Junta Suprema de Estado in AHN, Estado, Libro 2, pp. 98–99. See, too, Bernardo de Gálvez to José de Gálvez, New Orleans, Dec. 30, 1777, in Levaggi,

1996a, 238. For guidance to sources and further details, see Weber, 1992, 282–85, 289–91.

173. Romero Vargas, 1995, 91–98, 155.

174. Campillo y Cosío, 1789, 14 ("preferir el dominio a las ventajas y utilidades del comercio, y trato amigable con las naciones bárbaras, fue causa de malograr las conquistas hechas y de no hacer otras no menos importantes").

175. This in 1783, wherein he exempted Cuba and Puerto Rico. Quoted in Oltra and Pérez Samper, 1987, 237–38 ("Debe V.M. deshacerse de todas sus posesiones en el continente de ambas Américas, conservando tan sólo las islas de Cuba y Puerto Rico en la parte Septentrional, y alguna otra que pueda convenir en la parte meridional, con objeto de que nos sirvan como escala o depósito para el comercio español"). For the context of Aranda's advice, see, too, Navarro García, 1997a, 1–13.

176. Among them the conde de Campomanes, José de Abalos, Gaspar de Jovellanos, and Manuel Godoy. See Pagden, 1995, 118–25, 194; Ezquerra, 1962, 212–25; Campomanes, 1988, 355.

177. Malaspina, "Examen político de las costas del noroeste de la América," Malaspina, 1885, 367 ("no por una Bula arbitraria que corra de un polo al otro, sino por tratados auténticos con las demás potencias de Europa"). Ramos Pérez, 1994, 197–214. Seed, 1992, 207, suggests that Spaniards stopped asserting their rights under the papal donation in the late sixteenth century, "with the end of papal universality," but some Spaniards still invoked the papal bull in the late seventeenth and early eighteenth centuries. See Weber, 1992, 152, 158.

178. Lucena Giraldo, 1996, 265–75; Spain had recognized foreign possession of other spaces earlier, of course, such as English rights to North America above Charleston, in the Treaty of Madrid of 1670. Weber, 1992, 179.

179. The marqués de Grimaldi to Viceroy Bucareli, 1773, quoted in Archer, 1986, 25. Guirao de Vierna, 1989, 274–75; Weber, 1998, 14–15; Martínez de Gorla, 1986, 15–20. Navarro García, 1994, 15–21, offers a masterful overview of Spain's colonizing strategies. For a tortured argument that Spain possessed these lands but still needed to establish its legitimacy, see Pérez de Uriondo, 1969–72, 632.

180. Malaspina, 1995, 144 ("cebo"; "una frontera que, consumiendo para su defensa un millón de pesos, no abriga más que una propiedad de cien mil, debe precisamente evitarse"), and 113–15 for his views on California.

181. Rubí, 1982, 30 ("lo que debe llamarse dominio y verdaderas posesiones Del Rey").

182. Malaspina, 1995, 146, who consulted the French edition.

183. For the forts in Patagonia, see chap. 4.

184. For the debate in Spain into the 1600s, see Williams,

1990, 103–04, Muldoon, 1994, 29–30, 62–75, and Levaggi, 1993, 85. There seemed little debate, however, that Spain possessed the right to subsurface minerals. Seed, 2001, 57–62, 69–71.

185. Seed, 1995, 69–97, offers a fine analysis of the *requerimiento* and a brief introduction to its successor, the "Royal Orders for New Discoveries" of 1573, which spelled out Spanish expectations that Indians must become vassals of the Spanish crown and be instructed in Catholicism. See, too, Gibson, 1978, 13, for the *requerimiento* "as a kind of generalized capitulation or *pacto* in advance for American Indians."

186. See, for example, Levaggi, 2000, 26–27 and 31–70, 79–101, for this pattern in the Chaco over the course of several centuries. See below n.199, for Levaggi's analysis and my disagreement with it.

187. Vargas Machuca, 1892, 2:11–13. See, too, Lázaro Ávila, 1999, 652–54.

188. Jones, 1982, xii and 1, respectively.

189. Spaniards and Lipanes came to agreements in 1749 and 1774 (verbal, apparently), but bands of Lipanes began to enter into agreements as supplicants between 1787 and 1799; Mescaleros made agreements in 1781 and 1787. Levaggi, 2002, 238–55, reproduces the texts. See, too, the conditions imposed on the Gileño Apaches in ibid., 255–60.

190. For the text, see Levaggi, 2002, 250–55, and for additional context see Moorhead, 1968, 209–10; 212.

191. There were several *capitulaciones* between Spaniards and Apaches at this time. One signed by two Mescaleros, Patule and Quemado, "alias Inddafindilchi y Yl-lydé," May 17, 1787, is in the report of Joseph Antonio Rengel, apparently extracting a report by Capt. Domingo Díaz, in a lengthy *carpeta* on the Mescaleros, copied at Arizpe, Oct. 15, 1787, by Pedro Garrido y Durán, in AGN, Provincias Internas, tomo 112, exped. 1, microfilm at University of Texas, Austin.

192. Spaniards employed other synonyms, too, such as *concordia, paces, pactos, arreglos,* and *convenios.* Levaggi, 2000, 25–26. Concha to Jacobo Ugarte, July 13, 1790, SANM, roll 12, frames 289–91, spelled out seven articles of agreement ("puntos arreglados") in a peace solicited by Gileño Apaches ("paz que solicitaron y propusieron los Apaches"). Gibson, 1978, 3–4, 9, noted that Anglophone writers often misunderstood the word *capitulación,* mistranslating it as "capitulation" or "surrender," and argues that it was used interchangeably with "treaty." Pietschmann, 1987, 249–62, however, suggests that in the sixteenth century, *capitulación* often signified an agreement between parties of unequal strength and points to still-unresolved disagreements among scholars about the various meanings of that word. Was it a contract? Was it a concession? (It could have either meaning depending on the context.) What did it mean in the 1700s? Treaties of 1784 with various peoples in

southeastern North America used *artículos.* Treaties of 1792 and 1793 used the word *tratado.* For sources, see below.

193. Gibson, 1978, 2, caught the spirit of this Spanish legal stance when he wrote, "Spaniards understood Indian peoples to be royal subjects, ready for Christianization and exploitation, but inappropriate for the kinds of bargaining and negotiation that might have resulted in treaties." By "treaties," Gibson meant formal written agreements between nations. Gibson recognized that Spain entered into verbal contracts with Indians but sought to explain why Spaniards throughout America, in contrast to the English and French, negotiated so few *written* treaties. His explanation appears to be based on a false premise, for scholars have found a substantial number of written treaties in Spanish America, and some of those appear, as I argue below, to be between equals. See, too, Kinnaird, 1979, 39–48, Levaggi, 1993, 88–89, and Levaggi, 2002, 99, 264–65, and *passim,* both of whom address Gibson directly.

194. Roulet, 2004, 328–40.

195. For antecedents, which gave Mapuche *indios amigos* a special juridical status, see Méndez Beltrán, 1987, 218–21 (which looks at their exemption from forced labor in 1622, except for royal service), Zapater, 1989, Ruíz-Esquide Figueroa, 1993, 24–29, and Levaggi, 2002, 65–75. Several versions of the language of the Treaty of 1641, signed for Spain by the marqués de Baides, have come down to us, including that of Rosales, 1877–1988, 3:184–85, an eyewitness to the proceedings. The versions vary in particulars and, because Spaniards recorded the sense of the conversations in ways most favorable to them, the recorded terms of the treaty should not be read too literally. I have taken the quotation from the version of the pact that appears in Abreu y Bertodano, 1740–52, 4:416 ("Que no han de ser encomendados a los Españoles, sino que han de estar en cabeza de su Majestad; y debajo de su Real amparo, reconocerle vasalaje como a su señor"). Korth, 1968, 175–76, asserted that Araucanians achieved *de jure* independence in 1641 but doesn't explore the apparent contradiction that they also swore vassalage. León Solís, Silva Galdames, and Téllez Lúgaro, 1997, 22, sees Mapuches as direct vassals of the crown, not under the dominion of local elites. A tall, light-skinned cacique, Chicaguala, whose mother was Spanish, played a key role in the negotiations. Foerster G., 1991, 197–99. For a fresh interpretation, Gascón, 2003, which links Mapuche initiatives to a volcanic eruption in 1640 and Spanish reactions to a smallpox epidemic of 1639 that killed many of their Indian allies.

196. Córdoba y Figueroa, 1862, 29 ("se hacen paces con ellos como con potencia extraña"), a *maestre de campo,* writing before 1740. For the ongoing exemption from

tribute in Chile, where the *encomienda* lingered until 1791, see González Pomes, 1966, 48. For the *parlamentos,* see Méndez Beltrán, 1982, 107–73, and Levaggi, 2002, chaps. 3, 5.

197. The compendium is that of Abreu y Bertodano, 1740–52, 4:416. The other exception may be the Chichimecas. When the Chichimeca war died down in the late 1500s, Spaniards began to exchange food and clothing for "peace treaties," but they were apparently not written instruments, and we do not know if they offered Chichimecas a degree of autonomy. Powell, 1952, 187, 217. Lázaro Ávila, 1999, 652. For the usual conditions of a Spanish treaty with Indians in the Habsburg era, see Bushnell, 2001, 302–04.

198. O'Higgins, 1942–1943, no. 103, p. 34 ("tenían la culpa, porque además de agasajarles muy mezquinamente había algunos que ni aún se asomaban a sus casas a saludarles"). For "their lands" ("sus tierras") vs. "ours" ("las nuestras"), see ibid., 48. I am basing my description of the protocol for traveling in the Araucanía on Capt. O'Higgins's lengthy journey and valuable report. For de facto independence, see also chap. 3 above, where I note that officials in 1804 declared that missionaries entered the Araucanía only by invitation of the Indians. See, too, my discussion of *capitanes de amigos* in chap. 6.

199. The remarkably prolific Argentine legal scholar Abelardo Levaggi and the Spanish historian Carlos Lázaro Ávila see greater continuity between Habsburg and Bourbon treaties than I do. Levaggi, the leading student of this subject, has explored treaties in a series of articles and two books (Levaggi, 2000, and Levaggi, 2002). The books contain the texts of remarkable numbers of treaties; I regret not having had them when I began this study in the early 1990s. His earlier articles remain valuable because they contain some information and analysis that are not in the books. Levaggi acknowledges that many of the early treaties were probably verbal, but he suggests that written treaties may also have been numerous under the Habsburgs yet have been lost over time. He suggests further that the Bourbon treaties of peace did not represent an innovation but rather the more consistent application of much-violated royal intent as expressed in the Royal Orders for New Discoveries of 1573. The goal of the 1573 laws, it seems to me, however, was to persuade the natives to become vassals of the crown, to reduce them to tribute-paying Christians, not to treat with Indians as distinct nations with the right to retain their autonomy. Ordenanzas de su Magestad hechas para los nuevos descubrimientos, conquistas y pacificaciones [July 13, 1573], in *Colección,* 1864–84, 16:181–87. See, too, Seed, 1995, 95–96. In practice, Spaniards did carry out what Amy Bushnell has called a "conquest by contract," creating legal instruments by

which the native "lords of the land" served as corulers and received gifts, but also by which their role was to organize Indian labor and collect tribute. Bushnell, 1989, 134–44; Bushnell, 2001, 302. Levaggi, 1993, 90, makes light of the distinction between written and unwritten treaties, arguing that "the custom of entering into treaties of peace occurred on all the Indian frontiers, and for the entire Spanish period." (See, too, Levaggi, 2002, 31–37.) The content and spirit of *most* of those early agreements, however, seem qualitatively different from those of the late eighteenth century, particularly those in southeastern North America, which I describe below and which Levaggi himself has ably analyzed. Taken together, their content and their written form suggest that these later North American treaties were agreements between nations rather than terms of surrender. In a useful historiographical discussion (Lázaro Ávila, 1996, 15–22) and then in a more fully developed essay (Lázaro Ávila, 1999, 645–73), Lázaro Ávila extrapolates from the "ambience of consensus" between Spaniards and Araucanians ("ámbito de consenso") in seventeenth-century Chile to imagine a Habsburg "policy of consensus" ("política de consenso") that evolved under the Bourbons, who placed greater emphasis on commerce. I view the case of the Araucanians, like that of Chichimecas, as exceptional in the Habsburg era. In both cases, Indians possessed power that led Spaniards to make concessions. I see Bourbons as having been more willing to respond pragmatically to local situations, their strategy informed by the belief that trade and gifts were effective alternatives to military conquest in areas where conquest seemed beyond reach.

200. See especially Prucha, 1994.

201. Martens, 1795, 23–24, whose work appeared in 1788 and echoes a practice well understood among nations, and summarized earlier by Vattel, 1759, 1:10 (bk. 1, chap. 1, pp. 6, 7) and 1:172 (bk. 2, chap. 12, p. 155). For Iberian antecedents, see Gibson, 1978, 5. For the divisibility of sovereignty, see Chiaramonte, 1997, 151, and for application of this principle to treaties with Indians in Argentina, see Ratto, 2003a, 14.

202. Cantillo, 1843, for example, contains no treaties with Indians.

203. Capt. Fernando de Leyba to Gov. Louis de Unzaga, June 6, 1771, quoted in Arnold, 2000, 81; Croix to José Rubio, Valle de Santa Rosa, Feb. 12, 1778, quoted in Levaggi, 2002, 256 ("una muchedumbre de bárbaros dispersos, y sin cabeza, pues cada indio es una república libre").

204. Sors, 1921–23, no. 46, 340 ("monstruo de muchas cabezas").

205. The terms of the 1805 agreement, signed at the site of the future fort, are in Levaggi, 2000, 162–64. See, too, the Mapuche presence at this meeting, in Silva

Galdames, 2001, who places the *parlamento* that produced this treaty at San Carlos and says that Levaggi mistakenly put it at the site of the new fort of San Rafael (p. 18 n.6). Silva Galdames is mistaken. The garrison of San Carlos moved to the Diamante in 1805, where it was renamed San Rafael. Gil de Barraquero, 1980, 1:81. See Nacuzzi, 1998, 168–77, for "caciques duales."

206. Jacobo Ugarte to Juan Bautista de Anza, Oct. 5, 1786, in Thomas, 1932, 334–35, spells out the strategy. For context, see Moorhead, 1968, 148–49, and John, 1975, 710. See n. 214 below for Kavanaugh's contrary interpretation.

207. "Convenio de paz con la nación Navajó," Santa Fe, Aug. 21, 1819, art. 1, *Gaceta Extraordinaria del Gobierno de Mexico,* vol. 10, no. 144, Oct. 27, 1819 ("general de la nación Navajó para que tenga este gobierno de Nuevo México a quien dirigirse en lo que ocurra, y ella quien la gobierne y dirija").

208. Matorras to the king, Salta, June 20, 1773, AGI, BA, 143, "el famoso anciano"; "Primer Caporal o Gefe de las Naciones de Indios del Gran Chaco."

209. See, for example, how Spaniards understand Paikín's relationship with Lachirikin, in Brizuela, 1969–72, 274, 275, 279, 282. For elaboration of this point, see chap. 6 below.

210. The treaty has been published on a number of occasions, most recently in Levaggi, 2000, 79–86 ("Viva el Rey de España y de las Indias, Carlos Tercero"), who also provides context, as does Gullón Abao, 1993, 80–100. I have also drawn from another eyewitness, Brizuela, 1969–72, 278–79, 285–87, 300. Article 1 of the treaty promised Indians they would retain their lands. That was not inconsistent with the crown exercising dominion over those same lands, as implied by Miranda Borelli, 1984, 233–34. I have taken the distances from López Piacentini, 1979, 2:33. For Matorras's interest in protecting Indians from servitude, see the quotation in Vitar, 1997, 149, and Santamaría, 1999, 17–21, who (p. 14) mistakenly sees this treaty as "a kind of casebook for future negotiations with Indians" ("una suerte de vademécum para futuras negociaciones con los indios").

211. This is evident in the series of parlamentos held in Chile with Araucanians. See, too, the cases of Comanches and Pampas, in this chapter. Viceroy Avilés's misgivings about renewing treaties, noted by Levaggi, 2000, 162–63, seem exceptional.

212. Fray Antonio Lapa, quoted in Levaggi, 2000, 87 ("principal cacique de los demás"; "pidiéndome que el siguiente día hiciese la misma relación en presencia de los demás caciques").

213. In 1812, Pino, 1995, 52 and p. 42 of facsimile ("los nombramientos que reciben de su gobierno les son despreciables si no están confirmados por nuestros jefes a nombre del capitán grande"). I have substituted my translation.

214. Vitar, 2002, 411. Kavanagh, 1996, 125, argues that Comanche chiefs "were definitely not the creations of Spanish intervention" and that there is "no evidence of the direct involvement of Spaniards in Comanche political processes." The nature of Comanche political leadership, however, is dimly understood (Brooks, 2002, 168 n.10). By anointing individual Indian political leaders and treating with them, Spain may well have given them an advantage over competitors. In addition to the case of Paikín, mentioned above, see, for example, Rollings, 1992, 152–53, 159–62, 175, Saignes, 1990, 145–46, and Roulet, 2002, 88, who finds the emergence of a centralized leadership for Pehuenches de Malargüe in the space of a decade. For Spanish strategy, see Pedro de Nava, Instructions for Dealing with Apaches at Peace in Nueva Vizcaya, Chihuahua, Oct. 14, 1791, in Hendricks and Timmons, 1998, 103, art. 4. Acevedo, 1989–90, 604, describes how the Junta del Ramo de Sisa in Salta, Jan. 30, 1804, tried to ingratiate itself with the head of a small group of Matacos who helped free a Christian captive by, as the Junta said, "investing him with the position of captain of his people" ("investiéndolo en el carácter de capitán de los de su nación"). This was not an innovation of the late Bourbon era. See Gallup-Díaz, 2002, 286. And Spain was not alone in identifying and elevating individual leaders. Ferguson and Whitehead, 1992a, 13, and Hinderaker, 1996, 487–526. For an example of Spaniards promoting discord, see Rollings, 1992, 162.

215. Many sources discuss the philosophy behind the two *repúblicas* and the reasons for their failure. See, for example, Bakewell, 1997, 158–59. In some places, as in Yucatán, the idea of two *repúblicas* lasted until the end of the colonial period. Farriss, 1984, 376.

216. The treaty, dated Sept. 5, 1790, at Buenos Aires and a preliminary accord signed in Pampa territory on May 3 are reproduced in Levaggi, 2000, 130–37. Quotations are from both documents, on pp. 134–35 ("para evitar todo disturbio entre indios, y cristianos"; "españoles y otros guincas"; "cacique principal de todas las pampas, y cabeza de esta nueva república").

217. Levaggi, 2000, 137–43, for the aftermath of the treaty and the idea of equality between the two parties. Martínez Sierra, 1975, 1:255–69, examines these last years in detail, looking at plans for peaceful expansion put forth by Pedro Cerviño, Feliciano Chiclana, and Sebastián Undiano y Gastelú and the government's responses to them. He discusses Indian education on pp. 268–69. See, too, Barba, 1997, 65–71.

218. Levaggi, 2000, 158 (art. 1) ("señor y Soberano"). See Roulet, 2004, 313–48, for an elegant article on the meanings of treaties to Indians.

219. Pedro Carbonell y Pinto, Gov. of Panama, to José de Gálvez, Aug. 4, 1778 (reservado no. 4), AGI, Es-

tado, Audiencia de Guatemala ("manifestaron de vivir bajo la bandera de nuestro Católico monarca"). For the context of the Miskito treaty, see chap. 4 above; for treaties with Cunas in 1787 and 1789, see above in this chapter.

220. Prior to this, agreements with the Indians in New Mexico were apparently verbal. That seems to have been the case, for example, of an accord between Ute leaders and Gov. Tomás Vélez Cachupín of New Mexico in 1752. That agreement, the beginning of a long-lasting alliance, spoke to mutual protection, apprehension of criminals by both sides, trade, gifts, and hospitality and seems to have represented a respectful détente between two groups of roughly equal strength. Blackhawk, 1999, 81–91, 139–46. In 1762, during his second term, Vélez de Cachupín negotiated a second verbal accord with Comanche leaders. Levaggi, 2002, 265–66.

221. See article 18 in Anza's "Relación de los Sucesos ocurridos en la Provincia del Nuevo-México con motivo de la Paz concedida a la Nación Comanche ... desde 17 de Noviembre de 1785 hasta 15 de Julio de 86," AGN, Provincias Internas, tomo 65, exped. 7 ("toda su Nación al dominio del Rey"). Levaggi, 2002, 268–74, quotes at length from the preliminary negotiations, as recorded in another copy of the Spanish text from AGN, Guadalajara, 287. Thomas, 1932, provides translations of this treaty (329–31) and of Anza's own remarkable account of the forging of the Comanche peace (pp. 294–321). The terms of a treaty that eastern Comanches and the Texas governor Domingo Cabello apparently signed in 1785 are known to us only through Pedro de Nava's description of it to the viceroy, Chihuahua, July 23, 1799, and he does not report what it said about sovereignty. Faulk, 1964, 44–53, and Simmons, 1967, 21–22, reproduce the 1799 document. In Texas, Spaniards had made an earlier attempt to open negotiations with Comanches by signing a treaty with Taovayas and then using them as intermediaries. These treaties, negotiated in 1771 and 1774 by a former French trader, Athanase de Mézières, met opposition from Viceroy Bucareli and the leading officer in northern New Spain, Hugo O'Conor, who distrusted these new allies and refused to arm them. Bolton, 1914, 1:93–108, and docs. 83, 120, and 123, and Smith, 2000, 51–71, for a succinct overview. For the Spanish text of the treaty that Mézières signed with Taovayas on Oct. 27, 1771, see Levaggi, 2002, 266–67.

222. Extract of official reports of the governor of New Mexico, Chihuahua, Dec. 21, 1786, by Pedro Garrido y Durán, in AGN, Provincias Internas, tomo 65, exped. 9 ("subordinación y fidelidad"; "protección Del Rey"). This summary is translated in Thomas, 1932, 346–48.

223. Convenio de paz con la nación Navajó, Santa Fe,

Aug. 21, 1819, art. 10, *Gaceta Extraordinaria del Gobierno de Mexico*, vol. 10, no. 144, Oct. 27, 1819 ("en nombre del Soberano ... concede a la expresada tribu Navajó los terrenos que hasta ahora han disfrutado").

224. I have not tried to look comprehensively at all peace arrangements with powerful peoples. Others, such as Pehuenches on both sides of the Andes, could be included in this category.

225. For the Cunas, see above; for Ranqueles, see the treaty of 1796 signed at Córdoba, in Levaggi, 2000, 159, art. 9. For Navajos, see the "Convenio de paz con la nación Navajó," Santa Fe, Aug. 21, 1819, art. 13, *Gaceta Extraordinaria del Gobierno de Mexico*, vol. 10, no. 144, Oct. 27, 1819.

226. Levaggi, 1992, 292 ("naciones interiores"). See, above, chap. 2 n.32, for the meaning of *nación* at this time.

227. Intendente Martin Navarro to Antonio Valdés, New Orleans, Dec. 19, 1787, summarizing recent discussions with Indians, quoted in Levaggi, 1996b, 397.

228. For the *torrente* and other metaphors of natural disasters, see Hilton, 2002, 72, and pp. 90–94 for Spain's view of U.S. policy. See, too, Juan Gasiot's warnings, cited above in this chapter.

229. Aranda's diary for Aug. 3, 1782, reporting on his meeting with John Jay, in Yela Utrilla, 1925, 2:356 ("país de bárbaros"; "al cual era igual el derecho de nuestras dos partes, o igual la sinrazón de quererlo"). Emphasis added.

230. The Spanish texts of the 1784 treaties appear in Gómez del Campillo, 1944–45, 1:412–30, and in Levaggi, 1996b, 380–96, who has transcribed them from manuscript sources. English translations are conveniently found in Deloria and DeMallie, 1999, 1:122–30. The 1781 treaty with the Creeks is in Levaggi, 1996a, 238–41. Other treaties between Spaniards and southwestern tribes antedate these. Spanish authorities entered into a peace agreement with Alabamas and Creeks at Pensacola in Sept. 1761, in which Spaniards gave gifts and apparently opened the way to trade, but the treaty does not appear to have been written. Levaggi, 1996a, 229–33. See also Prucha, 1994, 24–25.

231. Artículos de convenio, trato y pacificación estipulados, y acordados por la nación española con los indios talapuches [Creeks], Pensacola, May 31–June 1, 1784, in Gómez del Campillo, 1944, 1:414–15, and Levaggi, 2002, 283–88 (arts. 4 and 1, respectively) ("nuestro Soberano, el Gran Rey de las Españas"; "súbditos y vasallos"; "aquellos puntos que son compatibles con nuestro carácter y circunstancias"). See, too, artículos convenidos ... con la nación chactá, Mobile, July 13–14, 1784, in Gómez del Campillo, 1944, 1:428 (art. 5).

232. Levaggi, 1991, 82, 90; Levaggi, 1996b, 382.

233. Tratado de amistad, Natchez, May 14, 1792, in Serrano y Sanz, 1912, 437, with Chickasaw and Choctaw leaders. This treaty, misdated 1790, is translated in

234. Hurt, 2002, 103–36; Weber, 1992, 274.

235. Treaty with the Creeks, Pensacola, June 14, 1781, in Levaggi, 1996a, 239 ("como buenos hijos a los Pies de su Padre y Protector"). Diario de Pedro Vial and Francisco Xavier Chávez, 1785, in Represa, 1990, 22–23 ("nuestro Padre"); John and Benavides Jr., 1994, 45–46. Roulet, 2004, 339–40. Matt Babcock reminds me that examples can be found in many Indian–European negotiations, as among Algonquians who used the Iroquois word *Onontio* to refer to the French governor as "father" in the sense of ally and protector. White, 1991, 38.

236. Obeyesekere, 1992, 15–16, reminds us that this idea lingered into our day in Euro-American thought.

237. Brading, 1971, 22–23, makes this point nicely.

238. For some tribes, for example, Choctaws, who saw people as either kin or enemies, turning Europeans into "fictive kin" was a necessary prelude to having peaceful dealings with them (O'Brien, 2002, 57), but "brothers" would have served that purpose if the goal was nothing more than kinship.

239. Galloway, 1989, 255. See, too, Arnold, 2000, 108–09, 144, on the Quapaws. Most of the southeastern tribes appear to have been matrilineal.

240. De la Cruz, 1969b–72b, 2:270 ("padre poderoso"; "seré de aquí adelante soldado fiel de ese rey grande … siendo tan poderoso, como padre, solicitándonos para hacernos bien"). The Ranqueles, of Pehuenche origin, were patrilineal. León Solís, 2001b, 24.

241. Defina, 1966, 61. Artículos de amistad, trato y comercio entre la nación española y la nación Chicacháá, Mobile, June 22–23, 1784, in Gómez del Campillo, 1944, 1:424 (art. 8).

242. The text in Spanish of this Treaty of Nogales, Oct. 28, 1793, is in Serrano y Sanz, 1916, 91–92, and in Levaggi, 2002, 296–98 ("naciones indias como una sola, bajo la protección de Su Majestad …"; "pacífica posesión de sus tierras"). Emphasis mine. For a detailed account, see Armillas Vicente, 1975–77, 225–66. An English translation is in Deloria and De-Mallie, 1999, 1:139–41. The treaty was read at the highest council in Spain, the Consejo de Estado. Assured that it would not adversely affect relations with the United States, whose neutrality Spain badly needed, Carlos IV approved the treaty. Session of March 7, 1794, Actas del Consejo de Estado, 1794 in AHN, Estado, Libro 7.

243. Campomanes, "Dictamen sobre los medios de asegurar el dominio de España en la Florida y Luisiana y sobre el proyecto para aumentar su comercio," San Lorenzo, Nov. 11, 1792, in Campomanes, 1996, 311–12 ("se desconfiarían y llamarían en su defensa a los americanos"). Campomanes wrote this from his position on the Consejo del Estado at the end of his distinguished career. Earlier in his career, in

1762, he had advocated expanding Spanish dominion in the Floridas through trade and missions. Campomanes, 1988, 29–30.

244. Gayoso de Lemos to Carondelet, Natchez, March 24, 1792, quoted in Holmes, 1965, 157.

245. For the Creeks' 1790 treaty with the United States and the Spanish response, including a new treaty of 1792 signed at New Orleans, see Levaggi, 1996b, 398–403. An English translation of the 1792 treaty appears in several places, including Deloria and DeMaille, 1999, 1:137–38. Choctaws seemed more circumspect. The group who signed a treaty with Spaniards at Mobile in 1784 sent a delegation of leaders who had not signed that treaty to negotiate with Americans in 1785. O'Brien, 2002, 56.

246. Carondelet to the Chiefs and Warriors of the Choctaws and Chickasaws here assembled [1793], trans. from the French. Kinnaird, 1946–49, vol. 4, pt. 3, pp. 140–41.

247. Alonso, 1995, 63.

248. Adelman and Aron, 1999, 830.

249. Berkhofer, 1978, 125. Emphasis added.

250. For the tightening of controls, see, for example, Brading, 1984, 1:389–439; Farriss, 1984, 355–65.

251. I refer here, of course, to the famous *requerimiento* and its successor, the Royal Orders for New Discoveries of 1573, which emphasized peaceful "pacification."

252. Levaggi, 1999, 302–12, has compared treaties in North and South America. He argues against the thesis that Spain employed treaties in imitation of its foreign rivals in North America. Influenced by Charles Gibson, I had advanced that argument in Weber, 1992, 230. Levaggi sees little difference between treaties in North America and treaties in South America and little change over time (see above n.199). He argues that Spanish treaties with Indians varied with local circumstances and foreign pressures, but that "las diferencias que hay entre los tratados de una y otra frontera son secundarias" (p. 312). Instead, he says, they consistently represented "la aplicación deliberada de un plan premeditado de la Corona" (p. 311). See, too, Levaggi, 1997, 103–18. Levaggi and I see the same phenomena but assess it differently.

253. Lynch, 1992, 80.

254. O'Higgins to Pedro de Acuña, Plaza de Los Angeles, March 17, 1793, in Levaggi, 1997, 116–17 ("solo convenía sujetarles por medios enteramente contrarios [a armas y su fuerza] y abandonando las ideas de conquista subrogar en su lugar las proporciones que darían el comercio y trato amigable con estas Naciones").

255. O'Higgins, "Descripción del Reyno de Chile," Madrid, Sept. 2, 1767, in Donoso, 1941, 440 ("tribus de salvajes"). See, too, Concha, 1949, 251.

256. For *capitanes de amigos,* see below, chap. 6. Licensing

traders who might enter Indian territory and serve as informants would not represent an innovation elsewhere in the empire, either. See Blackhawk, 1999, 165–68, for licensing New Mexico traders to the Ute country.

257. Malaspina, 1995, 146 ("inútilmente teñido el suelo de sangre española"; "se halla tranquila nuestra frontera con los araucanos, bajo de un sistema casi semejante al que han seguido las colonias inglesas"). See, too, p. 147. Malaspina based his judgments about northern New Spain on written sources, and his conclusions were somewhat out of date when he wrote this in the 1790s, upon return home. By then, officials in northern New Spain had turned to trade and treaties, and it, too, had become a more peaceful place. In suggesting the Bourbons' enchantment with things foreign, I do not mean to validate the old idea that Spanish reforms were entirely French-inspired, and I am mindful of the caveats in Kuethe and Blaisdell, 1991, 579–607. Navarro Floria, 1994a, 46, 56, 64, astutely observes the importance of the "emulation of the foreigner" ("la emulación del extranjero") for Bourbon policymakers.

258. Esteban Miró to Bernardo de Gálvez, New Orleans, April 15, 1784, quoted in Levaggi, 1996b, 379 ("poco exactos"). See, too, Bernardo de Gálvez to Gilberto Antonio Maxent, Havana, July 7, 1783, quoted in Levaggi, 1996b, 374. Williams, 1997, 79, argues for "the centrality of trust as an organizing theme in the language of Indian diplomacy" among Indians of North America's eastern woodlands (p. 127).

259. See, for example, Levaggi, 1996a, 229, and Levaggi, 1997, 113 n.11; Pedro de Nava, Instructions for Dealing with Apaches at Peace in Nueva Vizcaya, Chihuahua, Oct. 14, 1791, in Hendricks and Timmons, 1998, 102; fray Diego Bringas, Procurator of the College of Santa Cruz de Querétaro to the Comandante General, Chihuahua, March 15, 1796, in Matson and Fontana, 1977, 67.

260. Gálvez, 1951, art. 36 ("Nadie ignora las veleidades de todos los Indios y su mala fe, pero no siempre la han encontrado buena en nuestros procedimientos").

261. Mendinueta, 1910, quotations on pp. 565 and 559, respectively. The first quotation refers to both groups; the second to Guajiros ("disimulo de su independencia"; "contemporizando con ellos, sin afectar el ejercicio del dominio ni renunciar al incontestable derecho del Soberano"). Mendinueta y Múzquiz should not be confused with Pedro Fermín de Mendinueta, who governed New Mexico in 1767–78.

262. Pedro de Nava, Instructions for Dealing with Apaches at Peace in Nueva Vizcaya, Chihuahua, Oct. 14, 1791, in Hendricks and Timmons, 1998, 106, arts. 19 and 20.

263. Polo Acuña, 1999a, 21–22, quoting the campaign diary ("hombre ya no hay más ladrones"; "pues hombre, si me hurtan ahora, serás tú").

264. Bucareli to Arriaga, Sept. 26, 1774, in Velasco Ceballos, 1936, 1:179 ("General de su Nación"; "si no quieren verse sojuzgados y combatidos por el poder de las armas del rey").

265. Din and Nasatir, 1983, 146–54; Rollings, 1992, 169–72.

266. Saignes, 1990, 127 ("indios bárbaros"; "podamos sembrar y cultivar para tener frutos con que alimentarnos y vivir así en paz y quietud"), 133.

267. In 1805, quoted in Saignes, 1990, 142 ("inconstancia natural de los indios, a su propensión al robo y por último a su condición brutal").

268. In 1805, quoted in Saignes, 1990, 142 ("se llaman fronteras todas las tierras incógnitas ocupadas por los bárbaros y nuestras pertenencias siguen siempre extendiéndose con la población de nuevas misiones, y de las estancias que se van estableciendo más adelante por el interés de los buenos pastos y fértiles terrenos, como siempre se ha ejecutado desde la pacificación de este continente").

269. Santiago de Liniers, quoted in Saignes, 1990, 148 ("una guerra ofensiva a fuego y sangre"), who notes that this was the first *entrada general* against the Chiriguanos since 1735.

270. Saignes, 1990, 146–49.

271. Saignes, 1990, 156, finds no evidence of firearms among the Chiriguanos until 1813.

272. Tilly, 2003, 5, 8, 20–22, and *passim,* suggests that ideas in themselves are not powerful causes of collective violence. It may also be that they do not play a key role in preventing it.

Chapter 6. Crossing Borders

The epigraphs are from Francisco Balcarce to the marqués de Loreto, Frontera de Luján, May 16, 1784, AGN [Buenos Aires], IX, 1-6-2, folios 685–86 ("me dijo … a un cautivo llamado Pedro Pablo a quién le ha oído decir quería más bien andar entre los indios que venirse a los cristianos"), speaking of the captive Pedro Pablo Maldonado (reference through the extraordinary kindness of Eugenia Néspolo); Bernabéu, "Introducción," in Bernabéu Albert, 1999a, 6 ("las fronteras entre civilización y barbarie se han vuelto más cristalinas para vislumbrar indios 'salvajes' más occidentalizados de lo que se pensaba y súbditos del rey cuyas formas de vida eran parecidas a las de los pueblos indios que los rodeaban"); and Clendinnen, 2003, 12.

1. Levaggi, 2000, 134–36.

2. Declaración de Blas de Pedrosa, Dec. 8, 1786, AGN [Buenos Aires], IX, 1–5-3, folios 662–68. Copy courtesy of Raúl Mandrini. A portion of this is published as Appendix C in Lázaro Ávila, 1997, 116–19, who provides neither date nor source. Mariluz Urquijo, 1957, 64–65, relied on this document in sketching Pedrosa's life. I have not been able to identify Antemán, whose name Mariluz Urquijo read as Antenián.

3. Brown, 1979, 33, gives the distance as 775 kilometers; Jones, 1984, 53–54, 67.

4. Francisco Manuel de Herrera, quoted in Mariluz Urquijo, 1957, 66 ("con quienes es menester usar de mil cautelas para perpetuar la paz"), who provides no date but offers a fine discussion of this problem and a summary of Pedrosa's career.

5. *Real orden*, San Lorenzo, Nov. 15, 1792, in response to an *oficio* de la junta superior de hacienda del virreinato del Río de la Plata, Buenos Aires, May 10, 1792, in Solano, 1991, 271–73 ("para los casos en que haya precisión de trata con los indios pampas nunca falta un peón arriero o soldado que entienda su idioma").

6. Mariluz Urquijo, 1957, 68–69. The third *corralero*, Romero, apparently went out of business. Torre Revello, 1970, 73, quotes Izquierdo saying in 1794 that he had traded with Indians for twenty years. For *corrales*, see another contemporary, Gregory Funes (1748–1829), who says that Buenos Aires alone among Argentine cities developed the "casas de factoría con nombre de corrales" in the 1780s. He observed that the buyer of Indian goods is "siempre el corralero." Funes, 1856, 2:286.

7. Lastarria, "Declaraciones y expresas resoluciones soberanas que sumisamente se desean en beneficio de los Indios de las Provincias de la banda oriental del Río Paraguay, y de las márgenes del Paraná y Uruguay," Madrid, Aug. 31, 1804, in Lastarria, 1914, 121, who also notes the location of Pedrosa's store in the city's "primer barrio" and his relative prosperity ("salvajes comerciantes"; "Se van, y vuelven frecuentemente con sus mujeres").

8. Vignati, 1973, 78 ("pues todos los toldos no parecen viviendas de racionales, sino madrigueras de ratas").

9. Mariluz Urquijo, 1987, 381 ("la frontera con los indios, más que línea divisoria de dos enemigos, era un abismo que deslindaba dos opuestas concepciones de vida. El efímero enlace sexual o comercial que podía haber entre infieles y cristianos, no despejaba su incompatibilidad rotunda, su repulsión recíproca que sólo hubiera podido ser borrada por la acción evangelizadora. Y a fines del siglo XVIII ya habían desaparecido los grandes misioneros"). I am echoing here the celebrated American historian Frederick Jackson Turner's definition of frontier as "the meeting point between savagery and civilization," expressed in his famous essay of 1893, "The Significance of the Frontier in American History," in Weber and Rausch, 1994, 3.

10. Villar, 1993, 4 ("ficción político-militar"; "mundo … simbiótico"). He is writing of the nineteenth century, but his statement applies to the colonial era as well.

11. Socolow, 1992, 88, citing the manuscript version of Luis de la Cruz's diary of 1806.

12. Ortelli, 2003a, 71–110; Casanueva, 1992b, 192.

13. Martínez, 1994, 5–10, suggests a range of crossborder interactions, identifying four categories: alienation, coexistence, interdependency, and integration. Quijada, 2002, 106–10, offers a rich analysis of frontier theory and suggests the need to look beyond acculturation to the integration of frontier peoples.

14. Herren, 1992, tells the stories of some of these individuals, focusing on the 1500s and early 1600s.

15. See, for example, the testimony of one Andrés, Salta, Jan. 28, 1804, quoted in Acevedo, 1989–90, 603.

16. Guarda Geywitz, 1987, 93–157, is a fine study of Chilean captives that shows that the number diminished dramatically in the 1700s.

17. This often retold episode is recounted in detail in Lagos, 1908, 260–73. See especially p. 267.

18. Declaración de Blas Pedrosa, Dec. 8, 1786, AGN [Buenos Aires] IX, 1.5.3, folios 662–68 ("tienen infinitos cautivos"). Copy courtesy of Raúl Mandrini.

19. Mayo, 1985a, 240–41, tells the story of María. Socolow, 1992, 88, reports on a similar case. Schwartz and Salomon, 1999, 472, claim that Indians in the "Southern Cone," by which they mean Argentina and Chile, forbade captives to speak Spanish. For a similar case in northern New Spain of a captive who learned Spanish in captivity, see Stern, 1991, 267.

20. Menéndez, 1896–1900, 2:411–14, 424. Quotation on p. 414 ("aunque mal").

21. Lázaro Ávila, 1994, 197, makes this point about lack of official interest, which seems to me to have broad applicability. See the questions asked of Marcelino at Monclova, May 23, 1770, in Valdés, 1995, 251–53, and the questions posed of captives as transcribed in Mayo, 1985b. Operé, 2001, 27.

22. These gripping narratives of captivity of non-Indians by Indians, written to instruct, to entertain, to vilify, and to romanticize Indians, appeared as fiction, nonfiction, and combinations of the two and sold well. John Williams's *The Redeemed Captive, Returning to Zion* (1707), sold some one thousand copies within a week of its publication. The stories were usually written for or about women. For a systematic analysis and introduction to the vast literature, see Zabelle Derounian-Stodola and Levernier, 1993, chaps. 1– 3. For the appeal of captivity narratives, see Ebersole, 1995.

23. Stern, 1991, 267, and Socolow, 1992, 73–74 n.1, offer the literacy explanation. For published works in Spain and Spanish America, see Johnson, 1993, and Stolley, 1996. Sayre, 1997, 21–24, explores the cultural and religious differences between Francophone and Anglophone worlds with more subtlety than my summary suggests and notes that Catholic France and French America failed to produce a single Indian captivity narrative in the colonial era. Bauer, 1997, 685, describes a pirate captivity narrative in which Anglophones were the barbarians, but was this a popular genre in the Spanish colonial period? For Puritans, see Vaughan and Clark, 1981, 5–9. The didactic stories of punishment and redemption of the colonial era were supplanted in the 1800s by

fanciful thrillers; with the exception of Argentine writers, Spanish-American writers ignored the genre in the nineteenth century, too. Operé, 2001, 229. Operé, 2001, speculates that Hispanics, who had knowledge of Aztecs and Incas, had little interest in the more primitive Indians who took captives (p. 269), and he suggests the crown, which screened publications about Spanish America, might have discouraged the genre since "the story of a captive was a story of a failure that added nothing to the glorious record of an expansive Spain." (p. 26). Operé also discusses exceptions, including works published in the nineteenth century (chaps. 1, 2, 4), and points to the scarcity of novels in Spanish colonial America (pp. 227-43).

24. See, for example, Heard, 1973, 96-104, who finds few clear patterns in North America. Operé, 2001, 17, draws from examples in the colonial period and the nineteenth century alike and suggests the same for Spanish America.

25. Núñez de Pineda y Bascuñán, 1973, is an abridged but accessible edition. Bauer, 1998, 59-82, explains Pineda's motives and provides guidance to the literature. See, too, Adorno and Pautz, 1999, and Lázaro Ávila, 1995, 137-39.

26. Azara, 1923, 2:85, like other Spanish observers who knew Indians firsthand, believed this to be the case with "naciones salvajes" in general.

27. Testimony of one Andrés, Salta, Jan. 28, 1804, quoted in Acevedo, 1989-90, 604 ("los muchachos cautivos que encuentren para criarlos a su modo, y matar a los grandes"). Saeger, 2000, 80, notes that Abipones took Spanish males if they were young. Blackhawk, 1999, 99, finds that all but 8 of the 166 captives sold in Abiquiu, New Mexico, by Utes between 1754 and 1866 were children.

28. Sources abound. See, for example, García, 1999, 107-09, Jones, 1983, 91-94, Mayo, 1985a, 236-40, and Socolow, 1992, 83-87, on the Pampa; Azara, 1923, 2:12, describing Charrúas captive taking, and Azara, 1990, 120-25 on Mbayás. On Guaycuruan and Araucanian use of the dowry, see Palermo, 1994, 83, and Lázaro Ávila, 1994, 200, who also argues that historians have exaggerated the gender differential (p. 195). For a sophisticated analysis of women captured by Indians in New Mexico, see Brooks, 1997, 101-07.

29. As one of many examples, León Solís, 1990, 141-42, tells of "Aucas" using the captive Pedro Zamora to open negotiations with Buenos Aires in 1781.

30. Saeger, 2000, 80; Pedro Carbonell y Pinto, governor of Panama, to José de Gálvez, Aug. 4, 1778 (reservado no. 4), AGI, Estado, Audiencia de Guatemala.

31. Mayo, 1985a, 239. See, too, Socolow, 1992, 82.

32. Socolow, 1992, 79-80.

33. Jones, 1995, 137-38 (two Spanish boys for 28 and 30 pesos and a girl for 32 pesos). He finds a long tradi-

tion of the ransoming of captives in Nueva Vizcaya and New Mexico. Presidial soldiers received 240 pesos a year in 1787. Moorhead, 1975a, 219. Many sources discuss these values. For the Río de la Plata at this time, see Operé, 2001, 126-27.

34. Zavala, 1981, 281-86, 293-94, chronicles the establishment and life of this fund through 1792. The details need not concern us here, but this subject needs some scholarly attention. Jones, 1995, 143 n.45, who does not cite Zavala, traced the fund to a general order by Croix, dated June 8, 1780, asking for donations, and in so doing indirectly corrected Stern, 1991, 269 (whose work he also fails to cite), who put the beginning of this fund at 1784 and located it specifically in Texas. Zavala tells a somewhat different story. See León Solís, 1990, 137, for a Fondo de Cautivos in Buenos Aires.

35. Zavala, 1981, 282. Officials similarly expressed concern about increasing Indians' incentive by paying high prices for Christian captives. Operé, 2001, 127, gives an example from the Río de la Plata.

36. Levaggi, 2000, 138, quoting Juan Antonio Hernández ("enteramente poseídos de la vil avaricia"), an officer who helped broker that arrangement.

37. Guarda Geywitz, 1987, 120-22, who shows that in places that lacked Mercedarians bishops also authorized priests to collect alms for captives and that Mercedarians found other ways to raise funds to free American captives during the war of Arauco (p. 109). Martín de Codoni, 1997, 111, is a model study of "alms" given to the order in Tucumán, often in a will. Friedman, 1983, 114-15, indicates that two-thirds of the alms collected by the order in the late 1600s came from America. For the spread of the order in America, see the *New Catholic Encyclopedia* (New York: McGraw-Hill, 1967), 9:670, and the summary in Black, 1995, 48-54, a case study of one Mercedarian mission province.

38. We have a number of accounts of captives unwilling to return, among them Santamaría, 1998b, 175, who reports on what one officer described as the incredible resistance of captives he was trying to bring back from the Chaco. See, too, Levaggi, 1992, 309.

39. Manuel Rodríguez to Jacobo Ugarte, Presidio de San Juan Bautista, May 3, 1770, in Valdés, 1995, 250 ("perfecto ladrón de caballada"). Valdés reproduces Marcelino's testimony in the case (pp. 251-53). Zavala, 1981, 244-45, and Stern, 1991, 272, summarize this case.

40. Fray Diego Bringas, in Matson and Fontana, 1977, 119, who was scandalized by this. Called to my attention by Stern, 1991, 271. In Chile, too, Spaniards in the 1600s did not try to "rescue" acculturated captives. Villalobos R., 1992, 319, quoting Jerónimo de Quiroga.

41. Report of Athanase de Méziéres, Oct. 29, 1770, translated in Bolton, 1914, 1:216, called to my attention

by Stern, 1991, 270. See, too, Socolow, 1992, 98; Mayo and Latrubesse, 1993, 89–90; Lázaro Ávila, 1994, 203; Operé, 2001, 129–30.

42. And Christian Pueblo women as well. Brooks, 1999, 30.

43. Mayo, 1985a, 242. She was between two and four years old when Pampas captured her.

44. Gutiérrez, 1991, chaps. 5, 6, and 7, illuminate honor and shame in one frontier society.

45. Brooks, 2002, 99–103.

46. We know this today, of course, as the Stockholm syndrome.

47. Stern, 1991, 276–78; Stern, 1998, 175–77. Menchaca's defection to the Indians, however, probably owed much to the fact that his neighbors in San Antonio found him to be an unsavory character and had ostracized him even before Comanches captured him.

48. Dobrizhoffer, 1967–70, 2:140 ("y jamás temieron contaminarse las manos con sangre española, aunque ésta corriera por sus venas"). For another translation, see Dobrizhoffer, 1822, 2:142 ("little scrupulous about shedding the blood of Spaniards, though Spaniards themselves").

49. De la Cruz, 1969a-72a, 441 n.8 ("Tienen en sus tierras muchos españoles cautivos, unos y otros que se ocultan, y éstos son nuestros peores enemigos").

50. Teodoro de Croix to José de Gálvez, Chihuahua, June 29, 1778, reporting on the results of a Council of War, in Thomas, 1940, 201–02.

51. "Relacion del número de enemigos Apaches que han muerto," Sept. 30, 1787, included with Jacobo Ugarte to Viceroy Manuel Antonio Flores, Arizpe, Oct. 1, 1787, AGN, Provincias Internas, tomo 112 ("con el tiempo nos hubierán sido tan perjudiciales como ellos").

52. Zapater, 1981, 34, quoting *maestre de campo* Jerónimo de Quiroga, ca. 1690 ("aman tanto sus vicios, costumbres y libertad, que son perjudiciales entre nosotros. .. son peores que los más fieros bárbaros, porque son bárbaros con discurso"). Villalobos R., 1995, 71–72. For the phenomenon of Indianization and its varieties, see Hallowell, 1963, 523, whose neologisms, "transculturite" and "transculturalization" have entered the literature as descriptors of *individual* behavior. Hallowell reserved the words "acculturate" and "transculturate" for groups instead of individuals, a distinction that hardly required a new vocabulary in my view.

53. Ortelli, 2000, 193, drawing on Spanish-era sources, although her article treats the 1800s.

54. Or in Chile, as *capitanes de amigos.* Lázaro Ávila, 1994, 202. For an example of a former captive who was apparently employed on just one occasion, see the case of Francisca Bengolea, once held by the Ranqueles, who translated the treaty that the Ranquel cacique Carripilún signed at Córdoba in 1796. Levaggi, 2000, 158.

55. Oficio de la junta superior de hacienda del virreinato del Río de la Plata, Buenos Aires, Nov. 8, 1791, in Solano, 1991, 268 ("poseía con perfección el idioma de aquellos infieles"), and the crown's response, Aranjuez, April 18, 1792, in ibid., p. 270.

56. Acevedo, 1989–90, 598–99.

57. John and Benavides Jr., 1994, 27–28, 54–55, for his biography and guidance to other sources. The quotation, translated on p. 38, can be found in the published Spanish text of the diary of Vial (a French Indian trader in Spanish service) and Chaves, Nov. 15, 1785, in Represa, 1990. For the larger context, see John, 1975, 654–66. See, too, Mayo, 1985a, 241–42.

58. Quoted in Mariluz Urquijo, 1957, who cites AGN [Buenos Aires], Guerra y Marina, leg. 16, año 1792, IX-4-21-8 ("un trato puro, fiel, humanísimo y muy franco establecido por mucho tiempo").

59. John and Benavides Jr., 1994, 51. Diario de Pedro Vial y Francisco Xavier Chaves, Nov. 15, 1785, in Represa, 1990, 27–28 ("podrán ser duraderas sus Paces, siempre que se les trate con cariño y amor"; "sin olvidar a los muchachones"; "y amigos de que les den lo que equivale a las rapiñas, robo y hostilidades que hacen cuando están en guerra").

60. For the role of "cultural brokers" as anthropologists and ethnohistorians have seen them and the varieties of functions they have played, see Szasz, 1994, 3–20. As Szasz observes, "Cultural brokers often moved in the 'middle ground' explored by Richard White . . . but they have also moved between cultures when no 'middle ground' was readily apparent" (p. 20). James Merrell, 1999, has rich stories about these "go-betweens," who, he suggests, have often been forgotten in the history of English America.

61. León Solís, 1990, 97–105, makes this case for Chile, and logic suggests that it applied elsewhere, although we cannot quantify this trade since many traders operated illegally and never entered historical records.

62. Juan and Ulloa, 1978, 2:355–56; León Solís, 1990, 115. Río Cossa, 1935, 13, noted in Florida in 1787 that it had become possible to enter Creek villages with "un salvoconducto y un trato y contrato con toda la formalidad de la buena fe."

63. Depons, 1970, 1:221. Barrera Monroy, 2000, 144–71, provides an overview of smuggling in the Guajira peninsula. For other cases of Spanish–Indian trade during times of hostilities, see Brooks, 2002, 114, 119–20, 154; Casanueva, 1984, 5; Santamaría and Peire, 1993, 123; and Villalobos R., 1992, 298–302.

64. Chileans also used the disparaging word *conchavadores.*

65. See, for example, Moreno y Escandón, 1936, 575, and examples in chap. 5, above. Trading with the enemy was commonplace in English as well as Spanish America, of course, and smuggling, as one historian of North America has noted, is itself "a form of accommodation." Jennings, 1993, 201.

66. Ambrosio O'Higgins to the subdelegado de Curicó, quoted in Villalobos R., 1989b, 163, and Villalobos R., 1992, 309–10, urging that Spaniards not be allowed to cross the Andes from Chile to trade with Indians ("son ordinariamente facinerosos, pérfidos y malévolos, que huyendo aquí de la justicia van a inspirar de pronto entre los indios ideas diabólicas contra el gobierno y a la vuelta roban a los mismos indios, y les hacen otras mil iniquidades").

67. Pinto Rodríguez, 2000, 24, 40.

68. A Franciscan missionary of Río Bueno to his superior, April 22, 1783, quoted in Gay, 1846–52, 384 ("los indios obedecen sólo a su capitán o teniente y no a otro alguno"). Called to my attention by Villalobos R., 1992, 376.

69. These comparative figures are from Chile at that time. Villalobos R., 1982, 191.

70. Villalobos R., 1992, 368–71, quotation on p. 369 from an anonymous *informe* ("baja frontera"). I have depended here on Villalobos R., 1982, 187–95; Villalobos R., 1992, 371–82; and León Solís, 1990, 160–69, who disagree only on minor details. León Solís sees a greater proliferation of *capitanes* at the end of the colonial era (p. 166). See, too, Villalobos R. 1992, 375, and Silva Galdames, 1991, 34–35. The restructuring began in 1765, but an Araucanian revolt delayed its implementation.

71. Zapater, 1981, 37, in a frequently quoted passage from *maestre de campo* Jerónimo de Quiroga, ca. 1690 ("olvida el ser de cristiano, aprendiendo a ser infiel, casándose al uso de los indios con algunas mujeres, y bebiendo sobre apuesta con los indios"; "y lloraba entre ellas porque no podía apagar el fuego que encendía en todas ellas").

72. Amat, report to the crown, Dec. 6, 1769, quoted in Barros Arana, 1884–1902, 6:239 ("sin religión, y con plenitud de vicios, señaladamente el de la embriaguez"; "copiosísimas cantidades de vinos, cuchillos, fierro [hierro] y otros efectos prohibidos"). This language found its way into the *real cédula* to Agustín de Jáuregui, Gobernador y Capitán General del Reyno de Chile y Presidente de mi Audiencia de la Ciudad de Santiago. El Pardo, Feb. 6, 1774, ANSC, Fondos Varios, vol. 300, pieza 3.

73. There is a large literature on these types. See, for example, Sayre, 1997, 237–38; Van Kirk, 1980; and León Solís, 1990, 165.

74. Levaggi, 1989–90, 102–03, and Silva Galdames, 1991, 29–45, who reproduces a valuable letter from Ambrosio Benavides to Amigorena, dated 1779, that explains how the system worked.

75. Defina, 1966, 60–62.

76. The quotation is from Concha, 1949, 240, writing in 1794 and describing this custom among Comanches. This apparently had its origins in New Mexico with Anza in 1786. See Jacobo Ugarte to Juan Bautista de Anza, Oct. 5, 1786, and Pedro Ga-

rrido Durán's summary of Anza's negotiations with the Navajos in 1785–86, Chihuahua, Dec. 21, 1786, both in Thomas, 1932, 335, 347. For some years thereafter, Navajos had an interpreter living among them. See Joaquín del Real Alencaster to Salcedo, Santa Fe, May 15, 1805, SANM, no. 1828, roll 15, frames 591–93, containing a treaty signed on May 12, 1805, and the long career of interpreter José Antonio García in Flagler, 1997, 193, 194, 204, 210. See, too, John, 1975, 710. Officials in San Antonio apparently did not adopt such a system for Texas. Personal communication, Elizabeth A. H. John, April 11, 2001, although in 1813 Salcedo y Salcedo, 1990, 47, made a tantalizing reference to "tratantes" who traded Indians for pelts in Texas.

77. Instrucción, Col. Fernando de la Concha to his successor, Lt. Col. Fernando Chacón, Chihuahua, June 28, 1794, in AGN, Mexico, Historia, vol. 41, 327R–52, facsimile courtesy Ross Frank ("uno de los intérpretes, o otro sujeto de confianza"); translation in Concha, 1949, 247.

78. Stern, 1998, 164–65; Laws of 1563 and 1578, in the *Recopilación*, 1973, Libro 6, tit. 3, ley 21. Mörner, 1970, remains the essential work on this subject. Gálvez, 1873, 574 ("incorregibles, inobedientes y perjudiciales").

79. These reasons represent a composite from Stern, 1991, 274–80, Mayo and Latrubesse, 1993, 87–89, and Góngora, 1966, 5–6. All provide rich examples but take different tacks. Stern (like Mariluz Urquijo, 1987, 364, writing about the Charrúan territory along the Uruguayan–Portuguese border) tends to view these Spanish individuals as dysfunctional. Mayo and Góngora see Spanish society as dysfunctional, forcing individuals to flee. Among the many Indians who harbored fugitives, blacks and mestizos alike, were the Guajiros. Saler, 1980–88, 37.

80. Boccara, 1999b, 445, quoting fray Pedro de Angel de Espineira to the king, Concepción, Feb. 7, 1765 ("La pobreza que se experimenta cada día más y más en este obispado, en tanta manera que mucha de la gente de el, anhela pasarse y vivir en las tierras de los indios para hallar en ellas la abundancia de que carecen en las propias"). See, too, Casanueva, 1984, 3, and José Perfecto de Salas, 1750, quoted in Méndez Beltrán, 1987, 224.

81. Our present level of research does not allow us to differentiate between regions. Thomas Hall's suggestion that "voluntary migration into Indian societies by Spaniards" in southwestern America was "very rare" compared to Argentina does not seem sustainable. Hall, 1998, 158.

82. The quotation is from *Las ordenanzas de intendentes* for New Spain, in Fisher, 1929, 138, art. 60. For work as rehabilitation, see Pike, 1983, 148–53, and for validation of manual labor, see Floridablanca, 1867, 221, art. 52, and royal orders of May 18, 1783, available

in translation in Hargreaves-Mawdsley, 1973, 166. For one case study of the harsh treatment of the unemployed, see Góngora, 1966, 10–11. For the demoralizing poverty of soldiers on the frontier, see Moorhead, 1975, 196–200, 201–21, and Villalobos R., 1995, 73–87.

83. Teodoro de Croix to José de Gálvez, Sept. 23, 1778, in Bolton, 1914, 2:222, reporting that Lipan Apaches had learned the ingredients "perhaps, from some of our own people." John, 1975, 657, notes that Bernardo de Gálvez suspected Pedro Vial of teaching gun repair to Indians. Moreno y Escandón, 1936, 575, for renegade gun smugglers living among the Guajiros.

84. Ruiz López, 1952, 1:221 ("son por lo común los más ladinos y principales motores de alborotos y sublevaciones, a fin de mantenerse independientes y de vivir con toda libertad, sin estar sugetos a población alguna, más que en rancherías volantes"). "Ladino," as used here, suggests someone who is both astute and who speaks more than one language. See, too, Cerda-Hegerl, 1990, 46–47.

85. Avilés to the *capitán de amigos* Barros, Buenos Aires, Nov. 29, 1799, quoted in Levaggi, 2000, 163 ("algún español fugitivo los seduzca fingiendo que pretendemos hacerles algún perjuicio").

86. Marqués de Avilés to the king, Jan. 2, 1800, quoted in Acosta y Lara, 1961, 159 ("remediar y extinguir los frequentes robos, homicidios, contrabandos, destrozos de Ganados y otros graves delitos y desordenes que impunemente cometen los Vagos, delincuentes y forajidos de todas clases y condiciones, que sin respeto a las Leyes ni a la Religión infestan aquellos dilatados Campos"). See, too, the references to this melange of savages and bandits in the documents gathered in Lastarria, 1914, 60, 120, 201, 240.

87. Bernardo Suárez to Viceroy Antonio Olaguer Feliú, Dec. 27, 1797, quoted in Acosta y Lara, 1961, 136 ("las tolderías son el asilo de muchos delinquentes que amparados en ellas toman la voz y el nombre"). See, too, Mariluz Urquijo, 1987, 363–402, and Villegas, 1995, 95–96.

88. Declaración de Blas Pedrosa, Dec. 8, 1786, AGN [Buenos Aires] IX, 1.5.3, folios 662–68 ("espía"). Copy courtesy of Raúl Mandrini. Amigorena learned of a traitor named Lorenzo Vargas Machuca who scouted for the Ranqueles in 1784, helping them plan raids on Córdoba and San Luis. Amigorena, 1998, 69. See, too, Mayo, 1993, 91, and Saeger, 2000, 13–14, 16.

89. A point, for example, in a preliminary treaty with Callfilqui in 1790, and in a number of treaties with tribes in southeastern North America. Levaggi, 2000, 134, and Defina, 1966, 63–64.

90. John, 1975, 655–58.

91. Saavedra, 1989, 177, diary entry of May 11, 1781, at Pensacola.

92. *Recopilación,* 1973, Libro 6, tit. 2, ley 1 (a law of 1526 entitled, "Que los indios sean libres, y no sujetos a servidumbre") and Libro 3, tit. 4, ley 10 (1618). In New Spain, at the height of the Chichimeca War, in the late 1500s, officials permitted limited but not perpetual slavery of Indians seized in a "just war." Powell, 1952, 105–11. Long afterward, however, local officials in New Spain justified Indian slavery or overlooked it. Deeds, 2003, 71 and *passim,* for example. For a detailed chronicle of the ambiguity of these and subsequent laws as applied to New Spain, see Zavala, 1981. Araucanians were declared incorrigible exceptions, and their enslavement was permitted in just war in 1608 and again in 1625, but *cédulas reales* of 1610, 1674, 1683, and 1696 ended that exception and prohibited the enslavement of Araucanians in Chile, even if they were taken in a just war. The dates for these on-again, off-again decees vary with historians. See Villalobos R., 1992, 266–68, 279–85; Konetzke, 1953–62, vol. 3, book 1, 62–63; Hanisch Espíndola, 1981, 64; and Seed, 2001, 103.

93. *Real cédula,* Buen Retiro, Feb. 7, 1756, in Konetzke, 1953–62, vol. 3, book 1, 278 ("en ningún caso, lugar ni tiempo"). This royal order was to be sent to all viceroys, audiencias, and governors. The crown had a pattern of qualifying categorical prohibitions of slavery, permitting in particular enslavement of cannibals—a charge leveled at Indians who resisted domination. Seed, 2001, 103–05, 107–12. For Puritans, see Lepore, 1998, 154–67.

94. For Louisiana, where this became an issue in 1769 and 1787, see Zavala, 1981, 249, and Webre, 1984, 117–53. For the ongoing prohibition of Indian slavery, see Brinckerhoff and Faulk, 1965, 35 (tit. 10, art. 6), and Gálvez, 1873, 584, no. 38. For a contemporary (1787) statement of the need for black slaves for economic development, see Floridablanca, 1867, 229 (art. CVIII).

95. See, for example, Pedro de Nava to Fernando Chacón, Chihuahua, Oct. 19, 1797, paraphrased in Zavala, 1981, 298.

96. Zavala, 1981, 234–35, quoting from the Junta de Guerra of New Spain, July 15, 1691. West, 1949, 52, found that in the mines of seventeenth-century Parral, "Indians were rarely made perpetual slaves" but rather served for a set term, usually ten years. Whatever the practice, it is probably not correct to refer to Indians as "'justifiably' enslaved," as many writers do. See, for example, Deeds, 1989, 449. See, too, my discussion of the treatment of Apache prisoners of war in chap. 4.

97. Cramaussel, 1990–91, 73–89, observes that in practice the abuse of the *repartimiento* and *encomienda* made those legal institutions no different from slavery in Nueva Vizcaya. There and in northeastern Mexico the "enslavement" of Indians declined in the early eighteenth century as the numbers of missions in-

creased and the number of independent Indians diminished. Cuello, 1988b, 683–700.

98. Webre, 1984, 117–53, examines the gap between law and practice in Louisiana; Santa María, 1930, 2:447–50, offers a particularly vivid contemporary account of enslaving "salvajes" in Nuevo Santander in the 1790s. Brooks, 1999, 29–34, sees captive taking as a way to "redistribute resources . . . from the wealthy to the poorer orders of both societies" (p. 29).

99. Morelli, 1911, 3:133 ("salvajes"; "libertad y manumisión . . . fué debida únicamente a la clemencia del rey católico").

100. The use of *piezas* was commonplace. See, for example, Lorandi, 1988, 156, 162, who notes the expressions *piezas cobradas* and *piezas que cogeren* to refer to Indians as captured game. Croix to Bucareli, Chihuahua, Jan. 31, 1779, AGI, Guadalajara, 270, refers to a "grande collera de piezas." Felipe III, in 1618, ordered that "en ninguna forma se puedan repartir los Indios por piezas, como en algunas Provincias se ha hecho sin nuestra orden y voluntad." *Recopilación*, 1973, Libro 3, tit. 4, ley 10.

101. Juan and Ulloa, 1978, 2:354 ("de tales menudencias").

102. Opinion of the Fiscal Protector General de Naturales, Santiago, Nov. 28, 1777, ANSC, Archivo de la Capitanía General, vol. 637, 261 ("cierran enteramente la puerta a la compra de indios cuativos, asi como el uso de los rescates, prohibiendo que los compradores puedan servirse de ellos o tenerlos en sus casas, charcas, estancias o pueblos, aunque quieran los mismos indios"). The *fiscal protector* cited various laws in the *Recopilación*, among them Libro 6, tit. 2, leyes 7, 8, and 16; of those, in the quotation I provide he closely paraphrases law 7. These laws all prohibited the enslavement of Indians, which the *fiscal protector* apparently thought was encouraged by offers of ransom. Ley 7 (1618) addressed the practice of Guaycurúes and Spaniards buying and selling Indians taken in war in Tucumán, Río de la Plata, and Paraguay and ordered an end to these exchanges or "llamado rescates"—meaning "so-called ransoms" or "so-called exchanges" since the word *rescate* has both meanings in Spanish. Law 16 (1679) said clearly that in Chile "los Indios, Indias, y niños prisioneros no se pudiesen vender por esclavos." The *fiscal*'s use of "rescates" refers to the ransomed Indians themselves, a not uncommon neologism. Areces, López, and Regis, 1992, 159. Because of the multiple meanings of *rescate*, it could be argued that the Laws of the Indies prohibited buying and selling Indians and do not address the question of ransom directly, but it seems wrong to argue that the *Recopilación* "obliged Spanish [Spaniards] to ransom Indian captives enslaved by other Native groups." Magnaghi, 1990, 87–88, and Hämäläinen, 1998, 496, make that case, citing Libro 7, tit. 7, leyes 2, 3, and 17 of the *Recopilación*, which treat inspections of jails and do not

speak to the issue. Brooks, 2001, 156, and Brooks, 1997, 99, make the same assertion, citing the *Recopilación* but without reference to a specific law. The error seems to have made its way into the literature (see Tate, 1994, 232–33). Gutiérrez, 1991, 152, claims that the *Recopilación* stipulated that "ransomed Indians incurred debts that had to be repaid to their masters through work for an unspecified period," and he cites Libro 7 and laws 3 and 17, without indicating the title, but book 7 contains no such requirement.

103. Fray Joaquín Millán to Pedro Gregorio de Echeñique, Valdivia, May 12, 1781, quoted in Lagos, 1908, 286. Fray Joaquín referred to *leyes canónicas* of popes Paul III and Urban VII, and the "*Immensa Pastorum*" of Benedict XIV, dated Dec. 20, 1741. Some historians of New Mexico have concluded that the crown approved of the ransoming of captive Indian children, even with royal funds. See Brooks, 2002, 123, Thomas, 1932, 386 n.130, and Thomas, 1935, 13–14, who is often cited. Brooks and Thomas based their conclusion on an assertion attributed to a Jesuit, Juan Amando Niel, that the crown had ordered that royal funds be used to help Spaniards ransom Indian children lest Navajos murder their captives—a deed Niel claimed to have witnessed in 1694. Niel, 1856, 108. Niel, however, never visited New Mexico, and the commentary bearing his name appears to have been forged. Burrus, 1971, 417–18. Reference courtesy of John Kessell.

104. San Alberto to the Chiriguanos, Villa de Tarija, Oct. 23, 1787, in San Alberto, 1788, art. 23 ("Pero entended, que esto no es . . . rescate formal . . . de personas racionales . . . comprándolos, y vendiéndolos, como si fueran unas borricas"). See, too, Socolow, 1992, 82, and León Solís, 1990, 137–38. Black slaves did not fall into the category of rational persons.

105. Pedro Galindo Navarro to the comandante general, Chihuahua, Dec. 9, 1796, in Matson and Fontana, 1977, 74. See, too, ibid., 67, where fray Diego Bringas notes that Pimas would kill Apache prisoners if Spaniards did not buy them. See, too, ibid., 81–82. The Regulations of 1772 for the Interior Provinces of New Spain permitted Spaniards and their Indian allies to keep the spoils of war, but not human captives. Captives, the regulations said, had to be freed, converted, and instructed. For saving captives from cannibals, see Zavala, 1981, 230–31.

106. Sors, 1921–23, no. 48, 263 ("redimir las almas de la esclavitud del Demonio").

107. Morfi, 1967, 2:432, reporting on an idea advanced by Athanase de Mézières in 1778.

108. Adams and Chávez, 1956, 42.

109. Ibid. ("con la humanidad"; "para su cuidado y educación"). Sors, 1921–23, no. 45, 284, not the most objective interpreter of Jesuit actions, described a Jesuit plan to invite Araucanians into Chilean territory to sell their children or relatives.

110. Viana, 1958, 2:91 ("bajo la inteligencia de una absoluta libertad desde que fuesen adultos"). As is often
the case, Lieutenant Tova has the identical wording.
Tova Arredondo, 1993, 143. See, too, Malaspina,
1984, 311.

111. Felipe de Neve, "Relación concisa y exacta del estado en que ha encontrado las Provincias Internas,"
Arizpe, Dec. 1, 1783, AGI, Guadalajara 268, 43 ("la
feliz suerte"; "crian con igual amor, y cariño que si
fuesen sus propios hijos").

112. Ambrosio O'Higgins to Agustín de Jáuregui,
Santiago, Oct. 18, 1777, in ANSC, Archivo de la
Capitanía General, 637:252–54 ("a tierras nuestras";
"prohibido por los parlamentos y repetidas reales
ordenes").

113. Areces, López, and Regis, 1992, 165, who describe
an eighty-year period of peace beginning in 1632.

114. Santamaría, 1999, 19, gives examples from Jujuy and
notes the rising cost of black slaves in the eighteenth
century. See, too, Pifarré, 1989, 151, for the use of
purchased Chiriguano laborers at Tarija, Tomina,
and Santa Cruz.

115. Areces, López, and Regis, 1992, 161, contains explicit
contemporary statements to this effect.

116. See, for example, the cases in Zavala, 1981, 252–53.
For cases of officials invoking the law, see ibid., 243–
44, 255, and a case in 1820 in New Mexico, described
in Swadesh, 1974, 174. For a vivid if perhaps over-
heated picture of the impunity of local officials in
exploiting Indians in New Mexico, see Juan Sanz
de Lezaún, "An account of the lamentable happenings in New Mexico . . . 1760," in Hackett, 1923–37,
3:468–79.

117. For punishments to be meted out to officials buying and selling Indians, see the Consulta del Consejo de las Indias, Madrid, Feb. 1, 1715, in Konetzke,
1953–62, vol. 3, book 1, pp. 120–21.

118. Fray Pedro Serrano to Viceroy Cruillas, 1761, quoting fray Andrés Varo, in Hackett, 1923–37, 3:487. See,
for example, Hinojosa and Fox, 1991, 110, for an
episode in 1773. For the decline in official slave trading in New Mexico, which is based on the absence
of evidence from the 1700s, see Brugge, 1999, 106.
Doucet, 1988, 59–152, contains a fine discussion of
Indian slavery in Tucumán (his sources employ the
word "slave" between 1714 and 1761). See my discussion of *criados* as slaves below.

119. The quotation is from Andrews, 1980, 31. See, too,
Jones, 1984, 64. Jorge Gelman agrees with this assessment and notes a new need for manual labor in the
1820s and 1830s, at which time Argentines did turn
to Indians. In the southern part of the Banda Oriental, on the other hand, where cattle production
increased and the Spanish population was low in
the late colonial period, Gelman suspects a greater
use of Indian labor. Personal communication, May
3, 2001.

120. Brooks, 2002, 63–71.

121. Jacobo Ugarte to Viceroy Manuel Antonio Flores,
Arizpe, Oct. 1, 1787, in AGN, Provincias Internas,
tomo 112 ("párvulos"; "costumbres racionales").

122. Zavala, 1981, 307.

123. Jacobo Ugarte to Juan Bautista de Anza, Oct. 5, 1786,
in Thomas, 1932, 336.

124. Scholars have not located a copy of the treaty, but
a summary of it exists, translated and published in
Simmons, 1967, 21.

125. Jacobo Ugarte to Viceroy Manuel Antonio Flores,
Arizpe, Oct. 1, 1787, in AGN, Provincias Internas,
tomo 112 ("a la ciudad de Guadalajara en colleras,
a fin de que custodiados allí sin el riesgo de su fuga,
como era factible aqui"). Indians such as Utes and
Comanches who traded regularly with Spaniards
in New Mexico understood the market and brought
"little captive heathen Indians" to sell. Adams and
Chávez, 1956, 253.

126. In 1780, in Zavala, 1981, 292–93.

127. "If the slave is male, he is worth less," one priest observed in New Mexico in 1776. Adams and Chávez,
1956, 252, called to my attention by Magnaghi, 1990,
87. See, too, Gutiérrez, 1991, 186; Brooks, 1997, 97–
121; and Garavaglia, 1984, 29.

128. Amigorena, 1969–72, 213 ("quisieron más bien morir
que entregarse").

129. Torre Revello, 1958–59, 11–31.

130. After a successful foray into the Navajo country in
1805, for example, the veteran Indian fighter Lt. Antonio Narbona returned with thirty-three captives,
just three of them men, but he also brought back
the ears of a number of dead Navajo men to present
to the governor. McNitt, 1972, 44. See, too, Doucet,
1988, 114–16.

131. Garavaglia, 1984, 29; Santamaría, 1994b, 288, quoting
the governor of Salta. For the continued use of Indian captives in northern New Spain, see Deeds,
1989, 449, and Gutiérrez, 1991, 188.

132. Hanke, 1949, 139. The practice was widespread on
Indian frontiers. In 1798, for example, Arizpe's
twenty-five wealthiest households each contained
two Apache captives, and the local church commonly baptized captive Apache children. Officer,
1987, 75–76.

133. The idea that bonds of affection developed between
criados and their keepers is, of course, difficult to
prove but it has become part of the oral tradition of
New Mexico. Swadesh, 1974, 23; Jones, 1999, 223.
On earlier frontiers, Spanish soldiers with no women
of their own took Indian captives as mistresses and
wives, as in Chile. Cerda, 1990, 47–49. Guarda, 1980,
84, 94, a historian in the Benedictine Order, concluded that *criados* gained more than they lost and
claims ample evidence of "convivencia cordial y
cristiana relación mutua entre españoles y indios
de servicio."

134. Documents regarding the deposit of some eighty-five women and children in the Residencia after one episode in 1798 are in Acosta y Lara, 1961, 146–48 ("chusma de Chinas y niños de ambos sexos"). Documents refer to this as the Casa de Reclusión de la Residencia, or the Reclusión de la Residencia de las Chinas, or simply the Residencia. Miguel Lastarria, "Descripción topográfica y física: Noticias económicas y políticas de las referidas colonias hasta su estado actual … [y] plan para su nueva vigoroza organización y economía interior," Madrid, Dec. 31, 1804, in Lastarria, 1914, 273–74 ("personas pudientes, y de buenas costumbres"), notes that it was once a Jesuit residence and credits his employer, the marqués de Avilés, with distributing the captives to households; but the case of doña María, which I relate below, antedates the arrival of Avilés and suggests that the system was already in place.

135. Benito de la Matta Linares [writing on behalf of doña Marmól], to Viceroy Antonio Olaguer Feliú, Buenos Aires, Sept. 12, 1797, in Acosta y Lara, 1961, 133 ("propio, y debido"; "tener contentas tales gentes para que abrazen nuestra religión").

136. Ordenanzas de indios para el Tucumán, Viceroy Montesclaros, Nov. 8, 1614, quoted in Doucet, 1988, 65 ("como si fueran negros o mercaduría de comercio"), who provides a fine discussion of the legal definition of slavery (pp. 77–79).

137. Sors, 1921–23, no. 48, 261 ("esclavos"), 263, who vigorously defended the purchasing of Indian women and children. Laws regarding captives or ransomed Indians were not simply abstractions. See, for example, the viceroy to Diego de Vargas, Mexico, March 26, 1694, in Kessell, Hendricks, and Dodge, 1998, 2:94–95, who notes that women and children captives could not be "exchanged, or sold on any pretext" and that they should be freed once they become "domesticated," even if that occurred before they completed "the stated ten years."

138. Testamento, July 24, 1739, quoted in Doucet, 1988, 119 ("declaro que tengo una india de nación mocobí, mi esclava; declárola por tal y mando se le entregue a dicho mi hijo Joseph como todos los demás bienes"). See, too, Doucet, 1988, 109–14, 116–20, for the commerce in Indians by government officials and their treatment as slaves. No one in Tucumán, he says, was punished for enslaving Indians (82). For indios de depósito, used in Chile, see González Pomes, 1966, 15–16, 25–28, and Opinion of the Fiscal Protector General de Naturales, Santiago, Nov. 28, 1777, ANSC, Archivo de la Capitanía General, vol. 637, who described them as "depositarios." Brooks, 2002, 238, and Martin, 1996, 43, identify Indian servants listed as property in the estates of New Mexicans in the Spanish period. In a forthcoming book, Martina Will de Chaparro, who has studied wills in New Mexico, notes that some New Mexican criadas were

adults with children of their own. Only twice, however, did she find them referred to as esclavos, both times in the early 1810s, when the reference might have been to blacks. Since criados were subject to coercive labor, it is not surprising that some scholars ignore the distinction between de facto and de jure slavery and use "slave" as a synonym for criado, including Villalobos R., 1989, 205, Gutiérrez, 1991, 180–90, and Santamaría, 1999, 19. Brooks, 2001, 150, goes too far, however, in describing Indian criados as slaves, "legally speaking."

139. Testamento of Bernardino Pérez de Padilla, Hacienda del Pucará [Tucumán], May 27, 1739, quoted in Doucet, 1988, 118 ("María, india mocobí, que me ha servido más que una esclava, con todo amor, fidelidad, legalidad").

140. Alejandro Malaspina quoted in Cutter, 1991, 94, whose source is not clear.

141. C. Cutter, 1995, 42; Brooks, 2001, 156.

142. Zavala, 1981, 255–56.

143. Order of Pedro Gregorio de Echeñique, Valdivia, Aug. 19, 1779, Lagos, 1908, 285 ("vuelvan a la infidelidad, aunque los requieran sus parientes"), responding to a Franciscan's complaints. Guarda, 1980, 82–84, also discusses this order along with similar instructions issued in 1774 by the governor's predecessor. See, too, Sors, 1921–23, no. 48, 262.

144. The debate in the 1779 case is in Chiaramonte, 1989, 138–46. For sample treaties, see Levaggi, 2002, 239, 258. New Mexico governor Tomás Vélez Cachupín, known for his piety, stands among the apparent exceptions. See his letter to the viceroy, Santa Fe, June 27, 1762, in Thomas, 1940, 151–53.

145. Brooks, 2002, 238.

146. See, for example, Hinojosa and Fox, 1991, 105–20, and Guarda, 1980, 86.

147. Magnaghi, 1990, 91, Gutiérrez, 1991, 199–200, Cramaussel, 1995, 420, who draws her evidence from Parral, in Nueva Vizcaya in northern New Spain.

148. Weber, 1992, 308. The percentage of genízaros depends in part on how one defines the descendants of genízaros. For estimates later in the century, see Gutiérrez, 1991, 171, 180, who curiously puts them at 9,680 in 1793 and 7,000 in 1800. Frank, 2000, 176–80, argues that castas and genízaros in New Mexico became lumped together as españoles by 1800. In everyday use, however, the designation remained commonplace. See, for example, Brooks, 2001, 173.

149. Ventura Bustamante to Croix, June 20, 1780, quoted in Brooks, 2001, 150 (quotation), 167–69. Brooks conjectures that this community of genízaros, from the barrio of Analco in Santa Fe, consisted chiefly of detribalized Apaches.

150. García-Mariño Mundi, 1986, 21–28. Stein and Stein, 2003, 18.

151. Brooks, 2001, 164; Brooks, 1997, 109, 100, 116 n. 12. The numbers of genízaros in New Mexico were probably

higher than sources suggest. Baptismal records, used to good effect, do not give us a full picture since many baptismal books are no longer extant, and census records are notoriously inaccurate since respondents often identified themselves as of a higher caste than they actually were.

152. Brooks, 2001, 173; Weber, 1971, 23–31; Concha, 1949, 240. Hafen and Hafen, 1954, 263, note the importance of Manuel Mestas, a *genízaro*, as a trader and interpreter to the Utes.

153. Magnaghi, 1990, 89–91; Brooks, 2001, 171, 173. Gutiérrez, 1991, 150–56, 171–72, 179–90, and *passim*, sees *genízaro* as being synonymous with "slave."

154. White, 2000, 2, points to the use of this term as early as 1664 in New Mexico. Elsewhere, the standard modern spelling is *jenízaro*. See, too, Brooks, 2002, 127–28.

155. Dobyns and others, 1960, 230–58, explores the etymology and meaning of *nixora*, who were used commonly as household servants in Sonora (p. 253). See Matson and Fontana, 1977, 338, for "vendidos" and "nixoras" in the baptismal book at Caborca.

156. Hall, 1998, 160, suggests that *genízaros* had no counterpart in Argentine society, and it is true there were no communities of detribalized Indians employed to defend those provinces. The Río de la Plata region did, however, have detribalized Indians living in Spanish society; they simply were not called *genízaros.*

157. John, 1991a, 132; John, 1975, 698–99.

158. Beckerman, 1979, 25–26; the Diary of Sebastián José Guillén in Maracaibo, Dec. 4, 1772, in Alcácer, 1962, 275–76. Brooks, 1997, 112–13, provides several examples of women captives from New Mexico who served as emissaries or translators. Vitar, 1996, 160, for distrust.

159. Palma to Bucareli, Mexico, Nov. 11, 1776; Bucareli to José de Gálvez, Mexico, Nov. 26, 1776, and Feb. 27, 1777, translated in Bolton, 1930, 5:365–76, 395–97, 410–12. For context, see Weber, 1992, 156–58; for Palma and the nature of leadership in Yuma society, see Forbes, 1965, 173–84 and Santiago, 1998, 26–27, 71.

160. See chap. 5, n. 86.

161. Caballero y Góngora to José de Gálvez, Turbaco, July 9, 1787, quoted at length in Levaggi, 2002, 304 ("felices, y contentos a los Indios de este Pueblo bajo el suave yugo de S.M., que les observen a todos con su buena casa, sus sembrados, y comodidades"; "sin fausto, sin tropa, y con una confianza total").

162. This account draws from Romero Vargas, 1995, 197–202, who also looks at contradictory assessments of Briton by his contemporaries, and from the confusing García Peláez, 1943–44, 3:115–38, who paraphrases and quotes extensively from contemporary sources, including a *Gaceta* published in Cartagena, July 6, 1788. García, 1999, 111, relied solely on García

Peláez, 1943–44, and scrambles the chronology. For an account in English, see Floyd, 1967, 173–82.

163. Her concern about the other wives is suggested in a letter Briton wrote to her assuring her that when she returned to Tuapí Lagoon the other wives would be gone. Briton to María Rodríguez, Oct. 12, 1788, in García Peláez, 1943–44, 3:123–24.

164. Dictamen de Lic. Diego de Piloña, León, Dec. 7, 1788, quoted in García Peláez, 1943–44, 3:127 ("silvestres y semejantes a las fieras . . . sin ley, sin rey").

165. García, 1999, 116–18, summarizes the opposition to Briton and reports on a Spanish investigation into his death. Offen, 2002, 352, suggests that Briton united feuding Zambo and Tawira leaders against him.

166. Viceroy Amat to Gov. Jáuregui, Lima, April 27, 1774, refers to Jáuregui's invitation ("con el especioso título de embajadores destinar unos verdaderos rehenes de los cuatro butalmapus"). Quoted in Barros Arana, 1884–1902, 6:345. Campos Menchaca, 1972, 152–54, takes a more positive view.

167. Barros Arana, 1884–1902, 6:348 n.8.

168. Jáuregui to the minister of the Indies, Julián de Arriaga, Santiago, June 3, 1774, in Barros Arana, 1884–1902, 6:346 ("juraban ser fieles vasallos del rei nuestro señor prostraron todos ante el retrato de su real persona").

169. Vicente Carvallo y Goyeneche, quoted in Barros Arana, 1884–1902, 6:347 ("ellos no pueden representar a su nación porque ésta no tiene especie alguna de gobierno"; "principales caballeros de la ciudad, sin otro objeto que pedirles un par de reales para beber").

170. Ambrosio O'Higgins, the Marques de Osorno, Sept. 4, 1796, to Tomás O'Higgins, in O'Higgins, 1942–43, 101:45 ("usar de toda la prudencia, suavidad, dulzura y sagacidad que es necesario cuando se trata con este género de gentes, que a pesar de su barbaridad e idiotismo saben dar su estimación y confianza a quien les trata de aquel modo y yo logré completamente por su medio").

171. Frank, 2000, 34–57, 119–56.

172. León Solís, 1990, 102; 97–105.

173. Brown, 1979, 33–35. Miller Astrada, 1997, 68–84.

174. León Solís, 1990, 108–12, 123–27. Villalobos R., 1992, 340, for the alliance. Frank, 2000, 123, suggests that the Indian trade became less important to the growing New Mexico economy of the 1780s and 1790s, but his evidence is impressionistic. The Indian trade could, in theory, have risen in value at the same time that its *relative* importance decreased. The question requires more research.

175. John, 1975, 694–95; John, 1991a, 127. The interpreter was Andrés Courbière. For bathing and standards of cleanliness in Europe, see Braudel, 1981, 1:310, 329–30; in America, see Descola, 1968, 123, for problems of clean water, and Marc Simmons, "Misery

as a Factor in Colonial Life," in Simmons, 2001, 80, 86, 90.

176. Concha, 1949, 242.

177. For the impact of spending on just one area, see Frank, 2000, 132–39. The subject of independent Indians in Spanish towns needs further study. Usner, 1989, 104–28, looks at the phenomenon in New Orleans in its French and Spanish periods but concentrates on the French.

178. Carminati, 1995, 218, described the phenomenon of daily visits by heathen Indians at the coastal fort of Arauco, in Araucanian territory south of the Biobío, in 1755. For cases of workers coming for the season, see Mayo, 1985a, 235–43; Mayo and Latrubesse, 1993, 87–93; Radding, 1997, 109–12; Saignes, 1989, 13–51; Stern, 1991, 262–81; Zavala, 1981, 179–309; Teruel, 1994, 231, 236–39; and the other cases in this paragraph.

179. Deeds, 1989, 426–29, summarizes the literature admirably and adds her own voice to those who see a murkier pattern. See, too, Gelman, 1990, 241–79 (on p. 278 he identifies two peones as Indians, although their origin is unclear), and his theoretical observations in Gelman, 1999, 123–41.

180. Hackel, 1998, 125–26.

181. Carminati, 1995, 218, Méndez Beltrán, 1987, 216–19 and *passim*, who also finds them working as foresters. For demographic and economic growth in this area, see Cerda-Hegerl, 1990, 66–94. León Solís, 1990, 127, points to a labor shortage in southern Chile. Pinto, 2000, 25–26, provides guidance to recent studies that explore this question more deeply. See, too, Sors, 1921–23, no. 48, 261.

182. Azara, 1990, 116 ("medio civilizados"), 126–30.

183. Mateo de Saravia y Jáuregui quoted in Santamaría, 1994b, 288–89 ("la escasez de gente para el conchabo para la labranza ha obligado a sus moradores [Spaniards in Salta] a solicitar a los infieles para el conchabo de todo trabajo de a pie y de a caballo así en el campo como en la ciudad"). Although Buenos Aires grew faster than the province of Salta de Tucumán, the latter's economy still grew rapidly enough that it, too, suffered a labor shortage. López de Alborniz, 1997, 174–75. See, too, Halperín-Donghi, 1975, 61, and other sources on the Chaco cited below. For Chiriguanos, see Pifarré, 1989, 151–52.

184. Mateo de Saravia y Jáuregui to Santiago Liniers, Salta, Oct. 23, 1807, quoted in Acevedo, 1965, 392, who notes a much-ignored requirement that such labor required the approval of the *intendente* of Salta. Cuello, 1988b, 694–95, makes the point about the value of temporary labor in northeastern New Spain in the 1600s and early 1700s.

185. John, 1991a, 128. John, 1975, 711 n.24.

186. Francisco Balcarce to viceroy Juan José de Vertiz, Fuerte de Rojas, Dec. 19, 1779, AGN [Buenos Aires], IX, 1-5-1, folios 172–75, reporting on his interrogation

of an "indio de nación rancachel" ("a la tierra de cristianos"; "voluntariamente se venga a vivir con los cristianos siendo de nación contraria"). Reference courtesy of Sara Ortelli.

187. Juan and Ulloa, 1978, 2:361–62 ("muchos Indios, y Indias de estas naciones blancos, y rubios, como los mismos Españoles de aquel País"). See, too, Ruiz López, 1952, 1:222. This phenomenon of "passing" may have occurred elsewhere. By the first decade of the 1800s, observers reported that many light-skinned women could be found in the Comanche camps along the Louisiana frontier. Tate, 1994, 236. Haenke, 1942, 194–96, for poor Chileans.

188. Santamaría, 1995, 36 ("Este mismo espíritu de lucro, idéntico al de los españoles y mestizos"). For an especially penetrating discussion of the acculturation process on the pampa, see Quijada, 2002, 131–32.

189. Teruel, 1994, 236, 239.

190. Barfield, 1989, 2, who is eloquent on the emotional appeal of the nomadic life and hence its power to maintain itself against the forces of acculturation.

191. Brooks, 2002 ("Francisco el Comanche, Francisco Xavier de nación Aá, José María Gurulé de nación Caigua"). The fourth was a *genízaro;* see below. The four had traded with Comanches without a license and bad-mouthed Spaniards. See, too, Brooks, 2002, 196.

192. Azara, 1990, 115 ("pescan y trabajan con utilidad de esta ciudad, y aunque no sean católicos, pueden llamarse socios útiles)."

193. Azara, 1923, 2:68, 71 ("sin cambiar nada absolutamente"; "no quieren, en absoluto, ser cristianos, y si se los obligara empezarían otra vez la guerra"). See, too, Dobrizhoffer, 1967–70, 1:211–15, and Saeger, 2000, 18–19, 48.

194. Teruel, 1994, 239, quoting José Antonio Fernández Cornejo, who hired Matacos to harvest sugar in 1804. See, too, her analysis on p. 248.

195. North of the Biobío, in the jurisdiction of Penco near Concepción, independent Indians comprised 10 percent of the rural population in 1779 (León Solís, 1990, 130). Many were probably not Christians.

196. Indians fled missions, as we have seen, and *indios domésticos* also fled from onerous demands for tribute. By the early eighteenth century so many *retirados* had left the highlands of Peru for the trans-Andean lowlands that some officials supposed their departure explained the population decline in the Andean highlands. Lehnertz, 1974, 44–48. A shift eastward also occurred in the Central American highlands, where Hispanicized Indians fled to become what Spaniards called wild or untamed—*cimarrones* or *montaraces.* Izard, 1992–93, 172–73. Merrill, 2000, 653–54, sees Tarahumaras allying themselves with Apaches because they seemed more powerful than Spaniards in Nueva Vizcaya. See, too, Cruz, 2001, 155–58.

197. Morillo, 1969–72, 416 ("chusma"; "las verdades de

Jesucristo"; "las mentiras de Satanás"). See, too, 412, 415–18, 422. *Ladino* can also mean *mestizo,* but in this context it means an Indian who speaks Spanish along with his own language. See, too, Andrés Mestre, the governor of Tucumán, to José de Gálvez, Córdoba, Sept. 6, 1780, quoted in Vitar, 1996, 161.

198. Palermo, 1994, 71–72, 79–81.

199. Bernardo de Bonavia, Informe sobre las misiones de la provincia de Yucatán, 1804, quoted in Olmos Sánchez, 1986, 231 ("los indios bárbaros").

200. Instrucción, Col. Fernando de la Concha to his successor, Lt. Col. Fernando Chacón, Chihuahua, June 28, 1794, in AGN, Mexico, Historia, vol. 41, 327R–52, facsimile courtesy Ross Frank ("tampoco tienen intérprete señalado los Jicarillas, pero como hay muy raro entre ellas que deje de hablar algo el castellano, no es difícil entenderse"); translation in Concha, 1949, 241.

201. Acevedo, 1996, 293, writes of Indian groups in the northeastern Chaco, "semi convertidos, que ya no eran ni totalmente salvajes ni completamente cristianos"; his characterization would seem to apply to many places.

202. Polo Acuña, 1999b, 75 ("puente de contacto entre las autoridades españolas y los indios 'rebeldes'"). For the putatively Indian but highly mestizo community of Boronato, see Barrera Monroy, 2000, 69–71, and p. 189 for don Cecilio's visit to Spain.

203. Testimony taken in 1764 and quoted at length in Uribe, 1977, 129 ("festejarse con los despojos y muertes que hicieron"). See, too, Acevedo, 1996, 292, and Vitar, 1995, 58, quoting the bishop of Tucumán in 1768.

204. Croix to José de Gálvez, Arizpe, Jan. 23, 1780, quoted in Mirafuentes Galván, 1993, 113 ("porque el ejemplo de la absoluta libertad de los bárbaros les incita a buscar la propia, el parentesco que algunos tienen con los mismos bárbaros los obliga a la infidelidad"), whose work informs this paragraph.

205. The decree, issued by Mateo Antonio de Mendoza, San Felipe el Real, Jan. 11, 1755, is in Valdés, 1995, 242 ("indios amistados y mezclados con los inmediatos fronterizos gentiles y apóstatas"). See, too, Valdés and Dávila, 1998, nos. 378, 407, 428. The order of June 1, 1772, issued by Gov. Carlos de Aguero, is quoted in Sheridan, 2000, 264 ("traidor al rey"). For punishments meted out to two Indian towns in Nueva Vizcaya in the 1780s, see Vallebueno G., 2000, 674.

206. Officer, 1987, 56. See, too, the case described by Salcedo y Salcedo, 1990, 40.

207. Morfi, 1935, 316, called to my attention by Anderson, 1999, 132–33, who incorrectly assumes that Josecillo was a Spaniard. Other examples include Foerster G., 1996, 334, quoting the Sínodo of 1744; O'Crouley, 1972, 52; *real cédula* to the captain general of Guatemala, San Lorenzo, Nov. 19, 1787, in Pe-

ralta, 1898, 263. Ricklis, 1996, 145, quoting fray Juan Agustín de Morfi on the Karankawas in Texas; Antonio María Bucareli to Julián de Arriaga, Mexico, Oct. 27, 1772, in Velasco Ceballos, 1936, 1:70. Vitar, 1996, 154–61. For an interesting case, see Anderson, 1999, 114–15.

208. See, for example, León, 1997, 40 and 42, for two cases of Spaniards disguised as Indians in 1783 and 1781, respectively. For *indios reducidos* disguising themselves as Chimilas and Guajiros, see my introduction, and Rodríguez Gallardo, 1975, 42, for Pimas disguising themselves as Apaches. For the "sin" of dressing like Indians, see Brown, 2001, 36, who quotes the influential and often reprinted *Itinerario para párrocos de indios* by Alonso de la Peña Montenegro, first published in 1668.

209. Neve to Cristóbal Corvalán, Arispe, Dec. 10, 1783, no. 74 (copy of Jan. 26, 1784) AGI, Guadalajara, 519 ("facinerosos, y malhechores"; "no es facil averiguar los verdaderos autores por que executándolos disfrazados en traje de Apaches"). Documents could also fall into the wrong hands, as José de Gálvez warned. See Ortelli, 2003b, 340–41. For racial mingling and the limits of race, see Seed, 2001, 123–24, 131–32.

210. Stern, 1998, 168–69, tells the story of Juan José Peña, "an especially energetic career criminal" who moved back and forth between the Spanish and Indian worlds.

211. Valdés and Dávila, 1989; Teja, 1995, 123; Deeds, 1989, 431. In southeastern North America, most of the blacks who entered the Indian worlds in the eighteenth century came from English America. See Landers, 1995, 12–24.

212. Andrews, 1980, 4, 25; Studer, 1984, 340, provides a breakdown from the 1778 census that puts blacks at 3,837 and mulattos at 2,997 in a total population of 24,083.

213. For "muchos mestizos, mulatos y algunos negros fugitivos" among the Chiriguanos in 1728, see Calzavarini, 1980, 186. Fals Borda, 1979, 1:113A, notes the Chimilas' absorption of blacks and mestizos, many of whom, he says, became leaders. For Comanches (and Lipan Apaches), see Anderson, 1999, 133, 225. For Creeks and Cherokees, see May 1996, chap. 2, and her discussion of historical interpretations on pp. 19–24. Río Cossa, 1935, 13, writing in 1787, commented on the black slaves purchased from the British in St. Augustine by Florida Indians. For the ethnogenesis of Miskitos and the particular role of women in absorbing outsiders, see García, 1999, 97–102. Spaniards knew the Indianized descendants of blacks who lived among Caribs as "black Caribs." Whitehead, 1999, 430. Examples do not end here. See Lázaro Ávila, 1999, 646, for the Araucanía. Even the Huilliches, who lived at some remove from Spaniards and had been at war with them since the 1500s,

seem to have become a racially mixed group by the end of the 1700s. Silva Galdames, Schmidt Acharán, and Farga Hernández, 1991, 200 ("un conjunto de nativos, mestizos, mulatos y renegados"). Native Americans accommodated blacks into their societies in a variety of ways, of course, some absorbing them entirely and others, like the matrilocal Cherokees, who generally kept them as slaves and did not permit them to enter their clans. Perdue, 1979, 3–49, describes the evolution of slavery among the Cherokees in the colonial period.

214. Teodoro de Croix put the population at 6,460 in 1780. Jones, 1979, 93.

215. Merrill, 1994, 124–52, tells the story of the Calaxtrins' band, which was not unique in Nueva Vizcaya. See, too, Merrill, 2000, 623–68. Ortelli, 2003b, 159–89, 282–84, portrays Calaxtrin's band, along with others, as simple thieves. Although we have little literature on them, such groups certainly existed in other areas, such the Banda Oriental, where in 1767 Bougainville learned that band of over six hundred Spanish renegades and their Indian women and offspring reportedly lived in the no-man's-land between Spanish and Portuguese territory, trading stolen Spanish livestock for Portuguese weapons and clothing. Bougainville, 1921, 1:49–50, called to my attention by Street, 1959, 15. See, too, Street, 1959, 29, 51–52, 62–67, 119 n. 1, and Villegas, 1995, 86–87.

216. Mayo, 1993, 92.

217. Viedma, 1969c–72c, 3:677 ("casi no tienen, o reconocen a quién obedecer y temer: de modo que poco se diferencian de los indios salvajes"). See, too, Azara, 1943d, 3–6.

218. García, 1969b–72b, 4:263 ("era forzoso, pues, que reducidos a este género de vida, adquiriesen unas costumbres salvajes, y que, desconociendo la necesidades del hombre civilizado, se resintiesen de la indolencia e ignorancia de sus bárbaros vecinos"). This memoria also appears in Gelman, 1998, 77–99. García, 1969a–72a, 303 ("poco menos feroces e inciviles que los mismos indios"). See, too, Juan José de Vértiz, "Instrucción que debe observar el Comandante de la frontera, subinspector de las Milicias del Campo [May 5, 1779]," in Círculo Militar, 1973, 1:197, art. 30, and Wilde, 2003, 105–35. Contemporaries made the same point about Indianized Spaniards in remote areas elsewhere in the empire. See, for example, Alcedo y Bexerano, 1786–89, quoted in Lerner, 1971, 81–82.

219. Slatta, 1983, 8–15; Jones, 1984, 58–60; Socolow, 1998, 76–77. Slatta, and Gelman, 1990, 279, observe that *gauchos* may not have reached significant numbers until the 1800s, when the expansion of large ranches forced campesinos from their lands. Salvatore, 2003, generally avoids the term *gaucho*, which suggested social inferiority, and uses the more neutral *paysano* as

a synonym (pp. 11, 23, 131, 134), but not all of his *paysanos* were *gauchos*.

220. Rausch, 1984, 232; 241–42; Slatta, 1990, 161–63.

221. Vértiz y Salcedo, 1945, 149 ("de abominables costumbres, y dedicados a herir y matar gentes, robar caballadas y mujeres; y muchos de ellos con continuo trato con los infieles; por donde sabían nuestros movimientos cuando se dirijían a buscarlos en sus tierras, y siendo guias, o vaqueanos de ellos cuando venían a cometer a la frontera sus insultos").

222. Fray Manuel Gil, Mission Piray, 1776, quoted in Santamaría, 1994b, 281, and Santamaría, 1998a, 29 ("apóstatas de Santa Cruz, Vallegrande, fronteras de Tomina y Tarija"; "peores costumbres que los mismos bárbaros"; "sus latrocinios y maldades").

223. Sors, 1921–23, no. 46, 334 ("viven dispersos en las campañas"; "vida civil"; "así viven y mueren poco menos que los indios"), writing ca. 1780. See, too, León Solís, 1990, 101, 127, and Haenke, 1942, 195–96.

224. Antonio de Arévalo, 1773, quoted in Polo Acuña, 1999a, 26 ("desnudos como los indios a su libertad").

225. Jerónimo de Mendoza to the viceroy, May 24, 1766, quoted in Barrera Monroy, 2000, 177 ("no comprendo entre unos y otros cuales sean más bárbaros y de menos religión"). Barrera Monroy, 2000, for warning Guajiros (196) and for the town's ethnic composition (p. 69).

226. Instrucción, Col. Fernando de la Concha to his successor, Lt. Col. Fernando Chacón, Chihuahua, June 28, 1794, in AGN, Mexico, Historia, vol. 41, 327R–52, facsimile courtesy Ross Frank ("para adaptar [adoptar?] la libertad y desaliño que ven y notan en sus vecinos los indios bárbaros"); translation in Concha, 1949, 250; Simmons, 1979, 109–11; Weber, 1992, 332–33. See, too, Morfí, 1977, 13–14.

227. For a striking contemporary view of the land shortage in Chile, see Haenke, 1942 [Espinosa], 194.

228. See, for example, Robinson and Thomas, 1974, 8–14, Fals Borda, 1986, 4: 70A, and Castillero Calvo, 1995, 82. Sors, 1921–23, no. 45, 266, complained in 1780 that "las gentes dispersas por las campañas contribuyen con pocas limosnas a la Santa Cruzada." Brooks, 2001, 169. González de la Vara, 2002, 131–32. Officials in the Río de la Plata learned of this illegal commerce from escaped captives; see, for example, the declarations of Hipólito Bustos and María Paula Santana in Mayo, 1985b, 15, 21–22.

229. We have many accounts of soldiers consorting with and trading with putatively hostile Natives, but see Méndez Beltrán, 1987, 223–24. For foreman and Mbayás, see Santamaría, 1992, 144.

230. Góngora, 1966, 23–25.

231. Santamaría, 1998a, 15–34.

232. Paucke, 1942–44, 2:21, quoting a manuscript by a fellow Jesuit, Francisco Burges ("Los Españoles no desean otra cosa sino que los indios se mantengan sosegados para que ellos puedan ejercer en paz su

comercio. . . . no les importa nada si son paganos o cristianos").

233. Schwartz and Salomon, 1999, 481, offer this general rule. See, too, Alberro, 1992, 55–57, 224.

234. Molina, 1809, 319–20, writing of the 1760s. See, too, León Solís, 2002, 207, for an earlier example.

235. Urbina Burgos, 1986, 397. See, too, the governor's report in A. Santamaría, 1995, 272.

236. Urbina Burgos, 1986, 398, quoting Narciso de Santa María, Estado General . . . de Chiloé, March 14, 1755 ("la castellana, muy mal hablada y la beliche [Huilliche] . . . muy bien"). For another example, see Hackel, 1998, 128, who tells of some Spaniards speaking Indian languages in California in the 1790s and of some Indians speaking Spanish.

237. Foerster G., 1991, 202; Villalobos R., 1992, 262, 279, 314–26; Zapater, 1998, 128–29.

238. Súsnik, 1968, 216. See, too, Saignes, 1989, 13–51, for a suggestive analysis of the roles of mestizos in the Chiriguanía in the sixteenth and seventeenth centuries. For racial blending with another hostile group, the Guajiros, see Polo Acuña, 1999a, 24–29.

239. Increase Mather, quoted by Lepore, 1998, 7. See, too, 175. Nash, 1995, explains why racial mixing was "ideologically repugnant" to most white Americans (954), even as he sees the Anglo-Indian frontier as a "cultural merging ground and a marrying ground" (947). See, too, the masterful analysis by Elliott, 1994, 3–23.

240. Revillagigedo, 1966a, 86 ("mulatos y demás castas infectas"; "naturalmente inclinados a la ociosidad y a toda clase de vicios, necesitan para corregirlos en buen ejemplo de familias o gentes de mejores costumbres"). Concern for racial purity among elites seemed to increase in the late colonial period. See Twinam, 1999. For the problem of collecting tribute, see Pietschmann, 1998, 279.

241. Orders of viceroy Antonio Olaguer y Feliú, Feb. 7, 1797, quoted in Acosta y Lara, 1961, 155 ("cuñas del mismo palo"), meaning more literally "wedges from the same wood." Praise for the fighting prowess of frontiersmen came from many quarters: Juan and Ulloa, 1985, 2:81; *real cédula* to Agustín de Jáuregui, Gobernador y Capitán General del Reyno de Chile y Presidente de mi Audiencia de la Ciudad de Santiago. El Pardo, Feb. 6, 1774, ANSC, Fondos Varios, vol. 300, pieza 3; Moorhead, 1975, 178–80, 195–96. See, too, Serra y Canals in chap. 4, above.

242. Jorge Pacheco quoted in Mariluz Urquijo, 1987, 384 ("matadores, ladrones, bandidos, delincuentes, holgazanes que siempre vivieron sin religión, sin domicilio ni ley"). See, too, Street, 1959, 53.

243. Haedo, 1872, 455 ("porque para reñir con los indios no se necesitan evoluciones").

244. Alonso, 1995, 30.

245. Mariluz Urquijo, 1987, 366.

246. Capt. Jorge Pacheco to Viceroy Liniers, Buenos Aires, March 8, 1808 (a plan to colonize the frontier of the Banda Oriental), in Pivel Devoto, 1957, 272–73 ("civilización y la doctrina en lugar de los extragos, de las armas que nada sirven al progreso de la Religión").

247. Antonio Valdez to Higgins, April 3, 1789, quoted in Villar and Jiménez, 2000, 706 ("uso entre las naciones de estos infieles"). Roulet, 2002, 77 n.3. For correspondence regarding the five hundred mares, see Silva Galdames, 1998, 13–15. Documents spell Llanquetruz variously, including "Llanquitur." His biography is in Hux, 1991b, 7–14. See, too, chap. 4 above for Spaniards' deployment of the heads of Tarahumara "rebels," and Pedro de Allande y Saavedra to the king, ca. 1786, describing a campaign in 1782, in McCarty, 1976, 45. Offering rewards for Indians' heads dated back to the Habsburgs—see, for example, Deeds, 2003, 33. Smith, 1992, 7–24, an article whose scope is larger than its title suggests, surveys the subject of ear taking and notes that *bandeirantes* severed ears in Brazil. On at least one occasion authorities in New Granada paid a bounty for heads or ears. See Polo Acuña, 1999a, 21. Europeans appear to have learned about scalping from Indians. The practice seems to have been more widespread among Eastern woodland Indians in North America than elsewhere. For English awards for scalps in 1694, see Axtell, 1982, 142–43. See, too, Axtell, 1981, 16–32, and Axtell, 1981, 207–41. The Spanish governor of East Florida offered rewards to Seminoles for the scalps of Anglo-American invaders in 1812, rather than for their ears or heads. Cusick, 2003, 214. Smith, 1992, 6–24, makes clear that Indians took scalps in the Spanish period in northern New Spain (see, too, Kino, 1919, 2:169, and Pino, 1995, 51), but scalping did not become commonplace until Anglo-Americans and Eastern Indians moved into the region in the nineteenth century. Dobrizhoffer, 1967–70, 2:419, mentions Abipones taking heads and scalps; Garavaglia, 1984, 23, 29, writes of Indians and Spaniards taking scalps in the Chaco, but I have seen no study of this subject for South or Central America.

248. José de Gálvez to Agustín de Jáuregui, Aranjuez, July 3, 1777, ANSC, capitanía general, vol. 728 (1777) no. 9866 ("su cabeza presentado a nuestro comandante Dn Ambrosio Higgins"). The English of the era, of course, meted punishments no less brutal. See, for example, Axtell, 1982, 144–45.

249. That was the case, for example, with José Antonio Galán, one of the leaders of the Comunero Revolt of 1781 in Colombia. See, too, chap. 4 above for Viceroy Amat's treatment of Spanish criminals.

250. Socolow, 1992, 99.

251. Santamaría, 1994b, 292–94, discussing the province of Tucumán, but similar circumstances obtained on other frontiers.

252. Baud and van Schendel, 1997, 234, who focus on

modern political borders. Martínez, 1996, xiii, a life-long student of borderlands, suggests that the lives of borderlanders are shaped by the Janus-faced forces of "conflict and interdependence." See, too, Villalobos R., 1992, 311, for a pithy analysis, and see, too, Worcester, 1979b, 3.

253. Alonso, 1995, 68. See, too, 55–56, 63–64, 71. For the breakdown of the two *repúblicas* in Mexico City and environs, see Borah, 1983, 391. This was part of a broader collapse of boundaries in the colonial world, which Steve Stern, 1998, 53, refers to suggestively as "reverse colonization and massive social leakage."

254. Mendinueta, 1910, 445 ("gentes civilizadas"; "observarán su trato y costumbres; verán que disfrutan de ciertas conveniencias, bajo de un orden establecido, y se adelantará mucho por este medio, ya sea que obre con los indios el poderoso aliciente de la propia comodidad ó el espíritu de imitación").

255. The "Informe de don Miguel Constansó [Costansó] al Virrey," Mexico, Oct. 17, 1794, in Moncada Maya, 1994, 313, offers a classic statement of this philosophy by a military engineer based on his observations in California ("gente de razón"; "gente sin razón"; "hombres"; "vasallos útiles"; "que apenas conservan el menor accidente de Indios, pues criados entre españoles su lengua, sus usos y costumbres no se diferencían ya de las nuestras"). See, too, Ambrosio O'Higgins, Descripción del Reyno de Chile, Madrid, Sept. 2, 1767, in Donoso, 1941, 443, and Marmión, 1964, 450–51.

256. Manuel Centurión to the Council of the Indies, April 20, 1771, in González del Campo, 1984, 132 ("He facilitado 35 casamientos de españoles con indias principales de las naciones cariba, guaica y guaraúna"). This was not a novel idea. The governor of Chile in 1683 suggested intermarriage with Maphuches to amalgamate the races. Foerster G., 1996, 274. See, too, Capt. Lorenzo Cancio to José de Gálvez, Oct. 31, 1766, quoted in Hu-DeHart, 1981, 95, fray Junípero Serra's encouragement of marriage between soldiers and newly baptized Indians in California in Hurtado, 1999, 6, and Pedro Andrés García, Nov. 11, 1811, in Gelman, 1998, 89.

257. José de Gálvez to Agustín de Jáuregui, Aranjuez, May 9, 1777, ANSC, capitanía general, vol. 728 (1777) no. 9858 ("con mucha satisfacción"). See, too, Pérez de Uriondo, 1969–72, 2:628.

258. For a rich and cogent analysis of the difference between French and English policies, see Johnson, 1992, 15–25, whose scope is much larger than his title, and for Spanish–English difference, see Elliott, 1994, 8–12.

259. Aurrecoechea, 1964, 544–45 ("son unos árboles mejor para injertados que para esperar de ellos bueno y abundante fruto en su estado natural"; "resultan nuevas especies, todas de hombres de más robustos"). His work was published in Cádiz in 1814,

but Aurrecoechea served earlier as a government official in Venezuela. Vargas, 1944, 99, was less enthusiastic, suggesting that the results of interracial mixture were "tolerably good" ("pasaderas"). This was not an idiosyncratic view. Padre Joseph Sierra, himself a mestizo and the brother of the cacique Cecilio López Sierra, said Guajiros had absorbed the "fearsome races of mestizos, mulattos, zambos, etc. . . . which will make this nation more formidable and its conquest more difficult." Quoted in Polo Acuña, 1999a, 28 ("se multiplica la diversidad de razas temibles de mestizos, de mulatos, zambos, etc., las cuales unidos con los guajiros harán siempre más formidable esta nación, y más difícil cada día su conquista"). Polo Acuña places this in the last half of the eighteenth century but gives no date. Spanish fear that racial mixture would produce a more vigorous enemy could be heard in the sixteenth century. Powell and Powell, 1971, 220–21. Of course, some Spaniards of Aurrecoechea's era understood that cultural and racial mixture might lead back to savagery rather than toward civilization. See Quijada, 2002, 136–37, and Katzew, 2004, chap. 2 and *passim.*

Epilogue. Insurgents and Savages, from Inclusion to Exclusion

The epigraphs are from Pi Hugarte, 1993, 288 ("a mí me cupo la gloria de acabar con una horda de salvajes nómadas y feroces . . . hice lo que otros no pudieron hacer antes de mí"), and Comadrán Ruíz, 1955, 72 ("El exterminio de ese nuevo 'hombre libre' se cumplió en poco tiempo. La obra de tres siglos de 'esclavitud' se perdió en cincuenta años de 'libertad'").

1. Felipe made two appearances before the cabildo, accompanied the second time by Catemilla. Acuerdos, 1921–34, 2:277–78, 303, for sessions of Aug. 17 and Sept. 15, 1806 ("proteger a los Cristianos contra los colorados").

2. Sessions of Dec. 25 and Dec. 29, 1806 Acuerdos, 1921–34, 2:363–64, 373. The quotations are from the Dec. 25 meeting ("Hijos del Sol"; "Padres de la Patria"; "fidelidad, amor y patriotismo"; "fieles hermanos"). The medal was cast and presented early the following year. Session of Feb. 18, 1807, Acuerdos, 1921–34, 2:456–57. Zerda, 1934, 65. Molinari, 1963, 653, reproduces the inscription.

3. Hux, 1991a, 9–11, for Chulilaquín; Hux, 1991b, 5–29, for Carripilún.

4. Furlong Cardiff and others, 1953–59, with its index to articles in the *Telégrafo Mercantil del Río de la Plata* between 1800 and 1810, suggests that Indian raids had ceased or ceased to be. The only articles that treated Indian attacks were historical or literary. See, for example, 2:332, 334.

5. *Semanario de Agricultura, industria, y Comercio,* Oct. 22,

1806, reproduced in Furlong Cardiff and others, 1953–59, 2:458–59. *Razonamiento hecho por diez Caciques de las Pampas de Buenos-Ayres... 20 de Diciembre de este año de 1806, perorando por si y a nombre de otros seis Caciques inmediatos suyos...* (1806), a pamphlet identified in ibid., 2:456–57. *Minerva Peruana,* Jan. 5, 1807, and Feb. 28, 1807; *Gazeta de México,* May 20 and June 3, 1807 ("naciones salvajes").

6. *Semanario de Agricultura, industria, y Comercio,* Dec. 24, 1806, in Molinari, 1963, 653–54, a rambling editorial that misses the specific historical context of the Pampas' actions.

7. González Oropeza and Donis Ríos, 1989, 26, on concern about Guajiros in 1807–08, and Castillero Calvo, 1995, 383, on Miskitos in 1805.

8. Vancouver, 1984, 4:1509.

9. John, 1984b, 354–55; Weber, 1992, 295. For Florida, see Cusick, 2003, 213–23. Comandante General Nemesio Salcedo believed in 1813 that Comanches and Lipan Apaches would provide warnings about Anglo-Americans entering their territory. Salcedo y Salcedo, 1990, 38.

10. Quoted in Martínez Sarasola, 1992, 159 ("somos vástagos de un mismo tronco.... Amigos, compatriotas y hermanos"), who also recounts the 1810 expedition to the Pampa (pp. 160–63).

11. Martínez Sarasola, 1992, 170. The complicated infighting of these years is well summarized in English in Rock, 1987, 79–92. For earlier multilingual publications by Argentine leaders, see Molinari, 1963, 648–50.

12. Azcuy Ameghino, 1991, 16–24. The quotation, "indios bravos," is on p. 16, in Artigas to Capt. Ambrosio Carranza, Feb. 11, 1811. The bands of *indios bravos* reportedly numbered over four hundred on occasion. Guaraníes also joined Artigas, but he apparently did not include them among the *indios bravos.* See, too, Street, 1959, 273; Martínez Sarasola, 1992, 171–76. The Portuguese invaded Uruguay in Sept. 1816 and by 1817 had taken Montevideo. For Artigas and Indian equality, see Shumway, 1991, 61, called to my attention by James Brooks.

13. Henríquez Ureña, 1949, 108 ("yo también soy indio"). This frequently quoted passage (see, for example, König Eichstätt, 1990, 230, and Martínez Sarasola, 1992, 169) may have its origins in a popular biography of San Martín, Rojas, 1937, which contains invented dialogue. It does not appear in the classic biography of San Martín by Mitre, 1937.

14. The accord signed at San Carlos has not survived. Retellings of this well-known incident usually rely on Mitre, 1937, 2:135–40. Martínez Sarasola, 1992, 164–69; Levaggi, 2000, 173–75.

15. Guevara, 1910, is the classic account, but for fresh views, see Pinto Rodríguez, 2000, 45–56, 59, and the major articles by Téllez Lúgaro, 1998, 53–76, and Villar and Jiménez, 2003, 131–286. I am skating

over regional and ethnic differences. Pehuenches, for example, retained their loyalties to old colonial authorities; Mapuches along the coast and the *llanistas* of the central valley tended more toward the insurgents. Tribes divided by longtime enmity took different sides, and intertribal fighting intensified with the breakdown of colonial institutions. For Calfucurá the elder, see Hux, 1991a, 47–48.

16. Quoted in Collier, 1967, 214.

17. At a parlamento in Tapihue, Dec. 30, 1824, quoted in Pinto Rodríguez, 2000, 53 ("mis padres, que jamás me advirtieron que los españoles eran nuestros tiranos y que nos habían quitado nuestra libertad").

18. One Spanish official thought of enlisting the assistance of Lipan Apache warriors when he could not raise enough militia to defend Texas from an anticipated invasion by Hidalgo's forces. Almaraz, 1971, 111.

19. Arnade, 1957, 50–51; 214 n.50.

20. Hamill, 1966, 127–35.

21. Rausch, 1984, 169, 185, 244, here and elsewhere describes the *llaneros,* among whom were Indians; Cañizales Guédez, 1993, suggests that some Indians in Venezuela apparently joined the insurgents because they saw newly arrived Spanish troops as bloody outsiders who were annihilating the "casta primitiva," as Bolívar suggested (in a letter to J. Hodgson, Oct. 4, 1813, quoted on p. 139). Some "indios de flecha," however, fought alongside the royalists (ibid., pp. 127, 147, 178, 198, 207–08). Beckerman, 1979, 54, describes a Motilón brigade of mission Indians fighting for royalists. Lynch, 1973, 243–44. Earle, 1999, 51–53, 105, 107, 136, 141, 164–65, gives us glimpses of Hispanicized Indians fighting on both sides in New Granada.

22. Pino, 1995, 52 and 44 of the facsimile; John, 1984b, 362.

23. Saignes, 1990, 151, 156–57. The quotation, by Col. Mariano Diáz, is on p. 153 ("le contestó que con sus indios desharía todo aquello en un momento"). Chiriguanos who had fallen under missionary influence, on the other hand, tended to fight for the royalists. Pifarré, 1989, 280.

24. Fleming, 1967, 39–46.

25. König Eichstätt, 1984, 396–98, and König Eichstätt, 1990, 226–27, includes example of coins and illustrations in a fine analysis. See, too, Keen, 1971, 316–22.

26. Earle, 2001, 126–35.

27. José Miguel Carrera, quoted in Collier, 1967, 213, who also gives examples of a number of newspapers that incorporated the word "Araucano."

28. Pinto Rodríguez, 2000, 46. See, too, Casanova Guarda, 1999–2000, 23–32.

29. Bolívar's famous Jamaica letter, Sept. 6, 1815, in Bierck and Lecuna, 1951, 1:117, 105. For the Lautaro lodges and guidance to other sources, see Eyzaguirre, 1973, 1–17, who also seems to dispel the idea that the

group of Spanish-American Masons who founded a lodge in London named it after Lautaro.

30. Aurrecoechea, 1964, 544 ("observados de cerca y examinados a la luz de la imparcialidad, se los encuentra sólo como una especie de autómatas, o en el primer paso de la civilización"). Earle, 2001, 135–43.

31. Earle, 2001, 134–35, 141, is especially insightful on the contradictions within each discourse.

32. Earle, 2002, 775–805, explores this phenomenon, which she sees as beginning in Argentina with the Generation of 1837; for Chichimecs, see her pp. 783, 797.

33. Chap. IX, arts. 200–201, of the Constitution of Dec. 21, 1811, in Armellada, 1977, 17–18 ("ciudadanos que hasta hoy se han denominado Indios"; "del abatimiento y rusticidad en que los ha mantenido el antiguo estado de las cosas"; "les han perjudicado sobremanera, según ha acreditado la experiencia"). This was anticipated by a decree of Sept. 24, 1810. See Samudio A., 1992–93, 33, and Samudio A., 1996, 195–96.

34. Brading, 1971, 22–24, is particularly clear on this point. Through the nineteenth century, Venezuela would attempt on several occasions to return to the paternalistic Indian policy that its constitution of 1811 condemned. Armellada, 1977, 7–424, is a remarkable collection of documents pertaining to Venezuelan Indian policy. Venezuela's Indian heritage, however, has been of only marginal interest to Venezuelans and never a source of national identity, for reasons explained by Lombardi, 1982, 43–44, and suggested in Wright, 1990.

35. Emphasis added. Decrees of Oct. 15, 1810 ("los naturales que sean originarios de dichos dominios europeos o ultramarinos son iguales en derechos a los de esta península") and Feb. 9, 1811, in Armellada, 1959, 103 and 92–93, respectively.

36. Chap. 2, art. 5, of the Constitution of 1812 defined Spaniards as "todos los hombres libres nacidos y avecindados en los dominios de las Españas y los hijos de éstos," and chap. 4, art. 18, noted that "son ciudadanos aquellos españoles que por ambas líneas traen su origen de los dominios españoles de ambos hemisferios, y están avecindados en cualquier pueblo de los mismos dominios." For evolution at that time of the word "citizen," which formerly implied a resident of a city but now suggested a person with political rights, see König Eichstätt, 1984, 398–405, and García Godoy, 1998, 327–29. Equality did not extend to blacks, a fact analyzed by Anna, 1982, 258–61.

37. Much has been written about this subject. Armellada, 1959, reproduces the essential documents along with long quotes from the debates. Rieu-Millan, 1990, 108–37, provides a fine, brief overview and identifies the protagonists in the debates.

38. José Pablo Valiente in the debate of Jan. 23, 1811, in

Armellada, 1959, 32 ("su cortedad de ingenio, su propensión al ocio").

39. José Miguel Guridi de Alcocer in the session of Jan. 25, 1811, in Armellada, 1959, 34 ("no hubieron pasado de unos rudos"). See, too, Moreno Cebrian, 1975, 185. Anna, 1982, 261, suggests that delegates divided on this issue, with American-born Spaniards defending Indians and *peninsulares* displaying a deep belief in the inferiority of Indians. Rieu-Millan, 1990, 112, however, suggests that anti-Indian expressions were not widespread among the delegates from Spain.

40. Rieu-Millan, 1990, 146 ("las aptitudes naturales que les permitirían 'desindianizarse' para servir mejor los intereses de la sociedad moderna y dinámica proyectada"). See, too, Chust Calero, 1995, 179–202.

41. The influential *Nuevo sistema,* commonly attributed to José del Campillo and discussed in chap. 5 above, is the classic statement. Girvetz, 1950, 28–35. Scholars of this era of Latin American history, often oversimplifying, rightly see a continuity of enlightened and liberal thought. See, for example, Marichal, 1971, 107 (who argues that "the terms liberal and liberalism acquired . . . a political meaning" at Cádiz), and Martínez Torrón, 1992, 31. For the continuities with Indian policy, see Bushnell, 1983, 2; Saignes, 1990, 142; and the rich discussion in Portillo Valdés, forthcoming 2005, chap. 4. See, too, my discussion in chap. 3 above of the ill-fated attempt by Carlos IV to privatize the Guaraní, Moxos, and Chiquitos missions in 1803 and 1805.

42. See, for example, Collier, 1967, 216–17; Bushnell, 1983, 9–15; Safford, 1987, 88–89. In the Río de la Plata, *criollos* who had established a de facto independent government also assumed that Indians were "iguales a todas las demás clases en presencia de la ley." Azcuy Ameghino, 1991, 13, quoting an order of May 25, 1811, to governors and other authorities.

43. Borah, 1983, chap. 10.

44. Quoted in Gerbi, 1973, 78.

45. This frequently repeated story has been much studied. See, for example, Gullón Abao, 1993, 325; Amodio, 1991, 267–308; Samudio, 1992, 5–90; Samudio, 1996, 195–210; Laserna Gaitán, 1993, 25, 339; Farriss, 1984, 376–80; Hall and Weber, 1984, 5–32; González, 1998, 165.

46. Lynch, 1994, 381. On this point scholars agree: for example, Mörner, 1987, 62, and Shumway, 1991, 61.

47. See, for example, Lynch, 1973, 261–62, Gómez, 1988, 251–65; Samudio A., 1992–93, 26–32.

48. For the joyful response of some Indians in New Granada to Spain's fall, see Garrido, 1993, 304–12, and Cañizales Guédez, 1993, 200–201.

49. A petition of the Pueblo of Tocancipá, ca. 1812, quoted in Garrido, 1993, 303 ("hemos sido los más ínfimos esclavos . . . antes eramos protejidos y ahora no hay quién nos ampare").

50. Darwin, 1952, 361, called to my attention by Casanueva, 1992a, 31.

51. Schmidtmeyer, 1824, quotations on 319 and 310, respectively. He visited Chile in 1820. For the Constitution of 1822, see Pinto Rodríguez, 2000, 52–53, 79, 98–99.

52. O'Higgins to President Joaquín Prieto, 1830, quoted in Bengoa, 1996, 138 ("Yo considero a los Pehuenches, Puelches y Patagones por tan paisanos nuestros como los demás"). Pinto Rodríguez, 2000, 86–89, for the debate of the 1820s and 1830s over whether the Araucanians were a nation within Chile.

53. A decree of the congress, April 29, 1826, approved by the executive, May 1, 1826, in Armellada, 1977, 50–51 ("Las tribus de indígenas que habitan las costas de la Goagira, Darién y Mosquitos, y las demás no civilizadas que existen en el territorio de la República, serán protegidas y tratadas como colombinos").

54. Article 12 of the Plan of Iguala ("Todos los habitantes de él, sin otra distinción que su mérito y virtudes, son ciudadanos idóneos para optar cualquier empleo"), in Tena Ramírez, 1978, 115, and the law of Feb. 14 and Sept. 17, 1822, all in Dublán and Lozano, 1876–1912, 1:597, 629. For the internal debates and results, see González Navarro, 1991, 1:207–313. For an overview of the impact of these measures on communities of *indios domésticos* in northwestern Mexico, see Spicer, 1962, 334–40.

55. Mier, 1990, 317 ("se creen legítimos dueños de todo el Nuevo Mundo"; "chistosa"; "infelices dueños del país").

56. Casanova Guarda, 1999–2000, 37–43; Gallardo Porras, 2001, 127–29. Some contemporaries would continue to refer to Indians as citizens, for example, Col. Pedro Barnechea in 1825, quoted in Pinto Rodríguez, 2000, 98–99 ("ciudadanos chilenos"), but they appear to have been using the term loosely. Many firsthand sources testify to the continued use of coerced Indian labor in Hispanic households. See, for example, Orbigny, 1945, 2:714.

57. José Javier Bustamante, quoted in Pinto Rodríguez, 2000, 99 ("los medios de dulzura y prudencia para reducir, en cuanto sea posible, a la vida social a esos hombres selváticos").

58. Dublán and Lozano, 1876–1912, 3:10 ("tribus sublevados"; "¿Deben ser considerados como hijos de la gran familia mexicana, o como sus enemigos, para lanzarlos en el segundo caso, de los límites de ese Estado?"; "son mexicanos, porque nacieron y viven en la República. . . . El estado de barbarie en que yacen, les impide conocer los deberes universales, y los que les pertenecen como mexicanos"; "medios de dulzura y de prudencia"; "desgraciados"). Called to my attention by González Navarro, 1991, 1:264. See, too, Weber, 1982, 103.

59. DeLay, 2004, 338. For similar confusion in post-independence Argentina, see Ratto, 2003a, 14–26.

60. Fragment of a draft of a letter from Facundo Melgares to an unknown party, Santa Fe, Aug. 25, 1821, in SANM, no. 3010, roll 20, frames 740-41 ("faltarles los regalos a que estan acostumbrados empiezan a amenazar la provincia"). The unraveling was specific to individual bands and tribes. Park, 1979, 231, suggested that Apaches began to desert the *establecimientos de paz* as living conditions deteriorated in the 1810s, but his source (Ignacio Zúñiga) notes that the peace establishments did not deteriorate until Mexican independence, although the military did. Brinckerhoff, 1967, 5, 17, argues that Apaches de Paz remained peaceful, and Dobyns, 1976, 101–05, provides details about a group of Pinal Apaches who settled voluntarily near the presidio of Tucson as late as 1819 and received rations. Voss, 1982, 49, was probably correct in asserting a "lag between the disintegration of the presidial defense structure and the perception of the Apaches that they could once again raid successfully." See, too, Weber, 1982, 317 n.7.

61. Weber, 1982, 9–11, and McNitt, 1972, 66–91. For the Chaco, where Mocobíes and Tobas resumed raiding along the Paraná, particularly in the area of Santa Fe, see Martínez Sarasola, 1992, 176–84, Maeder, 1996, 73–79, and Saeger, 2000, 166.

62. Beaumont, 1828, 54. Beaumont arrived in Argentina in 1826. See, too, Head, 1967, 51–55, 65–73.

63. Beaumont, 1828, 55.

64. Rausch, 1993, 31–55; Armellada, 1974, 153–56, and Armellada, 1977, 56–58, for Bolívar's decrees of 1828 and other pieces of pro-mission legislation.

65. Weber, 1982, 43–68 (for Santa Anna, see p. 50); Escobar Ohmstede and Rabiela Rojas, 1992–93, 1:27.

66. Rodríguez, 1998, 23 ("de reducirlos vía la evangelización a aniquilarlos vía la guerra").

67. Levaggi, 2000, 177–78, for example, notes that none of the treaties signed with Indians in Argentina in the early independence period mentioned missions. This is not to say that missionaries were entirely neglected by these governments. In 1848, for example, the Chilean government did sign an agreement with Capuchin Franciscans. Pinto Rodríguez, 1988, 87. With or without government initiative, missionary orders continued to try to convert those Indians. For a synthesis of efforts in the Chaco, see Maeder, 1996, 89–93.

68. Pinto Rodríguez, 2000, 58–61.

69. Levaggi, 2000, 169–266.

70. McElhannon, 1949, 122–32, and Kavanagh, 1996, 196–98. See Rodríguez, 1998, 145–46, for examples from individual states. Everett, 1990, 24–28. The quotation, from Texas governor José Félix Trespalacios to Gaspar López, Nov. 8, 1822, is translated on p. 27.

71. Rodríguez, 1998, 147, makes this point about regrouping eloquently for Coahuila; Aboites Aguilar, 1991, 29, looks at local interests in Chihuahua.

72. Levaggi, 2000, 563 ("Por un lado, no reconoció que

los indígenas formasen comunidades jurídicas con categoría de nación (no Estados soberanos), y, por el otro, había firmado con ellos tratados de paz, que llevaban implícito ese reconocimiento").

73. Weber, 1982, 83–105; Kavanagh, 1996, 286–91; Velasco Ávila, 1998, 111. Blackhawk, 1999, 161–90, offers a case study of how these changes caused a long-standing New Mexico–Ute alliance to unravel during these years.

74. Escobar Ohmstede and Rabiela Rojas, 1992–93, 1:26–30, provides a splendid summary of Mexican efforts at defense against "nómadas" in the north. See, too, González Navarro, 1991, 1:263–79, and Velasco Ávila, 1998, 233–341, who sees the increased scope and intensity of Comanche raids in northern Mexico in the 1830s as a reaction to force that Anglo-Texans brought against them. No one shows the increasing brutality of Comanche raids of this era or explains them more convincingly than DeLay, 2004.

75. Much has been written about the expansion of the cattle industry during the 1810s and 1820s, but see especially Barba, 1997, 71–85, Navarro Floria, 1999, 257, and Gelman and Santilli, 2002, 81–107, which looks at regional differences and finds slowest growth in areas where Indian raids continued (105).

76. Rosas Segunda Memoria (n.d.), quoted in Bernal, 1997, 15 ("suplir la presente escasez de brazos en la campaña"; "tengo algunos peones indios pampas que me son fieles y son los mejores").

77. Rosas quoted in Bernal, 1997, 7, who takes this from an archival source without providing the date or person to whom Rosas directed the remark. For Rosas's preference for peace, in his own words, see Navarro Floria, 1999, 273–75. For smallpox, see Sulé, 1996, 57–62. See, too, Lynch, 1981, 40–41, 51–55 (the best biography of Rosas in English), and the brutal massacre of Pampas in the bullring in Buenos Aires in 1835, apparently to achieve political ends, described in Salvatore, 2003, 232.

78. Navarro Floria, 1999, 253–80, examines the extension of *proyectistas'* plans for peaceful expansion, and the internal debates over it, into the 1820s.

79. These paragraphs are informed by Jones, 1994, 103–23, Ratto, 1994b, 25–45, Ratto, 1994a, 1–34 (which distinguishes between *amigos* and *aliados*—a distinction that does not appear to have existed in the colonial period), Ratto, 1998, 241–65 (which looks at the sources of Rosas's funding and how it changed over time), and Ratto, 2003b, 191–222. For pacts made with Indians on the pampa in the Rosas era, see Levaggi, 2000, 203–44, who observes that Rosas favored verbal agreements (p. 222), and Ratto, 2003a, 21, who disagrees with Levaggi's explanation.

80. Francia to José Miguel Ibáñez, Jan. 21, 1815, quoted in Bouvet, 1992, 105 ("hasta haberlos exterminado, y arruinado enteramente"). Bouvet provides a splendid analysis.

81. A. G. Oxehufvud, quoted at length by another Swede, Bladh, 1970, 724–25, quotation, p. 726 ("fueron metidos como animales en un corral y allí se tiraron al suelo. Se les dió carne de un buey que había sido descuartizado y un poco de leña y un tizón con fuego"), called to my attention by Pi Hugarte, 1999, 157, who provides context.

82. Pi Hugarte, 1993, 287, and Pi Hugarte, 1999, 149–78, whose moving account I have relied on.

83. Saler, 1980–1988, 37; Heinen, 1980–1988, 603.

84. Feliciano Chiclana had warned at least as early as 1804 that the long peace had prepared Indians with weapons, supplies, and knowledge that would make them more formidable if war broke out again. Chiclana, 1945, 36. See, too, Barba, 1997, 69.

85. For the relationship between the exportation of ranching products, overwhelmingly dried cattle hides, expansion into Indian lands, and the oligarchy, see Barba, 1997, esp. 5–102, 115–43. No treatment of nineteenth-century Argentina fails to mention the celebrated Conquest of the Desert and its aftermath, but for the classic account of the campaign and events leading up to it, see Walther, 1976, 285–561. For a general account that represents Indian viewpoints, see Martínez Sarasola, 1992, 238–95, and the splendid essay by Villar, 1993, 13–16.

86. Both documents quoted in Lagos, 2002, 83–84 ("espero que no olvidará mandarme ... un par de chinitas de seis u ocho años"; "ser repartidos"). Guarda, 1980, 86–88, and Guarda, 2001, 384, notes the survival of this practice in Valdivia, Chile, up to the twentieth century, and the lack of opposition to it. My wife and I observed it in Bolivia in the 1990s. For the Chaco, see also Martínez Sarasola, 1992, 295–302, who sees operations there as "almost a copy" ("casi un calco") of the sweep of the Pampa and Patagonia, but I follow Levaggi, 2000, 557–58, and Lagos, 2002, 79–107, who point to the local elite's interest in preserving potential Indian labor. Efforts at making peace continued during these years, as best explored by Levaggi, 2000, 267–538, 538–60.

87. Bengoa, 1996, 170–325; Pinto Rodríguez, 2000, 161–82.

88. Rodríguez, 1998, 18.

89. Blas M. Flores, quoted in Rodríguez, 1998, 239 ("salvaje"; "como planta nociva"), who describes these expeditions (pp. 232–43) and the movement of Indians to reservations in the United States (pp. 259–67). See, too, González Navarro, 1991, 1:292–305.

90. Pinto, 2000, 53, quoting O'Higgins in 1819 ("ciudadanos chilenos y libres como los demás habitantes del Estado").

91. This document, written in English by O'Higgins, is reproduced in Collier, 1967, 369–71. O'Higgins apparently intended to bring his plan to the attention of British and U.S. leaders. North Americans' plans for Indian removal might have influenced him. See Sheehan, 1973, 243–75.

92. In suggesting competing discourses, I mean to convey that this rhetoric was not homogenous or without contradictions, even though one discourse became dominant. See, for example, the oscillations described by Garrido, 1993, 310, and the contending views in Gallardo Porras, 2001, 129–34. This happened earlier in some countries than in others. In Paraguay it began in the 1810s under Dr. Francia. Bouvet, 1992, 108–10.

93. The first quotation comes from "Comunicado de Arauco," published in *El Mercurio de Valparaiso,* Jan. 30, 1856 ("hordas salvajes"), and the second from a correspondent in Valdivia, "Una cuestión de primera importancia," *El Mercurio de Valparaiso,* July 5, 1859 ("el triunfo de la civilización sobre la barbarie, de la humanidad sobre la bestialidad"), both quoted in Pinto Rodríguez, 2000, 131, who explore this anti-indigenous discourse in rich detail.

94. Alberdi, 1969, 241 ("Quién casaría a su hermana o a su hija con un infazón de la Araucania y no mil veces con un zapatero inglés?"; "En América todo lo que no es europeo es bárbaro: no hay más división que esta: 10 el indígena, es decir el salvaje: 20 el europeo, es decir nosotros, los que hemos nacido en América y hablamos español, los que creemos en Jesucristo"), called to my attention by Shumway, 1991, 141, whose translations I have not relied on entirely.

95. Quoted in Pinto Rodríguez, 1996, 108 ("aunque nos llaman bárbaros conocemos lo que es justo").

96. Sarmiento, 1960, 2, called to my attention by Pratt, 1992, 186. See, too, pp. 183–85 for Pratt's analysis of Esteban Echeverría's poem "The Captive" (1837). For an interesting analysis of the depiction of the noble savage in nineteenth-century Latin American literature, see Virgillo, 1971, 254, who argues that the fictional savage finds salvation only by conforming "to the distorted society of the European and not the other way around, as Montaigne and later the French encyclopedists advocated."

97. Hernández, 1962, 101, whose epic poem appeared in two parts, in 1872 and 1879 ("Es tenaz en su bar barie / . . . el bárbaro sólo sabe / emborracharse y peliar [*sic*]").

98. *Plan para la defensa del estado de Coahuila invadido por los bárbaros* (Saltillo: Imprenta de Gobierno, 1849), 10, quoted in Rodríguez, 1998, 49 ("Este enemigo no merece el perdón; es inútil otorgárselo. Es un animal rabioso incapaz de domesticarse. Un sueño delirante, un quijotesco modo de pensar es pretender reducirlo a mision. Aquí no cabe escuchar la noble voz de la humanidad y de la clemencia: porque el rigor es necesario absolutamente"), who analyzes this discourse at length (pp. 40–53). See, too Velasco Ávila, 2000, 450–58.

99. Sarmiento, 1960. The quotations are on pp. 11 and 1, respectively. In a major article, Navarro Floria, 2001, 345–76, looks at the ways in which Argentine lawmakers embraced this view.

100. Pifarré, 1989, 285; Calzavarini, 1980, 219–25.

101. Bravo to the Minister of War, Feb. 14, 1845, quoted in Guardino, 1995, 185. For the use of "savage" to encompass all rural people who resisted the domination of the state, see Navarro Floria, 2001, 347.

102. Sarmiento's essay on José Victorino Lastarria's "Investigaciones sobre el sistema colonial de los españoles," Sept. 7, 1844, in Sarmiento, 2001, 2:165, called to my attention by Shumway, 1991, 255 ("gracias a esta injusticia, la América, en lugar de permanecer abandonada a los salvajes, incapaces de progreso, está ocupada hoy por la raza caucásica, la más perfecta, la más inteligente, la más bella y la más progresiva de las que pueblan la tierra"; "es preciso que seamos justos con los españoles; al exterminar a un pueblo salvaje cuyo territorio iban a ocupar, hacían simplemente lo que todos los pueblos civilizados hacen con los salvajes . . . absorbe, destruye, extermina").

103. Ibid., 166 ("no hay amalgama posible entre un pueblo salvaje y uno civilizado").

104. Beaumont, 1828, 58. The emphasis is Beaumont's.

105. Quijada, 2002, 138–41, is especially elocuente on the similarities and differences between the Bourbons and the Positivists.

106. Perry, 1996, 30. Burns, 1980, provides a concise and vivid introduction to this well-explored intellectual current in Latin America. See, too, Earle, 2002, 793–805.

Bibliography

Abad Pérez, Antolín. "Estadística franciscano-misionera en ultramar del S. XVIII: Un intento de aproximación." In *Los franciscanos en el Nuevo Mundo (siglo XVIII),* 125–56. Madrid: Editorial Deimos, 1993.

Abellán, José Luis. "Los orígenes españoles del mito del 'buen salvaje': Fray Bartolomé de Las Casas y su antropología utópica." *Revista de Indias* 36 (1976): 157–80.

Aboites Aguilar, Luis. "Poder político y 'bárbaros' en Chihuahua hacia 1845." *Secuencia* 19 (1991): 17–32.

————. *Norte Precario: Poblamiento y colonización en México (1760–1940).* Mexico: Colegio de Mexico/ Centro de Investigaciones y Estudios Superiores en Antropología Social, 1995.

Abreu y Bertodano, José Antonio, ed. *Colección de tratados de paz, alianza, neutralidad, garantía . . . hechos por los pueblos, reyes y principes, repúblicas y demas potencias de España . . . hasta el feliz reynado del rey N.S. don Felipe V.* 12 vols. Madrid: Antonio Morin, Juan de Zúñiga, y la Viuda de Peralta, 1740–52.

Acevedo, Edberto Oscar. "El virrey Arredondo y el proyectado avance de la frontera en el Chaco." *Revista de Historia Americana y Argentina* [Mendoza], no. 9–10 (1964–65): 45–61.

————. *La intendencia de Salta del Tucumán en el virreinato del Río de la Plata.* Mendoza, Argentina: Universidad Nacional de Cuyo, 1965.

————. "De intérpretes y cautivos." *Boletín de la Academia Nacional de la Historia* [Buenos Aires] 62–63 (1989–90): 597–605.

————. *La intendencia del Paraguay en el virreinato del Río de la Plata.* Buenos Aires: Ciudad Argentina, 1996.

————. *Controversias virreinales rioplatenses.* Buenos Aires: Ciudad Argentina, 1997.

Acosta y Lara, Eduardo F. *La guerra de los charrúas en la Banda Oriental: Período hispánico.* Montevideo: Impresores A. Monteverde, 1961.

Acuerdos. *Acuerdos del Extinguido Cabildo de Buenos Aires. Serie 4.* 9 vols. Buenos Aires: Archivo General de la Nación, 1921–34.

Adams, David B. "At the Lion's Mouth: San Miguel de Aguayo in the Defense of Nuevo León." *Colonial Latin American Historical Review* 9 (2000): 324–46.

Adams, Eleanor B., and Fray Angélico Chávez, eds. and trans. *The Missions of New Mexico, 1776: A Description by Fray Francisco Atanasio Domínguez.* Albuquerque: University of New Mexico Press, 1956.

Adelman, Jeremy. *Republic of Capital: Buenos Aires and the Legal Transformation of the Atlantic World.* Stanford: Stanford University Press, 1999.

Adelman, Jeremy, and Stephen Aron. "From Borderlands to Borders: Empires, Nation-States, and the Peoples in Between in North American History." *American Historical Review* 104 (1999): 814–41.

Adorno, Rolena, and Patrick Charles Pautz, eds. *Alvar Núñez Cabeza de Vaca: His Account, His Life, and the Expedition of Pánfilo de Narváez.* 3 vols. Lincoln: University of Nebraska Press, 1999.

Aguirre, Susan E. "Una alternativa al sistema de reducciones en la pampa a mediados del siglo XVIII." In *Congreso Nacional de Historia sobre la conquista del desierto,* 1:55–66. 4 vols. Buenos Aires: Academia Nacional de Historia, 1980.

Alberdi, Juan Bautista. *Las "Bases" de Alberdi [1852]. Edición crítica.* Edited by Jorge M. Mayer. Buenos Aires: Editorial Sudamericana, 1969.

Alberro, Solange. *Del gachupín al criollo, o de como los españoles de México dejaron de serlo.* Mexico: Colegio de Mexico, 1992.

Albers, Patricia. "Symbiosis, Merger, and War: Contrasting Forms of Intertribal Relationships Among Historic Plains Indians." In *Political Economy of the North American Indians,* edited by John H. Moore, 94–132. Norman: University of Oklahoma Press, 1993.

Alcácer, Antonio de. *El indio motilón y su historia.* Bogotá: Seminario Capuchino Puente Común, 1962.

Alcamán, Eugenio. "Los mapuche-huilliche de futahillimapu septentrional: Expansión colonial, guerras internas y alianzas políticas (1750–1792)." *Revista de Historia Indígena,* no. 2 (1997): 29–75.

Alcedo, Antonio de. *Diccionario geográfico histórico de las Indias Occidentales o América.* Edited by Ciriaco Pérez-Bustamante. 1st ed., 1786–89; 4 vols. Madrid: Atlas, 1967.

Alcedo y Bexerano, Antonio de. *Diccionario geográfico-histórico de América.* 5 vols. Madrid, 1786–89.

Alcocer, José Antonio. *Bosquejo de la historia del Colegio de Nuestra Señora de Guadalupe y sus misiones, año de 1788.* Edited by Rafael Cervantes. Mexico: Editorial Porrúa, 1958.

Aldridge, A. Owen. "The Concept of the Ibero-American Enlightenment." In *The Ibero-American Enlightenment,* edited by A. Owen Aldridge, 3–18. Urbana: University of Illinois Press, 1971.

Aldunate del Solar, Carlos. "El indígena y la frontera." In *Relaciones fronterizas en la Araucanía,* edited by Sergio Villalobos R. et al., 67–86. Santiago de Chile: Ediciones Universidad Católica de Chile, 1982.

Almaraz, Félix D. *Tragic Cavalier: Governor Manuel Salcedo of Texas, 1808–1813.* Austin: University of Texas Press, 1971.

Alonso, Ana María. *Thread of Blood: Colonialism, Revolution, and Gender on Mexico's Northern Frontier.* Tucson: University of Arizona Press, 1995.

Altman, Ida, and Reginald D. Butler. "The Contact of Cultures: Perspectives on the Quincentenary." *American Historical Review* 99 (1994): 478–503.

Alumni, José. *El Chaco, 1750–1950: Figuras y hechos de su pasado.* Resistencia, Argentina: n.p., 1951.

Álvarez Barrientos, Joaquín. *La novela del siglo XVIII.* Madrid: Ediciones Jucar, 1991.

Álvarez de Miranda, Pedro. *Palabras e ideas: El léxico de la ilustración temprana en España (1680–1760).* Madrid: Anejos del Boletín de la Real Academia Española, 1992.

Álvarez, Salvador. "Agricultores de paz y cazadores-recolectores de guerra: Los tobosos de la cuenca del Río Conchos en la Nueva Vizcaya." In *Nómadas y sedentarios en el norte de Mexico: Homenaje a Beatriz Braniff,* edited by Marie-Areti Hers et al., 305–54. Mexico: Instituto de Investigaciones Antropológicas, UNAM, 2000.

Alzate, José Antonio de. "Descripción de los indios de la Nueva España [ca. 1791]." In *La expedición Malaspina, 1789–1794.* Vol. 5, *Antropología y noticias etnográficas,* edited by Dolores Higueras Rodríguez and Juan Pimentel Igea, 75–83. Madrid: Ministerio de Defensa, Museo Naval, and Lunwerg Editores, 1993.

Amat y Junient, Manuel. "Historia geográphica e hidrográphica con derrotero general correlativo al Plan del Reyno de Chile, que remite a nuestro monarca el Señor don Carlos III ... su gobernador y capitán general Dn. Manuel de Amat y Junient [1760]." *Revista Chilena de Historia y Geografía*, no. 53–62 (1924–28): various.

Amich, José. *Historia de las misiones del convento de Santa Rosa de Ocopa.* Edited by Julián Heras. 1st ed., 1975; Iquitos, Peru: CETA, 1988.

Amigorena, José Francisco de. "Diario de la expedición contra los indios bárbaros tehuelches [1780]." In *Colección de obras y documentos relativos a la historia antigua y moderna de las provincias del Río de la Plata por Pedro de Angelis,* edited by Andrés M. Carretero, 4:203–20. 1st ed., 1836; 8 vols. Buenos Aires: Editorial Plus Ultra, 1969–72.

———. "Descripción de los caminos, pueblos, lugares, que hay desde la ciudad de Buenos Ayres a la de Mendoza, en el mismo reino [1787]." Edited by José Ignacio Avellaneda. *Cuadernos de Historia Regional* 4 (1988): 5–29.

———. "Diario de la Expedición que de orden del Señor gobernador intendente Marqués de Sobremonte acabo de hacer con las milicias de esta ciudad de Mendoza contra los indios Pampas [May 14, 1784]." In *Historia de los indios ranqueles: Orígenes, elevación y caída del cacicazgo ranquelino en la pampa central, siglos XVIII y XIX,* edited by Jorge Fernández C., 69–75. Buenos Aires: Instituto Nacional de Antropología y Pensamiento Latinoamericano, 1998.

Amodio, Emanuele. "Invasión y defensa de los resguardos indígenas en el Oriente de Venezuela (1770–1850)." *Montalban* 23 (1991): 267–308.

Anderson, Gary Clayton. *The Indian Southwest, 1580–1830: Ethnogenesis and Reinvention.* Norman: University of Oklahoma Press, 1999.

Anderson, Terry L., and Steven LaCombe. "Institutional Change in the Indian Horse Culture." In *The Other Side of the Frontier: Economic Explorations into Native American History,* edited by Linda Barrington, 103–23. Boulder: Westview Press, 1999.

Andrews, George Reid. *The Afro-Argentines of Buenos Aires, 1800–1900.* Madison: University of Wisconsin Press, 1980.

Anes, Gonzalo. *El siglo de las luces.* Historia de España dirigida por Miguel Artola, 4. Madrid: Alianza, 1994.

Anes y Álvarez de Castrillón, Gonzalo. *La corona y la América del siglo de las luces.* Madrid: Pons, 1994.

Anna, Timothy E. "Spain and the Breakdown of the Imperial Ethos: The Problem of Equality." *Hispanic American Historical Review* 62 (1982): 254–72.

Anónimo. "Viaje al Río de la Plata y Chile (1752–1756)." *Revista de la Junta de Estudios Históricos de Mendoza (segunda época),* no. 9, pt. 2 (1980): 359–76.

Anonymous. "Noticias de las provincias de Maracaibo y Barinas ... [Dec. 31, 1787]." In *Relaciones geográficos de Venezuela,* edited by Antonio Arellano Moreno, 413–33. Caracas: Academia Nacional de la Historia, 1964.

Anson, George. *A Voyage Round the World, in the Years MDCCXL, I, III, IV.* London: J. and P. Knapton, 1748.

Arbesmann, Rudolph. "The Contribution of the Franciscan College of Ocopa to the Geographical Exploration of South America." *The Americas* 1 (1945): 393–417.

Archer, Christon I. "The Deportation of Barbarian Indians from the Internal Province of New Spain, 1789–1810." *The Americas* 24 (1973a): 376–85.

———. "The Transient Presence: A Re-Appraisal of Spanish Attitudes toward the Northwest Coast in the Eighteenth Century." *BC Studies,* no. 18 (1973b): 3–32.

———. *The Army in Bourbon Mexico, 1760–1810.* Albuquerque: University of New Mexico Press, 1977.

————. "Spain and the Defense of the Pacific Ocean Empire, 1750–1810." *Canadian Journal of Latin American and Caribbean Studies* 11, no. 21 (1986): 15–41.

————. "The Voyage of Captain George Vancouver: A Review Article." *BC Studies,* no. 73 (1987): 43–61.

Archibald, Robert. *Economic Aspects of the California Missions.* Washington: Academy of American Franciscan History, 1978a.

————. "Indian Labor at the California Missions: Slavery or Salvation?" *Journal of San Diego History* 24 (1978b): 172–82.

Arcila Robledo, Gregorio. *Las misiones franciscanas en Colombia: Estudio documental.* Bogotá: Imprenta Nacional, 1950.

————. *Apuntes históricos de la Provincia Franciscana en Colombia.* Bogotá: Imprenta Nacional, 1953.

Arciniegas, Germán. *Latin America: A Cultural History.* Translated by Joan MacLean. New York: Knopf, 1967.

Areces, Nidia, Silvana López, and Elida Regis. "Relaciones interétnicas en Santa Fe la Vieja— Rescate con Charrúas." In *Reflexiones sobre el V Centenario,* 155–68. Rosario: Facultad de Humanidades y Artes, 1992.

Areces, Nidia R. "Concepción, frontera norte del Paraguay durante la gobernación intendencia, espacio de conflicto colonial." *Andes: Antropología e Historia,* no. 5 (1992): 39–70.

Arias Divito, Juan Carlos. *Las expediciones científicas españolas durante el siglo xviii: Expedición botánica de Nueva España.* Madrid: Ediciones Cultura Hispánica, 1968.

Arima, E. Y., et al. *Between Ports Alberni and Renfrew: Notes on West Coast Peoples.* Mercury Series Paper 121. Hull, Quebec: Canadian Ethnology Service, Canadian Museum of Civilization, 1991.

Ariza, Andrés de. "Comentarios de la rica y fertilísima Provincia del Darién. Año de 1774." *Hombre y Cultura* 2 (1971): 107–15.

Armellada, Cesáreo de. *La causa indígena americana en las Cortes de Cádiz.* Madrid: Editorial Cultura Hispánica, 1959.

————. "Fuero indígena Venezolano." *Montalban* 7 (1977): 7–424.

Armillas, Pedro. "La ecología del colonialismo en el Nuevo Mundo." *Revista de Indias* 43 (1983): 295–300.

Armillas Vicente, José Antonio. "Política Británica hacia las Floridas, después de la emancipación de los Estados Unidos, 1783–1804." *Separata de Estudios, Departamento de Historia Moderna, Zaragoza* (1975): 1–13.

————. "La gran confederación india: Interacción hispano-angloamericana con las naciones indias del sudeste norteamericano a fines del siglo XVIII." In *Estudios sobre política indigenista española en América: Simposio conmemorativo del V centenario del Padre Las Casas. . . .* 2:225–66. 3 vols. Valladolid: Seminario de Historia de América, Universidad de Valladolid, 1975–77.

Arnade, Charles W. *The Emergence of the Republic of Bolivia.* Gainesville: University of Florida Press, 1957.

Arnold, Morris. *The Rumble of a Distant Drum: The Quapaws and Old World Newcomers, 1673–1804.* Fayetteville: University of Arkansas Press, 2000.

Arnold, Morris S. *Unequal Laws unto a Savage Race: European Legal Traditions in Arkansas, 1686–1836.* Fayetteville: University of Arkansas Press, 1985.

Arredondo, Nicolás de. "Memoria a su sucesor don Pedro de Melo de Portugal y Villena, Buenos Aires, 16 de marzo de 1795." In *Memorias de los virreyes del Río de la Plata,* edited by Sigfrido Radaelli, 373–483. Buenos Aires: Editorial Bajel, 1945.

Artola, Miguel. "Campillo y las reformas de Carlos III." *Revista de Indias* 12 (1952): 685–714.

Ascasubi, Miguel. "Informe cronológico de las misiones del reino de Chile, hasta 1789 [Chillán, 31 octubre 1789]." In *Historia física y política de Chile . . . Documentos sobre la historia, la estadística y la geografía,* edited by Claudio Gay, 1:300–400. 2 vols. Santiago de Chile: Museo de Historia Natural, 1846.

August, Jack. "Balance-of-Power Diplomacy in New Mexico: Governor Fernando de la Concha and the Indian Policy of Conciliation." *New Mexico Historical Review* 56 (1981): 141–60.

Aurrecoechea, José María. "Memoria geográfica-económico-política del departamento de Venezuela [1814]." In *Relaciones geográficos de Venezuela,* edited by Antonio Arellano Moreno, 533–58. Caracas: Academia Nacional de la Historia, 1964.

Avilés, marqués de. "Memoria a su sucesor don Joaquín del Pino, Buenos Aires, 21 de mayo de 1801." In *Memorias de los virreyes del Río de la Plata,* edited by Sigfrido Radaelli, 495–536. Buenos Aires: Editorial Bajel, 1945.

Axtell, James. "Scalping: The Ethnohistory of a Moral Question." In James Axtell, *The European and the Indian: Essays in the Ethnohistory of Colonial North America,* 207–41. New York: Oxford University Press, 1981.

———. "The Scholastic Philosophy of the Wilderness." In James Axtell, *The European and the Indian: Essays in the Ethnohistory of Colonial North America,* 131–67. New York: Oxford University Press, 1982.

———. *The Invasion Within: The Contest of Cultures in Colonial North America.* New York: Oxford University Press, 1985.

———. "Columbian Encounters: 1992–1995." *William and Mary Quarterly* 52 (1995): 649–96.

———. *The Indians' New South: Cultural Change in the Colonial Southeast.* Baton Rouge: LSU Press, 1997.

Axtell, James, and William C. Sturtevant. "The Unkindest Cut, or Who Invented Scalping." In James Axtell, *The European and the Indian: Essays in the Ethnohistory of Colonial North America,* 16–35. New York: Oxford University Press, 1981.

Ayala, Manuel Josef de. *Diccionario de gobierno y legislación de Indias.* Edited by Milagros del Vas Mingo. 13 vols. Madrid: Instituto de Cooperación Iberoamericana. Ediciones de Cultura Hispánica, 1988–96.

Azara, Félix de. *Viajes por la América Meridional.* Edited by C. A. Walckenaer and G. Cuvier. Translated by Francisco de las Barras de Aragón. 1st ed. in French, 1809; 2 vols. Madrid: Calpe, 1923.

———. *Descripción e historia del Paraguay y del Río de la Plata.* Buenos Aires: Editorial Bajel, 1943a.

———. "Informe a la propuesta del virrey de Buenos Aires sobre la formación de un nuevo pueblo donde se juntan los ríos Diamante y Atuel [ca. 1805]." In *Memoria sobre el estado rural del Río de la Plata [1801] y otros informes,* edited by Julio César González, 219–26. Buenos Aires: Editorial Bajel, 1943b.

———. "Informe sobre el govierno y libertad de los indios guaraníes y tapes de la provincia del Paraguay, Madrid 1 de enero de 1806." In *Memoria sobre el estado rural del Río de la Plata [1801] y otras informes,* edited by Julio César González, 243–61. Buenos Aires: Editorial Bajel, 1943c.

———. *Memoria sobre el estado rural del Río de la Plata [1801] y otras informes.* Edited by Julio César González. Buenos Aires: Editorial Bajel, 1943d.

———. "Colonización del Chaco [Azara to Viceroy Antonio Olaguer Feliú, Buenos Aires, Feb. 19, 1799]." In *Colección de obras y documentos relativos a la historia antigua y moderna de las provincias del Río de la Plata por Pedro de Angelis,* edited by Andrés M. Carretero, 6:415–25. 1st ed., 1836; 8 vols. Buenos Aires: Plus Ultra, 1969–72.

———. *Descripción general del Paraguay.* Edited by Andrés Galera Gómez. Madrid: Alianza, 1990.

Azcuy Ameghino, Eduardo. *Artigas y los indios.* Montevideo: Ediciones Andresito, 1991.

Bakewell, Peter. *A History of Latin America.* London: Blackwell, 1997.

Barba, Fernando Enrique. *Frontera ganadera y guerra con el indio: La frontera y la ocupación ganadera en Buenos Aires entre los siglos XVIII y XIX.* La Plata, Argentina: Editorial de la Universidad Nacional de La Plata, 1997.

Barbier, Jacques A. "Charles III's Empire: Conjuncture and Structure." In *Charles III: Florida and the Gulf*, edited by Patricia Wickman, 2–18. Miami: Count of Gálvez Historical Society, 1990.

Barfield, Thomas J. *The Perilous Frontier: Nomadic Empires and China*. Cambridge, Mass.: Basil Blackwell, 1989.

Barickman, B. J. "'Tame Indians,' 'Wild Heathens,' and Settlers in Southern Bahia in the Late Eighteenth and Early Nineteenth Centuries." *The Americas* 51 (1995): 325–68.

Barnadas, Josep M. "The Catholic Church in Colonial Spanish America." In *Cambridge History of Latin America: Colonial Latin America*, edited by Leslie Bethell, 1:511–40. 2 vols. Cambridge: Cambridge University Press, 1984.

Barrera Monroy, Eduardo. *Mestizaje, comercio y resistencia: La Guajira durante la segunda mitad del siglo XVIII*. Bogotá: Instituto Colombiana de Antropología e Historia, 2000.

Barros Arana, Diego. *Historia jeneral de Chile*. 16 vols. Santiago de Chile: Rafael Jovier, 1884–1902.

Bartra, Roger. *Wild Men in the Looking Glass: The Mythic Origins of European Otherness*. Ann Arbor: University of Michigan, 1994.

Basso, Keith H. *Wisdom Sits in Places: Landscape and Language Among the Western Apache*. Tucson: University of Arizona Press, 1996.

Bataillon, Marcel. "Introducción á Concolorcorvo y su itinerario de Buenos Aires á Lima." *Cuadernos Americanos* 111 (1960): 197–216.

Baud, Michiel, and Willem van Schendel. "Toward a Comparative History of Borderlands." *Journal of World History* 8 (1997): 211–42.

Bauer, Ralph. "Creole Identities in Colonial Space: The Narratives of Mary White Rowlandson and Francisco Núñez Pineda y Bascuñán." *American Literature* 69, no. 4 (1997): 665–98.

———. "Imperial History, Captivity, and Creole Identity in Francisco Nuñez de Pineda y Bascuñán's *Cautiverio feliz*." *Colonial Latin American Review* 7, no. 1 (1998): 59–82.

Beaumont, J. A. B. *Travels in Buenos Ayres, and the Adjacent Provinces of the Río de la Plata. With Observations Intended for the use of Persons who Contemplate Emigrating to that Country . . .* London: James Ridgway, 1828.

Beckerman, Stephen. *Datos etnohistóricos acerca de los Barí (Motilones)*. Caracas: Universidad Católica Andrés Bello, 1979.

Beebe, Rose Marie, and Robert M. Senkewicz. *Tensions among the Missionaries in the 1790s*. [Bakersfield, Calif.]: California Mission Studies Association, 1996.

Beilharz, Edwin A. *Felipe de Neve, First Governor of California*. San Francisco: California Historical Society, 1971.

Benavides, Alonso de. *Fray Alonso de Benavides' Revised Memorial of 1634*. Edited and translated by Frederick W. Hodge, George P. Hammond, and Agapito Rey. Albuquerque: University of New Mexico Press, 1945.

Benedict, H. Bradley. "El saqueo de las misiones de Chihuahua, 1767–1777." *Historia Mexicana* 22 (1972): 24–33.

Benes, Ronald. "Anza and Concha in New Mexico, 1787–1793: A Study in New Colonial Techniques." *Journal of the West* 4 (1965): 63–76.

Bengoa, José. *Historia del pueblo mapuche: Siglo XIX y XX*. 1st ed., 1985; Santiago de Chile: Ediciones Sur, 1996.

Berkhofer, Robert F., Jr. *The White Man's Indian: Images of the American Indian from Columbus to the Present*. New York: Knopf, 1978.

Bernabéu Albert, Salvador, ed. *Historia, grafía e imágenes de Tierra Adentro: Nueve ensayos sobre el norte colonial*. Saltillo, Mexico: Archivo Municipal de Saltillo, 1999a.

———. "La Sombra Boltoniana: Albert Niesser y la Historia de los Dominicos de Baja California."

In *Historia, grafía e imágenes de Tierra Adentro: Nueve ensayos sobre el norte colonial,* edited by Salvador Bernabéu Albert, 91–133. Saltillo, Mexico: Archivo Municipal de Saltillo, 1999b.

———. "El diablo en California: Recepción y decadencia del maligno en el discurso misional jesuita." In *El septentrión novohispano: Ecohistoria, sociedades e imágenes de frontera,* edited by Salvador Bernabéu Albert, 139–76. Madrid: Consejo Superior de Investigaciones Científicas, 2000.

Bernal, Irma. *Rosas y los indios.* Concepción del Uruguay, Argentina: Búsqueda de Ayllú, 1997.

Bernstein, Harry. *Making an Inter-American Mind.* Gainesville: University of Florida Press, 1961.

Bethell, Leslie, ed. *Cambridge History of Latin America: Colonial Latin America.* 2 vols. Cambridge: Cambridge University Press, 1984.

Beverina, Juan. *El virreinato de las provincias del Río de la Plata: Su organización militar.* 1st ed., 1935; Buenos Aires: Círculo Militar, 1992.

Bindis, Ricardo. *Rugendas en Chile.* Santiago de Chile: Editorial Los Andes, 1989.

Bierck, Harold A., Jr., and Vicente Lecuna, eds. *Selected Writings of Bolivar.* 2d ed.; 2 vols. New York: Colonial Press, 1951.

Binnema, Theodore. *Common and Contested Ground: A Human and Environmental History of the Northwestern Plains.* Norman: University of Oklahoma Press, 2001.

Bitlloch, Eduardo, ed. *Tierra del Fuego en cuatro textos (del siglo xviii al xx).* Buenos Aires: Universidad de Buenos Aires, Facultad de Filosofía y Letras—Museo Etnográfico "Juan B. Ambrosetti," 1994.

Black, Nancy Johnson. *The Frontier Mission and Social Transformation in Western Honduras: The Order of Our Lady of Mercy, 1525–1773.* Leiden, Netherlands: E. J. Brill, 1995.

Blackhawk, Ned. "Violence Over the Land: Colonial Encounters in the American Great Basin." Ph.D. diss., University of Washington, 1999.

Bladh, Carlos Eduardo. "El Uruguay de 1831 a través del viajero sueco Carlos Eduardo Bladh." Translated by Julio Ricci. *Revista histórica* [Montevideo] 41, no. 121–23 (1970): 705–30.

Block, David. *Mission Culture on the Upper Amazon: Native Tradition, Jesuit Enterprise, and Secular Policy in Moxos, 1660–1880.* Lincoln: University of Nebraska Press, 1994.

Boccara, Guillaume. "Dispositivos de poder en la sociedad colonial-fronteriza chilena del siglo XVI al siglo XVIII." In *Del discurso colonial al proindigenismo: Ensayos de historia latinoamericana,* edited by Jorge Pinto Rodríguez, 29–41. Temuco, Chile: Ediciones Universidad de la Frontera, 1996a.

———. "Notas acerca de los dispositivos de poder en la sociedad colonial-fronteriza, la resistencia y la transculturación de los reche-mapuche del centro-sur de Chile (XVI–XVIIII)." *Revista de Indias* 56 (1996b): 659–95.

———. "El poder creador: Tipos de poder y estrategias de sujeción en la frontera sur de Chile en la época colonial." *Anuario de Estudios Americanos* 56 (1999a): 65–94.

———. "Etnogénesis mapuche: Resistencia y restructuración entre los indígenas del centro-sur de Chile (siglos XVI–XVIII)." *Hispanic American Historical Review* 79 (1999b): 425–61.

Bolton, Herbert E. "The Mission as a Frontier Institution in the Spanish American Colonies." In *New Spain's Far Northern Frontier: Essays on Spain in the American West,* edited by David J. Weber, 49–66. Albuquerque: University of New Mexico Press, 1979.

Bolton, Herbert Eugene, ed. and trans. *Athanase de Mézières and the Louisiana-Texas Frontier, 1768–1780.* 2 vols. Cleveland: Arthur H. Clark, 1914.

———. *Anza's California Expeditions.* 5 vols. Berkeley: University of California Press, 1930.

Boneu Companys, Fernando. *Gaspar de Portolá: Explorer and Founder of California.* Edited and translated by Alan K. Brown. Lérida, Spain: Instituto de Estudios Llerdenses, 1983.

Bonilla, Antonio. "Apuntes sobre el nuevo Mexico, Santa Rosa, Sept. 3, 1776." Bancroft Library, Berkeley, Bancroft M-M, 167.

Borah, Woodrow. *Justice by Insurance: The General Indian Court of Colonial Mexico and the Legal Aides of the Half-Real.* Berkeley: University of California Press, 1983.

Borges Morán, Pedro. *El envío de misioneros a América durante la época española.* Salamanca, Spain: Universidad Pontificia, 1977.

Borges, Pedro. "Estructura y características de la evangelización americana." In *Historia de la Iglesia en Hispanoamérica y Filipinas,* edited by Pedro Borges, 1:423–36. 2 vols. Madrid: Biblioteca de Autores Cristianos, 1992a.

———. "La expansión misional." In *Historia de la Iglesia en Hispanoamérica y Filipinas,* edited by Pedro Borges, 1:471–94. 2 vols. Madrid: Biblioteca de Autores Cristianos, 1992b.

———, ed. *Historia de la Iglesia en Hispanoamérica y Filipinas.* 2 vols. Madrid: Biblioteca de Autores Cristianos, 1992c.

———. "La metodología misional americana." In *Historia de la Iglesia en Hispanoamérica y Filipinas,* edited by Pedro Borges, 1:495–507. 2 vols. Madrid: Biblioteca de Autores Cristianos, 1992d.

———. "La nueva cristianidad indiana." In *Historia de la Iglesia en Hispanoamérica y Filipinas,* edited by Pedro Borges, 1:593–613. 2 vols. Madrid: Biblioteca de Autores Cristianos, 1992e.

———. "Primeros hombres, luego cristianos: La transculturación." In *Historia de la Iglesia en Hispanoamérica y Filipinas,* edited by Pedro Borges, 1:521–34. 2 vols. Madrid: Biblioteca de Autores Cristianos, 1992f.

Bougainville, Louis-Antoine de. *Viaje alrededor del mundo por la fragata del rey la "Boudeuse" y la fusta la "Estrella" en 1767, 1768 y 1769.* Translated by Josefina Gallego de Dantín. 1st French edition, 1771–72; 2 vols. Madrid: Calpe, 1921.

Bougainville, Louis-Antoine de, and Denis Diderot. *Voyage autour du monde la frégate la Boudeuse et la flûte l'Étoile.* 1st French edition, 1771–72; Paris: Union générale d'éditions, 1966.

Bouvet, Nora. "La política indígena del dictador supremo en la frontera norte paraguaya." *Suplemento Antropológico* [Asunción, Paraguay] 27 (1992): 93–124.

Brabo, Francisco Javier, ed. *Colección de documentos relativos a la expulsión de los jesuitas de la República Argentina y del Paraguay.* Madrid: José María Pérez, 1872.

Brading, D. A. *Miners and Merchants in Bourbon Mexico, 1763–1810.* Cambridge: Cambridge University Press, 1971.

———. "Bourbon Spain and its American Empire." In *Cambridge History of Latin America: Colonial Latin America,* edited by Leslie Bethell, 1:389–439. 2 vols. Cambridge: Cambridge University Press, 1984.

———. *The First America: The Spanish Monarch, Creole Patriots, and the Liberal State, 1492–1867.* Cambridge: Cambridge University Press, 1991.

Brandes, Stanley. "Los misiones de la Alta California como instrumentos de conquista." In *De palabra y obra en el nuevo mundo,* edited by Miguel León-Portilla et al., 2:153–72. 3 vols. Madrid: Siglo XXI/Junta de Extremadura, 1992.

Braudel, Fernand. *The Structures of Everyday Life: Civilization and Capitalism, 15th–18th Century.* 1st French edition, 1979; 3 vols. New York: Harper and Row, 1981.

Braund, Kathryn E. Holland. *Deerskins and Duffels: Creek Indian Trade with Anglo-America, 1685–1815.* Lincoln: University of Nebraska Press, 1993.

Bravo Guerreira, Concepción. "Las misiones de Chiquitos: Pervivencia y resistencia de un modelo de colonización." *Revista Complutense de Historia de América* 21 (1995): 29–56.

Brinckerhoff, Sidney B. "The Last Years of Spanish Arizona, 1786–1821." *Arizona and the West* 9 (1967): 5–20.

Brinckerhoff, Sidney B., and Odie B. Faulk, eds. and trans. *Lancers for the King: A Study of the Frontier Military System of Northern New Spain, With a Translation of the Royal Regulations of 1772.* Phoenix: Arizona Historical Foundation, 1965.

Brizuela, Joaquín. "Diario de la expedición hecha en 1774 a los países del Gran Chaco desde el Fuerte del Valle." In *Colección de obras y documentos relativos a la historia antigua y moderna de las provincias del Río de la Plata por Pedro de Angelis,* edited by Andés M. Carretero, 8A:239–301. 1st ed., 1836; 8 vols. Buenos Aires: Plus Ultra, 1969–72.

Brooks, James F. "'This Evil Extends Especially to the Feminine Sex': Captivity and Identity in New Mexico, 1800–1846." In *Writing the Range: Race, Class, and Culture in the Women's West,* edited by Elizabeth Jameson and Susan Armitage, 97–121. Norman: University of Oklahoma Press, 1997.

———. "Violence, Justice, and State Power in the New Mexican Borderlands, 1780–1880." In *Power and Place in the North American West,* edited by Richard White and John Findlay, 23–58. Seattle: University of Washington Press, 1999.

———. "'Lest We Go in Search of Relief to Our Lands and Our Nation': Customary Justice and Colonial Law in the New Mexico Borderlands." In *The Many Legalities of Early America,* edited by Christopher Tomlins and Bruce H. Mann, 150–80. Chapel Hill: University of North Carolina Press for the Omohundro Institute of Early American History and Culture, 2001.

———. *Captives and Cousins: Slavery, Kinship, and Community in the Southwest Borderlands.* Chapel Hill: University of North Carolina Press for the Omohundro Institute of Early American History and Culture, 2002.

Brown, Jonathan C. *A Socioeconomic History of Argentina, 1776–1860.* Cambridge: Cambridge University Press, 1979.

Brown, Michael F. "On Resisting Resistance." *American Anthropologist* 98, no. 4 (1996): 729–34.

Brown, Tracy L. "Conversion to Christianity in Eighteenth-Century New Mexico Pedagogy and Personhood in the Pueblo-Franciscan Encounter." *Catholic Southwest: A Journal of History and Culture* 12 (2001): 29–50.

Brugge, David M. "Captives and Slaves on the Camino Real." In *El Camino Real de Tierra Adentro,* edited by Gabrielle G. Palmer and Stephen L. Fosberg, 103–10. Santa Fe: Bureau of Land Management, 1999.

Brunet, José. "La iglesia en las Islas Malvinas durante el período hispano (1767–1810)." *Missionalia Hispánica* 26 (1969): 209–40.

Bruno, Cayetano. *La evangelización de la Patagonia y de la Tierra del Fuego.* Rosario: Ediciones Didascalia, 1992.

Bucareli y Ursúa, Francisco de. "Informe de Bucareli [1770]." *Revista de la Biblioteca Pública de Buenos Aires* 2 (1880): 265–389.

Burke, Michael E. *The Royal College of San Carlos: Surgery and Spanish Medical Reform in the Late Eighteenth Century.* Durham: Duke University Press, 1977.

Burnham, Philip. "Spatial Mobility and Political Centralization in Pastoral Societies." In *Pastoral Production and Society,* edited by L'équipe écologie et anthropologie des sociétés pastorales, 361–74. Cambridge: Cambridge University Press, 1979.

Burns, E. Bradford. *The Poverty of Progress.* Berkeley: University of California Press, 1980.

Burrus, Ernest. *Kino and Manje: Explorers of Sonora and Arizona.* St. Louis: Jesuit Historical Institute, 1971.

Bushnell, Amy Turner. "Ruling the Republic of Indians in Seventeenth-Century Florida." In *Powhatan's Mantle: Indians in the Colonial Southeast,* edited by Peter H. Wood, Gregory A. Waselkov, and M. Thomas. Hatley, 134–50. Lincoln: University of Nebraska Press, 1989.

———. *Situado and Sabana: Spain's Support System for the Presidio and Mission Provinces of Florida.* Anthropological Papers of the American Museum of Natural History, no. 74. New York: American Museum of Natural History, 1994.

———. "Spain's Conquest by Contract: Pacification and the Mission System in Eastern North

America." In *The World Turned Upside-Down: The State of Eighteenth-Century American Studies at the Beginning of the Twenty-First Century,* edited by Michael V. Kennedy and William G. Shade. Bethlehem, Penn.: Lehigh University Press, 2001.

———. "Gates, Patterns, and Peripheries: The Field of Frontier Latin America." In *Negotiated Empires: Centers and Peripheries in the Americas, 1500–1820,* edited by Christine Daniels and Michael V. Kennedy, 15–28. New York and London: Routledge, 2002.

———. "'None of These Wandering Nations Has Ever Been Reduced to the Faith': Missions and Mobility on the Spanish-American Frontier." In *The Spiritual Conversion of the Americas,* edited by James Muldoon, 142–68. Gainesville: University Press of Florida, 2004.

Bushnell, David. *Reform and Reaction in the Platine Provinces, 1810–1852.* Gainesville: University Press of Florida, 1983.

Bustamante, Carlos María de. *El indio mexicano, o avisos al Rey Fernando Séptimo para la pacificación de la América Septentrional.* Edited by Manuel Arellano Zavaleta. Mexico: Instituto Mexicano del Seguro Social, 1981.

Caamaño, Jacinto. "The Journal of Jacinto Caamaño." Edited by Henry R. Wagner and W. A. Newcombe. *British Columbia Historical Quarterly* 2 (1938): 189–222, 265–301.

Caballero y Góngora, Antonio. "Relación del estado del Nuevo Reino de Granada que hace el Arzobispo Obispo de Córdoba [Caballero y Góngora] á su sucesor El Excmo. Sr. D. Francisco Gil y Lemus, 1789." In *Relaciones de mando: Memorias presentadas por los gobernantes del Nuevo Reino de Granada,* edited by Eduardo Posada and Pedro María Ibáñez, 1:197–276. 2 vols. Bogotá: Biblioteca de Historia Nacional, 1910.

Caballero y Góngora, Antonio, et al. "Pacificación general de los indios de Darién, celebrada en 21 de julio de 1787." *Boletín de historia y antigüedades* 13 (1920): 197–202.

Calderón Quijano, José A. "Un incidente militar en los establecimientos ingleses en Rio Tinto (Honduras), en 1782." *Anuario de Estudios Americanos* 2 (1945): 761–84.

Calero, Luis F. *Chiefdoms Under Siege: Spain's Rule and Native Adaptation in the Southern Colombian Andes, 1535–1700.* Albuquerque: University of New Mexico Press, 1997.

Callahan, North. *Henry Knox: General Washington's General.* New York: Rinehart, 1958.

Callahan, William J. "Two Spains and Two Churches, 1760–1835." *Historical Reflections* 2 (1975): 157–81.

Calleja, Félix. *Informe sobre la colonia del Nuevo Santander y Nuevo Reino de León, 1795.* Mexico: José Porrúa e Hijos, 1949.

Calzavarini, Lorenzo-Giuseppe. *Nación Chiriguana: Grandeza y Ocaso.* Cochabamba, Bolivia: Los Amigos del Libro, 1980.

Campbell, Leon G. *The Military and Society in Colonial Peru, 1750–1810.* Philadelphia: American Philosophical Society, 1978.

Campillo y Cosío, José del. *Nuevo sistema de gobierno económico para la América.* Edited by Manuel Ballesteros Gaibrois. Oviedo, Spain: Grupo Editorial Asturiano, 1993.

Campillo y Cosío, Joseph del. *Nuevo sistema de govierno económico para la América.* Madrid: Imprenta de Benito Cano, 1789.

Campillo y Cossío [*sic*], José del. *Dos escritos políticos: Lo que hay de más y de menos en España/España despierta [1741].* Edited by Dolores Mateos Dorado. Oviedo, Spain: Junta General del Principado de Asturias, 1993.

Campomanes, Pedro Rodríguez, conde de. *Dictamen fiscal de expulsión de los jesuitas de España (1766–1767).* Edited by Jorge Cejuda and Teófanes Egido. Madrid: Fundación Universitaria Española, 1977.

———. *Reflexiones sobre el comercio español a Indias [1762].* Edited by Vicente Llombart Rosa. Madrid: Instituto de Estudios Fiscales, 1988.

―――. *Inéditos políticos*. Edited by Santos M. Coronas González. Oviedo, Spain: Junta General del Principado de Asturias, 1996.

Campos Menchaca, Mariano José. *Nahuelbuta*. Santiago de Chile: Editorial Francisco de Aguirre, 1972.

Canals Frau, Salvador. *Las poblaciones indígenas de la Argentina: Su origen, su pasado, su presente*. Buenos Aires: Editorial Sudamerica, 1973.

Cañizales Guédez, Emigdio. *El Indio en la independencia*. Serie Ensayos, 107. Caracas: Dirección de Cultura-APUCV, Universidad Central de Venezuela, 1993.

Cañizares-Esguerra, Jorge. *How to Write the History of the New World: Histories, Epistemologies, and Identities in the Eighteenth-Century Atlantic World*. Stanford: Stanford University Press, 2001.

Cano, Luis. "Franciscanos en Argentina, Paraguay y Uruguay." In *Franciscan Presence in the Americas: Essays on the Activities of the Franciscan Friars in the Americas, 1492–1900*, edited by Francisco Morales, 106–31. Potomac, Md.: Academy of American Franciscan History, 1983.

Cantillo, Alejandro del, ed. *Tratados, Convenios y Declaraciones de Paz y Comercio que han hecho con las Potencias Estranjeras los Monarcos Españoles de la Casa de Borbón, desde el año de 1700 hasta el día*. Madrid: Alegria y Charlain, 1843.

Carbia, Rómulo D. *Historia de la leyenda negra hispanoamericana*. Madrid: Consejo de Hispanidad, 1944.

Cardozo, Efraim. *El Chaco y los virreyes: La cuestión paraguayo-boliviana según documentos de los archivos de Buenos Aires y de Rio de Janeiro*. Asunción, Paraguay: Imprenta Nacional, 1934.

Cargill, Diane A., and Robert J. Hard. "Assessing Native American Mobility versus Permanency at Mission San Juan de Capistrano through the Use of Stable Isotope Analysis." *Bulletin of the Texas Archeological Society* 70 (1999): 199–213.

Carlson, Paul H. *The Plains Indians*. College Station: Texas A&M University Press, 1998.

Carminati, Tomás de. "Plazas y fuertes de la frontera de Arauco, Oct. 20, 1755." In *Relaciones Geográficas del Reino de Chile, 1756*, edited by Francisco Solano, 208–37. Madrid: Consejo Superior de Investigaciones Científicas, 1995.

Carneiro, Robert L. "The Chiefdom: Precursor of the State." In *The Transition to Statehood in the New World*, edited by G. Jones, 37–79. Cambridge: Cambridge University Press, 1981.

―――. "What Happened at the Flashpoint? Conjectures on Chiefdom Formation at the Very Moment of Conception." In *Chiefdoms and Chieftaincy in the Americas*, edited by Elsa Redmond, 18–42. Gainesville: University Press of Florida, 1998.

Carretero Collado, Leoncio. "Etnografía y cautividad en Nutka: Notas sobre presupuestos, métodos y resultados en la visión de los otros." In *Visión de los otros y visión de sí mismos*, edited by Fermín del Pino Díaz and Carlos Lázaro Ávila, 146–56. Madrid: Consejo Superior de Investigaciones Científicas, 1995.

Carril, Bonifacio del. *Monumenta Iconographica: Paisajes, ciudades, tipos, usos y costumbres de la Argentina, 1536–1860*. 2 vols. Buenos Aires: Emecé Editores, 1964.

Carrocera, Buenaventura de, ed. *Misión de los capuchinos en Cumaná*. Biblioteca de la Academia Nacional de la Historia. Fuentes para la historia colonial de Venezuela, 88–90. 3 vols. Caracas: Academia Nacional de la Historia, 1968.

―――. *Misión de los capuchinos en los llanos de Caracas*. Biblioteca de la Academia Nacional de la Historia. Fuentes para la historia colonial de Venezuela, nos. 111–13. 3 vols. Caracas: Academia Nacional de la Historia, 1972.

Carson, James T. *Searching for the Bright Path: The Mississippi Choctaws from Prehistory to Removal*. Lincoln: University of Nebraska Press, 1999.

Casanova Guarda, Holdenís. "Presencia franciscana en la Araucania: Las misiones del Colegio de Propaganda Fide de Chillan (1756–1818)." In *Misioneros en la Araucanía, 1600–1900: Un capítulo de historia fronteriza en Chile,* edited by Jorge Pinto Rodríguez et al., 121–97. Temuco, Chile: Ediciones Universidad de la Frontera, 1988.

———. "El rol del jefe en la sociedad mapuche prehispánica." In *Araucanía: Temas de historia fronteriza,* edited by Sergio Villalobos R. and Jorge Pinto, 31–46. Temuco, Chile: Ediciones de la Universidad de la Frontera, 1989a.

———. *Las rebeliones araucanas del siglo XVIII: Mito y realidad.* Temuco, Chile: Editorial Universidad de la Frontera, 1989b.

———. "La alianza Hispano–Pehuenche y sus repercusiones en el macroespacio fronterizo sur andino (1750–1800)." In *Araucanía y pampas: Un mundo fronterizo en América del Sur,* edited by Jorge Pinto Rodríguez, 72–92. Temuco, Chile: Ediciones Universidad de la Frontera, 1996a.

———. "La Araucanía colonial: Discursos, imágenes y estereotipos (1550–1800)." In *Del discurso colonial al proindigenismo: Ensayos de historia latinoamericana,* ed. Jorge Pinto Rodríguez, 43–84. Temuco, Chile: Ediciones Universidad de la Frontera, 1996b.

———. "Entre la ideología y la realidad: La inclusión de los mapuche en la nación chilena (1810–1830)." *Revista de Historia Indígena,* no. 4 (1999–2000): 9–48.

Casanueva, Fernando. "La evangelización periférica en el reino de Chile, 1667–1796." *Nueva Historia: Revista de Historia de Chile* 5 (1982): 5–30.

———. "Los Mapuches: Economía y guerra en una sociedad libre." *Mapuche—Apuntes* (1984): 1–36.

———. "Política, evangelización y rebeliones indígenas a fines del siglo XVIII: El caso sur Chileno." In *La América española en la época de las luces: Tradición, innovación, representaciones,* 229–47. Madrid: Ediciones de Cultura Hispánica, 1988.

———. "Chiloé, el jardín de la iglesia (notas para la historia de una evangelización colonial lograda)." In *IX Congreso Internacional de Historia de América,* 7–31. Seville: Asociación de Historiadores Latino Americanistas Europeos (AHILA), 1992a.

———. "Smallpox and War in Southern Chile in the Late Eighteenth Century." In *"Secret Judgments of God": Old World Disease in Colonial Spanish America,* edited by Noble David Cook and W. George Lovell, 183–213. Norman: University of Oklahoma Press, 1992b.

Castañeda, Antonia I. "Engendering the History of Alta California, 1769–1848: Gender, Sexuality, and the Family." In *Contested Eden: California Before the Gold Rush,* edited by Ramón A. Gutiérrez and Richard J. Orsi, 230–59. Berkeley: University of California Press, 1998.

Castillero Calvo, Alfredo. *Conquista, evangelisación, y resistencia: ¿Triunfo o fracaso de la política indigenista?* Panamá: Editorial Mariano Arosemena/Instituto Nacional de Cultura, 1995.

Castro, Américo. *The Spaniards: An Introduction to Their History.* Translated by Willard F. King and Selma Margaretten. Berkeley: University of California Press, 1971.

Castro, Concepción de. *Campomanes, estado y reformismo ilustrado.* Madrid: Alianza Universidad, 1996.

Castro Gutiérrez, Felipe. "De paternalismo autoritario al autoritarismo burocrático: Los éxitos y fracasos de José de Gálvez, 1764–1767." In *Mexico in the Age of Democratic Revolutions, 1750–1850,* edited by Jaime E. Rodríguez O., 21–33. Boulder and London: Lynne Rienner, 1994.

Cavazos Garza, Israel. *Breve historia de Nuevo León.* Mexico: Colegio de Mexico, 1994.

Cerda-Hegerl, Patricia. *Fronteras del Sur: La región del Bío Bío y la araucanía chilena, 1604–1883.* Temuco, Chile: Instituto Latinoamericano de la Universidad Libre de Berlin/Ediciones Universidad de la Frontera, 1990.

Cerezo Martínez, Ricardo. *La expedición Malaspina, 1789–1794.* Vol. 1, *Circunstancia histórica del viaje.* Madrid: Ministerio de Defensa, Museo Naval, and Lunwerg Editores, 1987.

Cervantes, Fernando. *The Devil in the New World: The Impact of Diabolism in New Spain.* New Haven: Yale University Press, 1994.

Cevallos, Pedro de. "Memoria a su sucesor don Juan José de Vértiz y Salcedo, Buenos Aires, 12 de junio de 1784." In *Memorias de los virreyes del Río de la Plata,* edited by Sigfrido Radaelli, 2–23. Buenos Aires: Editorial Bajel, 1945.

Chagnon, Napoleon A. *Yanomamö, the fierce people.* New York: Holt, Rinehart, and Winston, 1968.

Champagne, Duane. "Change, Continuity, and Variation in Native American Societies as a Response to Conquest." In *Violence, Resistance, and Survival in the Americas: Native Americans and the Legacy of Conquest,* edited by William B. Taylor and Franklin Pease G.Y., 208–25. Washington: Smithsonian Institution Press, 1994.

Chapa, Juan Bautista. *Texas and Northeastern Mexico, 1630–1690.* Edited by William C. Foster. Translated by Ned F. Brierley. Austin: University of Texas Press, 1997.

Chiaramonte, José Carlos. *La crítica ilustrada de la realidad: Economía y sociedad en el pensamiento argentino e iberoamericano del siglo XVIII.* Buenos Aires: Centro Editor de América Latina, 1982.

———. *La ilustración en el Río de la Plata: Cultura eclesiástica y cultura laica durante el Virreinato.* Buenos Aires: Puntosur Editores, 1989.

———. "La formación de los estados nacionales de Iberoamérica." *Boletín del Instituto de Historia Argentina y Americana "Doctor Emilio Ravignani,"* no. 15 (1997): 143–65.

Chiclana, Feliciano Antonio. "Actuación pública de Feliciano Antonio Chiclana [Dec. 29, 1804]." *Revista de la Biblioteca Nacional* [Buenos Aires] 13 (1945): 32–37.

Chiokoyhikoy. *Apocalypse of Chiokoyhikoy.* Edited by Robert Griffin and Donald A. Grinde, Jr. 1st ed., 1777; Quebec: Les Presses de L'Université Laval, 1997.

Chipman, Donald E., and Harriett Denise Joseph. *Notable Men and Women of Spanish Texas.* Austin: University of Texas Press, 1999.

Chust Calero, Manuel. "De esclavos, encomenderos y mitayos: El anticolonialismo en las Cortes de Cádiz." *Mexican Studies/Estudios Mexicanos* 11 (1995): 179–202.

Círculo Militar. *Política seguida con el aborigen, 1750–1819.* 2 vols. Buenos Aires: Comando General del Ejército, 1973.

Civrieux, Marc de. "Los Caribes y la conquista de la Guayana Española (etnohistoria kari'ña)." *Montalban* 5 (1976): 875–1021.

Clastres, Pierre. *Society Against the State: Essays in Political Anthropology.* Translated by Robert Hurley. New York: Zone Books, 1987.

———. *Investigaciones en antropología política.* 1st French edition, 1980; Barcelona: Gedisa, 1996.

Cleary, David. "Towards an Environmental History of the Amazon: From Prehistory to the Nineteenth Century." *Latin American Research Review* 35, no. 2 (2001): 65–96.

Clendinnen, Inga. "Disciplining the Indians: Franciscan Ideology and Missionary Violence in Sixteenth-Century Yucatan." *Past and Present* 94 (1982): 27–48.

———. *Dancing With Strangers.* Melbourne: Text Publishing, 2003.

Clifford, James. "Introduction: Partial Truths." In *Writing Culture: The Poetics and Politics of Ethnography,* edited by James Clifford and George E. Marcus. Berkeley: University of California Press, 1986.

Coatsworth, John H. "The Limits of Colonial Absolutism: The State in Eighteenth Century Mexico." In *Essays in the Political, Economic and Social History of Colonial Latin America,* edited by Karen Spalding, 25–51. Newark: University of Delaware, Latin American Studies Program, 1982.

Coker, William S., and Thomas D. Watson. *Indian Traders of the Southeastern Spanish Borderlands: Panton, Leslie & Company and John Forbes & Company, 1783–1847.* Pensacola: University of West Florida Press, 1986.

Colección de documentos inéditos relativos al descubrimiento, conquista y organización de las antiguas posesiones españolas de América y Oceanía. 42 vols. Madrid: various, 1864–84.

Collier, Simon. *Ideas and Politics of Chilean Independence, 1808–1833.* Cambridge: Cambridge University Press, 1967.

Comadrán Ruíz, Jorge. "En torno al problema del indio en el Río de la Plata." *Anuario de Estudios Americanos* 12 (1955): 39–74.

Comaroff, John, and Jean Comaroff. *Ethnography and the Historical Imagination.* Boulder: Westview Press, 1992.

Concha, Fernando de la. "Advice on Governing New Mexico, 1794." Edited and translated by Donald Worcester. *New Mexico Historical Review* 24 (1949): 236–54.

Concolorcorvo [Alonso Carrió de la Vandera]. *El Lazarillo: A Guide for Inexperienced Travellers between Buenos Aires and Lima, 1773.* Edited by Walter D. Kline. Bloomington: Indiana University Press, 1965.

———. "El Lazarillo de ciegos caminantes." In *Relaciones histórico-literarias de la América meridional . . . El lazarillo de ciegos caminantes,* edited by José J. Real Díaz, 246–407. Madrid: Ediciones Atlas, 1959.

Cook, Warren L. *Flood Tide of Empire: Spain and the Pacific Northwest, 1543–1819.* New Haven: Yale University Press, 1973.

Cooney, Jerry W. "North to the Yerbales: The Exploitation of the Paraguayan Frontier, 1776–1810." In *Contested Ground: Comparative Frontiers on the Northern and Southern Edges of the Spanish Empire,* edited by Donna J. Guy and Thomas E. Sheridan, 135–49. Tucson: University of Arizona Press, 1998.

Cooney, Jerry W., and Thomas L. Whigham. "Paraguayan Commerce with the Outside World, 1770–1850." In *The Political Economy of Spanish America in the Age of Revolution, 1750–1850,* edited by Kenneth J. Andrien and Lyman L. Johnson, 215–42. Albuquerque: University of New Mexico Press, 1994.

Cooper, John M. "The Araucanians." In *Handbook of South American Indians,* edited by Julian H. Steward, 2:687–760. Washington: Smithsonian Institution Press, 1946.

Cordero y Bustamante, Antonio. "Noticias relativas a la nación apache, que en el año de 1796 extendió en el Paso del Norte, el Teniente Coronel D. Antonio Cordero, por encargo del Sr. Comandante general Mariscal de Campo D. Pedro Nava." In *Geografía de las lenguas y carta etnográfica de México,* edited by Manuel Orozco y Berra, 369–83. Mexico: Impr. de J. M. Andrade y F. Escalante, 1864.

Córdoba, Antonio Santa Clara. *La orden franciscana en las repúblicas del Plata: Síntesis historica, 1536–1934.* Buenos Aires: Imprenta López, 1934.

Córdoba y Figueroa, Pedro de. "Historia de Chile." In *Colección de historiadores de Chile y documentos relativos a la historia nacional,* 1–316. Santiago de Chile: Imprenta del Ferrocarril, 1862.

Corrado, Alejandro, and Antonio Comajuncosa. *El colegio franciscano de Tarija y sus misiones.* Edited by Gerardo Maldini. 1st ed., 1884; 2 vols. Tarija, Bolivia: Editorial Offset Franciscana, 1990.

Corregido, Dolores Juliano. "Algunas consideraciones sobre el ordenamiento temporo-espacial entre los mapuches." *Boletín Americanista* 34 (1984): 125–52.

Cortés, José. *Views from the Apache Frontier: Report on the Northern Provinces of New Spain by José Cortés, Lieutenant in the Royal Corps of Engineers, 1799.* Edited and translated by Elizabeth A. H. John and John Wheat. Norman: University of Oklahoma Press, 1989.

Costello, Julia G. "Variability among the Alta California Missions: The Economics of Agricultural Production." In *Columbian Consequences.* Vol. 1, *Archaeological and Historical Perspectives on the Spanish Borderlands West,* edited by David Hurst Thomas, 435–49. Washington: Smithsonian Institution Press, 1989.

Couyoudmjian Bergamali, Ricardo. "Manuel José Orejuela y la abortada expedición en busca de los césares y extranjeros, 1780–1783." *Historia* [Universidad Católica de Chile] 10 (1971): 57–176.

Cramaussel, Chantal. "Encomiendas, repartimientos y conquista en Nueva Vizcaya." *Historias* 25 (1990–1991): 72–89.

———. "Los apaches en la época colonial." *Cuadernos del Norte* 21 (1992): 25–26.

———. "Ilegítimos y abandonados en la frontera norte de la Nueva España: Parral y San Barto-lomé en el siglo XVII." *Colonial Latin American Historical Review* 4 (1995): 404–38.

———. "De cómo los españoles clasificaban a los indios: Naciones y encomiendas en la Nueva Vizcaya central." In *Nómadas y sedentarios en el norte de Mexico Homenaje a Beatriz Braniff,* edited by Marie-Areti Hers et al., 275–303. Mexico: Instituto de Investigaciones Antropológicas, UNAM, 2000.

Crivelli Montero, Eduardo A. "Malones: ¿saqueo o estrategia? El objetivo de las invasiones de 1780 y 1783 a la frontera de Buenos Aires." *Todo es Historia,* no. 283 (1991): 6–32.

Cro, Stelio. *The Noble Savage: Allegory of Freedom.* Waterloo, Ontario: Wilfrid Laurier University Press, 1990.

Cruz, Enrique Normando. "La nueva sociedad de frontera: Los grupos sociales en la frontera de San Ignacio de Ledesma, Chaco Occidental, finales del siglo XVIII." *Anuario de Estudios Ameri-canos* 58 (2001): 135–83.

Cuello, José. "The Economic Impact of the Bourbon Reforms and the Late Colonial Crisis of Empire at the Local Level: The Case of Saltillo, 1777–1817." *The Americas* 44 (1988a): 301–23.

———. "The Persistence of Indian Slavery and Encomienda in the Northeast of Colonial Mex-ico, 1577–1723." *Journal of Social History* 21 (1988b): 683–700.

Cuesta Domingo, Mariano. "Descubrimientos geográficos durante el S. XVIII: Acción franciscana el la ampliación de fronteras." In *Los franciscanos en el Nuevo Mundo (siglo XVIII),* 293–342. Madrid: Editorial Deimos, 1993.

Curel, François de. *Arrivée en France de quatre sauvages Charruas, par le brick français Phaéton, de Saint-Malo.* Edited by José Joaquín Figueira. 1st ed., Paris, 1833; facsimile ed., Montevideo: Castro, 1959.

Cushner, Nicholas P. *Jesuit Ranches and the Agrarian Development of Colonial Argentina, 1650–1767.* Albany: State University of New York Press, 1983.

Cusick, James G. *The Other War of 1812: The Patriot War and the American Invasion of Spanish East Florida.* Gainesville: University Press of Florida, 2003.

Cutolo, Vicente Osvaldo. *Nuevo diccionario biográfico argentino, 1750–1930.* 7 vols. Buenos Aires: Edi-torial ELCHE, 1968–85.

Cutter, Charles R. *The Legal Culture of Northern New Spain, 1700–1810.* Albuquerque: University of New Mexico Press, 1995.

Cutter, Donald C., and Laurio H. Destefani. *Tadeo Haenke y el final de una vieja polémica.* Buenos Aires: Secretaría de Estado de Marina, Departamento de Estudios Históricos Navales, 1966.

Cutter, Donald C. *Malaspina in California.* San Francisco: John Howell Books, 1960.

———. *California in 1792: A Spanish Naval Visit.* Norman: University of Oklahoma Press, 1990.

———. *Malaspina and Galiano: Spanish Voyages to the Northwest Coast, 1791 and 1792.* Seattle: University of Washington Press, 1991.

D'Agostino, Peter R. "Orthodoxy or Decorum? Missionary Discourse, Religious Representations, and Historical Knowledge." *Church History* 72 (2003): 703–35.

d'Aquino Fonseca Gadelha, María. "Las misiones guaraní y el problema de las fronteras: 1610–1750." In *Fronteras, etnias, culturas: America Latina, siglos XVI–XX,* edited by Chiara Vangelista, 15–31. Quito: Abya-Yala, 1996.

Darwin, Charles. *Journal of Researches into the Geology and Natural History of the Various Countries Visited by the H.M.S. Beagle. A Facsimile Reprint of the First Edition.* 1st ed., 1839; New York: Hafner Publishing Co., 1952.

———. *Voyage of the Beagle.* 1st ed., 1839; London: Penguin Books, 1989.

Davidson, William V. "Geografía de los indígenas toles (jicaques) de Honduras en el siglo XVIII." *Mesoamérica: Revista del Centro de Investigaciones Regionales de Mesoamérica* 9 (1985): 58–90.

Davis, David Brion. *The Problem of Slavery in the Age of Revolution, 1770–1823.* Ithaca: Cornell University Press, 1975.

Dawson, Frank Griffith. "William Pitt's Settlement at Black River on the Mosquito Shore: A Challenge to Spain in Central America, 1732–87." *Hispanic American Historical Review* 63 (1983): 677–706.

———. "The Evacuation of the Mosquito Shore and the English Who Stayed Behind, 1786–1800." *The Americas* 55 (1998): 63–89.

de Armond, Louis. "Frontier Warfare in Colonial Chile." *Pacific Historical Review* 23 (1954): 125–32.

De la Cruz, Luis. "Descripción de la naturaleza de los terrenos . . . poseídos por los pehuenches [1806]." In *Colección de obras y documentos relativos a la historia antigua y moderna de las provincias del Río de la Plata por Pedro de Angelis,* edited by Andrés M. Carretero, 2:399–491. 1st ed., 1836; 8 vols. Buenos Aires: Plus Ultra, 1969a–72a.

———. "Viaje . . . de la Concepción de Chile . . . hasta la ciudad de Buenos Aires [1806]." In *Colección de obras y documentos relativos a la historia antigua y moderna de las provincias del Río de la Plata por Pedro de Angelis,* edited by Andrés M. Carretero, 2:1–399. 1st ed., 1836, 8 vols. Buenos Aires: Editorial Plus Ultra, 1969b–72b.

Deeds, Susan M. "Indigenous Responses to Mission Settlement in Nueva Vizcaya." In *New Latin American Mission History,* edited by Erick Langer and Robert Jackson, 77–108. Lincoln: University of Nebraska Press, 1995.

———. "Rural Work in Nueva Vizcaya: Forms of Labor Coercion on the Periphery." *Hispanic American Historical Review* 69 (1989): 425–49.

———. "Colonial Chihuahua: Peoples and Frontiers in Flux." In *New Views of Borderlands History,* edited by Robert H. Jackson, 21–40. Albuquerque: University of New Mexico Press, 1998.

———. *Defiance and Deference in Mexico's Colonial North: Indians Under Spanish Rule in Nueva Vizcaya.* Austin: University of Texas Press, 2003.

Defina, Frank. "Mestizos y blancos en la política india de la Luisiana y Florida del siglo XVIII." *Revista de Indias* 26 (1966): 59–77.

Del Rey Fajardo, José. "Las escoltas militares en las misiones jesuíticas de la orinoquía." *Boletín de la Academia Nacional de la Historia* [Caracas] 78, no. 311 (1995): 35–69.

DeLay, Brian Edward. "The War of a Thousand Deserts: Indian Politics in the Era of the U.S.–Mexican War." Ph.D. diss., Harvard University, 2004.

Deloria, Vine, Jr. *Red Earth, White Lies: Native Americans and the Myth of Scientific Fact.* Golden, Colo.: Fulcrum, 1997.

Deloria, Vine, Jr., and Raymond J. DeMallie, eds. *Documents of Indian Diplomacy: Treaties, Agreements, and Conventions, 1775–1979.* 2 vols. Norman: University of Oklahoma Press, 1999.

Demaría, Rafael M. *Historia de las armas de fuego en la Argentina; 1530–1852.* Buenos Aires: Ediciones Cabargon, 1972.

Depons, F., [François Raymond Joseph]. *Travels in South America during the years 1801, 1802, 1803, and 1804, Containing a Description of the Captain-Generalship of Caracas. . . .* 1st English edition, 1807; 2 vols. New York: AMS Press, 1970.

Descola, Jean. *Daily Life in Colonial Peru, 1710–1820.* New York: Macmillan, 1968.

Descola, Philippe. *The Spears of Twilight: Life and Death in the Amazon Jungle.* Translated by Janet Lloyd. New York: New Press, 1996.

Diccionario Porrúa: Historia, biografía y geografía de México. 3d ed., 2 vols. Mexico: Editorial Porrúa, 1971.

Dickason, Olive P. *The Myth of the Savage and the Beginnings of French Colonialism in the Americas.* Edmonton: University of Alberta Press, 1984.

Diderot, Denis. *Encyclopédie ou Dictionnaire raisonné des sciences, des arts et des métiers.* 17 vols., Paris: Briasson et al., 1751–1965.

Difrieri, Horacio. *Ensayo de geografía histórica.* Buenos Aires: Universidad del Salvador, 1980.

Dillehay, Tom D. *Araucanía: presente y pasado*. Santiago de Chile: Editorial Andrés Bello, 1990.

Din, Gilbert C., and Abraham P. Nasatir. *The Imperial Osages: Spanish–Indian Diplomacy in the Mississippi Valley*. Norman: University of Oklahoma Press, 1983.

Doblas, Gonzalo de. "Memoria histórica, geográfica, política y económica sobre la provincia de misiones de indios guaraníes [1785]." In *Colección de obras y documentos relativos a la historia antigua y moderna de las provincias del Río de la Plata por Pedro de Angelis*, edited by Andrés M. Carretero, 5:21–187. 1st ed., 1836; 8 vols. Buenos Aires: Plus Ultra, 1969–72.

Dobrizhoffer, Martin. *An Account of the Abipones, An Equestrian People of Paraguay*. Translated by Sara Coleridge. 1st ed., in Latin, 1783; 3 vols. London: John Murray, 1822.

Dobrizhoffer, Martín. *Historia de los Abipones*. Edited by Ernesto J. A. Maeder and Guillermo Furlong. 1st ed., in Latin, 1783; 3 vols. Resistencia, Argentina: Universidad Nacional del Nordeste, 1967–70.

Dobyns, Henry, et al. "What Were Nixoras?" *Southwestern Journal of Anthropology* 16 (1960): 230–58.

Dobyns, Henry F. *Spanish Colonial Tucson: A Demographic History*. Tucson: University of Arizona Press, 1976.

Donoso, Ricardo. *El marqués de Osorno don Ambrosio Higgins, 1720–1801*. Santiago de Chile: Universidad de Chile, 1941.

———. *Un letrado del siglo XVIII: El doctor José Perfecto de Salas*. 2 vols. Buenos Aires: Universidad de Buenos Aires, 1963.

Doucet, Gastón Gabriel. "Sobre cautivos de guerra y esclavos indios en el Tucumán: Notas en torno a un fichero documental salteño del siglo XVIII." *Revista de Historia del Derecho (Buenos Aires)* 16 (1988): 59–152.

Douthwaite, Julia V. *Exotic Women: Literary Heroines and Cultural Strategies in Ancien Régime France*. Philadelphia: University of Pennsylvania Press, 1992.

Dublán, Manuel, and José María Lozano, eds. *Legislación mexicana, o colección completa de las disposiciones legislativas expedidas desde la independencia de la República [1821–1912]*. 42 vols. Mexico: Imprenta del Comercio, 1876–1912.

Dueñas, Juan. "Carta y diario de Fr. Juan Dueñas misionero del Colegio de Ocopa que manifiesta el importantísimo camino de comunicación desde Manoa al pueblo de Cumbasa del Partido de Lamas." *Mercurio peruano de historia, literatura y noticias* 6, no. 194–96 (1792): 165–88.

Duggan, Marie Christine. "Market and Church on the Mexican Frontier." Ph.D. diss., New School for Social Research, 2000.

———. *The Chumash and the Presidio of Santa Barbara: Evolution of a Relationship, 1782–1823*. Santa Barbara: Santa Barbara Trust for Historic Preservation, 2004.

Dunaway, Wilma A. "Incorporation as an Interactive Process: Cherokee Resistance to Expansion of the Capitalist World-System, 1560–1763." *Sociological Inquiry* 66 (1996): 455–70.

Dussel, Enrique D. *Historia general de la iglesia en América Latina*. Vol. 1. Salamanca: Ediciones Sigueme, 1983.

DuVal, Kathleen. "The Education of Fernando de Leyba: Quapaws and Spaniards on the Border of Empires." *Arkansas Historical Quarterly* 60 (2001): 1–29.

Earle, Rebecca. "Creole Patriotism and the Myth of the 'Loyal Indian.'" *Past and Present* 172 (2001): 125–45.

———. "'Padres de la Patria' and the Ancestral Past: Commemorations of Independence in Nineteenth-Century Spanish America." *Journal of Latin American Studies* 34 (2002): 775–805.

Earle, Rebecca A. *Spain and the Independence of Colombia, 1810–1825*. Exeter: University of Exeter Press, 1999.

Ebersole, Gary L. *Captured by Texts: Puritan to Post-Modern Images of Indian Captivity*. Charlottesville: University of Virginia Press, 1995.

Ebright, Malcolm. "Breaking New Ground: A Reappraisal of Governors Vélez Cachupín and Mendinueta and Their Land Grant Policies." *Colonial Latin American Historical Review* 5 (1996): 195–233.

Ebright, Malcolm, Teresa Escudero, and Rick Hendricks. "Tomás Vélez Cachupín's Last Will and Testament, His Career in New Mexico, and His Sword with a Golden Hilt." *New Mexico Historical Review* 78 (2003): 284–321.

Echeverz, Fernando de. *Ensayos mercantiles para adelantar por medio de el establecimiento de vna Compañia de los fructos de el Reyno de Guathemala a beneficio de el publico, real haver, y diezmos ecclesiasticos.* . . . Guatemala: Sebastian de Arebalo, 1742.

Ellingson, Ter. *The Myth of the Noble Savage.* Berkeley: University of California Press, 2001.

Elliott, J. H. *The Old World and the New, 1492–1650.* Cambridge: Cambridge University Press, 1970.

———. *Britain and Spain in America: Colonists and Colonized.* Reading, England: University of Reading, 1994.

———. "The Old World and the New Revisted." In *America in European Consciousness, 1493–1750,* edited by Karen Ordahl Kupperman, 391–408. Chapel Hill: University of North Carolina Press, 1995.

Engelhardt, Zephyrin. *The Missions and Missionaries of California.* 4 vols. San Francisco: James H. Barry, 1908–15.

Engstrand, Iris H. W. *Spanish Scientists in the New World: The Eighteenth-Century Expeditions.* Seattle: University of Washington Press, 1981.

Ercilla y Zúñiga, Alonso de. *The Araucaniad: A Version in English Poetry of Alonso de Ercilla y Zúñiga's La Araucana.* Edited and translated by Charles Maxwell Lancaster and Paul Thomas Manchester. Nashville: Vanderbilt University Press, 1945.

Escandón, Patricia. "Los problemas de la administración franciscana en las misiones sonorenses, 1768–1800." In *Los franciscanos en el Nuevo Mundo (siglo XVIII),* 277–91. Madrid: Editorial Deimos, 1993.

———. *Historia general de Sonora.* Vol. 2, *De la conquista al estado libre y soberano de Sonora,* edited by Sergio Ortega Noriega, 249–74. 4 vols. 1st ed., 1985; 3d ed., Hermosillo, Mexico: Gobierno del Estado de Sonora, 1996.

Escobar Ohmstede, Antonio, and Teresa Rabiela Rojas, eds. *La presencia del indígena en la prensa capitalina del siglo XIX.* 4 vols. Mexico: INI and CIESAS, 1992–93.

Espiñeira, Pedro Angel de. "Relación del viaje y misión a los Pehuenches, 1758." In *Misioneros en la Araucanía, 1600–1900: Un capítulo de historia fronteriza en Chile,* edited by Jorge Pinto Rodríguez et al., 233–51. Temuco: Ediciones Universidad de la Frontera, 1988.

Espinosa y Tello, José. "Estudio sobre las costumbres y descripciones interesantes de la América del Sur." In *Viaje político-científico alrededor del mundo por las corbetas Descubierta y Atrevida al mando de los capitanes de navío D. Alejandro Malaspina y don José de Bustamante y Guerra, desde 1789–1794,* edited by Pedro Novo y Colson, 555–77. Madrid: Imprenta de la Viuda e Hijos de Abienzo, 1885.

Estala, Pedro de la, ed. *El viagero universal o noticia del mundo antiguo y nuevo.* 43 vols. Madrid: Imprenta Real, 1795–1801.

Esteva-Fabregat, Claudio. *Mestizaje in Ibero-America.* Translated by John Wheat. 1st ed., 1988; Tucson: University of Arizona Press, 1995.

Ethridge, Robbie, and Charles Hudson, eds. *The Transformation of the Southeastern Indians, 1540–1760.* Jackson: University Press of Mississippi, 2002.

Everett, Dianna. *The Texas Cherokees: A People Between Two Fires, 1819–1840.* Norman: University of Oklahoma Press, 1990.

Ewers, John C. "Symbols of Chiefly Authority in Spanish Louisiana." In *The Spanish in the Mississippi Valley, 1762–1804,* edited by John Francis McDermott, 272–86. Urbana: University of Illinois Press, 1974.

————. *Plains Indian History and Culture: Essays on Continuity and Change*. Norman: University of Oklahoma Press, 1997.

Eyzaguirre, Jaime. "Los libros y las nuevas ideas en Chile en el siglo XVIII." In *Miscelánea Vicente Lecuna, Homenaje Continental*, 144–55. Caracas: Fundación Vicente Lecuna, 1959.

————. *La Logia Lautarina y otros estudios sobre la independencia*. Buenos Aires: Editorial Francisco de Aguirre, 1973.

————. *Breve historia de las fronteras de Chile*. 1st ed., 1967; Santiago de Chile: Editorial Universitaria, 1997.

Ezpeleta, José de. "Relación del estado del Nuevo Reino de Granada que hace el Excmo. Sr. D. José de Ezpeleta á su sucesor el Excmo. Sr. D. Pedro Mendinueta, 1796." In *Relaciones de mando: Memorias presentadas por los gobernantes del Nuevo Reino de Granada*, edited by Eduardo Posada and Pedro María Ibáñez, 1:277–410. 2 vols. Bogotá: Biblioteca de Historia Nacional, 1910.

Ezquerra, Ramón. "La crítica española sobre América en el siglo XVIII." *Revista de Indias* 22 (1962): 159–283.

Fairchild, Hoxie Neale. *The Noble Savage: A Study in Romantic Naturalism*. New York: Columbia University Press, 1928.

Falkner, Thomas. *A Description of Patagonia and the Adjoining Parts of South America*. Edited by Arthur E. S. Neumann. 1st ed., 1774; facsimile, Chicago: Armann and Armann, 1935.

Falkner, Tomás. *Descripción de la Patagonia y de las partes contiguas de la América del Sur*. Edited by Raúl José Mandrini. Buenos Aires: Taurus, 2003.

Fals Borda, Orlando. *Historia doble de la costa*. Vol. 1, *Mompox y Loba*. Bogotá: Carlos Valencia Editores, 1979.

————. *Historia doble de la costa*. Vol. 4, *Retorno a la Tierra*. Bogotá: Carlos Valencia Editores, 1986.

Farriss, Nancy. *Crown and Clergy in Colonial Mexico, 1759–1821*. London: Athlone Press, University of London, 1968.

Farriss, Nancy M. *Maya Society Under Colonial Rule: The Collective Enterprise of Survival*. Princeton: Princeton University Press, 1984.

Faulk, Odie, ed. and trans. "Spanish-Comanche Relations and the Treaty of 1785." *Texana* 2 (1964): 44–53.

Faulk, Odie B. "The Presidio: Fortress or Farce?" In *New Spain's Far Northern Frontier: Essays on Spain in the American West*, edited by David J. Weber, 67–78. Albuquerque: University of New Mexico Press, 1979.

Fenn, Elizabeth A. "Biological Warfare in Eighteenth-Century North America: Beyond Jeffery Amherst." *Journal of American History* 86 (2000): 1552–80.

Fenn, Elizabeth Anne. *Pox Americana: The Great Smallpox Epidemic of 1775–82*. New York: Hill and Wang, 2001.

Ferguson, R. Brian. "A Reexamination of the Causes of Northwest Coast Warfare." In *Warfare, Culture, and Environment*, edited by R. Brian Ferguson, 267–328. Orlando: Academic Press, 1984.

————. "Explaining War." In *Anthropology of War*, edited by Jonathan Haas, 26–55. Cambridge: Cambridge University Press, 1990a.

————. "Blood of the Leviathan: Western Contact and Warfare in Amazonia." *American Ethnologist* 17 (1990b): 237–57.

————. *Yanomami Warfare: A Political History*. Santa Fe: School of American Research, 1995.

Ferguson, R. Brian, and Neil L. Whitehead. "The Violent Edge of Empire." In *War in the Tribal Zone: Expanding States and Indigenous Warfare*, edited by R. Brian Ferguson and Neil L. Whitehead, 1–30. Santa Fe: School of American Research, 1992a.

————, ed. *War in the Tribal Zone: Expanding States and Indigenous Warfare*. Santa Fe: School of American Research, 1992b.

Fernández C., Jorge. *Historia de los indios ranqueles: Orígenes, elevación y caída del cacicazgo ranquelino en la pampa central, siglos XVIII y XIX.* Buenos Aires: Instituto Nacional de Antropología y Pensamiento Latinoamericano, 1998.

Fernández, César A., ed. *Cuentan los Mapuches.* Buenos Aires: Ediciones Nuevo Siglo, 1995.

Fernández Guardia, Ricardo, ed. *Colección de documentos para la historia de Costa Rica recogidos por el Lic. D. León Fernández.* 10 vols. San José, Costa Rica: Archivo Nacional, 1881–1907.

Fernández, Juan Patricio. *Relación historial de las misiones del indios Chiquitos . . . [1726].* Edited by Daniel J. Santamaría. Jujuy, Argentina: Centro de Estudios Indígenas y Coloniales, Universidad Nacional de Jujuy, 1994.

Figueroa, Tomás de. "Diario puntual y manifiesto de las novedades ocurridas en la persecución de los indios rebeldes de la jurisdiccion de la plaza de Valdivia . . . 1792." In Benjamin Vicuña Mackenna, *El coronel don Tomás de Figueroa: Estudio crítico según documentos inéditos,* 16–77. Santiago de Chile: R. Jover, 1884.

Finegan, Caleb. "The East Florida Papers: Lists of Gifts to Indians, 1785–1788." Research paper, Vanderbilt University (paper in my possession courtesy of Jane Landers and the author), 1993.

Fireman, Janet R. *The Spanish Royal Corps of Engineers in the Western Borderlands, 1764 to 1815: Instrument of Bourbon Reform.* Glendale: Arthur H. Clark, 1977.

Fisher, Lillian Estelle. *The Intendant System in Spanish America.* Berkeley: University of California, 1929.

Fitzgerald, Frances. *America Revised: History Schoolbooks in the Twentieth Century.* New York: Vintage, 1980.

Fixico, Donald L., ed. *Rethinking American Indian History.* Albuquerque: University of New Mexico Press, 1997.

———. "Ethics and Responsibilities in Writing American Indian History." In *Natives and Academics: Researching and Writing about American Indians,* edited by Devon Mihesuah, 84–99. Lincoln: University of Nebraska Press, 1998.

Flagler, Edward K. "Relaciones interétnicas: Los españoles y los indios de Nuevo México durante la época colonial." In *Culturas hispanas en los Estados Unidos de América,* 39–56. Madrid: Ediciones de Cultura Hispánica, 1990.

———. *Defensores de la madre tierra: Relaciones interétnicas: Los españoles y los indios de Nuevo México.* Palma de Mallorca: Hesperus, 1997.

Fleming, E. McClung. "From Indian Princess to Greek Goddess: The American Image, 1783–1815." *Winterthur Portfolio,* no. 3 (1967): 37–66.

Fletcher, Richard. *The Barbarian Conversion from Paganism to Christianity.* New York: Henry Holt, 1998.

Florescano, Enrique, and Isabel Gil Sánchez, eds. *Descripciones económicas regionales de Nueva España. Provincias del Norte, 1790–1814.* Mexico: Instituto Nacional de Antropología e Historia, 1976.

Floridablanca, José Moñino y Redondo conde de. "Instrucción reservada que la junta de estado, creada formalmente por mi decreto de este día, 8 de julio de 1787, deberá observar en todos los puntos y ramos encargados á su conocimiento y exámen." In *Obras originales del Conde de Floridablanca,* edited by Antonio Ferrer del Río, 213–72. Madrid: M. Rivadeneyra, 1867.

Floyd, Troy S. *The Anglo-Spanish Struggle for Mosquitia.* Albuquerque: University of New Mexico Press, 1967.

Foerster G., Rolf. "Guerra y aculturación en la araucanía." In *Misticismo y violencia en la temprana evangelización de Chile,* edited by Jorge Pinto, Maximiliano Salinas, and Rolf Foerster, 169–212. Temuco, Chile: Ediciones Universidad de la Frontera, 1991.

———. *Historia de la evangelización de los mapuche.* Santiago de Chile: Instituto Nacional de Pastoral Rural, 1992.

———. *Jesuitas y Mapuches, 1593–1767.* Santiago de Chile: Editorial Universitaria, 1996.

Foerster G., Rolf, and Jorge Iván Vergara. "¿Relaciones interétnicas o relaciones fronterizas?" *Revista de Historia Indígena,* no. 1 (1996): 9–33.

Forbes, Jack D. "The Appearance of the Mounted Indian in Northern Mexico and the Southwest to 1680." *Southwestern Journal of Anthropology* 15 (1959): 189–212.

———. *Warriors of the Colorado: The Yumas of the Quechan Nation and Their Neighbors.* Norman: University of Oklahoma Press, 1965.

———. *Apache, Navaho, and Spaniard.* 1st ed., 1960; Norman: University of Oklahoma Press, 1994.

Fowler, Loretta. "The Great Plains from the Arrival of the Horse to 1885." In *Cambridge History of the Native Peoples of the Americas.* Vol. 1, *North America,* edited by Bruce G. Trigger and Wilcomb E. Washburn, pt. 2, 1–57. 2 parts. Cambridge: Cambridge University Press, 1996.

Frank, Ross. *From Settler to Citizen: New Mexican Economic Development and the Creation of a Vecino Society, 1750–1820.* Berkeley: University of California Press, 2000.

Frézier, Amedée. *A Voyage to the South-Sea and Along the Coasts of Chili and Peru, in the Years 1712, 1713, and 1714.* London: Jonah Bowyer, 1717.

Fried, Morton H. *The Notion of Tribe.* Menlo Park: Cummings, 1975.

Friedman, Ellen G. *Spanish Captives in North Africa in the Early Modern Age.* Madison: University of Wisconsin Press, 1983.

Frye, David. "The Native Peoples of Northeastern Mexico." In *Cambridge History of the Native Peoples of the Americas.* Vol. 2, *Mesoamerica,* Part 2, edited by Richard E. W. Adams and Murdo J. MacLeod, pt. 2, 89–135. 2 parts. Cambridge: Cambridge University Press, 2000.

Funes, Gregorio. *Ensayo de la historia civil de Buenos Aires, Tucuman y Paraguay.* Buenos Aires: 2d ed., 2 vols. Imprenta Bonaerense, 1856.

Furlong Cardiff, Guillermo, et al., eds. *Historia y bibliografía de las primeras imprentas rioplatenses, 1700–1850.* 4 vols. Buenos Aires: various, 1953–59.

Furlong, Guillermo. *Entre los pampas de Buenos Aires, según noticias de los misioneros jesuítas Matías Strobel, José Cardiel, Tomás Falkner, Jerónimo Rejón, Joaquín Camaño, Manuel Querini, Manuel García, Pedro Lozano y José Sánchez Labrador.* Buenos Aires: Talleres Gráficos San Pablo, 1938.

———. *Naturalistas argentinos durante la dominación hispánica.* Cultura Colonial Argentina, 7. Buenos Aires: Editorial "Huarpes," 1948.

———, ed. *Juan Camaño S.J. y su "Noticia de Gran Chaco" (1778).* Buenos Aires: Librería del Plata, 1955.

———. *Entre los Tehuelches de la Patagonia: Según noticias de los misioneros e historiadores jesuitas . . .* 1st ed., 1943; Buenos Aires: Ediciones Theoría, 1992.

Galbraith, Edith C. "Malaspina's Voyage Around the World." *California Historical Society Quarterly* 3 (1924): 215–37.

Galera Gómez, Andrés. *La ilustración española y el conocimiento del Nuevo Mundo: Las ciencias naturales en la expedición Malaspina (1789–1794): La labor científica de Antonio Pineda.* Madrid: Consejo Superior de Investigaciones Científicas, 1988.

Gallardo Porras, Viviana. "Héroes indómitos, bárbaros y ciudadanos chilenos: El discurso sobre el indio en la construcción de la identidad nacional." *Revista de Historia Indígena,* no. 5 (2001): 119–34.

Galloway, Patricia. "'The Chief Who Is Your Father': Choctaw and French Views of the Diplomatic Relation." In *Powhatan's Mantle: Indians in the Colonial Southeast,* edited by Peter H. Wood, Gregory A. Waselkov, and M. Thomas Hatley, 254–78. Lincoln: University of Nebraska Press, 1989.

———. *Choctaw Genesis, 1500–1700.* Lincoln: University of Nebraska Press, 1995.

Gallup-Díaz, Ignacio. "The Spanish Attempt to Tribalize the Darién, 1735–50." *Ethnohistory* 49 (2002): 281–317.

Gálvez, Bernardo de. "Noticias y reflexiones sobre la guerra que se tiene con los Apaches en la provincia de Nueva España." Edited by Felipe Teixidor. *Anales del Museo Nacional de Arqueología, Historia, y Etnografía* 3 (1925): 537–55.

———. *Instructions for Governing the Interior Provinces of New Spain, 1786.* Edited and translated by Donald E. Worcester. Berkeley: Quivira Society, 1951.

Gálvez, José de. "Instrucciones dadas en el año de 1784 al marqués de Loreto para el gobierno del virreinato de Buenos Aires." *Revista del Río de la Plata* 5 (1873): 556–95.

Gammalsson, Hialmar Edmundo. *El virrey Cevallos.* Buenos Aires: Editorial Plus Ultra, 1976.

Ganson, Barbara. *The Guaraní under Spanish Rule in the Río de la Plata.* Stanford: Stanford University Press, 2003.

Ganuza, Marcelino. *Monografía de las misiones vivas de Augustinos Recoletos (Candelarios) en Colombia.* 3 vols. Bogotá: Imprenta de San Bernardo, 1921.

Garate, Donald T., ed. "Captain Juan Bautista de Anza: Correspondence on Various Subjects, 1775." *Antepasados* 8 (1995): 1–328.

Garavaglia, Juan Carlos. "La guerra en el Tucumán colonial: Sociedad y economía en un área de frontera (1660–1760)." *HISLA* 4 (1984): 21–34.

———. "Campesinos y soldados: Dos siglos en la historia rural del Paraguay." In *Economía, sociedad y regiones,* 193–260. Buenos Aires: Editorial de la Flor, 1987.

———. "De la carne al cuero: Los mercados para los productos pecuarios (Buenos Aires y su Campaña, 1700–1825)." *Anuario del IEHS* 9 (1994): 61–96.

García Añoveras, Jesús María. "América Central: La evangelización." In *Historia de la Iglesia en Hispanoamérica y Filipinas,* edited by Pedro Borges, 2:241–58. 2 vols. Madrid: Biblioteca de Autores Cristianos, 1992.

García Belsunce, César A. "Los clérigos como agentes de la administración en el derecho indiano y patrio." In *Una Ventana al Pasado,* 17–42. Rosario: Instituto de Historia Política Argentina, 1994.

García Bernal, Manuela Cristina. "Política indigenista del reformismo de Carlos III y Carlos IV." *Temas Americanistas* 13 (1997): 8–16.

García, Claudia. "Interacción étnica y diplomacia de fronteras en el reino miskitu a fines del siglo XVIII." *Anuario de Estudios Americanos* 56 (1999): 95–121.

———. "Hibridación, interacción social y adaptación cultural en la Costa de Mosquitos, siglos XVII y XVIII." *Anuario de Estudios Americanos* 59 (2002): 441–62.

García Gavidia, Nelly. "Los indígenas venezolanos: De su demonización en la 'Historia de la nueva Andalucía' (1779) a la persecución actual por la ideología del progreso." In *Visión de los otros y visión de sí mismos,* edited by Fermín del Pino Díaz and Carlos Lázaro Ávila, 205–32. Madrid: Consejo Superior de Investigaciones Científicas, 1995.

García Godoy, María Teresa. *Las Cortes de Cádiz y América: El primer vocabulario liberal español y mejicano (1810–1814).* Seville: Diputación de Sevilla, 1998.

García-Mariño Mundi, Margarita. "Los jenízaros y el comercio indiano (1700–1750)." *Temas Americanistas* 6 (1986): 21–28.

García, Pedro Andrés. "Diario de un viaje a Salinas Grandes en los campos del sud de Buenos Aires [1810]." In *Colección de obras y documentos relativos a la historia antigua y moderna de las provincias del Río de la Plata por Pedro de Angelis,* edited by Andrés M. Carretero, 4:295–391. 1st ed., 1836; 8 vols. Buenos Aires: Editorial Plus Ultra, 1969a–72a.

———. "Memoria [to the junta superior gubernativa de Buenos Aires, Nov. 26, 1811]." In *Colección de obras y documentos relativos a la historia antigua y moderna de las provincias del Río de la Plata por Pedro de Angelis,* edited by Andrés M. Carretero, 4:261–92. 1st ed., 1836; 8 vols. Buenos Aires: Editorial Plus Ultra, 1969b–72b.

García Peláez, Francisco de Paula. *Memorias para la Historia del Antiguo Reino de Guatemala*. 2d ed.; 3 vols. Guatemala: Tipografía Nacional, 1943–44.

García Pérez, Rafael D. *El Consejo de Indias durante los reinados de Carlos III y Carlos IV*. Pamplona: EUNSA, 1998.

Gardoqui, Diego de. "S.M. concede fondos para agasajos y regalos de indios de la frontera de Cuyo y Córdoba." *Revista de la Junta de Estudios Históricos de Mendoza* 7 (1930): 355–56.

Garrido, Margarita. *Reclamos y respresentaciones: variaciones sobre la política en el Nuevo Reino de Granada, 1770–1815*. Bogotá: Banco de la República, 1993.

Gascón, Margarita. "'Los indios de chile se mueren de risa': El enemigo del siglo XVII según fuentes." Paper presented at the 51st Congreso internacional de americanistas, Santiago de Chile. 2003.

Gay, Claudio, ed. *Atlas de la Historia física y política de Chile*. Paris: E. Thunot, 1854.

————, ed. *Historia física y política de Chile . . . Documentos sobre la historia, la estadística y la geografía*. 2 vols. Paris: Imprenta de E. Thunot, 1846–52.

Gay, Peter. *The Enlightenment: An Interpretation*, 2 vols. New York: Knopf, 1966–1969.

Geary, Gerald J. *The Secularization of the California Missions (1810–1846)*. Washington: Catholic University of America, 1934.

Geiger, Maynard J. *The Life and Times of Fray Junípero Serra, O.F.M.* 2 vols. Washington: Academy of American Franciscan History, 1959.

Gelman, Jorge. "Sobre esclavos, peones, gauchos y campesinos: El trabajo y los trabajadores en una estancia colonial rioplatense." *Estructuras sociales y mentalidades en América Latina: Siglos XVII y XVIII*, 241–79. Buenos Aires: Fundación Simón Rodríguez/Editorial Biblos, 1990.

————. *Un funcionario en busca del estado: Pedro Andrés García y la cuestión agraria bonaerense, 1810–1820*. Quilmes, Argentina: Universidad Nacional de Quilmes, 1998.

————. "El fracaso de los sistemas coactivos de trabajo rural en Buenos Aires bajo el rosísmo, algunas explicaciones preliminares." *Revista de Indias* 59 (1999): 123–41.

Gelman, Jorge, and Daniel Santilli. "Una medición de la economía rural de Buenos Aires en la época de Rosas: Expansión ganadera y diferencias regionales." *Revista de Historia Económica* 20 (2002): 81–107.

Gerbi, Antonello. *The Dispute of the New World: The History of a Polemic, 1750–1900*. Pittsburgh: Pittsburgh University Press, 1973.

Gibson, Charles. *The Aztecs under Spanish Rule: A History of the Indians of the Valley of Mexico, 1519–1810*. Stanford: Stanford University Press, 1964.

————. *The Black Legend: Anti-Spanish Attitudes in the Old World and the New*. New York: Alfred A. Knopf, 1971.

————. "Conquest, Capitulation, and Indian Treaties." *American Historical Review* 83 (1978): 1–15.

Gil de Barraquero, María del Carmen. "La política de fronteras en la primera década del siglo XIX." In *La frontera interna de Mendoza* 1:67–88. 2 vols. Mendoza, Argentina: Gobierno de Mendoza, Archivo Histórico, 1980.

Gil y Lemos, Francisco. "Acuerdo de no agresión firmado entre los dirigentes cunas y las autoridades españolas . . . firmada el 25 de Oct. de 1789." *Hombre y Cultura* 3, no. 2 (1977): 155–62.

Gillespie, Alexander. *Gleanings and Remarks: Collected during Many Months of Residence at Buenos Aires and within the Upper Country*. Leeds: P. Dewhirst, 1818.

Girbal y Barceló, Narciso. "Noticia de los trages, supersticiones, y exercicios de los indios de la Pampa del Sacramento, y Montañas de los Andes del Perú." *Mercurio Peruano de Historia, Literatura y Noticias* 3, no. 78, 79 (1791): 73–90.

Girvetz, Harry K. *From Wealth to Welfare: The Evolution of Liberalism*. Stanford: Stanford University Press, 1950.

Godelier, Maurice. *The Enigma of the Gift.* Translated by Nora Scott. 1st ed., 1996; Chicago: University of Chicago Press, 1999.

Gómez Canedo, Lino. "Fray Rafael Verger en San Fernando de México, 1750–1782." *Humanitas [Universidad de Nuevo León]* 3 (1962): 551–75.

———. *Las misiones de Píritu: Documentos para su historia.* Biblioteca de la Academia Nacional de la Historia. Fuentes para la historia colonial de Venezuela, 83–84. 2 vols. Caracas: Academia Nacional de la Historia, 1967.

———, ed. *Sonora hacia fines del siglo XVIII: Un informe del misionero franciscano Fray Francisco Antonio Barbastro, con otros documentos complementarios.* Documentación Historica Mexicana, 3. Guadalajara, Mexico: Librería Font, 1971.

———. *La provincia franciscana de Santa Cruz de Caracas.* Biblioteca de la Academia Nacional de la Historia. Fuentes para la historia colonial de Venezuela, 121–23. 3 vols. Caracas: Academia Nacional de la Historia, 1974–1975.

———. *Sierra Gorda: Un típico enclave misional en el centro de México, siglos XVII–XVIII.* Pachuca, Mexico: Centro Hidalguense de Investigaciones Históricas, 1976.

———. "Franciscans in the Americas: A Comprehensive View." In *Franciscan Presence in the Americas: Essays on the Activities of the Franciscan Friars in the Americas, 1492–1900,* edited by Francisco Morales, 5–45. Potomac, Md.: Academy of American Franciscan History, 1983.

———. *Evangelización y conquista: Experiencia franciscana en hispanoamérica.* 1st ed., 1977; Mexico: Editorial Porrúa, 1988.

———. *Evangelización, cultura y promoción social: ensayos y estudios críticos sobre la contribución franciscana a los orígenes cristianos de México, siglos XVI–XVIII.* Edited by José Luis Soto Pérez. Mexico: Editorial Porrúa, 1993.

Gómez del Campillo, Miguel. *Relaciones diplomáticos entre España y los Estados Unidos según los documentos del Archivo Histórico Nacional.* 2 vols. Madrid: Consejo Superior de Investigaciones Científicas, 1944–1945.

Gómez Parente, Odilo. "Promoción indígena: Labor franciscana en Venezuela." *Montalban* 8 (1978): 473–974.

Gómez Pérez, María del Carmen. *El sistema defensivo americano: Siglo XVIII.* Madrid: MAPFRE, 1992.

Gómez, Thomás. "La evolución del mundo indígena en Nueva Granada y sus relaciones ane un aspecto del reformismo borbónico." In *La América española en la época de las Luces: Tradición, innovación, representaciones,* 251–65. Madrid: Ediciones de Cultura Hispánica, 1988.

Góngora, Mario. *Vagabundaje y sociedad fronteriza en Chile (siglos XVII a XIX).* Cuadernos del Centro de Estudios Socio-económicos. Santiago de Chile: Universidad de Chile, 1966.

———. "Aspectos de la 'ilustración Católica' en el pensamiento y la vida eclesiástica chilena, 1770–1814." *Historia* [Universidad Católica de Chile] 8 (1969): 43–73.

———. *Studies in the Colonial History of Spanish America.* Cambridge: Cambridge University Press, 1975.

González de Agüeros, Pedro. *Descripción historial de Chiloé (1791): Reedición facsimilar con un apéndice documental.* Edited by Isidoro Vázquez de Acuña. Santiago de Chile: Instituto de Investigaciones del Patrimonio Territorial de Chile, Universidad de Santiago, 1988.

González de la Vara, Martín. "La visita eclesiástica de Francisco Atanasio Domínguez al Nuevo México, 1776, y su relación." *Estudios de Historia Novohispana* 10 (1991): 267–88.

———. "¿Amigos, enemigos o socios?" *Relaciones: Estudios de Historia y Sociedad* 23 (2002): 107–34.

González del Campo, María Isabel. *Guayana y el gobernador Centurión (1766–1776).* Biblioteca de la Academia Nacional de la Historia. Fuentes para la historia colonial de Venezuela, 170. Caracas: Academia Nacional de la Historia, 1984.

González González, Alfonso F. *El oriente venezolano a mediados del siglo XVIII a través de la visita del gobernador Diguja.* Biblioteca de la Academia Nacional de la Historia. Fuentes para la historia colonial de Venezuela, 129. Caracas: Academia Nacional de la Historia, 1977.

González Luna, María Dolores. "La política de población y pacificación indígena en las poblaciones de Santa Marta y Cartagena, 1750–1800." *Boletín Americanista* 20 (1978): 87–118.

González, Michael J. "'The Child of the Wilderness Weeps for the Father of Our Country': The Indian and the Politics of Church and State in Provincial California." In *Contested Eden: California Before the Gold Rush,* edited by Ramón A. Gutiérrez and Richard J. Orsi, 147–72. Berkeley: University of California Press, 1998.

González Montero de Espinosa, María Luisa. *La ilustración y el hombre americano.* Madrid: Consejo Superior de Investigaciones Científicas, 1992.

González Navarro, Moisés. "Instituciones indígenas en el México independiente." In *La política indigenista en México,* edited by Alfonso Caso et al., 1:207–313. 1st ed., 1954; 1st new edition, 2 vols. Mexico: Instituto Nacional Indigenista, 1991.

González Oropeza, Hermann. *Atlas de la Historia Cartográfica de Venezuela.* 2d ed. Caracas: Enzo Papi Editor, 1987.

González Oropeza, Hermann, and Manuel Donis Ríos. *Historia de las fronteras de Venezuela.* Caracas: LAGOVEN, 1989.

González Pomes, María Isabel. "La encomienda indígena en Chile durante el siglo XVIII." *Historia* [Universidad Católica de Chile] 5 (1966): 7–97.

González Rissotto, Luis Rodolfo, and Susana T. Rodríguez Varese. "Las reducciones franciscanas y jesuíticas en la banda oriental del Uruguay." *Suplemento antropológico* [Asunción, Paraguay] 26 (1991): 229–51.

González Rodríguez, Jaime. "El sistema de reducciones." In *Historia de la Iglesia en Hispanoamérica y Filipinas,* edited by Pedro Borges, 1:535–48. 2 vols. Madrid: Biblioteca de Autores Cristianos, 1992a.

———. "La iglesia y la ilustración." In *Historia de la Iglesia en Hispanoamérica y Filipinas,* edited by Pedro Borges, 1:799–813. 2 vols. Madrid: Biblioteca de Autores Cristianos, 1992b.

González Salas, Carlos. *La evangelización en Tamaulipas: Las misiones novohispanas en la costa del Seno Mexicano, 1530–1831.* [Victoria, Mexico]: Universidad Autónoma de Tamaulipas, Instituto de Investigaciones Históricas, 1998.

Gorla, Carlos María. *Los establecimientos españoles en la Patagonia: Estudio institucional.* Seville: Escuela de Estudios Hispano-Americanos de Sevilla, 1984.

Gradie, Charlotte M. "Discovering the Chichimecas." *The Americas* 51 (1994): 67–88.

Grafton, Anthony. *New Worlds, Ancient Texts: The Power of Tradition and the Shock of Discovery.* Cambridge: Harvard University Press, 1992.

Grahn, Lance R. "Guajiro Culture and Capuchin Evangelization: Missionary Failure on the Riohacha Frontier." In *The New Latin American Mission History,* edited by Erick Langer and Robert Jackson, 130–56. Lincoln: University of Nebraska Press, 1995.

———. "Cuna–British Alliances and Caribbean Imperial Rivalries, 1680–1800." Paper presented at the Neale/Commonwealth Fund Conference, London. 1997.

———. "Chicha in the Chalice: The Cosmology of Missionary Failure in New Granada." In *Spiritual Encounters: Interactions between Christianity and Native Religions in Colonial America,* edited by Nicholas Griffiths and Fernando Cervantes, 255–75. Lincoln: University of Nebraska Press, 1998.

Gray, Edward G. *New World Babel: Languages and Nations in Early America.* Princeton: Princeton University Press, 1999.

Greene, Jack P. "Negotiated Authorities: The Problem of Governance in the Extended Polities of the Early Modern Atlantic World." In *Negotiated Authorities: Essays in Colonial Political and Constitutional History,* 1–24. Charlottesville: University of Virginia Press, 1994.

Griffen, William B. *Culture Change and Shifting Populations in Central Northern Mexico.* Tucson: University of Arizona Press, 1969.

———. *Apaches at War and Peace: The Janos Presidio, 1750–1858.* Albuquerque: University of New Mexico Press, 1988.

Griffiths, Nicholas, and Fernando Cervantes, eds. *Spiritual Encounters: Interactions between Christianity and Native Religions in Colonial America.* Lincoln: University of Nebraska Press, 1998.

Gruzinski, Serge. "La 'segunda aculturación': El estado ilustrado y la religiosidad indígena en Nueva España, 1775–1800." *Estudios de Historia Novohispana* 8 (1985): 175–201.

Guarda, Gabriel. "Los caciques gobernadores de Toltén." *Boletín de la Academia Chilena de la Historia* 78 (1968): 43–69.

———. "El servicio de las ciudades de Valdivia y Osorno, 1770–1820." *Historia* [Universidad Católica de Chile] 15 (1980): 67–178.

———. *"Flandes Indiano": Las fortificaciones en el reino de Chile, 1541–1826.* Santiago de Chile: Ediciones Universidad Católica de Chile, 1990.

———. *Nueva Historia de Valdivia.* Santiago de Chile: Universidad Católica de Chile, 2001.

Guarda Geywitz, Gabriel. "Los cautivos en la guerra de Arauco." *Boletín de la Academia Chilena de la Historia* 98 (1987): 93–157.

Guardino, Peter. "Barbarism or Republican Law? Guerrero's Peasants and National Politics, 1820–1846." *Hispanic American Historical Review* 75, no. 2 (1995): 185–213.

Guerra Moscoso, Sabrina. "La secularización de doctrinas en la audiencia de Quito y la participación indígena, siglo XVIII: Alangasí y Guano." *Historia Social y Económica de América* 13 (1996): 87–107.

Guest, Francis F. "New Look at the California's Missions [*sic*]." In *Some Reminiscences about Fray Junípero Serra,* edited by Francis J. Weber, 77–87. Santa Barbara: Knights of Columbus, 1985.

———. "Pedro Fages' Five Complaints Against Junípero Serra." *The Californians* 8 (1990): 39–41, 44–48.

———. *Hispanic California Revisited: Essays by Francis F. Guest, O.F.M.* Edited by Doyce B. Nunis Jr. Santa Barbara: Santa Barbara Mission Archive Library, 1996.

Guevara, Tomás. *Los araucanos en la revolución de la independencia.* Santiago de Chile: Imprenta de Cervantes, 1910.

Guirao de Vierna, Angel. "Notas para una comparación entre las expediciones a la Patagonia y a las del Noroeste americano." In *Culturas de la Costa Noroeste de América,* edited by José Luis Peset, 265–76. Madrid: Turner Libros, 1989.

Gullón Abao, Alberto José. *La frontera del Chaco en la gobernación del Tucumán (1750–1810).* Cádiz: Universidad de Cádiz, 1993.

Gunckel L., Hugo. "Fray Francisco Inalican, fraile franciscano mapuche." *Revista Chilena de Historia y Geografía,* no. 129 (1961): 140–57.

Gunnerson, Dolores A. *The Jicarilla Apaches: A Study in Survival.* DeKalb: Northern Illinois University Press, 1974.

Gutiérrez de la Concha, Juan. "Extracto de los sucesos acaecidos en el reconocimiento de la Costa NO [noroeste] de América en 1781 ..., Acapulco, Oct. 17, 1791." In *La expedición Malaspina, 1789–1794.* Vol. 5, *Antropología y noticias etnográficas,* edited by Dolores Higueras Rodríguez and Juan Pimentel Igea, 153–68. Madrid: Ministerio de Defensa, Museo Naval, and Lunwerg Editores, 1993.

Gutiérrez, Ramón A. *When Jesus Came, the Corn Mothers Went Away: Marriage, Sexuality, and Power in New Mexico, 1500–1846.* Stanford: Stanford University Press, 1991.

Guy, Donna J., and Thomas E. Sheridan. "On Frontiers: The Northern and Southern Edges of the Spanish Empire in the Americas." In *Contested Ground: Comparative Frontiers on the Northern and Southern Edges of the Spanish Empire,* edited by Donna J. Guy and Thomas E. Sheridan, 3–15. Tucson: University of Arizona Press, 1998.

Haas, Jonathan, and Winifred Creamer. "Warfare among the Pueblos: Myth, History, and Ethnography." *Ethnohistory* 44 (1997): 235–61.

Haas, Jonathan. "Warfare and the Evolution of Tribal Polities in the Prehistoric Southwest." In *Anthropology of War,* edited by Jonathan Haas, 171–89. Cambridge: Cambridge University Press, 1990.

Habig, Marion A., ed. *The San José Papers: The Primary Sources for the History of Mission San José y San Miguel de Aguayo from its Founding in 1720 to the Present. Part 1, 1719–1791; Part II, Aug. 1791– June 1809.* Translated by Benedict Leutenegger et al. 3 vols. San Antonio: Old Spanish Missions Historical Research Library at San José Mission, 1978–90.

Hackel, Steven W. "Land, Labor, and Production: The Colonial Economy of Spanish and Mexican California." In *Contested Eden: California Before the Gold Rush,* edited by Ramón A. Gutiérrez and Richard J. Orsi, 111–46. Berkeley: University of California Press, 1998.

———. "Sources of Rebellion: Indian Testimony and the Mission San Gabriel Uprising of 1785." *Ethnohistory* 50 (2003): 643–69.

Hackett, Charles Wilson, ed. *Historical Documents Relating to New Mexico, Nueva Vizcaya, and Approaches Thereto, to 1773.* 3 vols. Washington: Carnegie Institution, 1923–37.

Hadley, Diana, Thomas H. Naylor, and Mardith K. Schuetz-Miller, eds. *The Presidio and Militia on the Northern Frontier of New Spain: A Documentary History.* Vol. 2, Part 2, *The Central Corridor and the Texas Corridor, 1700–1765.* Tucson: University of Arizona Press, 1997.

Haedo, Felipe de. "Descripción de la Colonia del Sacramento y puertos del Río de la Plata al norte y sud de Buenos Aires, seguida de un plan para la conquista y población del Cabo de Hornos y sus pampas [Dec. 7, 1777]." *Revista del Río de la Plata* 3 (1872): 436–66.

Haenke, Thaddaeus Peregrinus [José de Espinosa y Tello]. *Descripción del Reyno de Chile.* Edited by Agustín Edwards. Santiago de Chile: Editorial Nascimento, 1942.

Hafen, LeRoy, and Ann W. Hafen. *Old Spanish Trail: Santa Fé to Los Angeles.* Glendale: Arthur H. Clark, 1954.

Hall, Emlen G., and David J. Weber. "Mexican Liberals and the Pueblo Indians, 1821–1829." *New Mexico Historical Review* 59 (1984): 5–32.

Hall, Thomas D. *Social Change in the Southwest, 1350–1880.* Lawrence: University Press of Kansas, 1989.

———. "Civilizational Change: The Role of Nomads." *Comparative Civilization Review* 24 (1991): 34–57.

———. "The Río de la Plata and the Greater Southwest: A View from World System Theory." In *Contested Ground: Comparative Frontiers on the Northern and Southern Edges of the Spanish Empire,* edited by Donna J. Guy and Thomas E. Sheridan, 150–66. Tucson: University of Arizona Press, 1998.

Hallowell, A. Irving. "American Indians, White and Black: The Phenomenon of Transculturalization." *Current Anthropology* 4 (1963): 519–31.

Halperín-Donghi, Tulio. *Politics, Economics and Society in Argentina in the Revolutionary Period.* Translated by Richard Southern. Cambridge: Cambridge University Press, 1975.

Hämäläinen, Pekka. "The Western Comanche Trade Center: Rethinking the Plains Indian Trade System." *Western Historical Quarterly* 29 (1998): 485–513.

———. "The Comanche Empire: A Study of Indigenous Power, 1700–1875." Ph.D. diss., University of Helsinki, 2001.

————. "The Rise and Fall of Plains Indian Horse Cultures." *Journal of American History* 90 (2003): 833–62.

Hamill, Hugh M., Jr. *The Hidalgo Revolt*. Gainesville: University of Florida Press, 1966.

Hanisch Espíndola, Walter. "Esclavitud y libertad de los indios de Chile, 1608–1696." *Historia* [Universidad Católica de Chile] 16 (1981): 5–65.

Hanisch, Walter. "Memorias sobre misiones jesuitas de 1794–1795 [1784–1785]." *Historia* [Universidad Católica de Chile] 25 (1990): 103–59.

Hanke, Lewis. *The Spanish Struggle for Justice in the Conquest of America*. Philadelphia: University of Pennsylvania Press, 1949.

Hargreaves-Mawdsley, W. N., ed. *Spain under the Bourbons, 1700–1833*. Columbia: University of South Carolina Press, 1973.

Haring, Clarence H. *The Spanish Empire in America*. New York: Oxford University Press, 1947.

Harris, Marvin. *The Rise of Anthropological Theory: A History of Theories of Culture*. New York: Thomas Y. Crowell, 1968.

Hausberger, Von Bernd. "La violencia en la conquista espiritual: Las misiones jesuitas de Sonora." *Jahrbuch für Geschichte von Staat, Wirtschaft und Gesellschaft Lateinamerikas* 30 (1993): 27–54.

Head, Francis Bond. *Journeys Across the Pampas and Among the Andes*. Edited by C. Harvey Gardiner. 1st ed., 1826; Carbondale: Southern Illinois University Press, 1967.

Heard, J. Norman. *White into Red: A Study of the Assimilation of White Persons Captured by Indians*. Metuchen, N.J.: Scarecrow Press, 1973.

Heinen, H. Dieter. "Los Warao." In *Los aborígenes de Venezuela*, edited by Walter Coppens, 3:585–689. 3 vols. Caracas: Fundación LaSalle, 1980–88.

Helms, Mary W. "The Cultural Ecology of a Colonial Tribe." *Ethnology* 8 (1969): 76–84.

————. *Asang: Adaptations to Culture Contact in a Miskito Community*. Gainesville: University of Florida Press, 1971.

Hemming, John. *Amazon Frontier: The Defeat of the Brazilian Indian*. London: Macmillan, 1987.

Hendricks, Rick, and W. H. Timmons. *San Elizario: Spanish Presidio to Texas County Seat*. El Paso: Texas Western Press, 1998.

Henríquez Ureña, Pedro. *Las corrientes literarias en la América Hispánica*. Mexico: Fondo de Cultura Económica, 1949.

Heras, Julián. "Los Franciscanos en el oriente Peruano." In *Franciscan Presence in the Americas: Essays on the Activities of the Franciscan Friars in the Americas, 1492–1900*, edited by Francisco Morales, 261–84. Potomac, Md.: Academy of American Franciscan History, 1983.

Herda, Phyllis S. "Ethnology in the Enlightenment: The Voyage of Alejandro Malaspina in the Pacific." In *Enlightenment and Exploration in the North Pacific, 1741–1805*, edited by Stephen Haycox, James K. Barnett, and Caedmon A. Liburd, 65–75. Anchorage and Seattle: Cook Inlet Historical Society and the University of Washington Press, 1997.

Hernández Aparicio, Pilar. "Las misiones franciscanas del Colegio de Santa Rosa de Ocopa, 1794–1820." In *Entre Puebla de los Angeles y Sevilla: Estudios americanistas en homenaje al Dr. José Antonio Calderón Quijano*, edited by María Justina Sarabia et al., 579–92. Seville: Escuela de Estudios Hispano-Americanos y Universidad de Sevilla, 1997.

Hernández Asensio, Raúl. "Caciques, jesuitas y chamanes el la frontera sur de Buenos Aires (1740–1753)." *Anuario de Estudios Americanos* 60 (2003): 77–108.

Hernández, Isabel. *Los indios de Argentina*. Madrid: Editorial MAPFRE, 1992.

Hernández, José. *Martín Fierro*. Garden City: Doubleday, 1962.

Hernández Sánchez-Barba, Mario. *La última expansión española en América*. Madrid: Instituto de Estudios Políticos, 1957.

Herr, Richard. *The Eighteenth-Century Revolution in Spain*. Princeton: Princeton University Press, 1958.

Herren, Ricardo. *Indios carapálidas: Españoles asimilados entre los indígenas de América.* Barcelona: Planeta, 1992.

Higueras, Dolores. "Cuestionarios científicas y noticias geográficas en la expedición Malaspina (1789–1784)." In *Cuestionarios para la formación de Relaciones Geográficas de Indias: Siglos XVI/XIX,* edited by Francisco Solano, cvii–cxxix. Madrid: Consejo Superior de Investigaciones Científicas, 1988a.

———. "The Malaspina Expedition (1789–1794): A Venture of the Spanish Enlightenment." In *Spanish Pacific from Magellan to Malaspina,* 147–63. Madrid: Ministerio de Asuntos Exteriores, 1988b.

Higueras Rodríguez, Dolores, and Juan Pimentel Igea, eds. *La expedición Malaspina, 1789–1794.* Vol. 5, *Antropología y noticias etnográficas.* 7 vols. Madrid: Ministerio de Defensa, Museo Naval, and Lunwerg Editores, 1993.

Hill, Lawrence. *José de Escandón and the Founding of Nuevo Santander: A Study in Spanish Colonization.* Columbus: Ohio State University Press, 1926.

Hilton, Sylvia L. "Movilidad y expansión en la construcción política de los Estados Unidos: 'Estos errantes colonos' en las fronteras españolas del Misisipí (1776–1803)." *Revista Complutense de Historia de América* 28 (2002): 63–96.

Hinderaker, Eric. "The 'Four Indian Kings' and the Imaginative Construction of the First British Empire." *William and Mary Quarterly* 53 (1996): 487–526.

———. *Elusive Empires: Constructing Colonialism in the Ohio Valley, 1763–1800.* New York: Columbia University Press, 1997.

Hinojosa, Gilberto M. "The Religious-Indian Communities: The Goals of the Friars." In *Tejano Origins in Eighteenth-Century San Antonio,* edited by Gerald E. Poyo and Gilberto Hinojosa, 61–84. Austin: University of Texas Press for the University of Texas Institute of Texan Cultures at San Antonio, 1991.

Hinojosa, Gilberto M., and Anne A. Fox. "Indians and Their Culture in San Fernando de Béxar." In *Tejano Origins in Eighteenth-Century San Antonio,* edited by Gerald E. Poyo and Gilberto Hinojosa, 105–22. Austin: University of Texas Press for the University of Texas Institute of Texan Cultures at San Antonio, 1991.

Hodgen, Margaret T. *Early Anthropology in the Sixteenth and Seventeeth Centuries.* Philadelphia: University of Pennsylvania Press, 1964.

Hoffman, Fritz L., and Olga Mingo Hoffman. *Sovereignty in Dispute: The Falklands/Malvinas, 1493–1982.* Boulder: Westview Press, 1984.

Holmes, Jack D. L. *Gayoso: The Life of a Spanish Governor in the Mississippi Valley, 1789–1799.* Baton Rouge: LSU Press for the Louisiana Historical Association, 1965.

———. "Spanish Regulation of Taverns and the Liquor Trade in the Mississippi Valley." In *The Spanish in the Mississippi Valley, 1762–1804,* edited by John Francis McDermott, 149–82. Urbana: University of Illinois Press, 1974.

Hornbeck, David. "Economic Growth and Change at the Missions of Alta California, 1769–1846." In *Columbian Consequences.* Vol. 1, *Archaeological and Historical Perspectives on the Spanish Borderlands West,* edited by David Hurst Thomas, 423–33. 3 vols. Washington: Smithsonian Institution Press, 1989.

Howe, James. *A People Who Would Not Kneel: Panama, the United States and the San Blas Kuna.* Smithsonian Institution Press Series in Ethnography Inquiry. Washington: Smithsonian Institution Press, 1998.

Hu-DeHart, Evelyn. *Missionaries, Miners, and Indians: Spanish Contact with the Yaqui Nation of Northwestern New Spain, 1533–1820.* Tucson: University of Arizona Press, 1981.

Huertas, Rafael. "Locura y norma social en el México ilustrado." In *El paraíso occidental: Norma y diversidad en el México virreinal,* edited by Salvador Bernabéu Albert, 155–64. Madrid: Instituto de México en España, 1998.

Humboldt, Alexander von. *Political Essay on the Kingdom of New Spain.* Translated by John Black. 3d ed., 4 vols. London: Longman, Hurst, Rees, Orme, and Brown, 1822.

Hurt, R. Douglas. *The Indian Frontier, 1763–1846.* Albuquerque: University of New Mexico Press, 2002.

Hurtado, Albert L. *Intimate Frontiers: Sex, Gender, and Culture in Old California.* Albuquerque: University of New Mexico Press, 1999.

Hux, Meinrado. *Caciques huilliches y salineros.* Buenos Aires: Ediciones Marymar, 1991a.

———. *Caciques pampa-ranqueles.* Buenos Aires: Ediciones Marymar, 1991b.

———. *Caciques puelches, pampas y serranos.* Buenos Aires: Ediciones Marymar, 1993.

Inglis, Richard. "The Spanish on the North Pacific Coast—An Alternative View from Nootka Sound." In *Spain and the North Pacific Coast: Essays in Recognition of the Bicentennial of the Malaspina Expedition, 1791–1792,* edited by Robin Inglis, 133–36. Vancouver: University of British Columbia and Vancouver Maritime Museum, 1992.

Irons, William. "Political Stratification among Pastoral Nomads." In *Pastoral Production and Society,* edited by L'équipe écologie et anthropologie des sociétés pastorales, 221–34. Cambridge: Cambridge University Press, 1979.

Izard, Miguel. "Poca subordinación y menos ambición." *Boletín Americanista,* no. 42–43 (1992–93): 159–82.

Jackman, Jarrell C. *Felipe de Goicoechea: Santa Barbara Presidio Comandante.* Santa Barbara: Anson Luman Press, 1993.

Jackson, Jack, and William C. Foster, eds. *Imaginary Kingdom: Texas as Seen by the Rivera and Rubí Military Expeditions, 1727–1767.* Austin: Texas State Historical Association, 1995.

Jackson, Robert H. "Population and the Economic Dimension of Colonization in Alta California: Four Mission Communities." *Journal of the Southwest* 33 (1991): 387–439.

———. "Northwestern New Spain: The Pimería Alta and the Californias." In *New Views of Borderlands History,* edited by Robert H. Jackson, 73–106. Albuquerque: University of New Mexico Press, 1998.

Jackson, Robert H., and Edward Castillo. *Indians, Franciscans, and Spanish Colonization: The Impact of the Mission System on California Indians.* Albuquerque: University of New Mexico Press, 1995.

Jara, Álvaro. *Guerra y sociedad en Chile y otros temas afines.* 1st ed., 1961; Santiago de Chile: Editorial Universitaria, 1990.

Jefferys, Thomas. *A Description of the Spanish Islands and Settlements on the Coast of the West Indians, Compiled From Authentic Memoirs . . .* London: St. Martin's Lane, 1762.

Jennings, Francis. *The Founders of America: How Indians Discovered the Land, Pioneered in It, and Created Great Classical Civilizations; How They Were Plunged into a Dark Age by Invasion and Conquest; and How They Are Now Reviving.* New York: W. W. Norton, 1993.

Jiménez, Juan Francisco. "Guerras inter-tribales y economía en la cordillera de los Andes, 1769–1798: El impacto de los conflictos sobre la economía de los pehuenche de Malargüe." *Revista Frontera [Temuco, Chile],* no. 16 (1997): 41–51.

———. "De malares y armas de fuego: Guerras intra-étnicas y transformaciones en la tecnología bélica en Araucanía y las Pampas, 1818–1830." In *Relaciones inter-étnicas en el Sur bonaerense 1810–1830,* edited by Daniel Villar, 49–77. Bahía Blanca, Argentina: Departamento de Humanidades, Universidad Nacional del Sur, and Instituto de Estudios Histórico-Sociales, Universidad Nacional del Centro de la Provincia de Buenos Aires, 1998.

Jiménez Núñez, Alfredo. "Etnohistoria de la Nueva Vizcaya." *Anales de la Universidad Hispalense* 27 (1967): 37–91.

John, Elizabeth A. H. *Storms Brewed in Other Men's Worlds: The Confrontation of Indians, Spanish, and French in the Southwest, 1540–1795.* College Station: Texas A&M University Press, 1975.

———, ed. and trans. "A Cautionary Exercise in Apache Historiography ['Notes and Reflections on the War with the Apache Indians in the Provinces of New Spain,' by Bernardo de Gálvez, ca. 1785–86]." *Journal of Arizona History* 25 (1984a): 301–15.

———. "Nurturing the Peace: Spanish and Comanche Cooperation in the Early Nineteenth Century." *New Mexico Historical Review* 59 (1984b): 345–69.

———. "Independent Indians and the San Antonio Community." In *Tejano Origins in Eighteenth-Century San Antonio,* edited by Gerald Poyo and Gilberto Hinojosa, 123–36. Austin: University of Texas Press for the University of Texas Institute of Texan Cultures at San Antonio, 1991a.

———, ed. "Views from a Desk in Chihuahua: Manuel Merino's Report on Apaches and Neighboring Nations, ca. 1804." Translated by John Wheat. *Southwestern Historical Quarterly* 95 (1991b): 139–76.

———, ed. "Governing Texas, 1779: The Karankawa Aspect." Translated by John Wheat. *Southwestern Historical Quarterly* 104 (2001): 561–80.

John, Elizabeth A. H., and Adán Benavides Jr., eds. and trans. "Inside the Comanchería, 1785: The Diary of Pedro Vial and Francisco Xavier Chaves." *Southwestern Historical Quarterly* 98 (1994): 27–56.

Johnson, Jerah. "Colonial New Orleans: A Fragment of the Eighteenth-Century French Ethos." In *Creole New Orleans: Race and Americanization,* edited by Arnold R. and Joseph Logsdon Hirsch, 12–57. Baton Rouge: Louisiana State University Press, 1992.

Johnson, John J. *A Hemisphere Apart: The Foundations of United States Policy toward Latin America.* Baltimore: Johns Hopkins University Press, 1990.

Johnson, John R. "The Chumash History of Mission Creek." *Noticias* 32 (1986): 20–37.

Johnson, Julie Greer. *Satire in Colonial Spanish America: Turning the World Upside Down.* Austin: University of Texas Press, 1993.

Jones, David S. "Virgin Soils Revisited." *William and Mary Quarterly* 60 (2003): 703–42.

Jones, Kristine L. "La Cautiva: An Argentine Solution to Labor Shortage in the Pampas." In *Brazil and Rio de la Plata: Challenge and Response,* edited by Luis Felipe Clay Mendez and Lawrence W. Bates, 91–98. Charleston, Ill.: Illinois Conference of Latin Americanists, 1983.

———. "Conflict and Adaptation in the Argentine Pampas, 1750–1880." Ph.D. diss., University of Chicago, 1984.

———. "Indian–Creole Negotiations in the Southern Frontier." *Revolution and Restoration of the Social Order in Nineteenth-Century Argentina,* edited by Jonathan C. Brown and Mark D. Szuchman, 103–23. Lincoln: University of Nebraska Press, 1994.

———. "Comparative Raiding Economies: North and South." In *Contested Ground: Comparative Frontiers on the Northern and Southern Edges of the Spanish Empire,* edited by Donna J. Guy and Thomas E. Sheridan, 97–114. Tucson: University of Arizona Press, 1998.

Jones, Oakah L., Jr. *Pueblo Warriors and Spanish Conquest.* Norman: University of Oklahoma Press, 1966.

———. *Los Paisanos: Spanish Settlers on the Northern Frontier of New Spain.* Norman: University of Oklahoma Press, 1979.

———. "Rescue and Ransom of Spanish Captives from the *Indios Bárbaros* on the Northern Frontier of New Spain." *Colonial Latin American Historical Review* 4 (1995): 129–48.

Jones, Sondra. "'Redeeming' the Indian: The Enslavement of Indian Children in New Mexico and Utah." *Utah Historical Quarterly* 67 (1999): 220–41.

Jovellanos, Gaspar Melchor de. *Obras publicadas é inéditas.* Edited by Cándido Nocedal and Miguel Artola. 5 vols. Madrid: Biblioteca de Autores Españoles, 1956.

Juan, Jorge, and Antonio de Ulloa. *Relación histórica del viaje a la América meridional.* Edited by José

P. Merino Navarro and Miguel M. Rodríguez San Vicente. 1st ed., 1748; facsimile, 2 vols. Madrid: Fundación Universitaria Español, 1978.

————. *Las "Noticias secretas de América."* Edited by Luis J. Ramos Gómez. 2 vols. Madrid: Consejo Superior de Investigaciones Científicas, 1985.

Juderías, Julián. *La leyenda negra: Estudios acerca del concepto de España en el extranjero.* 1st ed., 1914; Madrid: Editora Nacional, 1960.

Kagan, Richard L. "Prescott's Paradigm: American Historical Scholarship and the Decline of Spain." *American Historical Review* 101, no. 2 (1996): 423–46.

————. *Urban Images of the Hispanic World, 1493–1793.* New Haven: Yale University Press, 2000.

Katzew, Ilona. "La Virgen de la Macana." *Anales del Instituto de Investigaciones Estéticas* 72 (1998): 39–72.

————. *Casta Painting: Images of Race in Eighteenth-Century Mexico.* New Haven: Yale University Press, 2004.

Kavanagh, Thomas W. *Comanche Political History: An Ethnohistorical Perspective, 1706–1875.* Lincoln: University of Nebraska Press, 1996.

Keegan, John. *A History of Warfare.* New York: Alfred A. Knopf, 1994.

Keeley, Lawrence H. *War Before Civilization: The Myth of the Peaceful Savage.* New York: Oxford University Press, 1996.

Keen, Benjamin. *The Aztec Image in Western Thought.* New Brunswick, N.J.: Rutgers University Press, 1971.

Kellogg, Susan. *Law and the Transformation of Aztec Culture, 1500–1700.* Norman: University of Oklahoma Press, 1995.

Kendrick, John, ed. *The Voyage of the Sutil and Mexicana, 1792: The Last Spanish Exploration of the Northwest Coast of America.* Spokane: Arthur H. Clark, 1991.

————. *Alejandro Malaspina: Portrait of a Visionary.* Montreal: McGill-Queen's University Press, 1999.

Kenner, Charles L. *A History of New Mexican–Plains Indian Relations.* Norman: University of Oklahoma Press, 1969.

Kessell, John L., ed. and trans. "San José de Tumacácori—1773: A Franciscan Reports from Arizona." *Arizona and the West* 6 (1964): 303–12.

————, ed. and trans. "Anza Damns the Missions: A Soldier's Criticism of Indian Policy, 1772." *Journal of Arizona History* 13 (1972): 53–63.

————. *Kiva, Cross, and Crown: The Pecos Indians and New Mexico.* Washington: National Park Service, 1979.

Kessell, John L., Rick Hendricks, and Meredith D. Dodge, eds. *Blood on the Boulders: The Journals of Don Diego de Vargas, New Mexico, 1694–1697.* 2 vols. Albuquerque: University of New Mexico Press, 1998.

Kinnaird, Lawrence, ed. *Spain in the Mississippi Valley, 1765–94,* 4 vols. Annual Report of the American Historical Association, 1945. Washington: Government Printing Office, 1946–49.

————. "Spanish Treaties with Indian Tribes." *Western Historical Quarterly* 10 (1979): 39–48.

Kino, Eusebio Francisco. *Historical Memoir of Pimería Alta: A Contemporary Account of the Beginnings of California, Sonora, and Arizona, 1683–1711.* Edited and translated by Herbert Eugene Bolton. 2 vols. Berkeley: University of California Press, 1919.

Kleinpenning, Jan M. G. *Peopling the Purple Land: A Historical Geography of Rural Uruguay, 1500–1915.* Amsterdam: CEDLA, 1995.

Knack, Martha C. *Boundaries Between: The Southern Pauites, 1775–1995.* Lincoln: University of Nebraska Press, 2001.

Konetzke, Richard. *Colección de documentos para la historia de la formación social de Hispanoamérica.* 3 vols. Madrid: Consejo Superior de Investigaciones Científicas, 1953–62.

König Eichstätt, Hans-Joachim. "Símbolos nacionales y retórica política en la Independencia: El caso de la Nueva Granada." In *Problemas de la formación del estado y la nación en Hispanoamérica,* edited by P. D. Buillon, 389–405. Bonn: Lateinamerikanische Forschungen, 1984.

————. "La mistificación de la 'conquista' y del 'indio' en el comienzo de la formación de estados y naciones en hispanoamérica." *Boletín de la Academia Chilena de la Historia* 101 (1990): 221–34.

Kornfeld, Eve. "Encountering 'the Other': American Intellectuals and Indians in the 1790s." *William and Mary Quarterly* 52 (1995): 287–314.

Korth, Eugene H. *Spanish Policy in Colonial Chile: The Struggle for Social Justice, 1535–1700.* Stanford: Stanford University Press, 1968.

Kroeber, Clifton B., and Bernard L. Fontana. *Massacre on the Gila: An Account of the Last Major Battle Between American Indians, with Reflections on the Origin of War.* Tucson: University of Arizona Press, 1986.

Kuethe, Allan J. "The Pacification Campaign on the Riohacha Frontier, 1772–1779." *Hispanic American Historical Review* 50 (1970): 467–81.

————. *Military Reform and Society in New Granada, 1773–1808.* Gainesville: University Presses of Florida, 1978.

————. "La desregulación comercial y la reforma imperial en la época de Carlos III: Los casos de Nueva España y Cuba." *Historia Mexicana* 162 (1991): 265–92.

Kuethe, Allan J., and Lowell Blaisdell. "French Influence and the Origins of the Bourbon Colonial Reorganization." *Hispanic American Historical Review* 71 (1991): 479–607.

Kuethe, Allan J., and G. Douglas Inglis. "Absolutism and Enlightened Reform: Charles III, the Establishment of the *Alcabala,* and Commercial Reorganization in Cuba." *Past and Present: A Journal of Historical Studies,* no. 109 (1985): 118–43.

Kupperman, Karen Ordahl. *Indians and English: Facing Off in Early America.* Ithaca: Cornell University Press, 2000.

La Pérouse, Jean-François de Galaup de. *The Journal of Jean-François de Galaup de la Pérouse, 1785–1788.* Edited and translated by John Dunmore. 2 vols. London: Hakluyt Society, 1994.

La Vere, David. "Friendly Persuasions: Gifts and Reciprocity in Comanche–Euroamerican Relations." *Chronicles of Oklahoma* 71, no. 3 (1993): 322–37.

————. *The Caddo Chiefdoms: Caddo Economics and Politics, 700–1835.* Lincoln: University of Nebraska Press, 1998.

Lafora, Nicolás de. *Relación del viaje que hizo a los presidios internos situados en la frontera de la América Septentrional perteneciente al Rey de España. . . .* Edited by Vito Alessio Robles. Mexico: Editorial Pedro Robredo, 1939.

————. *The Frontiers of New Spain: Nicolás de Lafora's Description, 1766–68.* Edited and translated by Lawrence Kinnaird. Berkeley: Quivira Society, 1958.

Lafuente, Antonio. "Las expediciones científicas del setecientos y la nueva relación del científico con el estado." In *Ciencia y contexto histórico nacional en las expediciones ilustradas a América,* edited by Fermín Pino Díaz. Madrid: Consejo Superior de Investigaciones Científicas, 1988.

Lagos, Roberto. *Historia de las misiones del Colegio de Chillán: Propagación del Santo Evangelio entre los Araucanos.* Barcelona: Herederos de Juan Gili, 1908.

Landers, Jane. "Slave Resistance on the Southeastern Frontier: Fugitives, Maroons, and Banditti in the Age of Revolutions." *El Escribano* 32 (1995): 12–24.

Langer, Erick, and Robert Jackson, eds. *The New Latin American Mission History.* Lincoln: University of Nebraska Press, 1995.

Lanning, John Tate. *The Eighteenth-Century Enlightenment in the University of San Carlos de Guatemala.* Ithaca: Cornell University Press, 1956.

Larsen, Clark Spencer, et al. "Beyond Demographic Collapse: Biological Adaptation and Change in Native Populations of La Florida." In *Columbian Consequences.* Vol. 2, *Archaeological and Historical Perspectives on the Spanish Borderlands East,* edited by David Hurst Thomas, 2:409–28. 3 vols. Washington, D.C.: Smithsonian Institution Press, 1990.

Larson, Daniel O., John R. Johnson, and Joel C. Michaelsen. "Missionization among the Coastal Chumash of Central California: A Study of Risk Minimization Strategies." *American Anthropologist* 96, no. 2 (1994): 263–99.

Laserna Gaitán, Antonio Ignacio. "El franciscanismo en la defensa del patrimonio y de la dignidad humana del indígena durante el siglo XVIII en el Oriente Venezolano." *Chronica Nova,* no. 17 (1989): 131–45.

———. *Tierra, gobierno local y actividad misionera en la comunidad indígena del oriente venezolano: La visita a la provincia de Cumana de Don Luis de Chávez y Mendoza (1783–1784).* Biblioteca de la Academia Nacional de la Historia. Fuentes para la historia colonial de Venezuela, 219. Caracas: Academia Nacional de la Historia, 1993.

———, ed. *El viajero universal (1795–1801): La descripción de territorio Venezolano.* Granada: Universidad de Granada, 1994.

Lastarria, Miguel. *Colonias orientales del Río Paraguay o de la Plata.* Edited by Enrique Del Valle Iberlucea. Documentos para la Historia Argentina, 3. Buenos Aires: Compañía Sud-America de Billetes de Banco, 1914.

Lasuén, Fermín Francisco de. *Writings of Fermín Francisco de Lasuén.* Edited and translated by Finbar Kenneally. 2 vols. Washington: Academy of American Franciscan History, 1965.

Lavallé, Bernard. "Del indio al criollo: Evolución y transformación de una imagen colonial." In *La imagen del indio en la Europa moderna,* 319–42. Seville: Escuela de Estudios Hispano-americanos, 1990.

Lázaro Ávila, Carlos. "Un freno a la conquista: La resistencia de los cacicazgos indígenas americanos en la bibliografía histórico-antropológica." *Revista de Indias* 52 (1992): 589–609.

———. "Los cautivos en la frontera araucana." *Revista Española de Antropología Americana,* no. 24 (1994): 191–207.

———. "Las visiones condicionadas de Falcón y Pineda: Dos cautivos europeos ante la sociedad araucana." In *Visión de los otros y visión de sí mismos,* edited by Fermín del Pino Díaz and Carlos Lázaro Ávila, 127–39. Madrid: Consejo Superior de Investigaciones Científicas, 1995.

———. "Los tratados de paz con los indígenas fronterizos de América: Evolución histórica y estado de la cuestión." *Estudios de Historia Social y Económica de América* 13 (1996): 15–24.

———. *Las fronteras de América y los "Flandes indianos."* Madrid: Consejo Superior de Investigaciones Científicas, 1997.

———. "Conquista, control y convicción: El papel de los parlamentos indígenas en México, el Chaco y Norteamérica." *Revista de Indias* 59 (1999): 645–73.

LeBlanc, Steven A. *Prehistoric Warfare in the American Southwest.* Salt Lake City: University of Utah Press, 1999.

———. "Regional Interaction and Warfare in the Late Prehistoric Southwest." In *The Archaeology of Regional Interaction: Religion, Warfare, and Exchange across the American Southwest and Beyond. Proceedings of the 1996 Southwest Symposium.* Edited by Michelle Hegmon, 41–70. Boulder: University Press of Colorado, 2000.

Lehnertz, Jay Frederick. "Lands of Infidels: The Franciscans in the Central Montaña of Peru, 1709–1824." Ph.D. diss., University of Wisconsin, 1974.

Lejarza, Fidel de. *Conquista espiritual del Nuevo Santander.* Madrid: Consejo Superior de Investigaciones Científicas, 1947.

Lemann, Nicholas. "A Failed Dominion." *The Atlantic* (1992): 151–52.

León Solís, Leonardo. "La Corona española y las guerras intestinas entre los indígenas de Araucania, Patagonia y las Pampas, 1760–1806." *Nueva Historia: Revista de Historia de Chile* 5 (1982): 31–67.

———. *Malqueros y conchavadores en Araucanía y las Pampas, 1700–1800.* Temuco, Chile: Universidad de la Frontera, 1990.

———. "Guerras tribales y estructura social en la Araucanía, 1760–1780." *Revista de Ciencias Sociales* 39 (1994a): 91–110.

———. "Los araucanos y la amenaza de ultramar, 1750–1807." *Revista de Indias* 54 (1994b): 313–54.

———. "Raiguán, el *Calcu* de las Pampas, 1792–1796." *Boletín de Historia y Geografía,* no. 14 (1998): 167–96.

———. "Indios, piratas y corsarios en las costas de araucanía y patagonia, 1557–1790." *Boletín de Historia y Geografía,* no. 15 (2001a): 117–51.

———. *Los señores de la cordillera y las pampas: Los pehuenches de Malalhue, 1770–1800.* Mendoza, Argentina: Universidad de Congreso and Universidad de Malargüe, 2001b.

———. "Mestizos e insubordinación social en la frontera Mapuche de Chile, 1700–1726." In *Estudios Coloniales II,* edited by Julio Retamal A., 207–79. Santiago de Chile: Universidad Andrés Bello, 2002.

León Solís, Leonardo, Osvaldo Silva Galdames, and Eduardo Téllez Lúgaro. "La guerra contra el malón en Chile, Cuyo y Buenos Aires, 1750–1800." *Cuadernos de Historia* 17 (1997): 7–67.

León y Pizarro, Ramón García de. "Descripción de la ciudad de la Nueva Orán en el Valle de Senta, de la Pronvincia de Salta del Tucumán, por su fundador...." *Mercurio Peruano de Historia, Literatura y Noticias* 12, no. 606, 607 (1795): 193–210.

Leonis Mazzanti, Diana. "Control del ganado caballar a mediados del siglo xviii en el territorio indio del sector oriental de las Serranías de Tandil." In *Huellas en la Tierra: Indios, Agricultores y Hacendados en la Pampa Bonaerense,* edited by Raúl Mandrini and Andrea Reguera, 75–89. Tandil, Argentina: Instituto de Estudios Histórico Sociales, 1993.

Lepore, Jill. *The Name of War: King Philip's War and the Origins of American Identity.* New York: Alfred A. Knopf, 1998.

Lerner, Isaías. "The Diccionario of Antonio de Alcedo as a Source of Enlightened Ideas." In *The Ibero-American Enlightenment,* edited by A. Owen Aldridge, 71–93. Urbana: University of Illinois Press, 1971.

———. "Spanish Colonization and the Indigenous Languages of America." In *The Language Encounter in the Americas, 1492–1800: A Collection of Essays,* edited by Edward G. Gray and Norman Fiering, 281–92. New York and Oxford: Berghahn Books, 2000.

Leutenegger, Benedict, ed. and trans. "New Documents on Father José Mariano Reyes." *Southwestern Historical Quarterly* 71 (1968): 583–602.

———, ed. and trans. *Guidelines for a Texas Mission: Instructions for the Missionary of Mission Concepción in San Antonio (ca. 1760 [1788]).* Documentary Series no. 1. San Antonio: Old Spanish Missions Historical Research Library, 1976.

Leutenegger, Benedict, and Marion A. Habig, eds. and trans. *Management of the Missions in Texas: Fr. José Rafael Oliva's Views Concerning the Problem of the Temporalities in 1788.* Documentary Series no. 2. San Antonio: Old Spanish Missions Historical Research Library, 1978.

Levaggi, Abelardo. "Una institución chilena trasplantada al Río de la Plata: El 'Capitán de Amigos.'" *Revista de Estudios Histórico-Jurídicos* 13 (1989–90): 99–107.

———. "Notas sobre la vigencia de los derechos indígenas y la doctrina indiana." *Revista Complutense de Historia de América,* no. 17 (1991): 79–91.

———. "Tratados entre la Corona y los indios del Chaco." In *Homenaje a Ismael Sánchez Bella,* edited by Joaquín Salcedo Izu, 291–323. Pamplona, Spain: Biblioteca Jurídica, Universidad de Navarra, 1992.

————. "Los tratados entre la Corona y los indios, y el plan de conquista pacífica." *Revista Complutense de Historia de América* 19 (1993): 81–91.

————. "Aplicación de la política española de tratados a los indios de la Nueva España y sus confines: El caso de la Florida y tierras adyacentes (1700–1781)." *Anuario Mexicano de Historia del Derecho* 8 (1996a): 225–41.

————. "Aplicación de la política española de tratados a los indios de la Nueva España y sus confines: El caso de la Luisiana y las Floridas (1780–1790)." *Revista de Investigaciones Jurídicas* 20 (1996b): 371–403.

————. "Los tratados con los indios en la época borbónica: Reafirmación de la política de conquista pacífica." In *XI Congreso del Instituto Internacional de Historia del Derecho Indiano,* 103–18. Buenos Aires: Instituto de Investigaciones de Historia del Derecho, 1997.

————. "Los tratados hispano-indígenas en las fronteras septentrional y meridional de América. Análisis comparativo." In *México en el Mundo Hispánico: XXI Coloquio de Antropología e Historia Regional,* 302–12. Zamora, Mexico: Colegio de Michoacán, 1999.

————. *Paz en la frontera: Historia de las relaciones diplomáticas con las comunidades indígenas en la Argentina (siglos XVI–XIX).* Buenos Aires: Universidad del Museo Social Argentino, 2000.

————. *Diplomacia hispano-indígena en las fronteras de América: Historia de los tratados entre la Monarquía española y las comunidades aborígenes.* Madrid: Centro de Estudios Políticos y Constitucionales, 2002.

Lévi-Strauss, Claude. "Rousseau, The Father of Anthropology." *UNESCO Courier* 16 (1963): 10–14.

————. *The Savage Mind.* Chicago: University of Chicago Press, 1966.

Lindner, Rudi Paul. "Nomadism, Horses and Huns." *Past and Present* 92 (1981): 3–19.

Lipsett-Rivera, Sonya. "'Mira lo que hace el diablo': The Devil in Mexican Popular Culture, 1750–1856." *The Americas* 59 (2002): 201–19.

Llombart, Vicent. *Campomanes, economista y político de Carlos III.* Madrid: Alianza, 1992.

Lockhart, James, and Stuart B. Schwartz. *Early Latin America: A History of Colonial Spanish America and Brazil.* Cambridge: Cambridge University Press, 1983.

Lombardi, John V. *Venezuela: The Search for Order, the Dream of Progress.* New York: Oxford, 1982.

Longinos, José. *Diario de las expediciones a las Californias.* Edited by Salvador Bernabéu. Madrid: Doce Calles, 1994.

López de Alborniz, Cristina. "Productores rurales de San Miguel Tucumán." In *El Tucumán colonial y Charcas,* edited by Ana María Lorandi, 2:155–180. 2 vols. Buenos Aires: Universidad de Buenos Aires, Facultad de Filosofía y Letras, 1997.

López de Vargas Machuca, Tomás. *Atlas geográphico de la América septentrional y meridional dedicado a . . . don Fernando VI.* [Madrid?]: n.p., [1758].

López, François. *La república de las letras en la españa del siglo xviii.* Edited by Joaquín Álvarez Barrientos, 63–124. Madrid: Consejo Superior de Investigaciones Científicas, 1995.

López, José Francisco. "Report on the San Antonio Missions in 1792." Edited and translated by Marion A. Habig and Benedict Leutenegger. *Southwestern Historical Quarterly* 77 (1974): 486–98.

López Piacentini, Carlos Primo. *Historia de la Provincia del Chaco.* 5 vols. Resistencia, Argentina: Editorial Región, 1979.

López, Rafael, ed. *Estado general de las fundaciones hechas en la Colonia del Nuevo Santander por José de Escandón . . . documentos . . .* Publicaciones del Archivo General de la Nación, 14 and 15. 2 vols. Mexico: Talleres Gráficos de la Nación, 1929–30.

Lorandi, Ana María. "El servicio personal como agente de desestructuración en el Tucumán colonial." *Revista Andina* 6 (1988): 135–73.

Loreto, marqués de. "Memoria a su sucesor don Nicolás de Arredondo, Buenos Aires, 10 de febrero de 1790." In *Memorias de los virreyes del Río de la Plata,* edited by Sigfrido Radaelli, 200–371. Buenos Aires: Editorial Bajel, 1945.

Lowrie, Robert H. "Some Aspects of Political Organization among the American Aborigines." *Journal of the Royal Anthropological Institute of Great Britain and Ireland* 78, Parts I and II (1948): 11–24.

Lozano, Pedro. *Descripción corográfica del Gran Chaco Gualamba,* edited by Radamés A. Altieri. 1st ed., 1733; Tucumán, Argentina: Instituto de Antropología, 1941.

Lucena Giraldo, Manuel. *Laboratorio tropical: La expedición de limites al Orinoco, 1750–1767.* Caracas: Monte Avila, 1992a.

———. "La última búsqueda de el dorado: Las expediciones al Parime." *Ibero-Americana Pragensia* 21 (1992b): 67–86.

———. "El reformismo de frontera." In *El reformismo borbónico: Una visión interdisciplinar,* edited by Agustín Guimerá, 265–75. Madrid: Alianza, 1996.

Luengo Muñoz, Manuel. "Génesis de las expediciones militares al Darién en 1785–86." *Anuario de Estudios Americanos* 18 (1961): 333–416.

Luiz, María Teresañ Schillat Monika. *La frontera austral: Tierra del Fuego, 1520–1920.* Cádiz: Universidad de Cádiz, 1997.

Luna Moreno, Carmen de. "Alternativa en el S. XVIII: Franciscanos de la provincia del Santo Evangelio de México." In *Los franciscanos en el Nuevo Mundo (siglo XVIII),* 243–72. Madrid: Editorial Deimos, 1993.

Lynch, John. *Spanish Colonial Administration, 1782–1810. The Intendant System in the Viceroyalty of the Río de la Plata.* London: Athlone Press of the University of London, 1958.

———. *The Spanish American Revolutions, 1808–1826.* New York: W. W. Norton, 1973.

———. *Argentine Dictator: Juan Manuel de Rosa, 1829–1852.* Oxford: Clarendon Press, 1981.

———. *Bourbon Spain, 1700–1808.* Oxford: Basil Blackwell, 1989.

———. "The Institutional Framework of Colonial Spanish America." *Journal of Latin American Studies* 24 (1992): 69–81.

———. *Fray Juan de Santa Gertrudis and the Marvels of New Granada.* Institute of Latin American Studies Research Papers, 52. London: Institute of Latin American Studies, University of London, 1999.

Lyon, William H. "Social and Cultural Change Among the Navajo, Parts I & II." *New Mexico Historical Review* 78 (2003): 59–93, 167–84.

———, ed. *Latin American Revolutions, 1808–1826: Old and New World Origins.* Norman: University of Oklahoma Press, 1994.

Maas, Otto. "Estado de las misiones de la orden de S. Francisco, año de 1788 [Madrid]." In *Viajes de misioneros franciscanos á la conquista del Nuevo México: Documentos del Archivo General de Indias (Sevilla),* 187–208. Seville: Imprenta de San Antonio, 1915.

———. "Las órdenes religiosas de España y la colonización de América en la segunda parte del siglo XVIII. Estadística y otros documentos." *Estudios Franciscanos* 18–20 (1917–18): vol. 18 (Jan. 1917) 41–49; (Feb. 1917) 128–32; (March 1917) 209–22, (April 1917) 289–99; (May 1917) 366–75; (Junio) 445–56; vol. 19 (Julio 1917): 39–51; vol. 19 (Agosto 1917), 127–46; (Sept. 1917) 205–14; (Oct. 1917) 292–99; (Dec. 1917) 444–52; vol. 20 (Jan 1918) 56–63; (Feb. 1918) 117–30; (April 1918) 285–89.

MacLachlan, Colin M. *Spain's Empire in the New World: The Role of Ideas in Institutional and Social Change.* Berkeley: University of California Press, 1988.

MacLeod, Murdo J. *Spanish Central America: A Socio-economic History, 1520–1720.* Berkeley: University of California Press, 1973.

———. "Some Thoughts on the Pax Colonial, Colonial Violence, and Perceptions of Both." In *Native Resistance and the Pax Colonial in New Spain,* edited by Susan Schroeder, 129–42. Lincoln and London: University of Nebraska Press, 1998.

Maeder, Ernesto J. A. "La organización de la provincia de Chiquitos en la época postjesuítica:

Diferencias y semejanzas con la Provincia de Misiones de Guaraníes." *Revista de Historia del Derecho (Buenos Aires)* 16 (1988): 153–69.

———. "La producción ganadera en Misiones en la época post-jesuítica (1768–1810)." *Folia Histórica del Noreste* 9 (1990): 55–106.

———. *Misiones de Paraguay: Conflicto y disolución de la sociedad guaraní.* Madrid: MAPFRE, 1992.

———. "Un debate tardío sobre la libertad de los guaraníes de misiones." *Hispania Sacra* 46, no. (93) (1994): 191–205.

———. "Asimetría demográfica entre las reducciones franciscanas y jesuíticas de guaraníes." *Revista Complutense de Historia de América* 21 (1995): 71–84.

———. *Historia del Chaco.* Buenos Aires: Editorial Plus Ultra, 1996.

Maeder, Ernesto J. A., and Alfredo S. C. Bolsi. "La población de las misiones después de la expulsión de los jesuitas." In *A população missioneira: Fatores adversos e favoráves á reduçoes,* 127–55. Santa Rosa, Rio Grande do Sul: Anais do IV simposio nacional de estudos missioneiros, 1981.

Magaña-Mancillas, Mario A. "Las misiones domínicas en Baja California: Santo Domingo de la Frontera, 1775–1875." *Colonial Latin American Historical Review* 8 (Spring 1999): 185–206.

Magaña, Mario Alberto. *Población y misiones de Baja California: Estudio histórico demográfico de la misión de Santo Domingo de la Frontera: 1775–1850.* Tijuana, Baja California: Colegio de la Frontera Norte, 1998.

Magnaghi, Russell M. "Plains Indians in New Mexico The Genízaro Experience." *Great Plains Quarterly* 10 (1990): 86–95.

Malaspina, Alejandro. *Viaje político-científico alrededor del mundo por las corbetas Descubierta y Atrevida al mando de los capitanes de navío D. Alejandro Malaspina y don José de Bustamante y Guerra, desde 1789–1794.* Edited by Pedro de Novo y Colson. Madrid: Imprenta de la Viuda e Hijos de Abienzo, 1885.

———. *Viaje científico y político a la América Meridional, a las Costas del Mar Pacífico y a las Islas Marianas y Filipinas verificado en los años de 1789, 90, 91, 92, 93 y 94 a bordo de las corbetas Descubierta y Atrevida de la Marina Real, mandadas por los capitanes de navío D. Alejandro Malaspina y D. José F. Bustamante. Diario de viaje de Alejandro Malaspina.* Edited by Mercedes Palau, Aránzazu Zabala, and Blanca Sáiz. Madrid: Ediciones El Museo Universal, 1984.

———. *La expedición Malaspina, 1789–1794.* Vol. 2, Part 1, *Diario general del viaje.* Edited by Ricardo Cerezo Martínez. Madrid: Ministerio de Defensa, Museo Naval, and Lunwerg Editores, 1990.

———. "Descripción física de la costa noroeste." In *Varias expediciones a la costa noroeste,* edited by Fernando Monge and Margarita del Olmo, 163–235. Madrid: Historia 16, 1991a.

———. *Los "axiomas políticos sobre la América" de Alejandro Malaspina.* Edited by Manuel Lucena Giraldo and Juan Pimentel. Aranjuez, Spain: Ediciones Dos Calles, 1991b.

———. "Reflexiones políticas sobre las Costas Occidentales de la América al S. del Cabo Blanco de Martín de Aguilar y sobre las ocho Provincias Internas de Oriente, y Occidente." In *La expedición Malaspina, 1789–1794.* Vol. 7, *Descripciones y reflexiones políticas,* edited by Juan Pimentel Igea, 113–63. Madrid: Ministerio de Defensa, Museo Naval, and Lunwerg Editores, 1995.

———. *The Malaspina Expedition, 1789–1794: Journal of the Voyage.* Vol. 1, *Cadiz to Panama.* Edited by Andrew David et al. London: Hakluyt Society/Museo Naval, Madrid, 2001.

Maldi, Denise. "Guerreros del jaguar, centinelas de las Américas: Sociedades indígenas en la frontera setecientista—Río Guaporé/Itenez." In *Fronteras, etnias, culturas: America Latina, siglos XVI–XX,* edited by Chiara Vangelista, 33–49. Quito: Abya-Yala, 1996.

Mallon, Florencia. "The Promise and Dilemma of Subaltern Studies: Perspectives from Latin American History." *American Historical Review* 99 (1994): 1491–1515.

Malone, Patrick M. *That Skulking Way of War: Technology and Tactics Among the New England Indians.* Baltimore: Johns Hopkins University Press, 1991.

Mancall, Peter C. *Deadly Medicine: Indians and Alcohol in Early America*. Ithaca: Cornell University Press, 1995.

Mandrini, Raúl J. "La agricultura indígena en la región pampeana y sus adyacencias (siglos XVIII y XIX)." *Anuario del IEHS* 1 (1986): 11–43.

———. "Frontera y relaciones fronterizas en la historiografía Argentino–Chilena: A propósito de un reciente libro de Sergio Villalobos." *Boletín del Instituto de Historia Argentina y Americana "Doctor Emilio Ravignani,"* no. 3 (1991a): 139–45.

———. "Procesos de especialización regional en la economía indígena pampeana (s. XVIII–XIX): El caso del suroeste bonaerense." *Boletín Americanista* (1991b): 113–36.

———. "Indios y fronteras en el area pampeana (siglos XVI–XIX): Balance y perspectivas." *Anuario del IEHS* 7 (1992a): 59–73.

———. "Pedir con vuelta ¿Reciprocidad diferida o mecanismo de poder?" *Antropológicas, nueva epoca* 1 (1992b): 59–69.

———. "Las transformaciones de la economía indígena bonaerense, ca. 1600–1820." In *Huellas en la Tierra: Indios, Agricultores y Hacendados en la Pampa Bonaerense*, edited by Raúl Mandrini and Andrea Reguera, 45–74. Tandil, Argentina: Instituto de Estudios Historico Sociales, 1993a.

———. "Guerra y paz en la frontera bonaerense durante el siglo XVIII." *Ciencia Hoy* 4, no. 23 (1993b): 27–35.

———. "¿Sólo de caza y robos vivían los indios? Los cacicatos pampeanos del siglo XIX." *Siglo XIX, nueva época* 15 (1994): 5–24.

———. "Las fronteras y la sociedad indígena en el ámbito pampeano." *Anuario del IEHS* (1997): 23–34.

Mandrini, Raúl J., and Sara Ortelli. "Repensando viejos problemas: Observaciones sobre la araucanización de las pampas." *Runa* (1995): 135–50.

Manfredi, Dario. "El viaje de la fragata 'Astrea' (1786–88): Antecedente de la gran expedición científica de Alejandro Malaspina." *Revista de Historia Naval* [Madrid] 17 (1987): 69–95.

———. "Alejandro Malaspina: una biografía." In *Alejandro Malaspina: La América Imposible*, edited by Blanca Sáiz, 19–133. Madrid: Compañía Literaria, 1994.

Mantilla R., Luis Carlos. *Los Franciscanos en Colombia*. Vol. 3, *1700–1830*. 2 vols. Bogotá: Universidad de San Buenaventura, 2000.

Manuel, Frank. *The Eighteenth Century Confronts the Gods*. Cambridge: Harvard University Press, 1959.

Marchena Fernández, Juan. *Oficiales y soldados en el ejército de América*. Seville: Escuela de Estudios Hispanoamericanos, 1983.

———. *Ejército y milicias en el mundo colonial Americano*. Madrid: Editorial MAPFRE, 1992.

———. "De franciscanos, apaches y ministros ilustrados en los pasos perdidos del norte de Nueva España." *Los franciscanos en el Nuevo Mundo (siglo XVIII)*, 513–60. Madrid: Editorial Deimos, 1993.

Marfany, Roberto H. "Frontera con los indios en el sud y fundación de pueblos." In *Historia de la Nación Argentina*, edited by Ricardo Levene, vol. 4, pt. 1:307–33. 2d ed., Buenos Aires: Librería y Editorial El Ateneo, 1940.

Marichal, Juan. "From Pistoia to Cádiz: A Generation's Itinerary, 1786–1812." In *The Ibero-American Enlightenment*, edited by A. Owen Aldridge, 97–110. Urbana: University of Illinois Press, 1971.

Mariluz Urquijo, José María. "Los guaraníes después de la expulsión de los jesuítas." *Estudios Americanos* 6, no. 25 (1953): 323–30.

———. "Blas de Pedrosa, natural de Coruña y baqueano de la pampa." *Historia: Revista Trimestral de Historia Argentina, Americana y Española* 3, no. 9 (1957): 64–70.

———. "El levantamiento chiriguano de 1799 y la controversia sobre la legitimidad de la guerra." *Investigaciones y ensayos* [Academia Nacional de la Historia, Argentina] 1 (1966): 309–30.

————. *El virreinato del Río de la Plata en la época del Marqués de Avilés.* 2d ed.; Buenos Aires: Plus Ultra, 1987.

Marmión, Miguel. "Descripción Corográfico-Mixta de la Provincia Guayana . . . 1788." In *Relaciones geográficos de Venezuela,* edited by Antonio Arellano Moreno, 435–57. Caracas: Academia Nacional de la Historia, 1964.

Marshall, Peter J., and Glyndwr Williams. *The Great Map of Mankind: Perceptions of New Worlds in the Age of Enlightenment.* Cambridge: Harvard University Press, 1982.

Martens, Georg Friederich von. *Summary of the Law of Nations, Founded on the Treatise and Customs of the Modern Nations of Europe.* Translated by William Cobbett. 1st ed., 1788; Philadelphia: Thomas Bradford, 1795.

Martin, Cheryl English. *Governance and Society in Colonial Mexico: Chihuahua in the Eighteenth Century.* Stanford: Stanford University Press, 1996.

Martín de Codoni, Elvira. "La redención de cautivos en la Mendoza colonial." *Revista de la Junta de Estudios Históricos de Mendoza (tercera época)* 1 (1997): 99–116.

Martínez Cuesta, Ángel. *Historia de los Agustinos Recoletos.* Vol. 1, *Desde los orígenes hasta el siglo xix.* Madrid: Editorial Augustinus, 1995.

Martínez de Gorla, Dora Noemí. "El primer asentamiento de colonos en el Río Negro, en Patagonia." *Temas Americanistas* 6 (1986): 15–20.

Martínez Ferrer, Luis. "El Capitán Francisco Rodríguez Leyte (ca. 1589–1650) y la pacificación y evangelización del Oriente de Venezuela: El paso de las guerrras de conquista al régimen misional." *Boletín de la Academia Nacional de la Historia* [Caracas] 79, no. 316 (1996): 163–77.

Martínez Martín, Carmen. "Las reducciones de los pampas (1740–53): Aportaciones etnogeográficas al sur de Buenos Aires." *Revista Complutense de Historia de América* 20 (1994): 145–67.

Martínez, Oscar. *Border People: Life and Society in the U.S.–Mexico Borderlands.* Tucson: University of Arizona Press, 1994.

Martínez, Oscar J., ed. *U.S.–Mexico Borderlands: Historical and Contemporary Perspectives.* Wilmington, Del.: Scholarly Resources, 1996.

Martínez Sarasola, Carlos. *Nuestros paisanos los indios: Vida, historia y destino de las comunidades indígenas en la Argentina.* Buenos Aires: Emecé Editores, 1992.

Martínez Sierra, Ramiro. *El mapa de las pampas.* 2 vols. Buenos Aires: Ministerio del Interior, 1975.

Martínez Torrón, Diego. *Los liberales románticos españoles ante la descolonización americana.* Madrid: MAPFRE, 1992.

Mathes, W. Michael, ed. *Californiana IV: Aportación a la historiografía de California en el siglo XVIII.* 2 vols. Madrid: José Porrúa Turanzas, 1987.

Matson, Daniel S., and Bernard L. Fontana, eds. and trans. *Friar Bringas Reports to the King: Methods of Indoctrination on the Frontier of New Spain, 1796–97.* Tucson: University of Arizona Press, 1977.

Matson, Daniel S., and Albert H. Schroeder, eds. "Cordero's Description of the Apache—1796." *New Mexico Historical Review* 32 (1957): 335–56.

Mauss, Marcel. *The Gift: Forms and Functions of Exchange in Archaic Societies.* Translated by Ian Cunnison. 1st French ed., 1925; 1st English edition, 1954; New York: W. W. Norton, 1967.

Maxwell, Kenneth. *Pombal: Paradox of the Enlightenment.* Cambridge: Cambridge University Press, 1995.

May, Katja. *African Americans and Native Americans in the Creek and Cherokee Nations, 1830s to 1920s: Collision and Collusion.* New York: Garland, 1996.

Mayo, Carlos A. "El cautiverio y sus funciones en una sociedad de frontera: El caso de Buenos Aires, 1750–1810." *Revista de Indias* 45 (1985a): 225–34.

————. *Fuentes para la historia de la frontera: Declaraciones de cautivos.* Mar del Plata: Universidad Nacional del Mar del Plata, Facultad de Humanidades, Departamento de Historia, Publicaciones de Cátedra, 1985b.

————. "Landed But Not Powerful: The Colonial Estancieros of Buenos Aires (1750–1810)." *Hispanic American Historical Review* 71 (1991): 761–79.

Mayo, Carlos A., and Amalia Latrubesse. *Terratenientes, soldados y cautivos: La frontera, 1736–1815.* 1st ed., 1986; Mar del Plata: Universidad Nacional de Mar del Plata y Grupo Estado y Sociedad, 1993.

McCarty, Kieran. *A Spanish Frontier in the Enlightened Age: Franciscan Beginnings in Sonora and Arizona, 1767–1770.* Washington: Academy of American Franciscan History, 1981.

————, ed. and trans. "The Sonoran Prophecy of 1783." *Journal of the Southwest* 32 (1990): 316–20.

————, ed. and trans. *Desert Documentary: The Spanish Years, 1767–1821.* Tucson: Arizona Historical Society, 1976.

McCauley, Clark. "Conference Overview." In *Anthropology of War,* edited by Jonathan Haas, 1–25. Cambridge: Cambridge University Press, 1990.

McClelland, I. L. *Ideological Hesitancy in Spain, 1700–1750.* Liverpool: Liverpool University Press, 1991.

McElhannon, Joseph Carl. "Imperial Mexico and Texas." *Southwestern Historical Quarterly* 53 (1949): 117–50.

McNitt, Frank. *Navajo Wars: Military Campaigns, Slave Raids, and Reprisals.* Albuquerque: University of New Mexico Press, 1972.

Medina, José Toribio. *Medallas coloniales hispano-americanas.* Santiago de Chile: Impreso en casa del autor, 1900.

————. *Biblioteca Hispano-Chilena (1523–1817).* 1st ed., 1897–99; facsimile, 3 vols. Santiago de Chile: Fondo Histórico y Bibliográfico José Toribio Medina, 1963.

Medina, Miguel Ángel. *Los dominicos en América: Presencia y actuación de los dominicos en la América colonial española de los siglos XVI–XIX.* Madrid: Editorial MAPFRE, 1992.

Meek, Ronald L. *Social Science and the Ignoble Savage.* Cambridge: Cambridge University Press, 1976.

Meggers, Betty J. *Amazonia: Man and Culture in a Counterfeit Paradise.* Rev. ed. Washington: Smithsonian Institution Press, 1996.

Meigs, Peveril, III. *The Dominican Mission Frontier of Lower California.* University of California Publications in Geography, 7. Berkeley: University of California Press, 1935.

Mena, Filiberto de. "Descripción y narración historial de la antigua provincia del Tucumán escrita por don Filiberto de Mena en 1772 [1773]." In *La patria vieja: Cuadros históricos; guerra, política, diplomacia,* edited by Gregorio F. Rodríguez, 289–476. Buenos Aires: Compañía Sud-Americana de Billetes de Banco, 1916.

Méndez Beltrán, Luz María. "La organización de los parlamentos de indios en el siglo XVIII." *Relaciones fronterizas en la Araucanía,* edited by Sergio Villalobos et al., 107–73. Santiago de Chile: Ediciones Universidad Católica de Chile, 1982.

————. "Trabajo indígena en la frontera araucana de Chile." *Jahrbuch für Geschichte von Staat, Wirtschaft und Gesellschaft Lateinamerikas* 24 (1987): 213–49.

————. "La población indígena, su distribución espacial y el proceso de aculturación en la Araucanía (siglos XVII y XVIII): El recuento de 1796." *Memoria Americana: Cuadernos de Etnohistoria,* no. 3 (1994): 9–40.

Mendinueta, Pedro. "Relación del estado del Nuevo Reino de Granada, Guaduas, Dec. 1803." In *Relaciones de mando: Memorias presentadas por los gobernantes del Nuevo Reino de Granada,* edited by Eduardo Posada and Pedro María Ibáñez, 2:411–588. 2 vols. Bogotá: Biblioteca de Historia Nacional, 1910.

Menéndez, Fray Francisco. *Viajes de fray Francisco Menéndez a la Cordillera.* Edited by Francisco Fonck. 2 vols. Valparaíso, Chile: Carlos F. Niemeyer, 1896–1900.

Mercader Riba, Juan, and Antonio Domínguez Ortiz. "La época del despotismo ilustrado." *Historia social y económica de España y América*. Vol. 4, *Los Borbones: El siglo XVIII en España y América*, edited by J. Vicens Vives. Barcelona: Editorial Vicens-Vives, 1972.

Merino, Olga, and Linda A. Newson. "Jesuit Missions in Spanish America: The Aftermath of the Expulsion." In *Yearbook, Conference of Latin Americanist Geographers*, 133–48. Austin: University of Texas Press, 1995.

Merrell, James H. *Into the American Woods: Negotiators on the Pennsylvania Frontier*. New York: W. W. Norton, 1999.

Merrill, William L. *Rarámuri Souls: Knowledge and Social Process in Northern New Mexico*. Washington: Smithsonian Institution Press, 1988.

———. "Conversion and Colonialism in Northern Mexico: The Tarahumara Response to the Jesuit Mission Program, 1601–1767." In *Conversion to Christianity: Historical and Anthropological Perspectives on a Great Transformation*, edited by Robert W. Hefner, 129–63. Berkeley: University of California Press, 1993.

———. "Cultural Creativity and Raiding Bands in Eighteenth-Century Northern New Spain." In *Violence, Resistance, and Survival in the Americas: Native Americans and the Legacy of Conquest*, edited by William B. Taylor and Franklin Pease G. Y., 124–52. Washington: Smithsonian Institution Press, 1994.

———. "La economía política de las correrías: Nueva Vizcaya al final de la época colonial." In *Nómadas y sedentarios en el norte de Mexico: Homenaje a Beatriz Braniff*, edited by Marie-Areti Hers et al., 623–68. Mexico: Instituto de Investigaciones Antropológicas, UNAM, 2000.

Messía de la Zerda [Cerda], Pedro. "Relación del estado del Virreinato de Santafé, por el Excmo. Viceroy Bailío Frey Pedro Messía de la Zerda [Cerda] To Sr. D. Manuel Guirior, Santa Fe, Sept. 14, 1772." In *Relaciones de mando: Memorias presentadas por los gobernantes del Nuevo Reino de Granada*, edited by Eduardo Posada and Pedro María Ibáñez, 1:75–92. 2 vols. Bogotá: Biblioteca de Historia Nacional, 1910.

Métraux, Alfred. "Ethnography of the Chaco." *Handbook of South American Indians* 1:197–370. Washington: Smithsonian Institution Press, 1946.

———. "Tribes of the Eastern Slopes of the Bolivian Andes." *Handbook of South American Indians* 3:465–506. Washington: Smithsonian Institution Press, 1948.

Mier, Fray Servando Teresa de. *Historia de la Revolución de Nueva España Antiguamente Anáhuac*. Edited by André Saint-Lu and Marie Cécile Bénassy-Berling. 1st ed., 1813; Paris: Publications de la Sorbonne, 1990.

Miller Astrada, Luisa. *Salta Hispánica: Estudio Socio-económico (desde el siglo XVI hasta la primera década del sigo XIX)*. Buenos Aires: Ciudad Argentina, 1997.

Milliken, Randall. *A Time of Little Choice: The Disintegration of Tribal Culture in the San Francisco Bay Area, 1769–1810*. Menlo Park: Ballena Press, 1995.

Mills, Kenneth, and William B. Taylor, eds. *Colonial Spanish America: A Documentary History*. Wilmington, Del.: SR Books, 1998.

Mirafuentes Galván, José Luis. "Seris, apaches y españoles en Sonora: Consideraciones sobre su confrontación militar en el siglo XVIII." *Históricas* 22 (1987): 18–29.

———. "Las tropas de indios auxiliares: Conquista, contrainsurgencia y rebelión en Sonora." *Estudios de historia novohispana* 13 (1993): 93–114.

———. "Relaciones interétnicas y dominación colonial en Sonora." In *Nómadas y sedentarios en el norte de Mexico: Homenaje a Beatriz Braniff*, edited by Marie-Areti Hers et al., 591–612. Mexico: Instituto de Investigaciones Antropológicas, UNAM, 2000.

Miranda Borelli, José. "Tratados de paz realizados con los indígenas en la Argentina (1597–1875)." *Suplemento Antropológico* [Asunción, Paraguay] 19, no. 2 (1984): 233–84.

Mitre, Bartolomé. *Historia de San Martín y de la emancipación sudamericana.* 2 vols. Buenos Aires: La Cultura Popular, 1937.

Mociño y Losada, José Mariano. *Noticias de Nutka: Manuscrito de 1793.* Edited by Xavier Lozoya. Mexico: Universidad Nacional Autónoma de México, 1998.

Molina, Giovanni Ignazio. *The Geographical, Natural, and Civil History of Chili: Translated from the Original Italian of the Abbe Don J. Ignatius Molina....* 1st ed., 1782 and 1787, in Italian; 2 vols. London: Longman, Hurst, Rees, and Orme, 1809.

Molinari, José Luis. "Los indios y los negros durante las invasiones al Río de la Plata, en 1806–1807." *Boletín de la Academia Nacional de la Historia* [Buenos Aires] 34 (1963): 639–73.

Moncada Maya, José Omar. *El ingeniero Miguel Constanzó: Un militar ilustrado en la Nueva España del siglo XVIII.* Mexico: UNAM, 1994.

Monge, Fernando. "Sobre indios e ilustrados: La antropología y la expedición Malaspina en la costa noroeste (1791)." In *Culturas de la Costa Noroeste de América,* edited by José Luis Peset, 51–59. Madrid: Turner Libros, 1989.

———. *En la costa de la niebla: El paisaje y el discurso ethnográfico ilustrado de la expedición Malaspina en el Pacific.* Madrid: Consejo Superior de Investigaciones Científicas, 2002.

Monge, Fernando, and Margarita del Olmo, eds. *Varias expediciones a la costa noroeste.* Madrid: Historia 16, 1991.

Montesquieu, Baron de. *The Spirit of the Laws.* Edited by Thomas Nugent. 2 vols. in 1; New York: Hafner Press, 1949.

Moore, Mary Lu, and Delmar L. Beene, eds. "The Interior Provinces of New Spain: The Report of Hugo O'Conor, January 30, 1776." *Arizona and the West* 13 (1971): 265–82.

Moorhead, Max L. *The Apache Frontier: Jacobo Ugarte and Spanish–Indian Relations in Northern New Spain, 1769–1791.* Norman: University of Oklahoma, 1968.

———. *The Presidio: Bastion of the Spanish Borderlands.* Norman: University of Oklahoma Press, 1975a.

———. "Spanish Deportation of Hostile Apaches: The Policy and the Practice." *Arizona and the West* 17 (1975b): 205–20.

Morales, Francisco. "Secularización de doctrinas: ¿Fin de un modelo evangelizador en la Nueva España?" In *Los franciscanos en el Nuevo Mundo (siglo XVIII),* 465–96. Madrid: Editorial Deimos, 1993.

Morales Padrón, Francisco. "Mexico y la independencia de Hispanoamérica en 1781, según un comisionado regio: Francisco de Saavedra." *Revista de Indias* 29 (1969): 335–58.

Morales Valerio, Francisco. "Mexico: La evangelización del noroeste." In *Historia de la Iglesia en Hispanoamérica y Filipinas,* edited by Pedro Borges, 2:163–83. 2 vols. Madrid: Biblioteca de Autores Cristianos, 1992.

Morelli, Ciriaco Domingo Muriel. *Elementos de derecho natural y de gentes, por el presbítero Ciriaco Morelli [pseud].* Translated by Luciano Abeilla. 1st ed. in Latin, 1791; 3 vols. Buenos Aires: Imprenta de Coni Hermanos, 1911.

Moreno Cebrian, Alfredo. "El ocio del indio como razón teórica del repartimiento." *Revista de Indias* 35 (1975): 167–85.

Moreno, P. Josefina, and Alberto Tarazona, eds. *Materiales para el estudio de las relaciones inter-étnicas en la Guajira, siglo XVIII: Documentos y mapas.* Biblioteca de la Academia Nacional de la Historia. Fuentes para la historia colonial de Venezuela, 167. Caracas: Academia Nacional de la Historia, 1984.

Moreno y Escandón, Francisco Antonio. "Estado del virreinato de Santafé, Nuevo Reino de Granada, ... 1772." *Boletín de Historia y Antigüedades* 23 (1936): 547–616.

Morey, Nancy C., and Robert V. Morey. "Los Sáliva." In *Los aborígenes de Venezuela,* edited by Walter Coppens, 1:245–306. 3 vols. Caracas: Fundación LaSalle, 1980–88.

Morey, Robert V., and Donald J. Metzger. *The Guahibo: People of the Savanna.* Vienna: Stiglmayr, 1974.

Morfi, Juan Agustín. *Viaje de indios y diario del Nuevo México.* Edited by Vito Alessio Robles. Mexico: José Porrua y Hijos, 1935.

———. *History of Texas, 1673–1779.* Edited and translated by Carlos Eduardo Castañeda. 1st ed., 1935; 2 vols. New York: Arno Press, 1967.

———. *Account of Disorders in New Mexico, 1778.* Edited and translated by Marc Simmons. Isleta Pueblo, N.M.: Historical Society of New Mexico, 1977.

Morillo, Francisco. "Diario del viaje al río Bermejo [1780]." In *Colección de obras y documentos relativos a la historia antigua y moderna de las provincias del Río de la Plata por Pedro de Angelis,* edited by Andés M. Carretero, 8A:383–430. 1st ed., 1836; 8 vols. Buenos Aires: Plus Ultra, 1969–72.

Mörner, Magnus, ed. *The Expulsion of the Jesuits from Latin America.* New York: Alfred A. Knopf, 1965.

———. *La corona española y los foráneos en los pueblos de indios de América.* Stockholm: Latinamerika-institutet i Stockholm, 1970.

———. "The Indians as Objects and Actors in Latin American History." In *Natives and Neighbors in South America: Anthropological Essays,* edited by Harald O. Skar and Frank Salomon, 56–91. Göteborg, Sweden: Göteborgs Etnografiska Museum, 1987.

Morris von Bennewitz, Raúl. *Los plateros de la frontera y la platería Araucana.* Temuco, Chile: Universidad de la Frontera, 1997.

Mosse, George L. *Toward the Final Solution: A History of European Racism.* New York: Howard Fertig, 1978.

Mota Padilla, Matías de la. *Histora del reino de Nueva Galicia en América Septentrional [1742].* Guadalajara: Universidad de Guadalajara, Instituto Jalisciense de Antropología e Historia, 1973.

Moziño, José Mariano. *Noticias de Nutka: An Account of Nootka Sound in 1792.* Edited and translated by Iris Wilson. Seattle: University of Washington Press, 1970.

Muldoon, James. *The Americas in the Spanish World Order: The Justification for Conquest in the Seventeenth Century.* Philadelphia: University of Pennsylvania Press, 1994.

Muñoz Pérez, José. "Los proyectos sobre España e Indias en el siglo XVIII: El proyectismo como género." *Revista de Estudios Políticos* 81 (1955): 169–95.

Muro Orejón, Antonio, ed. *Cedulario americano del siglo xviii.* 3 vols. Seville: Escuela de Estudios Hispano-Americanos, 1956–77.

Mutis, José Celestino. *Archivo epistolar del sabio naturalista don José Celestino Mutis.* Edited by Guillermo Hernández de Alba. 4 vols. Bogotá: Editorial Kelly, 1968–75.

Nacuzzi, Lidia R. "Los grupos étnicos de Patagonia y sus transformaciones." In *Fronteras, etnias, culturas: America Latina, siglos XVI–XX,* edited by Chiara Vangelista, 51–62. Quito: Abya-Yala, 1996.

———. *Identidades impuestas: Tehuelches, aucas y pampas en el norte de la Patagonia.* Buenos Aires: Sociedad Argentina de Antropología, 1998.

Narváez y la Torre, Antonio de. "Relación, o informe de la provincia de Santa Marta, y Riohacha … [May 19, 1778]." In *Escritos de dos economistas coloniales: don Antonio de Narváez y la Torre y don José Ignacio de Pombo,* edited by Sergio Elías Ortiz, 17–65. Bogotá: Banco de la República, 1965.

Nash, Gary B. "The Image of the Indian in the Southern Colonial Mind." *Race, Class, and Politics: Essays on American Colonial and Revolutionary Society,* 35–64. Urbana: University of Illinois Press, 1986.

———. "The Hidden History of Mestizo America." *Journal of American History* 82, no. 3 (1995): 941–62.

Navarro Floria, Pedro. *Ciencia y política en la región norpatagónica: El ciclo fundador (1779–1806).* Temuco, Chile: Departamento de Humanidades, Facultad de Educación y Humanidades, Universidad de la Frontera, 1994a.

————. "Salvajes, bárbaros y civilizados: Los indios de la Patagonia y Tierra del Fuego ante la antropología de la Ilustración." *Cuadernos del Instituto Nacional de Antropología y Pensamiento Latino-americano* 15 (1994b): 113–40.

————. "Salvajes y bárbaros: La construcción de la idea de barbarie en la frontera sur argentina y chilena (siglos XVIII–XIX)." *Saber y Tiempo* 2 (1996): 101–12.

————. "Ciencia de frontera y mirada metropolitana: Las ciencias del hombre ante los indios de la Araucanía, las Pampas y la Patagonia (1779–1829)." *Cuadernos del Instituto Nacional de Antropología y Pensamiento Latinoamericano* 17 (1996–97): 115–43.

————. "'Formar patria a hombres que no la tienen': Pedro Andrés García, entre la frontera colonial y la política de conquista." *Revista Complutense de Historia de América* 25 (1999): 253–80.

————. "El *salvaje* y su tratamiento en el discurso político argentino sobre la frontera sur, 1853–1879." *Revista de Indias* 61, no. 222 (2001): 345–76.

Navarro García, Luis. *Don José de Gálvez y la Comandancia General de las provincias internas del norte de Nueva España.* Seville: Escuela de Estudios Hispanoamericanos, 1964.

————. "Campillo y el Nuevo Sistema: Una atribución dudosa." *Temas Americanistas* 2 (1983): 22–29.

————. *Hispanoamérica en el siglo xviii.* 2d ed. Seville: Universidad de Sevilla, 1991.

————. "Poblamiento y colonización estratégica en el siglo XVIII indiano." *Temas Americanistas* 11 (1994): 15–21.

————. "El falso campillo y el reformismo borbónico." *Temas Americanistas* 12 (1995): 5–14.

————. "La crisis del reformismo borbónico bajo Carlos IV." *Temas Americanistas* 13 (1997a): 1–8.

————. "El primer proyecto reformista de José de Gálvez." In *Entre Puebla de los Angeles y Sevilla: Estudios americanistas en homenaje al Dr. José Antonio Calderón Quijano,* edited by María Justina Sarabia et al., 387–402. Seville: Escuela de Estudios Hispano-Americanos y Universidad de Sevilla, 1997b.

————. *La política americana de José de Gálvez según su "Discurso y reflexiones de un vasallo."* Málaga, Spain: Editorial Algazara, 1998.

Naylor, Thomas H., and Charles W. Polzer, eds. *Pedro de Rivera and the Military Regulations for Northern New Spain, 1724–1729: A Documentary History of His Frontier Inspection and the Reglamento de 1729.* Tucson: University of Arizona Press, 1988.

Nentvig, Juan S. J. *Rudo Ensayo: A Description of Sonora and Arizona in 1764.* Edited and translated by Alberto Francisco Pradeau and Robert R. Rasmussen. Tucson: University of Arizona Press, 1980.

Neve, Felipe de. *Reglamento para el gobierno de la provincia de Californias, 1781.* Edited by Salvador Bernabéu Albert. Madrid: Doce Calles, 1994.

Newson, Linda. *The Cost of Conquest: Indian Decline in Honduras under Spanish Rule.* Boulder: Westview Press, 1986.

Niel, Juan Amando. "Apuntamientos que sobre el terreno hizo el Padre Juan Amando Niel de la Compañía de Jesús: Y pueden servir de explicación a las memorias que del Nuevo-Mexico y partes articas de la América Septentrional, nos dejó manscritas [manuscritas] el padre fray Gerónimo de Zarate Salmeron. . . ." In *Documentos para la historia de Méjico: Tercera Serie* 1:56–112. Mexico: Imprenta de J. R. Navarro, 1856.

Noel, C. C. "Opposition to Enlightened Reform in Spain: Campomanes and the Clergy, 1765–1775." *Societas* 3, no. 1 (1973): 21–43.

Noggler, Albert. *Cuatrocientos años de misión entre los araucanos.* Temuco, Chile: Editorial San Francisco, 1972.

Norris, Jim. *After the Year Eighty: The Demise of Franciscan Power in Spanish New Mexico.* Albuquerque: University of New Mexico Press and The Academy of American Franciscan History, 2000.

Núñez de Pineda y Bascuñán, Francisco. *Cautiverio feliz y razón individual de las guerras dilatadas del Reino de Chile.* Edited by Alejandro Lipshutz and Álvaro Jara. Santiago de Chile: Editorial Universitaria, 1973.

O'Brien, Greg. *Choctaws in a Revolutionary Age, 1750–1830.* Lincoln: University of Nebraska Press, 2002.

O'Brien, Jay, and William Roseberry. *Golden Ages, Dark Ages: Imagining the Past in Anthropology and History.* Berkeley: University of California Press, 1991.

O'Conor, Hugo. *The Defenses of Northern New Spain: Hugo O'Conor's Report to Teodoro de Croix, July 22, 1777.* Edited and translated by Donald C. Cutter. Dallas: Southern Methodist University Press/DeGolyer Library, 1994.

O'Crouley, Pedro Alonso. *A Description of the Kingdom of New Spain.* Edited and translated by Seán Galvin. 1st ed., in Spanish, 1774; San Francisco: John Howell, 1972.

O'Donnell, Hugo. *España en el descubrimiento, conquista y defensa del mar del sur.* Madrid: Editorial MAPFRE, 1992.

O'Higgins, Tomás. "Viaje del capitán D. Tomás O'Higgins, de orden del virrey de Lima, el marqués de Osorno [1796–97]." *Revista Chilena de Historia y Geografía,* no. 101, 103 (1942–43): 42–97, 30–82.

O'Phelan Godoy, Scarlett. "Rebeliones andinas anticoloniales: Nueva Granada, Peru y Charcas entre el siglo XVIII y el XIX." *Anuario de Estudios Americanos* 49 (1991): 395–440.

Oberg, Michael Leroy. *Dominion and Civility: English Imperialism and Native America, 1585–1685.* Ithaca: Cornell University Press, 1999.

Obeyesekere, Gananath. *The Apotheosis of Captain Cook: European Mythmaking in the Pacific.* Princeton and Honolulu: Princeton University Press and Bishop Museum Press, 1992.

Offen, Karl H. "British Logwood Extraction from the Mosquitia: The Origin of a Myth." *Hispanic American Historical Review* 80 (2000): 113–35.

———. "The Sambo and Tawira Miskitu: The Colonial Origins and Geography of Intra-Miskitu Differentiation in Eastern Nicaragua and Honduras." *Ethnohistory* 49 (2002): 319–56.

Officer, James E. *Hispanic Arizona, 1536–1856.* Tucson: University of Arizona Press, 1987.

Ojer, Pablo. *El Golfo de Venezuela: Una síntesis histórica.* Caracas: Instituto de Derecho Público de la Universidad Central de Venezuela, 1983.

Olaechea Labayen, Juan B. "Experiencias cristianos con el indio antillano." *Anuario de Estudios Americanos* 26 (1969): 65–114.

———. "La ilustración y el clero mestizo en América." *Missionalia Hispánica* 33 (1976): 165–79.

———. "La ciudadanía del indio en los dominios hispanos." *Cuadernos de Investigación Histórica* 5 (1981): 113–33.

———. *El indigenismo desdeñado: La lucha contra la marginación del indio en la América Española.* Madrid: Colecciones MAPFRE, 1992.

Olien, Michael D. "General, Governor, and Admiral: Three Miskito Lines of Succession." *Ethnohistory* 45 (1998): 277–318.

Oliveros de Castro, Maria Teresa. *La goajira.* Merida: Universidad de los Andes, 1975.

Olmos Sánchez, Isabel. "Consideraciones sobre la población indígena novohispana a finales del periodo colonial." *Estudios de Historia Social y Económica de América* 2 (1986): 217–41.

Oltra, Joaquín, and María Angeles Pérez Samper. *El conde de Aranda y los Estados Unidos.* Barcelona: PPU, 1987.

Operé, Fernando. *Historias de la frontera: El cautiverio en la América hispánica.* Mexico: Fondo de Cultura Económica, 2001.

Opler, Morris. "The Apachean Culture Pattern and Its Origins." In *Handbook of American Indians.* Vol. 10, *Southwest,* edited by Alfonso Ortiz, 368–92. Washington: Smithsonian Institution Press, 1983.

Orbigny, Alcides d'. *Voyage dans l'Amérique méridionale (le Brésil, la république orientale de l'Uruguay, la République argentine, la Patagonie, la république du Chili, la république de Bolivia, la république du Pérou), exécuté pendant les années 1826, 1827, 1828, 1829, 1830, 1831, 1832, et 1833.* 9 vols; Paris: Chez P. Bertrand, 1835–47.

————. *Viaje a la América meridional: Brasil, República del Uruguay, República Argentina, la Patagonia, República de Chile, República de Bolivia, República del Perú: Realizado de 1826 a 1833.* Translated by Alfredo Cepeda. 1st French ed., 1835–47; 4 vols.; Buenos Aires: Editorial Futuro, 1945.

Ortega y Medina, Juan A. *La evangelización puritana en Norteamérica.* Mexico: Fondo de Cultura Económica, 1976.

————. *Reflexiones históricas.* Mexico: Consejo Nacional para la Cultura y las Artes, 1993.

Ortelli, Sara. "La 'araucanización de las pampas': ¿Realidad histórica o construcción de los etnólogos?" *Anuario del IEHS* 11 (1996): 203–25.

————. "Marginalismo y relaciones interétnicas: Blancos e indios en la frontera rioplatense en el siglo XIX." *Revista Complutense de Historia de América* 26 (2000): 181–98.

————. "¿Quiénes eran los 'enemigos' en Nueva Vizcaya a fines del siglo XVIII?" In *Las fronteras hispanocriollas del mundo indígena latinoamericano en los siglos XVIII–IX. Un estúdio comparativo,* edited by Raúl J. Mandrini and Carlos D. Paz, 461–79. Tandil, Argentina: IEHS/CEHIR/UNS, 2002.

————. "La frontera pampeana en las últimas décadas del periodo colonial: Las delegaciones de indios y el comercio con Buenos Aires." In *Territorio, frontera y región en la historia de América: Siglos XVI al XX,* edited by Marco Antonio Landavazo, 71–110. San Nicolás de Hidalgo, Mexico: Universidad Michoacana de San Nicolás de Hidalgo/Editorial Porrúa, 2003a.

————. "Trama de una guerra conveniente: 'Apaches,' infidentes y abigeos en Nueva Vizcaya en el siglo XVIII." Ph.D. diss., Colegio de México, 2003b.

Osante, Patricia. *Orígenes del Nuevo Santander, 1748–1772.* Mexico: UNAM and the Universidad Autónoma de Tamaulipas, 1997a.

————. "Presencia misional en Nuevo Santander en la segunda mitad del siglo XVIII: Memoria de un infortunio." *Estudios de Historia Novohispana* 17 (1997b): 107–35.

Oses, Boris. "Los esfuerzos por integrar en pueblos a los araucanos en el siglo XVIII." *Revista de Indias* 21 (1961): 39–62.

Osterhammel, Jürgen. *Colonialism: A Theoretical Overview.* Translated by Shelley L. Frisch. Princeton, N.J.: Markus Wiener, 1997.

Outram, Dorinda. *The Enlightenment.* Cambridge: Cambridge University Press, 1995.

Oviedo Cavada, Carlos. "La defensa del indio en el sínodo del obispo Azúa de 1744." *Historia* [Universidad Católica de Chile] 17 (1982): 281–354.

Padden, Robert C. "Cultural Change and Military Resistance in Araucanian Chile, 1550–1730." *Southwestern Journal of Anthropology* 13 (1957): 103–21.

Pagden, Anthony. *The Fall of Natural Man: The American Indian and the Origins of Comparative Ethnology.* Cambridge: Cambridge University Press, 1982.

————. *Spanish Imperialism and the Political Imagination.* New Haven: Yale University Press, 1990.

————. "The Creation of Identity in Colonial Spanish America: c. 1520–1830." In Anthony Pagden, *The Uncertainties of Empire: Essays in Iberian and Ibero-American Intellectual History,* 1–93. Aldershot, Great Britain: Variorum, 1994a.

————. "The 'Defence of Civilization' in Eighteenth-Century Social Theory." In Anthony Pagden, *The Uncertainties of Empire: Essays in Iberian and Ibero-American Intellectual History,* 33–45. Aldershot, Great Britain: Variorum, 1994b.

————. "Liberty, Honour and Comercio Libre: The Structure of the Debates over the State of the Spanish Empire in the Eighteenth Century." In Anthony Pagden, *The Uncertainties of Empire:*

Essays in Iberian and Ibero-American Intellectual History, 1–22. Aldershot, Great Britain: Variorum, 1994c.

———. "The Reception of the 'New Philosophy' in Eighteenth-Century Spain." In Anthony Pagden, *The Uncertainties of Empire: Essays in Iberian and Ibero-American Intellectual History,* 126–40. Aldershot, Great Britain: Variorum, 1994d.

———. *Lords of All the World: Ideologies of Empire in Spain, Britain and France c. 1500–c. 1800.* New Haven: Yale University Press, 1995.

Palacio Atard, Vicente. "Spanish Enlightened Despotism." In *The Bourbon Reformers and Spanish Civilization,* edited and translated by Troy S. Floyd, 31–35. Boston: D. C. Heath, 1966.

Palau, Mercedes. "Alejandro Malaspina and His Vision of Colonial America Spain and the North Pacific Coast." In *Essays in Recognition of the Bicentennial of the Malaspina Expedition, 1791–1792,* edited by Robin Inglis, 125–32. Vancouver: University of British Columbia and the Vancouver Maritime Museum, 1992.

Palermo, Miguel Angel. "Reflexiones sobre el llamado 'complejo ecuestre' en la Argentina." *Runa* 16 (1986): 157–77.

———. "La innovación agropecuaria entre los indígenas pampeano-patagónicos: Génesis y procesos." *Anuario del IEHS* 3 (1988): 43–90.

———. "La compleja integración hispano-indígena del sur argentina y chileno durante el período colonial." *América Indígena* 51 (1991): 153–92.

———. *Documentos del Archivo General de Indias en el Museo Etnográfico: Catálogo y fichero analítico.* Buenos Aires: Universidad de Buenos Aires, Facultad de Filosofía y Letras-Museo Etnográfico "Juan B. Ambrosetti," 1992.

———. "El revés de la trama: Apuntes sobre el papel económico de la mujer en las sociedades indígenas tradicionales del sur argentino." *Memoria Americana: Cuadernos de Etnohistoria,* no. 3 (1994): 63–90.

Palóu, Francisco. *Historical Memoirs of New California.* Edited and translated by Herbert E. Bolton. 4 vols. Berkeley: University of California Press, 1926.

———. *Relación histórica de la vida y apostólicas tareas del venerable padre Fray Junípero Serra.* Edited by Miguel León-Portilla. Mexico: Editorial Porrúa, 1970.

Parejas Moreno, Alcides. "Don Lázaro de Ribera, gobernador de la provincia de Moxos, 1784–1792." *Anuario de Estudios Americanos* 33 (1976a): 949–62.

———. *Historia de Moxos y Chiquitos a fines del siglo XVIII.* La Paz: Instituto Boliviano de Cultura, 1976b.

Parejas Moreno, Alcides, and Virgilio Suárez Salas. *Chiquitos: Historia de una utopia.* Santa Cruz, Bolivia: Cordecruz and the Universidad Privada de Santa Cruz de la Sierra, 1992.

Park, Joseph F. "Spanish Indian Policy in Northern Mexico, 1765–1810." In *New Spain's Far Northern Frontier: Essays on Spain in the American West,* edited by David J. Weber, 217–36. Albuquerque: University of New Mexico Press, 1979.

Parras, Pedro Joseph. *Gobierno de los regulares de la América, ajustado religiosamente a la voluntad del Rey.... Para instrucción de los Prelados Generales, Provinciales, Visitadores y otros Delegados en las obligaciones de sus oficios respectivamente para con el Rey y para con sus súbditos.* 2 vols. Madrid: Joachín Ibarra, 1783.

Patch, Robert W. *Maya and Spaniard in Yucatan, 1648–1812.* Stanford: Stanford University Press, 1993.

Paucke, Florián. *Hacia allá y para acá (una estada entre los indios mocobíes, 1749–1767).* Edited and translated by Edmundo Wernicke. 3 vols. Tucumán, Argentina: Universidad Nacional de Tucumán, 1942–44.

Payne, Stanley G. *A History of Spain and Portugal.* 2 vols. Madison: University of Wisconsin Press, 1973.

Paz, Carlos Daniel. "'Como es su costumbre hacer casi cada año': Algunas consideraciones sobre las actividades económicas de los pueblos del Gran Chaco argentino. Siglo XVIII." In *Las fronteras hispanocriollas del mundo indígena latinoamericano en los siglos XVIII–IX: Un estúdio comparativo*, edited by Raúl J. Mandrini and Carlos D. Paz, 377–405. Tandil, Argentina: IEHS/CEHIR/UNS, 2002.

———. "'La mente de los bárbaros no siempre es bárbara': Consideraciones sobre el funcionamiento de la economía indígena chaqueña en el marco de los intentos de incorporación estatal." In *Territorio, frontera y región en la historia de América: Siglos XVI al XX*, edited by Marco Antonio Landavazo, 111–44. San Nicolás de Hidalgo: Universidad Michoacana de San Nicolás de Hidalgo/Editorial Porrúa, 2003.

Paz, Julián, Clotilde Olaran, and Mercedes Jalón, eds. *Catálogo de los manuscritos de América existentes en la Biblioteca Nacional*. 1st ed., 1933; rev. ed., Madrid: Ministerio de Cultura, 1992.

Pearce, Roy Harvey. *Savagism and Civilization: A Study of the American Mind*. 1st ed., 1953; Baltimore: Johns Hopkins University Press, 1965.

Peña, Gabriela Alejandra. *La evangelización de indios, negros y gente de castas en Córdoba del Tucumán durante la dominación española (1573–1810)*. Córdoba, Argentina: Facultad de Filosofía y Humanidades, Universidad Católica de Córdoba, 1997.

Peralta, Manuel M., ed. *Costa Rica y Costa de Mosquitos: Documentos para la historia de la jurisdicción territorial de Costa Rica y Colombia*. Paris: Imprimerie Générale Lahure, 1898.

Perdue, Theda. *Slavery and the Evolution of Cherokee Society, 1540–1866*. Knoxville: University of Tennessee Press, 1979.

———. *Cherokee Women: Gender and Culture Change, 1700–1835*. Lincoln: University of Nebraska Press, 1998.

Pérez Ayala, José Manuel. *Antonio Caballero y Góngora, Virrey y Arzobispo de Santa Fe, 1723–1796*. Bogotá: Imprenta Municipal de Bogotá, 1951.

Pérez de Ribas, Andrés. *History of the Triumphs of Our Holy Faith amongst the Most Barbarous and Fierce Peoples of the New World [1645]*. Edited and translated by Daniel T. Reff, Maureen Ahern, and Richard K. Danford. Tucson: University of Arizona Press, 1999.

Pérez de Uriondo, Dr. "Informe y dictamen del fiscal de Chile sobre las ciudades de los Césares, y los arbitrios que deberían emplear para descubrirlas [1782]." In *Colección de obras y documentos relativos a la historia antigua y moderna de las provincias del Río de la Plata por Pedro de Angelis*, edited by Andrés M. Carretero, 2:594–636. 1st ed., 1836; 8 vols. Buenos Aires: Editorial Plus Ultra, 1969–72.

Pérez, Joseph. "Tradición e innovación en América del siglo XVIII." In *La América española en la época de las Luces: tradición, innovación, representaciones*, 267–79. Madrid: Ediciones de Cultura Hispánica, 1988.

Pérez Magallón, Jesús. *Construyendo la modernidad: La cultura española en el tiempo de los novatores (1675–1725)*. Madrid: CSIS, 2002.

Perry, Claire. *Pacific Arcadia: Images of California, 1600–1915*. New York: Oxford University Press, 1999.

Perry, Richard J. *Western Apache Heritage: People of the Mountain Corridor*. Austin: University of Texas Press, 1991.

———. *From Time Immemorial: Indigenous Peoples and State Systems*. Austin: University of Texas Press, 1996.

Pfefferkorn, Ignaz. *Sonora: A Description of the Province*. Edited and translated by Teodore E. Treutlein. 1st ed., 1949; Tucson: University of Arizona Press, 1989.

Phelan, John Leddy. "Neo-Aztecism in the Eighteenth Century and the Genesis of Mexican Nationalism." In *Culture in History: Essays in Honor of Paul Radin*, edited by Stanley Diamond, 760–70. New York: Colombia University Press, 1960.

———. *The Millennial Kingdom of the Franciscans in the New World.* 1st ed., 1956; 2d ed., rev. Berkeley: University of California Press, 1970.

Phillips, George Harwood. *Indians and Intruders in Central California, 1769–1849.* Norman: University of Oklahoma Press, 1993.

Pi Hugarte, Renzo. *Los indios de Uruguay.* Madrid: Editorial MAPFRE, 1993.

———. *Historias de aquella "gente gandul": Españoles y criollos vs. indios en la Banda Oriental.* Montevideo: Ediciones Universitarias de Ciencias, Editorial Fin de Siglo, 1999.

Pietschmann, Horst. "Estado y conquistadores: Las capitulaciones." *Historia* [Universidad Católica de Chile] 22 (1987): 249–62.

———. "Actores locales y poder central: La herencia colonial y el caso de México." In *Nation Building in Nineteenth-Century Latin America: Dilemmas and Conflicts,* edited by Hans-Joachim König and Marianne Wiesebron, 257–80. Leiden, Netherlands: Research School CNWS, 1998.

Pifarré, Francisco. *Los Guaraní-Chiriguano, 2: Historia de un pueblo.* La Paz, Bolivia: Centro de Investigación y Promoción del Campesinado, 1989.

Pike, Ruth. *Penal Servitude in Early Modern Spain.* Madison: University of Wisconsin Press, 1983.

Pimentel Igea, Juan. *Malaspina y la Ilustración (pensamiento político, utopía y realidad colonial en Alejandro Malaspina).* Madrid: Instituto de Historia y Cultura Naval, Ministerio de Defensa, 1989.

———. "Los hombres tras el cristal: Antropología y noticias etnográficas en la expedición Malaspina." In *La expedición Malaspina, 1789–1794.* Vol. 5, *Antropología y noticias etnográficas,* edited by Dolores Higueras Rodríguez and Juan Pimentel Igea, 11–19. Madrid: Ministerio de Defensa, Museo Naval, and Lunwerg Editores, 1993.

Pimentel, Juan. *La física de la monarquía: ciencia y política en el pensamiento de Alejandro Malaspina (1754–1810).* Madrid: Doce Calles, 1998.

Pino Díaz, Fermín, and Angel Guirao de Vierna. "Las expediciones ilustradas y el estado español." In *Ciencia y contexto histórico nacional en las expediciones ilustradas a América,* edited by Fermín Pino Díaz, 19–69. Madrid: Consejo Superior de Investigaciones Científicas, 1988.

Pino Díaz, Fermín del. "Los estudios etnográficos y etnológicos en la expedición Malaspina." *Revista de Indias* 42 (1982): 393–465.

———. "Humanismo renacentista y orígenes de la etnología: a propósito del P. Acosta, paradigma del humanismo antropológico jesuita." *Humanismo y visión del otro en la España moderna: Cuatro estudios,* edited by Berta Ares, 379–429. Madrid: Consejo Superior de Investigaciones Científicas, 1992.

Pino, Pedro Baptista. *The Exposition on the Province of New Mexico, 1812.* Edited and translated by Adrian Bustamante and Marc Simmons. 1st ed., 1812; facsimile, Albuquerque: Rancho de las Golindrinas and the University of New Mexico Press, 1995.

Pinto Rodríguez, Jorge. "Frontera, misiones, y misioneros en Chile, y Araucania (1600–1900)." In *Misioneros en la Araucanía, 1600–1900: Un capítulo de historia fronteriza en Chile,* edited by Jorge Pinto Rodríguez et al., 17–120. Temuco, Chile: Ediciones Universidad de la Frontera, 1988.

———. "Del antiindigenismo al proindigenismo en Chile en el siglo XIX." In *Del discurso colonial al proindigenismo: Ensayos de historia latinoamericana,* edited by Jorge Pinto Rodríguez, 85–117. Temuco, Chile: Ediciones Universidad de la Frontera, 1996.

———. *De la inclusión a la exclusión: La formación del estado, la nación y el pueblo mapuche.* Santiago de Chile: Instituto de Estudios Avanzados, Universidad de Santiago, 2000.

Piqueras Céspedes, Ricardo. "Alfinger y Portolá: Dos modelos de frontera." *Boletín Americanista* 42–43 (1992–93): 107–21.

Pivel Devoto, Juan E. *Raíces coloniales de la revolución oriental, 1811.* 1st ed., 1952; 2d ed., Montevideo: Editorial Medina, 1957.

Poenitz, Edgar L., and Alfredo Poenitz. *Misiones, provincia guaranítica: Defensa y disolución, 1768–1830.* Posadas, Argentina: Universidad Nacional de Misiones, 1993.

Polo Acuña, José. "Los Wayúu y los Cocina: Dos caras diferentes de una misma moneda en la resistencia indígena en la Guajira, siglo XVIII." *Anuario Colombiano de Historia Social y de la Cultura*
26 (1999a): 7–29.

———. "Una mediación fallida: Las acciones del cacique Cecilio López Sierra y el conflicto
hispano-wayúu en la Guajira 1750–1770." *Historia Caribe* 2, no. 4 (1999b): 67–76.

Polt, John H. R. *Jovellanos and His English Sources: Economic, Philosophical, and Political Writings.* Philadelphia: American Philosophical Society, 1964.

———. *Gaspar Melchor de Jovellanos.* New York: Twayne, 1971.

Polzer, Charles W., and Thomas E. Sheridan, eds. *The Presidio and Militia on the Northern Frontier
of New Spain: A Documentary History.* Vol. 2, Part 1, *The Californias and Sinaloa-Sonora, 1700–1765.*
Tucson: University of Arizona Press, 1997.

Ponç i Fullano, Andreu. *Fr. Rafel Josep Verger i Suau.* Mallorca: Editorial Moll, 1990.

Poole, Stafford, and Roque Madrid. "War by Fire and Blood: The Church and the Chichimecas,
1585." *The Americas* 22 (1965): 115–37.

Porras Muñoz, Guillermo. *Iglesia y estado en Nueva Vizcaya, 1562–1821.* 1st ed., 1966; Mexico: Universidad Nacional Autónoma de México, 1980.

Portillo Valdés, José M. *Crisis Atlántica: Autonomía e independencia en la crisis del mundo hispano.* Barcelona: Marcial Pons, 2005.

Powell, Philip Wayne. *Soldiers, Indians, and Silver: North America's First Frontier War.* Berkeley: University of California Press, 1952.

———. *Mexico's Miguel Caldera: The Taming of America's First Frontier, 1548–1597.* Tucson: University of Arizona Press, 1977.

Powell, Philip Wayne, and María L. Powell, eds. *War and Peace on the North Mexican Frontier: A Documentary Record.* Vol. 1, *"Crescendo of the Chichimeca War" (1551–1585).* Madrid: José Porrúa Turanzas, 1971.

Powell, Phillip Wayne. *Tree of Hate: Propaganda and Prejudices Affecting United States Relations with
the Hispanic World.* New York: Basic Books, 1971.

Powers, Karen Viera. *Andean Journeys: Migration, Ethnogenesis, and the State in Colonial Quito.* Albuquerque: University of New Mexico Press, 1995.

Pratt, Mary Louise. *Imperial Eyes: Travel Writing and Transculturation.* London: Routledge, 1992.

Preston, Jean. *The Mosquito Indians and Anglo-Spanish Rivalry in Central America, 1630–1821.* Latin
American Studies Occasional Paper No. 48. Glasgow: University of Glasgow, 1987.

Priestley, Herbert Ingram. *José Gálvez, Visitor-general of New Spain (1765–1771).* Berkeley: University
of California Press, 1916.

Primo y Medina, María de los Angeles. "Los mocovíes argentinos durante la etapa franciscana."
Archivo Iberoamericano 46, no. 181–84 (1986): 885–900.

Prucha, Francis Paul. *Indian Peace Medals in American History.* Lincoln: University of Nebraska
Press, 1971.

———. *The Great Father: The United States Government and the American Indians.* 2 vols. Lincoln:
University of Nebraska Press, 1984.

———. *American Indian Treaties: The History of a Political Anomaly.* Berkeley: University of California
Press, 1994.

Quijada, Mónica. "Repensando la frontera sur argentina: Concepto, contenido, continuidades y
discontinuidades de una realidad espacial y étnica (siglos XVIII–XIX)." *Revista de Indias* 62
(2002): 103–42.

Radaelli, Sigfrido A., ed. *Memorias de los virreyes del Río de la Plata.* Buenos Aires: Editorial Bajel, 1945.

Radding, Cynthia. *Entre el desierto y la sierra: Las naciones o'odham y tegüima de Sonora, 1540–1840.*
Historia de los Pueblos Indígenas de México. Mexico: CIESAS/INI, 1995.

————. *Wandering Peoples: Colonialism, Ethnic Spaces, and Ecological Frontiers in Northwestern Mexico, 1700–1850*. Durham: Duke University Press, 1997.

————. "Cultural Boundaries between Adaptation and Defiance: The Mission Communities of Northwestern New Spain." In *Spiritual Encounters: Interactions between Christianity and Native Religions in Colonial America*, edited by Nicholas Griffiths and Fernando Cervantes, 116–35. Lincoln: University of Nebraska Press, 1998.

————. "From the Counting House to the Field and Loom: Comparative Frontier Economies in Sonora (Mexico) and Chiquitanía (Bolivia)." *Hispanic American Historical Review* 81 (2001): 45–87.

Ramenofsky, Ann F. "Historical Science and Contact Period Studies." In *Columbian Consequences*. Vol. 3, *The Spanish Borderlands in Pan-American Perspective*, edited by David Hurst Thomas, 3:437–52. 3 vols. Washington: Smithsonian Institution Press, 1991.

Ramírez, Fr. Francisco Xavier. *Coronicón sacro-imperial de Chile [1805]*. Edited by Jaime Valenzuela Márquez. Santiago, Chile: Dirección de Bibliotecas, Archivos y Museos, Centro de Investigaciones Diego Barros Arana, 1994.

Ramos, Hector R. Feliciano. *El contrabando inglés en el Caribe y el golfo de Mexico (1748–1778)*. Seville: Diputación Provincial de Sevilla, 1990.

Ramos Pérez, Demetrio. "El problema de los caribes de Guayana y los proyectos sobre el área del Cuchivero-Caura." *Estudios de Historia Venezolana*, 597–650. Caracas: Academia Nacional de la Historia, 1976a.

————. "Las misiones del Orinoco a la luz de sus pugnas territoriales (s. XVII y XVIII)." *Estudios de Historia Venezolana*, 507–40. Caracas: Academia Nacional de la Historia, 1976b.

————. "'Linea' y 'Frontera': De Tordesillas a la borbonización delimitadora." *Boletín de la Real Academia de la Historia* 191, no. 2 (1994): 197–214.

Ras, Norberto. *Crónica de la frontera sur*. Buenos Aires: Academia Nacional de Agronomía y Veterinaria, 1994.

Ratto, Silvia. "Indios amigos e indios aliados: Orígenes del 'Negocio Pacífico' en la Provincia de Buenos Aires (1829–1832)." *Cuadernos del Instituto Revignani* 5 (1994a): 1–34.

————. "El 'negocio pacífico de los indios': La frontera bonaerense durante el gobierno de Rosas." *Siglo XIX, nueva época*, no. 15 (1994b): 25–45.

————. "¿Finanzas públicas o negocios privados? El sistema de racionamiento del negocio pacífico de indios en la época de Rosas." In *Caudillismos rioplatenses: Nuevas miradas a un viejo problema*, edited by Noemí Goldman and Ricardo Salvatore, 241–65. Buenos Aires: Eudeba, 1998.

————. "Soberanos, 'clientes,' o vecinos?: Algunas consideraciones sobre la condición de los indígenas en la sociedad bonaerense." In *Conflicto, poder y justicia en la frontera bonaerense, 1818–1832*, edited by Daniel Villar, 9–42. Bahía Blanca and Santa Rosa, Argentina: Departamento de Humanidades, Universidad National del Sur, and Facultad de Ciencias Humanas, Universidad de la Pampa, 2003a.

————. "Una experiencia fronteriza exitosa: El negocio pacífico de indios en la provincia de Buenos Aires (1829–1852)." *Revista de Indias* 53 (2003b): 191–222.

Rausch, Jane M. *A Tropical Plains Frontier: The Llanos of Colombia, 1531–1831*. Albuquerque: University of New Mexico Press, 1984.

————. *The Llanos Frontier in Colombian History, 1830–1930*. Albuquerque: University of New Mexico Press, 1993.

"Real ordenanza para el establecimiento é instrucción de intendentes de ejército y provincia en el virreinato de Buenos Aires [1782]." In *Documentos referentes a la guerra de la independencia y emancipación política de la República Argentina* 1:29–95. 3 vols. Buenos Aires: Archivo de la Nación, 1914.

Recopilación de leyes de los Reynos de las Indias . . . 1st ed., 1681; 4 vols. Madrid: Editorial Cultural Hispánica, 1973.

Redmond, Elsa. *Tribal and Chiefly Warfare in South America.* Ann Arbor: Memoirs of the Museum of Anthropology, 1994.

Reeve, Frank D. "Navajo Foreign Affairs, 1795–1846." *New Mexico Historical Review* 46 (1971): 101–32, 223–52.

Reeve, Mary-Elizabeth. "Regional Interaction in the Western Amazon: The Early Colonial Encounter and the Jesuit Years: 1538–1767." *Ethnohistory* 41 (1994): 106–38.

Reff, Daniel T. *Disease, Depopulation, and Culture Change in Northwestern New Spain, 1518–1764.* Salt Lake City: University of Utah Press, 1991.

———. "The Jesuit Mission Frontier in Comparative Perspective: The Reductions of the Río de la Plata and the Missions of Northwestern Mexico, 1588–1700." In *Contested Ground: Comparative Frontiers on the Northern and Southern Edges of the Spanish Empire,* edited by Donna J. Guy and Thomas E. Sheridan, 16–31. Tucson: University of Arizona Press, 1998.

René-Moreno, Gabriel. *Catálogo del archivo de Mojos y Chiquitos.* 1st ed. 1888; La Paz: Librería Editorial Juventud, 1973.

Represa, Amando, ed. *La España ilustrada en el lejano oeste (viajes y exploraciones por las provincias y territorios hispánicos de Norteamérica en el siglo XVIII).* Valladolid: Junta de Castilla y León, Consejería de Cultura y Bienestar Social, 1990.

Requena, Francisco de. *Ilustrados y bárbaros: Diario de la exploración de límites al Amazonas (1782).* Edited by Manuel Lucena Giraldo. Madrid: Alianza, 1991.

Revillagigedo, Conde de. "Officio del Conde de Revillagigedo sobre secularización de curatos y separar de ellos a los Regulares [1754]." In *Instrucciones que los Virreyes de Nueva España dejaron a sus Sucesores,* 41–43. 2 vols. Mexico: Imprenta Imperial, 1867.

———. "Carta dirigida a la Corte de España contestando a la Real Orden sobre establecimientos de Misiones [Dec. 27, 1793]." In *Informe sobre las misiones, 1793, e Instrucción reservada al marqués de Branciforte, 1794,* edited by José Bravo Ugarte, 1–116. Mexico: Editorial JUS, 1966a.

———. "Instrucción reservada que del conde de Revilla Gigedo dió a su sucesor en el mando, marqués de Branciforte [1794]." *Informe sobre las misiones, 1793, e Instrucción reservada al marqués de Branciforte, 1794,* edited by José Bravo Ugarte, 117–390. Mexico: Editorial JUS, 1966b.

———. "Instruccion del Sr. Conde de Revillagigedo al Sr. Marqués de las Amarillas [Nov. 28, 1754]." In *Instrucciones y memorias de los virreyes novohispanos,* edited by Ernesto Torre Villar and Ramiro Navarro de Anda, 2:793–864. 2 vols. Mexico: Editorial Porrúa, 1991.

Reyes, Fray Antonio María de los. *Relaciones de las misiones de Sonora y Sinaloa (1784).* Edited by Roberto Ramos and Nicolás Vidales Soto. 1st ed., 1958; Culiacán Rosales, Sinaloa: Creativos, 2002.

Ricard, Robert. *The Spiritual Conquest of Mexico: An Essay on the Apostalate and the Evangelizing Methods of the Mendicant Orders in New Spain, 1523–1572.* Translated by Lesley Bryd Simpson. 1st ed. in French, 1933; Berkeley: University of California Press, 1966.

Ricklis, Robert. *The Karankawa Indians of Texas: An Ecological Study of Cultural Tradition and Change.* Austin: University of Texas Press, 1996.

Rico González, Victor, ed. *Documentos sobre la expulsión de los jesuítas y ocupación de sus temporalidades en Nueva España (1772–1783).* Mexico: Universidad Nacional Autónoma, Instituto de Historia, 1949.

Riekenberg, Michael. "'Aniquilar hasta su exterminio a estos indios . . .': Un ensayo para repensar la frontera bonaerense (1770–1830)." *Ibero-Americana Pragensia* 30 (1996): 61–75.

Rieu-Millan, Marie Laure. *Los diputados americanos en las cortes de Cádiz.* Madrid: Consejo Superior de Investigaciones Científicas, 1990.

Río Cossa, José del. *Descripción de la Florida Oriental hecha en 1787.* Edited by Agustín Barreiro. Madrid: Sociedad Geográfica Nacional, 1935.

Río, Ignacio del. *La aplicación regional de las reformas borbónicas en Nueva España: Sonora y Sinaloa, 1768–1787.* Mexico: Universidad Nacional Autónoma de Mexico, 1995.

Robinson, David J., and Teresa Thomas. "New Towns in Eighteenth-Century Northwest Argentina." *Journal of Latin American Studies* 6, no. 1 (1974): 1–33.

Rock, David. *Argentina, 1516–1987: From Spanish Colonization to Alfonsín.* 1st ed., 1985; Berkeley: University of California Press, 1987.

Rodríguez Gallardo, José Rafael. *Informe sobre Sinaloa y Sonora, 1750.* Edited by Germán Viveros. Mexico: Archivo Histórico de Hacienda, 1975.

Rodríguez, Martha. *La guerra entre bárbaros y civilizados: El exterminio del nómada en Coahuila, 1840–1880.* Saltillo, Mexico: Centro de Estudios Sociales y Humanísticos, 1998.

Roe, Frank Gilbert. *The Indian and the Horse.* Norman: University of Oklahoma Press, 1955.

Rojas, Ricardo. *El santo de la espada: Vida de San Martín.* Buenos Aires: Ediciones Rosso, 1937.

Rollings, Willard H. *The Osage: An Ethnohistorical Study of Hegemony on the Prairie-Plains.* Columbia: University of Missouri Press, 1992.

Román Gutiérrez, José Francisco. *Sociedad y evangelización en Nueva Galicia durante el siglo XVI.* Mexico: Colegio de Jalisco, Instituto Nacional de Antropología e Historia, and the Universidad Autónoma de Zacatecas, 1993.

Romero Vargas, Germán. *Las sociedades del Atlántico de Nicaragua en los siglos xvii y xviii.* Managua: Fondo de Promoción Cultural-BANIC, 1995.

Rosales, Diego de. *Historia general del reyno de Chile, Flandes indiano.* Edited by Benjamin Vicuña Mackenna. 3 vols. Valparaíso, Chile: Imprenta del Mercurio, 1877–88.

Roulet, Florencia. "De cautivos a aliados: Los 'Indios Fronterizos' de Mendoza (1780–1786)." *Xama* 12–14 (1999–2001): 199–239.

———. "Guerra y diplomacia en la frontera de Mendoza: La política indígena del comandante José Francisco de Amigorena (1779–1799)." In *Funcionarios, diplomáticos, guerreros: Miradas hacia el otro en las fronteras de pampa y patagonia (Siglos XVIII y XIX),* edited by Lidia R. Nacuzzi, 65–117. Buenos Aires: Sociedad Argentina de Antropología, 2002.

———. "Con la pluma y la palabra: El lado oscuro de las negociaciones de paz entre españoles e indígenas." *Revista de Indias* 64 (2004): 313–48.

Rousseau, Jean-Jacques. *The Social Contract and Discourse on the Origin of Inequality.* Edited by Lester G. Crocker. New York: Washington Square Press, 1967.

Rowe, John Howland. "The Renaissance Foundations of Anthropology." *American Anthropologist* 67 (1965): 1–20.

Rozat, Guy. *América, imperio del demonio: Cuentos y recuentos.* Mexico: Universidad Iberoamericana, 1996.

Rubí, Marqués de. "Dictámenes que de orden del exmo. sor. marqués de Croix, virrey de este reino, expone el mariscal de campo marqués de Rubí en orden a la mejor situación de los presidios... 1768." In *La frontera norte y la experiencia colonial,* edited by María del Carmen Velázquez, 29–82. Mexico: Secretaría de Relaciones Exteriores, 1982.

Rubin de Celis, Miguel. "An Account of a Mass of Native Iron, found in South-America." *Philosophical Transactions of the Royal Society of London* 78, no. 1 (1788): 37–42.

Rubio Mañé, Ignacio, ed. "El Teniente Coronel don Hugo O'Conor y la situación en Chihuahua, año de 1771." *Boletín del Archivo General de la Nación* [Mexico] 30 (1959a): 353–91.

———, ed. "Itinerario del teniente coronel don Hugo O'Conor de la ciudad de México a la Villa de Chihuahua [1771]." *Boletín del Archivo General de la Nación* [Mexico] 30 (1959b): 393–471, 649–65.

Ruíz-Esquide Figueroa, Andrea. *Los indios amigos en la frontera araucana.* Santiago de Chile: Dirección de Bibliotecas, Archivos y Museos, 1993.

Ruíz, José Francisco. *Report on the Indian Tribes of Texas in 1828.* Edited and translated by John C. Ewers and Georgette Dorn. New Haven: Yale University Library, 1972.

Ruiz López, Hipólito. *Relación histórica del viage, que hizo a los reynos del Perú y Chile el botánico D. Hipólito Ruiz en el año de 1777 hasta el de 1788, en cuya época regresó a Madrid.* Edited by Jaime Jaramillo-Arango. 2d ed.; 2 vols. Madrid: Real Academia de Ciencias Exactas, Físicas y Naturales, 1952.

Saavedra, Francisco de. *Journal of Don Francisco Saavedra de Sangronis during the Commission which He Had in His Charge from 25 June 1780 until the 20th of the Same Month of 1783.* Edited by Francisco Morales Padrón. Gainesville: University Presses of Florida, 1989.

Saeger, James Schofield. "Another View of the Mission as a Frontier Institution: The Guaycuruan Reductions of Santa Fe, 1743–1810." *Hispanic American Historical Review* 65 (1985): 493–517.

———. "Eighteenth-Century Guaycuruan Missions in Paraguay." In *Indian–Religious Relations in Colonial Spanish America,* edited by Susan E. Ramírez, 55–86. Syracuse: Maxwell School of Citizenship and Public Affairs, 1989.

———. "Warfare, Reorganization, and Readaptation at the Margins of Spanish Rule: The Chaco and Paraguay (1573–1882)." In *Cambridge History of the Native Peoples of the Americas.* Vol. 3, *South America,* edited by Frank Salomon and Stuart B. Schwartz, pt. 2, 257–86. 2 parts. Cambridge: Cambridge University Press, 1999.

———. *The Chaco Mission Frontier: The Guaycuruan Experience.* Tucson: University of Arizona Press, 2000.

Saenz de Santa María, Carmelo. "Inglaterra y el Reino de Goathemala: Influjo inglés en dos economistas guatemaltecos del periódo hispano, escasamente conocidos." *Revista de Indias* 43 (1982): 109–201.

Safford, Frank. "Politics, Ideology and Society." *Spanish America after Independence, c. 1820–c. 1870,* edited by Leslie Bethell, 48–122. Cambridge: Cambridge University Press, 1987.

Sahlins, Peter. *Boundaries: The Making of France and Spain in the Pyrenees.* Berkeley: University of California Press, 1989.

Saignes, Thierry. "Une frontière fossile: La cordillère chiriguano au XVIe siècle." 3d Cycle doctorate, Université de Paris, 1974.

———. "La guerra 'salvaje' en los confines de los Andes y del Chaco: La resistencia chiriguana a la colonización europea." *Quinto Centenario* 8 (1985): 103–23.

———. "Entre 'bárbaros' y 'cristianos': El desafío mestizo en la frontera chiriguano." *Anuario del IEHS* 4 (1989): 13–51.

———. *Ava y Karai: Ensayos sobre la frontera chiriguano (siglos XVI–XX).* La Paz, Bolivia: Hisbol, 1990.

Sáinz Ollero, Héctor. "Comprensión del otro y asimilación del otro: El reto de los chaqueños y el problema de la resistencia indígena en los textos jesuitas del siglo XVIII." In *Visión de los otros y visión de sí mismos,* edited by Fermín del Pino Díaz and Carlos Lázaro Ávila, 89–105. Madrid: Consejo Superior de Investigaciones Científicas, 1995.

Sáiz, Blanca. *Bibliografía sobre Alejandro Malaspina y acerca de la expedición Malaspina y de los marinos y científicos que en ella participaron.* Madrid: Ediciones el Museo Universal, 1992.

Saiz Díez, Félix. *Los colegios de propaganda fide en Hispanoamérica.* Madrid: Raycar, 1969.

Salcedo y Salcedo, Nemesio. *Instrucción reservada de don Nemesio Salcedo y Salcedo, Comandante General de Provincias Internas a su Sucesor [June 16, 1813].* Edited by Isidro Vizcaya Canales. Chihuahua, Mexico: Centro de Información del Estado de Chihuahua, 1990.

Saler, Benson. "Los Wayú (Guajiro)." In *Los aborígenes de Venezuela,* edited by Walter Coppens, 3:25–146. 3 vols. Caracas: Fundación LaSalle, 1980–88.

Salomon, Frank. "Testimonies: The Making and Reading of Native South American Historical

Sources." In *Cambridge History of the Native Peoples of the Americas.* Vol. 3, *South America,* edited by Frank Salomon and Stuart B. Schwartz, pt. 1:19–95. 2 parts. Cambridge: Cambridge University Press, 1999.

Salvatierra, Sofonías. *Contribución a la historia de Centroamérica (monografías documentales).* 2 vols. Managua: Tipografía Progreso, 1939–42.

Salvatore, Ricardo D. *Wandering Paysanos: State Order and Subaltern Experience in Buenos Aires during the Rosas Era.* Durham: Duke University Press, 2003.

Salzman, Philip C. "Inequality and Oppression in Nomadic Society." *Pastoral Production and Society,* edited by L'équipe écologie et anthropologie des sociétés pastorales, 429–46. Cambridge: Cambridge University Press, 1979.

Samudio A., Edda O. "El resguardo indígena en Mérida, siglos XVI–XIX." *Paramillo* 11–12 (1992–93): 5–90.

———. "Resguardo indígena en la legislación indiana y del siglo XIX: Proceso de institucionalizacion de las tierras de las comunidades indígenas en Merida." In *Hombre, tierra y sociedad,* edited by José del Rey Fajardo and Edda O. Samudio Azpurua, 159–259. Caracas: Universidad Católica del Tachira, 1996.

San Alberto, José Antonio de. *Carta que el illustrísimo señor D. Fr. Joseph Antonio de San Alberto, Arzobispo de la Plata, escribió a los indios infieles Chirihuanos [sic], con motivo de pasar los Comisionados de esta Villa de Tarija, a tratar de Treguas, o Paces solicitadas por ellos mismos, y obtenida antes la licencia del Exmo. Señor Marques de Loreto, Virrey de Buenos-Ayres [1787].* Buenos Aires: Real Imprenta de los Niños Expósitos, 1788.

Sánchez Agesta, Luis. *El pensamiento político del despotismo ilustrado.* 2d ed.; Seville: Universidad de Sevilla, 1979.

Sánchez-Blanco, Francisco. *La mentalidad ilustrada.* Madrid: Taurus, 1999.

Sánchez-Blanco Parody, Francisco. "Descubrimiento de la variedad humana y formación del espíritu moderno en la España del siglo XVI: El impacto del nuevo mundo." *Revista de Indias* 45 (1985): 181–99.

Sánchez Labrador, José. *El Paraguay Católico.* 3 vols. Buenos Aires, 1910–17.

Sánchez Labrador, Joseph. *Los indios pampas, puelches, y patagones según Joseph Sánchez Labrador.* Edited by Guillermo Furlong Cardiff. Buenos Aires: Viau y Zona, 1936.

Sandos, James A. "Between Crucifix and Lance: Indian–White Relations in California, 1769–1848." In *Contested Eden: California Before the Gold Rush,* edited by Ramón A. Gutiérrez and Richard J. Orsi, 196–229. Berkeley: University of California Press, 1998.

———. *Converting California: Indians and Franciscans in the Missions, 1769–1836.* New Haven: Yale University Press, 2004.

Santa María, Fray Vicente de. "Relación histórica de la colonia del Nuevo Santander [ca. 1795]." In *Estado general de las fundaciones hechas por D. José de Escandón en la Colonia del Nuevo Santander* 2:351–483. 2 vols. Mexico: Talleres Gráficas de la Nación, 1930.

Santamaría, Antonio Narciso de. "Isla de Chiloé, March 14, 1746." In *Relaciones Geográficas del Reino de Chile, 1756,* edited by Francisco Solano, 261–75. Madrid: Consejo Superior de Investigaciones Científicas, 1995.

Santamaría, Daniel J. "Fronteras indígenas del oriente boliviano: La dominación colonial de Moxos y Chiquitos, 1675–1810." *Boletín Americanista* 28 (1986): 197–228.

———. "La guerra guaykurú: Expansión colonial y conflicto interétnico en la cuenca del Alto Paraguay, siglo XVIII." *Jahrbuch für Geschichte von Staat, Wirtschaft und Gesellschaft Lateinamerikas* 29 (1992): 120–48.

———. *Del tabaco al incienso: Reducción y conversión en las misiones jesuítas de las selvas sudamericanas, siglos XVII y XVIII.* Jujuy, Argentina: CEIC, 1994a.

———. "Las relaciones económicas entre tobas y españoles en el Chaco Occidental, siglo XVIII." *Andes: Antropología e historia* 6 (1994b): 273–300.

———. "La iglesia en el Jujuy colonial, siglos XVII y XVIII." In *Jujuy en la historia: Avances de investigación II,* edited by Marcelo Lagos, 27–41. Jujuy, Argentina: Facultad de Humanidades y Ciencias Sociales, Universidad Nacional de Jujuy, 1995.

———. "Apóstatas y forajidos: Los sectores sociales no controlados en el Chaco, Siglo XVIII." In *Pasado y presente de un mundo postergado: Estudios de antropología, historia y arqueología del Chaco y Pedemonte Surandino,* edited by Ana Teruel and Jerez Omar, 15–34. San Salvador de Jujuy, Argentina: Universidad Nacional de Jujuy, Unidad de Investigación en Historia Regional, 1998a.

———. "Población y economía interna de las poblaciones aborígenes del Chaco en el siglo XVIII." *Andes: Antropología e Historia* 9 (1998b): 173–96.

———. "Paz y asistencialismo vs. guerra y esclavitud: La política reformista del gobernador Gerónimo de Matorras en el Chaco centro-occidental (1769–1775)." *Folia Histórica del Nordeste* 14 (1999): 7–32.

Santamaría, Daniel J., and Jaime A. Peire. "¿Guerra o comercio pacífico? La problemática interétnica del Chaco centro-occidental en el siglo XVIII." *Anuario de Estudios Americanos* 50, no. 2 (1993): 93–127.

Santiago, Mark. *The Red Captain: The Life of Hugo O'Conor, Commandant Inspector of the Interior Provinces of New Spain.* Tucson: Arizona Historical Society, 1994.

———. *Massacre at the Yuma Crossing: Spanish Relations with the Quechans, 1779–1782.* Tucson: University of Arizona Press, 1998.

Sanz, Francisco de Paula. *Viaje por el virreinato del Río de la Plata: El camino del tabaco.* Edited by Daisy Rípodas Ardanaz. Buenos Aires: Centro de Estudios Interdisciplinarios de Hispanoamérica Colonial, Librería Editorial Platero S.R.L., 1977.

Saranyana, Josep-Ignasi. "Métodos de catequisación." In *Historia de la Iglesia en Hispanoamérica y Filipinas,* edited by Pedro Borges, 1:549–68. 2 vols. Madrid: Biblioteca de Autores Cristianos, 1992.

Sarmiento, Domingo Faustino. *Life in the Argentine Republic in the Days of the Tyrants; or, Civilization and Barbarism.* Translated by Mrs. Horace Mann. 1st ed. in Spanish, 1845; New York: Hafner, 1960.

———. *Obras Completas.* 53 vols. San Justo, Argentina: Universidad Nacional de La Matanza, 2001.

Sarrailh, Jean. *La España ilustrada de la segunda mitad del siglo XVIII,* trans. Antonio Alatorre. 1st ed. in French, 1954; Mexico: Fondo de Cultura Económica, 1957.

Saunt, Claudio. *A New Order of Things: Property, Power, and the Transformation of the Creek Indians, 1733–1816.* Cambridge: Cambridge University Press, 1999.

———. "'The English Has Now a Mind to Make Slaves of Them All': Creeks, Seminoles, and the Problem of Slavery." In *Confounding the Color Line: The Indian–Black Experience in North America,* edited by James F. Brooks, 47–75. Lincoln: University of Nebraska Press, 2002.

Sayre, Gordon M. *Les Sauvages Américains: Representations of Native Americans in French and English Colonial Literature.* Chapel Hill: University of North Carolina Press, 1997.

Schiaffino, Santiago Lorenzo. *Origen de las ciudades chilenas: Las fundaciones del siglo XVIII.* Santiago de Chile: Editorial Andrés Bello, 1983.

Schilz, Thomas Frank, and Donald E. Worcester. "Spread of Firearms Among the Indian Tribes on the Northern Frontier of New Spain." *American Indian Quarterly* 11 (1987): 1–10.

Schmidt, James, ed. *What Is Enlightenment? Eighteenth-Century Answers and Twentieth-Century Questions.* Berkeley: University of California Press, 1996.

Schmidtmeyer, Peter. *Travels into Chile, over the Andes, in the Years 1820 and 1821, With some Sketches of the Productions and Agriculture; Mines and Metallurgy; Inhabitants, History, and other Features, of America, Particularly of Chile, and Arauco.* London: Longman, 1824.

Schroeder, Albert. *Apache Indians IV: A Study of the Apache Indians.* Parts IV and V. American Indian Ethnohistory: Indians of the Southeast. New York: Garland, 1974.

Schröter, Bernd. "La frontera en hispanoamérica colonial: Un estudio historiográfico comparativo." *Colonial Latin American Historical Review* 10, no. 3 (2001): 351–85.

Schuetz, Mardith K. "The Indians of the San Antonio [Texas] Missions, 1718–1821." Ph.D. diss., University of Texas at Austin, 1980.

Schwartz, Stuart B., and Frank Salomon. "New Peoples and New Kinds of People: Adaptation, Readjustment, and Ethnogenesis in South American Indigenous Societies (Colonial Era)." In *Cambridge History of the Native Peoples of the Americas.* Vol. 3, *South America,* edited by Frank Salomon and Stuart B. Schwartz, pt. 2, 443–501. 2 parts. Cambridge: Cambridge University Press, 1999.

Scott, James C. *Weapons of the Weak: Everyday Forms of Peasant Resistance.* New Haven: Yale University Press, 1985.

———. *Seeing Like a State: How Certain Schemes to Improve the Human Condition Have Failed.* New Haven: Yale University Press, 1998.

Secoy, Frank Raymond. *Changing Military Patterns of the Great Plains Indians.* 1st ed., 1953; Lincoln: University of Nebraska Press, 1992.

Sedelmayr, Jacobo. *Before Rebellion: Letters and Reports of Jacobo Sedelmayr, S.J.* Edited and translated by Daniel S. Matson and Bernard L. Fontana. Tucson: University of Arizona Press, 1996.

Seed, Patricia. "Taking Possession and Reading Texts: Establishing the Authority of Overseas Empires." *William and Mary Quarterly* 94 (1992): 183–209.

———. *Ceremonies of Possession in Europe's Conquest of the New World, 1492–1640.* Cambridge: Cambridge University Press, 1995.

———. *American Pentimento: The Invention of Indians and the Pursuit of Riches.* Minneapolis: University of Minnesota Press, 2001.

Selwyn, Jennifer D. "'Procur[ing] in the Common People These Better Behaviors': The Jesuits' Civilizing Mission in Early Modern Naples, 1550–1620." *Radical History Review* 67, no. 4 (1997): 4–34.

Serra y Canals, Francisco de. *El celo del español y el indiano instruido [1800].* Edited by Jorge Comadrán Ruíz. Buenos Aires: Facultad de Filosofía y Letras de la Universidad de Buenos Aires, Centro de Estudios Interdisciplinarios de Hispanoamérica Colonial/Librería Editorial Platero, 1979.

Serrano Álvarez, José Manuel. "Apuntes para una metodología del estudio del gasto militar en Indias." *Temas Americanistas* 15 (2002): 32–38.

Serrano y Sanz, Manuel, ed. *Documentos históricos de la Florida y la Luisiana, siglos XVI al XVIII.* Madrid: Librería General de Victoriano Suárez, 1912.

———. *España y los Indios Cherokis y Chactas en la segunda mitad del siglo XVIII.* Seville: Tip. de la Guía Oficial, 1916.

Service, Elman R. "Indian–European Relations in Colonial Latin America." *American Anthropologist* 57 (1955): 411–25.

Servín, Manuel P. "The Secularization of the California Missions: A Reappraisal." *Southern California Quarterly* 47 (1965): 133–50.

Sheehan, Bernard W. *Seeds of Extinction: Jeffersonian Philanthropy and the American Indian.* Chapel Hill: University of North Carolina Press, 1973.

Sheehan, Jonathan. "Enlightenment, Religion, and the Enigma of Secularization." *American Historical Review* 108 (2003): 1061–80.

Sheridan, Cecilia. *El "yugo suave del evangelio": Las misiones franciscanas de Río Grande en el periodo colonial.* Saltillo, Coahuila: Centro de Estudios Sociales y Humanísticos, 1999.

———. *Anónimos y desterrados: La contienda por el "sitio que llaman de Quauyla," Siglos XVI–XVIII.* Mexico: CIESAS, 2000.

Sheridan, Thomas E., ed. *Empire of Sand: The Seri Indians and the Struggle for Spanish Sonora, 1645–1803.* Tucson: University of Arizona Press, 1999.

Sheridan, Thomas E., and Thomas H. Naylor, eds. *Rarámuri: A Tarahumara Colonial Chronicle, 1607–1791.* Flagstaff: Northland Press, 1979.

Shoemaker, Nancy. "Categories." In *Clearing a Path: Theorizing the Past in Native American Studies,* edited by Nancy Shoemaker, 51–74. New York: Routledge, 2002.

Shumway, Nicolas. *The Invention of Argentina.* Berkeley: University of California Press, 1991.

Shweder, Richard A. "On Savages and Other Children." *American Anthropologist* 84 (1982): 354–66.

Silva Galdames, Osvaldo. "Guerra y trueque como factores de cambio en la estructura social. Una aproximación al caso mapuche." In *Economía y comercio en América Hispana,* edited by Guillerrmo Bravo Acevedo, 83–95. Santiago de Chile: Universidad de Chile, 1990.

———. "Acerca de los capitanes de amigos: Un documento y un comentario." *Cuadernos de Historia* 11 (1991): 29–45.

———. "Hombres fuertes y liderazgo en las sociedades segmentarias: Un estudio de casos." *Cuadernos de Historia* 15 (1995): 49–64.

———. "Fundamentos para proponer una distinción entre etnohistoria e historia indígena." *Revista de Historia Indígena,* no. 3 (1998): 5–16.

———. "Butanmapu mapuche en el parlamento pehuenche del fuerte de San Carlos, Mendoza, 1805." *Revista de Historia Indígena,* no. 5 (2001): 9–21.

Silva Galdames, Osvaldo, Marcela Schmidt Acharán, and María Cristina Farga Hernández. "Junta de los pehuenches de Malargüe con el Comandante General de Armas y Frontera de Mendoza, don Francisco José de Amigorena." *Cuadernos de Historia* 11 (1991): 199–209.

Silva Galdames, Osvaldo, and Eduardo Téllez Lúgaro. "Los Pewenche: Identidad y configuración de un mosaico étnico colonial." *Cuadernos de Historia* 13 (1993): 7–54.

Silvestre, Francisco. *Descripción del Reyno de Santa Fe de Bogotá, escrita en 1789 por D. Francisco Silvestre, Secretario que fué del Virreinato y antiguo Governador de la Provincia de Antioquia.* Bogotá: Ministerio de Educación Nacional, 1950.

Simmons, Marc, ed. and trans. *Border Comanches: Seven Spanish Colonial Documents, 1785–1819.* Santa Fe: Stagecoach Press, 1967.

———. *Spanish Government in New Mexico.* Albuquerque: University of New Mexico, 1968.

———. "Settlement Patterns and Village Plans in Colonial New Mexico." In *New Spain's Far Northern Frontier: Essays on Spain in the American West, 1540–1821,* edited by David J. Weber, 97–115. Albuquerque: University of New Mexico Press, 1979.

———. *Spanish Pathways: Readings in the History of Hispanic New Mexico.* Albuquerque: University of New Mexico Press, 2001.

Slatta, Richard W. *Gauchos and the Vanishing Frontier.* Lincoln: University of Nebraska Press, 1983.

———. *Cowboys of the Americas.* New Haven: Yale University Press, 1990.

———. "Spanish Colonial Military Strategy and Ideology." In *Contested Ground: Comparative Frontiers on the Northern and Southern Edges of the Spanish Empire,* edited by Donna J. Guy and Thomas E. Sheridan, 83–96. Tucson: University of Arizona Press, 1998.

Smith, Bernard. *European Vision and the South Pacific.* 2d ed.; New Haven: Yale University Press, 1985.

Smith, Carol A., ed. *Guatemalan Indians and the State: 1540–1988.* Austin: University of Texas Press, 1990.

Smith, F. Todd. *The Caddo Indians: Tribes at the Convergence of Empires, 1542–1854.* College Station: Texas A&M University Press, 1995.

————. *The Wichita Indians: Traders of Texas and the Southern Plains, 1540–1845*. College Station: Texas A&M University Press, 2000.

Smith, Ralph A. "The Spanish 'Piece' Policy in West Texas." *West Texas Historical Association Year Book* 68 (1992): 7–24.

Smith, Robert S. "English Economic Thought in Spain, 1776–1848." *South Atlantic Quarterly* 67, no. 2 (1968): 306–37.

Socolow, Susan Migden. "Spanish Captives in Indian Societies: Cultural Contact Along the Argentine Frontier, 1600–1835." *Hispanic American Historical Review* 72 (1992): 73–99.

————. "Women of the Buenos Aires Frontier, 1740–1810 (or the Gaucho Turned Upside Down)." In *Contested Ground: Comparative Frontiers on the Northern and Southern Edges of the Spanish Empire*, edited by Donna J. Guy and Thomas E. Sheridan, 67–82. Tucson: University of Arizona Press, 1998.

Solano, Francisco de. "Reformismo y cultura intelectual: La biblioteca privada de José de Gálvez, Ministro de Indias." *Quinto Centenario* 2 (1981): 1–100.

————, ed. *Cuestionarios para la formación de Relaciones Geográficas de Indias: Siglos XVI/XIX*. Madrid: Consejo Superior de Investigaciones Científicas, 1988.

————, ed. *Documentos sobre política lingüística en hispanoamérica, 1492–1800*. Madrid: Consejo Superior de Investigaciones Científicas, 1991.

Sors, Fr. Antonio. "Historia del Reino de Chile situado en la América Meridional [ca. 1780]." J. T. Medina, ed. *Revista Chilena de Historia y Geografía*, nos. 42, 43, 45, 46, 48, 49 (1921–23): 5–46; 163–199; 250–89; 330–67; 252–93; 49–86.

Sorsby, William. "Spanish Colonization of the Mosquito Coast, 1787–1800." *Revista de Historia de América*, no. 73–74 (1972): 145–53.

Soto Arango, Diana, Miguel Angel Puig-Samper, and Luis Carlos Arboleda, eds. *La ilustración en América Colonial: Bibliografía crítica*. Madrid: Ediciones Doce Calles/Consejo Superior de Investigaciones Científicas, 1995.

Sotos Serrano, Carmen. *Los pintores de la expedición Malaspina*. 2 vols. Madrid: Real Academia de la Historia, 1982.

Spell, Jefferson Rea. *Rousseau in the Spanish World before 1833: A Study in Franco-Spanish Literary Relations*. Austin: University of Texas Press, 1938.

Spicer, Edward H. *Cycles of Conquest: The Impact of Spain, Mexico, and the United States on the Indians of the Southwest, 1533–1960*. Tucson: University of Arizona Press, 1962.

————. *The Yaquis: A Cultural History*. Tucson: University of Arizona Press, 1980.

Steele, Arthur Robert. *Flowers for the King: The Expedition of Ruiz and Pavón and the Flora of Peru*. Durham: Duke University Press, 1964.

Stein, Stanley J. "Bureaucracy and Business in the Spanish Empire, 1759–1804: Failure of a Bourbon Reform in Mexico and Peru." *Hispanic American Historical Review* 61 (1981): 2–28.

Stein, Stanley J., and Barbara H. Stein. *Apogee of Empire: Spain and New Spain in the Age of Charles III, 1759–1789*. Baltimore: Johns Hopkins University Press, 2003.

Stern, Peter. "The White Indians of the Southwest." *Journal of the Southwest* 33 (1991): 262–81.

————. "Marginals and Acculturation in Frontier Society." In *New Views of Borderlands History*, edited by Robert H. Jackson, 157–92. Albuquerque: University of New Mexico Press, 1998.

Stern, Steve J. *Peru's Indian Peoples and the Challenge of Spanish Conquest: Huamanga to 1640*. Madison: University of Wisconsin Press, 1982.

————. "The Decentered Center and the Expansionist Periphery: The Paradoxes of Post-Colonial Encounters." In *Close Encounters of Empire: Writing the Cultural History of U.S.–Latin American Relations*, edited by Gilbert M. Joseph, Catherine C. LeGrand, and Ricardo D. Salvatore, 47–68. Durham: Duke University Press, 1998.

Stockel, H. Henrietta. "The Chiricahua Apaches and Catholicism on the Spanish Colonial Frontier." *Catholic Southwest: A Journal of History and Culture* 14 (2003): 51–64.

Stolley, Karen. "The Eighteenth Century: Narrative Forms, Scholarship, and Learning." In *Cambridge History of Latin American Literature*. Vol. 1, *Discovery to Modernism,* edited by Roberto González Echevarría and Enrique Pupo-Walker, 336–74. 3 vols. New York: Cambridge University Press, 1996.

Street, John. *Artigas and the Emancipation of Uruguay.* London: Cambridge University Press, 1959.

Studer, Elena F. S. de. *La trata de negros en el Río de la Plata durante el siglo XVIII.* Buenos Aires: Libros de Hispanoamérica, 1984.

Suárez, Teresa, and María Laura Tornay. "Poblaciones, vecinos y fronteras rioplatenses: Santa Fe a fines del siglo XVIII." *Anuario de Estudios Americanos* 60 (2003): 521–55.

Sulé, Jorge Oscar. *Rosas y la problemática del indio.* Buenos Aires: Instituto de Investigaciones Históricas Juan Manuel de Rosas, 1996.

Suria, Tomás de. "Diario de Tomás de Suria en su viaje a la costa noroeste con la expedición Malaspina, 1789–1794." In *Varias expediciones a la costa noroeste,* edited by Fernando Monge and Margarita del Olmo, 90–162. Madrid: Historia 16, 1991.

Suría, Tomás de. *Journal of Tomás de Suría of His Voyage with Malaspina to the Northwest Coast of America in 1791.* Edited by Henry R. Wagner and Donald C. Cutter. Fairfield, Wash.: Ye Galleon Press, 1980.

Súsnik, Branislava. *Chiriguanos I: Dimensiones etnosociales.* Asunción, Paraguay: Museo Etnográfico "Andrés Barbero," 1968.

———. *Dimensiones migratorias y pautas culturales de los pueblos del Gran Chaco y de su periferia: Enfoque etnológico.* Posadas, Argentina: Instituto de Historia, Facultad de Humanidades, Universidad Nacional del Nordeste, 1972.

Súsnik, Branislava, and Miguel Chase-Sardi. *Los indios del Paraguay.* Madrid: Editorial MAPFRE, 1995.

Swadesh, Frances León. *Los Primeros Pobladores: Hispanic Americans of the Ute Frontier.* Notre Dame: University of Notre Dame Press, 1974.

Sweet, David. "Misioneros Jesuitas e indios 'recalcitrantes' en la Amazonia colonial." In *De palabra y obra en el nuevo mundo,* edited by Miguel León-Portilla and others, 1:265–92. 3 vols. Madrid: Siglo XXI/Junta de Extremadura, 1992a.

———. "Native Resistance in Eighteenth-Century Amazonia: The 'Abominable Muras' in War and Peace." *Radical History Review* 53 (1992b): 49–80.

———. "The Ibero-American Frontier Mission in Native American History." In *The New Latin American Mission History,* edited by Erick Langer and Robert Jackson, 1–48. Lincoln: University of Nebraska Press, 1995.

Symcox, Geoffrey. "The Wild Man's Return: The Enclosed Vision of Rousseau's Discourses." In *The Wild Man Within: An Image in Western Thought from the Renaissance to Romanticism,* edited by Edward Dudley and Maximillian E. Novak, 223–47. Pittsburgh: University of Pittsburgh Press, 1972.

Szasz, Margaret Connell, ed. *Between Indian and White Worlds: The Cultural Broker.* Norman: University of Oklahoma Press, 1994.

Tamajuncosa [Comajuncosa], Antonio. "Descripción de las misiones, al cargo del Colegio . . . de Tarija [Feb. 6. 1800]." In *Colección de obras y documentos relativos a la historia antigua y moderna de las provincias del Río de la Plata por Pedro de Angelis,* edited by Andrés M. Carretero, 7:97–165. 1st ed., 1836; 8 vols. Buenos Aires: Plus Ultra, 1969–1972.

Tanck de Estrada, Dorothy. *Pueblos de indios y educación en el México Colonial, 1750–1821.* Mexico: Colegio de México, 1999.

Tanzi, Hector José. "El derecho de guerra en la América Hispana." *Revista de Historia de América*, no. 75–76 (1974): 79–139.

Tapson, Alfred J. "Indian Warfare on the Pampa during the Colonial Period." *Hispanic American Historical Review* 42 (1962): 1–28.

Tate, Michael. "Comanche Captives." *Chronicles of Oklahoma* 72 (1994): 228–63.

Taylor, Alan. *American Colonies: The Settling of North America.* New York: Viking, 2001.

Taylor, William B. "Between Global Process and Local Knowledge: Early Latin American Social History, 1500–1900." In *Reliving the Past: The Worlds of Social History,* edited by Oliver Zunz, 115–90. Chapel Hill: University of North Carolina Press, 1985.

———. "'. . . de corazón pequeño y ánimo apocado': Conceptos de los curas párrocos sobre los indios en la Nueva España del siglo XVIII." *Relaciones: Estudios de Historia y Sociedad* 10, no. 39 (1989): 5–68.

———. *Magistrates of the Sacred: Priests and Parishioners in Eighteenth-Century Mexico.* Stanford: Stanford University Press, 1996.

Teja, Jesús F. de la. *San Antonio de Béxar: A Community on New Spain's Northern Frontier.* Albuquerque: University of New Mexico Press, 1995.

———. "Spanish Colonial Texas." In *New Views of Borderlands History,* edited by Robert H. Jackson, 107–30. Albuquerque: University of New Mexico Press, 1998.

Téllez Lúgaro, Eduardo. "La población pehuenche de la cordillera chilena en tiempos de la dominación española." *Cuadernos de Historia* 7 (1987): 195–210.

———. "Espacios geoétnicos y confederaciones territoriales de la araucanía en tiempos de la guerra a muerte." *Revista de Historia Indígena,* no. 3 (1998): 53–76.

Tena Ramírez, Felipe. *Leyes fundamentales de México, 1808–1978.* 8th ed.; Mexico: Editorial Porrúa, 1978.

TePaske, John J. "French, Spanish, and English Indian Policy on the Gulf Coast, 1513–1763: A Comparison." In *Spain and Her Rivals on the Gulf Coast: Proceedings of the Second Gulf Coast History and Humanities Conference,* edited by Ernest F. Dibble and Earle W. Newton, 9–39. Pensacola: Historic Pensacola Preservation Board, 1971.

TePaske, John Jay. *The Governorship of Spanish Florida, 1700–1763.* Durham: Duke University Press, 1964.

Teruel, Ana A. "Zenta y San Ignacio de los Tobas: El trabajo en dos misiones del Chaco occidental a fines de la colonia." *Anuario del IEHS* 9 (1994): 227–52.

Thomas, Alfred B., ed. and trans. *Forgotten Frontiers: A Study of the Spanish Indian Policy of Don Juan Bautista de Anza, Governor of New Mexico, 1777–1787.* Norman: University of Oklahoma Press, 1932.

———, ed. and trans. *After Coronado: Spanish Exploration Northeast of New Mexico, 1696–1727.* Norman: University of Oklahoma Press, 1935.

———, ed. and trans. *The Plains Indians and New Mexico, 1751–1778: A Collection of Documents Illustrative of the History of the Eastern Frontier of New Mexico.* Albuquerque: University of New Mexico Press, 1940.

———. *Teodoro de Croix and the Northern Frontier of New Spain, 1776–1783.* Norman: University of Oklahoma Press, 1941.

Tibesar, Antonine, ed. and trans. *Writings of Junípero Serra.* 4 vols. Washington: Academy of American Franciscan History, 1955–66.

———. "Two Notes on the Jungle Missions in Peru in the Eighteenth Century." In *Franciscan Presence in the Americas: Essays on the Activities of the Franciscan Friars in the Americas, 1492–1900,* edited by Francisco Morales, 143–61. Potomac, Md.: Academy of American Franciscan History, 1983.

Tierney, Patrick. *Darkness in El Dorado: How Scientists and Journalists Devastated the Amazon*. W. W. Norton, 2000.

Tilly, Charles. *The Politics of Collective Violence*. Cambridge studies in contentious politics. Cambridge: Cambridge University Press, 2003.

Tiryakian, Josefina Cintrón. "Campillo's Pragmatic New System: A Mercantile and Utilitarian Approach to Indian Reform in Spanish Colonies of the Eighteenth Century." *History of Political Economy* 10 (1978): 233–57.

Todorov, Tzvetan. *The Conquest of America: The Question of the Other*. New York: Harper and Row, 1984.

Torgovnick, Marianna. *Gone Primitive: Savage Intellects, Modern Lives*. Chicago: University of Chicago Press, 1990.

Torre Curiel, José Refugio de la. *Vicarios en entredicho: Crisis y desestructuración de la provincia francis-cana de Santiago de Xalisco, 1749–1860*. Zamora and Guadalajara, Mexico: Colegio de Michoacán and the Universidad de Guadalajara, 2001.

Torre Revello, José. "Agasajos a los indios (1797)." *Boletín del Instituto de Investigaciones Históricas* [Buenos Aires] 22 (1937): 126–30.

———. "Aportación para la biografía del Maestre de Campo de Milicias y Comandante de Ar-mas y Frontera, Don José Francisco de Amigorena." *Revista de Historia Americana y Argentina* [Mendoza], no. 3–4 (1958–59): 11–31.

———. *La sociedad colonial (Páginas sobre la sociedad de Buenos Aires entre los siglos XVI y XIX)*. Buenos Aires: Ediciones Pannedille, 1970.

Tova, Antonio de. *62 meses a bordo: La expedición Malaspina según el diario del teniente de navío don An-tonio de Tova Arredondo, 2.º comandante de la Atrevida 1789–1794*. Edited by Lorenzo Sanfeliú Or-tiz. Madrid: Biblioteca de Camarote de la Revista General de Marina, 1943.

Tova Arredondo, Antonio. "Estada en Nutka [1791]." In *La expedición Malaspina, 1789–1794*. Vol. 5, *Antropología y noticias etnográficas*, edited by Dolores Higueras Rodríguez and Juan Pimentel Igea, 139–46. Madrid: Ministerio de Defensa, Museo Naval, and Lunwerg Editores, 1993.

Tovar Zambrano, Bernardo. "La historiografía colonial." In *La historia al final del milenio: Ensayos de historiografía colombiana y latinoamericana*, edited by Bernardo Tovar Zambrano, 1:21–134. 2 vols. Bogotá: Editorial Universidad Nacional, 1994.

Trias Mercant, Sebastián. "América y los misioneros franciscanos españoles del siglo XVIII: Un modelo antropológico-teológico." In *Mundo hispánico-nuevo mundo: Visión filosófica. Actas del VIII seminario de historia de la filosofía española e iberoamericana*, edited by Antonio Heredia Soriano, 97–115. Salamanca: Ediciones Universidad de Salamanca, 1995.

Trinchero, Hector Hugo. *Los dominios del demonio: Civilización y barbarie en las fronteras de la nación, El Chaco central*. Buenos Aires: EUDEBA, 2000.

Tristán, Esteban Lorenzo de. "Carta instructiva acerca de las Provincias Internas, y representación que hizo el ilustrísimo Señor Doctor Don Esteban Lorenzo de Tristán, del Consejo de S.M. y Dignísimo Obispo de la Ciudad de Durango [to Viceroy Manuel Antonio Flores, Durango, Sept. 9, 1788]." MS, Biblioteca de la Real Sociedad de Amigos de Tenerife (La Laguna, Tenerife). 1788.

Twinam, Ann. *Public Lives, Private Secrets: Gender, Honor, Sexuality, and Illegitimacy in Colonial Spanish America*. Stanford: Stanford University Press, 1999.

Ulloa, Antonio de. *Noticias Americanas: Edición Facsímile [1772]*. Edited by Miguel Molina Martínez. Granada: Universidad de Granada, 1992.

Undiano y Gastelú, Sebastián. In *Colección de obras y documentos relativos a la historia antigua y moderna de las provincias del Río de la Plata por Pedro de Angelis*, edited by Andrés M. Carretero, 2:493–512. 1st ed., 1836; 8 vols. Buenos Aires: Editorial Plus Ultra, 1969–72.

Urbina Burgos, Rodolfo. "Del período indiano de la cultura chilota." *Atenea,* no. 453–54 (1986): 385–402.

———. "Chiloé y la ocupación de los llanos de Osorno durante el siglo XVIII." *Boletín de la Academia Chilena de la Historia* 98 (1987): 219–69.

———. *Las misiones franciscanas de Chiloé a fines del siglo XVIII: 1771–1800.* Valparaíso, Chile: Instituto de Historia, Universidad Católica de Valparaíso, 1990.

Uribe, Carlos Antonio. "La rebelión Chimila en la provincia de Santa Marta, Nuevo Reino Granada, durante el siglo XVIII." *Estudios Andinos* 7, no. 13 (1977): 113–65.

Urruela V. de Quezada, María. "El indio en la literatura hispanoamericana: Un esbozo." *Boletín de la Academia Nacional de la Historia* [Caracas] 75, no. 299 (1992): 91–108.

Usner, Daniel H., Jr. "American Indians in Colonial New Orleans." In *Powhatan's Mantle: Indians in the Colonial Southeast,* edited by Peter H. Wood, Gregory A. Waselkov, and M. Thomas Hatley, 104–28. Lincoln: University of Nebraska Press, 1989.

———. *Indians, Settlers, and Slaves in a Frontier Exchange Economy: The Lower Mississippi Valley Before 1783.* Chapel Hill: University of North Carolina Press, 1992.

———. *American Indians in the Lower Mississippi Valley: Social and Economic Histories.* Lincoln: University of Nebraska Press, 1998.

Valdés, Carlos Manuel. *Historia de los pueblos indígenas de México.* Mexico: Centro de Investigaciones y Estudios Superiores en Antropología Social, 1995.

Valdés, Carlos Manuel, and Ildefonso Dávila. *Esclavos negros en Saltillo: Siglos XVII a XIX.* Saltillo, Mexico, 1989.

———, ed. *Fuentes para la Historia India de Coahuila.* Madrid: Fundación Histórica Tavera, Archivo Municipal de Saltillo, 1998.

Vallebueno G., Miguel. "Apaches y comanches en Durango durante los siglos XVIII y XIX." In *Nómadas y sedentarios en el norte de Mexico: Homenaje a Beatriz Braniff,* edited by Marie-Areti Hers et al., 669–82. Mexico: Instituto de Investigaciones Antropológicas, UNAM, 2000.

Van Kirk, Sylvia. *Many Tender Ties: Women in Fur-Trade Society in Western Canada, 1670–1870.* Winnipeg, Man.: Watson and Dwyer, 1980.

Vancouver, George. *A Voyage of Discovery to the North Pacific Ocean and Round the World, 1791–1795.* Edited by W. Kaye Lamb. 4 vols. London: Hakluyt Society, 1984.

Vangelista, Chiara. "Los payaguá entre Asunción y Cuiba: Formación y decadencia de una frontera indígena (1719–1790)." In *Conquista y resistencia en la historia de América,* edited by Pilar García Jordán and Miguel Izard, 151–66. Barcelona: Universitat de Barcelona, 1992.

———. "Los Guaikurú, Españoles y Portugueses en una región de frontera: Mato Grosso, 1770–1830." *Boletín del Instituto de Historia Argentina y Americana "Doctor Emilio Ravignani,"* no. 8 (1993): 55–76.

Varela, Gladys A., and Luz María Font. "La mujer indígena, protagonista de una historia de hombres." In *Los Hijos de la Tierra: Algunos capítulos de la historia indígena del Neuquén,* edited by Gladys A. Varela et al., 89–110. San Martín de los Andes, Argentina: Municipalidad de San Martín de los Andes, 1998.

Varese, Stefano. *Salt of the Mountain: Campa Asháninka History and Resistance in the Peruvian Jungle.* Norman: University of Oklahoma Press, 2002.

Vargas-Lobsinger, María. *Formación y decadencia de una fortuna: Los mayorazgos de San Miguel de Aguayo de San Pedro del lamo, 1583–1823.* Mexico: Universidad Nacional Autónoma de México, 1992.

Vargas Machuca, Bernardo de. *Milicia y descripción de las Indias.* Colección de libros raros o curiosos que tratan de América, 8–9. 1st ed., 1599; 2 vols. Madrid: Librería Victoriano Suarez, 1892.

Vargas, Pedro Fermín de. "Memoria sobre la población del Nuevo Reino de Granada [1791]." In

Pensamientos políticos y Memoria sobre la población del Nuevo Reino de Granada [1791], edited by Manuel José Forero, 85–110. Bogotá: Biblioteca Popular de Cultura Colombiana, 1944.

Vattel, M. de. *The Law of Nations; or the Principles of the Law of Nature Applied to the Conduct and Affairs of Nations and Sovereigns*. 1st French ed., 1758; 2 vols. London: J. Newbery, 1759.

Vaughan, Alden T., and Edward W. Clark, eds. *Puritans among the Indians: Accounts of Captivity and Redemption, 1676–1724*. Cambridge: Harvard University Press, 1981.

Vázquez de Acuña, Isidoro. "Evolución de la población de Chiloé (siglos xvi–xx)." *Boletín de la Academia Chilena de la Historia* 102 (1991–92): 403–57.

Velasco Ávila, Cuauhtémoc José. "La amenaza comanche en la frontera mexicana, 1800–1841." Ph.D. diss., Universidad Nacional Autónoma de México, 1998.

Velasco Ávila, Cuauhtémoc. "'Nuestros obstinados enemigos': Ideas y imágenes de los indios nómadas en la frontera noreste mexicana, 1821–1840." In *Nómadas y sedentarios en el norte de Mexico: Homenaje a Beatriz Braniff*, edited by Marie-Areti Hers et al., 441–59. Mexico: Instituto de Investigaciones Antropológicas, UNAM, 2000.

Velasco Ceballos, R., ed. *La administración de D. Frey Antonio María de Bucareli y Ursúa*. Publicaciones del Archivo General de la Nación, tomos 29–30. 2 vols. Mexico: Archivo General de la Nación, 1936.

Velázquez, María del Carmen. *El estado de guerra en Nueva España, 1760–1808*. Mexico: Colegio de Mexico, 1950.

———. *El marqués de Altamira y las provincias internas de Nueva España*. Mexico: Colegio de Mexico, 1976.

———. *Tres estudios sobre las provincias internas de Nueva España*. Mexico: Colegio de México, 1979.

———. "Don Matías de la Mota Padilla y su política de poblamiento." *Estudios de Historia Novohispana* 7 (1981): 79–98.

———, ed. *La frontera norte y la experiencia colonial*. Mexico: Secretaría de Relaciones Exteriores, 1982.

Ventura Beleña, Eusebio. *Recopilación sumaria de todos los autos acordados de la Real Audiencia y Sala del Crimen de esta Nueva España*. 1st ed., 1787; facsimile, 2 vols. Mexico: Universidad Autónoma de México, 1981.

Verde Casanova, Ana María. "Notas para el estudio etnológico de las expediciones científicas españolas a América en el siglo XVIII." *Revista de Indias* 40 (1980): 81–97.

Vértiz y Salcedo, Juan José. "Memoria a su sucesor marqués de Loreto, Buenos Aires, 12 de marzo de 1784." In *Memorias de los virreyes del Río de la Plata*, edited by Sigfrido Radaelli, 24–199. Buenos Aires: Editorial Bajel, 1945.

Viana, Francisco Xavier de. *Diario de viaje*. Edited by Homero Martínez Montero. 1st ed., 1849; 2 vols. Montevideo: Ministerio de Instrucción Pública y Previsión Social de Uruguay, 1958.

Vidal, E. E. *Picturesque illustrations of Buenos Ayres and Monte Video*. 1st ed., 1820; facsimile, Buenos Aires: Editorial Viau, 1943.

Vidal, Silvia M. "Kuwé Duwákalumi: The Arawak Sacred Routes of Migration, Trade, and Resistance." *Ethnohistory* 47 (2000): 635–67.

Vidal, Silvia M., and Alberta Zucchi. "Efectos de las expansiones coloniales en las poblaciones indígenas del Noroeste Amazónico (1798–1830)." *Colonial Latin American Review* 8, no. 1 (1999): 113–32.

Viedma, Francisco de. "Descripción y estado de las reducciones de indios chiriguanos [Cochabamba, Jan. 15, 1788]." In *Descripción geográfica y estadística de la provincia de Santa Cruz de la Sierra*, 223–70. Cochabamba, Bolivia: Amigos del Libro, 1969.

———. "Descripción geográfica y estadística de la provincia de Santa Cruz de la Sierra [March 2, 1793]." In *Colección de obras y documentos relativos a la historia antigua y moderna de las provincias del Río de la Plata por Pedro de Angelis,* edited by Andrés M. Carretero, 6:513–735. 1st ed., 1836; 8 vols. Buenos Aires: Editorial Plus Ultra, 1969a–72a.

———. "Descripción y estado de las reducciones de indios chiriguanos [Jan. 15, 1788]." In *Colección de obras y documentos relativos a la historia antigua y moderna de las provincias del Río de la Plata por Pedro de Angelis,* edited by Andrés M. Carretero, 6:736–94. 1st ed., 1836; 8 vols. Buenos Aires: Editorial Plus Ultra, 1969b–72b.

———. "Memoria dirigida al señor marqués de Loreto virrey y capitán general de las provincias del Río de la Plata [Buenos Aires, May 1, 1784]." In *Colección de obras y documentos relativos a la historia antigua y moderna de las provincias del Río de la Plata por Pedro de Angelis,* edited by Andrés M. Carretero, 3:635–84. 1st ed., 1836; 8 vols. Buenos Aires: Editorial Plus Ultra, 1969c–72c.

Vignati, Milcíades Alejo, ed. "Un diario inédito de Pablo Zizur [1781]." *Revista del Archivo General de la Nación* 3 (1973): 65–114.

Vilaplana, Hermenegildo. *Vida Portentosa del Americano Septentrional Apostol El. V.P. Fr. Antonio Margil de Jesús.* Mexico: Imprenta de la Bibliotheca Mexicana, 1763.

Villalobos R., Sergio. "Tipos fronterizos en el ejército de Arauco." In *Relaciones fronterizas en la Araucanía,* edited by Sergio Villalobos R. et al., 175–209. Santiago de Chile: Ediciones Universidad Católica de Chile, 1982.

———. "Guerra y paz en la araucanía: Periodificación." In *Araucanía: Temas de historia fronteriza,* edited by Sergio Villalobos R. and Jorge Pinto, 7–30. Temuco, Chile: Ediciones de la Universidad de la Frontera, 1989a.

———. *Los pehuenches en la vida fronteriza.* Santiago de Chile: Ediciones Universidad Católica de Chile, 1989b.

———. "Tres siglos y medio de vida fronteriza chilena." In *Estudios (nuevos y viejos) sobre la frontera,* edited by Francisco de Solano and Salvador Bernabeu, 289–359. Madrid: Consejo Superior de Investigaciones Científicas, 1991.

———. *La vida fronteriza en Chile.* Madrid: Editorial MAPFRE, 1992.

———. "Deficiencia de la historiografía Europea relativa a América: El caso de la frontera en Chile." *Historia* [Universidad Católica de Chile] 27 (1993): 553–66.

———. *Vida fronteriza en la araucanía: El mito de la guerra de arauco.* Santiago de Chile: Andrés Bello, 1995.

———. "El avance de la historia fronteriza." *Revista de Historia Indígena,* no. 2 (1997): 5–20.

Villar, Daniel. *Ocupación y control del espacio por las sociedades indígenas de la frontera sur de Argentina (siglo XIX).* Bahía Blanca, Argentina: Universidad Nacional de Sur, 1993.

Villar, Daniel, and Juan Francisco Jiménez. "Botín, materialización ideológica y guerra en las Pampas, durante la segunda mitad del siglo XVIII: El caso de Llanketruz." *Revista de Indias* 60, no. 220 (2000): 687–707.

———. "La tempestad de la guerra: Conflictos indígenas y circuitos de intercambio. Elementos para una periodización (Araucanía y las Pampas, 1780–1840)." In *Las fronteras hispanocriollas del mundo indígena latinoamericano en los siglos XVIII–IX: Un estúdio comparativo,* edited by Raúl J. Mandrini and Carlos D. Paz, 123–71. Tandil, Argentina: IEHS/CEHIR/UNS, 2002.

———. "Conflicto, poder y justicia: El cacique Martín Toriano en la cordillera y las pampas (1818–1832)." In *Conflicto, poder y justicia en la frontera bonaerense, 1818–1832,* edited by Daniel Villar, 131–286. Bahía Blanca and Santa Rosa, Argentina: Departamento de Humanidades, Universidad National del Sur, and Facultad de Ciencias Humanas, Universidad de la Pampa, 2003.

Villareal, Francisco Joaquín de. *Representación del reyno de Chile sobre la importancia, y necesidad de sujetar, y reducir a pueblos los indios araucanos. La impossibilidad de conseguirlo, preservando en la conducta passada; y la facilidad, con que puede lograrse, sin costo alguno del Real Erario, por medio de las providencias, que se expresan.* Madrid, 1741.

Villaseñor y Sánchez, José Antonio. *Theatro americano, descripción general de los reynos, y provincias de la Nueva-España, y sus jurisdicciones.* 2 vols. Mexico: Impr. de la viuda de d. J. Bernardo de Hogal, 1746–48.

Villava, Victorián de. "Apuntes para una reforma de España, sin trastorno del Gobierno Monárquico ni la Religion [1797]." In *Vida y escritos de Victorián de Villava,* edited by Ricardo Levene, lxxix–cxx. Buenos Aires: Instituto de Investigaciones Históricas, 1946.

Villegas, Juan. *Instrucciones para el Virrey Bucareli de Nueva España.* Montevideo: Universidad Católica del Uruguay, 1987.

———. "La evangelización del indio de la Banda Oriental del Uruguay (siglos XVI–XVII)." In *Cristianismo y mundo colonial: Tres estudios acerca de la evangelización de Hispanoamérica,* edited by Johannes Meier, 69–111. Münster: Aschendorffsche Verlagsbuchhandlung, 1995.

Viñuales, Graciela María. "El territorio y la ilustración: La fortificación de la frontera Chaco-Tucumana." In *Estudios sobre el territorio iberoamericano,* 207–31. Seville: Consejería de Cultura, 1996.

Virgillo, Carmelo. *The Ibero-American Enlightenment,* edited by A. Owen Aldridge, 243–55. Urbana: University of Illinois Press, 1971.

Vitar, Beatriz. "Las fronteras 'bárbaras' en los virreinatos de Nueva España y Perú (Las tierras del norte de México y oriente del Tucumán en el siglo XVIII)." *Revista de Indias* 55 (1995): 33–66.

———. "La otredad lingüística y su impacto en la conquista de las Indias." *Revista Española de Antropología Americana* 26 (1996): 143–65.

———. *Guerra y misiones en la frontera chaqueña del Tucumán (1700–1767).* Madrid: Consejo Superior de Investigaciones Científicas, 1997.

———. "Algunas notas sobre la figura de los líderes chaqueños en las postrimerías del siglo XVIII." In *Las fronteras hispanocriollas del mundo indígena latinoamericano en los siglos XVIII–XIX: Un estúdio comparativo,* edited by Raúl J. Mandrini and Carlos D. Paz, 407–28. Tandil, Argentina: IEHS/CEHIR/UNS, 2002.

Vives Azancot, Pedro A. "Entre el esplendor y la decadencia: La población de Misiones (1750–1759)." *Revista de Indias* 42 (1982): 469–543.

Voss, Stuart F. *On the Periphery of Nineteenth-Century Mexico: Sonora and Sinaloa, 1810–1877.* Tucson: University of Arizona Press, 1982.

Wade, Maria F. *The Native Americans of the Texas Edwards Plateau, 1582–1799.* Austin: University of Texas Press, 2003.

Walker, Charles. "Voces discordantes: Discursos alternativos sobre el indio a fines de la colonia." In *Entre la retórica y la insurgencia: Las ideas y los movimientos sociales en los Andes, siglo XVIII,* edited by Charles Walker, 89–112. Cusco, Peru: Centro de Estudios Regionales Andinos "Bartolomé de Las Casas," 1996.

Wallace, Anthony F. C. *Jefferson and the Indians: The Tragic Fate of the First Americans.* Cambridge: Belknap Press of Harvard University, 1999.

Wallace, Ernest, and E. Adamson Hoebel. *The Comanches: Lords of the South Plains.* Norman: University of Oklahoma Press, 1952.

Walther, Juan Carlos. *La conquista del desierto.* 1st ed., 1948; 3d ed., Buenos Aires: Editorial Universitaria de Buenos Aires, 1976.

Ward, Bernardo. *Proyecto económico.* Edited by Juan Luis Castellano Castellano. Madrid: Instituto de Estudios Fiscales, 1982.

Watson, Thomas D. "A Scheme Gone Awry: Bernardo de Galvez, Gilberto Antonio de Maxent, and the Southern Indian Trade." *Louisiana History* 17 (1976): 5–17.

Weber, David J. *The Taos Trappers: The Fur Trade in the Far Southwest, 1540–1846.* Norman: University of Oklahoma Press, 1971.

————. *The Mexican Frontier, 1821–1846: The American Southwest Under Mexico.* Albuquerque: University of New Mexico Press, 1982.

————. *The Spanish Frontier in North America.* New Haven: Yale University Press, 1992.

————. "Conflicts and Accommodations: Hispanic and Anglo-American Borders in Historical Perspective, 1670–1853." *Journal of the Southwest* 39 (1997): 1–32.

————. "The Spanish Moment in the Pacific Northwest." In *Terra Pacifica: People and Place in the Northwest States and Western Canada,* edited by Paul Hirt, 3–24. Pullman: Washington State University Press, 1998.

Weber, David J., and Jane M. Rausch, eds. *Where Cultures Meet: Frontiers in Latin American History.* Wilmington, Del.: Scholarly Resources, 1994.

Webre, Stephen. "The Problem of Indian Slavery in Spanish Louisiana, 1769–1803." *Louisiana History* 25 (1984): 117–36.

West, Elizabeth H., ed. and trans. "Bonilla's Brief Compendium of the History of Texas [1772]." *Southwestern Historical Quarterly* 8 (1904): 3–78.

West, Elizabeth Howard. "The Indian Policy of Bernardo de Gálvez." *Proceedings of the Mississippi Valley Historical Association* 8 (1914–15): 95–101.

West, Elliott. *Contested Plains: Indians, Goldseekers, and the Rush to Colorado.* Lawrence: University of Kansas Press, 1998.

West, Robert C. *The Mining Community in Northern New Spain: The Parral Mining District.* Ibero-Americana, 30. Berkeley: University of California Publications, 1949.

Whigham, Thomas. *The New Latin American Mission History,* edited by Erick Langer and Robert Jackson, 157–88. Lincoln: University of Nebraska Press, 1995.

Whitaker, Arthur P. "Changing and Unchanging Interpretations of the Enlightenment in Spanish America." *Proceedings of the American Philosophical Society* 114 (1970): 256–71.

Whitaker, Arthur P., et al. *Latin America and the Enlightenment.* 1st ed., 1942; Ithaca: Cornell University Press, 1961.

White, Hayden. "The Noble Savage Theme as Fetish." In *First Images of America: The Impact of the New World on the Old,* edited by Fredi Chiapelli, 1:121–35. 2 vols. Berkeley: University of California Press, 1976.

White, Richard. *The Roots of Dependency: Subsistence, Environment, and Social Change among the Choctaws, Pawnees, and Navajos.* Lincoln: University of Nebraska Press, 1983.

————. *The Middle Ground: Indians, Empires, and Republics in the Great Lakes Region, 1650–1815.* Cambridge: Cambridge University Press, 1991.

White, Richard Alan. "The Political Economy of Paraguay and the Impoverishment of the Missions." *The Americas* 31 (1975): 417–33.

White, Robert R. "New Mexican Genízaros and Turkish Janissaries." *Taos Lightnin'* 6 (2000): 1–4.

Whitehead, Neil L. *Lords of the Tiger Spirit: A History of the Caribs in Colonial Venezuela and Guyana, 1498–1820.* Dordrecht, Holland: Foris Publications, 1988.

————. "Carib Ethnic Soldiering in Venezuela, the Guianas, and the Antilles, 1492–1820." *Ethnohistory* 37, no. 4 (1990): 357–85.

————. "Native Peoples Confront Colonial Regimes in Northeastern South America (c. 1500–1900)." In *Cambridge History of the Native Peoples of the Americas.* Vol. 3, *South America,* edited by Frank Salomon and Stuart B. Schwartz, pt. 2, 382–442. 2 parts. Cambridge: Cambridge University Press, 1999.

Whitehead, Neil Lance. "The Snake Warriors—Sons of the Tiger's Teeth: A Descriptive Analysis of Carib Warfare, ca. 1500–1820." In *Anthropology of War,* edited by Jonathan Haas, 146–70. Cambridge: Cambridge University Press, 1990.

Whitehead, Neil Lancelot. "The Ancient Amerindian Polities of the Amazon, the Orinoco, and the Atlantic Coast: A Preliminary Analysis of Their Passage from Antiquity to Extinction." In *Amazonian Indians from Prehistory to the Present: Anthropological Perspectives,* edited by Anna Roosevelt, 33–53. Tucson: University of Arizona Press, 1994.

Wilde, Guillermo. "¿Segregación o asimilación? La política indiana en América meridional a fines del período colonial." *Revista de Indias* 69 (1999): 619–44.

———. "Los guaraníes después de la expulsión de los jesuitas: Dinámicas políticas y transacciones simbólicas." *Revista Complutense de Historia de América* 27 (2001): 69–106.

———. "Orden y ambigüedad en la formación territorial del Río de la Plata a fines del siglo XVIII." *Horizontes Antropológicos,* no. 19 (2003): 105–35.

Williams, Caroline A. "Resistance and Rebellion on the Spanish Frontier: Native Responses to Colonization in the Colombian Chocó, 1670–1690." *Hispanic American Historical Review* 79, no. 3 (1999): 397–424.

Williams, John Hoyt. "The Deadly Selva: Paraguay's Northern Indian Frontier." *The Americas* 33 (1976): 1–24.

Williams, Robert A., Jr. *The American Indian in Western Legal Thought: The Discourses of Conquest.* New York: Oxford University Press, 1990.

———. *Linking Arms Together: American Indian Treaty Visions of Law and Peace, 1600–1800.* New York: Oxford University Press, 1997.

Wood, Peter H. "The Changing Population of the Colonial South: An Overview by Race and Region, 1685–1790." In *Powhatan's Mantle: Indians in the Colonial Southeast,* edited by Peter H. Wood, Gregory A. Waselkov, and M. Thomas Hatley, 35–103. Lincoln: University of Nebraska Press, 1989.

Worcester, Donald E. "The Navaho During the Spanish Regime in New Mexico." *New Mexico Historical Review* 26 (1951): 101–18.

———. *The Apaches: Eagles of the Southwest.* Norman: University of Oklahoma Press, 1979a.

———. "The Significance of the Spanish Borderlands to the United States." In *New Spain's Far Northern Frontier: Essays on Spain in the American West,* edited by David J. Weber, 1–13. Albuquerque: University of New Mexico Press, 1979b.

Wortman, Miles L. *Government and Society in Central America, 1680–1840.* New York: Columbia University Press, 1982.

Wright, J. Leitch, Jr. *The Only Land They Knew: The Tragic Story of the American Indians in the Old South.* New York: Free Press, 1981.

Wright, Robert E. "How Many Are 'A Few'? Catholic Clergy in Central and Northern New Mexico, 1780–1851." In *Seeds of Struggle/Harvest of Faith: The Papers of the Archdiocese of Santa Fe Catholic Cuarto Centennial Conference on the History of the Catholic Church in New Mexico,* edited by Thomas J. Steele, Paul Rhetts, and Barbe Awalt, 219–61. Albuquerque: LPD Press, 1998.

Wright, Winthrop R. *Café con Leche: Race, Class, and National Image in Venezuela.* Austin: University of Texas Press, 1990.

Yela Utrilla, Juan F. *España ante la independencia de los Estados Unidos.* Rev. ed.; 2 vols. Lérida, Spain: Gráficos Academia Mariana, 1925.

Zabelle Derounian-Stodola, Kathryn, and James Arthur Levernier. *The Indian Captivity Narrative, 1550–1900.* New York: Twayne, 1993.

Zahino Peñafort, Luisa. "La cuestión indígena en el IV Concilio Provincial Mexicano." *Relaciones: Estudios de Historia y Sociedad* 12 (1990): 5–31.

Zapater, Horacio. "Una nueva fuente para la etnohistoria chilena: La crónica de Jerónimo de Quiroga." *Revista Chilena de Historia y Geografía,* no. 149 (1981): 24–40.

————. "La expansión araucana el los siglos XVIII y XIX." In *Relaciones fronterizas en la Araucanía*, edited by Sergio Villalobos R. et al., 89–105. Santiago de Chile: Ediciones Universidad Católica de Chile, 1982.

————. "Parlamentos de paz en la guerra de Arauco, 1612–1626." *La Araucanía: Temas de historia fronteriza*, edited by Sergio Villalobos R. and Jorge Pinto, 47–82. Temuco, Chile: Ediciones de la Universidad de la Frontera, 1989.

————. *Los aborígenes chilenos a través de cronistas y viajeros*. 1st ed. 1978; Santiago de Chile: Editorial Andrés Bello, 1998.

Zaragoza, Gonzalo, and Ricardo García Cárcel. "La polémica sobre la conquista española de América: Algunos testimentos en el siglo XVIII." In *Ilustración española e independencia de América: Homenaje a Noël Salmon*, 374–79. Barcelona: Universidad Autónoma, 1979.

Zavala, Silvio. "The Frontiers of Hispanic America." In *New Spain's Far Northern Frontier: Essays on Spain in the American West, 1540–1821*, edited by David J. Weber, 179–99. Albuquerque: University of New Mexico Press, 1979.

————. *Los esclavos indios en Nueva España*. 1st ed., 1968; Mexico: Colegio Nacional Luis González Obregón, 1981.

————. *América en el espíritu francés del siglo XVIII*. 1st ed., 1949; Mexico: Colegio Nacional, 1983.

Zerda, Wellington F. *Los indios y las invasiones inglesas*. Buenos Aires: Privately printed, 1934.

Zorraquín Becú, Ricardo. *La organización política argentina en el período hispánico*. Buenos Aires: Emecé, 1959.

Zusman, Perla. "Entre el lugar y la linea: La constitución de las fronteras coloniales patagónicas (1780–1792)." *Fronteras de la Historia* [Bogotá], no. 6 (2001): 37–59.

Index